ECOLOGY OF FRESHWATER AND ESTUARINE WETLANDS

ECOLOGY OF FRESHWATER
AND ESTUARINE WETLANDS

EDITED BY

Darold P. Batzer and Rebecca R. Sharitz

UNIVERSITY OF CALIFORNIA PRESS

Berkeley   Los Angeles   London

University of California Press, one of the most distinguished university presses in the United States, enriches lives around the world by advancing scholarship in the humanities, social sciences, and natural sciences. Its activities are supported by the UC Press Foundation and by philanthropic contributions from individuals and institutions. For more information, visit www.ucpress.edu

University of California Press
Berkeley and Los Angeles, California

University of California Press, Ltd.
London, England

© 2006 by the Regents of the University of California

Library of Congress Cataloging-in-Publication Data

Ecology of freshwater and estuarine wetlands / edited by Darold P. Batzer and Rebecca R. Sharitz.
    p. cm.
   Includes bibliographical references and index.
   ISBN 0-520-24777-9 (case : alk. paper)
   1. Wetland ecology. I. Batzer, Darold P. II. Sharitz, Rebecca R.
   QH541.5.M3E266 2006
   577.68—dc22

                                   2006018049

Manufactured in the United States of America
10   09   08   07   06
10   9   8   7   6   5   4   3   2   1

The paper used in this publication meets the minimum requirements of ANSI/NISO Z39.48-1992 (R 1997) *(Permanence of Paper)*. ∞

Cover photograph: Waterfowl at the Modoc Wildlife Refuge. Photo by Frank Balthis.

This book is dedicated to the memories of
Robert G. Wetzel and Harold O. Batzer

CONTENTS

LIST OF CONTRIBUTORS

DAROLD P. BATZER, Department of Entomology, University of Georgia, Athens, Georgia 30602

PAUL I. BOON, Sustainability Group, Victoria University (St. Albans campus), P.O. Box 14428, Melbourne City Mail Centre, Victoria 8001, Australia

MARK M. BRINSON, Biology Department, Howell Science Complex, N-108, East Carolina University, Greenville, North Carolina 27858

ROBERT COOPER, Warnell School of Forest Resources, University of Georgia, Athens, Georgia 30602

C. RHETT JACKSON, Warnell School of Forest Resources, University of Georgia, Athens, Georgia 30602

WOLFGANG J. JUNK, Max-Planck-Institute for Limnology, Working Group Tropical Ecology, 24306 Plön, Postbox 165, Germany

RANDY K. KOLKA, USDA Forest Service–North Central Research Station, 1831 Hwy. 169 E., Grand Rapids, Minnesota 55744

IRVING A. MENDELSSOHN, Wetland Biogeochemistry Institute and Department of Oceanography and Coastal Sciences, School of the Coast and Environment, Louisiana State University, Baton Rouge, Louisiana 70803

STEVEN C. PENNINGS, Department of Biology and Biochemistry, University of Houston, Houston, Texas 77204

BRUCE A. PRUITT, Nutter & Associates Inc., 1073 S. Milledge Avenue, Athens, Georgia 30605

REBECCA R. SHARITZ, University of Georgia, Savannah River Ecology Laboratory, P.O. Drawer E, Aiken, South Carolina 29802

D. ERIC SOMERVILLE, Nutter & Associates Inc., 1073 S. Milledge Avenue, Athens, Georgia 30605

JAMES A. THOMPSON, West Virginia University, Division of Plant and Soil Sciences, 1090 Agricultural Sciences Building, P.O. Box 6108, Morgantown, West Virginia 26506

KARL MATTHIAS WANTZEN, Institute of Limnology, University of Konstanz, 78457 Konstanz, Postbox M659, Germany

ROBERT G. WETZEL, William R. Kenan Distinguished Professor, Department of Environmental Sciences and Engineering, The University of North Carolina, Chapel Hill, North Carolina 27599 (to communicate about Chapter 8, contact D. Batzer).

SCOTT A. WISSINGER, Department of Biology, Allegheny College, Meadville, Pennsylvania 16335

JOY B. ZEDLER, Botany Department and Arboretum, University of Wisconsin, Madison, Wisconsin 57306

PREFACE

Wetland ecology as an organized field has a relatively recent history. With college courses on wetland ecology proliferating, creating a textbook for students was an unfilled need and became the primary objective for this book. Initial chapters address the physical wetland environment. Chapters 2 and 3 cover geomorphology, biogeochemistry, soils, and hydrology in wetlands. Chapter 4 addresses how hydrology and chemistry constrain wetland plants and animals and the strategies employed by biota to cope with stress. Middle chapters focus on the ecology of key organisms. Chapter 5 covers microbial ecology, especially how most chemical cycles in wetlands are mediated by bacteria. Plants are the most important organisms in wetlands, and Chapter 6 covers plant ecology, presenting perhaps the most complete discussion in this book of how wetlands function biotically. Chapter 7 describes animal roles in the community and ecosystem ecology of wetlands. Chapter 8 covers ecosystem ecology, describing how biofilms growing on plant and sediment substrata hold a focal position in wetland ecosystem dynamics. Final chapters focus on applied ecology. Chapter 9 addresses wetland regulation and assessment using the framework developed in the United States. Chapter 10 covers wetland restoration, emphasizing how ecological theory should be incorporated into the restoration process. Chapter 11 describes how flood pulses control the ecology of most wetland complexes (river floodplains, tidal marshes) and how human regulation of flood pulses threatens wetland biotic integrity. Chapter 12 further develops threats to wetlands and addresses the danger to wetlands of a changing global climate.

1

ECOLOGY OF FRESHWATER AND ESTUARINE WETLANDS
An Introduction

Darold P. Batzer and Rebecca R. Sharitz

WHAT IS A WETLAND?

The study of wetland ecology can entail an issue that rarely needs consideration by terrestrial or aquatic ecologists, and that is the need to define the habitat. What exactly constitutes a wetland may not always be clear. Thus, it seems appropriate to begin by defining the word *wetland*. The Oxford English Dictionary says, "Wetland (F. wet a. + land n.)—an area of land that is usually saturated with water, often a marsh or swamp." While covering the basic pairing of the words *wet* and *land*, this definition is rather ambiguous. Does "usually saturated" mean at least half of the time? That would omit many seasonally flooded habitats that most would consider wetlands. Under this definition, it also seems that lakes or rivers could be considered wetlands. A more refined definition is clearly needed for wetland science or policy.

Because defining *wetland* is especially important in terms of policy, it is not surprising that governmental agencies began to develop the first comprehensive definitions (see Chapter 9). One influential definition was derived for the U. S. Fish and Wildlife Service (USFWS) (Cowardin et al. 1979):

Wetlands are lands transitional between terrestrial and aquatic systems where the water table is usually at or near the surface or the land is covered by shallow water. Wetlands must have one or more of the following three attributes: (1) at least periodically, the land supports predominately hydrophytes; (2) the substrate is predominantly undrained hydric soil; and (3) the substrate is nonsoil and is saturated with water or covered by shallow water at some time during the growing season of each year.

FIGURE 1.1

Although the residents of this house might beg to differ, this area would not be a jurisdictional wetland in the United States because hydric soils and wetland vegetation are lacking. Photo courtesy of the Kentucky Division of Water.

This USFWS definition emphasizes the importance of hydrology, soils, and vegetation, which you will see is a recurring theme in wetland definitions. The U. S. Army Corps of Engineers (USACE), the primary permitting agency for wetlands of the United States, adopted a slightly different wording:

> The term "wetlands" means those areas that are inundated or saturated by surface or ground water at a frequency and duration sufficient to support, and that under normal circumstances do support, a prevalence of vegetation typically adapted for life in saturated soil conditions. Wetlands generally include swamps, marshes, bogs, and similar areas.

This definition also incorporates hydrology, soils, and vegetation but is more restrictive than the USFWS definition. The USACE definition requires all three features to be present, while the USFWS Cowardin definition indicates that only one of the three conditions needs to occur. Despite its exclusive nature, the USACE definition has been adopted as the authority to define legal (or jurisdictional) wetlands of the United States.

However, as ecologists, we must realize that legal definitions may not cover all habitats that function ecologically as wetlands. For example, mud flats devoid of vegetation, floodplains that primarily flood in winter outside the "growing season," and flooded areas of floodplains where anoxic soil conditions do not develop (Figure 1.1) are all probably *ecological* wetlands but may not fit the legal definition. In Georgia, we have seen floodplains repeatedly covered by as much as 1 m of water, yet competent delineators following USACE criteria determined that these habitats did not meet the legal definition of a

TABLE 1.1. Estimated Relative Economic Values per Hectare of
Services Provided by the World's Ecosystems

Ecosystem Type	US$ ha^{-1}yr^{-1}
Estuaries	22,832
Swamps/floodplains	19,580
Coastal sea grass/algae beds	19,004
Tidal marsh/mangrove	9,990
Lakes/rivers	8,498
Coral reefs	6,075
Tropical forests	2,007
Coastal continental shelf	1,610
Temperate/boreal forests	302
Open oceans	252

NOTE: From Constanza et al. (1997).

wetland (B. Pruitt, personal conversation). However, the determination that these flood-plains were legally "terrestrial" did not affect the responses of soil-dwelling arthropods and herbaceous plants that were covered by the water nor the functioning of waterfowl or fish that were swimming and feeding in those habitats. While definitions serve a purpose, especially for regulation (see Chapter 9), ecologists should not be constrained by definition when studying wetlands. Nonetheless, for ecologists seeking a biologically useful definition for wetlands, we recommend the simple, straightforward, yet inclusive, definition put forward by Paul Keddy (2000):

A wetland is an ecosystem that arises when inundation by water produces soils dominated by anaerobic processes and forces the biota, particularly rooted plants, to exhibit adaptations to tolerate flooding.

WHY ARE WETLANDS IMPORTANT?

Wetlands comprise only about 6% of the earth's surface, but ecologically they are disproportionately important. For example, 25% of the plant species in Malaysia occur in only one wetland type, peat swamps (Anderson 1983), and almost 10% of the world's fish fauna occurs in the Amazon basin (Groombridge and Jenkins 1998). Because wetlands support both terrestrial and aquatic biota, they are unusually diverse (Gopal et al. 2000). Those taxa unique to wetlands will contribute significantly to the overall diversity of regions containing numerous wetlands. Besides supporting the plethora of plants and animals of interest to ecologists and nature enthusiasts, wetlands provide an assortment of ecosystem services of considerable value to all people.

FIGURE 1.2

Wetland occurrence (dark-shaded areas) in the state of Minnesota prior to European settlement (left map) and in the 1970s (right map). From Tiner (1984).

Constanza et al. (1997) estimated the economic values of services provided by the world's ecosystems and found that on a per-hectare basis, estuaries and freshwater floodplains/swamps were the world's two most valuable ecosystem types (Table 1.1). The values of these wetlands to people stem primarily from their roles in nutrient cycling, water supplies, disturbance (flood) regulation, and waste treatment. However, recreation, food production, and cultural (aesthetic, artistic, educational, spiritual, or scientific) values were also important (Constanza et al. 1997). Many of these services are accomplished by wetland biota (microbes, plants, animals). However, despite the value of wetlands, there is a long history of humans destroying or degrading the world's wetland resources.

WETLAND LOSS AND DEGRADATION

The emergence of the field of wetland ecology coincided with the realization in the latter decades of the twentieth century that wetland habitats were disappearing at an alarming rate. By the 1970s, it was estimated that almost half of the wetlands in the lower 48 states of the United States had been filled or drained (Tiner 1984). Productive farmland can be produced by draining wetlands, and hence agriculture was the primary historical threat to wetlands. For example, Figure 1.2 shows the original extent of wetlands (shaded dark) in the state of Minnesota prior to European settlement (early 1800s) and the extent in the latter 1900s. While considerable wetland acreage remains in the forested northeastern portions of Minnesota, most of the wetlands in the agricultural south and west were destroyed. A similar pattern of destruction developed throughout the world. However, more recently in the United States, urban and rural development have eclipsed agriculture as the major threats to wetlands (Dahl 2000).

One doesn't need to be an ecologist to recognize the negative impacts of complete wetland loss. However, recently, the more subtle threat of losing certain wetland functions is now being recognized, and assessing functional change requires the skills of trained ecologists. Concerns have developed about conversion of one wetland type to another. The latest survey of wetlands in the United States (Dahl 2000) indicates that many forested wetlands are being converted into scrub/shrub habitats, often from silvicultural practices. While it may be heartening to know that the wetlands have not been eliminated and that scrub/shrub wetlands are themselves valuable, the functional change associated with such conversion needs to be assessed. In wetland restoration (Chapter 10), we now recognize that not just acreage needs to be conserved or replaced but also important wetland functions. The common past practice of replacing lost wetlands, regardless of type, with small permanent ponds is being discouraged. Instead, mitigation plans that replace functions actually lost are now required.

WHAT THIS BOOK COVERS

Wetland ecology incorporates the interactions of biota (plants, animals, microbes) with the unique physical and chemical environment present in wetlands. Wetlands are foremost geologic features, and geomorphology coupled with climate forms the template on which wetland ecology occurs (Figure 1.3). Hydrology is the factor most influenced by geomorphology and climate, and hydrology is also the primary conduit for the control of the physico-chemical environment and the biotic interactions in wetlands. The contents of this book are organized in recognition of these facts.

The initial chapters address physical aspects of wetland environments. Chapters 2 and 3 present the basics of geomorphology, biogeochemistry, soils, and hydrology in wetlands. Readers will find these straightforward chapters to be a useful foundation to better interpret later chapters on ecology and policy, as the themes of geomorphology, biogeochemistry, and especially hydrology are repeatedly revisited. Chapter 4 addresses how abiotic factors, specifically hydrology and chemistry, constrain wetland plants and animals, and the chapter elaborates on the physiological and ecological strategies employed by biota to cope with those stresses.

The middle chapters of this book focus on the ecology and functioning of key organisms. The discussion of the physical aspects of wetland biogeochemistry in Chapters 2

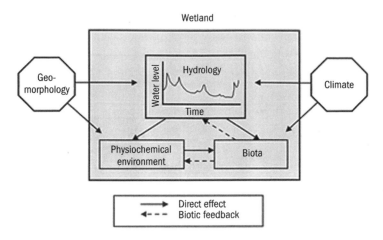

FIGURE 1.3

Schematic indicating the important factors influencing wetland biota. Modified from NRC (1995).

through 4 lead logically to the microbial themes presented in Chapter 5 because most chemical cycles in wetlands are mediated by microbes, especially bacteria. Plants are the most important organisms in wetlands and probably the best studied. Chapter 6 has the daunting task of covering plant ecology and presents perhaps the most complete discussion in this text of how wetlands function biotically. Chapter 7 presents animal ecology. While animals may be the most charismatic organisms in wetlands, most research has focused on individual taxa (population studies). Animal roles in the community and ecosystem ecology of wetlands are less well known, and Chapter 7 attempts to synthesize the available information on those themes. Chapter 8 focuses on ecosystem ecology, presenting the perhaps controversial notion that algal periphyton (biofilm that grows on plant and sediment substrata) holds a focal position in wetland ecosystem dynamics.

The final chapters focus on applied ecology. Chapter 9 addresses how wetlands are regulated and assessed, based on the regulatory framework developed in the United States. Chapter 10 examines wetland restoration, and given the ecological theme of this book, this chapter emphasizes how ecological theory can and should be incorporated into the restoration process. Chapter 11 addresses an important aspect of wetland conservation, describing how flood pulses control the ecology of most large wetland complexes (river floodplains, tidal marshes) and how human regulation of flood pulses is a primary threat to wetland biotic integrity. Chapter 12 further develops the theme of threats to wetlands. It addresses the greatest emerging danger to wetlands, a changing global climate, returning full circle to the original premise of this book that climate and geomorphology form the basis for all wetland functioning (Figure 1.3).

2

WETLAND GEOMORPHOLOGY, SOILS, AND FORMATIVE PROCESSES

Randy K. Kolka and James A. Thompson

The soil is where many of the hydrologic and biogeochemical processes that influence wetland function and ecology occur. A complete understanding of wetland formation, wetland ecology, and wetland management requires a basic understanding of soils, including soil properties, soil processes, and soil variability. In this chapter, we will discuss how soils and landscapes influence the local hydrologic cycle to lead to the development of wetland hydrology. We then will examine some fundamental soil properties and how they lead to and respond to the development of wetland hydrology. Finally, we will consider specific types of wetland ecosystems and discuss their general distribution, origin, hydrology, soil, and vegetation.

WETLAND GEOMORPHOLOGY AND WETLAND SOILS

Landscape geomorphology influences how water moves over or through the soil, and thus hillslope hydrology and local hydrologic budgets affect soil properties and determine the formation of wetland soils. Surface topography is a particularly important factor controlling surface and subsurface water flow and accumulation. While many landscapes are complex and irregular, there exist distinct and repeating patterns of hillslope elements, which occur in most geomorphic settings. A typical hillslope profile (Fig. 2.1) can be segmented into summit, shoulder, backslope, footslope, and toeslope landscape positions. The summit is the relatively flat area at the top of the slope. The shoulder is the steeply convex portion at the top of the slope. This surface shape favors the shedding of water and relatively drier soil conditions. The backslope is

7

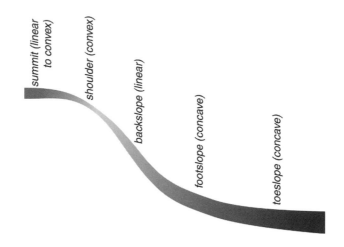

summit (linear to convex)

shoulder (convex)

backslope (linear)

footslope (concave)

toeslope (concave)

FIGURE 2.1

Typical hillslope cross section illustrating landscape positions of summit, shoulder, backslope, footslope, and toeslope.

a linear portion of the slope and is not present in all hillslopes. At the bottom of the slope are the more concave footslope and toeslope positions, with the footslope being more steeply sloping than the toeslope. On such a typical hillslope, the quantity of water stored in the soils increases with proximity to the base of the hillslope in response to the accumulation of surface and subsurface flow from upslope positions. The cross-slope geometry of the land also influences water redistribution and accumulation at the hillslope scale (Fig. 2.2). Concave contours promote convergent water flow, focusing surface and subsurface runoff to lower hillslope positions. Conversely, convex contours lead to divergent water flow. Across the landscape, we can identify various landforms that represent different combinations of profile and contour curvatures (Fig. 2.2), each of which affects the redistribution and storage of water. This, in turn, influences soil properties and wetland functions. Hillslope hydrologic processes and wetland water budgets are discussed in greater detail in Chapter 3.

SOIL PROPERTIES

Soils represent the zone of biogeochemical activity where plants, animals, and microorganisms interact with the hydrologic cycle and other elemental cycles. A typical soil contains both mineral and organic materials as well as the adjacent water-filled and air-filled pore space. The physical and chemical properties of a soil may influence the processes that lead to wetland formation and function. Furthermore, wetland formation and function may influence some of the physical and chemical properties of soils, especially soil color. Important soil physical properties include soil texture, soil structure, bulk density, porosity, and pore size distribution. These directly affect hydrologic conductivity and water storage and availability.

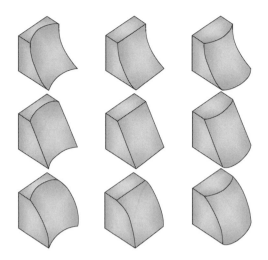

FIGURE 2.2
Diagrams illustrating concave, convex, linear, and combination contour curvatures typical of hillslopes.

Color is the most apparent soil morphological property, and it often indicates much about the composition and the hydrologic conditions of a soil. Soil scientists quantify soil color using the Munsell color system, which uses three quantities—hue, value, and chroma—to define a color. *Hue* refers to the spectral color: red (R), yellow (Y), green (G), blue (B), and purple (P) or neutral (N), which has no hue. These five principal hues (not including neutral), plus the intermediate hues, such as yellow-red (YR) or blue-green (BG), are used in the Munsell notation, with numbers placed before the hue letter(s) to designate four subdivisions within each of the ten major hues. A progression of Munsell hues from reds to yellows is: 5R, 7.5R, 10R, 2.5YR, 5YR, 7.5YR, 10YR, 2.5Y, 5Y. *Value* is a number between zero and ten that indicates the lightness or darkness of color relative to a neutral gray scale. A value of zero is pure black, and a value of ten is pure white. *Chroma* is a number that designates the purity or saturation of the color. A high chroma indicates a pure color, meaning that there is one clearly dominant hue. A low chroma indicates that the color is a mixture of more than one hue. This is often illustrated when a small child uses a set of watercolor paints and, invariably, does not rinse the brush when changing colors. The resulting dull, drab, and muted colors have low chroma. For soils, chroma can range from zero to about eight. The format for writing a Munsell color is "hue value/chroma"—such as 10YR 3/5.

Iron oxides and organic matter are the two primary coloring agents within most soils. Iron oxides give the soil a red, orange, or yellow color. Consequently, most soils are yellow-red in hue. Organic matter makes the soil brown or black, with a low value and low chroma. The majority of the soil, though, is made up of aluminosilicate minerals, which are white to gray in color. In the absence of iron oxides or organic matter, soil color is dull and grayish and has a low chroma. Such gray colors may be observed because iron oxides were never present in the soil, but more commonly, gray colors arise because iron oxides have been reduced, become soluble, and translocated within the soil, usually because of saturated and anaerobic conditions. Uniform low-chroma gray, or gley, colors are typical of prolonged saturated and anaerobic conditions in the soil. A mottled color pattern is often seen in soils that are wet for part of the year. The alternating patterns of red (high chroma) and gray (low chroma) colors indicate that some of the iron has been reduced or depleted (exposing the gray colors) and has been concentrated in the red patches.

The mineral fraction of a soil contains particles of various sizes. Clay particles are, by definition, those that are smaller than 0.002 mm in diameter. Silt particles are greater than 0.002 mm but less than 0.05 mm. The largest soil particles are sand particles, which are greater than 0.05 mm but less than 2.0 mm. Any particles greater than 2.0 mm are collectively termed *coarse fragments*. The most important aspect of soil particle size is the influence it has on surface area and pore size distribution. Clay particles have a high specific surface area, or surface area per gram of soil (up to 8,000,000 cm^2 g^{-1}), whereas the larger sand particles have a low specific surface area (<1000 cm^2 g^{-1}). Most of the soil biogeochemical reactions occur at these particle surfaces, so soils with greater clay content tend to be much more reactive.

The relative proportions of these three soil particle size separates determine the texture of a soil. For convenience, soil scientists have defined 12 different soil textural classes that cover various ranges in sand, silt, and clay content (Fig. 2.3). Soil texture influences almost every other property of a soil. Additionally, soil texture is a relatively stable soil property that does not readily change over time or in response to soil management. Soils within each textural class possess many similar characteristics and can be treated and managed in the same way.

In most soils, the individual sand, silt, and clay particles are aggregated together to form secondary soil particles, or peds. The peds give the soil stability, and the spaces between the peds form the large pores that promote faster water movement, greater gas exchange, and easier root penetration. The combination of texture and structure control the bulk density, porosity, and pore size distribution of a soil. The bulk density is the mass of soil per total volume of soil, and it is inversely related to the total porosity, which is the volume of pores per total volume of soil. In general, a sandy soil has a higher bulk density and a lower porosity than a clayey soil. However, the pores within a sandy soil tend to be larger, while the pores in a clayey soil are smaller. A soil with more well-developed structure has greater total porosity, lower bulk density, and more large pores.

This internal architecture of the soil influences the water relations of the soil. For example, soils with relatively high sand content (sands, loamy sands, sandy loams) tend to have rapid infiltration and percolation rates, good aeration, and low water storage capacity. This is primarily due to the high proportion of large pores and low surface area associated with the sandy soil (Fig. 2.4a). Conversely, finer-textured soils tend to have slow rates of infiltration and percolation and poor aeration, mainly because of the lack of large pores that readily transmit water (Fig. 2.4b). However, finer-textured soils that have well-developed structure, and therefore have more large pores as created by the voids between individual peds, may also have rapid infiltration and percolation rates and good aeration (Fig. 2.4c). Clayey soils have a high water storage capacity, but many of the small pores hold water too tightly to be readily available to plants.

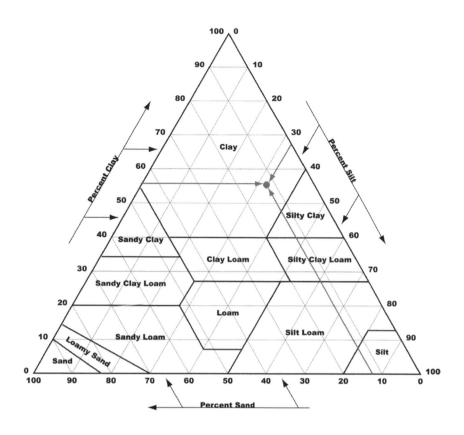

FIGURE 2.3
The soil textural triangle, illustrating the twelve soil textural classes.

The minerals that make up the clay particles in the soil—mostly secondary aluminosilicates, are also more chemically active than the predominant minerals of the silt and sand particles, which are mostly silica. Clay particles have a much higher cation exchange capacity, which gives clayey soils a greater ability to retain plant nutrients. The high surface area and cation exchange capacity of clay particles also promotes interactions between clay and organic matter particles, which fosters greater organic matter retention in finer-textured soils.

Along with soil texture, the other prominent property that greatly influences soil properties and processes is soil acidity, as quantified by pH. Soil acidity mainly influences the solubility of various elements in the soil, particularly plant nutrients. At low pH values (<5.8), the availability of certain plant nutrients, such as phosphorus, nitrogen, calcium, and magnesium may be limited. Microbial activity is also diminished when soil acidity is high. Conversely, aluminum and manganese availability is increased and may reach levels toxic to some plants. At high pH values (>7.5), the availability of phosphorus, iron, manganese, copper, and zinc is limited. The pH of a soil is controlled by the relative amounts of acidic (H^+ and Al^{3+}) versus nonacidic (Ca^{2+}, Mg^{2+}, K^+, Na^+) elements retained within the cation exchange capacity of a soil. If the soil parent materials are low in nonacidic cations,

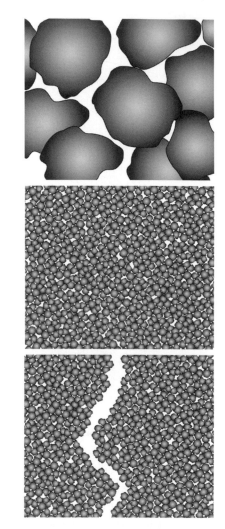

A

B

C

FIGURE 2.4
(A) Interparticle voids are relatively large between sand particles, creating numerous macropores. (B) These interparticle voids are much smaller between finer soil particles. (C) Structural development creates macropores between peds, which allows for greater water and air movement even in clayey soils.

the resulting soil will also be low in nonacidic cations. Rainfall and organic matter decomposition deposit acidic cations to the soil, while groundwater influx tends to be a source of nonacidic cations. Areas receiving groundwater discharge are often less acidic than areas that receive most of their water through precipitation. Leaching and plant uptake remove nonacidic cations and concentrate acidic cations within the cation exchange complex.

The soil property most commonly associated with wetland soils is increased organic matter content. The prolonged saturated and anaerobic conditions in wetland soils slow organic matter decomposition and lead to organic matter accumulation. Organic matter, specifically humus, in a mineral soil promotes aggregation and structural stability, lowers bulk density, increases porosity, and leads to higher infiltration and percolation rates. Organic matter also contains significant amounts of plant nutrients (in unavailable forms), which can be converted to available forms during organic matter decomposition. The complex humus molecules also add to the cation exchange capacity of the soil.

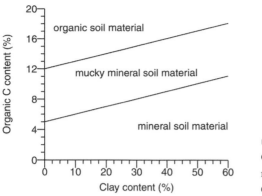

FIGURE 2.5

Organic soil materials are defined by the relationship between clay content and organic C content.

If the organic C content is greater than 12% to 18%, depending on the clay content (Fig. 2.5), the soil material is considered organic. Soils dominated by organic soil materials have a low bulk density, high porosity, and a high water holding capacity; however, water movement through organic soil materials is generally slow. While the nutrient content of the organic soil materials is high, much is not in available forms. The cation exchange capacity of organic soil materials is high, but the exchange complex is dominated by acidic cations, such that the pH of organic soil materials is generally low.

SOIL PROFILES

Soils properties differ with depth. Water movement over and through the soil (a) adds and removes materials, such as through erosion and deposition; (b) alters materials, such as through organic matter decomposition; and (c) redistributes materials within the profile, such as clay accumulation in the subsoil. These processes naturally lead to the development of layers within the soil. These layers are not depositional—they form in place as the soil develops from the parent material. The various soil horizons found with depth within a soil are approximately parallel to the soil surface. Each horizon will differ in its color, texture, structure, or other soil properties from the layers immediately below or above. These layers strongly affect the flow and distribution of soil water (Chapter 3) and the distribution of biological activity such as root growth; bacterial, fungal, and mycorrhizal growth (Chapter 5); and animal burrowing and feeding (Chapter 7).

Soil horizons are named in reference to their most important distinguishing characteristics. The master horizons, of which there are six, are designated by capital letters (Table 2.1). Lowercase letters sometimes follow the master horizon designations; these subordinate distinctions (Table 2.2) specify other important characteristics of the horizon. At the soil surface, many wetland soils have an O horizon composed of vegetative detritus (leaves, needles, twigs, etc.) in various states of decay along with living vegetative matter. Wetland soils in warm, humid climates with high biological activity will typically have thinner O horizons, while in cool and cold humid climates, the O horizons tend to be

TABLE 2.1   The Six Master Horizons and the Distinguishing Characteristics of Each

O	Layer dominated by *organic material*
A	*Mineral* layer formed at the surface (or below an O or another A horizon) characterized by *accumulation of humified organic matter;* or having properties resulting from cultivation or other agricultural activities
E	*Mineral* layer characterized by an *eluvial loss* of silicate clay, iron, and/or aluminum, leaving a concentration of sand- and silt-sized particles of quartz and/or other resistant minerals
B	*Mineral* layer dominated by one or more of the following: (a) *illuvial accumulation* of silicate clay, iron, aluminum, humus, carbonates, gypsum, and/or silica; (b) carbonate removal; (c) nonilluvial coatings or residual concentration of iron and/or aluminum sesquioxides; (d) structure development; (e) brittleness
C	*Mineral* layer that has been mostly *unaffected by pedogenic processes*
R	Hard *bedrock* layer

TABLE 2.2   Subordinate Soil Horizon Distinctions

a	Highly decomposed organic material (sapric)	n	Accumulation of sodium
b	Buried genetic horizons in a mineral soil	o	Residual accumulation of sesquioxides
c	Concretions or nodules	p	Plowing or similar disturbance
d	Physical root restriction (e.g., dense basal till, plow pans, and mechanically compacted zones)	q	Accumulation of secondary silica
e	Organic material of intermediate decomposition (hemic)	r	Weathered or soft bedrock
f	Frozen soil (permanent ice)	s	Illuvial accumulation of sesquioxides and organic matter
g	Strong gleying	ss	Presence of slickensides
h	Illuvial accumulation of organic matter	t	Accumulation of silicate clay
i	Slightly decomposed organic material (fibric)	v	Plinthite
j	Jarosite	w	Development of color or structure but with no illuvial accumulation
jj	Cryoterbation	x	Fragic or fragipan characteristics
k	Accumulation of pedogenic carbonates	y	Accumulation of gypsum
m	Continuous or nearly continuous cementation	z	Accumulation of salts more soluble than gypsum

thicker. The first mineral soil layer is the A horizon, which is often synonymous with the topsoil. A horizons can be of any texture but are usually loamy or sandy relative to subsoil materials. A horizons are characterized by darker colors (low value, low chroma) due to high organic matter content.

Depending on the characteristics of the parent material from which a soil profile was formed as well as other soil-forming factors, there may be one or more B horizons below the A horizon. The B horizons are the subsoil and are normally characterized by the accumulation of materials translocated from upper portions of the soil profile. Common B horizon types are those that feature high contents of clay (Bt), organic material (Bh), or iron (Bs) that have been removed from the A horizon through eluviation by infiltrating water and concentrated by illuviation in the B horizon. Weakly developed B horizons (Bw) and gleyed B horizons (Bg) are also common. Below the solum, or combined A and B horizons, is often found the C horizon(s), which are composed of less-weathered parent material. The physical, chemical, and mineralogical characteristics of the parent materials can have a profound effect on the properties of overlying soil horizons (Table 2.3). If consolidated bedrock is found within the soil profile, it is considered an R horizon. Between the A and B horizons, some soils feature a light-colored E horizon from which clay particles and organic matter have been eluviated.

Not every soil has all six master horizons. O horizons are not common, especially in disturbed or managed soils, such as agricultural land, where any horizons within the plow layer are mixed to form an Ap horizon. E horizons are found mainly in more highly weathered soils in warmer and moister climates. Young soils, typified by alluvial floodplain soils, or soils formed from parent materials highly resistant to weathering often lack a B horizon and feature an O or A horizon directly overlying C horizons.

Profile data from several seasonally saturated soils (Table 2.4) illustrate just a few of the variable horizon sequences that are commonly observed in and near wetland environments. Soils that experience prolonged saturation at or near the soil surface may develop thick O horizons, as is seen in the pocosin soil (Table 2.4). Below the highly decomposed (sapric) plant material (Oa horizons), there is little soil development in the mineral parent materials. These horizons are gleyed (Cg horizons) because of the near-continuous saturated and anaerobic conditions. Wet mineral soils in some environments, such as in poorly drained soils in drainageways (Table 2.4), show an accumulation in organic matter to greater depths, forming several black (low value, low chroma) A horizons, with gleyed (Bg) horizons below. Distinct redox concentrations throughout these horizons are further evidence of prolonged saturated and anaerobic conditions. Upland soils can also have water tables at or near the surface, especially if they occur in depressional landscape positions (Table 2.4). Impermeable subsoil horizons, such as the fragipan (Btx horizons), further contribute to the development of saturated and reducing conditions in such soils by promoting perched water tables. The Btg horizon immediately above the fragipan is evidence of the seasonally saturated conditions at a depth of 20 cm in this soil.

TABLE 2.3 Types of Soil Parent Materials, Their Characteristics, and Their Relationship to Soil Profile Properties

Soil Parent Material Type	General Description of Origin	Typical Geomorphic Position	Typical Soil Properties
Residuum	Weathered in place from underlying rock	Uplands—ridgetops and hillslopes	Highly variable; profiles typically include A, E, B, and C horizons
Colluvium	Weathered from chunks of upslope soil and bedrock carried by gravity; transport usually triggered by slope disturbance processes	Toes of hillslopes	Highly variable; profiles typically include A, E, B, and C horizons
Alluvium	Waterborne materials such as river sediment deposits	Floodplains	Sandy or silty; no B horizon
Lacustrine	Material formed by sediment deposition on lake bottoms	Current and former lake beds	Silty or clayey
Aeolian	Wind-deposited material	Downwind of current and former desert environments	Sandy or silty
Glacial till	Material overrun by a glacier	Anywhere affected by glaciation	Mixed sands, silts, and gravels; may be very dense with poor drainage
Glacial outwash	Material deposited by glacial meltwater	Broad glacial plains	Mixed sands and gravels; typically very porous; high conductivity
Marine	Material deposited by marine processes	Coastal plains	Mixed layers of sands and clays

The Btx horizons are not gleyed, but the macropores are lined with depleted (high value, low chroma) soil material.

SOIL PROCESSES

The shallow water tables and saturated soil conditions that are required for technical standards of wetland hydrology and hydric soil conditions initiate a series of biogeochemical

Horizon	Depth (cm)	Matrix Color	Redox Concentrations[a]	Redox Depletions[a]
Pocosin				
Oa1	0–5	7.5YR 3/2		
Oa2	5–60	7.5YR 3/1		
Oe	60–85	2.5YR 3/2		
Oa3	85–202	5YR 3/2		
A	202–228	5Y 3/1		
Cg1	228–237	5Y 3/1		
Cg2	237–240	5Y 4/1		
Drainageway				
Ap	0–20	10YR 2/1	c f 7.5YR 4/6	
A2	20–53	N 2/0	f f 7.5YR 4/6	
A3	53–64	10YR 2/1	f f 7.5YR 4/6	
Bg1	64–88	2.5Y 4/2	m f 7.5YR 4/6	
Bg2	88–102	2.5Y 6/2	m f 7.5YR 4/7	
Bg3	102–155	2.5Y 6/2	m c 7.5YR 4/6	c m 5BG 5/1
Upland depression				
A	0–8	10YR 3/1		
E	8–20	10YR 6/2		
Btg	20–46	10YR 6/2	c m 7.5YR 5/8	c m 10YR 4/1
Btx1	46–71	10YR 4/3	m m 7.5YR 5/6	m m 10YR 6/2
Btx2	71–117	7.5YR 4/4	m m 7.5YR 5/6	m m 10YR 6/1
R	117+			
Terrace				
A	0–9	10YR 3/1		
Bw	9–22	10YR 5/3	c m 5YR 4/6	
C1	22–59	2.5Y 6/4	c m 5YR 4/6	c m 2.5Y 7/2
C2	59–85	2.5Y 6/4	c m 5YR 4/6	c m 5Y 7/2
Cg1	85–179	2.5Y 7/2	c m 7.5YR 6/4	
Cg2	179–210	2.5Y 7/1	f f 7.5YR 6/4	

[a]First letter indicates abundance (f = few, c = common, m = many); second letter indicates size (f = fine, m = medium, c = coarse).

processes that create the special ecological environment of wetland systems and control the functions and values of wetlands. The biology of biogeochemical processes is primarily mediated by the microbial community, and that perspective is covered in detail in Chapter 5. Here, we focus on the geology and chemistry of biogeochemical reactions in wetland soils.

There is a general progression that occurs as a soil becomes saturated. As the water tables rise, air that is held in the soil pores is displaced by water (although a small fraction of pores retain entrapped air such that the degree of saturation never reaches 100%). The rate of oxygen diffusion into the soil is greatly diminished in a saturated soil. If temperature and bioavailable carbon are not limiting, microbes quickly deplete the oxygen that is trapped in the pores or dissolved in the soil solution of a saturated soil. Subsequently, the activity of facultative and obligate anaerobic microbes increases. These microbes function either as autotrophs, which may reduce Fe and Mn and employ the electron in ATP production; or as heterotrophs, which oxidize organic material and use Fe and Mn as electron acceptors during respiration.

Oxidation-Reduction Reactions

In theory, the utilization of available oxidants dictates preferential use of the species that provides the greatest amount of energy to the microbes. In the soil system, the order of electron acceptor preference is:

$$O_2 > NO_3^- > Mn(III \text{ or } IV) > Fe(III) > SO_4^{2-} > H^+$$

The half-reactions that represent the reduction of each of these species are used to calculate the electrode potential associated with each reaction (Table 2.5). For a hypothetical reduction half-reaction:

$$Ox + ne^- + mH^+ \leftrightarrow Red + {}^m/_2 H_2O$$

The electrode potential, *Eh,* is calculated as:

$$Eh = Eh°D\frac{RT}{nF} \times \ln \frac{(Red)}{(Ox) \, \xi \, (H^+)^m}$$

where Ox and Red are the oxidized and reduced species, respectively, $Eh°$ is the standard electrode potential, R is the gas constant, T is the absolute temperature, F is the Faraday constant, and values in parentheses are activities.

Redox potentials at which reduction of O_2, NO_3^-, Mn(III or IV), Fe(III), SO_4^{2-}, and H^+ occur in the soil are not as discrete as the calculated electrode potentials (Table 2.5), with significant overlap among the observed ranges. This occurs because of the nature of redox potential and its measurement: (a) the calculated electrode potential is an equilibrium potential, but the soil system does not reach oxidation-reduction equilibrium because of the constant additions and losses of oxidants and reductants within the system (Bohn et al. 1985); (b) the potential that is measured by the platinum electrode represents multiple oxidation-reduction reactions occurring in the soil at the electrode surface; and (c) each reaction is a function of concentration of reactants and activity of selective microbes that facilitate oxidation and reduction reactions around the electrode. Therefore, electrode potentials and redox potentials are not equivalent.

TABLE 2.5

TABLE 2.5   Order of Utilization of Electron Acceptors in Soils and Measured
Potential of These Reactions in Soils

Reaction	Electrode Potential, pH$_7$	Measured Redox Potential in Soils
	V	V
$\frac{1}{2} O_2 + 2e^- + 2H^+ \leftrightarrow H_2O$	0.82	0.6 to 0.4
$NO_3^- + 2e^- + 2H^+ \leftrightarrow NO_2^- + H_2O$	0.54	0.5 to 0.2
$MnO_2 + 2e^- + 4H^+ \leftrightarrow Mn^{2+} + 2H_2O$	0.4	0.4 to 0.2
$FeOOH + e^- + 3H^+ \leftrightarrow Fe^{2+} + 2H_2O$	0.17	0.3 to 0.1
$SO_4^{2-} + 6e^- + 9H^+ \leftrightarrow HS^- + 4H_2O$	-0.16	0 to -0.15
$H^+ + e^- \leftrightarrow \frac{1}{2} H_2$	-0.41	-0.15 to -0.22
$(CH_2O)_n \leftrightarrow {}^n/_2 CO_2 + {}^n/_2 CH_4$	—	-0.15 to -0.22

NOTE: After Bohn et al. (1985).

Certain microbes catalyze the reduction of Fe(III) and Mn(III or IV) oxides, hydroxides, and oxyhydroxides (collectively "oxides"). When these microbes, such as *Micrococcus lactilyticus* and *Thiobacillus thiooxidans* (Zajic 1969), contact Fe and Mn "oxides" on soil particle surfaces, they reduce the Fe(III) or Mn(III or IV) to Fe(II) and Mn(II). The more soluble Fe(II) and Mn(II) ions readily dissolve into the soil solution (Fischer 1988). Depending on hydraulic and chemical gradients in the soil solution, the Fe^{2+} or Mn^{2+} may: (a) remain in the vicinity of the original soil particle surface until oxidizing conditions return; (b) become adsorbed to the cation exchange sites in the soil; (c) be translocated locally until an oxidizing environment is encountered and is reprecipitated as an Fe or Mn "oxide" mineral; or (d) be leached from the soil system. Depending on the fate of the reduced Fe or Mn, various morphological features may develop, such as low-chroma mottles in a high-chroma matrix, high-chroma mottles in a low-chroma matrix, or a gleyed soil.

According to Ponnamperuma (1972), soil saturation and development of anoxic conditions causes (a) a decrease in redox potential; (b) neutralization of pH; (c) changes in specific conductance and ion strength; (d) changes in certain mineral equilibria; (e) ion exchange reactions; and (f) sorption and desorption of ions. In a mixed system, such as the soil, the dominant redox couple determines the redox potential (Ponnamperuma 1972). The order of oxidant utilization and associated potential of these reactions in soils (Table 2.5) indicates the redox potential that may be expected when that reaction is controlling the redox chemistry of a soil.

Redoximorphic Feature Formation
There are several theories explaining the formation of redoximorphic features under different hydrologic regimes (Veneman et al. 1976, Fanning and Fanning 1989, Vepraskas 1992). The location of saturated and aerated soil zones, and therefore the source of Fe(III)

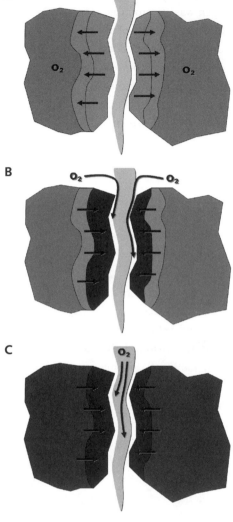

FIGURE 2.6

Models of redoximorphic feature formation.
(A) Within a saturated and reduced pore, an
adjacent soil is the site of Fe(III) reduction,
and an aerated and oxidized matrix is the site
of Fe(II) oxidation. (B) Saturated and reduced
matrix is the site of Fe(III) reduction, and an
aerated and oxidized pore is the site of Fe(II)
oxidation. (C) Saturated and reduced matrix is
the site of Fe(III) reduction, and an oxidized
rhizosphere is the site of Fe(II) oxidation. See
insert for color version.

reduction within the soil, relative to pores or the soil matrix distinguishes between the hypothesized mechanisms of redoximorphic feature formation. Models of redoximorphic feature formation can be divided into two basic categories (Fig. 2.6): (a) within a saturated and reduced pore, an adjacent soil is the site of Fe(III) reduction, and an aerated and oxidized matrix is the site of Fe(II) oxidation (Fig. 2.6a); or (b) a saturated and reduced matrix is the site of Fe(III) reduction, and an aerated and oxidized pore is the site of Fe(II) oxidation (Fig. 2.6b). Both of these types of redoximorphic features are readily observed in seasonally saturated soils (Table 2.4). The redox depletions in the third Bg horizon of the drainageway soil and the Btx horizons of the upland depression soil (Table 2.4) formed when the macropores between the peds were strongly reducing and Fe was translocated away from the pore (Fig. 2.6a). Most of the redox concentrations in the subsoil horizons of the drainageway, upland depression, and terrace soils (Table 2.4) were formed when oxygen was reintroduced via macropores and reduced Fe reoxidized along the pore (Fig. 2.6b). A special case of this second mechanism of redoximorphic feature formation is seen prominently in dark A horizon materials, such as the upper horizons of the drainageway soil (Table 2.4). Roots of some wetland plants transport O_2 down to the roots. This can create an oxidized rhizosphere in which reduced Fe from the surrounding saturated soil will oxidize and precipitate around the root (Fig. 2.6c). This is often the only type of redoximorphic feature seen in surface horizons of wetland soils with thick, dark A horizons.

Organic Matter Decomposition and Accumulation

Organic matter is an important component to all wetland systems because it is the energy source for the microbial activity that drives the development of anaerobic and reducing conditions. The subsequent soil biogeochemical processes often lead to the accumulation of greater amounts of soil organic matter that, along with the presence of Fe-based redoximorphic features, is the property most commonly associated with wetland soils.

Soil microorganisms (bacteria and fungi) play the most significant role in organic matter decomposition in soils. In well-drained, aerobic soils, the rate of organic matter decomposition is often much greater than the rate of organic matter deposition from above- and below-ground biomass (leaves, stems, roots, macroorganisms, microorganisms). As a result, the equilibrium level of soil organic matter can be quite low (e.g., <2%). However, under anaerobic conditions that develop in saturated wetland soils, the aerobic decomposers no longer function, and the facultative and obligate anaerobic microorganisms are left to decompose organic matter. These organisms do not derive as much energy when electron acceptors other then O_2 are used (Table 2.5), and organic matter decomposition can occur at a much slower rate in saturated and anaerobic soils (but see Chapter 5). Consequently, organic matter inputs can be much greater than outputs, and the equilibrium level of soil organic matter is higher in wetland soils (see pocosin and drainageway soils in Table 2.4).

DIFFERENTIATION OF WETLAND SOILS

While organic matter accumulation is typical of wetland soils, not all wetland soils have accumulated enough organic matter to have an organic soil horizon at the soil surface. The presence of an O horizon or black A horizon at the soil surface is commonly associated with wetland soils. Other morphological properties that develop in seasonally saturated soils include Mn concentrations, Fe concentrations, and Fe depletions.

Hydric soils, which along with hydrophytic vegetation and wetland hydrology are identifying characteristics of wetlands, are specifically defined as soils that formed under conditions of saturation, flooding, or ponding long enough during the growing season to develop anaerobic conditions in the upper part (Federal Register 1994). From this definition, the United States Department of Agriculture (USDA) Natural Resources Conservation Service

BOX 2.2 FIELD INDICATORS OF HYDRIC SOILS

NOTE: From *Federal Interogency Committee for Wetland Delineation* (1989).

1. Organic soils[a]

2. Histic epipedons[a]

3. Sulfidic material[b]

4. Aquic or peraquic moisture regime[a]

5. Direct observation of reducing soil conditions with α-α dipyridyl indicator solution

6. Gleyed, low-chroma, and low-chroma/mottled soils

    a. Gleyed soils

    b. Low-chroma soils and mottled soils

7. Iron and manganese concretions

[a]As defined in *Keys to Soil Taxonomy* (USDA 2003).
[b]As evidenced by hydrogen sulfide, or rotten egg odor.

(NRCS) developed a set of mandatory technical criteria for hydric soils (http://soils.usda.gov/use/hydric/criteria.html). These criteria (Box 2.1) serve mainly as a means to retrieve a list of likely hydric soils from a database of soil information; however, the criteria can also be used as indicators for identification of hydric soils in the field. Hydric soil lists are developed and updated using these criteria and can be used in conjunction with published soil survey reports to generate preliminary inventories of hydric soils in an area (http://soils.usda.gov/use/hydric/). It is important to note that on-site field verification of the presence of hydric soils is required because soil survey maps cannot represent all soils within an area, only soil bodies that are large enough to be delineated at the scale of the map (usually larger than 1.2 ha). Also, being placed on a hydric soil list does not guarantee that a soil is indeed hydric. It only indicates that the range in properties associated with a given soil in a map unit overlap with those of the technical criteria.

Most hydric soil determinations are based on field indicators. The 1987 Federal Manual for Delineating Wetlands lists a series of field indicators intended to be used as general guidelines for field identification of hydric soils (Box 2.2). More detailed and specific field indicators (NRCS 2002) have been developed for on-site identification and delineation of hydric soils. These indicators (Box 2.3) are observable soil morphological properties that form when the soil is saturated, flooded, or ponded long enough during the growing season to develop

BOX 2.3 FIELD INDICATORS OF HYDRIC SOILS IN THE UNITED STATES

NOTE: NRCS 2002.

ALL SOILS

A1 *Histosol or Histel[a]*—Soil classifies as a Histosol (except Folist) or as a Histel (except Folistel).

A2 *Histic Epipedon[a]*—Soil has a histic epipedon.

A3 *Black Histic*—Soil has a layer of peat, mucky peat, or muck 20 cm (8 in) or more thick starting within the upper 15 cm (6 in) of the soil surface having hue 10YR or yellower, value 3 or less, and chroma 1 or less.

A4 *Hydrogen Sulfide*—Soil has hydrogen sulfide odor within 30 cm (12 in) of the soil surface.

A5 *Stratified Layers*—Soil has several stratified layers starting within the upper 15 cm (6 in) of the soil surface. One or more of the layers has value 3 or less with chroma 1 or less, and/or it is muck, mucky peat, peat, or mucky modified mineral texture. The remaining layers have value 4 or more and chroma 2 or less.

A6 *Organic Bodies*—Soil has 2% or more organic bodies of muck or a mucky modified mineral texture, approximately 1 to 3 cm (0.5 to 1 in) in diameter, starting within 15 cm (6 in) of the soil surface.

A7 *5-cm Mucky Mineral*—Soil has a mucky modified mineral surface layer 5 cm (2 in) or more thick starting within 15 cm (6 in) of the soil surface.

A8 *Muck Presence*—Soil has a layer of muck that has a value 3 or less and chroma 1 or less within 15 cm (6 in) of the soil surface.

A9 *1-cm Muck*—Soil has a layer of muck 1 cm (0.5 in) or more thick with value 3 or less and chroma 1 or less starting within 15 cm (6 in) of the soil surface.

A10 *2-cm Muck*—Soil has a layer of muck 2 cm (0.75 in) or more thick with value 3 or less and chroma 1 or less starting within 15 cm (6 in) of the soil surface.

SANDY SOILS

S1 *Sandy Mucky Mineral*—Soil has a mucky modified sandy mineral layer 5 cm (2 in) or more thick starting within 15 cm (6 in) of the soil surface.

S2 *2.5-cm Mucky Peat or Peat*—Soil has a layer of mucky peat or peat 2.5 cm (1 in) or more thick with value 4 or less and chroma 3 or less starting within 15 cm (6 in) of the soil surface underlain by sandy soil material.

S3 *5-cm Mucky Peat or Peat*—Soil has a layer of mucky peat or peat 5 cm (2 in) or more thick with value 3 or less and chroma 2 or less starting within 15 cm (6 in) of the soil surface underlain by sandy soil material.

(continued)

BOX 2.3 (CONTINUED)

_____

S4 *Sandy Gleyed Matrix*[b]—Soil has a gleyed matrix that occupies 60% or more of a layer starting within 15 cm (6 in) of the soil surface.

S5 *Sandy Redox*—Soil has a layer starting within 15 cm (6 in) of the soil surface that is at least 10-cm (4 in) thick and has a matrix with 60% or more chroma 2 or less with 2% or more distinct or prominent redox concentrations as soft masses and/or pore linings.

S6 *Stripped Matrix*—Soil has a layer starting within 15 cm (6 in) of the soil surface in which iron/manganese oxides and/or organic matter have been stripped from the matrix, exposing the primary base color of soil materials. The stripped areas and translocated oxides and/or organic matter form a diffuse splotchy pattern of two or more colors. The stripped zones are 10% or more of the volume; they are rounded and approximately 1 to 3 cm (0.5 to 1 in) in diameter.

S7 *Dark Surface*—Soil has a layer 10 cm (4 in) or more thick starting within the upper 15 cm (6 in) of the soil surface with a matrix value 3 or less and chroma 1 or less. At least 70% of the visible soil particles must be covered, coated, or similarly masked with organic material. The matrix color of the layer immediately below the dark layer must have chroma 2 or less.

S8 *Polyvalue Below Surface*—Soil has a layer with value 3 or less and chroma 1 or less starting within 15 cm (6 in) of the soil surface underlain by a layer(s) where translocated organic matter unevenly covers the soil material, forming a diffuse splotchy pattern. At least 70% of the visible soil particles in the upper layer must be covered, coated, or masked with organic material. Immediately below this layer, the organic coating occupies 5% or more of the soil volume and has value 3 or less and chroma 1 or less. The remainder of the soil volume has value 4 or more and chroma 1 or less.

S9 *Thin Dark Surface*—Soil has a layer 5 cm (2 in) or more thick entirely within the upper 15 cm (6 in) of the surface, with value 3 or less and chroma 1 or less. At least 70% of the visible soil particles in this layer must be covered, coated, or masked with organic material. This layer is underlain by a layer(s) with value 4 or less and chroma 1 or less to a depth of 30 cm (12 in) or to the spodic horizon, whichever is less.

S10 *Alaska Gleyed*—Soil has a dominant hue N, 10Y, 5GY, 10GY, 5G, 10G, 5BG, 10BG, 5B, 10B, or 5PB, with value 4 or more in the matrix, within 30 cm (12 in) of the mineral surface, and underlain by hue 5Y or redder in the same type of parent material.

LOAMY AND CLAYEY SOILS

F1 *Loamy Mucky Mineral*—Soil has a mucky modified loamy or clayey mineral layer 10 cm (4 in) or more thick starting within 15 cm (6 in) of the soil surface.

(continued)

BOX 2.3 (CONTINUED)

F2 *Loamy Gleyed Matrix*[b]—Soil has a gleyed matrix that occupies 60% or more of a layer starting within 30 cm (12 in) of the soil surface.

F3 *Depleted Matrix*[c]—Soil has a layer with a depleted matrix that has 60% or more chroma 2 or less that has a minimum thickness of either (a) 5 cm (2 in), if 5 cm (2 in) is entirely within the upper 15 cm (6 in) of the soil, or (b) 15 cm (6 in) and starts within 25 cm (10 in) of the soil surface.

F4 *Depleted Below Dark Surface*—Soil has a layer with a depleted matrix that has 60% or more chroma 2 or less starting within 30 cm (12 in) of the soil surface that has a minimum thickness of either (a) 15 cm (6 in) or (b) 5 cm (2 in), if the 5 cm (2 in) consists of fragmental soil material such as gravel, cobbles, or stones. The layer(s) above the depleted matrix has value 3 or less and chroma 2 or less.

F5 *Thick Dark Surface*—Soil has a layer at least 15-cm (6 in) thick with a depleted matrix that has 60% or more chroma 2 or less (or a gleyed matrix) starting below 30 cm (12 in) of the surface. The layer(s) above the depleted or gleyed matrix has hue N and value 3 or less to a depth of 30 cm (12 in) and value 3 or less and chroma 1 or less in the remainder of the epipedon.

F6 *Redox Dark Surface*—Soil has a layer at least 10-cm (4 in) thick entirely within the upper 30 cm (12 in) of the mineral soil that has (a) a matrix value 3 or less and chroma 1 or less and 2% or more distinct or prominent redox concentrations as soft masses or pore linings, or (b) a matrix value 3 or less and chroma 2 or less and 5% or more distinct or prominent redox concentrations as soft masses or pore linings.

F7 *Depleted Dark Surface*—Soil has redox depletions, with value 5 or more and chroma 2 or less, in a layer at least 10-cm (4 in) thick entirely within the upper 30 cm (12 in) of the mineral soil that has (a) a matrix value 3 or less and chroma 1 or less and 10% or more redox depletions, or (b) a matrix value 3 or less and chroma 2 or less and 20% or more redox depletions.

F8 *Redox Depressions*—Soil is in closed depression subject to ponding, 5% or more distinct or prominent redox concentrations as soft masses or pore linings in a layer 5 cm (2 in) or more thick entirely within the upper 15 cm (6 in) of the soil surface.

F9 *Vernal Pools*—Soil is in closed depressions subject to ponding, presence of a depleted matrix in a layer 5-cm (2 in) thick entirely within the upper 15 cm (6 in) of the soil surface.

F10 *Marl*—Soil has a layer of marl that has a value 5 or more starting within 10 cm (4 in) of the soil surface.

F11 *Depleted Ochric*—Soil has a layer 10 cm (4 in) or more thick that has 60% or more of the matrix with value 4 or more and chroma 1 or less. The layer is entirely within the upper 25 cm (10 in) of the soil surface.

F12 *Iron/Manganese Masses*—Soil is on floodplains, with a layer 10 cm (4 in) or more thick with 40% or more chroma 2 or less, and 2% or more distinct or prominent

(continued)

BOX 2.3 (CONTINUED)

redox concentrations as soft iron/manganese masses and diffuse boundaries. The layer occurs entirely within 30 cm (12 in) of the soil surface. Iron/manganese masses have value 3 or less and chroma 3 or less; most commonly, they are black. The thickness requirement is waived if the layer is the mineral surface layer.

F13 *Umbric Surface*—Soil is in depressions and other concave landforms with a layer 25 cm (10 in) or more thick starting within 15 cm (6 in) of the soil surface in which the upper 15 cm (6 in) must have value 3 or less and chroma 1 or less, and the lower 10 cm (4 in) of the layer must have the same colors as above or any other color that has a chroma 2 or less.

F14 *Alaska Redox Gleyed*—Soil has a layer that has dominant matrix hue 5Y with chroma 3 or less, or hue N, 10Y, 5GY, 10GY, 5G, 10G, 5BG, 10BG, 5B, 10B, or 5PB, with 10% or more redox concentrations as pore linings with value and chroma 4 or more. The layer occurs within 30 cm (12 in) of the soil surface.

F15 *Alaska Gleyed Pores*—Soil has a presence of 10% hue N, 10Y, 5GY, 10GY, 5G, 10G, 5BG, 10BG, 5B, 10B, or 5PB with value 4 or more in the matrix or along channels containing dead roots or no roots within 30 cm (12 in) of the soil surface. The matrix has dominant chroma 2 or less.

F16 High Plains Depressions—Soil is in closed depressions subject to ponding, with a mineral soil that has chroma 1 or less to a depth of at least 35 cm (13.5 in) and a layer at least 10-cm (4 in) thick within the upper 35 cm (13.5 in) of the mineral soil that has either (a) 1% or more redox concentrations as nodules or concretions, or (b) redox concentrations as nodules or concretions with distinct or prominent corona.

[a]As defined in *Keys to Soil Taxonomy* (USDA 2003).

[b]Soils that have a gleyed matrix have the following combinations of hue, value, and chroma, and the soils are not glauconitic: (a) 10Y, 5GY, 10GY, 10G, 5BG, 10BG, 5B, 10B, or 5PB with value 4 or more and chroma 1; or (b) 5G with value 4 or more and chroma 1 or 2; or (c) N with value 4 or more; or (d) (for testing only) 5Y, value 4 or more, and chroma 1.

[c]The following combinations of value and chroma identify a depleted matrix: (a) a matrix value 5 or more and chroma 1 with or without redox concentrations as soft masses and/or pore linings; or (b) a matrix value 6 or more and chroma 2 or 1 with or without redox concentrations as soft masses and/or pore linings; or (c) a matrix value 4 or 5 and chroma 2 and has 2% or more distinct or prominent redox concentrations as soft masses and/or pore linings; or (d) a matrix value 4 and chroma 1 and has 2% or more distinct or prominent redox concentrations as soft masses and/or pore linings.

anaerobic conditions in the upper part. Some indicators can be applied to all soil types, while others can only be applied to sandy soils or only to loamy and clayey soils. The variety of soil morphologies by which hydric soil conditions can be expressed is evidenced by the length of this list of indicators. However, the indicators are regionally specific, so not all of these indicators are applicable in all places. Normally, within a region, there are a small number of indicators that can reasonably be expected to be used in most circumstances.

Use of the indicators is comparative. After exposing and describing a soil profile to a depth of at least 50 cm, the descriptions of the field indicators are then compared with the field description. For example, the thick organic layers of the pocosin soil (Table 2.4) more than adequately meets the requirements of indicator A1, which requires a minimum of 40 cm of organic soil material in the upper 80 cm of soil. A thinner (20–40 cm) accumulation of organic soil materials at the surface might meet the requirements of indicator A2 or A3. Even less organic soil material at the surface may express indicator A7, A8, A9, or A10. The drainageway soil (Table 2.4) also has an accumulation of organic matter but not organic soil materials. Below the thick, dark A horizons is a layer with a depleted matrix. For this loamy soil, indicator F6 applies. If the surface horizon were thinner, indicators F3 or F4 may have applied. If the surface horizon had hue N like the second A horizon, the requirements of indicator F5 would have been met.

For soils without organic soil materials or thick, dark surfaces, it is the subsoil color that most often is the reliable indicator of seasonally saturated and reducing conditions. Specifically, the presence of gleyed matrix colors or the presence of a depleted (high value, low chroma) matrix is often used to identify hydric soils. Depending on the exact Munsell value and chroma, the presence of redoximorphic features may be required along with a depleted matrix. For the upland depression soil (Table 2.4), the Btg horizon, which starts at a depth of 20 cm, has a depleted matrix and meets indicator F3. This horizon has redox concentrations, but the relatively high value means that they are not required to meet this indicator. Conversely, when examining the terrace soil (Table 2.4), the presence of redox concentrations starting at a depth of 9 cm is not enough to meet any hydric soil indicator. This soil does experience high water table conditions during the year, as evidenced by the high value and low-chroma colors deeper in the profile, but prolonged saturated and reducing conditions do not occur close enough to the surface to meet the definition of a hydric soil.

SPECIFIC WETLAND TYPES: FORMATIVE PROCESSES, GEOMORPHOLOGY, AND SOILS

Wetland types vary in their geomorphology, soils, and the processes that lead to their presence in the landscape. In the previous section, we discussed the fundamental properties and processes that lead to wetland soil development. In this section, we introduce the three basic geomorphical settings and the types of wetlands that exist in those settings, specifically in North America. Those three basic geomorphical settings are depressional wetlands, nondepressional wetlands, and estuarine systems (Fig. 2.7).

Wetlands resulting from depressions are the most common types of wetlands found in North America, from bogs in Alaska to cypress domes in Florida. Although depressional wetlands are found in the highest number, they do not represent the greatest area of wetlands (see the next section on nondepressional wetlands). Most depressional wetlands are relatively small, ranging in size from less than a hectare to perhaps as large as several hundred hectares but most being at the low end of this range. Depressional wetlands result from "filling in" or the process known as *terrestrialization,* whereby depressions that were once water bodies or low areas in the landscape have accumulated organic matter and filled the depression. Depressional wetlands may or may not have groundwater influences depending on their relationship with the regional groundwater table. Many types of depressional wetlands are associated with "perched" water table conditions whereby the water table is local in origin and is mainly fed by only precipitation and runoff (both surface and subsurface runoff). Perched water tables result from a hydrologically limiting layer present in the soil such as a highly decomposed organic horizon or a clay-enriched mineral soil horizon. Vegetation can vary from forested to marsh and soils can either be organic or inorganic depending on the climate and geomorphic setting in the landscape (Table 2.6).

Bogs

DISTRIBUTION AND ORIGIN.   *Bogs* are isolated depressional wetlands generally found in northern glaciated climates such as the Great Lakes area, Canada, and Alaska. The origin of bogs is related to glacial processes that have left depressions in the landscape. Many of the depressions left behind following glaciation are those from ice that broke off the receding glacier; the ice block was then covered with sediment; and ultimately it melted, creating the depression. These geomorphic features are known as *ice block depressions* and represent numerous wetlands in glaciated landscapes, although they do not represent the most wetland area (see fens in the nondepressional wetlands section). Other depressions include those created from the irregular deposition of glacial till and outwash creating both high and low spots in the landscape. Following glaciation, most of these systems were small open water bodies that began to fill in with vegetation. Because of the cool climate and low redox conditions that resulted from the ponded water, biomass production was greater than decomposition, and organic soils began to develop. Shallow areas filled in first, followed by the deeper areas. In some bog systems today, open water still is present, and the process of terrestrialization is continuing.

HYDROLOGY, SOILS, AND VEGETATION.   Bogs are the result of perched water table conditions and have no current connection with regional groundwater systems. Evidence suggests that initially some bog systems were connected to regional groundwater systems but through time and the accumulation of organic matter ultimately separated from the regional groundwater (Mitsch and Gosselink 2000). Because bogs are perched, precipitation and upland

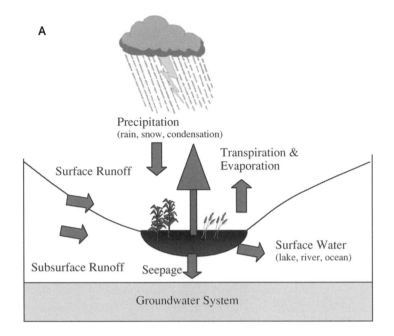

A

Precipitation
(rain, snow, condensation)

Transpiration &
Evaporation

Surface Runoff

Subsurface Runoff

Seepage

Surface Water
(lake, river, ocean)

Groundwater System

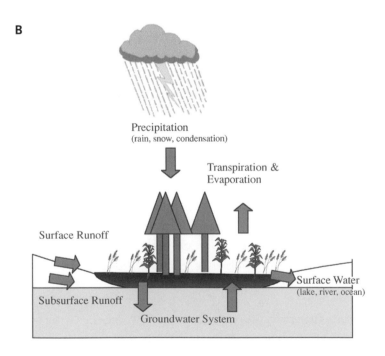

B

Precipitation
(rain, snow, condensation)

Transpiration &
Evaporation

Surface Runoff

Subsurface Runoff

Surface Water
(lake, river, ocean)

Groundwater System

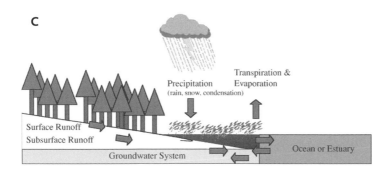

FIGURE 2.7

Typical wetland geomorphic positions including (A) depressional, (B) nondepressional, and (C) tidal or estuarine.

runoff are the main sources of water to these systems. Bogs are convex or slightly domed in the middle, leading to runoff from the center of the bog to the edge. Upland runoff also flows to the bog edge, creating a hydrologically active zone around the bog called the *lagg*. In the typical bog condition, the lagg surrounding a bog eventually coalesces at the downstream end of the wetland and is the headwater of a stream that exits the bog. Because of the influence of relatively low pH precipitation and the organic acids that result from decomposition in bogs, soil water and stream waters exiting bogs are low in pH (3.5–4.5), cations, and other nutrients while being high in dissolved organic carbon.

Bogs generally have deep organic soils with deposition as great as 10+ m and accumulation rates as high as 100+ cm per 1000 years (Glaser et al. 1997). In general, bog soil horizons tend to be more compacted and hydrologically limiting with depth because of the weight of overlying soil. Bog soils provide a history of the vegetation present over time. Because climates and water tables have been changing since the last glacial period, vegetation communities have also changed. Through the use of pollen analysis, partial decomposition of plant material, and carbon dating, past vegetation communities can be reconstructed (Klimanov and Sirin 1997). Bog vegetation can vary in stature with conditions from relatively open to forested. *Sphagnum* moss species dominate the ground vegetation in bogs with a few grasses, forbs, and woody shrubs also common. Forested bogs are also common with similar understory vegetation as that found in open bogs with black spruce *(Picea mariana)* and tamarack *(Larix laricina)* being common tree species. Because of the low pH and nutrient poor conditions present in bogs, only a small suite of plants can exist, and species richness tends to be low. Although species richness within a bog is low, they support many unique species, and thus bogs can significantly add to the overall richness across bog-dominated landscapes.

Prairie Potholes

DISTRIBUTION AND ORIGIN. *Prairie potholes* are isolated wetlands and lakes found in the northern Great Plains from southern Alberta and Saskatchewan across the eastern Dakotas

TABLE 2.6   Example Morphology, Color, pH, and Texture for Depressional Soils

Horizon	Depth (cm)	Matrix Color	pH	Texture
Northern bog				
Oi	0–15	5YR 4/4	Ext. Acid	O
Oa1	15–30	10YR 2/1	Ext. Acid	O
Oa2	30–115	5YR 2/2	Ext. Acid	O
Oa3	115–135	10YR 2/1	Ext. Acid	O
Oa4	135–150	5YR 2/2	Ext. Acid	O
Oe	150–200	5YR 3/3	Ext. Acid	O
Prairie pothole				
Ap	0–25	N 2/0	Neu.	SiCL
A1	25–55	N 2/0	Neu.	SiCL
A2	55–90	5Y 3/1	S. Alk.	SiCL
Cg	90–200	5Y 5/1	Mod. Alk.	SiCL
Carolina bay				
A	0–15	10YR 3/1	V.S. Acid	L
Btg	15–85	10YR 6/1	Str. Acid	C
BCg1	85–135	N 7/0	V.S. Acid	SCL
BCg2	135–180	N 7/0	V.S. Acid	SCL
C	180–200	N 7/0	V.S. Acid	SCL
Cypress dome				
Oa	0–30	N 2/0	Str. Acid	O
A	30–60	10YR 4/1	Neu.	S
Eg	60–110	10YR 4/2	Neu.	S
Btg/Eg	110–140	2.5Y 5/2	Mod. Alk.	SL
Btg	140–185	2.5Y 5/2	Mod. Alk.	SL
2C	185–200	10YR 7/2	Mod. Alk.	S
Seasonal wetland				
A	0–25	10YR 3/1	V.S. Acid	LS
Bg1	25–50	10YR 5/1	V.S. Acid	LS
Bg2	30–40	2.5Y 5/2	V.S. Acid	LS
2Bg3	40–65	2.5Y 5/2	V.S. Acid	SL
2C	65–200	7.5YR 4/4	Str. Acid	SL

NOTE: Soil pH categories include Ultra Acid (<3.5), Extremely (Ext.) Acid (3.5–4.4), Very Strongly (V.S.) Acid (4.5–5.0), Strongly (Str.) Acid (5.1–5.5), Moderately (Mod.) Acid (5.6–6.0), Slightly (S.) Acid (6.1–6.5), Neutral (Neu.) (6.6–7.3), Slightly Alkaline (S. Alk.) (7.4–7.8), Moderately Alkaline (Mod. Alk.) (7.9–8.4), Strongly Alkaline (Str. Alk) (8.5–9.0), and Very Strongly Alkaline (V.S. Alk.) (>9.0). Texture includes organic (O), sand or sandy (S), silt or silty (Si), clay or clayey (C), and loam or loamy (L).

and western Minnesota and Iowa. The origin of prairie potholes is similar to that of bogs where low spots and ice block depressions were left behind following glaciation. Also, like bogs, most of these systems were open water bodies that began to fill in with vegetation, but many still have open water. Because the climate in the northern Great Plains is dryer and more susceptible to extended periods of drought than regions where bogs are found further east, prairie potholes tend to be mineral soil wetlands. Organic matter accumulation in prairie potholes is not as great as in bogs, and soils tend to be enriched in organic matter but not meeting the definition of an organic soil.

HYDROLOGY, SOILS, AND VEGETATION. Unlike bogs, prairie potholes tend to be associated with groundwater and typically have no outlet or stream exiting the wetland. Prairie potholes are concave with most of the hydrologic output through evapotranspiration and/or recharge of the regional groundwater. In general, most wetlands, including prairie potholes, are water discharge areas instead of groundwater recharge areas. Groundwater recharge generally occurs in upland environments in most landscapes as well as in depressional wetlands such as prairie potholes when water tables are below the soil surface and upland runoff and direct precipitation are greater than what is being discharged from evapotranspiration demands. Prairie potholes have shown to be both groundwater recharge and discharge areas and in some cases can be both depending on the climate of a particular year or season (Winter and Rosenberry 1995).

The connection to groundwater and mineral soils that are commonly carbonate rich generally leads to the nutrient-rich, circum-neutral, and higher pH surface and soil waters in prairie potholes. Mineral soils present in prairie potholes have accumulated significant organic matter since glaciation and have deep dark horizons near the surface. Soil scientists in the United States call these soils *Mollisols*, or mineral soils that have accumulated significant organic matter in the upper horizons but do not meet the organic content (12–18%) and/or depth (40 cm) criteria for a Histosol.

As described by the name, prairie potholes have prairie vegetation, which commonly is suites of grasses and forbs that tend to get shorter in stature from east to west (i.e., tall grass prairie in the east and short grass prairie in the west) following the precipitation gradient that decreases from east to west.

Carolina Bays

DISTRIBUTION AND ORIGIN. *Carolina bays* are isolated, closed depressional wetlands found along the eastern U.S. Coastal Plain and Piedmont from Florida to Maryland but are concentrated in the Carolinas. The origin of Carolina bays is speculation because of the mature (old) landscapes (nonglaciated) where they are found. Theories range about the origin of the depressions, from meteor showers to sink holes. However the depressions formed, they are typically elliptical in shape with their long-axis oriented in a northwest to southeast direction. Some research suggests that their oval nature and orientation are the result of wind and wave action that has occurred during past wetter climates when they held open water (Sharitz and Gibbons 1982). Supporting evidence for the theory includes sandy ridges around the southeastern rims of Carolina bays that may be a result of previous beaches that formed during these wetter times. Associated with their uncertainty in origin is an uncertainty in age. Through various dating methods, Carolina bay age has been found to range from 250,000 ybp (year before present) to 10,000 ybp (Sharitz and Gibbons 1982).

HYDROLOGY, SOILS, AND VEGETATION.   Carolina bays are concave, closed systems that may or may not be connected to regional groundwater. Carolina bays that are connected to regional groundwater tend to have different hydrology, vegetation, and soil properties than those that are connected to perched water tables resulting from clay-enriched horizons present at depth in the soil profile (Sharitz 2003). Bays that are not connected to regional groundwater tables tend to have more variable hydrology with distinct drying and wetting cycles and less soil carbon accumulation, and are more likely to support forested communities. Carolina bays that are connected to groundwater tend to have more consistent water tables and more carbon accumulation, and support shorter stature vegetation communities. Soils can either be organic or mineral, with those bays connected to groundwater having a more likely chance of being organic. Mineral soils tend to be sandy in nature and are likely the result of surficial fluvial and marine deposits on stream terraces that occurred when ocean water levels were much lower than they are today.

Cypress Domes

DISTRIBUTION AND ORIGIN.   *Cypress domes* are found embedded in low spots of the pine flatwoods region of Florida and southern Georgia. The term *dome* in the context of cypress domes refers to the appearance of a dome when observed from afar because trees in the center of wetland are typically taller than those on the edge. The soil surface is not domed as in bogs. Although there has been some conjecture on the reason why productivity is greater in the center than at the edge, no conclusive research has explained the phenomena (Mitsch and Gosselink 2000).

HYDROLOGY, SOILS, AND VEGETATION.   Cypress domes are generally disconnected from regional groundwater with inputs mainly from precipitation and upland runoff. Typically, cypress domes are wettest during the summer growing season and driest during fall and spring, reflecting the precipitation patterns of the region. Although soils in cypress domes can range from sandy to clayey, typically a hydrologically limiting layer exists in the soil profile. Organic soils do accumulate in cypress domes and in some cases have the depth necessary to be considered a Histosol. As indicated by the wetland type, cypress domes are forested, typically with pondcypress *(Taxodium distichum* var. *nutans)*, black gum *(Nyssa sylvatica)*, slash pine *(Pinus elliottii)*, hardwood shrubs, and forbs.

Seasonal Wetlands

DISTRIBUTION AND ORIGIN. Seasonal wetlands include depressions that meet jurisdictional wetland requirements but do not easily fit within the description of depressional wetlands discussed previously. As suggested by the term, *seasonal wetlands* are depressions that are only wet during various times in the average climate year. Mitsch and Gosselink (2000) describe several types of depressional wetlands that are seasonal in nature, including vernal pools found in the western United States and Mexico and playas found in the south central United States. Other seasonal depressional wetlands exist from the Great Lakes to the northeastern United States (Palik et al. 2003). The origin of seasonal wetlands in glaciated areas is mainly the result of landscape variability associated with glacial deposition. The deposition of till and outwash following glaciation left a heterogeneous landscape with numerous low spots even in higher portions of the landscape. In nonglaciated regions, geology and depositional/erosional environments control where in the landscape seasonal wetlands occur.

HYDROLOGY, SOILS, AND VEGETATION. Generally, seasonal wetlands are small, concave, and found in various landscape positions and are likely to have perched water tables if high in the landscape and possibly groundwater connections, at least at times, if low in the landscape. Hydrologic outputs are through evapotranspiration and groundwater recharge during high runoff periods such as in the spring. Mineral soils are typically found in seasonal wetlands because water is not ponded long enough to lead to the redox conditions that are more typical in more saturated types of wetlands. Vegetation varies from forested to marsh depending on the periodicity of saturation, length of saturation, and climate of the area. Seasonal wetlands in the west tend to be dominated by marshes, while seasonal wetlands in the Great Lakes and eastern United States are more likely to have forested vegetation.

NONDEPRESSIONAL WETLANDS

Like depressional wetlands, nondepressional wetlands are common across North America. Nondepressional wetlands include those wetlands that occur on upland slopes, near to streams or lakes, or otherwise have connections to groundwater (Fig. 2.7). Nondepressional wetlands develop due to a number of factors including a close connection to the regional groundwater table, being near an open water body, or a hydrologically limiting layer present in the soil. Nondepressional wetlands can cover huge expanses of land, as found in northern Minnesota, Canada, and parts of Russia. Although depressional wetlands are the most numerous, nondepressional wetlands cover the most area. As in most wetland types, soils can vary from mineral to organic (Table 2.7).

Northern Fens

DISTRIBUTION AND ORIGIN. Northern fens occur across the glaciated region of the northern Great Lakes states, Canada, and Alaska. Commonly, fens occur where glaciation left behind large areas of flat land such as till plains that are connected to the regional

TABLE 2.7 Example Morphology, Color, pH, and Texture for Nondepressional Soils

Horizon	Depth (cm)	Matrix Color	pH	Texture
Northern fen				
Oa	0–15	5YR 2/1	Str. Acid	O
Oe1	15–180	5YR 2/2	Med. Acid	O
Oe2	180–200	5YR 3/3	Med. Acid	O
Southern marsh				
Oa	0–20	7.5YR 3/2	S. Acid	O
Oe1	20–70	5YR 3/2	S. Acid	O
Oe2	70–200	7.5YR 3/2	S. Acid	O
Pocosin				
Oi	0–10	N 2/0	Ext. Acid	O
Oa1	10–30	N 2/0	Ext. Acid	O
Oa2	30–140	5YR 2/2	Ext. Acid	O
Oa3	140–165	5YR 2/2	Ext. Acid	O
2Cg1	165–180	10YR 3/2	Ext. Acid	S
2Cg2	180–200	10YR 4/1	Ext. Acid	S
Riverine				
A	0–10	10YR 4/2	Str. Acid	SL
Bg1	10–25	10YR 6/2	V.S. Acid	S
2Cg1	25–75	10YR 5/1	V.S. Acid	L
2Cg2	75–105	10YR 5/1	V.S. Acid	SiL
3Cg	105–200	10YR 6/1	V.S. Acid	S
Freshwater				
shoreline wetlands				
Oa	0–10	N 2/0	Neu.	O
A	10–35	10YR 2/2	S. Alk.	LS
Cg1	35–95	10YR 6/1	S. Alk.	S
2Cg2	95–200	10YR 5/1	S. Alk.	SiL

NOTE: Soil pH categories include Ultra Acid (<3.5), Extremely (Ext.) Acid (3.5–4.4), Very Strongly (V.S.) Acid (4.5–5.0), Strongly (Str.) Acid (5.1–5.5), Moderately (Mod.) Acid (5.6–6.0), Slightly (S.) Acid (6.1–6.5), Neutral (Neu.) (6.6–7.3), Slightly Alkaline (S. Alk.) (7.4–7.8), Moderately Alkaline (Mod. Alk.) (7.9–8.4), Strongly Alkaline (Str. Alk) (8.5–9.0), and Very Strongly Alkaline (V.S. Alk.) (>9.0). Texture includes organic (O), sand or sandy (S), silt or silty (Si), clay or clayey (C), and loam or loamy (L).

groundwater system. In heterogeneous glaciated landscapes, both bogs and fens can be present and in many cases can both be part of the same wetland complex. As compared with bogs that generally develop through the terrestrialization process, fens develop through the process of "paludification," which occurs when microtopographic low areas of mineral soil or sediment become inundated, decomposition slows because of anaerobic conditions, and organic material begins to build. Over time, the low areas fill and connect with other low areas, and ultimately a blanket of peat forms over the entire area.

HYDROLOGY, SOILS, AND VEGETATION.   Northern fen hydrology is controlled by the flow of groundwater. Although precipitation and upland runoff contribute to fen inputs, groundwater is the dominant source of water to the system. Generally, groundwater in glaciated landscapes is relatively high in pH and nutrient rich because of its association with calcium carbonate–rich (calcareous) glacial deposits. Ecologists term these nutrient rich systems either as *rich* fens, or *minerotrophic* fens. However, some groundwater is associated with glacial deposits that are low in nutrients such as sandy outwash deposits and, hence, lead to lower pH, less-nutrient-rich fens with water chemistry and vegetation that can resemble bogs. Depending on the level of nutrients ecologist term these systems *intermediate, transitional, acidic,* or *poor* fens (Mitsch and Gosselink 2000). Organic soils in fens are typically shallower than those found in bogs but can be >5 m in depth. More typically, organic soil depths range from 50 cm to several meters. Vegetation communities will vary across the gradient of both nutrient and inundation conditions and can be open, low in stature to forested. Like bogs, many fens are dominated with *Sphagnum* species on the soil surface. In rich fens, open conditions will typically include various species of sedges, grasses, and forbs, while forested systems will typically include those species and tree species such as northern white cedar *(Thuja occidentalis),* tamarack, birch species (*Betula* spp.), and willow species (*Salix* spp.).

Southern Swamps and Marshes

DISTRIBUTION AND ORIGIN.   Across the southeastern United States are both large and small expanses of wetlands that are connected to regional groundwater systems and not necessarily riverine in nature. Both swamps (forested) and marshes (nonforested) exist across the region (Mitsch and Gosselink 2000). Probably the best known of these wetlands is the Florida Everglades. The swamps and marshes in the southeastern United States are found in low spots in the landscape or where water becomes ponded because of relatively impermeable soil or geologic layers.

HYDROLOGY, SOILS, AND VEGETATION.   Typically, more inundated conditions for longer periods lead to marsh vegetation, whereas water tables that dry down periodically lead to forested systems. Soils can range from organic to mineral. Wetlands with a greater degree and longer soil saturation tend to form organic soil layers, so peat soils will be found more commonly in marshes than in swamps. Vegetation in marshes is comprised of grasses, grass-like plants (e.g., sedges and rushes), and numerous forbs. Vegetation in swamps is similar to riverine wetlands found in the Southeast and include bald cypress *(Taxodium distichum),* black gum, green ash *(Fraxinus pennsylvanica),* and red maple *(Acer rubrum).*

Pocosins

DISTRIBUTION AND ORIGIN. *Pocosins* are freshwater wetlands found on the Atlantic Coastal Plain from Virginia to Florida, with the largest concentration occurring in North Carolina (Sharitz and Gibbons 1982). They have no characteristic shape and can range in size from less than a hectare to thousands of hectares. Pocosin origin is thought to have occurred following the last glaciation period 10,000 to 15,000 ybp. The ice sheet from the Wisconsinan glacial period led to falling ocean levels that subsequently led to increased downcutting of Coastal Plain streams. When the glacier receded, ocean water levels rose again, and streams were essentially blocked from flowing into the ocean. Stream flows were slowed, allowing for deposition of organic materials in the interstream areas. The blocking of the streams also led to shallow water tables across the Coastal Plain. The combination of shallow water tables, organic deposition, and the process of paludification led to the development of pocosins in the interstream areas of the Coastal Plain.

HYDROLOGY, SOILS, AND VEGETATION. Much like northern bogs, pocosins are typically raised in the middle and are perched from the regional groundwater. Initial development was a direct result of groundwater interaction, but since the last glacial period, peat has accumulated to the point where the peatland has separated from the regional groundwater. Perched water moves slowly out of the raised peatlands to surrounding areas, including, in some cases, being the headwaters of streams. Soils tend to be organic, and peat can be up to several meters deep. Mineral subsoils tend to be layered marine sediment ranging from clays to sands. Vegetation communities typically include broadleaf evergreen shrubs and pond pine *(Pinus serotina)*.

Atlantic White Cedar Swamps

DISTRIBUTION AND ORIGIN. Atlantic white cedar swamps exist near the Atlantic Coast from southern Maine to the Gulf Coast, with the greatest concentration existing in New Jersey, North Carolina, and Florida. Their origin is related to the hydrology associated with the growth of Atlantic white cedar. In the typical glaciated case, Atlantic white cedar swamps are really fens with Atlantic white cedar present *(Chamaecyparis thyoides)*. Outside the glaciated region, Atlantic white cedar can be found from peatland to mineral soil environments including stream floodplains.

HYDROLOGY, SOILS, AND VEGETATION. Atlantic white cedar swamps have moderate hydrology. They are not as saturated as marsh systems but are somewhat wetter than swamps (such as red maple swamps in the Northeast) (Mitsch and Gosselink 2000). Atlantic white cedar swamps are seasonably flooded, with some of that flooding occurring during the growing season. Atlantic white cedar swamps generally occur on peat soils but also exist where groundwater intersects mineral soils. As suggested by its name, Atlantic white cedar is a dominant tree species, but commonly, others such as red maple, gray birch *(Betula populifolia*), black spruce, and eastern hemlock *(Tsuga canadensis)* in the North and bald cypress and redbay *(Persea borbonia)* in the South also occur.

Riverine Wetlands

DISTRIBUTION AND ORIGIN. Riverine wetlands occur across North America wherever there are wetlands associated with streams. Others term these types of wetlands as *riparian wetlands* or *floodplain wetlands,* but not all riparian areas or floodplains are wetlands, and not all riparian areas are associated with streams and rivers; lakes, for example, also have riparian areas. Riverine wetlands can be tens of kilometers wide on major river systems but more typically are found in a narrow zone next to the stream. As stream size increases and stream slope decreases, the potential for wetland occurrence increases because water movement is slowed, both in the stream and from the surrounding landscape. Generally, the wetland position in the landscape is controlled by the surficial geology that affects the channel forming fluvial processes that govern where wet soil conditions can persist.

HYDROLOGY, SOILS, AND VEGETATION. Typically, streams are connected to the regional groundwater system, and wetlands next to the stream have water inputs from groundwater, precipitation, and upland runoff. In addition, wetlands near streams may also receive water inputs from overbank flows when stream flooding occurs. Soils range from organic to mineral, but usually, because of only periodic inundation, soils are mineral with relatively high concentrations of organic matter. Soils are also typically coarse textured because of the influence of fluvial processes that leads to the removal of fine-textured particle sizes as streams shift in their floodplains. Vegetation varies tremendously depending on the climate, the connectivity to groundwater, the chemistry of the receiving groundwater, and disturbance history of the watershed. Some of the more commonly known riverine wetland ecosystems are the cypress-tupelo swamps and bottomland hardwood systems in the southeastern United States, red maple swamps in the northeastern United States, northern white cedar and green ash swamps in the Great Lakes states, cottonwood *(Populus deltoides)* dominated wetlands near streams in the midwestern United States, and salt cedar *(Tamarix gallica)* wetland areas in the Southwest.

Freshwater Shoreline Wetlands

DISTRIBUTION AND ORIGIN. Typically, we think of shoreline wetlands associated with lakes in the glaciated region of North America; however, shoreline wetlands also exist around impoundments and reservoirs across the continent. In glaciated regions, lake distribution is related to glacial features such as heterogeneous deposition, ice block depressions, and moraine features that impounded water following glacial recession. Lakes can be either isolated, closed depressions like some wetland types, or a source of water for streams like other wetland types. Lakes in closed systems are referred to as *seepage lakes,* while those that are sources of surface water are termed *drainage lakes.*

HYDROLOGY, SOILS, AND VEGETATION.   Wetlands associated with seepage and drainage lakes can be either sources or sinks for lake water, but typically, wetlands associated with seepage lakes are sinks for lake water, whereas wetlands associated with drainage lakes are sources of water to the lake. Wetlands associated with seepage lakes are typically driven by lake water "seeping" into the surrounding terrestrial landscape. Upland runoff and precipitation also contribute to seepage lake wetlands, but generally, wetland water levels are controlled by lake water levels. Drainage lake wetlands typically are areas where significant upland runoff and/or groundwater contributes to the lake and hydrologic gradients exist from the wetland to the lake. Freshwater shoreline wetland soils can be either mineral or organic depending on the period of inundation, with longer inundation periods leading to the more likely occurrence of organic soils. Vegetation also is variable depending on the hydrology, with less inundated conditions generally leading to forested wetlands and more inundated conditions leading to marsh systems.

ESTUARINE SYSTEMS

DISTRIBUTION AND ORIGIN.   Estuarine wetlands are distinguished from other types of wetlands because of the influence of oceanic tides on the hydrology of the wetlands. In North America, estuarine wetlands are found at the terrestrial edge of coasts of the Atlantic and Pacific oceans, and the Gulf of Mexico. Estuarine wetlands result from the periodic inundation of salt water as the tides rise and fall.

HYDROLOGY, SOILS, AND VEGETATION.   Estuarine wetlands have hydrologic inputs from direct precipitation, subsurface runoff from associated uplands, and groundwater, and some marshes have surface runoff inputs from freshwater streams draining to the ocean (Fig. 2.7); however, the largest influence on hydrology is the daily tidal input. Three geomorphic settings describe the typical estuarine wetland (Rabenhorst 2001). *Estuarine marshes* are formed in mineral alluvial sediment deposited by freshwater streams entering estuaries, a typical delta situation. Soils are typically silty to clayey in nature but may contain lenses of organic soils if there are prolonged periods where mineral deposition does not occur (Table 2.8). *Submerging coastal marshes* are found behind barrier islands in a lagoon setting and form in both organic and mineral sediment. Soils can be either organic or mineral, and both can be present in close proximity. Also, soils will typically be layered because of sediment deposition during significant weather events such as hurricanes (Table 2.8). *Submerged upland marshes* are found along all coasts and are the result of rising water levels over the past several thousand years. Marsh soils have formed over underlying terrestrial soils (Table 2.8). As a result of

TABLE 2.8   Example Morphology, Color, pH, and Texture for Estuarine Soils

Horizon	Depth (cm)	Matrix Color	pH	Texture
Estuarine marsh				
Ag	0–35	5Y 3/2	Neu.	SiL
Cg1	25–75	5Y 4/1	Neu.	SiL
Cg2	75–200	5Y 4/2	Neu.	SiCL
Submerging coastal marsh				
Oe	0–30	10YR 3/1	S. Acid	O
Cg1	30–55	10YR 5/1	Neu.	S
Cg2	55–200	2.5Y 5/1	Neu.	S
Submerged upland marsh				
Oi	0–15	10YR 4/2	Neu.	O
Oe	15–30	10YR 3/3	Neu.	O
Oa	30–55	10YR 2/1	Neu.	O
Ag	55–60	5Y 2/1	Neu.	SiL
Eg	60–90	10YR 5/1	Neu.	SiL
Btg1	60–120	5Y 4/1	Neu.	SiCL
Btg2	120–200	10YR 5/1	Neu.	SiCL

NOTE: Soil pH categories include Ultra Acid (<3.5), Extremely (Ext.) Acid (3.5–4.4), Very Strongly (V.S.) Acid (4.5–5.0), Strongly (Str.) Acid (5.1–5.5), Moderately (Mod.) Acid (5.6–6.0), Slightly (S.) Acid (6.1–6.5), Neutral (Neu.) (6.6–7.3), Slightly Alkaline (S. Alk.) (7.4–7.8), Moderately Alkaline (Mod. Alk.) (7.9–8.4), Strongly Alkaline (Str. Alk) (8.5–9.0), and Very Strongly Alkaline (V.S. Alk.) (>9.0). Texture includes organic (O), sand or sandy (S), silt or silty (Si), clay or clayey (C), and loam or loamy (L).

greater inundation from rising sea levels, organic soils have typically developed with organic soil depth greatest at the seawater interface with a narrowing toward the upland interface (Rabenhorst 2001). All three wetland types are marshes consisting of salt tolerant grass or grass-like vegetation (e.g., sedges and rushes). Along the Gulf Coast, mangroves are also an important vegetation component of some marshes. Marsh vegetation is an important contributor of organic matter to the soils and slows the velocity of receding tides, allowing for mineral and organic deposition originating from outside the marsh.

CONCLUSIONS

In the first part of the chapter, we introduced the geomorphic conditions and soil processes that lead to the development of wetland soils. *Wetlands,* as suggested by the term, are wet. Soils that are permanently or periodically saturated with water develop differently than upland soils because of the biogeochemical reactions and microbial interactions in low oxygen conditions.

Although there are numerous exceptions, wetlands are commonly found in lower parts of the landscape where water is focused as a result of geomorphic processes. Alternatively, water can be perched higher up in the landscape as a result of impermeable soil layers being present. Typically, groundwater is very different chemically than water derived from surface or subsurface runoff. A connection to regional groundwater can influence both the vegetation communities and the biogeochemical processes occurring in wetlands. Groundwater-influenced wetlands also tend to have more consistent hydrology than those fed by only precipitation and runoff.

In the second part of the chapter, we introduced three groups of wetlands based on their geomorphology. Depressional wetlands develop in dips or holes in landscape where water is either focused or groundwater connections exists. Terrestrialization, or filling in of water bodies with organic material is an important process in depressional wetland development. Examples of depressional wetlands include bogs, prairie potholes, Carolina bays, cypress domes, and seasonal wetlands. Nondepressional wetlands occur as a result of numerous geomorphic and hydrologic conditions ranging from river flooding to groundwater influences. In some cases such as northern fens and pocosins, paludification—or blanketing an entire area with organic material—is an important wetland process. Other nondepressional wetlands include southern swamps and marshes, Atlantic white cedar swamps, riverine wetlands, and freshwater shoreline wetlands. Finally, we discussed three geomorphic types of estuarine wetlands or wetlands that are influenced by ocean tides. Estuarine marshes develop on alluvial sediment deposits of streams entering the ocean. Submerging coastal marshes are found in lagoon settings behind barrier islands. Submerged upland marshes occur where coastal marshes are creeping farther inland as a result of rising ocean levels.

It is important to realize that these broad groups of wetlands we have presented do not encompass all wetlands on the planet or even in North America. However, understanding the soil, geomorphic and hydrologic processes that lead to the development of the wetlands presented in this chapter should lead to an understanding of wetland development anywhere.

3

WETLAND HYDROLOGY

C. Rhett Jackson

The commonly used phrase "wetland hydrology" should be considered shorthand for "hydrology, as it relates to wetlands," as there is no special subdiscipline of hydrology for wetlands. The principles and processes of hydrology can be applied to uplands, wetlands, streams, lakes, and groundwater. This chapter presents basic principles of hydrology that can applied to understand and explain annual, seasonal, and daily water level dynamics (the hydropattern or hydroperiod) of wetlands and to illuminate physical and chemical water quality processes occurring in wetlands. The text assumes the reader has only a cursory knowledge of hydrology.

The hydroperiod of a wetland is one of the dominant controls on wetland plant and animal communities as well as on primary productivity and decomposition. *Hydroperiod* is a statistically ill-defined term that refers to the general seasonal pattern of surface inundation depth. Nuttle (1997) says "the pattern of water-level fluctuations in a wetland is its hydroperiod," and this simple definition could also be an argument for the term *hydropattern*. Recently, several researchers, mostly working on Everglades restoration, have suggested that hydropattern would be a better term for the overall water level time series of a wetland and that hydroperiod should refer only to the dates and duration of surface inundation (e.g., Acosta and Perry 2001, 2002; King et al. 2004). While hydroperiod, used in its broadest sense, is still the dominant term in wetland literature, this chapter will use hydropattern from this point forward. Classification or description of wetlands by hydropattern has become a common framework from which to explore and explain wetland ecology.

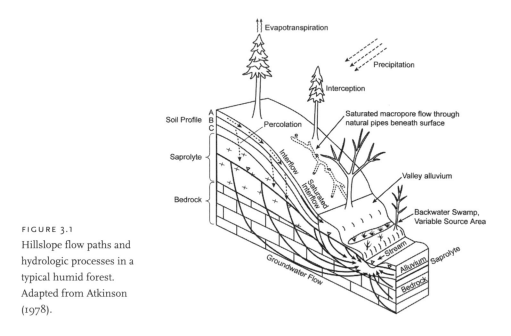

FIGURE 3.1
Hillslope flow paths and
hydrologic processes in a
typical humid forest.
Adapted from Atkinson
(1978).

HILLSLOPE HYDROLOGIC PROCESSES

Hillslope hydrology is a subbranch of hydrology devoted to describing and explaining how water moves through the terrestrial landscape into surface waters. The effects of land management activities, such as cropping, silviculture, forest conversion (clearing and stump removal), and development, on downstream surface waters are best understood through the prism of hillslope hydrology. Furthermore, a wetland's water budget and its resulting hydroperiod are best understood by framing a wetland with respect to the dominant hydrologic processes in the contributing watershed. Hillslope hydrology encompasses interception, infiltration, Horton overland flow, interflow, percolation, evapotranspiration, groundwater flow, and variable source area runoff (Fig. 3.1).

INTERCEPTION

Except in barren and denuded environments, falling rain first strikes vegetative surfaces (leaves, branches, stems, trunks, or vegetative detritus) before hitting the ground. Depending on the humidity within the canopy, a certain amount of the water temporarily sorbed onto vegetative surfaces evaporates before dripping to the ground. This process, well known to all children who play outdoors and use trees for temporary cover, is called *interception*. The amount of water a canopy can intercept is a function of *leaf area index,* or the ratio of vegetative surface area to the underlying ground surface area. Leaf area indices range from as little as 1.0 for short grasses and desert scrub, around 3.0 to 4.0 for grasslands and savannahs, 5.0 to 8.0 for temperate deciduous forests, and 8.0 to 18.0 for conifer forests and rainforests (Reichle 1981; Barbour et al. 1998; Perry 1994). In deciduous forests, interception

TABLE 3.1.   Interception as Absolute Annual Amounts and as Percentage of
Annual Precipitation from Various Locations around the World

Location	Forest Type	Precipitation (mm)	Interception as %P	Interception (mm)
Amazon	rainforest	281	9	25
Southwest India	cashew	300	31	93
E. Puerto Rico	rainforest	575	42	242
S. Appalachians, USA	mature White pine	203	9	18
S. Appalachians, USA	hardwoods	203	12	24
S. Appalachians, USA	35-yr White pine	203	19	39
S. Appalachians, USA	10-yr White pine	203	15	30
S. I. New Zealand	mixed forest	260	24	62
N. Appalachians, USA	hardwoods	130	13	17
SE U.K.	Corsican pine	79	35	28
Norfolk, U.K.	mixed pines	60	36	22
Wales, U.K.	Sitka spruce	187	27	50
Holland	Oak forest	31	22	7
S. Scotland, U.K.	Sitka spruce	160	30	48
Northumberland, U.K.	mature Sitka spruce	100	49	49
Northumberland, U.K.	Sitka spruce—pole timber	100	29	29
S. Scotland, U.K.	Sitka spruce	97	32	31
Scotland, U.K.	Sitka spruce	213	28	60
NE Scotland, U.K.	Scots pine	64	42	27

NOTE: Adapted from Dingman (1994); data from multiple published sources.

varies seasonally with the changing leaf cover, and in all forests, leaf area index and interception vary with stand age and condition. On an annual basis, interception is greater in coniferous forests than in deciduous forests in the same climatic region.

The quantity of rainfall intercepted during individual storms is small, in the range of 0.7 to 2.0 mm (Shuttleworth 1992). However, since humid climatic regions often experience 50 to 90 rainfall events per year, annual interception totals comprise a significant fraction of annual rainfall (Table 3.1).

Human alterations of the landscape, through urbanization, agriculture, and forestry, have direct impacts on interception. By removing the overhead canopy and reducing leaf area indices, timber harvest reduces interception and increases the amount of precipitation reaching the ground. Along with reduced evapotranspiration (discussed later), this usually contributes to elevated water tables and higher base flows for several years following forest harvest.

There are rare geographic exceptions to the relationship between leaf area indices and interception. In cloud forests, or areas where dense fog is common, fog drip occurs in a process that could be considered negative interception. In such areas, tree canopies act as mist nets that condense cloud water. This condensation is perceived as fog drip, and it results in a net increase in precipitation. Removal of the canopy in fog-drip areas leads to a lowering of water tables and a reduction in stream flows (Harr 1982).

INFILTRATION, SOIL PHYSICS, AND SOIL WATER STORAGE

Infiltration is the movement of water into the ground, and the hydrology and water quality of a watershed is controlled to a large degree by the infiltration characteristics of the surface soils. While infiltration rates in wetlands themselves are typically low, infiltration rates across the landscapes surrounding wetlands can have a strong effect on the routing of water to the wetlands. In forested humid landscapes, most rainfall that is not intercepted by the canopy infiltrates into the ground, where it either enters the vegetative root system to be used in evapotranspiration or it travels by subsurface pathways to surface waters (streams, wetlands, or lakes) found at the base of slopes. Infiltration rates in forested soils tend to be quite high—higher than all but extreme rainfall rates—so the hydrology of forested hillslopes tends to be dominated by subsurface processes. Human land-use activities that compact or denude soils reduce infiltration rates, often reducing them so much that they are exceeded by commonly experienced rainfall rates. When rainfall rates exceed infiltration rates, the excess water runs off the soil surface, rapidly carrying sediment and contaminants to surface waters and increasing storm flows. Maintenance of good hydrologic and water-quality conditions in surface waters is largely a matter of maintaining high infiltration rates.

The physics of infiltration are complicated. Infiltration rates in soils are affected by soil porosity, structure, texture, moisture content, the amount of organic material on the soil surface, vegetation, layering of soils, vertebrate and invertebrate activity in the topsoil, landscape position, groundwater dynamics, and even air temperature. For given soil conditions, the potential infiltration rate decreases asymptotically over time during a wetting event (Fig. 3.2).

Infiltration is driven by two forces: gravity and soil capillarity. Gravity remains constant during infiltration, but soil capillary forces pulling water into the soil diminish as the soil gets wetter. The shape of the maximum infiltration rate curve matches the shape of the curve of total force (gravity + capillarity) driving infiltration over time (Fig. 3.2).

Soil organic cover, or the lack of it, strongly affects infiltration rates. Organic cover protects soils from the kinetic energy of raindrops. When organic cover is removed, raindrop energy breaks up surface soil aggregates, and the resulting smaller soil particles clog the surface pores, creating a crust on the soil surface. The final infiltration rate of a crusted soil is usually a small fraction of the final infiltration rate for the same soil with organic cover in place.

Soils absorb water in the same way that sponges and paper towels absorb water. A water molecule is composed of two hydrogen atoms attached by covalent bonds to a single oxygen

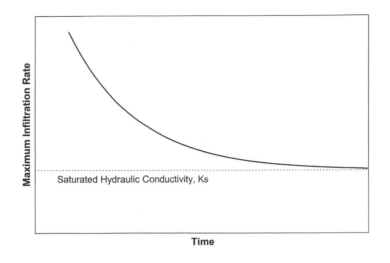

FIGURE 3.2

General behavior of maximum infiltration rates over time. When rainfall exceeds the maximum infiltration rate at any time, overland flow occurs.

atom. The hydrogen atoms are not arranged symmetrically on the water molecule; rather, the water molecule features a 104.5° bond angle. Therefore, the water molecule is *polar* with the oxygen atom displaying negative charge and the hydrogen atoms displaying positive charge. The polarity of the water molecule accounts for the high surface tension of water, as water molecules tend to form weak chains of molecules attracted by *cohesion* of the negative side of one molecule to the positive side of another molecule. *Capillarity* is driven by the adhesion of polar water molecules to charged surfaces and cohesion of polar water molecules to one another. Capillarity is really electromagnetic attraction. Water adheres to soils because soil particles tend to feature negatively charged surfaces. If soil particles were uncharged, the root zone would not be able to hold water, and plant life would exist only on the margins of surface waters.

Electrostatic attraction is inversely proportional to the square of the distance between charged particles or surfaces. Therefore, narrow soil pores hold water more tightly than do large soil pores. This is why sandy soils (large pore sizes) drain more quickly than soils with high clay contents (small pore sizes). Wetlands usually feature slowly moving surface waters that allow the settling of clays, silts, and fine organic particles, so very fine-textured soil layers tend to develop on the bottoms of wetlands. Such fine-textured soils create low infiltration rates and impede the loss of wetland surface water to the underlying groundwater system. In essence, once a wetland forms, it evolves in ways that increase its wetness or hydroperiod.

Understanding the dynamics between soil water movement and soil characteristics requires a basic knowledge of soil physical properties. Some of the major soil characteristics that hydrologists and wetland scientists consider with respect to soil hydrologic behavior are porosity, bulk density, texture, and the soil moisture release curve or moisture characteristic curve. The soil matrix is composed of soil particles, air, and water, and the relative amounts of air and water are constantly shifting as soil wets and dries. Soil porosity (n) is the ratio of the void space (air volume + water volume) to the total soil volume:

$$n = (\text{volume void space})/(\text{total soil volume})$$

or

$$n = \frac{(V_a + V_w)}{(V_a + V_w + V_p)} = \frac{(V_a + V_w)}{V_s} \qquad \text{(Eq. 1)}$$

where

V_a = volume of air,

V_w = volume of water,

V_p = volume of soil particles, and

V_s = total soil volume.

Porosity is sometimes expressed as a dimensionless fraction (e.g., 0.5) or as a percentage (e.g., 50%). Bulk density is the dry mass of soil divided by the total soil volume:

$$\rho_b = (\text{dry mass of soil})/(\text{total soil volume}) \qquad \text{(Eq. 2)}$$

Bulk density has units of mass/volume or g/cm³. Bulk density and porosity are directly related. Soils with high porosity have low bulk density and vice versa. If the particle density is known or assumed, then porosity and bulk density can be calculated from one another as

$$n = 1 - \frac{\rho_b}{\rho_s} \qquad \text{(Eq. 3)}$$

where

ρ_b = bulk density (g/cm³), and

ρ_s = particle density (g/cm³).

The particle density for most soils is typically assumed to be 2.65 g/cm³. Undisturbed vegetated soils in humid environments tend to have high porosities and low bulk densities that contribute to high infiltration rates.

Soil particles are grouped into three size classes, sand, silt, and clay, based on different physical and chemical behavior of particles in these classes (Chapter 2). Soil *texture* is the mix of sand, silt, and clay in a particular soil (see textural triangle in Chapter 2). Texture strongly affects water storage and transmission properties of a soil as discussed below.

Water in soil moves from areas of high energy to areas of low energy. Many forms of energy, such as kinetic, thermal, and osmotic, are negligible in most soil and groundwater flow situations. Typically, only potential energy and pressure energy are considered in soil water and groundwater movement:

$$\text{Soil water energy} = \text{potential energy} + \text{pressure energy} \qquad \text{(Eq. 4)}$$

The pressure in a standing column of water increases linearly with depth, but the total energy stays constant because the potential energy decreases as the pressure energy increases. Hydrologists and hydraulic engineers use the concept of *hydraulic head,* which is the energy per specific weight of fluid and has units of length, to describe the amount of energy in water (Eq. 5). For example, the pressure head below a 10-m water column is 10 meters.

$$\text{head} = \text{energy}/(\text{specific weight}) \qquad \text{(Eq. 5)}$$

$$\text{Total hydraulic head, } H = \text{potential head} + \text{pressure head} \qquad \text{(Eq. 6)}$$

where

$$H = z + \psi.$$

Below the water table, water molecules are under compression, and pressure head is considered to be positive. In unsaturated soil, water molecules are under tension as they are being pulled downward by gravity and pulled upward by electrostatic attraction to soil particles. Pressure head is negative for unsaturated soils. The drier the soil, the greater the negative pressure in the soil. The relationship between a soil's moisture content and its pressure is called the *soil moisture characteristic curve* or the *soil moisture release curve.* Examples of soil moisture release curves for different textural classes of soils are shown in Figure 3.3.

Sandy soils tend to drain quickly because of large pore spaces, and clayey soils tend to drain slowly because of small pore spaces. Neither sandy nor clayey soils are ideal for plant growth because of their water-holding characteristics. Sandy soils drain too quickly for plant roots to access much water, and clayey soils hold water so tightly that plants can not access much of the water held in clay soils. Soil scientists use the concept of *field capacity* to describe the water held in a soil after rapid gravitational drainage, and field capacity corresponds to water held at approximately −1.0 m negative pressure head (or, as soil scientists would say, 0.1 bars of tension). Sandy soils hold relatively little water at field capacity, whereas clays are nearly saturated at field capacity. At the other end of the soil moisture release curve, soil scientists define *wilting point* as the water held at approximately −150 m of pressure head (soil scientists would call this 15 bars of tension), which is about the maximum tension plants can apply to extract water from soil. A sandy soil will be nearly bone dry at the wilting point, whereas a clay soil will still hold significant amounts of water. The difference in water storage between field capacity and wilting point

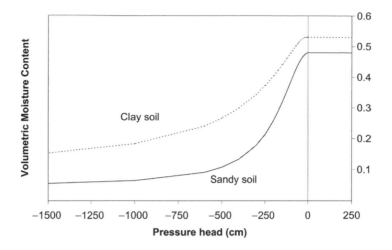

FIGURE 3.3
Representative soil moisture release curves.

is often called *dynamic soil storage* or *maximum plant-available water*. Loamy soils, composed of similar amounts of sands, silts, and clays, have the greatest dynamic soil storage and feature optimal moisture dynamics for plant growth.

Soil water moves from areas of high hydraulic head to areas of low hydraulic head by the route of least hydraulic resistance according to Darcy's law.

Darcy's law in one direction for saturated soils:

$$Q_x = -K_{sx}A\frac{\partial H}{\partial x}$$ (Eq. 7)

where

Q_x = volume of flow per unit time (L³/t),

K_{sx} = saturated hydraulic conductivity of the soil (L/t),

A = cross-sectional area of flow (L²), and

$\partial H/\partial x$ = hydraulic gradient, the rate of change of head over distance (unitless ratio).

Darcy's law says that the volume of water per unit time that moves from one region to another in soils is proportional to the area of flow and to the *hydraulic gradient,* defined as the rate of change of hydraulic head over distance. The hydraulic gradient can be considered the driving force for soil and groundwater movement. The flow of water in soil is also proportional to the *hydraulic conductivity* of the soil, which defines the rate of water movement across a flow cross section under a unit hydraulic gradient. The hydraulic conductivity is an intrinsic flow property of soils and bedrock that is affected by porosity,

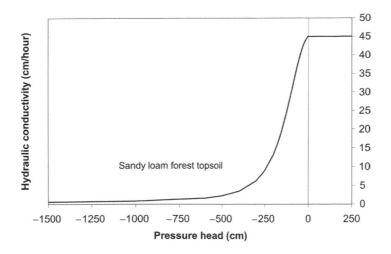

FIGURE 3.4
Typical hydraulic conductivity versus pressure head relationship.

texture, structure, and macropore networks. Hydraulic conductivities of natural soils and rock vary over twelve orders of magnitude (Freeze and Cherry 1979). Spatial variations of hydraulic conductivities strongly control the hydrology of hillslopes and wetlands.

When a soil is saturated and the pressure head is positive, hydraulic conductivity is constant and referred to as the *saturated hydraulic conductivity*. Hydraulic conductivity rapidly decreases as soils dry. For unsaturated conditions, there is a relationship between hydraulic conductivity and pressure head, as shown in Figure 3.4. As do the moisture release curves, conductivity versus pressure curves vary with soil porosity, texture, structure, and macropore networks.

Darcy's law can be modified to describe both saturated and unsaturated flow by substituting conductivity as a function of pressure head into the equation.

$$Q_x = -K_x(\psi)\frac{\partial H}{A\partial x} \qquad \text{(Eq. 8)}$$

The terms are the same as in Equation 7, except that now the hydraulic conductivity is not a constant but is a function of the pressure head in the soil. Dividing both sides of Equation 7 by the cross-sectional area of flow *(A)* produces the equation for *specific flux,* or *Darcy velocity, q.* The specific flux is the average flow rate across the entire flow cross section.

$$q_x = -K_x(\psi)\frac{\partial H}{\partial x} \qquad \text{(Eq. 9)}$$

However, water can not flow through the soil particles themselves, only through the wetted portion of the pore space. The *pore velocity* is the average velocity of water molecules and can be calculated by dividing the specific flux by the volumetric moisture content.

where

q_x = specific flux or Darcy velocity in the x direction, the average rate of water flow assuming water flows through the entire flow cross section (which it does not). Specific flux has units of velocity (L/t).

$$\text{pore velocity} = q/(\theta_v) \qquad \text{(Eq. 10)}$$

where

θ_v = volumetric moisture content = V_w/V_s.

The pore velocity describes the average rate of movement of a solute, such as a contaminant or a tracer, being carried by soil water.

In many hydrologic investigations, soil and groundwater movement can be simplified to one- or two-dimensional systems, but groundwater can move in any direction, and some wetlands reside in fully three-dimensional subsurface flow systems. Furthermore, some wetlands may receive or discharge soil water as both unsaturated and saturated flow, making simple hydrologic characterization difficult or impossible. Three-dimensional saturated/unsaturated flow problems are analyzed by a differential equation called *Richards' equation* (Richards 1931). Richards' equation is a generalization of Darcy's law coupled with the continuity equation as follows:

$$\frac{\partial}{\partial X_i}\left(Ki(\psi)\frac{\partial H}{\partial X_i}\right) = C(\psi)\frac{\partial \psi}{\partial T} \qquad \text{(Eq. 11)}$$

$$C = \frac{\partial \theta}{\partial \psi}$$

where

θ = volumetric moisture content.

Richards' equation simply says that at any point and time, flow will move in the direction where the product of the conductivity and the hydraulic gradient are greatest. For most transient analyses of groundwater flow, Richards' equation can not be solved analytically, so finite-element or finite-difference models of Richards' equation are used to describe soil and groundwater flow systems. Finite-element and finite-difference models are different techniques to transform differential equations into sets of algebraic equations that can be solved iteratively on computers.

When considered in the light of soil physical properties and Richards' equation, the temporal dynamics of maximum infiltration rates and the variability of infiltration rates across soil and cover types are more easily understood. At the beginning of a rainfall or ponding event, there is a large pressure head gradient between the just-wetted soils at the surface and the drier soils below. In essence, capillary forces pull water from the wet surface into the drier soils below. The sharp interface between high moisture contents and low moisture contents is called the *wetting front*. As the wetting front advances deeper into the soil, the pressure gradient at the surface approaches o. At this point, flow at the soil surface is driven only by gravity. In other words, infiltration is driven by the potential head gradient in the vertical direction, which is equal to 1 when there is no vertical variation in moisture content or pressure. If the rainfall rate is less than the saturated hydraulic conductivity of the soil, then equilibrium will be reached when the soil reaches a moisture content and a pressure at which the hydraulic conductivity equals the rainfall rate. If the rainfall rate exceeds the saturated hydraulic conductivity of the soil, the infiltration rate will approach the saturated hydraulic conductivity, and the excess rainfall will flow over the soil surface (see the section on Horton overland flow). Maintaining high infiltration rates and minimizing surface runoff involves keeping an organic cover on the soil, avoiding soil compaction, and maintaining a healthy soil ecosystem with plants, macroinvertebrates, and even small mammals that create macropore networks with high flow capacities.

Soils and their hydrologic characteristics vary with depth, and soil profiles usually exhibit distinct layers with different textures, structures, chemistry, and biology in each layer. These layers strongly affect the flow and distribution of soil water and the distribution of biological activity such as root growth, fungal and mycorrhizal growth, and animal burrowing and feeding. At the soil surface, there is typically an O horizon composed of vegetative detritus (leaves, needles, twigs, etc.) in various states of decay along with living vegetative matter. In warm humid climates with high biological activity, O horizons are thin, whereas O horizons in cool and cold humid climates are thick. Vernacular names for the O horizon include litter layer, duff, and mulch. The first mineral soil layer is the A horizon, which people often call *topsoil*. In upland soils, the A horizon usually features loam, sandy loam, or loamy sand textures; dark color (due to high organic content); high porosity; and high saturated hydraulic conductivity. A deep, uncompacted, natural A horizon with an intact O horizon typically supports very high infiltration rates. Thus, wetlands in forested humid landscapes typically drain watersheds where Horton overland flow (discussed below) is rare and where most water reaches streams and wetlands by subsurface pathways or by variable source area runoff (also discussed below).

Depending on the characteristics of the parent material from which a soil profile was formed, there may be a B horizon(s) below the A horizon. B horizons typically feature high contents of either clays (most common), organic material, or iron that translocated out of the A horizon by infiltrating water and concentrated by *illuviation* in the B horizon. B horizons tend to have relatively low saturated hydraulic conductivities. Between the A and B horizons, some soils feature a light-colored E horizon from which fine particles and humus have been transported by infiltrating water into the B horizon. Below these surface horizons lie C horizons composed of less-weathered parent material. Depending on the parent material and the weathering history, C horizons may be either more or less conductive of water than the B horizon. Young soils, typified by alluvial floodplain soils, often lack a B horizon and feature an A horizon directly overlying C horizons.

Building upon a soil taxonomy developed by the Russian scientist V. V. Dokuchaiev in the early twentieth century (Glinka 1927), soil scientists of the United States Department of Agriculture (USDA) have developed a soil classification system that roughly encompasses all soils found in the world (USDA 1999). The USDA soil classification system defines twelve soil orders. Most older wetland soils are *Histosols,* which are organic soils composed of mucks or peats created by the deposition and decomposition of plant material (Rabenhorst and Swanson 1999; USDA 1999). Mucks contain fine, highly decomposed organic matter, whereas peats contain fibrous and partially decomposed plant detritus. The deep histic O horizons overlie C horizons usually without intervening A or B horizons. The relatively slow decomposition and relatively high primary productivity of wetlands contributes to the accumulation of high levels of organic matter in the soils beneath the wetlands. Decomposed organic matter clogs the soil pores and also holds water strongly. Therefore, a typical histic O horizon of a well-developed wetland Histosol drains water very slowly. In turn, the low hydraulic conductivity of the organic muck contributes to the hydrologic conditions that create or maintain wetland conditions.

Not all wetland soils are Histosols. Younger wetlands formed on floodplains often feature relatively young Entisols or Enceptisols, and other wetlands may form in Alfisols and Ultisols. Nevertheless, due to surface fining and organic matter accumulation, the soils underlying most wetlands become less conductive to water over time.

From a hillslope and wetland hydrology perspective, a basic understanding of soil properties and profiles is useful for diagnosing the flow connections between a wetland and its surrounding environment as well as for understanding where wetlands occur and how they form (Chapter 2).

OVERLAND FLOW

When precipitation rates exceed soil infiltration rates, the excess rainfall runs over the ground surface, creating *surface runoff,* called *Horton overland flow* by hydrologists (Horton 1933). Over short distances, this surface runoff will travel as a dispersed film, but after traveling tens of meters, it will concentrate into small channels due to microtopographic effects and scour caused by the flow itself. Horton overland flow is rare in humid forested environments because litter cover, high soil organic content, and biological activity in the topsoils (due to roots, invertebrates, small mammals) all combine to create very high infiltration rates. Horton overland flow may become common when soils are compacted and litter layers removed. Horton overland flow scours and transports sediment and any other pollutants found on the ground surface, creating water-quality problems in the receiving waters. At the extreme, Horton overland flow carves rills and gullies and then deposits large amounts of sediment on floodplains and in streams and wetlands (Richter and Markewitz 2001).

The fundamental hydrologic shift engendered by watershed urbanization is the frequent and widespread occurrence of Horton overland flow on pavements, rooftops, and compacted soils that have little to no infiltration capacity. This alteration of the infiltration capacity of the landscape results in higher peak flow rates and stormflow volumes and also produces large storm flows in the summer and early fall when forested basins normally produce no significant runoff events due to dry soil conditions. Overland flows from urban areas typically carry high concentrations of fertilizers, pesticides, oils and grease, and heavy metals, while overland flows from row-crop agricultural areas typically carry fertilizers, pesticides, and sediment. Thus, overland flow is an important source of contaminants to wetlands.

EVAPOTRANSPIRATION

Hydrologists usually lump *evaporation,* water moving from a water body to the atmosphere, with *transpiration,* water moving from plant tissue to the atmosphere, into a single metric called *evapotranspiration.* In most analyses of wetland water budgets, however, it makes sense to consider evaporation and transpiration separately.

Evaporation is the change of state of liquid water, either from an open water body or from the ground, into vapor and the transfer of this vapor to the atmosphere. Evaporation is an energy-driven process that occurs when molecules of liquid water attain enough kinetic energy to overcome surface tension and escape from the water surface. Accurate monitoring and estimation of evapotranspiration is difficult and one of the most problematic issues in water budgeting.

Most of the energy that drives evaporation comes from solar radiation and sensible heat transfer (exchange of heat) from the atmosphere. As a result, evaporation varies by season and time of day. The energy it takes to evaporate a gram of water is quite large and is known as the *latent heat of vaporization,* which is about 580 cal/g at 30°C. At the small scale, evaporation and condensation are always occurring simultaneously in the air over a water layer. The evaporation rate depends on the humidity in the air and also on the wind speed. As the humidity of the air increases, so does the partial pressure of water vapor in the air, and it becomes more difficult for water to evaporate. At a given temperature and solar radiation, evaporation is greatest on a windy, dry day and lowest on a still, humid day. In other words, the evaporation increases with increasing vapor pressure deficit (VPD):

$$VPD = e_s - e_a = e_s (1 - RH) \qquad \text{(Eq. 12)}$$

where

e_s = maximum, or saturated vapor pressure,

e_a = actual vapor pressure, and

RH, relative humidity = e_a/e_s.

Basically, this equation means that drier air has a greater moisture deficit. In 1802, English chemist John Dalton developed mass transfer equations of the following form for predicting free water evaporation (Dingman 1994):

$$E = 1.26 \times 10^{-4} \, v_a \, (e_s - e_a)$$ (Eq. 13)

where

E = evaporation in cm/day, and

v_a = wind speed 2 m above water surface, cm/s.

Evaporation from an open water body is called *potential evapotranspiration* (PET) because it is not limited by water availability. Potential evapotranspiration is typically measured using a United States Weather Bureau Class A pan (Shaw 1988), which is a circular aluminum pan 1.22 m in diameter and 25.4 cm high with an operating water depth between 17.5 and 20 cm. Annual PET varies relatively predictably across the United States (Farnsworth and Thompson 1982) and varies relatively little from year to year (Dingman 1994). PET data for particular areas can be obtained from the National Weather Service as well as from many state climatological data programs.

Evaporation from soils is complicated because water supply is limited, and water is bound to soil by capillary forces. After the first few milliliters of water evaporate from soil near the surface, vapor must diffuse out of the pores. By setting up pressure gradients between dry surface soils and wetter soils below, evaporation can cause upward vertical unsaturated flow. Evaporation from soil is a very slow process after the top few centimeters become dry. If the soil is covered by an organic litter layer, then evaporation from soil is further inhibited. Therefore, water loss from the subsurface soils to the atmosphere occurs primarily through plant transpiration.

Plants use atmospheric carbon dioxide (a trace component of the air with a concentration of about 300 ppm and rising) as the source of carbon for building plant tissue. To access carbon dioxide, leaves of plants contain small gas chambers that exchange gas with the atmosphere through openings called *stomata*. When a stoma is closed, the air in the gas compartment becomes nearly saturated with water vapor, and when the stoma is open, this high humidity air is exchanged with lower humidity air, causing a net loss of water. Stomata close when cell wall turgor pressure drops due to water deficits in leaves. This transfer of water from leaves to the atmosphere is called *transpiration*, and it is a necessary by-product of the plant's need for carbon dioxide. Transpiration also drives the movement of water from the roots to the canopy and thus allows delivery of essential soil nutrients to plant tissue. Like evaporation, transpiration rates are partly controlled by vapor pressure deficit and wind, but transpiration is also controlled by the supply of water in the soil, leaf area index, solar radiation, and air temperature. Because of ample water supplies and typically lush vegetation, transpiration can be a major source of water movement from wetlands.

The actual evapotranspiration (AET) from the landscape on any day is almost always less than the PET for that day. On an annual basis, AET is typically in the range of 50% to 90% of PET, with higher ratios of AET/PET in wet climates and lower ratios in arid climates. One simple way to estimate AET is by multiplying PET measured in pans by

TABLE 3.2.   Gross Watershed Water Budgets for Various Locations in the United States

Location	Precipitation, cm	Stream Flow, cm	Actual Evapotranspiration (AET), cm
Atlanta, GA	130	90	40
Seattle, WA	100	50	50
Olympic Mountains, WA	300	250	50
Tucson, AZ[a]	30	0	90

[a]AET in and around Tucson, Arizona, exceeds precipitation due to irrigation using groundwater or water imported from the Colorado River.

the pan coefficient, which is the ratio of annual AET to annual PET as follows:

$$AET = Cp \times PET \qquad\qquad (\text{Eq. 14})$$

where

$$Cp = \text{Pan coefficient} = \text{annual AET/annual PET.}$$

Annual AET can be estimated using a simplified basin water budget. Assuming that transwatershed human and groundwater exchanges are negligible when compared with surface flows leaving the basin, then long-term average annual precipitation and runoff data can be used to estimate annual AET as follows:

$$P = AET + R \qquad\qquad (\text{Eq. 15a})$$

or

$$AET = P - R \qquad\qquad (\text{Eq. 15b})$$

where

AET = average annual actual evapotranspiration in cm,

P = average annual rainfall in cm, and

R = average annual flow discharge expressed as a depth in cm.

This equation says that over the long term (a long-term record renders negligible any changes in soil or surface water storage), precipitation becomes either evapotranspiration or runoff. The partitioning of precipitation into evapotranspiration or runoff varies greatly with climate type (Table 3.2).

Predicting and modeling evapotranspiration based on physical principles is difficult because of the complexities of evapotranspiration processes, differences in water usage between vegetative communities, the strong control exerted by soil moisture availability, and the temporal dynamics of the physical forcing functions (humidity, temperature, solar insolation, wind, etc.). More physically realistic evapotranspiration equations are based on energy budget considerations. An energy budget model is based on measuring all major incoming and outgoing energy fluxes as well as changes in energy storage, and then solving for the energy used in evapotranspiration. The Penman-Monteith equation (Monteith 1965) combines energy budget and mass-transfer concepts and also accounts for canopy conductance, and it is commonly used for estimating actual evapotranspiration. The Penman-Monteith equation was modified from the Penman equation (Penman 1948) for predicting evaporation from lakes, and these equations ignore smaller energy flux terms such as changes in heat storage and energy carried by water flowing into and out of the water body. With calibration of the conductance terms, the Penman-Monteith equation has accurately estimated evapotranspiration in many environments (e.g., Calder 1977, 1978; Lindroth 1985; Dolman et al. 1988; Stewart and Gay 1989; Lemeur and Zhang 1990).

The Penman-Monteith and other energy-budget models require a lot of data that may not be available for a given site and time period. The empirical Thornthwaite model of potential evapotranspiration is a commonly used index model that uses only temperature data to predict PET (Thornthwaite and Hare 1965). The idea of an index model is that hot days typically have higher solar radiation and vapor pressure deficit, and thus higher PET, while cool days typically have lower solar radiation and vapor pressure deficit, and thus lower PET. The Thornthwaite equation predicts monthly PET as follows:

$$Et = 1.6 \left[\frac{10 Ti}{I} \right]^a \qquad \text{(Eq. 16)}$$

where

Et = potential evapotranspiration in cm/month,

Ti = Mean monthly air temperature (degrees C),

I = annual heat index = $\displaystyle\sum_{i=1}^{12} \left[\frac{Ti}{5} \right]^{1.5}$, and

$a = 0.49 + 0.179 I - 7.71 \times 10^{-5} I^2 + 6.75 \times 10^{-7} I^3$.

Another relatively simple way to estimate AET is with a soil-factor (F_s) and crop-factor (F_c) model that accounts for soil moisture and plant conditions.

$$AET = F_s\, F_c\, PET \qquad \text{(Eq. 17)}$$

The soil factor varies between 0, when the soil is at wilting point, and 1, when the soil is at field capacity. Various equations have been developed to relate the soil factor to soil moisture content (Shuttleworth 1992), but the simplest of these equations assumes a linear relationship:

$$Fs = \frac{(\theta - \theta_{wp})}{(\theta - \theta_{fc})} \qquad \text{(Eq. 18)}$$

where

$$\theta = \text{current moisture content,}$$

$$\theta_{fc} = \text{moisture content at field capacity, and}$$

$$\theta_{wp} = \text{moisture content at wilting point.}$$

A soil moisture accounting model can be developed to track soil moisture and AET over time. This is how some golf courses and more sophisticated farmers optimize irrigation. The crop factor is a function of growth stage, and various empirical crop factor relationships can be found in the agricultural literature (Shuttleworth 1992). These models are all appropriate for estimating AET and PET from wetlands, and the appropriate model choice depends on data availability.

INTERFLOW

Interflow is shallow, lateral subsurface flow moving nearly parallel to the soil surface over an impeding soil or bedrock horizon. Interflow during or just following rainfall is analogous to Horton overland flow because interflow occurs when a wetting front delivers water through a soil horizon faster than the lower horizon can accept water. Hydraulic conductivities of soils tend to decrease with depth, and conductivities and other hydraulic properties may feature abrupt changes at the interfaces of soil layers. As infiltrating water reaches a soil layer that impedes percolation, such as a dense clay B horizon, then some of the soil water will begin to flow laterally downslope over the impeding horizon. During storms, interflow can occur as saturated or unsaturated flow. Interflow during storms will not occur until after the wetting front has crossed the topsoil and encountered the impeding horizon (Zaslavsky and Sinai 1981a, 1981b; Wallach and Zaslavsky 1991). Therefore, a threshold rainfall amount, typically in the range of 50 mm, is necessary before interflow becomes an important part of stormflow processes (Newman et al. 1998; Freer et al. 2002; Tromp van Meerveld and McDonnell, in review).

Interflow also occurs as unsaturated flow during drying conditions between rainstorms and thus serves to redistribute moisture and solutes from upslope to downslope (Hewlett and Hibbert 1963; Jackson 1992). The unsaturated drainage of shallow soils by interflow supports base flows in streams and wetlands. Because interflow occurs in the upper soil layers where organic content and biological activity are high, many biochemical transformations of materials dissolved or suspended within interflow may occur. Travel times associated with interflow are in the order of hours to months, depending on slope position and soil moisture.

PERCOLATION

Soil water that has infiltrated, avoided root uptake and transpiration, and passed through the topsoil now flows downward through the *vadose zone*, driven mostly by gravity but partly by horizontal and vertical pressure gradients developed during hillslope drying and moisture redistribution. The vadose zone is comprised of the soil and rock between the ground surface and the water table. The vadose zone is usually unsaturated but that may become saturated for short periods of time during rainfall events. The downward movement of soil water to the underlying water table is called *percolation*, and percolating water that reaches the water table is called *recharge*. Below ridgetops, the depth to the water table may be large, so travel times for percolating water may be months, even years. Near the base of hillslopes, where the water table is near the ground surface, percolation travel times are relatively short. The vadose zone beneath the root zone, and the percolating water within it, act to buffer stream flows and wetland hydropatterns from changes in climatic conditions. During wet periods, the vadose zone stores rainfall and minimizes stormflow response, and during dry periods, the percolating water supplies recharge to aquifers and help support base flows in streams.

GROUNDWATER FLOW

Infiltration, percolation, and interflow are all special forms of groundwater flow. Groundwater hydrology encompasses the subsurface movement of water as both unsaturated flow in the vadose zone and saturated flow beneath the water table. Ironically, in most humid natural environments, surface water hydrology, encompassing the behavior of wetlands, streams, rivers, and lakes, is strongly associated with groundwater flow processes because surface waters receive most of their flow from various groundwater flow paths. This discussion of groundwater flow, however, will focus on saturated flow systems and their relationships to surface waters, particularly wetlands. Laypeople often say "water flows downhill," and residents of arid environments often say "water flows toward money," but it is most accurate to say that "water flows from high head to low head," as described by Darcy's law. Surface water bodies such as wetlands, streams, and rivers are located at local low points in the landscape, and in humid environments, they generally act to drain groundwater from the surrounding landscape.

The hydraulic head of groundwater is measured using wells or piezometers (Fig. 3.5). The elevation of the equilibrium water surface in a well is the total hydraulic head associated with the screened section of the well, and it defines the water table at that point. The *water table* is the three-dimensional surface defined by water standing in wells or piezometers in that area. Above the water table, soil water is held in tension, and thus the pressure head is negative. Below the water table, groundwater is under positive pressure. Another way to define the water table is the surface at which water pressure (or pressure head) equals zero. Water tables are partly controlled by surface topography and tend to form a muted reflection of the surface topography.

The earth is approximately 4.6 billion years old, and the hydrologic cycle has been running for about 4 billion years. Consequently, the fractured surface mantle is full of

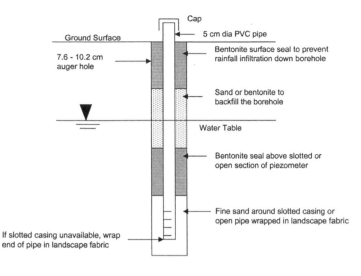

FIGURE 3.5
Well schematic.

circulating water down to a depth of about 10 km. In humid environments, this ground-water is constantly recharged and leaks into the surface water system from hillsides. In arid environments, saturated groundwater systems occur at depths where evaporation losses and drainage to local surface water bodies are minimal. The movement of ground-water and its exchanges with surface waters occur at all spatial and temporal scales. Wetlands generally occur where the saturated groundwater system approaches the soil surface due to topographic, geologic, or soil conditions.

An *aquifer* is any geologic medium that will transmit usable quantities of water to a well, so aquifers have relatively high saturated hydraulic conductivities and porosities. Conversely, an *aquitard* is a geologic medium with limited transmission of water, and an *aquiclude* is a geologic medium that essentially moves no water because either the porosity or the saturated hydraulic conductivity are practically 0. The low conductivity Histosols formed below wetlands typically act as thin aquitards.

There are two general types of aquifers: surficial (unconfined) and confined, although many aquifers are semiconfined (Fig. 3.6). In a *surficial aquifer,* the water table is usually open to the atmosphere through the air-filled pore spaces in the vadose zone. The entire overlying landscape is a recharge zone for surficial aquifers. When a surficial aquifer is recharged by percolation, the zone of saturation expands to the same extent that the water table rises. Surficial unconfined aquifers continually drain to local surface water bodies and provide stream flow between storms. As water drains out of the surficial aquifers, water tables drop, and the rate of discharge from aquifers to streams diminishes. That is why base flows slowly and continuously drop between storms.

A *confined aquifer* is sandwiched between two aquitards or aquicludes. Water fully saturates a confined aquifer, and the zone of saturation does not change as pressure changes

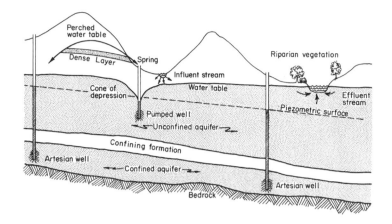

FIGURE 3.6

Aquifer types and surface water interactions. From Hewlett (1982). Reprinted by permission of the University of Georgia Press.

in the aquifer. Water levels of wells drilled into a confined aquifer form a *potentiometric surface.* Where the potentiometric surface rises above the ground surface, the aquifer is artesian, and wells will flow without the aid of a pump in these areas. Typically, a confined aquifer outcrops somewhere on the landscape, meaning that the geologic strata bearing the aquifer contacts the land surface at some location. These outcrop areas are *recharge areas* for the confined aquifer because recharge from above the aquifer is limited by the overlying aquitard. Usually, hydrologic connections between confined aquifers and surface water are limited and damped, but in some cases, rivers cut into confined aquifers, and thus interactions are direct and rapid.

At base flow, streams and rivers typically flow at velocities ranging from 0.3 to 1.5 m/sec. Even a river 300 km long would only take from 2 to 11 days to completely drain if there were no continuous inputs of water. Groundwater is what sustains streams, rivers, and many wetlands between rainfall events.

Groundwater flow paths are complicated and three-dimensional (Fig. 3.7). Recharge water that reaches the water table below ridgetops takes a deep and circuitous path to streams that may take many years. Ridgetop recharge water may not flow to the local surface water network but rather may enter the regional flow network and travel to the ocean or a large lake without ever entering the stream and wetland system. Recharge water that reaches the water table near a stream, on the other hand, will travel a relatively fast (on the order of days or weeks) and shallow route to the stream. Consequently, geochemical transformations of groundwater vary by flow path. For example, the chemistry of shallow groundwater near the valley floor is affected by rapid microbial transformations and may undergo denitrification processes. Deep groundwater travels in a medium with little organic carbon, and biological interactions with groundwater chemistry are minimal.

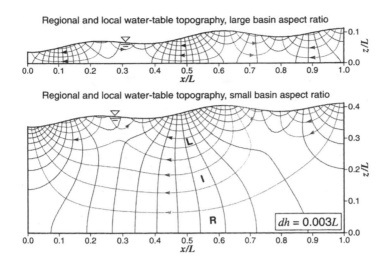

FIGURE 3.7
Local and regional groundwater flow nets. From Hornberger et al. (1998). Reprinted with permission of The John Hopkins University Press.

VARIABLE SOURCE AREA RUNOFF OR SATURATED SURFACE RUNOFF

Where water tables lie close to the ground surface, such as in low-lying areas near streams, in low portions of floodplains, and around wetlands, the water tables may rise to the ground surface during rainfall. When the soil becomes saturated, additional rainfall runs across the soil surface to surface waters, and runoff from this mechanism is called *variable source area runoff*, or *saturated surface runoff* (e.g., Betson 1964; Hewlett and Hibbert 1967; Ragan 1967; Dunne and Black 1970a, 1970b; Dunne et al. 1975). These runoff source areas are "variable" in that the saturated areas expand and contract with climatic and groundwater conditions. Variable source areas are fed by groundwater and interflow, and the water table position in these areas is partly controlled by water levels in the nearby surface waters. Variable source areas are responsible for most of the storm flow from undeveloped forested watersheds in humid climates. From a hydrologist's viewpoint, most wetlands are variable source areas.

SUMMARY OF HILLSLOPE FLOW PROCESSES

These categorizations and descriptions of flow processes are conceptually useful, and they allow for ready and simple explanations of how hydrology differs between mountain hillsides, Piedmont hillsides, Coastal Plain hillsides, and glacial landscapes. With basic information on soils and topography, a hillslope's dominant hydrologic processes can be inferred (Fig. 3.8). Furthermore, this simple reductionist view of hillslope flow processes can guide the development of a wetland water budget and illuminate a wetland's biogeochemical controls.

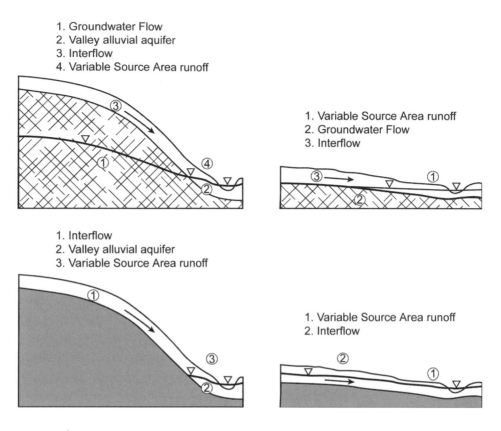

1. Groundwater Flow
2. Valley alluvial aquifer
3. Interflow
4. Variable Source Area runoff

1. Variable Source Area runoff
2. Groundwater Flow
3. Interflow

1. Interflow
2. Valley alluvial aquifer
3. Variable Source Area runoff

1. Variable Source Area runoff
2. Interflow

FIGURE 3.8
Examples of how hillslope topography, soils, and lithology affect relative importance of possible hillslope flow pathways.

FIGURE 3.9
Hydrographs for two rivers in Georgia for water years 1997 and 1998. One is a free-flowing Piedmont river and the other is the outflow of the Okefenokee Swamp complex in the Lower Coastal Plain. (A) Hydrograph of the Middle Oconee River in Athens, Georgia, which drains a basin of 392 square miles of mostly forested uplands with few floodplain wetlands. (B) Hydrograph of the Suwannee River with drains 1,260 square miles dominated by the Okefenokee Swamp. Flows are in cubic feet per second from USGS gauges 02217500 and 02314500.

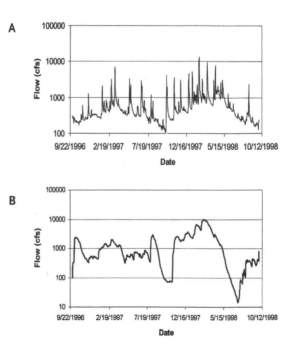

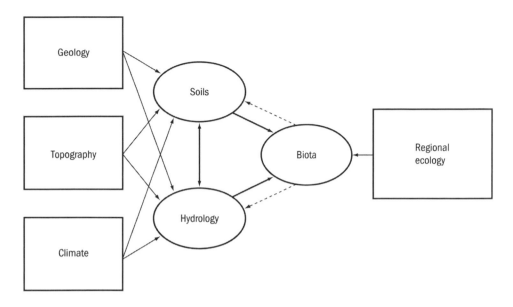

FIGURE 3.10
Abiotic and biotic influences on wetlands.

No unmanaged hydrologic system is static. Stream flows, groundwater levels, soil moisture, and wetland water levels are always either increasing due to recent rainfall or decreasing due to drainage and evapotranspiration (Fig. 3.9). Due to local hydraulic controls, such as beaver dams, some wetlands may experience relatively long periods of time with low water level fluctuations, but inflows and outflows are always in transition.

GEOMORPHIC CONTROLS ON WETLAND HYDROLOGY

Wetlands occur where hydrologic conditions driven by climate, topography, geology, and soils cause surface saturation of sufficient duration to form hydric soils and competitively favor hydrophylic vegetation (Fig. 3.10). From a geomorphic standpoint, wetlands occur in a relatively limited set of positions (Table 3.3), including on floodplains, on glacial terrain, in high water table areas or groundwater discharge areas, and on continental margins.

From a geologic perspective, wetlands are constantly being destroyed, shifting locations, and being created. Almost all wetlands are Holocene features less than 12,000 years old (formed since the last episode of continental glaciation), and some wetlands, such as beaver swamps, have life spans of just a few decades. Some areas of wetland concentrations, such as the lower Mississippi Valley and the Amazon, are ancient, but the wetland features themselves are constantly shifting due to river and sediment dynamics. The primary drivers of natural wetland destruction and creation are eutrophication, sedimentation,

TABLE 3.3.   Geomorphic Classification of Major Wetland Types
with Notes and Examples

Stream and River Associated	
Floodplain or alluvial wetlands	Hydrology of floodplain wetlands is affected variously by high water tables, frequent overbank flow, or backwater effects of hydraulic impediments to stream flow. Floodplain wetlands tend to occur in depressions formed by fluvial action.
High floodplain water table	Wetlands occur anywhere the water table lies at or near the floodplain surface for significant duration.
Overflow channels	An example is a backwater swamp.
Abandoned oxbows	Relict river bends isolated from current channel.
Paleo-channel features	Relict low spots in floodplains created by formerly active flow paths.
Beaver swamps	Created in small and medium streams.
Accidental swamps	Created when humans inadvertently inhibit the drainage of a stream with road crossings with insufficient culvert capacity or the placement of railroad grade fills across valleys.
Ill-defined stream and river channels	Created by low dams, drainage blockages. Also common where mountain river systems drain into low gradient areas and overbank flow is frequent and of long duration (e.g., Pantanal, Amazon).
Lacustrine	
Lake fringes	Lakes with low water level variation develop wetland fringes.
Lake deltas	Wetlands form where sediment-laden streams enter lakes.
Dying lakes	Small alpine lakes eventually become alpine wetlands and then flat meadows.
Glacial	
Glacial till	Bogs, fens, and tundra are examples of wetlands that form on flat, infiltration-limited topography common in glacial till deposits.
Glacial outwash	Prairie potholes and kettles form where relict blocks of ice left depressions in the glacial outwash. Kettles only become wetlands if regional water tables intersect kettle bottoms for a period of time sufficient for fines and organic matter to accumulate and seal the wetland bottom. Wide flat outwash channels feature a variety of wetland types.

TABLE 3.3. *(continued)*

Groundwater Associated	
Lower Coastal Plains	Low-lying flat areas of coastal plains typically feature near-surface water tables caused by the hydraulic control of the ocean, and these areas feature a variety of isolated depressional wetlands (cypress domes and gum swamps) and linear, seasonally wet areas (hardwood bottoms) as well as large contiguous wetland areas (pocosins, Tate's Hell Swamp in Florida, Okefenokee Swamp in Georgia).
Hillslope seeps	Geologic discontinuities may force hillslope ground water and/or interflow to exit the side of the hill and thus create wetland conditions.
Regional discharge areas	Desert oases are examples.
Limestone dissolution areas	May occur in a variety of geomorphic settings including mountain ridgetops.
Marine Associated	
Freshwater marshes	
Estuarine fringe	
Saltwater marshes	
Miscellaneous Inland Depressions	
Wind-carved depressions	Most common in arid areas. Some may form wetlands such as playas.
Paleo-marine features	A variety of inland depressions left by ancient marine processes. Examples include California's vernal pools.
Man-made depressions	Old quarries and borrow pits commonly form wetlands after sufficient time for hydric soil development and hydrophilic plant colonization.
Animal-made depressions	Buffalo wallows are an example.

NOTE: Figure 3.11 provides some examples of wetlands associated with streams and rivers.

erosion, glaciation, climate change, declines or ascensions in water tables, and sea level change. Obviously, these factors are not independent.

Every wetland is a unique actualization of many abiotic and biotic factors, including geologic and geomorphic history, topography, connections to the local and regional hydrologic system, connections to local and regional ecosystems, time since formation, and disturbance history. For example, although they will share obvious similarities, no two beaver swamps are identical. Paraphrasing Gertrude Stein, "a wetland is not a wetland is not a wetland." Consequently, wetlands defy simple classification. Wetland scientists have tried vegetative and geomorphic classification systems (Cowardin et al. 1979), hydrologic classification systems (e.g., Cowardin et al. 1979; Bridgham et al. 1996; Reinelt et al. 2001), hydrogeomorphic classification systems (Ramsar Convention Bureau 1991; Brinson 1993), water chemistry and hydrology classification systems (Warner and Rubec 1997), and others. While all these systems have value, none has provided robust classification and description for all wetlands. What, then, is the value of the geomorphic classification presented in Table 3.3? This table illustrates that, regardless of the biotic and structural diversity found in the world's wetlands, there are only a few general landscape locations in which wetlands occur and a few processes by which wetlands are formed. Such a geomorphic understanding of wetlands helps explain and describe the spatial and temporal context of wetlands within the biogeography of a region. Furthermore, a simple geomorphic view of wetlands is instructive for setting regional and national wetland management policies as well as for designing created wetlands. With the exception of the polar environments, wetlands occur all over the world, on all continents, and in all climates, but almost all occur in the few landscape positions listed in Table 3.3.

Wetlands are relatively abundant on active floodplains because the water table draining to the stream or river is near the floodplain surface and because overbank flows from the stream or river may cause periodic inundation. Floodplains are dynamic and complex features that over time collect a variety of relictual fluvial features (e.g., Hupp 2000; Leigh et al. 2004), some of which are conducive to wetland formation. Floodplain wetland features can be transformed immediately by large floods or other natural disturbances (e.g., Johnson et al. 2000). Figure 3.11 illustrates the variety of wetland and fluvial features that may be found on a large river floodplain. Depending on its geomorphic history, a floodplain may have several levels, including an active floodplain that receives overbank flows during floods and several terraces comprising the paleo floodplain. Terraces are usually relatively high above the water table and rarely, if ever, receive overbank flow. Thus, wetlands tend to occur on active floodplain areas and less so on terraces.

Natural lakes with muted water level fluctuations have wetlands on low-slope lake margins, in coves, and on sediment deltas where streams and rivers discharge. Conversely, management of man-made reservoirs for water supply and flood control usually results in large yearly water level fluctuations that do not favor wetland formation on reservoir margins. Reservoirs, therefore, usually feature wetlands only in delta areas. A comparison of lacustrine wetlands between natural and man-made lakes illustrates how water level dynamics can control wetland formation and characteristics.

Continental glaciers are powerful agents of wetland creation. Glacial till, compacted by the weight of the overlying ice, tends to have very low hydraulic conductivity. In locations where precipitation exceeds evapotranspiration over much of the year, relatively flat till

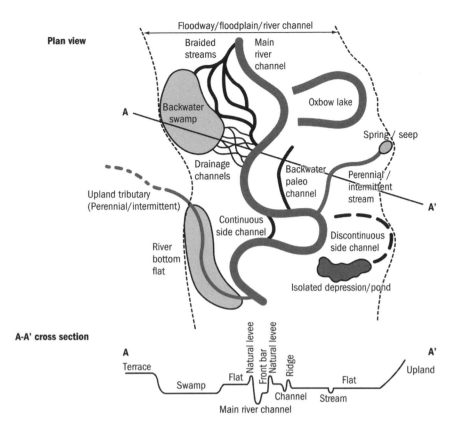

Plan view

Floodway/floodplain/river channel

Braided streams

Main river channel

Backwater swamp

A

Oxbow lake

Spring/seep

Drainage channels

Backwater paleo channel

Perennial/intermittent stream

Upland tributary (Perennial/intermittent)

A'

Continuous side channel

Discontinuous side channel

River bottom flat

Isolated depression/pond

A-A' cross section

A

Terrace

Natural levee

Front bar

Natural levee

Ridge

A'

Upland

Flat

Flat

Swamp

Channel

Stream

Main river channel

FIGURE 3.11

Varieties of floodplain wetland features. Figure courtesy of Masato Miwa, Hydrologist, International Paper. Modified from Mitsch and Gosselink (2000) and Hodges (1998).

deposits form wetlands in even slight depressions due to the restricted percolation rates of till soils. Outwash soils, typically sands and gravels discharged from a glacier but not compacted by it, have high hydraulic conductivities that would suggest these soils are unlikely places for wetland formation. Flat outwash channels, however, often act as conduits for regional groundwater flow, and water tables lie at or near the ground surface. Therefore, outwash channel features are often wetland areas. In addition, kettles or potholes left by blocks of ice calved from retreating glaciers often become wetlands. The Upper Midwest of the United States, including Wisconsin, Minnesota, the Dakotas, Nebraska, and Iowa, features numerous small and large wetlands created on glacial till and outwash features.

Many if not most wetlands are hybrids in terms of their geomorphic origins and controls. Floodplains contain many wetlands partly because of shallow water tables, so floodplain wetlands could be considered groundwater-associated wetlands. Furthermore, groundwater-associated wetlands of coastal plains are influenced by sea level controls on groundwater dynamics, so they could be considered marine associated. Still, it is difficult to think of a wetland that does not fit into one or more of these simple geomorphic categories.

Some wetlands, such as the Carolina bays of the U.S. eastern seaboard are difficult to classify. Carolina bays are carbonate dissolution features that occur on marine deposits in both the upper and lower coastal plains overlying geologic units containing carbonate. Many Carolina bays are perched well above the normal surficial water table and located far outside of floodplains and the area of marine influences on groundwater. Carolina bays could be considered either groundwater associated (due to the groundwater processes that caused the carbonate dissolution) or paleo-marine features (given their landscape position).

The distinction between marine-associated wetlands and many wetlands of groundwater origin is blurry. The marine environment is the ultimate discharge point for aquifer systems, and sea level provides the base hydraulic control for aquifer discharge. As a result, many low-gradient coastal plain areas feature very shallow water tables, and thus wetlands are common in topographic depression in coastal plains. Hydrologic inputs to coastal plain wetlands are precipitation and possibly surface flow and groundwater inputs, but the dominant hydrologic control on coastal plain wetlands is seasonally high water tables. In the continental interior, groundwater-dominated wetlands occur where large regional groundwater systems discharge or connect to flat valley bottoms.

Marine-associated fresh water marshes receive most of their water from river flow that has backed up and spread out due to the hydraulic control exerted by the tidal systems into which they discharge. Water exchange in salt water marshes is predominantly by tidal exchange. In between, brackish marshes receive both river and tidal inputs.

Wetlands are a product of a landscape's geologic and geomorphic history as well as its current hydrologic behavior. A landscape's hydrologic behavior is driven by topography, soils, climate, vegetation, and land use. Once formed, wetlands can modify local or regional hydrology. For example, depressional flow-through wetlands, such as beaver ponds, temporarily store flood flows and reduce peak flows downstream. They also trap sediments, thus altering stream dynamics.

There have been many efforts to develop systematic evaluations of the hydrologic functions and values of wetlands (e.g., Adamus and Stockwell 1983; Bardecki 1984; Carter 1986; Hruby et al. 1995; Smith et al. 1995; Brinson and Rheinhardt 1998), but the hydrologic functions of wetlands have in some cases been overstated. Floodplain wetlands are often cited as providing flood water storage and flood mitigation, but any part of the floodplain does the same thing, and this is not a function peculiar to jurisdictional wetlands. Bullock and Acreman (2003) extensively reviewed the literature on hydrologic functions of wetlands and found "generalised and simplified statements of wetland function are discouraged because they demonstrably have little practical value." They concluded "apparently similar wetlands are driven by very different hydrologic processes; almost invariably, some data need to be collected at a site to identify its functional role."

WETLAND WATER BUDGETS

Quantitative or semiquantitative water budgets provide useful insight into the hydrodynamic and geochemical behavior of a wetland. However, an accurate quantitative water budget is time consuming, expensive, and usually beyond the scope of most wetland studies. Nevertheless, relatively simple hydrologic data collection and analysis can provide a rough and useful quantification of a wetland's water budget. Water budgeting is based on the simple physical principle of *conservation of mass*, or *continuity*, which says that the mass (or volume) of inputs to a system must equal the mass (or volume) of outputs plus the change in internal system storage over any period of time. The continuity equation

$$\text{inputs} = \text{outputs} + \text{changes in storage},$$

when applied to a freshwater wetland, yields

$$P + G_{in} + OF_{in} + SF_{in} + OBF_{in} = ET + G_{out} + SF_{out} + OBF_{out} + dV \qquad \text{(Eq. 19)}$$

where

P = volume of precipitation falling on wetland,

G_{in} = volume of groundwater flow into wetland,

G_{out} = volume of groundwater flow leaving wetland,

OF_{in} = volume of overland flow into wetland,

SF_{in} = volume of stream flow into wetland,

SF_{out} = volume of stream flow leaving wetland,

OBF_{in} = volume of overbank flow into wetland,

OBF_{out} = volume of overbank flow leaving wetland,

ET = evapotranspiration, and

dV = change in volume of water stored in wetland.

Depending on the goal of the investigation, a wetland water budget can be more finely or more coarsely partitioned. Groundwater flow can be separated into interflow and surficial aquifer flow, and overland flow can be separated into variable source area runoff and Horton overland flow from upslope. Stream flow and overbank flow could be considered separately or together. The first step in creating a water budget is identifying the possible water inputs and outputs (Table 3.4). The second step is to decide the time scales of interest, as this will directly affect the choice of monitoring and analytical methods, and the third step is to identify and collate the climate and streamflow data available for characterizing regional hydrology such as amounts, seasonality,

TABLE 3.4.   Possible Sources and Losses of Water for Wetlands

Possible Water Sources	Possible Water Losses
Precipitation	Evapotranspiration
Stream flow	Stream flow
River overflow during floods	River return flow following floods
Groundwater	Groundwater
Variable source area runoff	Tides
Horton overland flow	Human withdrawals
Tides	
Human inputs	

and variability in precipitation, evapotranspiration, stream flow, and water table levels.

Water budgets can be applied conceptually with general information about climate and landscape conditions. It is obvious that the water budget of a wetland located on a perennial stream is dominated by streamflow input and output, and such a wetland will stay saturated year-round. A desert playa wetland generally receives water only from rainfall, and the wetland is inundated only for a short period of time until evapotranspiration removes the water. A floodplain backwater swamp may be fed in most seasons and most years by the regional water table and by hillslope interflow, but during a flood period, the wetland's water may be completely exchanged with river overflow water. Depending on the river and floodplain characteristics, it may be months or years between flood events that reach the wetland. A wetland's water budget has direct implications for biogeochemical cycling, as discussed in Chapter 5.

Outside of the tropics, there is always strong seasonality to evapotranspiration demands. Therefore, even if monthly precipitation is relatively constant, wetland water budgets and water levels usually exhibit seasonality. When seasonality of precipitation or snowmelt also affects a wetland's water budget, the tendency for seasonal behavior is enhanced. The information provided by a water budget depends on the time scale of the data and the analysis.

HYDROPATTERN

The *hydropattern* (commonly called *hydroperiod*—see chapter introduction) is the typical or average behavior of a wetland's water level time series. Wetland hydropatterns are important ecologically because most aquatic organisms live within the water column, and their life histories must be synchronized to the inundation periods of a wetland. In general, the hydropattern is "the seasonal pattern of the water level of a wetland and is like a hydrologic signature" (Mitsch and Gosselink 2000, describing *hydroperiod*). It is difficult to describe a complex and annually variable time series with simple mathematical terms, so a large number of metrics can be used to characterize a wetland's hydropattern (Table 3.5). Nuttle (1997) recommended that hydropattern measurements incorporate the following four distinct attributes of the water level time series: average water level for a period, intensity or amplitude of fluctuation, cyclic periods embedded in fluctions, and timing of fluctuations with respect to life histories of interest. Similarly, Wissinger (1999) proposed that "biologically relevant" classifications of wetland hydropatterns should include the following components:

1. Permanence (permanent, semipermanent [dry in some years], temporary),
2. Predictability of drying and filling,
3. Phenology (seasonal timing) of drying and filling,
4. Duration of the dry and wet phases, and
5. Harshness during both phases.

Wetland hydropatterns vary hugely between wetlands of different types and climates and also vary within wetlands of the same type and climate. Wissinger (1999) neatly summarized the many types of hydropatterns observed in North American wetlands (Figure 3.12), and Mitsch and Gosselink (2000) provided excellent examples of various hydropattern behaviors.

Hydropattern is a dominant driver of wetland ecology. Permanently inundated wetlands usually support fish (and other top predators such as bullfrogs), the presence of which precludes the existence of many amphibian species and alters macroinvertebrate community structure. Conversely, wetlands with very short hydroperiods are not wet long enough for many amphibians to breed and mature beyond their larval stage (e.g., Pechman et al. 1989; Snodgrass et al. 2000; Ryan and Winne 2001). Broad differences in hydropatterns are reflected in different macroinvertebrate community structures (e.g., King et al. 1996; Wissinger et al. 1999; Brooks 2000; Acosta and Perry 2001; Boix et al. 2001), but small differences in hydropatterns do not perceptibly alter macroinvertebrate communities (Batzer et al. 2004). The greatest amphibian and macroinvertebrate richness is usually found in wetlands with long, but not perennial, hydroperiods (Whiles and Goldowitz 2001; Paton and Crouch 2002). Hydropatterns affect plant communities not only through length of inundation, but also through depth of inundation (e.g., David 1996; Newman et al. 1996b; Baldwin et al. 2001; Steven and Toner 2004). Water levels of some wetlands are managed to create optimal conditions for plants that produce high-quality food for waterfowl. Hydropatterns also affect decomposition rates of organic material (e.g., Battle and Golladay 2001; see also Chapter 5).

Wetland hydropatterns can be observed simply and inexpensively with a staff gauge visited on a regular schedule, but staff gauge observations have several drawbacks. Staff gauges provide no information on water level dynamics occurring between visits, and human observers have trouble maintaining a precisely regular visitation schedule. Automatic water level monitoring, using any of a variety of water level sensing and data recording technologies, can provide continuous water level data sampled at short intervals but at a

TABLE 3.5. Some Metrics for Characterizing Wetland Hydropatterns

Metric	Notes
Duration of inundation period	Usually expressed in months or weeks, this metric is the average annual duration of surface saturation.
Start and end dates of surface inundation	Wetlands may have equivalent durations of surface inundation, but these periods may occur at different times of year. The temporal relationship of the inundation period to the life histories of plants, macroinvertebrates, waterfowl, and amphibians has obvious repercussions for wetland ecology.
Stage duration curve	A curve that relates the fraction of time the wetland water level equals or exceeds a given stage. The statistical analog in stream hydrology is the flow-duration curve. This curve does not yield information about the number of times water level rises and drops across a specific level.
Stage excursion frequency	A histogram showing the number of events per year during which any given range of stages is equaled or exceeded.
Stage recurrence curve	A curve describing the annual probability of exceedence or the average return period of all observed peak annual stages. The statistical analog in stream hydrology is the peak flow recurrence curve.
Mean water level fluctuation	The idea behind the mean water level fluctuation is to characterize how much the water level rises and falls—the "flashiness" of the water levels. The highest and lowest water levels are recorded for specified time intervals, usually two weeks or a month. The metric is not independent of the sampling frequency (Reinelt et al. 2001).
Monthly or seasonal mean water level	
Graphical analysis of wetland water level and/or water table level dynamics over time.	A plot of water level over time.

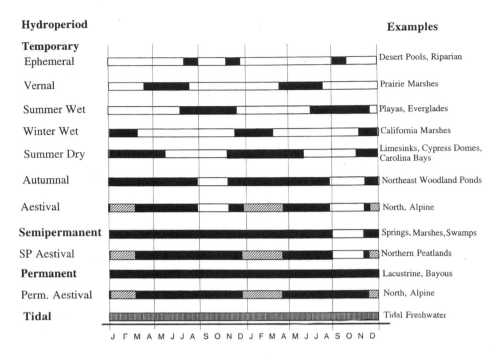

Hydroperiod

Temporary
Ephemeral — Desert Pools, Riparian
Vernal — Prairie Marshes
Summer Wet — Playas, Everglades
Winter Wet — California Marshes
Summer Dry — Limesinks, Cypress Domes, Carolina Bays
Autumnal — Northeast Woodland Ponds
Aestival — North, Alpine
Semipermanent — Springs, Marshes, Swamps
SP Aestival — Northern Peatlands
Permanent — Lacustrine, Bayous
Perm. Aestival — North, Alpine
Tidal — Tidal Freshwater

J F M A M J J A S O N D J F M A M J J A S O N D

Examples

FIGURE 3.12
Summary of hydropatterns observed in North America. Dark blocks represent inundation, hatched blocks represent iced conditions, and white areas represent dry periods. Reprinted from Wissinger (1999) with the permission of John Wiley & Sons.

higher monetary cost. Automatic sampling equipment measurements must be checked regularly for sensor drift, temperature effects on measurements, and power supply status. Equipment failure for any of a number of reasons may leave data gaps unless redundant sampling equipment is installed. Automatic water level monitoring systems are usually installed in a piezometer and thus provide information on water depth when the wetland is inundated and water table depth when the wetland is dry.

Richter (1997) used a corrosion-protected steel rod, a float, and button magnets to create a cheap, simple staff gauge that records maximum and minimum water levels occurring between visits. Richter's gauges provide an inexpensive and easy way to improve on the information provided by staff gaging, but corrosion of the steel rod is inevitable, and Richter's gauges have a life span of only two to three years, depending on care of construction and harshness of the monitoring environment. Euliss and Mushet (1996) developed a more corrosion-resistant but also more sophisticated and costly version of a maxima/minima recorder.

Nonrecording piezometers are inexpensive, easy to install, and provide information on shallow water table dynamics when the wetland is not inundated. A small diameter tube cut to the same length as the piezometer can be left inside the piezometer to provide information on the highest water level since the last visit. Finger paint or water-finding paste can be streaked on the tube prior to insertion into the piezometer, and the highest smearing or color change of the paint or paste indicates the previous high water level. Alternatively, cork dust can be placed in the piezometer, and the dust will leave a ring on the inside tube at the highest water level since the previous visit.

Bridgham et al. (1991) developed a steel rod oxidation methodology to quantify relative differences in water table depth in wetland soils. Steel rods are inserted into the ground and left in place for an extended time period. Where the rod is oxidized, water levels have risen and fallen, allowing oxygen into the soil and causing oxidation of the rod. Where the rod is free of rust, it is assumed that the soil has been nearly continuously saturated. This technique allows a semiquantitative evaluation of relative wetness and dryness of surface soils.

HYDRAULICS AND WATER QUALITY

Hydraulics is the study of the physics of water bodies, both moving *(hydrodynamic)* and static *(hydrostatic)*. The hydraulics of wetlands affect sediment deposition, biogeochemical cycling, and wetland hydropattern.

Wetlands are slow water environments, so when surface waters enter a wetland carrying sediment particles, some of the sediment will settle out along with nutrients or pollutants adsorbed to the sediment particles. The amount and type of sediment that will settle out depends on the size distribution of sediment particles transported to the wetland and the residence time of the wetland. Larger sediment particles fall faster than smaller sediment particles because the mass of the particle increases with the cube of the particle radius, while the friction forces acting on a particle moving through a liquid increase with the square of the particle radius (Table 3.6). The fall velocity of a spherical particle in liquid is described by Stoke's law:

$$v = (g/18v)(\rho_s - \rho)d_p^2 \qquad \text{(Eq. 20)}$$

where

v = particle fall velocity in water, cm/s,

g = acceleration of gravity, 981 cm/s^2,

ρ_s = density of sediment, g/cm^3,

ρ = density of water, 1.0 g/cm^3,

d_p = particle diameter (cm), and

ν = absolute viscosity of water, a function of temperature, cm^2/s.

Stoke's law says that fall velocity increases with the difference between the particle density and the fluid density and that the fall velocity increases with the square of the

TABLE 3.6. Settling Velocities of Soil Particles at 10°C.

Particle Type	Assumed Diameter (mm)	Velocity (mm/s)	Approximate Travel Time per Meter
Coarse sand	1	100	10 s/m
Fine sand	0.1	8	2 min/m
Silt	0.01	0.154	2 hour/m
Clay	0.0001	0.0000154	750 days/m

particle radius. For example, sand particles are relatively large and settle rapidly in water, while clay particles are very small and may remain in suspension for months (Table 3.6).

Wetlands receiving streamflow-carrying sediments usually display spatial patterns in soil texture. Because sands settle rapidly, soils near the stream discharge point tend to be sandier, whereas soils in slack coves of the wetland tend to have fine-textured soils. Over time, deltas form where streams enter wetlands. The amount and type of sediment entering and exiting a wetland strongly controls plant successional processes and the evolution of wetland morphology. Sediment deposition and organic matter accumulation cause shallow lakes to become wetlands and wetlands to become meadows.

The *residence time* of a wetland is the average time a water molecule spends in a wetland from the time it enters to the time it leaves. A short residence time means that water is flushed quickly and undergoes relatively little biogeochemical transformation in the wetland, while a long residence time means the opposite. Conceptually, residence time is easy to calculate:

$$R_t = V/Q \qquad \text{(Eq. 21)}$$

where

R_t = Residence time of wetland, seconds,

V = volume of water in wetland, m³, and

Q = outflow rate of wetland, m³/s.

A large wetland with relatively small outflow, such as the Okefenokee Swamp in Georgia, will have a very long residence time. Such a wetland will be a sink for pollutants that enter the wetland, such as mercury from atmospheric deposition (George and Batzer, submitted). Conversely, a small beaver pond on a relatively large stream will have a very short residence time.

For a given average water depth, more and finer sediment particles will settle in a wetland with longer residence time (more time for particles to settle out). For a given residence time, more and finer sediment particles will settle in a wetland with shallower average depth (decreased settling distance). In most wetlands with surface waters flowing through them, the residence time is spatially variable, with lower residence times in relatively unobstructed and fast flow paths and longer residence times in backwater areas (Ferguson 1998). Residence time is also temporally variable, as neither wetland water volumes nor outflow rates are constant over time.

Biogeochemical processes in wetlands are strongly affected by residence time. Nutrient cycling is dependent on residence time because of the time scales associated with food webs. Sufficient time is needed for the various trophic levels to collect and transform nutrients. If water flows through the system faster than nutrients can be assimilated and cycled, then nutrient sequestration and transformation is not possible. For these reasons, residence time is one of the main design factors in constructed wetlands for stormwater and wastewater treatment.

Hydraulic engineers describe wetlands, ponds, and lakes by their *stage-storage-discharge relationships* (e.g., Dingman 1994; Ferguson 1998), which define the volume of water stored in a wetland and the wetland outflow for any given water depth (stage). Hydraulic relationships are usually monotonic, meaning that for any stage, there is only one possible outflow rate and one possible storage volume, although this assumption breaks down when there are backwater effects of surface waters downstream. The outlet configuration of a wetland strongly affects the stage-storage-discharge relationship. For example, if all other hydrologic factors are equal, a wetland that drains over a long beaver dam will have quite a different hydropattern characteristics from the same wetland draining through a small culvert. In the case of the beaver dam, a slight rise in stage produces a large increase in outflow rate, so the wetland water level changes very little during a storm. When the wetland drains through a culvert, the stage must rise much higher to achieve the same discharge rate, so the water level fluctuation during a storm is large. There are infinite possible outlet configurations for wetlands, and each will alter a wetland's hydropattern.

EFFECTS OF LAND USE CHANGES ON WETLAND HYDROLOGY

Land use activities adjacent to wetlands can affect wetland habitat by altering inputs of sunlight, sediment, organic debris, nutrients, and dissolved carbon, and sometimes contaminants such as pesticides, heavy metals, and organic chemicals. Vegetation and soil alteration in a wetland's watershed predominantly affects the wetland through altered hydrology and sediment contributions. Some activities may directly alter outlet hydraulics and thus change a wetland's hydropattern. Depending on the details of the activity, abiotic effects of human actions may make a wetland wetter, drier, flashier, sunnier, or more nutrient rich, and these abiotic changes may alter the biology of the system. Basic hydrologic concepts can be applied to predict likely effects of landscape alteration around and above a wetland. There is also a body of literature that has examined effects of forestry, agriculture, and urbanization on wetlands in various settings.

Clear-cutting a wetland's watershed reduces interception and evapotranspiration sufficiently to cause water table rise for one to five years following harvest (Riekerk 1985, 1989a, 1989b; Aust and Lea 1992; Crownover et al. 1995; Dube et al. 1995; Lockaby et al. 1997; Sun et al. 2000; Bliss and Comerford 2002). This water table rise increases inundation periods and reduces dry periods in wetlands in the affected basins. Compared with typical rotation lengths for commercial timber (as little as 22 years in the southeastern United States and as much as 70 years in the Pacific Northwest), the hydropattern effects of canopy removal are relatively short lived. If the canopy of a forested wetland is cut without removing the canopy in the contributing basin, an opposite hydropattern effect may occur because direct evaporation from the wetland will increase.

Observed effects of this hydropattern change on plants and macroinvertebrates are mixed because the hydrologic effect is difficult to divorce from light effects or nutrient effects of adjacent silviculture. For example, Batzer et al. (2000) studied wetlands in commercial pine plantations and found that wetlands surrounded by smaller trees had greater light levels, water temperatures, pH, herbaceous plant cover and biomass, terrestrial invertebrate diversities and numbers, and water flea numbers. These wetlands also had lower specific conductivities and aquatic oligochaete numbers than wetlands surrounded by mature trees. Hydrologic differences were not detectable, and it was hypothesized that these differences were driven by differences in nutrient concentrations and light. Even without fertilization of newly planted trees, timber harvest usually results in a temporary release of nutrients, principally nitrogen (Riekerk 1985).

The effects of agricultural practices on nearby wetlands are difficult to generalize. Irrigation of agricultural lands may increase or decrease inundation periods of adjacent wetlands, depending on whether irrigation water is pumped from the surficial aquifer, a confined aquifer, or a nearby stream (Bolen et al. 1989; Smith and Haukos 2002). Tilled fields increase surface runoff and thus increase water level fluctuations in receiving wetlands (Euliss and Mushet 1996). Tilled fields also increase sedimentation in receiving wetlands (Martin and Hartmann 1987; Luo et al. 1997, 1999).

Azous and Horner (2001) provide many case studies from the Puget Sound basin of the U.S. Pacific Northwest on the effects of urbanization on wetlands. In general, urbanization increases water level fluctuations and nutrient concentrations of wetlands. The biotic response to these abiotic drivers is usually reduced plant and amphibian species richness and diversity. In many urbanized wetlands of the Puget Sound, hardy invasive plant species outcompete native vegetation.

Undisturbed vegetative buffers are required or recommended by many state and local laws as well as by some forestry and agricultural best management practice manuals to mitigate the effects of land use change on wetlands. Vegetative buffers provide a number

TABLE 3.7. Benefits of Forested Buffers around Wetlands and Considerations
about Width and Function

Function	Necessary Width	Notes
Sediment, nutrient filtration	Width varies depending on upslope conditions. More is better (10 m to 30 m)	Most important during construction to minimize sediment input during excavation, grading, and grass establishment; also helps keep sediment, fertilizers, and pesticides from upslope activities out of wetlands.
Minimization of direct human impact	15 m is usually adequate.	People living near wetlands may landscape down to the edge or dump yard waste and garbage in the buffer or the wetland.
Organic debris input	Narrow buffer (~3 m) will suffice.	Leaves, twigs, pine needles, etc., can be important drivers of wetland ecology.
Large woody debris recruitment	$1/2$ Mature tree height (12–20 m)	Pieces of large wood provide habitat complexity, substrate for macroinvertebrates, cover for amphibians, roosts for waterfowl, and haul-out and sunning areas for turtles.
Wildlife habitat	Benefits increase out to 100 m.	Many birds and amphibians depend on terrestrial habitat adjacent to wetlands. Important remnant habitat after basin development.
Bank stability	3 m will suffice.	Sometimes valuable on certain wetland features with well-defined banks (e.g., sand rims on Carolina Bays, streambanks on floodplain wetlands)
Shade (water temperature)	15 m is generally sufficient.	More important on forested wetlands where light limits primary productivity. Peripheral shade is unimportant for marshes and open water wetlands.

TABLE 3.7. (*continued*)

Function	Necessary Width	Notes
Social (children playing)	>12 m	A narrow buffer grows a lot of blackberries and briers due to light effects. Hard to play in narrow buffer.
Aesthetics	Eye of the beholder	After development, wetland and stream buffers are often the only natural areas left in the landscape.

of benefits to wetlands (Table 3.7). Federal law provides some protection against direct alterations of wetlands, but federal law provides no buffer protections. Horner et al. (2001) provide guidelines for maintaining wetland functions in developing basins, and Booth et al. (2002) provide guidelines for protecting the natural hydrology of developing basins. All such guidelines include buffers as a necessary protection for wetlands. The buffers themselves provide little to no protection against hydrologic change, but they minimize the other abiotic influences associated with human land use activities.

4

ABIOTIC CONSTRAINTS FOR WETLAND PLANTS AND ANIMALS

Irving A. Mendelssohn and Darold P. Batzer

Wetland habitats can be stressful places for plants and animals to live, although most wetland organisms are well adapted to cope with the environmental challenges posed. The two most important abiotic factors influencing wetland biota are hydrology and the chemistry of soils and water. The extremely variable and unpredictable nature of hydrology and chemistry in wetlands can profoundly influence the structure and productivity of resident flora and fauna. In this chapter, we first address how hydrology constrains plant and animal populations, and discuss some of the ways biota have become adapted for life in hydrologically diverse wetlands. We couple our discussion of hydrology with the constraints imposed by low oxygen levels because the two factors are intimately intertwined. We continue the chapter with a discussion of the constraints imposed by salinity and describe adaptations of plants and animals for life in saline wetlands.

HYDROLOGY

In general, the dominant environmental factor affecting the structure and function of wetlands, fresh and saline, is hydrology (Mitsch and Gosselink 2000). Thus, it is not surprising that the flooding and drying of wetland habitats is a primary constraint on the distribution and productivity of wetland plants and animals. Although both excessive flooding and drying can stress wetland plants and animals, plants in general seem more affected by flooding constraints, and animals seem more affected by drying constraints.

Interestingly, however, to deal with either flooding or drying, plants and animals have tended to employ many of the same basic tactics.

CONSTRAINTS IMPOSED BY FLOODING ON WETLAND PLANTS

Although all wetland plants are certainly flood tolerant, dramatic differences in flood tolerance occur among wetland species. As a result, excessive duration and depth of flooding can influence the distribution and growth of some species more than others. The three major impacts of flooding for plants are (1) root oxygen deficiency, (2) soil phytotoxin accumulation, and (3) postanoxic injury. Before we can appreciate the adaptations of wetland plants to these potential stresses, it is first important to review the mechanisms responsible for their impacts.

Root Oxygen Deficiency

Organisms adapted to live in air receive life-sustaining energy through aerobic respiration, which requires oxygen as a terminal electron acceptor and a carbon source (e.g., glucose) as an electron donor. Plants are no exception to this rule. The roots of plants that grow in terrestrial soils receive their oxygen from the soil, which is in equilibrium with oxygen in the atmosphere, approximately 21%. Aerobic respiration is an energy efficient process that produces approximately 36 moles of adenosine triphosphate (ATP), the energy currency of the cell, for each mole of glucose oxidized during aerobic respiration (Fig. 4.1).

What happens when the soil becomes flooded? The oxygen that was present in the soil rapidly disappears, as it is used in respiration by soil microbes and roots. Replenishment of the soil oxygen from the atmosphere is inhibited because of a very slow diffusion rate in water—10,000 times less than in air. The absence of oxygen in the soil can create a root oxygen deficiency in a few hours, depending on the degree of flooding. This oxygen deficiency is termed *hypoxia,* which has been biochemically defined as the oxygen concentration at which the production of ATP from aerobic respiration is less than maximum. As the extent of hypoxia becomes greater, the root oxygen deficiency worsens, and the production of ATP decreases. Since ATP is required for life-sustaining processes, such as nutrient uptake, metabolite synthesis, and transport processes, a reduction in plant growth occurs that may reduce the competitive ability of the plant or even result in death. The inability to maintain energy status has also been linked to cell acidosis, the decrease in cytoplasmic pH resulting from lactate fermentation, which occurs in the first stages of plant response to anoxia (the absence of oxygen). Cytoplasmic acidosis impairs cell function, such as energy production, and results in cell death. Both cytoplasmic acidosis and cellular energy deficiencies are primary impacts of root oxygen deficiencies resulting from plant flooding.

However, there are other impacts as well. One is the production of potentially toxic metabolites produced during anaerobic metabolism (carbon metabolism in the absence

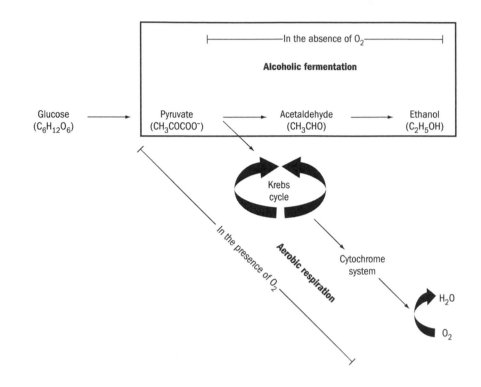

FIGURE 4.1

General pathways of plant carbon metabolism as a function of the presence or absence of oxygen.

of oxygen). As hypoxia worsens, there is a point at which an alternate pathway of carbon metabolism is induced. The alternate pathway, which is most active during the complete absence of oxygen or at very low oxygen concentrations, is called *alcoholic fermentation* (Fig. 4.1). Alcoholic fermentation is the generation of ethanol from pyruvate, which is formed during glycolysis. Alcoholic fermentation, which is analogous to lactate fermentation in animals, allows carbon metabolism to proceed even when aerobic respiration has stopped. This process also produces some energy, 2 moles of ATP per mole of glucose oxidized, but about 16 times less than aerobic respiration. A negative impact from alcoholic fermentation can result because the ethanol produced in alcoholic fermentation is toxic if it accumulates to high enough levels in root cells where it can solubilize phospholipid membranes. However, since ethanol is a small molecule, it readily diffuses from the roots of most plants, especially wetland plants. For example, 98% of the ethanol produced in rice roots diffuses into the rooting medium (Jackson et al. 1982). Acetaldehyde is an intermediary metabolite in alcoholic fermentation that is also highly toxic, and lactic acid, which forms from lactate fermentation, can also induce a cascade of negative impacts.

Another impact of root oxygen deficiency to the plant is a carbohydrate deficiency. Carbohydrates are used for the synthesis of structural materials like cellulose and lignin and for metabolites needed for cellular processes such as carbon skeletons for nitrogen assimilation. The diffusion of ethanol from plant roots, although preventing ethanol toxicity, is a loss of carbon that could be used for these processes. Also, it is well known that some cells increase glucose metabolism under hypoxia; this is referred to as the Pasteur effect. The Pasteur effect allows for greater ATP production per unit time but at the expense of considerable carbon consumption. Carbon deficiencies can also occur because of reduced carbon transport to the roots due an inhibition of phloem loading in the leaves and from lower photosynthetic rates during flooding.

Soil Phytotoxin Accumulation

When an aerobic soil becomes flooded, rapid changes in the biogeochemistry of the soil occur. The first change is the depletion of oxygen, as discussed previously. However, this is only the beginning of a cascade of microbially mediated biogeochemical events, each setting the stage for the next (see Chapters 2 and 5). Soil bacteria have evolved to use elements, in addition to oxygen, as terminal electron acceptors in respiration. Bacteria that can utilize oxygen or other oxidized elements are called *facultative anaerobes,* that is, they can thrive in both aerobic and anaerobic environments. These bacteria can use oxidized manganese (Mn^{4+}) and iron (Fe^{3+}) as electron acceptors in their respiration. The electrons come from the carbon source that the bacteria are metabolizing. As a result, the manganese and iron are reduced to manganese (Mn^{3+}) and ferrous iron (Fe^{2+}), which are much more soluble in water than their oxidized forms. These reduced forms can accumulate in flooded soil to levels that are toxic to plants. After most of the iron and manganese are biochemically reduced, a group of bacteria that are active only under anaerobic conditions, obligate anaerobes, are responsible for the reduction of sulfate (SO_4^{2-}) and carbon dioxide (CO_2) to toxic hydrogen sulfide (H_2S) and methane (CH_4). Hydrogen sulfide is even more toxic to living cells than hydrogen cyanide. During the anaerobic decomposition of carbon in the soil, a number of organic compounds are produced that can be toxic as well. Organic acids such as formic, acetic, proprionic, and butyric are generated from the incomplete decomposition of organic matter and can cause growth reductions in plants. These compounds may also stimulate callus formation in the air space tissue that prevents or reduces oxygen transport to the roots (Armstrong et al. 1996).

Postanoxic Injury

The reexposure of plant tissues to aerobic conditions after periods of anoxia due to inundation can result in severe damage. This impact has been termed *postanoxic injury* and can result from a number of causes. Reexposure of tissues to oxygen can produce superoxide radicals (e.g., O_2^-, as O_2 is metabolically reduced to H_2O). Also, the rapid oxidation of anaerobically accumulated metabolites, like ethanol, can cause a rise in the production of toxic intermediates like acetaldehyde (Crawford 1992). Hence, the reestablishment of an aerobic state after flooding can have impacts commensurate with the flooding itself.

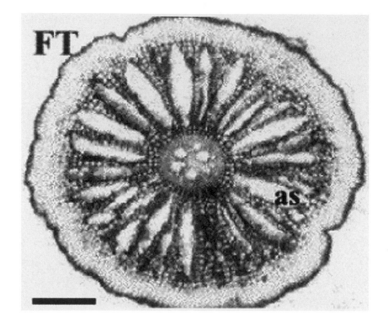

FIGURE 4.2

Cross section of a flooded root of cattail *(Typha domingensis)*. The lysigenous air space tissue (aerenchyma) is apparent in the root cortex. From Chabbi et al. (2000), with permission.

ADAPTATIONS OF WETLAND PLANTS TO FLOODING IMPACTS

Plants possess many adaptations to flooding that can be organized into two primary categories: (1) anatomical-morphological and (2) biochemical-physiological. Both classes of adaptations are important to plant survival in flooded environments.

Anatomical-Morphological Adaptations

The primary adaptation that flood tolerant plants utilize to cope with flooding stress is aerenchyma, or air space tissue. Aerenchyma is a tissue type maintaining air spaces that act like a straw, moving oxygen from the atmosphere through plant leaves and stem and into belowground roots and rhizomes (underground stems). Some of this oxygen leaks into the soil surrounding the roots. The oxygen that diffuses out of the root can create an oxidized zone around the root, which has been termed an *oxidized rhizosphere*. The oxidized rhizosphere can also assist in flood tolerance as described below. Most anatomical and morphological adaptations allow the plant to avoid oxygen stress by providing oxygen from the atmosphere.

AERENCHYMA.   Aerenchyma tissue can occupy as much as 60% of a flood tolerant plant's cross-sectional volume (Fig. 4.2), while nonflood-tolerant plants may only have from 2% to 7% aerenchyma volume. The holes that comprise the aerenchyma are called *lacunae*,

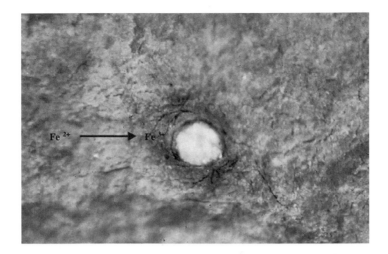

FIGURE 4.3
A cross section of the root of the swamp tree, green ash *(Fraxinus pennsylvanica)*, growing in a soil medium. The oxidized iron rhizosphere is clearly identified by the orange (iron oxide) color surrounding the root. Photo by Bill Good. See insert for color version.

which are constitutive (present regardless of flooding condition) in some plants or specific organs and inducible (develop on flooding) in others. The lacunae form in three primary ways: (1) the lysis or death of living cells, (2) the separation of the cell walls of adjoining cells, and (3) expansion of intercellular spaces from the cell division of surrounding cells (Seago et al. 2004). The plant hormone ethylene plays an important role in aerenchyma formation, as it does in a number of adaptations to flood tolerance. The primary function of aerenchyma is to provide oxygen for aerobic respiration in flooded belowground structures and to create the oxidized rhizosphere. However, the presence of this tissue also reduces the number of living cells and hence reduces the oxygen demand. It also provides a means by which toxic, volatile root metabolic products, like ethanol and acetaldehyde, can diffuse from plant roots to the atmosphere. In addition, carbon dioxide that is produced in the root and the soil can diffuse up the plant to the leaves, where it may be used in photosynthesis. Finally, the oxidized rhizosphere (Fig. 4.3) provides a zone in which potentially toxic compounds can be detoxified. For example, hydrogen sulfide, which has been shown to be toxic to mangroves and salt marsh grasses (Koch et al. 1990), can be oxidized to nontoxic sulfate in the oxidized rhizosphere (McKee et al. 1988). The oxidized rhizosphere helps plants avoid phytotoxins in flooded soils and also can precipitate soluble and potentially toxic forms of iron and manganese (Fig. 4.4) (Mendelssohn and Postek 1982).

PRESSURIZED FLOW.   For many flood-tolerant plants, the oxygen in the aerenchyma tissue moves to the roots via diffusion, a relatively slow process. However, in many plants that grow in the deepest water and have the greatest flood tolerance, oxygen movement occurs via convective or pressurized flow. For example, in the Florida Everglades, the highly flood-tolerant

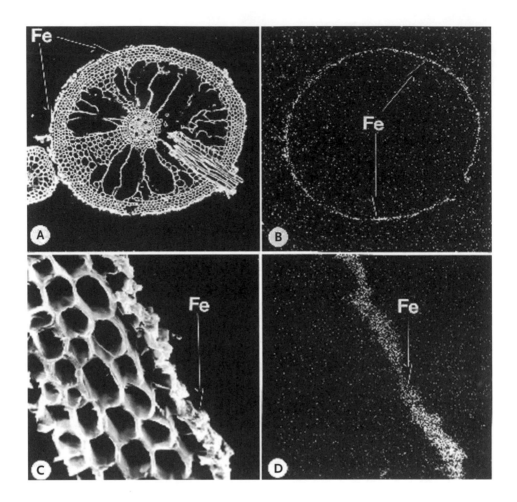

FIGURE 4.4

X-ray microanalysis of smooth cordgrass *(Spartina alterniflora)* roots. (A) Secondary electron image of a
root cross section from *Spartina*, x 210. (B) Iron area map of the cross section shown in image A
showing the presence of the element iron around the root periphery. (C) Secondary electron image of a
root cross section showing particulate deposition on the epidermal cell surface, x1,150. (D) Iron area
map of the cross section shown in image C showing the presence of iron localized at the epidermal cell
surface. From Mendelssohn and Postek (1982), with permission.

southern cattail *(Typha domingensis)* exhibits a rate of oxygen movement much greater than
other wetland plants, such as sawgrass *(Cladium jamaicense)*, in which air movement is by
diffusion (Sorrel et al. 2000). Pressure gradients are created within the plant by a variety of
mechanisms that result in the mass flow of air through the plant. This results in a greater capacity for oxygen movement to the roots of wetland plants that possess pressurized flow. For
example, the rooted, floating aquatic species *Nuphar* can transport as much as 22 l per day
of air through one petiole (Dacey 1981). Thus, plants with pressurized flow are less likely to
experience root oxygen deficiencies and will have greater flood tolerance (Chabbi et al. 2000).

FIGURE 4.5
Hypertrophied lenticels on the stem of one-year-old plants of tupelo *(Nyssa sylvatica)*. From Keely (1979), with permission.

FIGURE 4.6
Adventitious roots of spikerush *(Eleocharis cellulosa)* produced after four months of flooding.

LENTICELS. Plants must possess a means by which atmospheric oxygen can enter the interior tissues. Oxygen can diffuse into leaf tissue through stomates, used primarily for carbon dioxide intake and water loss. However, trunks and other woody structures of trees possess lenticels, small slits or pores on the stem or trunk that allows gas exchange to living interior cells. In flood-tolerant trees, the lenticels become hypertrophied, raised structures, often corky, of loosely packed cells (Fig. 4.5). The hypertrophied lenticels provide an enhanced pathway for oxygen to diffuse into aerenchyma within the plant as well as to allow the loss of volatile root metabolites in the opposite direction. Flood tolerant trees such as green ash *(Fraxinus pennsylvanica)* and black willow *(Salix nigra)* rely on lenticels during periods of high water. Also, flood-tolerant saltwater mangroves possess lenticels on their modified aerial roots (discussed below) for the same reason. Lenticels are integral to the flood tolerance of many plant species.

ADVENTITIOUS ROOTS. Another morphological adaptation of flood-tolerant plants is a rapid production of adventitious roots (Fig. 4.6). Adventitious roots are roots that arise from mature tissue like a stem or trunk, and not from embryonic tissue, like the radicle (embryonic root). Adventitious roots can be seen on the trunks of floodplain trees during and immediately after spring flooding. These roots, which have been called *water roots,* are important in oxygen and nutrient uptake from the aerobic flood waters. Other adventitious roots (e.g., soil water roots) grow in the surface soil. They contain aerenchyma and are likely able to function in nutrient uptake.

BARRIERS TO ROOT OXYGEN LOSS. The roots of some wetlands plant have a suberized hypodermis, a ring of cells 2 to 3 layers thick, just interior to the epidermis (Seago et al. 2000). The outermost cell layer, called the *exodermis,* has thickened cell walls (casparian bands) that prevent the loss of substances like oxygen from the root (Perumalla et al. 1990; Peterson and Perumalla 1990) (Fig. 4.7).

MODIFIED ROOTS. One of the most amazing morphological adaptations to flooding are the modified roots found in a number of flood-tolerant trees. These structures often account for a considerable proportion of the biomass of the tree. Mangroves, trees that grow in tropical, saline, intertidal environments, possess modified roots in the form of pneumatophores and prop roots. The black mangrove (*Avicennia* species) possess a modified root called the *pneumatophore* (Fig. 4.8a), which has lenticels, aerenchyma, and adventitious roots. The pneumatophores are pencil-like woody structures that arise vertically from underground horizontal roots (cable roots) and, via surface lenticels and internal aerenchyma, allow the movement of air to soil adventitious roots. Interestingly, air movement into the aerenchyma is facilitated indirectly by the ebb and flow of the tides (Scholander et al. 1965). Prop roots (Figure 4.8b) occur in many of the red mangroves (*Rhizophora* species). Prop roots, or stilt roots, are aerial roots that extend from the trunk of the tree downward into the soil, where adventitious roots develop. The prop roots are covered with

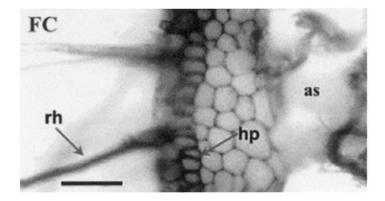

FIGURE 4.7
Cross section of a flooded sawgrass *(Cladium jamaicense)* root showing the thickened cell walls of the hypodermis (hp). Root hairs (rh) are also apparent. From Chabbi et al. (2000), with permission. See insert for color version.

lenticels that allow air to enter the prop root and move to the adventitious roots where oxygen is used by the roots and diffuses into the soil (McKee et al. 1988; McKee 1996).

One of the most interesting of the modified roots is the "knee" (Fig. 4.9) of the cypress tree, *Taxodium distichum*, a species that dominates deep water swamps in the southeastern part of the United States. Depending on the age of the tree and the hydrology and fertility of the swamp, cypress knees can grow in excess of 2 m in height. The knees project from the soil where they connect with horizontal roots, in a manner similar to pneumatophores. Several possible functions of cypress knees have been suggested, but a comprehensive investigation to determine their function has not been conducted. Nonetheless, it has been suggested that cypress knees support the tree by (1) providing a conduit for oxygen transport to underground roots, (2) aiding the physical support of these shallow-rooted trees, and (3) supplying carbohydrates to metabolizing cells under flooded conditions. The function of oxygen transport, which originally received the most attention, does not appear valid. Knees do not possess lenticels, so they have no obvious entry path for oxygen. Also, aerenchyma tissue is not present in the knee, although the wood of knees is not very dense. Measurements of gaseous diffusion through the knee have demonstrated little movement (Kurz and Demaree 1934; Pulliam 1992). For these reasons, knees do not appear to function as an aeration mechanism as do pneumatophores. Evidence is also weak for carbohydrate storage and other functions. Physical structural support is certainly a logical function in that knees may provide extra stability for these trees in a similar way as do buttresses.

Buttresses, or expanded trunk bases, occur in a number of flood-tolerant trees, such as bald cypress and swamp tupelos, *Nyssa* species. These swollen trunks are similar to root buttresses of tropical forest trees. Based on theoretical assessments, buttresses appear to provide mechanical support for trees that may be exposed to asymmetrical stresses during development or from environmental events such as storms (Warren et al. 1988; Ennos 1993).

FIGURE 4.8

(A) Pneumatophores of the black mangrove *(Avicennia germinans)* are modified roots that transport oxygen via surface lenticels to submerged roots. (B) Prop roots of the red mangrove *(Rhizophora mangle)* serve a similar function as well as functioning in support.

SHOOT RESPONSES.   Upon submergence, many flood-tolerant species exhibit accelerated rates of shoot elongation (Voesenek and Blom 1999). This allows the shoots to reach the air and for oxygen transport and photosynthesis to proceed. The plant hormone ethylene, which accumulates during flooding, is responsible, in addition to auxins (growth hormones), for the rapid stem elongation. Other shoot responses to flooding include stomatal closure to prevent excess water loss (often seen in less flood-tolerant trees), leaf senescence to reduce

FIGURE 4.9
Knees of the bald cypress (*Taxodium distichum*) like the prop roots of mangroves are modified roots. However, the function of cypress knees is still unknown, although physical support is likely.

the amount of living tissue, nutrient relocation to provide nutrients to growing organs, reduction in growth rate for some species to reduce energetic needs, and others.

Metabolic-Physiological Adaptations

What happens if the anatomical-morphological adaptations that were previously discussed are not sufficient to provide adequate oxygen to support aerobic respiration in flooded plant organs? Flood-tolerant plants, just like animals, are adapted to these periods of hypoxia or even anoxia. Flood-tolerant plants can compensate for the energy deficiencies that result from cessation of aerobic respiration and can maintain carbon metabolism via alcoholic fermentation. Plants show an induction in alcoholic fermentation that generates some ATP, as mentioned earlier, and also maintains electron transport and thus carbon metabolism. However, this induction alone does not provide flood tolerance because of both the limited ATP that is produced and the potential for ethanol toxicity and carbon deficiency. Many flood-tolerant plants accelerate the rate of alcoholic fermentation (Pasteur effect) and thus are able to compensate for the generally low ATP production that occurs during anoxia (Saglio et al. 1980; Ricard et al. 1994). This capacity to compensate for lower energy production from alcoholic fermentation has been well documented in rice, where an induction of alcoholic fermentation maintains root energy status (Drew 1992). Evidence for this metabolic adaptation has been documented in noncrop wetland species as well (Mendelssohn et al. 1981; Smits 1990; Joly and Brandle 1995; Blom and Voesenek 1996). As discussed, postanoxic injury can occur as a result of reactive oxygen radicals that form when anaerobic tissue is reexposed to the atmosphere (Crawford 1992). It is thought that flood-tolerant species are better protected against free radicals by the accumulation of antioxidants like ascorbic acid or by the activation of enzymes like superoxide dismutase that remove these radicals (Monk et al. 1987).

A comprehensive tolerance to flooding requires the integration of both physiological and morphological adaptations. Young plants or plants growing in nonflooded conditions may not yet possess the anatomical adaptations, like aerenchyma, for flood adaptation. Hence, on flooding, these plants must adapt physiologically until anatomical adaptations are induced, if they are to survive. This integration of anatomical and physiological adaptations has been demonstrated in *Spartina patens,* a brackish marsh grass native to the United States (Burdick and Mendelssohn 1990). On flooding, the roots of young plants of this species initially exhibit an increase in the potential for alcoholic fermentation, as indicated by an acceleration in the activity of alcohol dehydrogenase (ADH), the enzyme that catalyzes the terminal step in alcoholic fermentation. Root aerenchyma development is minimal during this initial stage of flooding. However, over a 30-day period, aerenchyma development is induced until approximately 50% of the root volume is composed of air space. As the aerenchyma develops over this period, ADH activity decreases by 75%, indicating that the air space tissue provides sufficient oxygen to reduce dependency on root anaerobic metabolism. Nonetheless, even after 60 days of flooding, ADH activity remains twice as high in flooded roots as in roots in drained soil, suggesting that aerenchyma development in this species does not completely eliminate oxygen deficiencies. This example of flooding response in this brackish marsh grass demonstrates the dependency on both physiological and anatomical adaptations. This integrated response has also been demonstrated in other plant species such as *Zea* and *Isotes* (Drew et al. 1985; Sorrell 2004).

CONSTRAINTS IMPOSED BY FLOODING ON WETLAND ANIMALS

When assessing flooding constraints on animals, the terrestrial and aquatic faunas must be considered separately. Many terrestrial animals, such as canopy-dwelling birds and insects, are not stressed by flooding. Ground-dwelling terrestrial animals (mammals, invertebrates) are more at risk for drowning during floods, but many can simply relocate to higher ground. Aquatic animals (fish, amphibians, invertebrates) actually rely on flooded conditions, but when hydrologic conditions begin to affect dissolved oxygen levels, like plants, they too can become stressed.

Some significant differences exist between plants and animals in the nature of oxygen stress, however. For wetlands plants, a lack of oxygen in the root zone is the primary problem, and oxygen levels in the water column are less of an issue. In contrast, for aquatic animals, levels of oxygen in the water column are more important than the dynamics in soils. Wetland aquatic animals are virtually excluded from soils by anoxic conditions, unless they create burrows or tubes to maintain contact with the surface. Thus, aquatic animals mostly occupy the water column or the upper layers of the soil substratum.

Fluctuations of oxygen levels in wetland waters can be volatile. They can be influenced by abiotic factors such as temperature and wind action, and biotic factors such as decomposition and photosynthesis. During a warm, still night, oxygen in water can plummet to very low levels as microbial and animal respiration uses up available oxygen, and supplies are not replenished because of an absence of photosynthesis, an absence of mixing, and the reduced solubility of oxygen in warm water. On the other hand, on a sunny, wind-swept afternoon, oxygen levels in waters can become high as mixing and photosynthesis saturate or even supersaturate the water with oxygen. It is the episodes of extremely low oxygen levels, even if infrequent and brief, that stress wetland animals. The inability of many aquatic animal groups to cope with oxygen stress prevents them from occupying wetlands. This is why many aquatic invertebrate groups that thrive in streams, rivers, and lakes such as the stoneflies (Plecoptera), mayflies (Ephemeroptera), and caddisflies (Trichoptera) are poorly represented in wetlands. Similarly, only a few groups of fish are able to survive in oxygen-poor wetland waters.

In northern latitudes, even those fish tolerant of low oxygen levels can be stressed by a phenomenon called *winterkill*. Contrary to what some believe, winterkill does not require a water body to freeze completely. Instead, it usually develops when snow cover is deep and persists late into the spring, preventing sunlight from penetrating into the water column beneath the ice. In the absence of light, the photosynthetic rate of algae below the ice is dramatically slowed, yet oxygen-depleting decomposition processes continue. Eventually, oxygen levels become so low that fish begin to die.

ADAPTATIONS OF WETLAND ANIMALS TO FLOODING IMPACTS

Terrestrial Animals

Most terrestrial animals that occupy wetlands (mammals, birds, invertebrates) are little affected by flooding beyond perhaps the need to move to higher ground and thus have no special adaptations for flood tolerance. However, some of the more sedentary invertebrates have developed some interesting strategies to cope with flooding. For the short duration floods that occur in tidal wetlands, animals such as fiddler crabs can retreat to air-filled burrows during high tides and others can simply tolerate being submersed for relatively short periods of time. Certain ants *(Crematogaster)* use their large heads to block the entrance to their nests during high tides. Other insects hide in air-filled spaces in plants.

Terrestrial animals in floodplain wetlands have to deal with longer-term habitat inundation. Braccia and Batzer (2001) found that many terrestrial invertebrates of floodplains could withstand relatively long-term flooding (weeks or months) inside pieces of dead wood, where they apparently accessed pockets of air. Certain floodplain millipedes, normally considered terrestrial organisms, can function beneath the water by using plastron respiration to extract oxygen from water (Adis et al. 1997). Ground beetles, millipedes, and centipedes will move onto floating pieces of wood during floods, essentially

FIGURE 4.10
Response of a wetland ant colony to flooding. The colony congeals into a mass and either floats by itself or adheres to emergent plants materials or wood until flood waters subside. Photo by Jennifer Henke.

using the wood as lifeboats (Braccia and Batzer 2001). When colonies of ants in freshwater wetlands become flooded, they create their own lifeboats by congealing into large balls composed of literally thousands of individuals (Fig. 4.10). The balls of ants float or adhere to above-water substrates, and the individuals on the outside, which are exposed to water, cyclically migrate into the center of the swarm to survive. With the invasion of the imported fire ant into the southern United States, these floating swarms of stinging ants are a hazard to unwitting wetland researchers.

Aquatic Animals

Animals use many of the same basic strategies as plants to cope with low oxygen levels. As mentioned earlier, plants frequently develop air channels of aerenchyma tissue to deliver atmospheric oxygen to their roots. Similarly, air breathing is also quite common in aquatic wetland animals. Beetle adults and most water bugs will collect air under their wings or along surfaces of their bodies (Fig. 4.11). The organisms carry this air supply with them under water and extract their oxygen needs from it. If the surface of the air bubble has significant contact with water and the water is sufficiently oxygenated, additional oxygen can diffuse into the bubble from the water as oxygen concentrations in the bubble decline. This *physical gill* enables the organisms to extract more oxygen from the bubble than it originally contained (Eriksen et al. 1996). Other insects (mosquito larvae, diving beetle larvae, water scorpions) use siphon tubes to breathe surface air, and the aptly named rat-tailed maggot (Diptera: Syrphidae) has a telescoping siphon that can extend six times its body length. Several species of wetland fish will gulp surface air or use the

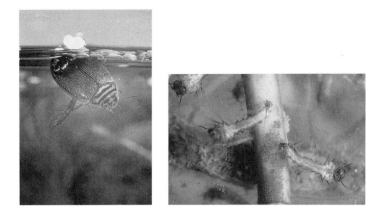

FIGURE 4.11

Mechanisms for aquatic invertebrates to breathe air. Dysticidae beetle adults (left) collect air bubbles from the surface and retain the bubble under their leathery wing covers on top of their respiratory spiracles. *Coquillettidia* mosquito larvae (right) have respiratory siphons that are modified to access oxygen in aerenchyma tissue of emergent plants root (e.g., *Typha*) and remain attached to these plants throughout their larval development. Beetle photo by Gordon Guyer.

water of the surface film when the oxygen level in the main water column becomes too low, and they use this oxygen supply until conditions improve.

In perhaps the best example of an animal using the strategies of plants, some insect larvae will exploit the air supply found in plant aerenchyma. The siphons of *Coquillettidia* and *Mansonia* mosquito larvae are modified into structures that pierce plant roots to access the oxygen in the aerenchyma, and unlike other mosquitoes, these larvae do not have to risk constantly revisiting the water's surface to satisfy their oxygen demands (Fig. 4.11). In another example of animals exploiting plant adaptations, benthic midge larvae will congregate around plants roots (Entrekin et al. 2001) presumably to use the oxidized rhizosphere associated with many hydrophytes.

Mobility is one clear advantage that animals have over plants in terms of dealing with oxygen stress. Aquatic animals that must extract their oxygen needs from the water can simply search out areas where oxygen is not limiting. When oxygen stress develops, fish will congregate in areas of flow where mixing occurs or rest near the water's surface where oxygen levels are higher. Even sedentary midge larvae will leave benthic sediments when conditions are excessively harsh and crawl up plant stems or woody debris to access the more highly oxygenated water near the surface. Conversely, some wetland animals deal with oxygen stress by drastically reducing their activity. Fiddler crabs will become virtually inactive in their submersed burrows if oxygen level become too low and will remain that way until conditions improve (Vernberg and Vernberg 1972).

Many wetland animals are physiologically adapted to tolerate low oxygen conditions. Just as plants will utilize anaerobic metabolism as a respiratory pathway when oxygen is limiting (see earlier discussion), many wetland animals will do the same. Common wetland fishes such as carp (van Ginneken et al. 1998), killifish (Rees et al. 2001), and cichlids (Muusze et al. 1998), and wetland invertebrates such as midge larvae (Augenfeld 1963) and the marine periwinkle (Greenway and Storey 2001) all will switch to anaerobic metabolism in response to anoxia. An assortment of wetland invertebrates (certain midge larvae, aquatic worms, crustaceans, backswimmers, clams, and nematodes) possess forms of haemoglobin or other respiratory pigments (Eriksen et al. 1996, Mitsch and Gosselink 2000). Midge haemoglobin differs from the form found in vertebrates in that it has a higher affinity for oxygen and will release oxygen only in hypoxic conditions (Eriksen et al. 1996). Walshe (1950) determined that midge haemoglobin contained only about a nine-minute supply of oxygen, so its purpose may not be to counteract long-term anoxia. Midge larvae live in tubes and pump oxygenated water through them by undulating their bodies. The haemoglobin may simply permit breaks in pumping to occur without causing the larvae undue stress. Water fleas can use oxygen bound to haemoglobin to sustain efficient aerobic metabolism under hypoxic conditions for up to an hour (Pirow et al. 2001), so for these organisms, the pigment may be a more important stress relief than for midges. Haemoglobin in backswimmers (Hemiptera: Notonectidae) enables them to use smaller air bubbles, reducing buoyancy problems associated with large bubbles (Wells et al. 1981). The relative importance of respiratory pigments to wetland animals for tolerating anoxic conditions remains equivocal.

For fish in wetlands, low oxygen conditions may pose problems for egg survival, and parental care of progeny by these fish is especially common. Sunfish (Centrarchidae) create nests and fan the eggs to keep them oxygenated and silt free. Some wetland fish orally manipulate their eggs to ensure the environment is suitable for development. Mosquitofish are live-bearers, and the females incubate the eggs inside their bodies until they hatch and are mobile. These behaviors will confer multiple benefits to progeny, but relieving oxygen stress may have been an important factor in their evolution.

CONSTRAINTS IMPOSED BY DRYING ON WETLAND PLANTS

Adaptations of wetland plants to drought have been poorly investigated because soil moisture deficiency is a relatively rare occurrence in most wetlands (although species-specific differences in tolerance to soil moisture deficiency can be important). Many wetland tree species have been shown to be more impacted by drained soil conditions than by continuously flooded conditions (e.g., Elcan and Pezeshki 2002). This is especially true for swamp species such as bald cypress *(Taxodium distichum)* and water tupelo *(Nyssa aquatic)* in which flooding can be stimulatory to growth. This implies a trade-off between flood tolerance and drought tolerance whereby those species exhibiting the greatest flood tolerance are often the least tolerant of drier conditions. Keeley (1979) shed light on this hypothesis when he investigated population differentiation of *Nyssa sylvatica*, a broadleaf deciduous tree, along a flood frequency gradient in the southeastern United States. He found that floodplain populations were similar to upland populations in physiology and biomass allocation when under drained conditions but similar to swamp populations when under flooded conditions. Because flooding is considered such a strong environmental stressor, why do floodplain populations not always possess adaptations to maximize flood tolerance so that when flooding occurs they are initially better adapted? Keeley answered this question by suggesting that flooding adaptations—for example, oxygen transport—carry a "cost" for survival under drained conditions. It is likely that this cost involves a high degree of water loss under drought conditions in flood-tolerant plants. Swamp trees are known to have a relatively porous cambium, which allows internal aeration of the stem during flooding events. Most xeric trees have a dense cambium, probably in part as an adaptation to water loss. Hence, a porous cambium, which would afford an advantage to the tree during flooded conditions, becomes a detriment during dry conditions. Keeley thus hypothesized that plants under continuously hydric conditions, where oxygen is limiting and water is not, have been selected for increased aeration of stems and roots, among other factors. Consequently, most swamp plants are more impacted by drought than upland plants and should be at a competitive disadvantage under dry conditions. Herbaceous wetland species also exhibit this trade-off between flood tolerance and competitive ability as demonstrated in cattails (Grace and Wetzel 1981).

Although the impact of soil drying is often simply a deficiency in soil moisture, severe drought can result in the extensive oxidation of the soil, which can lead to plant mortality due to drought-related factors other then moisture deficiency. This is especially true in saline wetland ecosystems, where oxidation of metal sulfides such as pyrite can lead to a cascading suite of stressors. Such a severe drought occurred in the Mississippi River Delta Complex of the northern Gulf of Mexico in 1999 and 2000, when approximately 200,000 acres of salt marsh were impacted as a result of record low precipitation, low fresh water supply from the Mississippi River, and low water levels in the north-central Gulf of Mexico (McKee et al. 2004). Although the exact cause of the extensive plant mortality may never be known with certainty, it appears that because of excessive water loss from the marsh soil and resulting soil oxidation, soil acidification, as a consequence of the oxidation of metal sulfides, promoted a release of metals, such as Al, Fe, and Mn, that were toxic to the dominant marsh plant, *Spartina alterniflora*. These stressors may have interacted with a soil moisture deficit, which was likely exacerbated by somewhat elevated soil salinities, contributing to the overall stress on the vegetation (Mendelssohn unpublished data). This case study of large-scale salt marsh mortality demonstrates that the impacts of soil drying on wetland vegetation may be much more complex than a simple water deficiency.

In some freshwater wetlands, drought-stricken plants are subjected to the additional stress of fire (Sutter and Kral 1994; see review in Keddy 2000). Laubhan (1995) found that timing and intensity of fires could affect wetland plant regeneration, with summertime fires being destructive to plants because seed production was curtailed, while spring-time fires actually enhanced diversity of annual plants. *Panicum* grasses in wetlands of the southeastern United States can be harmed by winter fires followed by inundation (Kirkman and Sharitz 1993). Certain woody wetland plants are strongly affected by fire, and relative fire tolerances of plants can be an important factor structuring plant communities in fire-influenced wetlands (Kirkman et al. 2000; see Chapter 6).

ADAPTATIONS OF WETLAND PLANTS TO DRYING IMPACTS

Plants have adapted to drought by either avoiding the stress or tolerating it. Avoidance mechanisms include control of water loss, improved water uptake, efficient water conduction, and water storage (Larcher 1995). Wetland grasses reduce water loss by leaf curling, which reduces the transpirational surface area and shields the stomates from wind, which accelerates transpiration. Many wetland species such as mangroves and some herbaceous species have thickened and waxy cuticles, which reduce water loss. The abscission of leaves is another way of reducing the overall transpirational surface area, albeit at the expenses of photosynthetic leaf surface area. Probably the most effective means of avoiding water stress is with water storage organs such as underground rhizomes or the succulent stems and leaves of some halophytes. Succulence greatly retards drought stress and allows plants to photosynthesize without excessive water loss. Deep roots that can tap the water table or dense surface roots that can exploit short periods of rain are mechanisms to maximize water uptake.

When plants cannot avoid drought, they must tolerate it to survive. Desiccation tolerance varies with species and is genetically determined. Tolerance mechanisms include cytoplasmic tolerance to desiccation (a variety of metabolic responses determine this adaptive response), dormancy during dry periods, and reduced body size and prostrate growth form, to name a few (Larcher 1995). Lichens are probably some of the most desiccation-tolerant species that can be found in wetlands. Most wetland plants exposed to regular inundation are relatively desiccation intolerant and therefore do not compete well with more terrestrial species under dry conditions. If soil drying is extreme enough to cause plant mortality and drought persists, species composition changes may occur (see Chapter 6).

The ability of plant seeds to remain viable through long periods of drought is another valuable adaptation for life in highly variable wetlands. Weinhold and van der Valk (1989) examined survival of plant seeds in 82 wetlands in the U.S. northern plains that had different drainage histories; 30 were natural and undrained, while the rest had been drained for agricultural purposes for 5, 10, 20, 30, 40, or 70 years. Over the first 5 years of drainage, seed numbers actually accumulated markedly (mostly mudflat annuals), although fewer species occurred compared with natural wetlands (Table 4.1). Thereafter, seed numbers declined steadily. However, even after 30 years of drainage, the number of species occurring remained relatively high. In the wetlands drained for 70 years, a handful of wetland seeds still remained viable, although it was not possible to determine whether the seeds had persisted for 70 years or had been somehow introduced more recently (Weinhold

TABLE 4.1. Persistence of Seeds in Wetlands Drained for
Different Periods of Time

Class	Duration						
	0 yrs	5 yrs	10 yrs	20 yrs	30 yrs	40 yrs	70 yrs
Seeds/m²	3600	7000	1400	1200	600	300	160
Species/wetland	12.3	7.5	5.4	5.0	7.4	3.2	2.1

NOTE: Data from Weinhold and van der Valk (1988).

and van der Valk 1989). Nonetheless, it is clear that the seeds of many wetland plants are well equipped to survive prolonged drought conditions.

Many wetland plants (e.g., cattails) do not have propagules that can endure prolonged flooded or dry conditions but instead rely on aerial dispersal of seeds to rapidly colonize wetland substrates exposed by drought. In Chapter 6 on plant ecology, Sharitz and Pennings describe how variation in seed adaptation (seed bank species, dispersal species, germination requirements) has been incorporated into the ecological models used to predict plant community structure (see environmental sieve model). This same variation is also being considered in efforts to restore plant communities in degraded wetlands (Galatowitsch and van der Valk 1994).

CONSTRAINTS IMPOSED BY DRYING ON WETLAND ANIMALS

Most fish and aquatic invertebrates can not tolerate the dewatering that frequently occurs in wetlands, and thus only a relatively small subset of these organisms occurs in wetlands. While amphibians flourish in wetlands, aquatic larval forms remain very susceptible to drying stress. The degree to which habitat drying affects wetland animals varies from habitat to habitat. Wissinger (1999) suggests that a classification of wetland hydroperiod that is biologically relevant to animals would include:

1. Duration of flooding (permanent, semipermanent, temporary),
2. Predictability of flooding (seasonal, cyclical, unpredictable),
3. Phenology of flooding and drying (spring, summer, autumn, and/or winter), and
4. Harshness of dry and wet phases (temperature extremes, moisture levels).

For example, fish can survive and reproduce in permanently flooded ponds, but most will be eliminated from habitats that dry periodically (annually or cyclically). Salamanders can successfully reproduce in wetlands that flood for months at a time, but not in ones that remain flooded for only a few weeks. If stressful dry periods occur very predictably, as they do in some seasonal (vernal) pools, it enables numerous species to evolve life history strategies timed to that schedule. However, if flooding and drying occur

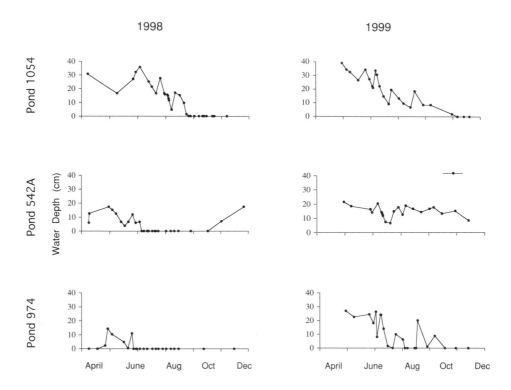

FIGURE 4.12

Spatial and temporal variability in hydroperiods of three small woodland ponds in northern Minnesota (based on staff gauge readings from April to November). Pond 1054 would be classified as vernal because it floods each spring and dries over the summer. In 1999, heavy summer rains extended the hydroperiod into the late summer. Pond 542A would be classified as autumnal in 1998. It flooded in autumn, and the hydroperiod extended through the winter and spring before drying in summer. The next year, that same pond would be classified as a permanent pond because it remained flooded all year. Pond 974 was vernal in 1998 and was intermittently flooded the next year. Numerical pond names were assigned by the USDA Forest Service, Forest Sciences Laboratory, Grand Rapids, Minnesota.

unpredictably, it is more difficult for animals to evolve coping mechanisms, and only a few opportunistic species will exploit such habitats. The seasonality of flooding also affects animals in temporary wetlands. Wiggins and associates (1980) maintain that animals in vernal pools (spring-flooded; Fig. 4.12) are subjected to more stress than animals in autumnal pools (those that flood from autumn through early summer; Fig. 4.12). In vernal pools, wintering animals must cope with both drying and extreme cold, whereas animals wintering in autumnal pools do not have to cope with this combination of stresses. In wetlands in xeric prairies and deserts, stresses from drying might be especially harsh, whereas in humid forested wetlands, drought stress can be relatively benign (Wissinger 1999). In tidal wetlands, where dry phases are short (hours) and very predictable (twice daily), drying might not pose a particularly significant constraint on marine animals.

Wetland animals, like plants, can either cope with drought by tolerating the disturbance or by avoiding it. Tolerance can involve either physiological or behavioral mechanisms, while avoidance typically involves behavioral or life history adaptations.

Desiccation Tolerance

In perhaps the most exhaustive review and synthesis of the adaptations of aquatic animals to habitat drying, Wiggins and associates (1980) used animals' dispersal capabilities and their abilities to tolerate or avoid drought to assign them to four ecological categories. *Group 1* organisms tolerate drought but lack active dispersal. They remain in the wetlands year-round and must avoid desiccation during dry phases either by burrowing into moist sediments or employing a drought-resistant stage. Prominent examples of Group 1 organisms include flightless invertebrates such as mollusks (clams and snails), annelids (worms and leeches), and crustaceans. Many crustacean groups such as fairy shrimps (Anostraca), clam shrimps (Conchostraca), and tadpole shrimps (Notostraca) occur exclusively in temporary water wetlands (Wissinger 1999), and they have drought-resistant eggs that can persist for years, even in arid environments. A few vertebrates would also fit this category. Mudminnows (Esociformes) burrow into moist mud to avoid drought conditions, and embryos of some wetland killifish (Cyprinodontiformes) enter a desiccation-resistant diapause stage that enables survival over multiple months of drought (Podrabsky et al. 2001).

Group 2 and *Group 3* organisms of Wiggins and associates (1980) probably could have been combined into a single category of animals able to tolerate drought and actively disperse. These organisms, mostly insects, aerially colonize the wetlands to oviposit and have life stages that aestivate and winter in dry basins (typically as eggs or larvae). The only major difference between Group 2 and 3 is that Group 2 organisms oviposit during the spring and in water, whereas Group 3 organisms oviposit in the summer and on moist, exposed substrates. Group 2 and 3 organisms include numerous flies (Diptera), beetles (Coleoptera), some mayflies (Ephemeroptera), dragonflies and damselflies (Odonata), caddisflies (Trichoptera), and mites (Acarina, which are external parasites of the insects). Perhaps the best-known animals in this group are mosquitoes in the genus *Aedes*. Adult female mosquitoes lay their eggs along the edges of drying ponds (Group 3), and the desiccation-resistant eggs will persist in dry basins until the next flood event (even if it takes years). The eggs then hatch, and the larvae complete development rapidly. As a bet-hedging strategy, some eggs will not hatch during the first flood but will persist until subsequent events. This ensures that if the initial flood is not of sufficient duration for larvae to complete development, the egg batch has subsequent chances for success. Although Wiggins and associates (1980) included only invertebrates in their categorization for Groups 2 and 3, some salamanders use a similar strategy of drought resistance and active dispersal. They enter the wetlands from surrounding uplands and lay their drought-resistant eggs in dry basins prior to annual flooding. The eggs hatch once inundated. The salt marsh fish *Fundulus heteroclitus* also deposits its eggs on plant stems or inside empty mussel shells in the high marsh, and the eggs then develop while exposed to air, eventually hatching during subsequent high spring tides (Kneib 1997a).

Desiccation Avoidance

Group 4 organisms of Wiggins and associates (1980) do not have a desiccation-resistant stage but instead are capable of active dispersal. As wetlands dry, these animals must leave or else perish. After leaving the basin, they colonize permanent water habitats, or in the case of some amphibians, the surrounding uplands. When wetland basins reflood the next year, the animals return to breed. The primary reason that Group 4 organisms inhabit temporary wetlands is to reproduce in the food-rich and relatively predator-free environment. Prominent examples of Group 4 organisms include water bugs (Hemiptera), some beetles, and most wetland amphibians. Some water bugs and beetles have life histories specially adapted for migration between temporary and permanent waters, and Wissinger (1997) refers to this strategy as *"cyclic colonization."* For example, the adults of some water boatmen (Corixidae) winter in permanent water bodies (ponds, lakes) but fly to temporary water wetlands once they fill in spring. Upon arrival, the wing muscles of females histolyze, and the energy and internal body space vacated is used to maximize egg production. These adults subsequently die. The progeny develop quickly, and if the duration of the flood is sufficiently long, multiple generations of flightless forms can develop, enabling population levels to grow rapidly. However, as the wetland dries, flight-capable individuals are produced, and they fly back to permanent water bodies, completing the cycle.

Hydroperiod Generalists

From the previous discussion, one might come to the conclusion that wetland animals are highly specialized to cope with fluctuating hydroperiods. However, Batzer and colleagues (2004) argue that rather than specializing for a specific hydroperiod, many wetland macroinvertebrates instead are generalists. Hydroperiods of temporary water wetlands often vary greatly both spatially and temporally (see the extent of natural hydrologic variation exhibited in Fig. 4.12), and animals that successfully exploit these habitats must cope with a wide range of environmental conditions. In their study of seasonal woodland ponds in northern Minnesota, they found that virtually all of the macroinvertebrates had some capability to survive drought, but few responded to hydroperiod variation (i.e., most could exploit the full range of hydroperiods that were available, from ephemeral to virtually permanent). Further, Williams (1996) questions how much of a constraint drying really poses for aquatic animals. He notes that desiccation resistance has evolved repeatedly in an assortment of animal taxa, many unrelated, and therefore the constraints imposed by drying are probably not difficult for aquatic animals to overcome. Nonetheless, one of the major environmental transitions shaping animal communities in wetlands is between permanently flooded habitats (lakes, ponds) and temporarily flooded wetlands (ephemeral, seasonal, or semipermanent habitats) (Wellborn et al. 1996; see Chapter 7).

SALINITY

Although hydrology is the dominant abiotic factor affecting wetland structure and function, it is salinity that differentiates freshwater and tidal estuarine wetlands, and one tidal wetland type from another (e.g., fresh marsh from brackish or brackish marsh from salt marsh). Even in nontidal inland wetlands, variation in salinity can be an important ecological factor. Within saline wetlands, salinity, in conjunction with hydrology and biotic interactions, often controls horizontal structure (i.e., plant zonation) and functional responses like productivity and community development (see Chapter 6). In coastal habitats, the most important salt is NaCl. In inland wetlands, NaCl can also accumulate, but other salts such as $CaCO_3$ (alkali) might be more important. Hence, salinity, along with hydrology, is a "keystone" variable controlling plant and animal responses as well as wetland structure and function.

CLASSIFICATION OF PLANTS TO SALINITY BASED ON GROWTH RESPONSE

The majority of terrestrial plants can be classified as glycophytes—that is, plants that use fresh water and cannot survive chronic levels of salt. Most freshwater marsh species are glycophytes. When exposed to increasing salinity, the growth of glycophytes decreases relatively quickly (Fig. 4.13). However, the rate of the growth decrease is species specific. In contrast, halophytes are plants that grow and complete their life cycle in elevated salinities. In fact, some halophytes show growth stimulation at low salinity levels (e.g., 3–5 ppt for the salt marsh grass *Spartina alterniflora*). Others maintain their growth rate or exhibit a slow decrease in growth at lower salinities followed by a more rapid decrease as salinity increases further (Fig. 4.13). Halophytes can be divided into two types: (1) facultative and (2) obligate. *Facultative halophytes* are plants that do not require salt for growth and survival but can tolerate salt and may even have stimulated growth at low salinities. These plants, which include salt marsh and mangrove species, are presumably excluded from freshwater habitats by competitively superior fresh marsh species (Bertness and Ellison 1987). *Obligate halophytes* require salt to grow and survive. Obligate halophytes are restricted to certain algae and sea grasses. No tidal marsh species are true obligate halophytes.

CONSTRAINTS IMPOSED BY SALINITY ON WETLAND PLANTS

Wetland plants exhibit differential tolerances to salinity. Fresh marsh species are sensitive to low salinities, while salt marsh species exhibit tolerance to salinities equal to or

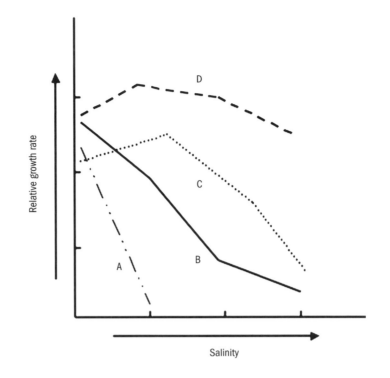

FIGURE 4.13

Although glycophytes (represented by growth curve A) can be separated from halophytes (B, C, and D) by the former's high sensitivity to increasing salinity, species-specific differences in salt tolerance also exist among halophytes. Species D is little affected by increased salinity and represents the expected growth response for a succulent. Species C is moderately affected by salinity and could indicate a species with salt glands. Species B is likely a brackish marsh plant with less developed adaptations to salinity. After Figure 5 in Pearcy and Ustin 1984, with kind permission of Springer Science and Business Media.

greater than seawater. However, even within a given marsh type, plant species exhibit different salt tolerances. For example, in fresh marshes of the southeastern United States, the broad leaf monocot bulltongue *(Sagittaria lancifolia)* is more tolerant of salt than the grass maidencane *(Panicum hemitomon)* (Howard 1995). In salt marshes, glasswort *(Salicornia* spp.) is more salt tolerant than cordgrass species *(Spartina* spp.) (Pearcy and Ustin 1984).

Why are plants negatively affected by elevated salinities? Three primary impacts result when plants are exposed to salinities beyond their tolerance limits: (1) osmotic, (2) toxic ion, and (3) nutrient uptake.

OSMOTIC EFFECT. Plants may experience an osmotic stress when exposed to salt. The osmotic stress causes a water deficiency to occur in the plant. Thus, marsh plants can have their roots immersed in water, but elevated salinities can prevent its uptake. For this reason, the osmotic effect induced by salinity is called *physiological drought*, that is, water is available in the soil, but the plant can not use it.

The ability of a plant to take up water is determined by its water potential (ψ_{plant}) relative to that of the soil (ψ_{soil}). The ψ is a measure of the chemical energy of water and as such provides an index of water availability, whether in the plant or in the soil. Just as ions move by diffusion from areas of high ion availability (chemical activity) to areas of low ion availability, water moves from sites of high water potential (high water availability) to sites of low water potential (low water availability). Therefore, in order for water to move from the soil into the plant, the ψ_{soil} must be greater than the ψ_{plant}. Because the ψ of pure water, which has the highest chemical energy and therefore the greatest availability, is arbitrarily set at 0, water with lower chemical energies than pure water have ψ's less than 0 (negative). By convention, water potential is measured in pressure units of megapascals (MPa). If the ψ_{soil} is -0.5 MPa and the ψ_{plant} is -1.0 MPa, then water will move by diffusion into the plant.

Water potential comprises several individual components. These include osmotic potential (ψ_π), pressure potential (ψ_p), matric potential (ψ_m), gravitational potential (ψ_g), and electrical potential (ψ_e) (i.e., $\psi = \psi_\pi + \psi_p + \psi_m + \psi_g + \psi_e$). The osmotic potential, which has a negative value except for pure water, is primarily determined by the concentration and ionization constant of solutes present in the water. The matric potential, which is primarily due to the sorption of water molecules onto soil and cell surfaces, also is a negative value. For plants, the osmotic potential and the pressure potential (a measure of hydrostatic pressure, which can be positive or negative) are generally most important in determining ψ_{plant}, while for soil, the matric and osmotic potentials are most important. Hence, plant cells that contain appreciable salt ions and saline soils will have relatively negative osmotic potentials and thus relatively negative water potentials. Saline soils have relatively low (negative) water potentials because of high salt content in the soil and the very negative osmotic potential of seawater (about -2.5 MPa). Plants growing in seawater must, therefore, possess a more negative water potential than that of the soil to take up water. Plants growing in saline soils can have ψ's between -2.5 and -3.5 MPa (Jefferies et al. 1979). If this plant response cannot be attained, water uptake will be impeded and the plant will experience water deficits—an osmotic stress. The inability of the plant to remain hydrated causes several impacts to the plant, including reduced cell elongation due to loss of turgor (cell pressure) and reduced photosynthesis due to stomatal closing and a reduced capacity for photosynthesis in the mesophyll chloroplasts (chlorophyll containing organelles located in the photosynthetic cell layers between the upper and lower epidermis of the leaf).

TOXIC ION EFFECT. The dominant ions in seawater are sodium and chloride, both of which can exert toxic effects on plant metabolism. Although it can be difficult to unequivocally distinguish between toxic ion effects and osmotic effects, very low Cl^- levels can impact glycophytes, even before an osmotic effect can occur. Chloride accumulation in the cytoplasm can disrupt protein synthesis and enzyme activity (Britto et al. 2004). Sodium can exert its toxic ion effect by inhibiting the uptake of Ca^{2+}, which is required for membrane integrity and structure and a variety of enzymatic pathways (Cramer et al. 1985).

NUTRIENT UPTAKE EFFECT. Ions comprising salt water can competitively inhibit the uptake of similarly charged ions that are needed by the plant for growth. Sodium inhibition of ammonium uptake is a prime example. An increase in salinity from 5 to 50 g l^{-1} caused a decrease in the efficiency of ammonium uptake, as indicated by a significant increase in apparent K_m (half-saturation constant) from 2.7 to 17.6 μmoles L^{-1} of NH$_4^+$–N in *Spartina alterniflora* (Bradley and Morris 1991a). Hence, the efficiency of ammonium uptake can dramatically decrease at high salinities. This decrease in ammonium uptake coupled with the use of nitrogen for compatible solute production, an adaptation to stress under elevated salinities, exacerbates the nitrogen deficiency in many tidal salt marshes (Cavalieri and Huang 1981).

ADAPTATIONS OF WETLANDS PLANTS TO SALINITY IMPACTS

Wetland plants that grow in salt-influenced environments possess a suite of anatomical and physiological adaptations that enable them to not only survive but to thrive in saline habitats. Adaptations for salinity, as for drought, can be classified into avoidance and tolerance strategies. However, salinity tolerance in plants is arguably the best example of an integrated adaptation that requires the synergistic effects of a number of anatomical, morphological, physiological, and metabolic plant responses.

Avoidance Strategies

Salt-tolerant wetland plants possess a variety of mechanisms for avoiding high internal levels of salt in the plant. These mechanisms can be classified into two types: (1) exclusion and (2) excretion. *Exclusion mechanisms* prevent high concentrations of potentially detrimental ions from entering the plant in the first place, while *excretion mechanisms* emphasize the elimination of the salts once they enter the plant. Both exclusion and excretion can occur in the same plant species.

EXCLUSION. Some halophytes exclude, or at least impede, the uptake of potentially toxic salt ions (e.g., Na$^+$ and Cl$^-$) at the root surface while allowing physiologically essential ions, such as K$^+$, to enter. This results in a Na/K specificity whereby Na/K ratios are lower in the plant tissue than in the interstitial water. Although there is some debate concerning how ubiquitous this trait is among halophytes and the quantitative importance of this mechanism for salt tolerance (Flowers et al. 1977; Luttge 2002), support for the "filtration" capacity of halophytes exists. For example, indirect evidence for this effect was described for *Spartina alterniflora* (Smart and Barko 1980). One might expect that if a plant

FIGURE 4.14
Salt crystals excreted on the leaf surface of smooth cordgrass, *Spartina alterniflora*, by salt glands.

is selectively taking up K^+ over Na^+, the interstitial water around the roots should have a greater Na/K ratio than in adjacent unvegetated soils and that this ratio would increase with larger plants and more root biomass. Indeed, this was the case for *S. alterniflora*, suggesting that some Na exclusion at the root surface occurs in this species. In fact, estimates are that from 91% to 97% of the theoretical maximum uptake of salts is excluded by this species (Bradley and Morris 1991b). Certain species of mangroves also have been identified as excluders of salt (Atkinson et al. 1967; Luttge 2002). For example, the mangrove *Rhizophora mucronata* has more than five times less Cl^- ion in its xylem sap than does the mangrove *Aegialitis annulata* when grown under similar conditions (Atkinson et al. 1967).

EXCRETION. The excretion of salts is a relatively ubiquitous adaptation for living in saline habitats (Fig. 4.14). The primary organ of excretion is the salt gland. Although plants in at least 10 families have salt glands, the structure of the salt gland can vary greatly from 2 cells *(Spartina)* to as many as 40 cells *(Aegialitis)* (Breckle 2002). The simple two-celled salt gland of *Spartina* and other salt marsh grasses consists of a basal cell that accumulates the salt and a cap cell from which the salt is excreted (Fig. 4.15). Because salt is accumulated in the basal cell against a concentration gradient, energy is required. Thus, salt excretion from salt glands is a cost to the plant. The loss of salt from plant leaves can also occur by (1) leaching from cracks on the leaf surface, (2) guttation via hydathodes (glands than expel water), (3) death and removal of salt-saturated organs, and (4) salt hairs, modified epidermal cells, that expel salt.

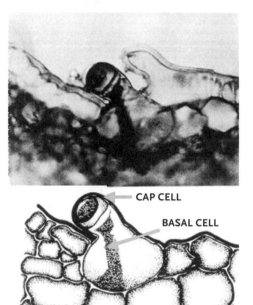

SALT GLAND OF
AELUROPUS LITTORALIS

CAP CELL

BASAL CELL

FIGURE 4.15
The two-celled salt gland of the grass,
Aeluropus littoralis, with one basal cell for salt
accumulation and one cap cell for salt
excretion. From Waisel (1972), with
permission.

DILUTION. Some of the most salt-tolerant species use succulence as a means of diluting the
salt and avoiding the salt stress. Genera such as pickleweed *Salicornia* and turtleweed *Batis,*
which are often found in hypersaline salt pans, are highly succulent (Fig. 4.16). In this case,
the salt that is taken up by the plant is diluted by water in the cytoplasm. It has been shown
for the white mangrove *(Laguncularia racemosa)* that a fourfold increase in leaf succulence
(0.20–0.85 kg m^{-2}) allowed for only a twofold increase in Cl$^-$ concentration (350–700 mM),
while the actual leaf chloride content increased tenfold (130–1220 mmol m^{-2}) (Kinzel 1982;
Luttge 2002). Because it is the concentration of the ion, and not the amount, that determines salt stress, succulence is an important means of avoiding high salinities.

Tolerance Strategies
Some adaptations to salinity allow the plant to better endure the effects of elevated salinities. It should be emphasized that although the avoidance and tolerance strategies are
described separately in this discussion, plants utilize mechanisms within both strategy
types simultaneously to cope with saline environments.

COMPARTMENTALIZATION. Many halophytes exhibit the ability to sequester toxic ions
like Na$^+$ and Cl$^-$ in the cell vacuole, thereby reducing the concentrations of these ions

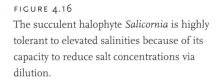

FIGURE 4.16

The succulent halophyte *Salicornia* is highly tolerant to elevated salinities because of its capacity to reduce salt concentrations via dilution.

in the cytoplasm where most life-sustaining metabolic activities takes place (Harvey et al. 1976). For example, the halophyte *Suaeda maritima* sequesters in the vacuole 94% and 95% of the Na^+ and Cl^-, respectively, found in mesophyll cells. More importantly, Na^+ and Cl^- concentrations in the vacuole are four and six times greater, respectively, than in the cytoplasm (Flowers 1985). Hence, it is clear that this halophyte can dramatically reduce toxic ion concentrations in the cytoplasm by compartmentalization of these ions in the cell vacuole. However, there is a cost to the plant. Transporting salt from the cytoplasm to the vacuole against a concentration gradient once again requires energy to fuel membrane-bound ATPases (enzymes that hydrolyze ATP to generate energy).

OSMOTIC ADJUSTMENT. Although compartmentalization is an important tolerance strategy, it would not be successful in promoting plant growth and survival in saline environments if it were not for the ability of cells to synthesize cytoplasmic organic solutes. As the cell vacuole sequesters more and more Na and Cl ions, the vacuolar water potential becomes more negative than that of the cytoplasm. As a result, water moves from the cytoplasm to the vacuole and, if allowed to proceed, will cause dehydration and plasmolysis of the cell. Salt-adapted plants, however, prevent this by synthesizing non-toxic organic osmotica in the cytoplasm (known as *compatible solutes* because they do not negatively affect cellular metabolism as would Na^+ and Cl^-). These organic solutes comprise four categories: (1) amino acids and amides, (2) quarternary ammonium compounds, (3) sugar alcohols (polyols), and (4) sugars. Tidal marsh grasses, such as *Spartina alterniflora*, accumulate high concentrations of glycine betaine (Cavalieri and Huang 1981), a quaternary ammonium compound, and of dimethylsulfoniopropionate (DMSP) (Otte and Morris 1994), a compound similar to glycine betaine but with sulfur replacing nitrogen, and lower levels of the amino acid proline. Elevated salinities induce higher levels of prolinc and, and to a lesser extent, glycine betaine. Because both of these compounds contain approximately 12% nitrogen, their synthesis represents a considerable nitrogen drain to the plant. Experimental evidence, in fact, indicates that where salt marsh salinities are high, the inherent nitrogen limitation to growth is exacerbated by the synthesis of these compounds (Cavalieri and Huang 1981).

In mangroves, sugar alcohols such as pinitol are important compatible solutes, while freshwater and oligohaline marsh plants accumulate sugars such as sucrose and fructose in response to elevated salinities. There is some question as to the exact functions of all of these compatible solutes. For example, proline is likely to play a bigger role in protein (enzyme) stabilization in contrast to osmoregulation. In fact, some of the compounds that accumulate in response to salt may be stress metabolites that form as a result of metabolic disturbance and serve as sinks for reducing power generated by these pathways (Greenway and Munns 1980).

CONSTRAINTS IMPOSED BY SALINITY ON WETLAND ANIMALS

Animals in Estuarine Wetlands

Salinity seems to be a less important constraint on estuarine animals than plants (Lin et al. 2003). The mobility of animals versus plants is likely one reason; as mentioned earlier, many animals can simply move to avoid harsh conditions, while rooted plants must find ways to cope. Another reason may be the fact that the ancestors of most estuarine plants evolved terrestrially and then invaded tidal wetlands, while the ancestors of most estuarine animals (mollusks, crustaceans, fish) evolved in marine environments. Thus, plants had to develop methods to tolerate salt, while animals were already preadapted to deal with saline environments. It is interesting to note that much of the variation in fish assemblages across a range of salinities in a Texas coastal wetland could be explained by fish of marine origin exploiting the lower, brackish areas and fish of freshwater origin exploiting the higher, fresher areas (Gelwick et al. 2001).

While insects comprise the majority of species in most terrestrial and aquatic environments, and freshwater wetlands as well, this group is very poorly represented in estuarine environments (with the exception of some herbivorous leafhoppers and grasshoppers that feed on the above-water portions of estuarine plants). It seems unlikely, however, that salinity is the major factor preventing insect communities from exploiting estuarine wetlands. In inland saline wetlands, where salinities greatly exceed those found in estuarine wetlands, insects can thrive. Some suspect that because marine invertebrates were already entrenched, insects have been excluded from marine habitats by competition (Daly et al. 1998).

In the Suisun Marsh of California's Sacramento River estuary, many tidal salt marshes have been isolated from tidal action by man-made dikes. Most are now managed as waterfowl habitat and are flooded on the same schedules used for freshwater waterfowl marshes of the region. While the water remains brackish (salinities up to 18 ppt) and salt marsh vegetation still persists (e.g., pickleweed [*Salicornia*]), an animal community more reflective of freshwater marshes develops (e.g., mallards and other dabbling ducks;

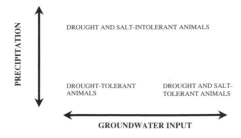

FIGURE 4.17

Adaptation of the wetland continuum concept, illustrating the effect on animals of the combined influences of ionic concentration caused by variation in groundwater input (*x*-axis) and hydroperiod caused by variation in precipitation level (*y*-axis). Simplified and redrawn from Euliss et al. (2004).

chironomid midges, hydrophilid beetles, and other typical freshwater insects) (Batzer et al. 1993) rather than an animal community that normally occurs in tidally influenced salt marshes. This community, however, is less rich in species than in most freshwater marshes, probably because of the saline conditions. In these manipulated salt marshes, it appears that hydrology is a more important factor than salinity for structuring animal communities, and it may follow that in salt marshes, the twice daily tidal fluctuations in hydrology may be more important than salinity.

Animals in Inland Saline or Alkaline Wetlands

In some inland wetlands, salt levels can vary dramatically (Lovvorn et al. 1999; Euliss et al. 2004), at times even more so than in estuarine habitats. For example, in the Prairie Pothole region of the central North American plains, some wetlands are filled by precipitation and primarily lose water to groundwater recharge, resulting in ion concentrations being very low. In contrast, other pothole wetlands are fed by ion-rich groundwater and lose water almost exclusively to evapotranspiration, and ion concentrations can become very high (up to 10 times the salinity of the oceans). In a paradigm termed the *wetland continuum concept,* Euliss and colleagues (2004) maintain that the ionic differences caused by this variation in the hydrologic relation to groundwater, combined with the influence of precipitation patterns on hydroperiod length, largely structure the biological expression of animals in individual prairie potholes (Fig. 4.17). Hydroperiod and salinity levels co-vary as deluge periods result in longer hydroperiods and more dilute water, and periods of drought both reduce hydroperiods and increase salinity levels. When extreme saline conditions develop, the only animals that flourish are salt-tolerant species like brine shrimp *(Artemia salina),* which can also tolerate temporary drying.

The hypersaline conditions found in prairie pothole wetlands do not develop in many wetland complexes, and variation in ionic concentration on animals in these other inland wetlands may be less important. Benbow and Merritt (2004) found that even saline changes induced by road salt application were insufficient to cause significant changes in the invertebrate faunas of roadside wetlands of Michigan, probably because those taxa had a relatively broad salt tolerance. Batzer and colleagues (2004) found that natural variation in conductivity, alkalinity, and pH among seasonal woodland ponds of Minnesota

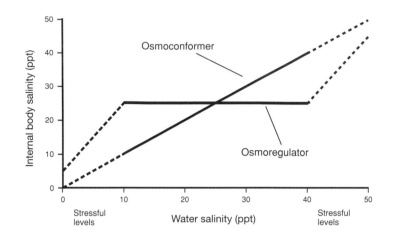

FIGURE 4.18

Hypothetical internal body salinities of an osmoconforming or osmoregulating estuarine animal in relation to salinities in the surrounding water. As water salinities get low (approaching fresh) or high (hypersaline), both kinds of organisms will be stressed.

was insufficient to affect invertebrates, and companion work (unpublished) on amphibians in those same wetlands came to the same conclusion. In inland wetlands, variation in ion concentration may be only important to animals in situations where extremes in condition develop.

ADAPTATIONS OF WETLAND ANIMALS TO SALINITY IMPACTS

Wetland animals have developed two physiological strategies to cope with saline conditions: (1) osmoregulation and (2) osmoconformity. *Osmoregulators* have special organs (glands, gills) to excrete excess salt and thus can maintain the internal chemical and water (osmotic) composition of their bodies and cells (Vernberg and Vernberg 1972; Fig. 4.18), employing a strategy analogous to plant excretion. However, the internal osmotic potential of osmoregulators may still vary somewhat depending on local conditions.

Alternatively, animal *osmoconformers* do not physiologically regulate their body chemistry per se, but instead, the osmotic conditions in their internal cell environment mirror the external environment (Fig. 4.18). However, these animals can still maintain osmotic conditions within a narrow range by tracking optimal salinity conditions in their environment. The ability to migrate to avoid undesirable environmental extremes in salinity is especially important to osmoconformers (Lin et al. 2003) but is probably also useful for osmoregulators.

5

BIOGEOCHEMISTRY AND BACTERIAL ECOLOGY OF HYDROLOGICALLY DYNAMIC WETLANDS

Paul I. Boon

I was fortunate to have spent my childhood in the Hawkesbury Sandstone region of New South Wales, just north of Sydney, Australia. The climate is warm temperate, the country characterized by rugged sandstone gorges and nutrient-poor soils, and the vegetation sclerophyllous and taxonomically diverse (Benson and Howell 1990). The many small streams and temporary pools in the valleys provided us with a fascinating diversion after school. Other than catching tadpoles and frogs, we were obsessed with two missions: to dam the streams to make the pools larger and more permanent, and to bolster their meager aquatic flora by introducing exotic plants such as elodea, water hyacinths, and water lilies. The aim was to create a "real" wetland, like the ones we had seen in English natural-history books back in school. Had we had access to newts, toads, and sticklebacks, undoubtedly we would have introduced them as well.

It is now clear that we utterly misunderstood the landscape in which we lived. Our Eurocentric education had not prepared us for an unruly environment of thin poor soils, shadeless gum trees, prickly hard-leaved shrubs, and pools that filled only after violent thunderstorms or mysteriously and unreliably from beneath the ground. As the poet A. D. Hope (1973) put it in his poem "Australia," we were where "second-hand Europeans pullulate timidly on the edge of alien shores." Our misunderstanding raises two paradoxes. First, many of the early explorers had understood very well the contrary nature of the Australian landscape. In 1818, an exasperated John Oxley, exploring in northwestern New South Wales, reported that the area "must at all times be impassable. In wet seasons it is a bog; in dry ones there is no water" (Rolls 1981). Second, our conception of the English countryside and its streams, pools, and wetlands was also in serious error. We did not know that aquatic systems, even in well-watered temperate England, dried out episodically. But this was hardly new knowledge. The Reverend Gilbert White reported that the ponds in his village of Selbourne in Hampshire (U.K.) had dried up in 1781 after a severely hot summer and an unusually dry spring and winter, and again earlier in 1775 (White 1789).

As an adult, I now study wetland ecology from a microbial and botanical perspective but suggest that some of the problems listed earlier have shaped modern perceptions about the biogeochemistry and microbial ecology of wetlands. Too often, studies fail to acknowledge that wetlands are by nature incredibly dynamic habitats in terms of hydrology and that episodic wetting and drying has a profound influence on chemical reactions and microbial ecology.

CHAPTER THEMES
HYDROLOGIC VARIABILITY

This chapter addresses three main themes. The first theme relates directly to the introductory homily: hydrologic dynamism in wetlands. Hydrologically dynamic wetlands are those with water levels that fluctuate widely and, in the most severe cases, dry out completely. For most purposes, *hydrologically dynamic wetlands* might just as accurately be called *temporary wetlands,* and the two terms are used interchangeably throughout the chapter. Note, however, that the phenomenon of wetting a dry wetland is not ecologically the same disturbance as that of drying a filled wetland (Kingsford et al. 1999).

Hydrologically dynamic wetlands are found across the world but are especially common where the climate is highly seasonal, such as in the monsoonal wet-dry tropics, Mediterranean lands with hot dry summers and cool wet winters, and arid and semiarid regions. Regions with these climates encompass much of Africa, Asia, the Middle East, North and South America, and Australia (Finlayson and Moser 1991; Britton and Crivelli 1993; Brendonck and Williams 2000). Indeed, 37% of Africa, 66% of the Middle East, and 69% of Australia are classified as arid or semiarid (Williams 1998b). But, as Reverend White's natural-history studies indicated over 200 years ago, hydrologically dynamic wetlands are common even in the cool temperate zones of Europe and North America (see also Finlayson and Moser 1991, Brinson and Malvarez 2002, and Palik et al. 2003 for more recent expositions). Boreal regions in extreme northerly latitudes, with their alternating freeze-thaw conditions, also support hydrologically dynamic wetlands, due mainly to seasonal changes in the level of the water table (Finlayson and Moser 1991). Despite their ubiquity, aquatic systems that exhibit a high degree of hydrologic dynamism have not been well studied in the limnological literature (Williams 1988); recent studies, however, are in the process of turning around this neglect (e.g., Puckridge et al. 2000; McMahon and Finlayson 2003).

FIGURE 5.1

Raftery Swamp, central Victoria, during its dry phase. Photograph was taken in October 2002.

FIGURE 5.2

Raftery Swamp, central Victoria, during its wet phase. Photograph was taken in November 1992. The aquatic plants visible are *Triglochin* sp. and *Potamogeton* sp.

Figures 5.1 and 5.2 illustrate the great difference in the wet and dry phases of a hydrologically dynamic wetland. The site is Raftery Swamp, a temporary wetland on the floodplain of the Goulburn River in central Victoria (Australia).

Hydrologically dynamic wetlands are not limited to inland regions but are abundant also in coastal areas, where the periodicity of wetting and drying is driven not by weather and/or groundwater but by tidal cycles. Mangroves, salt marshes and, brackish-water coastal swamps fall into this category. I do not cover in detail these coastal wetlands, but concentrate on wetlands that are found in inland areas. One area of overlap between these inland wetlands and marine-dominated coastal wetlands is salinity. Inland wetlands are not always fresh, and saline wetlands and lakes are a common feature of many inland regions, especially those with endorheic drainage patterns (Williams 1998b; Bailey et al. in press).

BIOGEOCHEMISTRY AND BACTERIAL ECOLOGY

The second theme is biogeochemistry and bacterial ecology. Since I limit the review mostly to bacteria, it is more accurate to use the term *bacterial ecology* than the more general *microbiology*. Differences between the two terms are discussed later. Limiting the review to bacteria is a constraint enforced mainly by space, and the neglect of other microbes is not intended to underestimate their importance. Aquatic viruses, for example, have been recognized for over a decade as playing a major role in controlling the abundance of bacteria in aquatic systems. Maranger and Bird (1995), Fuhrman (1999), Wommack and Colwell (2000), and Weinbauer (2004) have reviewed the ecological role of viruses in aquatic systems.

Another group of important aquatic microbes is the fungi, which play critical roles in the decomposition of wetland plants and as food for detritivorous consumers (Findlay et al. 2002; Buchan et al. 2003). They may have important roles also in solubilizing iron in aquatic systems, perhaps through their production of low-molecular-weight organic compounds called *siderophores* (Baakza et al. 2004). Hyde and associates (1998) and Wong and colleagues (1998) reviewed the ecological role of fungi in aquatic systems. Zooplankton have been well covered in the general limnological literature (e.g., Lampert and Sommer 1997), even if there have been relatively few studies of zooplankton dynamics in temporary systems (e.g., see Tan and Shiel 1993). Vymazal (1995) has exhaustively reviewed the algae of wetlands.

Although wetlands are the focus habitat for this chapter, many advances in bacterial ecology have come from oceanographic and marine studies (Azam et al. 1983; Thingstad and Rassoulzadegan 1999; Kirchman 2000), and these are introduced as necessary. For example, the microbiology of coastal marine wetlands such as mangroves, salt marshes, and seagrass beds has been relatively well covered in the literature (e.g., Moriarty and Boon 1986; DeLaune and Patrick 1990; Alongi and Sasekumar 1992; Pollard et al. 1993; Alongi 1996; Dame and Allen 1996). In comparison, there are comparatively few comprehensive reviews of the bacterial ecology of inland freshwater wetlands (e.g., Boon 2000a). The topic is not well covered even in existing monographs on wetlands (e.g., see the otherwise excellent text by Mitsch and Gosselink 2000).

INTEGRATING MICROBIAL ECOLOGY WITH BROADER-SCALE WETLAND ECOLOGY

The third theme is one of integration and synthesis. As Moore (1990) noted, "The underlying ecological unity of wetlands is best appreciated when they are viewed as ecosystems . . . in which the flow of energy through and the cycling of chemical elements within the system form the basis for understanding its ecological structure and function." Ten years ago, Pedros-Alio and Guerrero (1994) argued that the fields of microbial ecology and "mainstream" ecology (i.e., ecology dealing with metazoans) had become increasingly divorced. To a large extent this is still true, as seen in the cursory treatment that many ecological textbooks give to microbiological and biogeochemical phenomena. Conversely, most general microbiological texts continue to have strongly medical overtones and fail to address the diversity of bacteria found in natural systems or their ecological significance. The exceptions are Atlas and Bartha (1993) and Madigan and colleagues (1997).

Thus, an important aim of this chapter is to link the biogeochemistry and bacterial ecology of temporary wetlands with the wetland's most important physical driving force: its hydrology. Bacterial diversity and wetland hydrology are introduced briefly in order to provide essential background material., the ways in which hydrology controls biogeochemical processes are illustrated by referring to the processes of organic-matter decay and nutrient regeneration and cycling in temporary wetlands. To extend these arguments, I show how bacterial populations and communities interact with a critical physical component (soil) and a critical biological component (aquatic plants) in temporary wetlands.

A PRIMER ON WETLAND BACTERIOLOGY
BACTERIAL BIODIVERSITY

Prokaryotes and Eukaryotes

The discipline of microbiology involves the study of organisms—both prokaryotic and eukaryotic—that are not visible to the naked eye. In contrast, bacteriology refers to one particular set of microscopic and prokaryotic organisms—the bacteria. The division between prokaryotic and eukaryotic organisms is one of the greatest evolutionary discontinuities of life on Earth (Margulis and Schwartz 1988). Table 5.1 shows the primary differences between these two main groups of cellular organisms.

The visually dominant life forms on Earth are eukaryotic: plants, animals, fungi, and protistans (e.g., protozoa). In contrast, the prokaryotes, comprising all the bacteria, are being overwhelmingly microscopic and their importance not so readily apparent (Margulis and Schwartz 1988). As summarized in Table 5.1, prokaryotes are organisms whose cell contents are not compartmentalized by intracellular membranes. They lack the membrane-bound organelles (e.g., nucleus, mitochondria, and plastids, such as chloroplasts) found in eukaryotic organisms. Despite their lack of intracellular membranes, prokaryotic cells are not merely disorganized sacks of chemicals; their nucleic material, for example, is aggregated in the nucleoid, a fibrous, DNA-rich region visually quite distinct in electron micrographs of bacterial cells. The DNA of prokaryotic cells forms a circular molecule, unlike the linear chromosomes of eukaryotic cells. Moreover, prokaryotes usually divide by simple division and not by the mitosis evident in eukaryotes. Prokaryotic cells are not

TABLE 5.1.   Major Differences between Prokaryotic and Eukaryotic Cells

Characteristic	Prokaryotes	Eukaryotes
Size	Mostly small (1–10 μm)	Mostly large (10–100 μm)
Nucleic material	DNA in nucleoid, not membrane-bound and not coated with protein	DNA in membrane-bound nucleus containing chromosomes made up of DNA, RNA, and protein
Cell division	Direct cell division, usually by binary fission	Cell division by mitosis
Tissue development	Usually single celled and with no tissue differentiation	Single- or multicelled, often with tissue development
Cell walls	Cell walls usually present and composed of peptidoglycan in the Bacteria	Cell walls present in plants and fungi, composed of cellulose and other materials such as chitin
Requirement for oxygen	Diverse requirements for oxygen, some forms being strictly anaerobic, others facultative and some obligately aerobic	Almost always aerobic, with the exception of some protozoa
Metabolic diversity	Enormous variation in metabolic pathways	Limited range of metabolic pathways (e.g., Embden-Meyerhof glucose metabolism, Krebs cycle oxidation, cytochrome electron transport chains)
Energy generation	Mitochondria absent and enzymes for oxidative processes bound to cell membranes	Enzymes for oxidation of organic acids packaged into mitochondria
Photosynthesis	Enzymes for photosynthesis not packaged into organelles; photosynthesis may be oxygenic or anoxygenic	Membrane-bound plastids contain photosynthetic pigments, and all photosynthetic species produce oxygen
Flagella	Flagella simple in structure and chemical composition	Flagella composed of a complex 9+2 construction, with many proteins
Resistant stages	Heat-, desiccation-, and radiation-resistant endospores produced in many species	Endospores not produced; if spores are produced, they are usually for reproduction and dispersal

NOTE: Adapted from Margulis and Schwartz (1988).

only nearly always much smaller than eukaryotic cells, but rarely differentiate into discernible tissues. Prokaryotes are also predominantly unicellular organisms, although some do form colonies with a degree of cellular specialization (e.g., cyanobacteria with their nitrogen-fixing heterocysts and gliding myxobacteria with their fruiting bodies).

Prokaryotes differ from eukaryotic cells in other ways. They are nearly always surrounded by a cell wall but, unlike the cellulose-based cell walls of plants and chitin-based cell walls of fungi, bacterial cell walls are usually comprised of peptidoglycan, a complex of long-chain sugars cross-linked by bridges of amino acids. Prokaryotic cells often have flagella, but again, they are structurally and chemically unlike the flagella of eukaryotes. Bacterial flagella move the cell by rotating like a propeller, whereas flagella in eukaryotes whip backwards and forwards to effect propulsion. Some prokaryotes produce endospores, which are not a means of reproduction (as in fungi) but a survival mechanism. Endospores allow bacteria to persist, in a dormant state, under extremes of heat, pressure, desiccation, and radiation. Some protistans also produce dormant stages (e.g., the oocysts of flagellated protozoa), but they are not as resistant to environmental extremes as bacterial endospores.

Bacteria and Archaea

The prokaryotes are comprised of two quite dissimilar groups, or Domains: the Domain Archaea or archaebacteria, and the Domain Bacteria or eubacteria (Woese and Fox 1977). The terminology can get confusing, so in this chapter I use *bacteria* (lowercase *b*) to refer to both the archaebacteria and eubacteria. When it is important to distinguish between the two Domains, the capitalized forms (Bacteria and Archaea) are used.

The Bacteria includes the vast majority of known prokaryotes and consists of all those microbes we normally consider as "bacteria." Medical examples include *Escherichia coli,* the common gut microbe; *Salmonella typhi,* the cause of typhoid fever; and *Staphylococcus aureus,* the cause of golden-staph skin infections. In contrast, the Archaea is made up of only three main groups: the obligately halophilic prokaryotes (growing at salt concentrations of 8–32%), the sulfur-dependent extreme thermophiles, and the obligately anaerobic methanogens (Atlas and Bartha 1993; Williams and Embley 1996). The methanogens are particularly relevant to us, since they are responsible for the terminal pathway for organic-matter decomposition in freshwater environments (Boon 2000b). Methanogens, however, are not a taxonomically coherent group, and genetic studies have shown them to be as dissimilar from each other as are the major groups of the eukaryotes from each other.

Archaea differ fundamentally from Bacteria in a number of key biochemical characteristics (Margulis and Schwartz 1988; Williams and Embley 1996). Their lipids are ether-linked, where those in Bacteria are ester-linked. This difference allows us to calculate the abundance of the two groups of prokaryotes in environmental samples: Boon and associates (1996) used the ratio of ester-linked to ether-linked lipids to infer the relative abundance of methane-producing bacteria in a temporary wetland in central Victoria. The cell walls of archaebacteria lack the peptidoglycan of eubacteria, and their ribosomes have a distinctive shape, quite unlike that of Bacteria or eukaryotic cells. Also, the archaebacteria can not form resistant endospores, whereas a wide range of Bacteria have this ability (e.g., *Bacillus,* responsible for anthrax; and *Clostridium,* various species of which are responsible for gas gangrene, tetanus, and botulism).

The two Domains of prokaryotes include an incredible diversity of organisms (Table 5.2). There are many perspectives from which to gauge the diversity of prokaryotes, and Table 5.2 uses a mixed taxonomic-physiological approach. The important distinctions among autotrophic, chemolithotrophic, and heterotrophic bacteria are discussed later in the chapter when I examine the ways in which bacteria obtain their carbon and energy supplies. Note that blue-green algae, or cyanobacteria, are actually prokaryotic organisms and not eukaryotic algae like diatoms and green algae. They are the sole group of photosynthetic prokaryotes that can undertake oxygen photosynthesis, other than the more restricted prochlorophytes. Other photosynthetic bacteria do not generate oxygen as a result of their photosynthesis. For those readers wishing to pursue this topic further, Madigan and associates (1997) offer a good introductory text to read for a more detailed overview of bacterial diversity.

WHY SHOULD WE BE INTERESTED IN BACTERIA?

Perhaps the best way to show the importance of bacteria in hydrologically dynamic wetlands is to examine their roles in wetland structure, function, and value. *Structure* refers to the abundance and taxonomic composition of populations—at all levels from bacteria to vertebrates—in wetlands. *Function* refers to the processes that are mediated by bacterial populations or communities, and *value* refers to the benefits that human communities extract from wetlands. Let us look at structure first, by analyzing some papers on bacterial abundance and species diversity.

Bacterial Abundance and Community Composition

Bacteria are probably the most abundant organisms in wetlands. Studies of bacterial numbers in some floodplain wetlands in southern Australia have shown that it is not uncommon to find bacterial numbers exceeding 10 to 100×10^{10} L^{-1} in the water column (Boon 1991a). By comparison, nearby rivers typically contained only 1 to 10×10^9 cells L^{-1} in the water column. Sediments contain even more bacteria. Fenchel (1992), for example, calculated that a core of sediment 10 cm deep and covering 1 cm^2 would contain 4×10^{10} bacterial cells, 1×10^8 algal cells, 1×10^4 heterotrophic flagellates and amoebae, and 1 to 4×10^3 ciliates.

The only organisms that could approach bacteria in terms of abundance are viruses (Maranger and Bird 1995). There are few reports on viral abundances in freshwater wetlands, with most studies having been undertaken on the oceans. Farnell-Jackson and Ward (2003), however, did report that the number of planktonic viruses in a riverine wetland

TABLE 5.2.   Broad Groups of Prokaryotes That Have Been Identified
in the Domains Bacteria and Archaea

Major Groups	Representative Species
Archaea	
Methanogens	*Methanobacillus*
	Methanobacterium
	Methanococcus
Sulfur-dependent extreme thermophiles	*Desulfurococcus*
	Sulfolobus
	Thermococcus
Extreme halophiles	*Halobacterium*
	Natronococcus
Bacteria	
Photoautotrophic bacteria (e.g., cyanobacteria, green sulfur bacteria, and purple sulfur bacteria)	Cyanobacteria: *Anabaena, Microcystis, Nostoc*
	Green sulfur bacteria: *Chlorobium, Chloroflexus, Chloropseudomonas*
	Purple sulfur bacteria: *Chromatium, Thiospirillum, Thiocapsa*
Photoheterotrophic bacteria (e.g., purple nonsulfur bacteria and green nonsulfur bacteria)	Purple nonsulfur bacteria: *Rhodospirillum, Rhodopseudomonas*
	Green nonsulfur bacteria: *Chlorobium*
Chemolithotrophic bacteria (e.g., nitrifying bacteria, methane-oxidizing bacteria, sulfur-oxidizing bacteria, and iron-oxidizing bacteria)	Nitrifying bacteria: *Nitrosomonas, Nitrobacter*
	Methane-oxidizing Bacteria: *Methylomonas*
	Sulfur-oxidizing bacteria: *Sulfolobus, Thiobacillus*
	Iron-oxidizing bacteria: *Ochrobium, Siderocapsa*
Chemoorganotrophic bacteria (e.g., the heterotrophs)	Myxobacteria: *Myxococcus*
	Spirochetes: *Spirochaeta, Treponema*
	Actinomycetes: *Actinomyces, Streptomyces*
	Gram-negative aerobic cocci and rods: *Agrobacterium, Azotobacter, Pseudomonas, Rhizobium*
	Gram-negative facultative anaerobic rods: *Escherichia, Salmonella, Proteus*
	Gram-negative anaerobic bacteria: *Bacteroides*
	Rickettsias: *Chlamydia, Rickettsia*
	Gram-positive cocci: *Staphylococcus, Streptococcus*
	Endospore-forming cocci and rods: *Bacillus, Clostridium*
	Gram-positive, non–spore-forming rods: *Lactobacillus*

NOTE: Adapted from Atlas and Bartha (1993) and Madigan and associates (1997).

varied from 2 to 4×10^8 particles L^{-1}, and changes seemed to be linked with variations in bacterial abundance.

Although it is relatively easy to determine the total number of bacteria in wetlands, describing quantitatively the composition of the bacterial community and the abundance of different species is more problematic. There are very real difficulties when we try to apply the species concept to bacteria, and these arise primarily from the definition of what constitutes a bacterial species (O'Donnell et al. 1994). Indeed, some microbiologists have argued that the term *species* can not be applied to bacteria (e.g., Cowan 1962).

The classic definition of a bacterial species refers to a limited number of easily observable traits, such as shape, staining reaction (e.g., Gram negative or Gram positive), and phenotypic signatures (e.g., the pattern of sugar utilization or fermentation products). More recently, molecular criteria have been applied, including the $G+C$ ratio in bacterial DNA, the extent of DNA:DNA hybridization across strains, and studies of ribosomal RNA. The molecular approaches, in particular, have demonstrated many weaknesses in the existing classification schemes based on bacterial morphology and metabolic reactions (Boon 2000 a). For example, *Listeria pneumophila,* a causative agent of pneumonia, was previously classified as a single bacterial species, but it is now known that different strains vary by more than 50% in the homology of their nucleotide sequences (Selander 1985). As May (1994) points out, this is greater than the genetic dissimilarity between mammals and fish.

Despite these conceptual limitations, great advances have been made recently in describing the structure of bacterial populations and communities in aquatic systems. In most part, advances have been tied to the development of powerful new molecular methods (Morris et al. 2002). Two examples demonstrate this point.

EXAMPLE 1. Hewson and Fuhrman (2004) used automated rRNA intergenic spacer analysis (ARISA) to study the diversity of aquatic bacteria along an estuarine gradient in Moreton Bay, Queensland (Australia). They found that some bacterial groups were specific to distinct parts of the gradient from estuary to bay to ocean, in contrast to the general assumption that bacterial communities were relatively homogeneous in well-mixed coastal waters.

EXAMPLE 2. Galand and associates (2003) used denaturing gradient gel electrophoresis (DGGE) and restriction fragment length polymorphism (RFLP) analysis to unravel the structure of methanogenic communities in boreal oligotrophic fens in Finland. They showed that different microsites in the wetland supported quite different methanogenic populations, and that novel species of methanogenic bacteria (i.e., currently unidentified gene sequences) were common at all sites and sediment depths.

It is not difficult to envisage the next decade seeing a revolutionary increase in our understanding of bacterial diversity in wetlands. It is likely that these studies will confirm the notion that there is more diversity of species in wetlands at the bacterial level than at any other taxonomic level in a given habitat (e.g., see Torsvik et al. 1990 for an analogous case with terrestrial soils).

Bacterial Diversity and Wetland Function

The second approach to gauging the importance of bacteria to wetlands is to examine the roles they play in wetland function, that is, in mediating key ecological processes. This approach is intimately linked with the physiological diversity of aquatic bacteria. Unlike most metazoans, which are totally reliant on oxygen, heterotrophic bacteria can use a wide range of substances as oxidants or alternative electron acceptors (Table 5.1). For example, different groups of bacteria can use nitrate (the denitrifiers), sulfate (the sulfate-reducing bacteria), and even metals (such as iron and manganese) as electron acceptors (oxidants) to oxidize organic matter (Table 5.2). Details on these terms and biogeochemical processes are discussed later in the chapter.

Aquatic bacteria can metabolize a wide range of organic materials as carbon and/or energy sources. These compounds include, for example, the complex carbohydrates found in wood (e.g., degradation of cellulose by *Cytophaga*) and a diverse range of toxic or xeno-biotic compounds (Francis 1994). Wetland bacteria have been shown to be capable of degrading complex chlorinated solvents that would otherwise pollute the groundwater (Lorah and Voytek 2004), diesel fuel and other hydrocarbons (Boopathy 2003), and pesticides (Kao et al. 2002). They also interact significantly with a very wide range of elements, including heavy metals and metalloids (Wackett et al. 2004).

Aquatic bacteria can undertake these ecological functions under extreme environmental conditions, ranging from the highly reducing environments colonized by methanogens, the highly saline systems (NaCl at >4 mol L^{-1}) colonized by halobacteria, and the extremely acidic environments (pH <1) colonized by the sulfur-oxidizing *Sulfolobus* (Boon 2000a). Extreme temperatures ($>80°C$) are tolerated, indeed required, by some aquatic prokaryotes in both the Domains Bacteria (e.g., *Thermus*) and Archaea (e.g., *Thermoplasma*).

The combination of importance at both the structural and functional levels of organization means that bacteria also dominate the functional diversity of temporary wetlands. Palmer and colleagues (1997) reviewed the role of sediment bacteria in ecosystem-scale processes in fresh waters and concluded that bacteria were at least as, and possibly more, diverse than any other group of organisms. This conclusion is consistent with earlier work on taxonomic diversity in terrestrial soils (Torsvik et al. 1990). Palmer and colleagues (1997) also argued that bacteria occupied more "functional roles" than any other group of organisms. Partly, this importance is a function of bacteria occurring in all wetland habitats, including the water column, sediments, root zone (rhizosphere), submerged and emergent leaf surfaces (phyllosphere), and on the surface and in the guts of aquatic animals.

As shown later, almost all nutrient-cycling processes in wetlands are mediated by bacteria. Bacteria play a critical role (along with fungi in running-water systems) in the decay of organic matter in aquatic environments, conditioning leaves and providing nutrient-rich food for detritivorous invertebrates. In fact, the conditioning role that bacteria and fungi play in degrading plant material has led to their other functions in aquatic systems being underestimated (Gessner et al. 1999). Nevertheless, the fact that aquatic food webs are overwhelmingly detrital (meaning that plant matter is not consumed by herbivores while it is alive, but rather only after it has died and been partly degraded by microbes) is a clear indication of the functional role of bacteria in wetland ecosystems (Wetzel 1995). Bacteria have an almost unassailable position as key functional organisms in wetlands, since they alone are capable of assimilating dissolved organic carbon, the form that dominates the pool of organic carbon in aquatic systems (Wetzel 1995).

A related indication of the key functional position of bacteria in wetlands is their role as secondary producers. In temperate-region eutrophic lakes, the rate of bacterial gross production can exceed 100 g C m^{-2} year^{-1} and, in some cases, bacterial production is at least half that of phytoplankton primary production (Riemann and Sondergaard 1986; see Pedros-Alio and Guerrero 1994 for other examples). Stanley and associates (2003) even showed that bacterial carbon demands were greater than could be provided by phytoplankton production alone in a wetland in the southeastern United States. In seagrass beds, which might be a reasonable surrogate for freshwater wetlands densely colonized by submerged vascular plants, bacterial productivity was 9% to 31% of the primary production of the seagrasses (Moriarty and Boon 1986). There are few data on the productivity of bacteria in wetlands, but one large study of riverine wetlands in southeastern Australia showed the bacteria had extremely fast doubling times (specific growth rates often >0.10 hour^{-1}) and very high productivity (>100 µg C L^{-1} hour^{-1}) (Boon 1991a).

High productivity, combined with the small size and thus high surface area-to-volume ratio of bacteria, means that aquatic bacteria dominate the uptake and release of dissolved organic matter and nutrients in wetlands. Again, many key data are lacking for specific wetlands, but studies of eutrophic lakes have shown that simple monomers, such as glucose and amino acids, can have turnover times as short as 0.5 hours (Riemann and Sondergaard 1986). Bacteria are also intimately involved in the secretion of extracellular enzymes that degrade complex particulate organic materials in wetlands into the simple monomers (Boon 1991b; Chrost 1991).

The high productivity of heterotrophic bacteria has implications for the structure of food webs in wetlands. Planktonic bacteria in the water column provide food for a diverse range of zooplankton (Boon and Shiel 1990). On the basis of work undertaken on oceanic systems, they would seem also to play a major role in the transformation and liberation of nutrients via the microbial loop whereby bacteria are voraciously consumed by bacteriovorus zooplankton (Azam et al. 1983). Their ecological function in sediments may be quite different, but bacteria are still likely to be important as a food source for benthic protozoa and metazoans (Kemp 1990).

Finally, bacteria can have quite unexpected ecological functions in wetlands. Gereta and Wolanski (1998), for example, showed that bacterial by-products helped flocculate suspended material in saline, eutrophic wetlands in the Serengeti National Park (Tanzania), improving light penetration into the waters that were so turbid that the euphotic zone was less than 1 cm deep.

Bacteria and Wetland Values

The third approach for gauging the importance of bacteria in wetlands is to examine their role in the benefits (or lack of benefits) that humans extract from wetlands, that is wetland values. Three examples indicate the way in which bacteria affect the human use of wetlands.

EXAMPLE 1. A large number of human infections and diseases are water borne (Leclerc et al. 2002; Theron and Cloete 2002), and some, like the mosquito-transmitted malaria and yellow fever, have an immediate link with wetlands. Brackish-water wetlands also have been implicated in the spread of gastrointestinal pathogens, enterococcal bacteria, and *Vibrio cholerae,* the causative agent of cholera along beaches in southern California (Grant et al. 2001; Jiang 2001).

EXAMPLE 2. Bacteria can alter the toxicity of heavy metals in aquatic systems. There is, for example, some evidence that sulfate-reducing bacteria in estuarine wetlands increase the solubility, toxicity, and availability of mercury (King et al. 2002). We have already seen the capacity of bacteria to metabolize complex anthropogenic pollutants, such as hydrocarbon fuels and pesticides. And, as shown later, bacteria are central to the production of sulfuric acid in acid-sulfate soils of coastal wetlands.

EXAMPLE 3. Pathogenic bacteria may be responsible for the mass death of waterbirds in wetlands. Avian botulism, for example, is caused by toxins produced by Clostridium botulinum type C, and kills thousands of birds annually across the globe (Rocke et al. 1999; Rocke and Samuel 1999; Barras and Kadlec 2000). Other mass deaths of waterbirds have been reported that may involve causes other than Clostridium, including the toxins produced by cyanobacteria (Murphy et al. 2000) and enterocolic bacteria (Leon-Quinto et al. 2004).

APPROACHES TO STUDYING WETLAND BACTERIA AND BIOGEOCHEMICAL PROCESSES

Earlier, I noted that many of the difficulties with quantifying bacterial community structure in natural environments were being solved by the application of powerful new molecular methods. Since the use of new methods is such an important issue, it is timely to sidetrack briefly to look at some of the key technical issues in aquatic bacteriology.

The study of bacteria traditionally has been limited to culture-based techniques, and the key problem with this approach is that only a small fraction of the bacteria that occur in aquatic systems can be grown in the laboratory as pure cultures (Jannasch and Jones 1959). Pure-culture methods, while they have their place in microbiology in order to isolate new species (Buck 1979), are totally unsuited for enumerating bacteria in natural environments (e.g., see Scholz and Boon 1993a, 1993b for wetland examples).

If plating methods are inappropriate for enumerating native bacteria, what methods are suitable? The manual edited by Hurst (1997) provides a detailed overview of the different techniques available in environmental microbiology, including biogeochemical analysis. Its coverage is now dated for some molecular techniques but remains topical for most other purposes. The recent text edited by Persing (2004) will prove invaluable for this purpose. Other useful, but now old, texts include those by Jones (1979), Austin (1990), and Kemp and associates (1993). Boon (2000a) summarized current information on approaches for quantifying bacterial biodiversity in wetlands, including immunological and nucleic acid–based methods, biomarker techniques, substrate-utilization approaches, and methods for measuring biomass and productivity. Although this review is still reasonably topical for all but the most recent molecular approaches, constant surveillance is required to remain familiar with the latest developments (e.g., Theron and Cloete 2000; Persing 2004). There are still issues to be solved with even well-established techniques, such as bacterial enumeration via epifluorescence microscopy (Buesing and Gessner 2002) and the isolation of pure strains from environmental samples (Stevenson et al. 2004).

Our understanding of the numbers and roles played by bacteria in wetlands has not come only from better analytical tools. Conceptual advances, as opposed to methodological developments, are also important; this topic has been reviewed recently by Morris and colleagues (2002).

THE HYDROLOGY OF TEMPORARY WETLANDS
WHY IS HYDROLOGY IMPORTANT?

Components of a Wetland's Water Regime
Hydrology is such a powerful controller of wetland ecosystems that there are many excellent reviews in the scientific literature (Gosselink and Turner 1978; Orme 1990; Gilman 1994; Vymazal 1995; Wheeler 1999; Cronk and Fennessy 2001; see Chapter 3). However, because hydrology, biogeochemistry, and bacterial ecology are inextricably linked, I take the liberty of reviewing pertinent aspects of hydrology here.

The term *wetland hydrology* covers a multitude of attributes. Bedford (1996) identified three core hydrologic variables:

- Source of the water, specifically the relative inputs from precipitation, surface water, and groundwater;
- Quality of water, primarily the ionic content (salinity and cation-anion ratios), supplemented by other water-quality variables such as nutrient concentration, pH, and suspended load (or turbidity); and

- Spatial and temporal characteristics of the wetland's wetting and drying cycle. This is a complex variable that includes the frequency, duration, and timing of inundation; the rate of water rise and fall; the maximum water depth; and so on. Bedford (1996) termed this factor *wetland hydrodynamics.*

The first of these variables—source of the water—has long been recognized as a key factor in controlling the type of wetland that develops under a given climatic regime (Cronk and Fennessy 2001; Brinson and Malvarez 2002). Bogs, for example, are peat-accumulating wetlands with no discernible inflows or outflows of surface water, whereas fens are peat-accumulating wetlands that receive some drainage from their surrounding catchment (Mitsch and Gosselink 2000). Other wetland types receive water from their parent river: wetlands on the floodplains of large (usually lowland) rivers commonly receive their water when their parent river is in flood. As discussed later, many wetlands in boreal, semiarid and Mediterranean regions are surface expressions of shallow unconfined groundwater, and changes in the level of the surrounding water table have a large impact on the level of water in these types of wetland that are hydraulically connected with the groundwater.

Clearly, the source of the inundating water plays a significant role in influencing the second of Bedford's (1996) variables—water quality. Moore (1990) discussed the ways in which energy patterns, nutrient cycling, and water quality were controlled by wetland hydrology. For example, since raised ombrotrophic bogs receive all their water via precipitation, they have no external supply of nutrients other than that provided by rainfall. As a result, they are relatively nutrient-poor wetlands, characterized by low concentrations of plant nutrients and exchangeable cations. In contrast, mineralotrophic fens, which lay at lower points in the landscape, receive water that has passed through mineral soil and are relatively enriched in plant nutrients (Mitsch and Gosselink 2000).

Not all wetlands receive their water as surface flows. Wetland systems subject to movements of the groundwater have been termed *rheotrophic,* and in these cases, the groundwater can be responsible for the importing of organic carbon and nutrients (Moore 1990). Clearly, groundwater-fed wetlands may experience vastly different ionic and nutrient relationships to wetlands that are inundated by surface waters. The relative importance of surface and ground waters has been demonstrated clearly with communities of the swamp paperbark tree (*Melaleuca halmaturorum,* Myrtaceae) in wetlands of southern Australia. The trees utilizes both relatively fresh surface water and more variably saline groundwater, the ratio of use depending on the prevailing weather, the presence of surface waters, and the position of the water table (Mensforth and Walker 1996).

Although hydrology is probably the single most important determinant for the establishment and maintenance of specific wetland types, it is a mistake to consider wetlands as merely passive players in their water relationships. As Vymazal (1995) pointed out, the biotic components of wetlands control their hydrology through a variety of mechanisms, including the generation of peat, sediment trapping, shading, and altered rates of evapotranspiration.

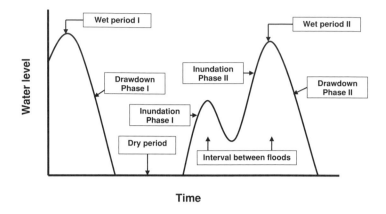

FIGURE 5.3

Some key aspects of the hydrodynamics of temporary wetlands. Adapted from Boulton and Brock (1999).

The third of Bedford's (1996) three hydrologic variables—wetland hydrodynamics—is the most complex. Figure 5.3 shows some key aspects of wetland hydrodynamics and the way in which the water levels vary with time in a temporary wetland. The shape of the annual hydrograph is important (e.g., rise times and fall times), but so too are long-term characteristics, such as the frequency and reliability of floods over the period of decades to centuries (Blanch et al. 1999a, 1999b; Boulton and Brock 1999). Long-term hydrodynamics are especially significant for long-lived species that might recruit only rarely (e.g., clonal plant species, such as reeds).

Ecological Significance of Wetting and Drying

The stylized hydrograph of Figure 5.3 allows a number of questions to be raised about the ecological significance of the hydrodynamics of temporary wetlands:

- How long is the wetland dry between wet periods? Obligately submerged plant taxa can survive only short periods of drying. Conversely, prolonged and complete drying may be required for sediment oxidation, liberation of potential electron acceptors, and changes in crystal mineralogy that affect phosphorus adsorption and release.
- How quickly does the water rise? Does it rise so quickly that submerged aquatic plants cannot extend their leaves fast enough to remain in the photic zone?
- How deep is the water? If water is deeper than about 2 m, it is difficult for even the tallest emergent aquatic plants to keep some aerial organs exposed to permit root aeration, and the plants may drown if the water remains at this level for appreciable periods. With the death of emergent plants, the aeration of below-ground organs will fail, and oxic zones around the rhizosphere may disappear. Submerged plants may become light limited if the water is too deep, especially

if it is also turbid. The death of these plants may also affect the supply of oxygen to the roots and rhizomes, and ultimately the oxygen status of the sediments and the survival of obligately aerobic bacteria in otherwise highly reducing sediments.

· How long does the wetland retain water? If the wet period is too short, aquatic plants will not achieve their maximum biomass or lay down long-lived desiccation-resistant propagules. This will have implications for the supply of organic substrates to wetland bacteria. If the sediments are submerged for only short periods, anoxia may not to develop, and plant material will be degraded primarily by oxic decay processes rather than anoxic ones.

· How quickly does the water level drop during the dry period? Does it recede slowly, allowing fringing herbage to remain green for an appreciable time and provide a food resource for waterbirds, or does it drop rapidly and the wetland dry quickly due to evaporative losses?

· In what season does the wetland fill with water? Is filling a natural event over the rainy season (e.g., in winter-spring in temperate and Mediterranean climates, in the "summer" in monsoonal climates) or an unnatural and out-of-season event related to the anthropogenic maintenance of high river water levels for irrigation supply? Aseasonal filling in autumn or winter may create conditions too cold for wetland plants, animals, and bacteria, and biogeochemical processes may be far slower than had the wetland filled in spring or summer (e.g., see Boon et al. 1997).

It is clear from Figure 5.3 that hydrologically dynamic wetlands can be dry for long periods and, under some circumstances, may fill only for short periods. Some temporary wetlands, of course, may be almost permanently inundated and dry out only rarely. To avoid confusion over terminology, the simplified classification of wetlands shown in Table 5.3 is used to distinguish among wetlands along this hydrodynamic spectrum. The scheme is based on Paijmans and associates (1985) and Boulton and Brock (1999). Williams (1998a) proposed a simpler system for classifying temporary wetlands into two main groups: intermittent wetlands that contained water at more-or-less predictable times, and episodic wetlands, which contained water unpredictably and not as part of an annual rainfall cycle.

ECOTONES IN HYDROLOGICALLY DYNAMIC WETLANDS

The variability in hydrodynamics inevitably leads to variability in the ecology of temporary wetlands, both in time and space. This means that temporary wetlands are intrinsically ecotonal environments. Ecotones are zones of transition between adjacent ecological systems, and the clear hydrologic shifts across various spatial and temporal scales create a series of ecotonal environments in a hydrologically dynamic wetland. The importance of the ecotonal nature of coastal and estuarine wetlands has recently been stressed by Levin and associates (2001).

TABLE 5.3.   Simplified Classification of Temporary Wetlands

	Predictability and Duration of Filling
Ephemeral	Filled only after unpredictable rainfall and runoff; surface water dries within a couple of days of filling and seldom supports macroscopic aquatic life
Episodic	Dry most of the time, with rare and very irregular wet phases that may persist for months; annual inflow is less than minimum annual loss in nine years out of ten
Intermittent	Alternately wet and dry, but less frequently and less regularly than seasonal wetlands; surface water persists for months to years after filling
Seasonal	Alternately wet and dry every year, according to season; usually fills in the wet part of the year and dries predictably every year during the dry season; surface water persists for months, long enough to support macroscopic aquatic life; biota adapted to desiccation
Permanent	Predictably filled although water levels may vary across seasons and years; annual inflow is greater than minimum annual loss in nine years out of ten; may dry during extreme droughts; biota generally can not tolerate desiccation

NOTE: Adapted from Boulton and Brock (1999) and Paijmans and colleagues (1985).

Holland (1996) identified a number of lateral boundaries with their associated ecotones in freshwater wetlands:

·   Upland/high marsh wetland ecotone;

·   High marsh wetland/low marsh wetland ecotone;

·   Low marsh wetland/open water ecotone;

·   Sediment/open water ecotone; and

·   Anaerobic/aerobic sediment ecotone.

To these five ecotonal systems, we can add the ecotone beneath the wetland. This is an important addition since many wetlands are intimately connected to the groundwater that underlies them. Temporary wetlands in the Swan Coastal Plain (Western Australia), for example, are overwhelmingly surface expressions of a shallow unconfined groundwater aquifer (Froend et al. 1993). Water levels in these wetland types vary markedly according to changes in the level of the water table, the latter being controlled by climate and, increasingly, the degree to which groundwater is abstracted for human use (Balla and Davis 1993).

FIGURE 5.4
Groundwater less than 0.5 meters below the sediment surface at a wetland in central Victoria. Cracks in the clay soil are also evident. The photograph was taken during the drought of April 1998.

Figure 5.4 shows that groundwater can be only a few centimeters below the soil surface in a wetland that appears thoroughly dry, even to the point where the sediments have commenced to crack. The ecological significance of this ecotone—the hyporheic zone—has been reviewed recently for streams and rivers (Boulton et al. 1998), but it seems to be a neglected topic in wetland ecology, other than for riparian wetland systems (Storey et al. 1999).

BIOGEOCHEMICAL CYCLES IN TEMPORARY WETLANDS
IMPORTANCE OF WETTING AND DRYING

With the prior sections giving a background to microbiology and water regimes, let us now try to integrate our knowledge of the bacteriology, biogeochemistry, and hydrologic phenomena operating in wetlands. One of the main changes that takes place when a dry wetland becomes inundated with water is that the desiccated and aerated sediments become waterlogged and quickly devoid of oxygen (Ponnamperuma 1972, 1984). The sediments thus change from being oxic (where free oxygen is present as O_2) to being anoxic (where free oxygen is absent). Another term for *anoxic* is *anaerobic*; the former term is often limited to describe just the environment, whereas the latter can refer to either environmental conditions or the physiology of the resident bacteria. One other term worth introducing is *reducing*. This term is not synonymous with anoxic, as anoxic refers merely to the absence of oxygen, whereas reducing refers to the presence of reduced compounds in the sediment and thus a specific aspect of the sediment's redox potential. Let us look at this topic next, since the biogeochemical impact of alternating dry (oxic) and wet (anoxic) conditions is best explained in terms of changes in the reduction-oxidation (redox) chemistry of wetland sediments.

REDOX REACTIONS AND POTENTIAL

What Are Redox Reactions?

Reduction-oxidation (or redox) reactions dominate the biogeochemical processes taking place in wetland sediments. Reduction and oxidation refer to the transfer of electrons from a donor to an acceptor: one substance is oxidized by another which, in turn, is reduced. Redox reactions, therefore, require the presence of an electron donor (the reduced material that becomes oxidized) and an electron acceptor (the oxidant that, by accepting electrons from the electron donor, becomes reduced). Since the reactions are reversible, the reduced and oxidized forms constitute a conjugate pair, or redox couple.

Organic compounds provide the source of reduced (i.e., oxidizable) material for most wetland bacteria. This organic material can be produced either within the wetland (e.g., phytoplankton, periphyton, macrophytes), in which case it is known as *autochthonous* material. If the organic matter is produced outside the wetland (e.g., inputs of terrestrial material from plants fringing the wetland or as dissolved material supplied via the groundwater) it is called *allochthonous* organic matter. The oxidant, or electron acceptor, varies according to environmental conditions and the physiological capacity of the organism, also as described later. In fact, the ability of different types of bacteria to use different substances as oxidants is the basis of much of their physiological diversity.

The tendency of a substance to donate electrons is measured by its standard reduction potential (Harold 1986). Table 5.4 shows the standard reduction potential of the biogeochemically important redox pairs in wetland sediments. The values shown are $E_o{}^I$, which refers to so-called "standard conditions." This means that all components are present at a concentration of 1 mole L^{-1}, the pH is 7, and there is one atmosphere of pressure. The more electropositive the redox pair (e.g., O_2/H_2 at $+0.820$ mV), the more powerful it acts as an oxidant. The more negative the value, the more powerful the redox pair acts as a reductant, and the farther apart are any two half-reactions, the more energy can be released from their reaction. The free-energy yield of a reaction is thus related directly to the difference in reduction potential:

$$\Delta G^{oI} = -nF \, \Delta E_o{}^I$$

where

ΔG^{oI} = free-energy yield under standard conditions at pH 7,

n = number of electrons transferred,

F = Faraday constant (96.48 kJ V^{-1}), and

$\Delta E_o{}^I$ = Difference in reduction potentials, that is, reduction potential ($E_o{}^I$) of the electron-accepting couple minus $E_o{}^I$ of the electron-donating couple.

TABLE 5.4. Reduction Potentials for Some Biogeochemically
Important Redox Pairs

Redox Pair	Eo^I (mV)
O_2/H_2O	+0.820
Mn^{4+}/Mn^{2+}	+0.800
Fe^{3+}/Fe^{2+}	+0.770
NO_3^-/N_2	+0.740
NO_3^-/NO_2^-	+0.430
SO_4^{2-}/HS^-	−0.220
CO_2/CH_4	−0.240
$2H^+/H_2$	−0.420

NOTE: Adapted from Madigan and associates (1997).

The values shown in Table 5.4 can be used to predict the stability and direction of redox reactions in natural environments. For example, the standard reduction potential for the reduction of O_2 to water is +0.820 mV, whereas the reduction of Fe^{3+} to Fe^{2+} is +0.770 mV. This means that, under standard conditions, the Fe^{3+}/Fe^{2+} couple will tend to reduce O_2 to water rather than vice versa. This means also that an aqueous mixture of Fe^{3+}, Fe^{2+}, and O_2 is unlikely to be at equilibrium. The degree to which the mixture is not at equilibrium can be quantified using the equation above, since it indicates the free-energy change of the oxidation-reduction reaction involving these two half-reactions.

The sequence in which various redox reactions take place in a wetland sediment is controlled largely by their relative reduction potential and the related free-energy change of their oxidation-reduction reactions (Krumbein and Swart 1983; Hedlin et al. 1998; Catallo et al. 1999). When the oxidant with the greatest free-energy yield is exhausted, oxidation continues using the next most efficient oxidant and so on until the supply of organic material has been exhausted or possible oxidants are no longer available. This pattern has been shown a number of times in aquatic sediments (e.g., Patrick and Jugsujinda 1992; Hedlin et al. 1998; Ratering and Conrad 1998). What this pattern means in practical terms is that metabolic waste products produced under anaerobic conditions contain some of the free energy that would have been liberated had they been degraded fully by aerobic respiration. These waste-product compounds can then be used by other microbes, and this cascade then forms the basis of an entire sediment food web (Fenchel 1978).

We have noted that, by convention, standard reduction potentials are given for conditions in which the oxidized and reduced forms are at the same concentration (1 mole L^{-1}), at pH 7 and at 1 atmosphere of pressure. This assumption hardly ever holds in nature, and half-reactions may be coupled if the concentrations are greatly different, even though the potential difference is unfavorable. For example, H_2 is taken up so voraciously by methanogenic bacteria that this reduces the H_2 concentration to the point where H^+ can function as an electron acceptor (i.e., an oxidant) even though the E_o' for the $2H^+/H_2$ couple is very low, at -0.420 mV. When this occurs, H^+ can be used as an electron acceptor to produce H_2 in fermentation reactions (Madigan et al. 1997).

Catallo and associates (1999) gave an excellent overview of the importance of redox in aquatic sediments and its implications for biogeochemical cycles. They noted that redox controls a wide range of processes in wetlands, including the biogeochemistry of key elements, such as carbon, hydrogen, nitrogen, and sulfur as well as that of many trace elements. Redox conditions also influence the health and distribution of wetland plants, bacterial and meiofaunal ecology, transformations of pollutants and trace metals, and the preservation of the "chemical fossils" used in diagenesis studies.

Measuring Redox Potential in Wetland Sediments

We have seen that redox potential is a measure of the oxidation states of various oxidation-reduction couples in the environment. Since natural systems are rarely at equilibrium, redox potential is commonly measured in wetland sediments with an inert electrode, usually platinum, which integrates all the redox couples together. A reference electrode acts to complete the circuit for redox measurements. The measurement of redox potential in complex, nonequilibrial natural systems suffers inherently from a number of shortcomings, and these are especially severe when the soil is dry and well aerated. The method is most suitable for waterlogged, reducing conditions, where the system is well poised and measurements are reasonably stable (Bohn 1971).

Quantitative measurements of redox potential (at pH 7 and corrected for the type of reference electrode) are commonly divided into four categories: oxidized soils have a redox of $>+400$ mV, moderately reduced soils are $+100$ to $+400$ mV, reduced soils from -100 to $+100$ mV, and highly reduced soils from -300 to -100 mV (Bohn 1971). The boundary between oxidizing and reducing conditions is commonly marked by the Fe^{2+}/Fe^{3+} couple, which at pH 7 corresponds to a redox potential of $+270$ mV. The division, however, is strongly dependent on soil pH. A correction factor of about -60 mV per pH unit is often applied to correct for sediments at nonneutral pH.

Too much emphasis should not be given to the precise value of redox measurements in wetland sediments or other natural environments. As Bohn (1971) noted: "The instability and irreproducibility of mixed potentials indicate that measurement of redox potential down to the last millivolt in natural systems has little significance." Where redox measurements are especially useful is in allowing the broad distinction among oxic (O_2 present), anoxic (O_2 absent), and reducing conditions. Vershinin and Rozanov (1983) also commented incisively on the utility of redox measurements and concluded that field measurements should not be interpreted in terms of very slight differences in observed redox values.

Aerobic Metabolism and Alternative Electron Acceptors

Since oxygen is such a strong oxidant, it allows bacteria to completely degrade organic substances to carbon dioxide, with the maximum yield of energy. It also permits almost all organic materials to be decomposed, with the possible exception of some xenobiotic substances produced in modern industrial processes (Krumbein and Swart 1983). Oxygen, however, is poorly soluble in water and is rapidly consumed by aerobic metazoans and bacteria in the sediments. For example, at 10°C, the solubility of oxygen in pure water at atmospheric pressure is only about 11 mg L^{-1}, and it falls to about 7.5 mg L^{-1} at 30°C. This means that oxygen penetrates only shallowly into waterlogged sediments and quickly becomes unavailable to the microbiota in deeper layers (e.g., see Ponnamperuma et al. 1967). The situation is even more severe with salinized wetlands, since the solubility of oxygen in water falls as the salt content increases. Nevertheless, the poor solubility and diffusibility of oxygen in water and its rapid consumption by aerobic organisms is responsible for the rapid shift from aerobic to anaerobic conditions when wetlands soils are flooded.

In the absence of oxygen, a wide range of different bacteria can use a suite of alternative electron acceptors to oxidize organic material, largely in order of their potential energy yield (Table 5.4). Since the alternative electron acceptors are not as electropositive as the O_2/H_2O couple, they do not release as much energy as when oxygen is used as the oxidant (as in aerobic metabolism). This difference accounts for the finding that organic matter usually decays more rapidly under aerobic than under anaerobic conditions (e.g., see D'Angelo and Reddy 1999) and why, under some conditions, organic matter can be preserved for long periods in anoxic wetland sediments. The preservation of human remains in peat bogs is one example. With some oxidants, such as Mn^{4+} and Fe^{3+} and to a lesser extent NO_3^-, there is little difference in electropositivity compared with oxygen, meaning that the free-energy yield is almost as good as when aerobic metabolism takes place.

The availability and use of alternative electron acceptors allows bacteria to respire and grow when or where oxygen is not present, if there are reserves of organic material to act as carbon and energy sources. Because of their similarity to aerobic respiration, these anaerobic metabolic processes using inorganic alternative electron acceptors as oxidants are collectively often referred to as *anaerobic respiration*. Some biogeochemists do not agree with this terminology and limit respiration to aerobic reactions (e.g., Gottschalk 1986).

Fermentation

Under many circumstances, bacteria can use organic compounds as both the electron donor and the electron acceptor. This is the basis of *fermentation* reactions. In fermentation reactions, phosphorylation (i.e., the production of ATP) occurs at the substrate level during fermentation, unlike the case with anaerobic respiration, where the generation of ATP is contingent on a proton motive force and membrane-bound electron transport chains. Fermentation thus yields far less energy from a given organic substrate than does respiration (Gottschalk 1986). Moreover, the organic compounds broken down in fermentation reactions can not be metabolized fully to carbon dioxide. Thus, the amount of cellular material generated by fermentation of a given amount of substrate is quite low, and large amounts of organic compounds are formed as waste products.

Perversely, this "inefficient" production of waste products is what makes fermentation so important in the overall process of organic-matter decomposition in anoxic sediments. Since fermentative bacteria release large amounts of simple, low-molecular-weight organic substrates as metabolic waste products, these compounds can be used subsequently by other anaerobic bacteria that are incapable themselves of oxidizing complex organic substrates. These bacteria include key groups, such as sulfate-reducing bacteria and methanogens. Fermentation reactions also often produce H_2, for example, during pyruvate- and formate-forming mixed-acid fermentations (Krumbein and Swart 1983). Like the low-molecular-weight organic compounds generated by fermentative bacteria, the hydrogen is rapidly used by methanogens, and this forms the basis of a rapid H_2 cycle in aquatic sediments.

Iron and Manganese

Since the oxidized forms of iron and manganese are almost as electropositive as oxygen, they are potentially powerful oxidants (Table 5.4). The reduction of ferric iron (Fe^{3+}) to ferrous iron (Fe^{2+}) is likely to be a very important biogeochemical reaction in wetland sediments not only because of the favorable reduction potential (especially under acid conditions), but also because ferric iron is usually abundant in soils and sediments. A number of studies has shown that iron-reducing bacteria are common in natural systems and that the dissimilatory reduction of Fe^{3+} contributes significantly to the overall metabolism of carbon in aquatic sediments (e.g., see Lovley 1987, 1993; Roden and Wetzel 2002; Thamdrup 2000).

A fascinating aspect of dissimilatory iron reduction is that, under the range of circumneutral pH commonly encountered in wetlands, Fe^{3+} oxides are highly insoluble (see Warren and Haack 2001 for a complete review). This means that the reduction process involves an interaction of the bacterial cell not with dissolved electron acceptors (as is the case with oxygen, nitrate, and sulfate), but with a particulate phase that is not transported into the cell (Lovley 1987; Roden and Wetzel 2002).

Because the reduction potential is so positive, iron reduction can be linked to the oxidation of a wide range of organic substrates, and these compounds can be oxidized fully to carbon dioxide if the pH is appropriate (Thamdrup 2000). Also, because of the high reduction potential associated with iron reduction, sulfate reduction and methane production are almost completely inhibited by the addition of Fe^{3+} to aquatic sediments (Lovley and Phillips 1987; see also Yao and Conrad 2000). This inhibition takes place because the iron-reducing bacteria rapidly consume the H_2 and low-molecular-weight organic substrates (e.g., acetate) produced by fermentative bacteria. By virtue of this voracious consumption, the iron-reducing bacteria maintain the concentrations of these compounds at concentrations too low for sulfate-reducing or methanogenic bacteria to compete effectively with them (Lovley and Phillips 1987; Ratering and Conrad 1998; Roden 2003).

A very wide range of bacteria can oxidize organic matter by linking it with the reduction of Fe^{3+} to Fe^{2+} (Thamdrup 2000). Some fermentative bacteria channel only a small part of the electron flow from the organic matter to Fe^{3+}, thus using iron as an electron sink. Other bacteria more or less completely oxidize the organic matter with Fe^{3+} as the sole electron acceptor; in these cases, the reduction of the iron is linked to an electron transport chain and thus to ATP generation. The types of iron-reducing bacteria isolated so far are taxonomically diverse and include *Bacillus, Shewanella,* and *Geobacter.* For those seeking extra detail on iron cycling, see the reviews by Ponnamperuma and associates (1967), Thamdrup (2000), and Warren and Haack (2001).

The dynamics of manganese reduction should be similar to those of iron, since manganese oxides are also abundant in soils, have a low solubility in water at circumneutral pH, and precipitate in a form that is either poorly crystallized or amorphous (Warren and Haack 2001). The reduction potential for the Mn^{4+}/Mn^{2+} couple is also very nearly as electropositive as those for oxygen and iron. However, it has been difficult to demonstrate convincingly that manganese reduction is quantitatively important for carbon flow in natural aquatic environments (Krumbein and Swart 1983; Madigan et al. 1997; but see also Lovley 1991). Part of the difficulty is that manganese oxides rapidly react abiologically with Fe^{2+} and other reduced compounds in aquatic sediments, making it difficult to separate biological from merely chemical transformations (Thamdrup 2000).

Denitrification and Nitrate Reduction

The next electron acceptor of interest is nitrate. Nitrate is used as the alternative electron acceptor by denitrifying bacteria, which reduce NO_3^- to N_2O or N_2 gas (Seitzinger 1988). Since nitrate is a good oxidant (E_o^I for the NO_3^-/N_2 couple is +0.740 mV), most organic substrates can be oxidized entirely to CO_2 with a useful yield of energy. The complete aerobic oxidation of glucose, for example, yields 2,870 kJ per mole of glucose, and denitrification yields an only slightly lower 2,669 kJ (Gottschalk 1986). The two reactions, respectively, are:

$$C_6H_{12}O_6 + 6\,O_2 \rightarrow 6\,CO_2 + 6\,H_2O \qquad \Delta G^{o\prime} = -2{,}870 \text{ kJ mole}^{-1}$$

$$C_6H_{12}O_6 + 4.8\,NO_3^- + 4.8\,H^+ \rightarrow 6\,CO_2 + 2.4\,N_2 + 8.4\,H_2O \qquad \Delta G^{o\prime} = -2{,}669 \text{ kJ mole}^{-1}$$

Denitrification has been reported to commence in soils at a redox potential of about +200 mV (Bohn 1971). Almost all of the denitrifying bacteria use oxygen in preference to nitrate as their electron acceptor when both are available because of oxygen's higher reduction potential. In most cases, nitrate is required to induce denitrification, and the enzymes active in nitrate reduction are inhibited strongly by oxygen (Gottschalk 1986). Denitrifying bacteria are thus facultative in their reliance on oxygen, undertaking aerobic respiration when oxygen is available and switching to anaerobic respiration when it is not. Because of this effect of oxygen, denitrification occurs mostly when sediments are anoxic. It can take place, however, in anaerobic microsites in otherwise oxic soils.

Perhaps the greatest ecological significance of denitrification in wetlands is that it represents a net loss of nitrogen as N_2O or N_2 gas from the ecosystem. Denitrification-mediated losses of nitrogen from temporary wetlands will be controlled strongly by the relative extent and duration of the wet and dry phases. Since denitrification occurs primarily under anoxic conditions, it is most rapid when the wetland has been flooded for some time, free oxygen in the sediments has been exhausted, and sediments have become mildly reducing. However, nitrification—the bacterial process responsible for the production of nitrate—can take place only in the presence of free oxygen, that is, it is obligately aerobic process. (Nitrification is discussed in greater detail later in the chapter.) This means that nitrate will be produced in sediments only when they are aerated, when the wetland is dry and the soil pores are open and well aerated. Some nitrate can be produced in sediments when the wetland is flooded, but only soon after flooding when oxygen is still available or, later in the wet phase, in the spatially limited aerobic zones near the sediment-water interface, and around the roots and rhizomes of aquatic plants or the holes of burrowing animals.

Alternating wetting and drying cycles should maximize the loss of gaseous N_2 from temporary wetlands via the close coupling of nitrification during the dry phase and denitrification during the wet phase. Reddy and Patrick (1975) demonstrated such a pattern with flooded soils, with the greatest losses of nitrogen (24% of soil nitrogen) occurring when terrestrial soils were subjected to alternating aerobic and anaerobic conditions. In comparison, 7% of the soil nitrogen was lost in continuously aerobic soils (when the limiting step was denitrification) and almost none in continuously anaerobic soils (when the limiting step was nitrification). Alternating aerobic and anaerobic periods as short as 2 days each were sufficient to allow the rapid loss of nitrogen from the soils. The rapidity of bacterial responses to alternating aerobic-anaerobic and wet-dry cycles is clearly an important factor in the ecological significance of wetting and drying cycles discussed earlier.

In addition to its use as an alternative electron acceptor in denitrification, nitrate can be used to oxidize complex organic compounds via the reduction of nitrate to nitrite only (nitrate-nitrite respiration) or via the reduction of nitrate or nitrite to ammonium (dissimilatory reduction to ammonium) (Gottschalk 1986; Simon 2002). These processes may be quite common in waterlogged sediments that are highly reducing and have an abundant supply of organic substrates (Boon et al. 1986). They are especially significant from an ecosystem-scale perspective because they retain nitrogen in the wetland system, unlike the case with coupled nitrification-denitrification.

Sulfate Reduction

With the depletion of nitrate, sulfate becomes the next most important inorganic electron acceptor in aquatic systems. As sulfate is a relatively poor oxidant (E_o^I for the SO_4^{2-}/H_2S couple is -0.220 mV), sulfate-reducing bacteria can use only a limited range of organic chemicals as electron donors, including volatile fatty acids (e.g., lactate, acetate, propionate) and some alcohols, including ethanol. As we have seen earlier, these simple, low-molecular-weight compounds are produced primarily as waste products by fermentative bacteria. Since the free-energy change is so low with sulfate as the oxidant, few ATP can be generated or NADH reduced. This means that sulfate-reducing bacteria must reduce large amounts of sulfate to grow, and even then, they grow only slowly (Gottschalk 1986). The reaction for sulfate reduction of acetate is:

$$CH_3COO^- + SO_4^{2-} + 3\ H^+ \rightarrow 2\ CO_2 + H_2S + 2\ H_2O \qquad \Delta G^{\circ\prime} = -57.5\ kJ\ reaction^{-1}$$

Sulfate reduction is an obligately anaerobic process. Bohn (1971) concluded that it commenced at a redox potential of about -150 mV in soils, indicating highly reducing conditions. It is possible, however, for obligately anaerobic biogeochemical processes to take place in otherwise oxic soils, if anaerobic microsites are present. Small oxygen-free microsites may occur, for example, in the central zones of large particles of organic detritus, where the oxygen present in the external environment is metabolized more quickly than it can diffuse into the inner interstices of the particle. Jorgensen (1977) has shown convincingly that bacterial sulfate reduction can take place inside small particles in otherwise oxidized sediments. Again, this phenomenon means that too much reliance should not be placed on measurements of the redox potential of bulk sediments when inferring the presence or absence of specific biogeochemical processes.

Sulfate reduction is a dissimilatory process, where anaerobic bacteria use sulfate as an electron acceptor to oxidize organic matter. It is timely here to differentiate between dissimilatory and assimilatory reactions. In assimilatory reactions, small amounts of sulfate are taken up and reduced by bacteria for anabolic (or biosynthetic) reactions, such as to synthesize amino acids and proteins. Assimilatory reduction is not linked to the production of ATP, but often to the use of ATP in the synthesis of compounds used in cellular construction. During dissimilatory sulfate reduction, sulfate is used as a respiratory oxidant, and large amounts of sulfate are reduced in order that the organic material (that is, the electron donor) can be oxidized. Thus, dissimilatory reduction is a catabolic process resulting in the degradation of organic matter, and assimilatory reduction is an anabolic process resulting in the synthesis of cellular materials.

A similar distinction is necessary when discussing dissimilatory nitrate reduction (i.e., denitrification, nitrate respiration, etc.) versus assimilatory nitrate reduction and with dissimilatory and assimilatory iron reduction. In the case of nitrogen, for example, assimilatory nitrogen uptake is responsible for the uptake of nitrogen to be used to synthesize proteins and nucleic acids. Dissimilatory reduction is the degradative process whereby the nitrate is used in a respiratory role, with large amounts of nitrate being reduced and respired away in order to oxidize the organic matter acting as the electron donor. Tiedje and colleagues (1981) discussed the differences between assimilatory and dissimilatory nitrate reduction, with a survey of methods for discriminating between the two.

A note also should be made with regard to the term *alternative* as the electron acceptor for sulfate-reducing bacteria. These bacteria are obligate anaerobes (unlike the oxygen-facultative denitrifiers) and, strictly speaking, do not have the luxury of using oxygen preferentially and sulfate as an alternative when oxygen becomes in short supply. In fact, sulfate-reducing bacteria are killed when exposed to oxygen. This has interesting implications for the survival of sulfate-reducing bacteria in oxic sediments during the dry phase of a temporary wetland.

Sulfate reduction is important in wetlands for at least four reasons. First, by using the waste products of fermentative bacteria as electron donors, sulfate-reducing bacteria keep the concentrations of these compounds low in aquatic sediments. This makes possible fermentation reactions that would be otherwise energetically unfavorable. Second, sulfate-reducing bacteria produce S^{2-} as a metabolic end product; sulfide is significant in the formation of acid-sulfate soils and as a plant toxicant. Third, sulfate reduction has been linked with the release of phosphorus from aquatic sediments, probably via the displacement of phosphorus from insoluble Fe^{2+} mineral phases by the S^{2-} (Baldwin and Mitchell 2000a).

The fourth, and most important reason for us, is that sulfate is abundant is seawater (about 28 mmol L^{-1}) but far less abundant in fresh waters. Sulfate reduction, therefore, is the dominant anaerobic decay processes in marine and coastal environments where sulfate supply is rarely limiting (at least in the upper layers of the sediment). This is the fundamental difference between anaerobic carbon metabolism in fresh waters and marine systems; in the latter, sulfate reduction is the most important terminal process for anaerobic decay (Capone and Kiene 1998). A different process—methanogenesis—becomes operative in freshwater systems, as described next. Although sulfate is usually found only in low concentrations in fresh waters, increased sulfur loads originating from water and atmospheric pollution mean that the modest role currently played by sulfate reduction might become progressively more important with time (Lamers et al. 1998, 2002).

Methanogenesis

Since sulfate is generally not abundant in freshwater environments, it quickly becomes depleted by any sulfate-reducing bacteria that are present in the sediments. Rather than sulfate reduction, the terminal route for anaerobic decomposition in freshwater sediments is the production of methane (Capone and Kiene 1998; Segers 1998). Boon (2000b), for example, calculated that methanogenesis accounted for at least 30% to 60% of the total benthic carbon flow in a temporary wetland in northeastern Victoria (Australia). Happell and Chanton (1993) estimated that 49% of carbon mineralization in swamp forests in Florida was by nonmethanogenic processes that produced carbon dioxide and the remainder by methanogenic processes that produced both carbon dioxide and methane. Rates of methane production are, however, highly variable across wetlands: Segers (1998) reported them to range by over three orders of magnitude, according to wetland type, temperature, and latitude.

Methanogens are members of the Archaea, the group of prokaryotes that includes the obligate halophiles and obligate thermophiles. Methanogens are obligate anaerobes and are rapidly killed by exposure to oxygen. With few exceptions, they compete with sulfate-reducing bacteria for the simple, low-molecular-weight organic compounds, such as acetate, produced as fermentation waste products, as well as for H_2. Given a good supply of sulfate, sulfate-reducing bacteria almost always outcompete methanogens for these substrates (Kristjanson and Schonheit 1983; Kuivila et al. 1988; Reddy and D'Angelo 1994; Ratering and Conrad 1998). This competitive ability arises from the difference in reduction potential of the two electron acceptors and accounts for the dominance of sulfate reduction in marine wetlands and methanogenesis in freshwater wetlands.

Methane can be generated via three different classes of reaction. All take place only under highly reducing conditions. The first reaction uses CO_2, $HCOO^-$, or CO to produce methane. The typical reaction is:

$$CO_2 + 4\,H_2 \rightarrow CH_4 + 2\,H_2O \qquad \Delta G^{ol} = -131 \text{ kJ reaction}^{-1}$$

Second, methane can be produced via reduction of the methyl group of methyl-containing compounds, such as methanol. The typical reaction is:

$$4\,CH_3OH \rightarrow 3\,CH_4 + CO_2 + 2\,H_2O \qquad \Delta G^{ol} = -319 \text{ kJ reaction}^{-1}$$

Third, methane can be produced via the cleavage of acetate to methane plus carbon dioxide:

$$CH_3COO^- + H_2O \rightarrow CH_4 + HCO_3^- \qquad \Delta G^{ol} = -31 \text{ kJ reaction}^{-1}$$

One important caveat must be made regarding the use of standard free energy yields (ΔG^{ol}) to compare the relative likelihood of different anaerobic reactions in wetland sediments. As noted earlier, the calculation of ΔG^{ol} assumes 1 molar concentration of both the oxidized and reduced forms, a pressure of 1 atmospheric, and a pH of 7. These assumptions rarely hold in aquatic ecosystems, and environmental variations can greatly modify the free-energy yield that occurs under natural conditions. In the case of methanogenesis, for example, the ΔG^{ol} for methane production from $H_2 + CO_2$ and from acetate are, respectively, -131 and -31 kJ reaction^{-1}. However, under conditions more typical of fresh waters, the ΔG is more likely to be about -3 and -25 kJ reaction^{-1}, respectively (Madigan et al. 1997). This alters completely the theoretical energetic benefits of the two routes for methane production. Similar considerations hold for iron reduction in sediments of different pH values.

Other Inorganic Electron Acceptors

In addition to the common inorganic electron acceptors, O_2, Fe^{3+}, Mn^{4+}, NO_3^-, SO_4^{2-}, and CO_2, a number of other oxidized inorganic compounds can be used as oxidants by bacteria in aquatic systems. Arsenic and selenium, for example, support the growth of various bacteria via the reduction of SeO_4^{2-} to SeO_3^{2-} and, eventually, to Se° (metallic selenium) in polluted streams and wetlands. Warren and Haack (2001) and Wackett and associates (2004) provided a fascinating overview of the interactions of bacteria with diverse metallic and metalloid elements. A number of low-molecular-weight organic compounds can also act as electron acceptors in anaerobic respiration, including fumarate and trimethylamine oxide; further details are provided in Gottschalk (1986) and Madigan and colleagues (1997).

Phosphine Evolution

So far, we have spoken mainly about the use of the common alternative electron acceptors by bacteria to metabolize organic matter in wetlands. It should be possible also for PO_4^{2-} to be reduced to phosphine (PH_3) at a redox potential similar to that at which methanogenesis takes place (Catallo et al. 1999). This transformation would be interesting for two reasons. First, it would represent a gaseous phase for phosphorus cycling; the absence of a phosphorus equivalent to denitrification is often cited as a major difference between the two nutrient cycles in aquatic systems. Second, phosphine generation might explain one of the most puzzling phenomena associated with wetlands.

Phosphine is a colorless gas, analogous to ammonia, and when combined with impurities such as P_2H_2 is spontaneously flammable. The luminous flame produced when phosphine burns is the basis of Holmes's signal, a device used for signaling at sea. Canisters of calcium phosphide (Ca_3P_2) are attached to wooden floats, pieced at both ends so that they fill with water, then thrown overboard, upon which they generate the warning light (Partington 1947). Nowadays, phosphine is often used to fumigate grain supplies and kill insect pests. The fact that phosphine is spontaneously flammable has been used by some to explain the will-of-the-wisps and other strange lights alleged to be associated with wetlands. In fact, the Thai newspaper *The Nation* carried an article on this topic in October 2003. The Deputy Permanent Secretary of the Thai Science Ministry, Saksit Tridech, claimed that the Naga fireballs, seen over the Mekong River at the end of Buddhist Lent, were not a supernatural phenomenon but, instead, the result of phosphine evolution and combustion at the river surface (see http://www.100megsfree4.com/farshores/n03naga.htm, accessed August 4, 2004).

There are only a couple of papers on phosphine production in aquatic systems. In an often-cited report, Devai and associates (1988) noted the evolution of phosphine from sewage treatment facilities in Hungary. Devai and DeLaune (1995) reported a phosphine emission rate of 0.4 to 6.5 ng m^{-2} h^{-1} from coastal brackish-water wetlands and salt marshes in the southern United States. Presumably, though, there is rarely sufficient phosphate in wetland sediments to support substantial rates of phosphine evolution. But, if phosphine production can explain will-of-the-wisps and other ghostly lights, wetland biogeochemistry might not be the dry topic it first appears.

Summary of Biogeochemical Processes

The various reactions important in oxidizing organic matter in wetlands are summarized as Figure 5.5. This figure should be interpreted in the light of the summary of reduction

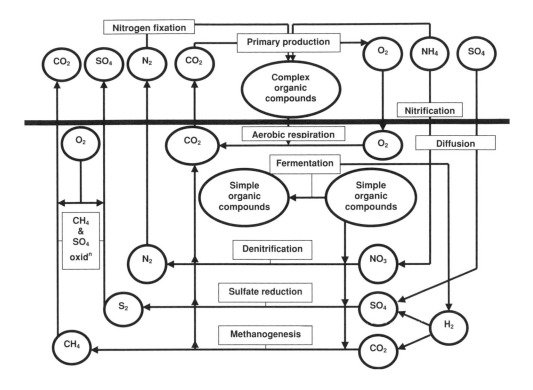

FIGURE 5.5
Biogeochemical pathways in wetland sediments associated with the decomposition of organic matter. The thick horizontal line indicates the sediment-water interface.

potentials (Table 5.4) and the main decomposition processes shown in Table 5.5. Similar schematic summaries have appeared in earlier reviews of sediment biogeochemistry (e.g., Fenchel and Blackburn 1979; Reddy et al. 1988; Catallo et al. 1999). A key issue with these simple representations is that the biogeochemical cycles are often shown as a linear progression, with aerobic processes dominating in the upper sediments and anaerobic processes down the soil profile in concert with changes in sediment redox. Such presentations imply a constant water level with a simple downward trend in carbon and nutrient cycles. What is far more likely to occur in hydrologically dynamic wetlands is that the theoretical vertical profile of biogeochemical processes varies in time and space as the wetland wets and dries, ecotonal zones shift up and down, and rooted angiosperms and burrowing animals allow the penetration of oxygen deep into the sediment profile.

Chemolithotrophy, Heterotrophy, and Autotrophy
It is apparent from Figure 5.5 that the reduced inorganic compounds produced as respiratory waste products by anaerobic decomposition themselves can be used as energy

TABLE 5.5. Diversity of Electron Acceptors Used by Aquatic Bacteria as a Function of Increasing Reduction Potential

Reduction Potential	Type of Respiration	Electron Acceptor	Product
Electronegative	Carbonate respiration	CO_2	CH_3-COO^-
	Sulfur respiration	S^0	HS^-
	Methanogenesis	CO_2	CH_4
	Sulfate reduction	SO_4^-	HS^-
	Denitrification	NO_3^-	NO_2^-, N_2O, N_2
	Iron respiration	Fe^{3+}	Fe^{2+}
Electropositive	Aerobic respiration	O_2	H_2O

NOTE: Adapted from Madigan and associates (1997).

sources by aquatic microbes. For example, methane produced by methanogenic bacteria is a potential source of both energy and cellular carbon for aquatic bacteria. Similarly, reduced ferrous iron (Fe^{2+}) is a potential energy source if it can be oxidized back to ferric iron (Fe^{3+}), even at circumneutral pH (Neubauer et al. 2002).

To investigate these processes further, it is important to remember that the biochemical pathway by which bacteria obtain their energy may differ from that in which they obtain their carbon for biosynthetic reactions. Most bacteria obtain their energy and their cellular carbon from the oxidation of organic compounds. They are called *chemoorganotrophs*, or *heterotrophs*. The aerobes, denitrifying bacteria and sulfate-reducing bacteria discussed previously are all heterotrophic bacteria, since organic materials (e.g., plant litter) are oxidized to liberate energy and as a source of carbon for cellular biosynthesis. Metazoan animals also are heterotrophic; for example, humans obtain both their energy and carbon requirements from the food that they eat.

However, some bacteria can use reduced inorganic compounds, rather than organic compounds, as their source of energy. This second physiological type of microbes are called *chemolithotrophs* (see Table 5.2). As we have seen in the earlier discussion on redox reactions, the free-energy yield of a redox reaction is related directly to the difference in reduction potentials of the reductant and oxidant. Important chemolithotrophic bacteria include the nitrifiers (which oxidize ammonium or nitrite) and the methanotrophs (which oxidize methane). Both groups of bacteria use oxygen to oxidize the reduced inorganic compounds. While chemolithotrophs use reduced inorganic compounds for their energy source, other types of bacteria can use inorganic carbon as their source of carbon. The bacteria that fix carbon dioxide as their sole source of carbon for cellular biosynthesis are called *autotrophs*. Autotrophs, representing a third type of bacterial physiology, obtain the energy needed to fix carbon dioxide from a range of sources. Organisms that use light as an energy source for carbon fixation are called *photoautotrophs*; cyanobacteria, eukaryotic algae, and vascular plants fall into this category. Many chemolithotrophic bacteria are also autotrophic. For example, the nitrifying bacteria use the energy liberated in the oxidation of ammonium or nitrite to fix carbon dioxide into cellular material. This reaction is discussed in detail later.

The fourth major nutritional group is the *photoheterotrophs,* which use light as an energy source but organic materials as their carbon source. Finally, there are the *mixotrophs,* which are able to assimilate organic compounds as carbon sources but use inorganic compounds as electron donors (i.e., as energy sources). An example of mixotrophy is the bacteria that use H_2 as their energy source but, being unable to fix carbon dioxide, use organic compounds as their carbon source.

An important group of chemolithotrophic bacteria in wetlands is the methanotrophs, which obtain their energy by oxidizing the methane produced by methanogens in the sediments. They are autotrophic since they use this energy to fix carbon dioxide into cellular material (note that some methane is also incorporated into their cellular biomass). Despite being known for at least 100 years, there are still major gaps in our understanding of the physiology and molecular biology of methanotrophic bacteria (Wood et al. 2004). Since they use oxygen to oxidize methane, methanotrophs are obligately aerobic and limited to the epilimnion or oxic regions of the sediment, such as surface sediments at the water-sediment interface, around plant roots, or the holes of burrowing animals (Boon and Lee 1997). Methanotrophs oxidize much of the methane produced deeper in the sediments and limit the transfer of this greenhouse-active gas to the atmosphere. Happell and Chanton (1993), for example, showed that benthic methanotrophs in northern Florida swamp forests oxidized nearly one-half of the methane diffusing to the surface sediments from deeper anoxic zones. When the wetland was dry, the methanotrophs consumed atmospheric methane from the air. This voracious consumption of methane by methanotrophs means that a simple comparison of carbon dioxide emissions with methane emissions will underestimate markedly the importance of methanogenesis to total carbon flux in wetland sediments (e.g., see Boon 2000b).

Nitrification is another important chemolithotrophic reaction in wetlands. Nitrifying bacteria obtain their energy to fix carbon dioxide by oxidizing ammonium to nitrate, or nitrate to nitrite. Like methanotrophy, nitrification occurs only under oxic conditions in freshwater sediments (redox >300 mV according to Reddy and D'Angelo 1994). Nitrification is important in wetlands for three reasons. First, it provides the nitrate that allows denitrification to occur in the anaerobic zones of the sediments. Second, the initial oxidative step converts the positively charged ammonium ion (NH_4^+), which is readily adsorbed onto negatively charged clay particles, to the negatively charged nitrate or nitrite ions, which are not retained on clay lattices. Since they are repulsed by clay particles, nitrate and nitrite are easily leached from wetland soils by downwards-percolating waters. Third, nitrification is another oxygen-demanding process in the water column and sediments, and it contributes to the deletion of oxygen by microbes and other aerobic organisms.

Reactions for the oxidation of ammonia to nitrite and nitrite to nitrate by nitrifying bacteria are:

$$NH_3 + 1.5\ O_2 \rightarrow NO_2^- + H^+ + H_2O \qquad \Delta G^{o\prime} = -287\ kJ\ reaction^{-1}$$

$$NO_2 + 0.5\ O_2 \rightarrow NO_3^- \qquad \Delta G^{o\prime} = -76\ kJ\ reaction^{-1}$$

Other reduced compounds used as energy sources by chemolithotrophic bacteria include Fe^{2+} and S_2^-. A wide range of chemolithotrophic bacteria (e.g., *Beggiatoa, Thiobacillus, Thioploca, Thiothrix,* and *Thermothrix*) grow by oxidizing reduced sulfur compounds in the presence of oxygen.

In all cases of chemolithotrophy in wetland environments, there is a close nexus between the various anaerobic and aerobic biogeochemical processes. The anaerobic processes of organic-matter decomposition generate the reduced inorganic substances (e.g., methane, ammonium, ferrous iron, sulfide), and these energy-rich substances are then oxidized by chemolithotrophic bacteria in the water column or oxic zones of the sediment (Fig. 5.5). As we have seen before, this coupling may be manifest spatially in the wet phase of a temporary wetland in different zones of the sediment, or temporally across the alternating wet-dry phases in hydrologically dynamic systems.

It should be apparent that a limited number of elements—nitrogen, manganese, iron, and sulfur—dominate biogeochemical decomposition processes in temporary wetlands. This is because these elements can exist in a range of oxidation states. In the case of nitrogen, oxidation states range from the highly oxidized (nitrate, with an oxidation state of $+5$) to the highly reduced (oxidation state of -3 for organic nitrogen in the form $R-NH_2$). By convention, N_2 gas is ascribed an oxidation state of 0. Similarly, sulfur exists in highly oxidized ($+6$: sulfate) and highly reduced (-2: organic sulfur in the form R-SH and sulfide, H_2S) forms. Phosphorus does not exist in a number of oxidation states; its biogeochemical cycling arises more from complex sorption-desorption mechanisms than from redox reactions. These reactions are discussed later.

Anomalous Microbial Reactions

It is timely here to digress slightly and mention some of the "anomalous" microbial populations and transformations that have been reported recently in the literature. The traditional concept of biogeochemical processes (e.g., Fig. 5.5) restricts aerobic microbes, such as nitrifying and methane-oxidizing bacteria, to oxic environments or the oxic-anoxic interfaces around plant roots and the holes of burrowing animals. Similarly, processes such as denitrification, sulfate reduction, and methanogenesis are traditionally believed to be limited to anaerobic zones, either as the reducing bulk sediment or anaerobic microsites in oxic sediments.

There is now convincing evidence that some processes, thought in the past to be obligately aerobic, can occur under anoxic conditions. For example, ammonium oxidation has been reported in anoxic marine sediments; the process is probably mediated by unidentified members of the Planctomycetales, a type of Bacteria (Freitag and Prosser 2003). These bacteria undertake the so-called *ammanox* reaction, oxidizing ammonium with nitrite as the electron acceptor and liberating N_2 gas as the waste product (Schouten et al. 2004). Likewise, the putatively anaerobic process of denitrification has been observed to occur under aerobic conditions that are not explicable by the existence of anaerobic microsites (Takaya et al. 2003). Moreover, there are numerous reports of the survival of supposedly anaerobic prokaryotes, such as methanogens and sulfate reducers, in well-aerated soils (Fetzer et al. 1993; Peters and Conrad 1995; see also Boon et al. 1997 and Oquist and Sundh 1998). This phenomenon raises the interesting question as to how such obligately anaerobic microbes can survive in conditions where they should rapidly die, especially as they are thought to be incapable of forming desiccation-resistant endospores.

BIOGEOCHEMICAL PROCESSES IN THE WATER COLUMN

So far, we have concentrated on the sediments of hydrologically dynamic wetlands. Let us turn our attention to the water column, since the large biogeochemical demand that sediments have for oxygen has many implications for biogeochemical processes that take place in the overlying water. Figure 5.6 shows some results we have obtained for a shallow (<2 m) floodplain wetland in a part of northeastern Victoria (Australia) with a strongly seasonal climate. The wetland, Ryans Billabong, is densely vegetated with a mix of emergent rushes and sedges, and submerged angiosperms (mainly *Vallisneria* sp.). In summer, the water column is thermally stratified during the day and homogeneous (mixed) during the night, a type of stratification known as *polymixis*. The daytime stratification is driven by high air temperatures (>35°C), clear skies, and intense solar radiation, characteristics common in arid, semiarid, and Mediterranean regions. The nighttime mixing is a result of wind action and the loss of energy from the water column into the sky during the clear, cool nights.

A high oxygen demand is created both in the sediments and the water column by aerobic respiration and chemolithotrophic reactions, such as nitrification and methanotrophy. The results of this demand are evident in the very low (<1 mg L^{-1}) concentrations of dissolved oxygen in the water column during the night. During the daytime, however, concentrations of dissolved oxygen increase (to >10 mg L^{-1}) as a result of the rapid photosynthesis of planktonic algae, benthic algal mats, and submerged aquatic plants.

At the same time as these changes in oxygen concentrations are taking place, there are very strong dynamics in methane cycling (Fig. 5.6). The concentration of dissolved methane in the water column is often high, a result of rapid methanogenesis in the sediments (e.g., see Ford et al. 2002). The close spatial relationship of abundant dissolved oxygen and abundant dissolved methane allows methanotrophic bacteria to grow in the water column and on the sediment surface. These chemolithotrophic bacteria may be extremely

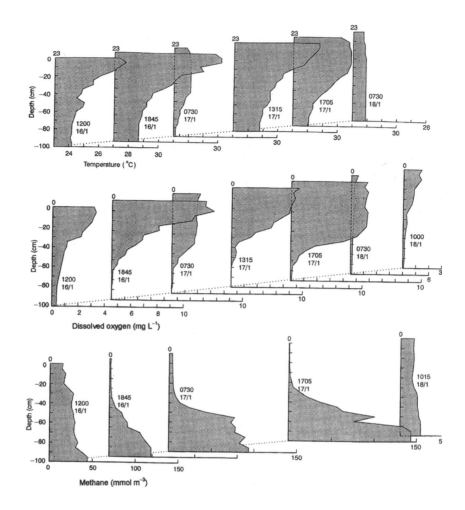

FIGURE 5.6

Vertical profiles of temperature, dissolved oxygen, and dissolved methane down the water column of Ryans Billabong, northeastern Victoria (36°07′S, 146°58′E) at six different times of day (1200 h, 1845 h, 0730 h, 1315 h, 1705 h, and 0730 h) from January 16–18, 1995. Redrawn from Ford and colleagues (2002).

abundant, accounting for about 10% to 50% of all planktonic bacteria in the wetland (Ross et al. 1997). It is likely that the oxygen demand created by their oxidation of methane, like that of ammonium oxidation by nitrifying bacteria, also contributes to planktonic oxygen depletion. Hamilton and associates (1997), for example, showed the strong effect of methanotrophy on oxygen consumption in the Pantanal wetland of the Paraguay River, South America.

The rapid photosynthesis by plants, resulting in the high daytime concentrations of dissolved oxygen in the water column, also causes substantial shifts in pH. Morris and colleagues (2003a, 2003b), for example, reported that the pH of a shallow, densely vegetated lake in central Victoria varied by up to 2 pH units across the day, in response to diel variations in photosynthesis and respiration. If the pH were to rise above about 8 during the daytime, it is possible for ammonium to be converted to ammonia (pKa = 9.2) and nitrogen lost from the wetland via volatilization across the water-atmosphere interface (Reddy and D'Angelo 1994). Such losses would add to the loss of N_2O and N_2 gases that occurs as a result of denitrification in the sediments. It is also possible for pH shifts to affect phosphorus dynamics via impacts on carbonate chemistry. These are discussed later.

Having reviewed the various biogeochemical pathways that operate in temporary wetlands, let us turn our attention to the specific effects that wetting and drying have on the decay of organic matter in these types of hydrologically dynamic water bodies. I concentrate in the dynamics of leaf-litter decay, since aquatic vegetation is such an evident and important component of temporary wetlands.

ORGANIC-MATTER DECAY IN TEMPORARY WETLANDS

DISTINGUISHING ORGANIC-MATTER BREAKDOWN FROM DECOMPOSITION

It is worth distinguishing between the breakdown of leaf litter and the biogeochemical process of organic-matter decomposition. The term *breakdown* is probably best used when describing the gradual loss of mass from plant litter constrained in leaf packs or other mesh bags. This loss of plant material is a complex function of physical fragmentation, leaching of dissolved organic substances, and conversion of organic carbon to inorganic forms such as carbon dioxide and methane (Boulton and Boon 1991). In contrast, *decomposition* involves mineralization of the organic matter. The term *mineralization* has been used widely in the biogeochemical literature to mean the conversion of organic substrates to gaseous inorganic forms of carbon, specifically carbon dioxide and methane (e.g., see Oquist and Sundh 1998; D'Angelo and Reddy 1999; Marschner and Kalbitz 2003). Analogously, *nutrient regeneration* refers to the conversion of complex organic forms of nitrogen and phosphorus (e.g., proteins, nucleic acids, ATP, etc.) to their simple inorganic forms, such as ammonium and orthophosphate, during decomposition.

EFFECTS OF WETTING AND DRYING ON ORGANIC-MATTER DECOMPOSITION

The effects of wetting and drying on decomposition processes in soils and sediments are well understood, and a summary of the key experiments is provided here. It has been known for nearly half a century that wetting a dry soil results in an immediate flush of mineralization, evident in a rapid but short-lived evolution of carbon dioxide (Stevenson

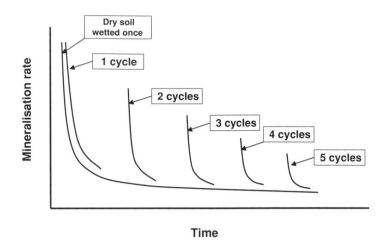

FIGURE 5.7

Effect of repeated wetting and drying on organic-matter decomposition in wetland sediments. Redrawn from Birch (1958).

1956; Birch 1958; Soulides and Allison 1961; Sorensen 1974; Orchard and Cook 1983). Figure 5.7 typifies the results obtained by Birch (1958) in one of the earliest demonstrations of the effect of wetting previously dry soils. Although Birch worked on terrestrial soils, the results are likely to be applicable to sediments from temporary wetlands that experience alternating wet and dry phases.

Figure 5.7 shows that the cycle of decomposition under alternating wet-dry cycles is one of rapid initial mineralization immediately after wetting, followed by a decrease in the mineralization rate and progressively smaller emissions of carbon dioxide with every subsequent wetting and drying cycle. This means that only a portion of the total amount of organic matter in a dry soil is decomposed after a single wetting event. Two factors are probably responsible. First, although a part of the carbon dioxide liberated is derived from the decay of the soil humus, most comes from the degradation of soil microbes themselves (Marumoto et al. 1982a, 1982b; Salonius 1983). Once these microbes have died and been mineralized to carbon dioxide, the microbial populations must build up again during subsequent wet-dry cycles to permit a subsequent flush of carbon dioxide with the next inundation event. Second, it seems that the bacteria mediating the decay quickly become limited by nitrogen availability (Birch 1958). This nutrient limitation is consistent with the known dynamics of nitrogen limitation and regeneration by aquatic bacteria, discussed later.

Birch (1958) also showed that more organic matter was mineralized when soils were oven dried than when they were gently air dried. Earlier, Birch and Friend (1956) found that drying at high temperatures increased the decomposition of soil humus and enhanced carbon dioxide production when an East African soil was dried and wetted. This response could have implications for organic-matter decomposition in temporary wetlands. Since many temporary wetlands are found in monsoonal, Mediterranean, or arid or semiarid environments, the baking that their organic matter receives during the dry season could lead to the accelerated loss of soil carbon during subsequent inundation events. Also, it has been shown that exposure to ultraviolet radiation affects the rate of leaf-litter decay, especially by promoting the rate at which dissolved compounds are leached from particulate detritus (Mans et al. 1998). The effect of ultraviolet radiation may bolster that of high temperatures in accelerating the rate at which soil organic matter decomposes in temporary wetlands in tropical, Mediterranean, and desert regions.

Earlier, we saw that inundating a dry soil causes the soil pores to be filled with water, resulting in poor diffusion of oxygen into the sediment and the gradual replacement of oxic by anoxic (even reducing) conditions. As the wetland dries out, the waterlogged soils become dry, and oxic conditions again replace the reducing conditions that typify the wetland during its flooded phase. How does this pattern of alternating wet-dry and oxic-anoxic conditions affect the relative rates of aerobic and anaerobic decomposition? Reddy and Patrick (1975) attempted to answer this question by examining the effects of alternating oxic and anoxic conditions on organic-matter mineralization in wetted soils. They used permanently wet soils bubbled with air or argon to create aerobic and anoxic conditions, respectively, that cycled over periods of 2 to 128 days. Permanently anaerobic and highly reducing conditions (redox of -300 mV) generated only about one-half the amount of carbon dioxide produced in the other treatments. This means that organic-matter decomposition was markedly slower under anaerobic conditions. However, there was little difference in the total amount of decomposition between the fully aerobic incubations (redox of $+600$ mV) and those incubations that experienced alternating aerobic and anaerobic conditions. Carbon dioxide accounted for most of the soil organic matter that was mineralized, and methane emissions were minor except under permanently anaerobic conditions. Under these situations, methane was a major product of organic-matter decomposition.

To extend our analysis on the effects of wetting and drying on the decomposition of soil organic matter, let us look at one detailed study undertaken on methane emissions from temporary wetlands in southeastern Australia (Boon et al. 1997; Boon 2000b). We used four approaches to quantify the effect of wetting and drying on anaerobic decomposition in a range of floodplain wetlands: (1) field observations on methane emissions following natural flood events, (2) artificially manipulating water levels in small wetlands under field conditions, (3) large-scale mesocosm studies, and (4) laboratory incubations of wetland sediments.

Artificially flooding the small wetlands when they were dry resulted in methane being evolved within three days of inundation. Methane fluxes from these temporary wetlands could exceed 2 to 3 mmol m^{-2} h^{-1}, which was about the same as emissions from nearby permanent wetlands. Methane emissions depended greatly on the season of flooding, with almost no methane being evolved after a winter flood. The in vitro production of methane slowly decreased as wetland sediments were dried in the air, and there was no detectable methane production from sediments that had been drying for more than two months.

Similar results have been reported for wetland sediments in other climates. Ratering and Conrad (1998), for example, demonstrated that draining water of rice-paddy soils from the Po River Valley (Italy) markedly decreased methane emissions. It was postulated that this was due to two processes. First, the rate and spatial extent of methane oxidation probably increased as the sediments became increasingly aerated, resulting in more methane being intercepted by methanotrophic bacteria before it could enter the atmosphere (e.g., see also Henckel et al. 2001). Second, methanogenesis may have been inhibited by the rapid regeneration of alternative electron acceptors (especially ferric iron and sulfate) from their reduced precursors as the sediments were drained, oxygen diffused into them, and iron-reducing and sulfate-reducing bacteria outcompeted methanogenic bacteria for carbon substates (Ratering and Conrad 1998).

The effect of water table fluctuations on methane emissions from peatlands in boreal and other cool-climate regions is also quite well understood (Moore and Knowles 1989; Moore and Dalva 1997; Grunfeld and Brix 1999; Blodau and Moore 2003). In these cases, the wetting and drying effect again seems to be a function of rapid methanogenesis and rapid methanotrophy occurring under anaerobic and aerobic conditions, respectively.

The consistent picture that has developed from these diverse studies on terrestrial soils, rice paddies, and natural wetlands is that there is a flush of inorganic carbon (mainly carbon dioxide) when dry soils or sediments are inundated. With ongoing inundation, the wetlands evolve progressively more methane. Carbon dioxide emissions, however, remain high since a number of methanogenic pathways generate some or, in the case of acetate cleavage, equal amounts of carbon dioxide and methane for each molecule of organic compound metabolized. There is a net production of methane from wetlands during their flooded phase and either no production, or even methane uptake from the atmosphere by methanotrophic bacteria, during their dry phase or when the water table has been lowered substantially.

Our analysis of the effects of wetting and dying on the biogeochemical process of organic-matter decomposition leads naturally to the topic of whether wet and dry cycles have any effect on the breakdown of the leaf litter that comprises so much of the organic matter that enters temporary wetlands.

EFFECTS OF WETTING AND DRYING ON LEAF-LITTER BREAKDOWN

Diversity of Plant Inputs to Temporary Wetlands

Since freshwater wetlands are among the most productive of all ecosystems, there is often abundant plant detritus available to be broken down by microbes and invertebrates (Westlake 1963; Vymazal 1995; Wetzel 2001). For example, the net productivity of emergent herbaceous C4 plants, such as *Cyperus,* in freshwater wetlands can range from 6 to

9 kg m^{-2} year^{-1}, and the productivity of C3 plants, such as *Phragmites,* is only slightly less. The productivity of woody plants associated with wetlands is also high, commonly in the range of 0.5 to 1.6 kg m^{-2} year^{-1} (Vymazal 1995).

It is easy to see how a hydrologically dynamic wetland accumulates a diverse range of plant material over its alternating wet and dry phases. Terrestrial plants, especially grasses and forbs, grow on the dry wetland floor during the dry phase, and leaf and other material (e.g., bark and wood) is blown into the wetland basin from surrounding terrestrial areas. This material partly degrades in situ and contributes to the pool of humic material in the soil. But not all the plant material is fully decomposed. and substantial amounts may have accumulated on the wetland floor by the time the wetland refloods. For example, we (Nias, Boon, and Bailey, unpublished data) found from 0.75 to 1.6 kg DW m^{-2} of terrestrial detritus (leaves and bark, mainly) on the dry floodplain floor of Raftery Swamp in central Victoria (Figs. 5.1 and 5.2).

The flooding of a temporary wetland drowns the fully terrestrial species, adding to the detritus in the wetland basin. Submerged and emergent aquatic plants germinate as the wetland fills, grow throughout the inundation phase, and are subject to ongoing decomposition as they mature, senesce, and die. The submerged portions of the aquatic plants also support a diverse and productive suite of attached algae and microbes, the epiphyton. Other biofilms develop on submerged wood during the wet phase. As the wetland dries again, this complex mixture of partly degraded allochthonous and autochthonous plant litter, comprising material from terrestrial trees, grasses and forbs, aquatic vascular plants, and algae, remains on the wetland floor.

Does Wetting and Drying Accelerate Leaf-litter Breakdown?

In contrast to the consistent picture that has emerged from studies of organic-matter decomposition and the generation of carbon dioxide and methane, there is less certainty about the effects of wetting and drying on the breakdown of leaf litter. Because temporary wetlands can be expected to have such a diverse input of plant material, let us first examine the literature on how the leaves of terrestrial and semiaquatic trees break down, then the sparse literature on the effects of wetting and drying on the breakdown of the more aquatic taxa. An attempt at a synthesis, collating some ideas on how methodological limitations have confounded the question, concludes the section.

A number of reports, usually using plant matter constrained in litter bags, has shown more rapid mass loss of leaf material or cellulose sheets in seasonally flooded sites than in nearby unflooded areas or permanently wet areas (e.g., Brinson 1977; Bell et al. 1978; Day 1982; Peterson and Rolfe 1982; Yates and Day 1983; Glazebrook and Robertson 1999). Battle and Golladay (2001), for example, examined the rate of leaf-litter decay of cypress (*Taxodium* sp.) and gum *(Nyssa sylvatica)* under three different hydrologic regimes in wetlands on the Gulf Coastal Plain of Georgia. Leaves decayed more rapidly in a site that was subject to multiple flooding/exposure than in sites that were either permanently inundated or flooded and dried only once annually.

On the other hand, many studies have not demonstrated a positive effect of wetting and drying of leaf-litter breakdown, and these are summarized briefly to show the variety of responses. Day (1983) showed that the breakdown of red maple *(Acer rubrum)* was initially accelerated by wetting, but subsequent repeated wetting and drying had no effect. Tate and Gurtz (1986) examined the decay of elm leaves *(Ulmus americana)* in three prairie streams in Kansas and found that leaves broke down faster in the perennial stream than in the two intermittent streams. Taylor and Parkinson (1988) found that wetting and drying did not affect leaching from pine needles *(Pinus contorta* × *Pinus banksiana)* or aspen leaves *(Populus tremuloides)*. Leaf material subjected to repeated wetting and dying decayed more quickly initially, but the effect was lost after two to three months.

Boulton (1991) found that leaves of the terrestrial riparian tree *Eucalyptus viminalis* decayed more rapidly when kept permanently submerged than under exposed conditions in the Lerderderg River, a temporary stream in western Victoria (Australia). In this case, it seemed that permanent inundation was required to leach away polyphenolic compounds that inhibited decay. Gessner (1991) reported only little overall effect of drying on mass loss from alder *(Alnus glutinosa)* leaves in Europe, but did find differences in the time course for decay across various wetting and drying treatments. Francis and Sheldon (2002) found that an alternate wet-dry cycle did not affect the leaf breakdown rate of river red gum *(Eucalyptus camaldulensis)* litter on the floodplain of the Darling River in semiarid eastern Australia. Brinson and associates (1981) also reported that some plant species decayed more rapidly in dry than in periodically wet sites. Other studies also have generated equivocal results (e.g., Baker et al. 2001 for leaf decay in floodplain wetlands of Arkansas).

There are comparatively few reports on the effect of wetting and drying on the breakdown of freshwater aquatic plants. Neckles and Neill (1994) examined the decay of litter from the emergent wetland macrophyte *Scolochloa festucacea* in a prairie marsh in Canada. Flooding increased the rate at which mass was lost from material kept above the ground, probably because of increased water availability. In contrast, flooding resulted in a slowing of the decay rate of buried material because it led to anoxic conditions in the sediments. Ryder and Horwitz (1995) conducted one of the few studies to specifically examine the influence of hydrology on the decay of aquatic leaf material in a seasonal (Mediterranean) wetland. Using leaf packs of the emergent vascular macrophytes *Baumea articulata* and *Typha orientalis* in a wetland on the Swan Coastal Plain near Perth (western Australia), they reported that material exposed to seasonal inundation decayed more quickly than material kept permanently wet.

The work of Herbst and Reice (1982) is often cited as an example of how fluctuating water regimes accelerate the decay of leaves in aquatic systems. It is worth looking at this paper in some detail because it is cited so frequently. They reported that the decay of common reed, *Phragmites australis,* and *Eucalyptus rostrata* (perhaps misidentified *Eucalyptus camaldulensis;* P. S. Lake, pers. com.) in the temporary Upper Tanninim River (Israel) was halted when the river became dry and recommenced when the river reflooded. However, the decay rate on the second inundation was "not discernably faster than during the initial flow period." The authors concluded that "the alternate wetting and drying of leaf material in intermittent streams does not enhance the decomposition process" (Herbst and Reice 1982).

The picture that emerges is that it can not be said that wetting and drying always leads to quicker leaf breakdown than would occur under more constant hydrologic conditions. Part of the confusion arises from the methods used in the various studies, and the problems are both analytical and statistical. Many researchers collected fresh leaves from terrestrial trees but dried them prior to the experiment in order to obtain a common starting point in the mass-loss kinetic. Sometimes, the drying treatment was severe: oven drying at elevated temperatures. Although this is a common treatment in leaf-decay studies (Boulton and Boon 1991), there is abundant evidence that drying alters both the rate of leaf breakdown and the relative importance of leaching of soluble compounds from leaf material (Gessner and Schwoerbel 1989; Gessner 1991; Taylor and Barlocher 1996; Taylor 1998). Drying also changes the chemical composition of leaves, altering their susceptibility to leaching and enzymatic decay (Serrano and Boon 1991; Baldwin 1999), especially in terms of the polyphenolic compounds that exert a great influence over the decay rate (Lake et al. 1985; Gallardo and Merino 1993).

In addition to these analytical problems, many studies that have purported to show an effect of wetting and drying on leaf breakdown have a flawed experimental design and are spatially or temporally confounded and frequently have no replication at the appropriate treatment level. Confounding makes it impossible to separate the putative effect of wetting and drying from other environmental impacts. For example, studies using dry upland sites in comparison with episodically inundated lowland sites are spatially confounded. Studies conducted over a change in seasons, when a previously inundated system dries out, confound the wet and dry phases of the wetland with seasonal shifts in temperature and oxygen regimes (e.g., see Barlocher et al. 1978). Spatial confounding is also apparent where different techniques have been applied to material in the wet sites and in the dry sites (e.g., Brinson 1977). Often, there is no replication at the appropriate treatment level: one dry or wet site is frequently compared with one hydrologically variable site. All that can be said with this type of experimental design is that the two sites differed in decay rates, and no inferences can be drawn as to the impact of different hydrologic regimes.

The timing with which leaves become available for breakdown in temporary wetlands, and the degree to which this is mimicked in the experimenters' manipulations, may be a critical factor in the response to wetting and drying. Water stress is the major factor controlling the fall of leaves from eucalyptus forests, woodlands, and riparian corridors in southern Australia (Briggs and Maher 1983; Boulton and Suter 1986; Bunn 1986). A peak in litter fall that coincides with a seasonally dry period means that the greatest input of leaf litter from trees would occur when streams were least likely to flow and wetlands most likely to be dry. Under these conditions, leaf material derived from terrestrial trees fringing temporary wetlands would be almost completely air-dry before being broken down during the wet phase of the wetland. Laboratory treatments should be designed to mimic these characteristics if accurate rates are to be obtained for leaf-litter decay during this phase of the wetland's wet-dry cycle. However, some leaf material may enter a temporary wetland while the leaves are alive and still green, such as with terrestrial plant material blown in during storms. In this case, laboratory manipulations should again be careful to maintain the original condition of the leaves—alive, green, and not dried. In the case of studies purporting to measure the decay rate of submerged taxa, it is difficult to see how meaningful rates could be obtained with dried material of any sort unless the plants survived until the complete drawdown of the wetland.

NUTRIENT UPTAKE AND RELEASE IN TEMPORARY WETLANDS
NITROGEN RELEASE FROM DECOMPOSING PLANT MATERIAL

Sources of Nitrogen to Wetlands

Nitrogen can enter a wetland via a number of sources. Nitrogen-fixing prokaryotes, such as cyanobacteria, can convert atmospheric N_2 to amino acids and eventually protein. Nitrogen can enter the wetland via precipitation, in overland flows when the wetland floods, or as inputs from groundwater. Decomposition of plant material is another potential source, the one that is of most interest to us most in this chapter. As has been shown earlier, the organic material that enters temporary wetlands can have diverse origins. It can include terrestrial litter as well as material from aquatic macrophytes and even, in some cases, appreciable amounts of aquatic algae (periphyton and/or phytoplankton, sometimes even benthic mats). Ammonium is the ultimate inorganic form of nitrogen produced during the decay of this organic material and is derived from a number of sources, including the hydrolytic deamination of amino acids, degradation of nucleic acids, and metabolism of methylamines by methanogenic prokaryotes (Reddy and D'Angelo 1994).

Nitrogen Regeneration by Aquatic Bacteria

Under aerobic conditions, any ammonium regenerated on the decomposition of these compounds would be rapidly oxidized by nitrifying bacteria to nitrate. This phenomenon has been reported in a number of studies of wetted sediments and soils (Kadlec 1962; Reddy and Patrick 1975; Scholz et al. 2002). Under anaerobic conditions, however, ammonium can not be nitrified (other than by the ammanox reaction noted earlier), and ammonium tends to accumulate in the sediments (e.g., see Reddy and Patrick 1975; De Datta 1981). The accumulation of ammonium could be manifest in a number of ways, including increases in the concentration of ammonium in the sediment pore water or the overlying water column, or as increases in the fractions adsorbed (exchangeable or fixed) onto clays in the sediments.

There is a clear relationship between the amounts of nitrogen assimilated by bacteria and that released during the decomposition of organic detritus. The ratio between these two processes is largely a function of the C:N ratio of the organic detritus being decomposed, the C:N ratio of the bacterial cells undertaking the decomposition, and the efficiency of bacterial growth (Blackburn 1983). This relationship can be expressed as:

$$\frac{N_{assimilated}}{N_{decomposed}} = \frac{C:N_{detritus} \times E_{growth}}{C:N_{bacteria}}$$

When $N_{assimilated}$ is greater than $N_{decomposed}$ (i.e., the ratio of the two is >1), the bacteria need to take up additional nitrogen from the external environment in order to maintain their current C:N ratio. Only if $N_{assimilated}$ is less than $N_{decomposed}$ (i.e., the ratio is <1) is there excess nitrogen available from decomposition to be regenerated (that is, mineralized) as ammonium.

We can assume values of about 6:1 for the C:N ratio of bacterial cells and 0.3 for the growth efficiency (E_{growth}) of anaerobic bacteria (Blackburn 1983). (Growth efficiency is the proportion of carbon incorporated into cellular biomass as a function of the total amount of organic carbon taken up by the cell; the remainder is respired away as carbon dioxide.) It is thus clear that bacteria need to take up additional nitrogen from the external environment if they are degrading organic detritus with a C:N ratio of more than about 20:1. Under anaerobic conditions, this nitrogen can only be ammonium. As submerged aquatic plants have a C:N ratio slightly lower than this (e.g., 15:1 by weight for *Vallisneria americana*; Morris et al. 2003b), it is possible for small amounts of ammonium to be regenerated under anaerobic conditions with this source of organic matter. The yield of ammonium is, however, still quite meager, as 75% of the nitrogen in the detritus is required to maintain bacterial C:N ratios, and only about 25% could be released to the external environment. The situation with terrestrial material is quite different. Leaves of sclerophyllous plants can have C:N ratios of higher than 100:1 (e.g., Glazebrook and Robertson 1999, for eucalyptus species). Under these circumstances, bacteria need to take up very large amounts of external nitrogen, as the detrital material provides only about 20% of the nitrogen required for balanced growth. Goldman and colleagues (1987) provided a fuller discussion of this topic. In such cases, the bacteria degrading terrestrial plant litter are more likely to be a sink for nutrients than a source of nutrients for other biota. And since the bacteria are so small, with a large surface area to volume ratio and a rapid growth rate, they would present a very formidable competitor for any available nutrients.

Given these calculations, it is difficult to see how large amounts of inorganic nitrogen could be mineralized by the bacterial decomposition of plant detritus in hydrologically dynamic wetlands. Organic nitrogen may be leached from plant detritus, especially during a drying phase on the wetland floor, but if this takes place, there is even less nitrogen available to support bacterial growth on the remaining substrate when the wetland refloods. The microbes must then draw additional amounts of nitrogen from the external environment. In other words, they must take up nitrogen from the surrounding water or sediments. As has been shown for other aquatic systems (Azam et al. 1983; Kemp 1990), it is likely that nutrient regeneration occurs primarily when these nutrient-rich bacteria are consumed by metazoan animals with a higher C:N ratio and lower growth efficiencies. The consumption of bacteria with a concomitant regeneration of nutrients by the bacterivores has been termed the *microbial loop*, largely on the basis of oceanographic research. In the case of temporary wetlands, the consumers of bacteria could include zooplankton (Boon and Shiel 1990) and larger bactivorous animals such as chironomids (Bunn and Boon 1993). Likely differences between marine and freshwater versions of the microbial loop have been discussed recently by Sinsabaugh and Foreman (2003).

Let us now turn to the cycling of phosphorus in temporary wetlands, where there are very strong effects of wetting and drying on patterns of nutrient liberation and uptake.

PHOSPHORUS DYNAMICS IN TEMPORARY WETLANDS

Phosphorus is present in wetlands in a wide variety of forms, including organic and inorganic, dissolved, adsorbed, and particulate. Unlike nitrogen, phosphorus does not have a number of different oxidation states and is not liable to be lost from the wetland via metabolic gas-producing processes such as denitrification (excepting possibly via phosphine). Nevertheless, the dynamics of phosphorus cycling in hydrologically dynamic aquatic systems are astonishingly complex. There are two main types of mechanisms regulating the uptake and release of phosphorus in hydrologically dynamic wetlands (McComb and Qiu 1998):

1. Physico-chemical reactions dominated by sorption-desorption processes and controlled largely by pH and redox conditions; and
2. Biological processes dominated by bacterial activity.

Wetting and Drying Effects on Physicochemical Reactions

To draw together these complex interactions, McComb and Qiu (1998) devised a conceptual model of the processes involved in phosphorus uptake and release when wetland sediments were dried and rewetted. This is shown, in a modified form, in Figure 5.8.

Much early limnological research addressed the complex physicochemical roles in phosphorus cycling of sorption-desorption reactions (Mortimer 1941; Williams et al. 1971). These and subsequent studies showed that, under acid conditions, phosphorus was fixed mostly as aluminium and ferric phosphates; in alkaline soils, calcium and magnesium were more important for phosphorus retention (Reddy and D'Angelo 1994). Wetting and drying seems to affect the physicochemical aspects of phosphorus cycling in two main ways: (1) by modifying redox conditions, and (2) modifying the physical properties of the minerals responsible for binding phosphorus, such as changes in the iron crystallinity or the coating of inorganic adsorption sites by organic humic materials. Of these two mechanisms, the former is probably the most important (McComb and Qiu 1998).

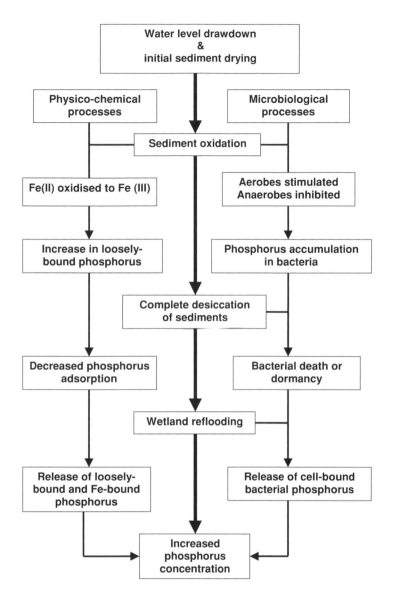

FIGURE 5.8.
Conceptual model of the effects of wetland drying and reflooding on sediment phosphorus dynamics. Adapted from McComb and Qiu (1998).

Redox conditions markedly alter the ability of phosphorus to bind to minerals. The binding occurs primarily via interactions with both iron and sulfide, and the reduction of ferric oxyhydroxide and ferric phosphate to the more soluble ferrous forms increases phosphorus availability under anaerobic conditions (De Groot and Van Wijck 1993). As well, the sulfide produced under anaerobic conditions by sulfate-reducing bacteria allows the formation of ferrous sulfides, which preclude the adsorption of phosphorus by any available iron (Reddy and D'Angelo 1994; Baldwin and Mitchell 2000; but see also Golterman 1995). In calcareous systems, phosphorus is immobilized when it coprecipitates with $CaCO_3$, although even here absorption onto iron hydroxides is probably equally or more important than a reaction with divalent cations (Golterman 1988; Olila and Reddy 1997). The different types of reaction that involve phosphorus under acid and alkaline conditions suggest that it may be possible for phosphorus to be precipitated and remobilized alternately each day and night in response to diel fluctuations in the pH (and thus carbonate chemistry) of the water column. As we have seen earlier, pH exerts a strong control on the volatilization of ammonia from wetlands.

Wetting and Drying Effects on Biological Processes

The biological aspects of phosphorus cycling in wetland sediments are, overwhelmingly, mediated by bacteria (Bostrom et al. 1988; Gachter and Meyer 1993). Wetland bacteria mediate phosphorus dynamics by assimilating and releasing inorganic phosphorus as part of their growth cycles, excreting extracellular enzymes to hydrolyze organic phosphorus to inorganic forms, and creating the anoxic conditions that favor the reduction of ferrous to ferric iron. They also are critical in the uptake of any phosphorus leached from leaves that fall into wetlands (Qiu et al. 2002). There are also some indications that the growth of aquatic bacteria may be limited by the availability of phosphorus, although the effect is likely to be site specific and vary among different suites of bacteria (Sundareshwar et al. 2003; see also Waiser 2001 and Bodelier and Laanbroek 2004). There are also indications that bacteria in aquatic sediments alternately take up and release phosphorus under fluctuating aerobic and anaerobic conditions (Khoshmanesh et al. 1999).

Large amounts of phosphorus are sequestered in bacterial biomass, and this may become available as the wetland dries and the bacteria die. Qiu and McComb (1995), for example, reported that drying killed about three-quarters of the microbial biomass in wetland sediments, a result that confirmed the conclusions of Sparling and associates (1985) that microbial lysis was the major factor contributing to increases in the phosphorus content of soils on drying. Grierson and associates (1998) and Turner and colleagues (2003) also have reported that the initial flush of inorganic phosphorus released from previously dry soils was largely a function of mineralization of microbial biomass. This pattern is also consistent with the role played by bacterial lysis in the evolution of carbon dioxide when soils are wetted and dried.

EFFECTS OF WETTING AND DRYING ON NUTRIENT RELEASE FROM TEMPORARY WETLANDS

In Australia, it is almost a mantra among wetland managers that periodically drying and then reflooding a hydrologically dynamic wetland increases the rate at which organic matter decays and that this then translates into a flush of nutrients from the wetland sediments into the overlaying water column. What empirical evidence is there that this sequence of events really takes place?

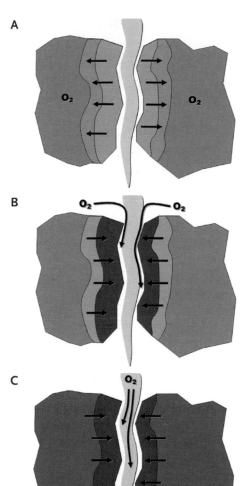

FIGURE 2.6

Models of redoximorphic feature formation.
(A) Within a saturated and reduced pore, an
adjacent soil is the site of Fe(III) reduction, and
an aerated and oxidized matrix is the site of
Fe(II) oxidation. (B) Saturated and reduced
matrix is the site of Fe(III) reduction, and an
aerated and oxidized pore is the site of Fe(II)
oxidation. (C) Saturated and reduced matrix is
the site of Fe(III) reduction, and an oxidize
rhizosphere is the site of Fe(II) oxidation.

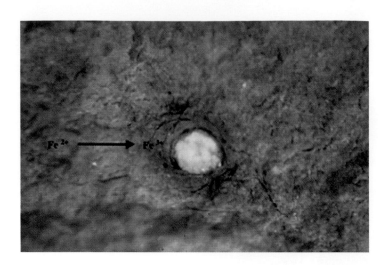

FIGURE 4.3

A cross section of the root of the swamp tree, green ash *(Fraxinus pennsylvanica)*, growing in a soil medium. The oxidized iron rhizosphere is clearly identified by the orange (iron oxide) color surrounding the root. Photo by Bill Good.

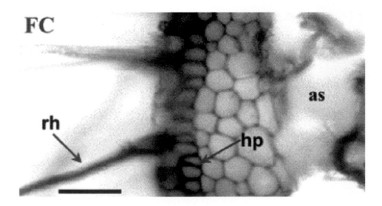

FIGURE 4.7

Cross section of a flooded sawgrass *(Cladium jamaicense)* root showing the thickened cell walls of the hypodermis (hp). Root hairs (rh) are also apparent. From Chabbi et al. (2000), with permission.

FIGURE 4.6
Adventitious roots of spikerush *(Eleocharis cellulosa)* produced after four months of flooding.

FIGURE 4.9
Knees of the bald cypress *(Taxodium distichum)* like the prop roots of mangroves are modified roots. However, the function of cypress knees is still unknown, although physical support is likely.

FIGURE 4.10

Response of a wetland ant colony to flooding. The colony congeals into a mass and either floats by itself or adheres to emergent plants materials or wood until flood waters subside. Photo by Jennifer Henke.

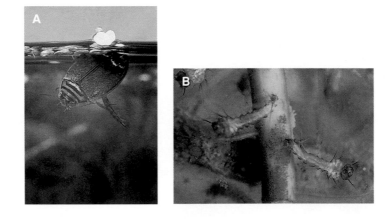

FIGURE 4.11

Mechanisms for aquatic invertebrates to breathe air. Dysticidae beetle adults (left) collect air bubbles from the surface and retain the bubble under their leathery wing covers on top of their respiratory spiracles. *Coquillettidia* mosquito larvae (right) have respiratory siphons that are modified to access oxygen in aerenchyma tissue of emergent plants root (e.g., *Typha*) and remain attached to these plants throughout their larval development. Beetle photo by Gordon Guyer.

FIGURE 4.14
Salt crystals excreted on the leaf surface of smooth cordgrass, *Spartina alterniflora*, by salt glands.

FIGURE 4.16
The succulent halophyte *Salicornia* is highly tolerant to elevated salinities because of its capacity to reduce salt concentrations via dilution.

FIGURE 5.1

Raftery Swamp, central Victoria, during its dry phase. Photograph
was taken in October 2002.

FIGURE 5.2

Raftery Swamp, central Victoria, during its wet phase. Photograph
was taken in November 1992. The aquatic plants visible are
Triglochin sp. and *Potamogeton* sp.

FIGURE 5.4
Groundwater less than 0.5 meters below the sediment surface at a
wetland in central Victoria. Cracks in the clay soil are also evident.
The photograph was taken during the drought of April 1998.

FIGURE 6.16
Northern bog and lake with ericaceous shrubs and conifer trees in
northern Michigan. Courtesy of K. E. Francl.

FIGURE 6.27

Salt marsh along a tidal creek with saltmarsh cordgrass
(Spartina alterniflora) at creek's edge on Sapelo Island, Georgia.

FIGURE 10.6

Michelle Peach (UW–Madison, pers. com.) attempted to reproduce
tussocks by creating mounds; however, the dry summer led tops to
become dominated by cottonwood seedlings, while cattails filled in the
bottoms, which were at the level of groundwater. Photo by M. Peach.

We have seen that there is good evidence that wetting a dry soil or sediment does result in a short-term release of carbon dioxide as organic matter in the soil, mainly dead microbes, is decomposed. The effect is, however, relatively short lived and soon becomes limited by the supply of nitrogen and the relatively small size of the pool of dead microbial cells available to be decomposed. We have also seen that the evidence for wetting and drying accelerating the breakdown of leaf litter is equivocal at best and, in any case, the bacterial decay of terrestrial plant material is unlikely to be directly responsible for nitrogen regeneration. Wetting and drying, however, does have strong effects on phosphorus cycling, mediated by both physicochemical and microbiological processes. Given the complexity of the effects of wetting and drying on organic-matter decay and nutrient cycling, there is ample opportunity for equally intricate relationships between wetland hydrology and gross patterns of nutrient release from temporary wetlands.

In this section, we look at the literature to see whether there is robust evidence for the proposition that drying and flooding a temporary wetland necessarily results in the release of nutrients into the water column. As with leaf-litter decay, it is worthwhile first to examine the methodological approaches that can be employed to address the problem.

Methodological Issues

In general, two approaches have been used to determine whether nutrients are released when a temporary wetland dries then refloods:

1. Field-based observations of nutrient concentrations in sediments or the overlying water column throughout the hydrologic cycle; and

2. Laboratory experiments in which wetland sediments are dried and inundated under controlled conditions, possibly also being exposed to different oxygen regimes after flooding.

There are obvious advantages and disadvantages to both approaches. Field-based methods include all the "real life" factors involved in nutrient transformations and fluxes, but at the risk of the individual processes being confounded and results difficult to interpret unequivocally. Confounding makes it difficult to unravel the processes that are really important from those that are peripheral. For example, nutrients may be released from sediments into the water column on inundation, but their assimilation by plants could result in no *net* increase in the measured concentrations of nutrients being observed in the overlying water. This type of artifact could be excluded if the increase in nutrient concentrations occurred before plants had time to respond to the inundation event, but the possibility that there were other types of uptake (e.g., back onto the sediments) cannot be eliminated so readily. Conversely, an apparent release of nutrients may be observed during flooding but might not be related at all to a release from the sediments. The release could be linked, for example, to the decay of aquatic plants (Jacoby et al. 1982) or the simple resuspension of sediment particles (Fabre 1988).

What also has to be demonstrated is that high concentrations of nutrients in the water column of a recently flooded wetland are not a simple function of nutrients being imported with the floodwaters (e.g., see Sanchez-Carrillo et al. 2000 and Sanchez-Carrillo and Alvarez-Cobelas 2001 for a temporary wetland in Spain). Nutrient imports could be particularly important during the first overland flows of the season, when the floodwaters are loaded with nutrients and other materials derived from the catchment (Serrano 1994). Serrano and associates (1999), for example, showed that phosphorus loads into temporary wetlands in the Donana National Park of southern Spain were highest in the initial filling periods after the first rains. In her case, nutrients were apparently leached from the surrounding terrestrial soils and vegetation by the first rains that broke the dry season, and less effectively during subsequent storms. Qiu and colleagues (2002) reported a similar process for phosphorus leaching from leaf detritus in wetlands in western Australia, a region also enjoying a Mediterreanean climate. Conversely, however, changes in nutrient concentrations apparent in the drawdown phase must be separated from simple evaporative concentration. The distinction between concentrations and amounts needs to be observed at all times or conservative tracers (such as salt) used to normalize changes in nutrient concentrations.

In contrast to the case with field-based trials, laboratory-based experiments allow the individual environmental factors to be controlled and potential sources of confounding to be limited. But this control comes at the real cost of reduced realism. At least four sets of factors may compromise the realism of laboratory-based observations. First, laboratory experiments are usually conducted at a very small spatial scale, and there are considerable problems with scaling up to the field situation. Second, intrusive manipulations are often necessary to collect and incubate sediments under controlled laboratory conditions, and this quickly modifies the existing redox potentials and other critical aspects of the sediments. Third, the natural environment was formerly an open system, with connections to the atmosphere, surface waters, and groundwaters; this is irrevocably converted to a fully closed system in the laboratory or glasshouse, by virtue of the necessary use of experimental enclosures. Finally, small-scale laboratory experiments, moreover, mostly exclude animals, including burrowing invertebrates that bioturbate and aerate the sediments and are central in regenerating nutrients from microbial biomass (e.g., see Bird et al. 2000).

Biogeochemists undertaking laboratory experiments also are faced with crucial questions relating to the choice of sediments. In some cases, sediments are collected from different sites within a wetland to encompass the natural variation in inundation regimes (e.g., Baldwin et al. 2000; Watts 2000). In others, they are taken from a single location, bulked, and then subsampled and finally exposed to different wetting and drying cycles (e.g., Reddy and Patrick 1975). For all their precision, the critical problem with laboratory-based approaches is to show how they relate to the real conditions that exist in the wetland.

Does Wetting and Drying Liberate Nutrients from Wetland Soils?
Many laboratory studies have shown that drying and rewetting does result in the rapid release of phosphorus from soils and sediments. Using sediment cores from a small

wetland in western Australia, Qiu and McComb (1994, 1995), for example, found that inorganic phosphorus was released from sediments after drying, with more being released under anaerobic than aerobic conditions. Turner and associates (2003) found that wetting a dried pasture soil released large amounts of phosphorus, mainly in the organic form and mainly as a result of the lysis of bacterial cells.

A range of other laboratory and field-based studies, however, do not present unequivocal evidence for phosphorus release on drawdown and subsequent inundation of aquatic environments. Examples include Schoenberg and Oliver (1988) for the Okefenokee Swamp in Georgia; Fabre (1988) for the Puyvalador Reservoir in Pyrenees, France; Jacoby and colleagues (1982) for Long Lake in Washington; and McComb and Qiu (1998) for some Western Australian wetlands. There were highly variable responses to inundation after partial or complete drying across a range of temporary wetlands in semiarid regions of southern Australia (van der Wielen, unpublished data, cited in Tucker et al. 2003).

Let us next look at three published papers to see whether reflooding a dried wetland did result in a net release of nutrients from the sediments into the water column. Reports from Mediterranean and semiarid zones are used as examples, due to the ubiquity of temporary wetlands in these climatic regions. Example 1 is a paper by Briggs and associates (1985), which is often cited by Australian natural-resource managers to demonstrate the positive effect of wetting and drying on nutrient liberation from temporary wetlands. The Briggs group collected dry soils from a lake and a temporary wetland in semiarid New South Wales (Australia) and immersed them in tanks in a glasshouse. Concentrations of nitrate and inorganic phosphorus increased after 4 days of wetting, but the response was short lived, and there was no further net increase in nutrient concentrations up to 130 days of inundation. Field observations, on water samples collected approximately monthly for 1 to 2 years after the sites were flooded, were equivocal as to nutrient release; there were generally no statistically significant effects of a wetting and drying phase or water level on nitrate or inorganic phosphorus concentrations. Since wetting and drying accounted for about 15% of the total variance in nutrient concentrations in both locations, environmental factors other than wetting and drying were contributing strongly to the observed variations in nutrient concentrations in the two sites. Interestingly, Mitchell and Baldwin (1999) also reported that there was no flush of inorganic nitrogen from desiccated lake-bed sediments of inland southeastern Australia when they were rewetted.

Example 2 is another study undertaken in southeastern Australia. Scholz and colleagues (2002) reported on the effect of drying and wetting on nutrient release from a range of hydrologically dynamic deflation-basin wetlands in semiarid western New South Wales. There was only a small, if any, response in the concentrations of total nitrogen or total phosphorus to flooding across the range of sites and, in the cases where increases were observed, the major source of nutrients was often the input from the riverine floodwaters. Only one wetland, Lake Bijiji, showed a clear response in total nitrogen concentrations to flooding, where concentrations increased from approximately 1 to 3 mg N L^{-1} over three months of flooding. Ammonium accounted for only a very minor component

($<$0.05 mg N L^{-1}) of the nitrogen pool after flooding, but nitrate concentrations rose markedly and peaked within a month of flooding in all sites. In some cases, nitrate peaked within a week of inundation, and this was presumably a response related to rapid nitrification in the recently flooded sediments. The effects of inundation on the release of bioavailable phosphorus were very unclear.

Example 3 comes from Spain. Sanchez-Carrillo and Alvarez-Cobelas (2001) monitored wetlands in the semiarid Tablas de Daimiel National Park. Concentrations of dissolved inorganic nitrogen and total nitrogen peaked immediately after flooding of a dry wetland basin, but, especially in the case of nitrogen, most of the increase in wet years could be attributed to runoff from the catchment. Surface inflows of nitrogen, for example, ranged from nearly 9 to 66 g m^{-2} yr^{-1}, whereas internal loadings accounted for 27 to 78 g m^{-2} yr^{-1}. Nitrogen loadings during the initial inundation phase were overwhelmingly derived from external sources. In contrast to the case with nitrogen, the internal loading was more important for phosphorus than were any external loads from the surrounding environment (cf. Serrano et al. 1999).

There are strong parallels between the putative effects of wetting and drying on nutrient liberation from recently flooded temporary wetlands with those on the effects of wetting and drying on leaf-litter breakdown. In both cases, entrenched generalizations do not seem to be warranted by the empirical, scientific literature. Far from providing strong evidence that flooding a (dry) temporary wetland reliably causes the net liberation of nutrients into the water column, most studies present a very equivocal response that can not be applied to both nitrogen and phosphorus across all hydrodynamic cycles. Moreover, there is little good evidence that any nutrients that are liberated necessarily derive directly from the sediments. Other sources may be responsible, as outlined next.

NUTRIENT INPUTS FROM OTHER SOURCES

Although most attention in the literature has been directed to the regeneration of nitrogen from decomposing plant material and the importance of adsorption-desorption phenomena in phosphorus cycling, there are at least two other possibilities for nutrients to be released when temporary wetlands are flooded or drained:

1. Fecal inputs from waterbirds roosting or breeding in temporary wetlands as they fill, and
2. Decomposition of fish stranded by the falling water levels.

Waterbird Feces
Temporary wetlands in the process of being filled are critical sites for breeding waterbirds, especially in arid, semiarid, and Mediterranean climates where permanent water bodies may be rare and sparsely distributed (Kingsford et al. 1999, 2004; Roshier et al. 2001; Kingsford and Norman 2002; Taft et al. 2002). In fact, it is now clear that, at least

for waterfowl, the best breeding in arid and semiarid regions occurs when a dry wetland is inundated (Crome 1986, 1988; Briggs and Thornton 1999). This use of temporary wetlands during their filling phase by waterbirds could have interesting implications for nutrient cycling.

A number of studies has demonstrated the importance of waterbird feces to the nutrient budgets of various aquatic systems. Portnoy (1990), for example, estimated that gulls (*Larus* spp.) contributed 52 kg P yr^{-1} to Gull Pond, a 44-hectare pond in the Cape Cod area of the northern United States. This compared with a phosphorus loading to the pond of 67 kg P yr^{-1} from sewage and only 2 kg P yr^{-1} from rainfall. The contribution from the waterbirds represented a loading of about 1.2 kg P $ha^{-1} yr^{-1}$. Earlier, Ruess and associates (1989) showed that defecation from Lesser Snow Geese *(Chen caerulescens caerulescens)* contributed significantly to the mineral nutrition of plants in the nitrogen-limited salt marsh flats of La Perouse Bay (Canada). Purcell and Goldsborough (1995) demonstrated that waterfowl feces increased the biomass of phytoplankton in a prairie wetland in Manitoba (Canada). In Hickling Pond in the United Kingdom, increases in the abundance of Black-headed Gulls *(Larus ridibundus)* had led to fish kills and the replacement of submerged plants by phytoplankton (Moss and Leah 1982). Post and colleagues (1998) concluded that waterfowl contributed nearly 40% of the nitrogen and 75% of the phosphorus entering areas of a wetland used for bird roosting in New Mexico's Bosque del Apache National Wildlife Refuge.

Is it possible that breeding waterbirds could contribute significantly to the nutrient budget of a temporary wetland as it fills with water? For the sake of argument, let us assume that a 1-meter deep, 1,000-hectare wetland supports a population of 2,500 breeding pairs of geese-sized waterbirds for 6 months of the year. Also assume that the birds excrete nitrogen and phosphorus at rates of 6.8 and 2.1 g $bird^{-1} day^{-1}$, respectively (Manny et al. 1975). The annual nitrogen and phosphorus inputs from the 5,000 adult birds sum to about 6,000 kg N and 2,000 kg P, or loadings of about 6 kg N $ha^{-1} yr^{-1}$ and 2 kg P $ha^{-1} yr^{-1}$. This loading would translate to total nitrogen and total phosphorus concentrations in the water column of 0.6 mg N L^{-1} and 0.2 mg P L^{-1}. Such a loading could be sustained year after year, if birds returned to breed annually at the same wetland.

The calculation assumes that the waterbirds feed outside the wetlands and defecate only in them, but this may not be an unrealistic assumption for birds such as ibis, which commonly feed on adjacent farmlands and roost only in the wetlands. Indeed, Post and associates (1998) showed that Lesser Snow Geese and Ross' Geese *(Chen rossii)* translocated large quantities of nutrients from farm fields, where they fed, to wetlands, where they roosted.

Death of Stranded Fish
Although it is hardly considered in reviews of the impact of animals on aquatic nutrient cycles (Vanni 2002), it is possible also for carrion to contribute significantly to nutrient dynamics in freshwater systems (Minshall et al. 1991,; Parmenter and Lamarra 1991).

Carrion inputs may even influence rates of primary productivity (Wold and Hershey 1999). Richey and associates (1975), for example, calculated that a run of land-locked sockeye salmon *(Oncorhynchus nerka)* contributed over 40 kilograms of phosphorus to a short stream in California and Nevada, possibly increasing the inorganic phosphorus concentration by about 5 μg L^{-1}. It may be possible that significant amounts of nitrogen and phosphorus are liberated in temporary wetlands when their resident fish are stranded by falling water levels. Certainly, massive fish kills have been reported to occur in temporary lakes and wetlands when their water levels drop rapidly (e.g., see Ruello 1976 for Lake Eyre in southern Australia), and manipulating water levels is a favored means for controlling noxious fish in southeastern Australia.

Let us use carp *(Cyprinus carpio)* as an example to estimate the magnitude of nutrient release attributable to the death and decay of fish in a temporary wetland. Carp are a noxious introduced fish in southern Australia, and their biomass can exceed 3,000 kg ha^{-1} in lakes and wetlands (Koehn et al. 2000). If we assume a lowish biomass of 500 kg ha^{-1} and a nitrogen content of 10% dry mass (Parmenter and Lamarra 1991), the amount of nitrogen sequestered in carp biomass is 50 kg N ha^{-1}. These fish will die when a temporary wetland dries out. Many of the stranded fish will be scavenged by birds such as sea eagles and terrestrial carrion eaters such as foxes. But if only 10% of the decaying biomass remains on the wetland floor, a total nitrogen concentration of 0.5 mg N L^{-1} is possible when the wetland (assumed to be 1-meter deep) refills.

Unlike the case with breeding waterbirds, the release of nutrients from stranded fish could not occur annually, as it takes some time for a carp biomass of 500 kg ha^{-1} to be achieved. Although nutrients in the decaying fish were derived from the wetland in the first instance, this does not negate the argument that decomposed fish biomass could contribute to a flush of nutrients in the water column upon the wetland reflooding. The situation with phosphorus probably differs from that of nitrogen, as substantial amounts of phosphorus are retained in fish bones after the flesh has decayed (Parmenter and Lamarra 1991).

INTEGRATION AND SYNTHESIS: BIOGEOCHEMISTRY, HYDROLOGY, AND SEDIMENTS IN TEMPORARY WETLANDS

The final parts of this chapter draw together various aspects of the microbiology and biogeochemistry of sediments in temporary wetlands, and links them with other ecological phenomena involving broader-scale aspects of wetland structure and function, especially with soil formation and plant dynamics. Soils are considered first.

A good review of the significance of wetting and drying cycles in the formation of wetland soils is Buol and Rebertus (1988). They noted that the characteristics of wetland soils change markedly on wetting, and the change in oxygen status of the soil (with related redox changes) is one of the earliest biogeochemical effects of inundation. Depending on the source of the water (precipitation, overland flow, or groundwater), the downwards percolation of water also moves dissolved compounds downwards until the water table is reached or upwards until they precipitate on the soil surface. The heat capacity of the soil is also affected by inundation, with wet soil retaining its heat better over the night and further into cool periods later in the year. The color of the soil also changes. In the absence of substantial organic-matter contents, iron oxides largely control the color of the wetted soil, and mottled red-yellow colors indicate the segregation of iron into zones with different redox potentials. Wetland soils that are grey or whitish frequently occur when organic contents are low and the iron has been reduced and leached, leaving the inherent colors of the quartz and clay minerals. Gley colors (olive, bluish-grey, etc.) indicate the presence of ferrous iron and a long period of saturation with little soil-water movement, preventing the leaching of this material.

There are at least three main areas where wetting and drying cycles affect the structure and/or condition of wetland sediments:

1. Surface cracking and gilgai formation;
2. Wetland salinization; and
3. Pyrite oxidation and acid-sulfate soils.

In all cases, there are implications for wetland biogeochemistry and the composition of microbial communities, although the implications range from the relatively weak (as in the case of gilgai) to the very strong (as with acid-sulfate soils, where bacteria are the causative biological agent).

SURFACE CRACKING AND GILGAI FORMATION

Many soils in semiarid and subhumid climatic zones are vertisols, soils with a high content of expansive clays such as illite, montmorillonite, and smectite (FitzPatrick 1980; Gibbons and Rowan 1993). These clays expand when wet and contract when dry, causing the soils to crack deeply. In some cases, the shrinking and swelling of the clays is sufficient to cause the formation of gilgai, gently undulating mound-and-depression landforms created as a direct result of the characteristics of cracking clay soils. Topsoil falls into the deep cracks when the soil is dry, adding even more expansive clay material to the middle and lower horizons, ready to become activated when the soil is wetted. Water preferentially trickles down the cracks, penetrating deeply into the soil, allowing the subsoil to swell and create pressure zones, which thrust the soil profile upwards and allow the characteristic low mounds of gilgai landscapes to form (Gibbons and Rowan 1993).

Figure 5.9 shows the sorts of cracks that can develop when a cracking clay soil in a wetland is dried. In some cases, cracks can be over 10 centimeters wide and up to a meter deep (FitzPatrick 1980). The cracks trap organic detritus, provide shelter for animals during the dry phase of the wetland, and facilitate the movement of water deep into the soil when it floods. Cracking clay soils have a poorer water-content-below-wilting-point

FIGURE 5.9
Surface cracks in a cracking clay soil in a southeastern Victorian wetland during its dry phase. The lens cap provides a scale.

than most other soil types, and this commonly adds a further limitation to plant growth over summer. When the soils are wetted, however, the porosity of the soil becomes very low, exacerbating soil anoxia via decreases in oxygen diffusion and limiting the growth and extension of the sediment by plant roots (Gibbons and Rowan 1993). This, in turn, has implications for the relative importance of aerobic versus anaerobic bacterial metabolism in the sediments, as discussed in the last section of this chapter.

WETLAND SALINIZATION

There are two broad types of wetland salinization (Williams 1998b; Bailey et al. in press), of which secondary salinization is the one of most interest to us. Secondary salinization refers to the conversion of fresh aquatic systems to saline ones as a result of human activity; primary salinization refers to the natural occurrence of saline water bodies, such as salinas and salt lakes. Secondary salinization almost always results from disturbance to the hydrologic balance of an existing landscape, due either to clearing the original deep-rooted, perennial vegetation and replacing it with shallow-rooted annuals or to permanently flooding soils as a result of the application of additional water through irrigation (Hatton and Nulsen 1999).

There is a high risk of secondary salinization when temporary wetlands are drawn down if underlying groundwater is saline, as has been reported with Big Mussel Lagoon, a temporary wetland in semiarid southern Australia (Tucker et al. 2003). Keeping the wetland permanently filled with water ensures that the hydrostatic head excludes groundwater and maintains a nearly fresh water column, despite the wetland sitting only a meter or so above a water table with a salinity approaching that of seawater. Should the wetlands be drained, however, the hydrostatic head is lost, and saline groundwater flows into the wetland depression from the surrounding soils. Even if the wetland floor were above the water table or if soil porosity were such that it did not permit mass flow of saline groundwater, the water tables are so close to the surface that capillary action would draw salts to the soil surface. Salts accumulate on the surface and in the soil profile, and the soil becomes progressively more salinized over time.

The ecological impact of salinization of wetlands is usually considered in terms of general osmotic effects and specific ionic toxicity arising from the NaCl component (Bailey et al. in press). Salinization of freshwater wetlands, however, could have quite severe biogeochemical impacts, even if these have been barely considered by either biogeochemists or those charged with managing salinized landscapes. For example, the saline groundwaters in southeastern Australia are largely of marine origin and contain appreciable amounts of sulfate. Since methanogenesis is inhibited by high sulfate concentrations, it is possible that sulfate reduction could replace methanogenesis as the terminal route for carbon metabolism in even slightly salinized wetlands. The production of phytotoxic H_2S could have serious effects on plant health, as discussed later. Although the direct toxic and indirect osmotic effects of salinity are likely to have a far greater ecological impact than a shift among anaerobic decomposition pathways, the biogeochemical impacts should not be ignored.

ACID-SULFATE SOILS

Acid-sulfate soils are soils that produce sulfuric acid (H_2SO_4) when exposed to the air. They are common in coastal areas across the globe (e.g., see van Breemen 1975 for an account from Thailand). In Australia, potential and/or actual acid sulfate soils are found along almost the entire coastline, with the main exception being the steep limestone cliffs of the Great Australian Bight (Sammut 2000). The key component of acid-sulfate soils is pyrite (FeS_2), a highly insoluble crystalline form of iron sulfide produced (usually within the past 10,000 years) by the reaction of ferrous sulfide (FeS) with sulfur. The ferrous sulfide in turn was produced in coastal wetlands, such as mangroves, paperbark swamps, and salt marshes, by sulfate-reducing bacteria oxidizing the abundant organic material produced in these highly productive environments (Fig. 5.5).

Sulfuric acid is produced from pyrite in a complex set of reactions involving both physical and microbiological phenomena (Atlas and Bartha 1993; Madigan et al. 1997). At neutral pH, pyrite is spontaneously oxidized on contact with air. This reaction is important because it leads to the initial development of acidic conditions, under which ferrous iron is relatively stable in the presence of oxygen. Once the pH drops below about 4.5, autooxidation with atmospheric oxygen slows appreciably and stalked iron bacteria in the genus *Metallogenium* are primarily responsible for pyrite oxidation. As the pH drops further, to below 3.5, acidophilic *Thiobacillus* bacteria become the major oxidizers. The abiotic and the microbiological steps both produce sulfate and H$^+$, with the overall reaction being:

$$2 \text{ FeS}_2 + 7.5 \text{ O}_2 + 7 \text{ H}_2\text{o} \rightarrow 2 \text{ Fe(OH)} + 4 \text{ H}_2\text{SO}_4$$

The sulfuric acid moves through the soil, stripping iron, aluminium, and manganese, as well as dissolving, in the worst cases, heavy metals such as cadmium (DeLaune and Smith 1985). This noxious mixture makes the soil highly toxic and, combined with the very low pH (<3), renders plant growth impossible. Sufficient sulfuric acid can be produced that it seeps into adjacent waterways, resulting in drastic reductions in pH, massive fish kills, and the death of estuarine invertebrates, including economically important species such as shellfish.

Because of the low hydraulic gradients and often peaty substrata, swampy soils, the natural drainage of wetlands tends to occur very slowly. Artificial drainage, however, often results in the rapid and extensive production of sulfuric acid, especially following prolonged dry weather and further lowering of the water table (Walker 1972). Acid-sulfate soils generally do not present a serious management problem as long as they are kept waterlogged. They become problematic when drains are dug through wetlands, causing the water table to drop rapidly and surface soils to dry out and become aerobic. Large spoil heaps, raised along the edges of the drains, also can produce acid for many years after the drain has been excavated. The release of sulfuric acid from these spoil dumps typically occurs after drought-breaking rains, which raises the water table back to its original (predrought or predrainage) level and washes the acid and dissolved metals out of the surface layers of the soil (Wilson et al. 1999). In many cases, reverting to the earlier hydrologic regime is not sufficient to cure the problem, as large volumes of acid may remain in the soil, and there may have been irreversible changes to the soil structure due to drying and oxidation (White et al. 1997).

The biogeochemical implications of acid-sulfate soils for hydrologically dynamic wetlands are obvious. If potential or actual acid-sulfate soils are present, it may be unacceptable to instigate a strong wetting and drying cycle because of the risk of severe damage to downstream, often estuarine, ecosystems should the wetland drain completely and the sediments start to oxidize. Johnston and associates (2003), for example, reported that some extensive fish kills in the Clarence Estuary of northern New South Wales (eastern Australia) were caused by an oxygen-depletion event which was, in turn, caused by anoxic and iron-rich surface waters draining from two acid-sulfate soil backswamps.

In inland situations, the formation of acid-sulfate soils may be linked with secondary salinization, since wetting and drying cycles play a major role in facilitating many of the conditions that lead to the formation of both secondary salinization and acid-sulfate soils (Fitzpatrick et al. 1996). Initially, sulfates, sulfides, iron oxides, and sodium chloride accumulate in the soil profile in sensitive sites as the soil becomes waterlogged by rising water tables. As with coastal acid-sulfate soils, acidification then occurs under oxidized conditions, usually created as the water table drops and the soils dry out. This acidification leads to massive soil degradation and, in the worst cases, the formation of hard impenetrable crusts of iron on the soil surface. On wetting, the sulfidic conditions destroy soil microaggregrates by dissolving the iron oxides (e.g., goethite and hematite) that bind soil clay particles together. Wetting further increases salinization, leading to flocculation of soil particles and low soil strength. On redrying, the salt and iron minerals crystallize on the soil surface by evaporation, forming hard surface layers due to clays clogging the soil pores and the cementation of iron and silica compounds. This leads to poor germination of seeds and a decrease in the rate of water infiltration. The latter then leads to an increase in overland flow and possible consequences for channel erosion and downstream sedimentation.

INTEGRATION AND SYNTHESIS: BIOGEOCHEMISTRY, HYDROLOGY, AND AQUATIC PLANTS IN TEMPORARY WETLANDS

The second demonstration of synthesis shows how the aquatic plants that grow in temporary wetlands interact with bacteria to influence the biogeochemistry of these hydrologically dynamic environments. Other than uptake and release of nutrients (Graneli and Solander 1988; Gophen 2000), topics not covered in this chapter, there are four main ways in which wetland plants interact with microbes to modify the biogeochemistry of wetland sediments:

Aeration of belowground organs, particularly
1. modification of sediment redox conditions, and
2. venting metabolic gases to the atmosphere; and

Production of organic matter, particularly
1. the range of different types of organic matter generated by various groups of plants under different water regimes, and
2. the substantial amounts of material produced via primary production and available for bacterial decomposition.

Since the last two points have been examined already, let us concentrate on the ability of aquatic plants to aerate their belowground organs and the biogeochemical implications of this flux of oxygen.

PLANTS, SEDIMENT REDOX POTENTIAL AND WETLAND BACTERIA

To cope with sediment anoxia, almost all wetland plants have an elaborate internal anatomy (air-space tissue, or aerenchyma) that permits air to flow through the plants to belowground organs (Jackson and Armstrong 1999; Colmer 2003; see Chapter 4). Aerenchyma in stems and roots can occupy up to 60% of the internal volume of a wetland plant (Armstrong 1982).

Air flows through these internal air spaces either via passive diffusion or via convective flow, the latter a function of temperature and humidity differences across the inside and outside of the aerial portions of the plant, especially between influx green culms and dead or broken efflux culms (Sorrell et al. 1994; Brix et al. 1996). Convective flow is often up to two orders of magnitude more effective than diffusion in moving oxygen from aerial to belowground organs (Aldridge and Ganf 2003). Accordingly, plant species with well-developed convective-flow mechanisms can survive into deeper water, and survive more prolonged waterlogging, than can taxa that rely on diffusion alone or in which convective flow is poorly developed.

A portion of the oxygen that moves down the shoots and stems and into the subterranean organs of wetland plants diffuses into the *rhizosphere,* the soil immediately surrounding the roots and rhizomes. This loss of oxygen creates a band of aerobic conditions in an otherwise anaerobic, often reducing, environment (Brix et al. 1996). The flux of oxygen can increase the redox potential of the sediments by at least 100 mV and sometimes over 200 mV (Boon and Sorrell 1991; Muller et al. 1994; Aldridge and Ganf 2003). Just as species capable of convective flow are able to live in deeper water than those that rely on simple diffusion, emergent aquatic plants such as reeds *(Phragmites),* rushes *(Juncus),* spikerushes *(Eleocharis),* and cattail *(Typha)* have a much greater effect on sediment redox than do submerged taxa such as the pondweeds (e.g., *Potamogeton*) (Chen and Barko 1988; Boon and Sorrell 1991).

The oxygen that diffuses radially from the belowground organs of emergent aquatic plants modifies the relative rates of aerobic and anaerobic microbial processes in the sediments (Sorrell and Boon 1994; Boon and Sorrell 1995; Brix et al. 1996; Beckett et al. 2001). For example, studies with peat (Watson et al. 1997), rice (Gilbert and Frenzel 1998; Le Mer and Roger 2001; Conrad 2002) and reeds such as *Phragmites* (Grunfeld and Brix 1999) have all shown that methane oxidation occurs rapidly in the aerated rhizosphere of wetland plant roots.

The loss of oxygen across the root-rhizome surface into the surrounding anaerobic sediments also could have a number of other biogeochemical effects. For example, Aldridge and Ganf (2003) showed that aeration of the root zone increased the adsorption of phosphorus onto sediment particles. Aeration of the rhizosphere also affects the cycling of iron: Weiss and colleagues (2003) reported that Fe^{2+}-oxidizing bacteria were found in 92% of plant specimens, representing 25 species of wetland plants across the Mid-Atlantic region of the United States. Bacteria capable of reducing Fe^{3+} accounted for about 12% of all bacteria in the rhizosphere of wetland plants, whereas they comprised <1 % of the bacteria in the bulk soil away from the plant roots. Subsequent work (Weiss et al. 2004) indicated that the rhizosphere was a site of intense iron cycling and that the rapidity of iron oxidation and reduction was related strongly to the presence of plant roots and rhizomes in the sediments.

Root aeration and its effects on sediment bacteria creates a positive feedback loop with plant health, mediated via the production and oxidation of hydrogen sulphide (H_2S). Hydrogen sulfide is highly toxic to many aquatic organisms, including benthic animals and many species of aquatic plants. As described earlier, hydrogen sulfide is produced by anaerobic sulfate-reducing bacteria using sulfate as the terminal electron acceptor to oxidize organic material under reducing conditions (Fig. 5.5). Sulfide or ferrous iron toxicity is widely reported for rice (e.g., *suffocation disease* in Taiwan, *akiochi* in Japan, *straighthead disease* in the United States), and sulfide has been shown to play a major role in structuring coastal salt marsh communities (Armstrong 1982). The "dieback" disease of *Phragmites* stands has been linked, at least in part, to sulfide toxicity (van der Putten 1997; Chambers et al. 1998; Armstrong and Armstrong 2001).

The significance of sulfide toxicity in formerly freshwater wetlands that have been drained and subjected to intrusions of sulfate-rich saline groundwater has been noted earlier. It has been shown with coastal salt marshes along the coast of Britain that sulfide was an important factor in controlling the distribution of higher plants, being responsible, for example, in the exclusion of *Puccinellia maritima* from certain locations (Ingold and Havill 1984).

There is also some evidence that the bacterial communities in the rhizosphere of wetland plants alters as the plant community becomes less healthy, commonly as a result of plant dieback and decreases in belowground aeration. Micsinai and associates (2003) reported that healthy stands of the reed *Phragmites australis* around Lake Velencei (Hungary) supported a bacterial community dominated by facultatively fermentative bacteria, whereas less healthy stands supported a more saprophytic community, possibly including pathogenic species. Santruckova and associates (2001) also detected microbiological changes as reed stands declined, primarily decreases in redox potential that resulted in less aerobic microbial activity and a lower proportion of aerobic bacteria, a decrease in the rate of denitrification, and an increase in the rate of methanogenesis.

VENTING METABOLIC GASES TO THE ATMOSPHERE

An interesting phenomenon is that the "internal wind" of oxygen from the aerial organs to the belowground organs is responsible also for venting metabolic waste products, such as methane, from wetland sediments to the atmosphere. Because their convective flow mechanisms are so effective in internal aeration, emergent vascular plants, such as *Phragmites, Typha,* and *Eleocharis,* act as simple and efficient conduits to the atmosphere for methane produced deep in the sediment (Chanton and Dacey 1991; Boon 2000b). The flux through emergent plant organs decreases the concentration of dissolved methane in sediment interstitial waters and can account for 30% to 70% of the total methane flux into the atmosphere (Sorrell and Boon 1994; Boon and Sorrell 1995).

ACKNOWLEDGMENTS

This chapter is dedicated to the late Professor Bill Williams, who long sought to have recognized the value of temporary aquatic systems in arid, semiarid, and Mediterranean regions of the world. Dr. Sanchez-Carrillo kindly provided me with many reports of her work on temporary wetlands in Spain. Drs. Andrew Boulton and Brian Sorrell kindly read and commented incisively on an early draft. An anonymous reviewer also provided valuable comments. Monash University is thanked for providing resources during my sabbatical of late 2003.

6

DEVELOPMENT OF WETLAND PLANT COMMUNITIES

Rebecca R. Sharitz and Steven C. Pennings

Plant communities in different types of wetlands vary greatly in species composition, species richness, and productivity. They are influenced to varying degrees by a long list of abiotic factors including hydrologic conditions, position on the landscape, substrate, fertility, climate, environmental stress, and disturbance, and also by a variety of biotic interactions including competition, facilitation, and herbivory. They range from highly productive herbaceous marshes dominated by a few robust perennial species to infertile but species-rich wet meadows; from boreal bogs and other peatlands with mosses and evergreen shrubs to tropical wet grasslands and palm savannas; from nutrient-poor wetland communities of isolated depressions that gain water primarily from rainfall to river floodplain communities that are flooded by nutrient-rich river water and overland runoff; and from coastal marshes that experience regular flooding with salt water to seasonal freshwater ponds in shallow depressions that frequently dry completely. This diversity of wetland types presents a challenge to both students and professional scientists. Is it helpful to think about "wetland plant communities" in general, or is it the case that students of boreal bogs have little to discuss with students of mangrove forests?

Certainly, each type of wetland has some unique features. Nevertheless, there are general processes that shape plant communities in all wetlands, and we believe that one can gain a better understanding of wetland plant communities by first discussing general principles and only then considering how these principles apply to different wetland types. Accordingly, this chapter begins by presenting general concepts about how plant communities in wetlands are structured by abiotic and biotic factors. It then discusses

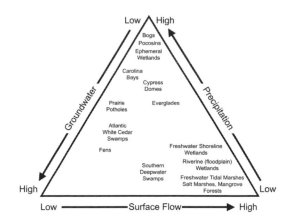

FIGURE 6.1
The relative contribution of three water sources (precipitation, groundwater discharge, and surface inflow) to wetlands. As there may be much variation in the relative importance of different water sources within many of the wetland types, their locations are approximate and often overlap. Modified from Brinson (1993b).

the general factors mediating plant growth and primary productivity in wetlands. The chapter concludes with descriptions of major wetland types, illustrating how the general principles we have discussed apply to particular habitat types.

IMPORTANCE OF HYDROLOGIC CONDITIONS

Hydrologic conditions such as the source, depth, flow rate, and timing of water presence are the fundamental determinants of the structure and productivity of wetland plant communities. Hydrologic conditions determine the chemical and physical aspects of the ecosystem, which then influence the biotic components (see Chapter 3). In turn, the vegetation may influence the hydrologic conditions through evapotranspiration and by reducing surface flow rates.

There are three main sources of water for wetlands—precipitation, groundwater discharge, and surface water inflows, although the water entering any particular wetland will often come from more than one of these sources (Fig. 6.1). The position of the wetland on the landscape dictates the amount and quality of precipitation, groundwater, and surface water that it will receive. The relative contributions of these different sources of water in large part determine the nature of the plant community that develops because nutrient levels are related to water source. Northern bogs, Carolina bays, pocosins, and other seasonal or ephemeral wetlands (see habitat descriptions in Chapter 2) that receive most of their moisture from rainfall are typically nutrient poor (oligotrophic) because precipitation is very low in nutrients. Fens that are groundwater fed tend to be more nutrient rich because groundwater accumulates dissolved minerals from bedrock. Cypress domes and prairie potholes typically have more surface water inputs and may also be somewhat more rich in nutrients. Other freshwater marshes and swamps, river floodplains, and coastal tidal salt marshes that receive surface flows are typically quite nutrient-rich (eutrophic) systems because water moving across the surface of the ground picks up large amounts of dissolved minerals and particulate matter from the soil. These, of course, are broad generalizations, and specific site conditions strongly influence not only water source and amount, but also soil and nutrient conditions in wetlands. For example, fens can range from very nutrient poor peatlands to relatively nutrient-rich ecosystems, depending on relative amounts of groundwater and/or surface water inputs in addition to precipitation. Similarly, southern swamps and marshes occur across a range of geomorphic, hydrologic, and soil conditions (see Chapter 2) and can differ greatly in vegetation characteristics. In addition, the landscape position, climate, and local environmental conditions that determine the type of wetland that is present also create the hydrologic and geochemical gradients within the wetland that mediate the local distributions of different plant species.

The presence of water in wetlands profoundly affects the plant community. Typical wetland plant communities have lower species richness than most plant communities found on drier soils, and wetland and nonwetland habitats usually have few plant species in common. Waterlogged soils are low in oxygen and often experience other chemical conditions that are absent in dry soils (see Chapters 2 and 5). Because these conditions are highly stressful for nonadapted species (see Chapter 4), flooded or saturated soil conditions strongly select for water-tolerant plant species and exclude flood-intolerant species. There are about three hundred thousand species of vascular plants on Earth, but relatively few have adapted to growth in waterlogged soils (see Chapter 4). As a result, wetlands typically contain unique but relatively low-diversity floras.

Although all wetlands, by definition, have waterlogged soils, the hydrologic conditions vary considerably among different wetland types, with corresponding effects on plant diversity. Wetlands that are flooded or saturated for long periods generally have lower plant species richness than wetlands that are flooded less frequently or for shorter durations. Flowing water may allow plant species richness in wetlands to increase by reducing anaerobic conditions and renewing minerals. Highly variable hydroperiods that occur in many wetlands may result in more environmental heterogeneity and promote establishment of a greater array of plant species. In wetlands such as lakeshore marshes, river floodplains, or coastal tidal marshes, erosion and sediment deposition caused by flowing waters may create additional niches that allow diverse plant communities to establish. Finally, wetlands that are flooded with saline water (salt marshes and mangroves) typically have lower plant diversity than adjacent freshwater wetlands because plants face the twin stresses of waterlogged soils and high salinities (Odum 1988).

Variable hydrologic conditions not only characterize certain wetlands but are necessary to maintain the plant communities. Shallow depressional wetlands such as prairie potholes, playas, and Carolina bays, which receive water mostly from precipitation or local runoff, may be completely dry during summer months or contain no water at all in dry years. Many herbaceous plants in these wetlands may require episodic dry periods for seeds to germinate and seedlings to establish. Many forested wetlands, including bottomland hardwood forests and riparian or floodplain forests, are flooded only periodically (although deepwater forested swamps may experience longer inundation). Here again, prolonged flooding limits seed germination and seedling establishment, and eventually kills most woody plants. Under these conditions, forested wetlands are replaced by wet meadows or marshes that are dominated by more flood-tolerant herbaceous species. Tidal marshes cycle between flooded and exposed conditions on a daily basis and are dependent on these hydrologic fluctuations.

Hydrologic conditions also affect the primary productivity of wetlands because plant productivity is mediated by the physiological stresses or benefits that result from the duration and frequency of flooding. In general, wetlands with water that is stagnant or continuously deep have lower productivity, whereas those with flowing water have higher productivity because flowing water tends to supply nutrients and flush toxins from the soils. The link between water movement and productivity has been well documented in studies of forested wetlands (e.g., Mitsch and Rust 1984; Megonigal et al. 1997). Numerous studies have shown that nutrient poor peatlands such as bogs generally have lower productivity than do fens that receive some groundwater or surface water flows (e.g., Szumigalski and Bayley 1996; Bedford et al. 1999; Bedford and Godwin 2003). The influence of hydrologic conditions on productivity of freshwater marshes is less consistent. Some studies have shown that productivity is stimulated in marshes with flowing water (e.g., Odum et al. 1984); whereas, other studies have suggested that fluctuations in surface water conditions may serve as a stress to macrophyte communities. In coastal ecosystems, productivity of salt marsh plants is greatest close to creeks, where tidal action has a greater influence on soil chemistry (delivering nutrients and flushing toxins such as sulfides) and at sites with greater tidal amplitudes (Turner 1976; Pennings and Bertness 2001).

Hydrologic conditions vary not only between wetlands, but also within individual wetlands. As a result, there may be predictable gradients in species composition and productivity along physical gradients within wetlands. For example, across lake shorelines, where hydrologic conditions change with elevation, different zones of vegetation often are found. Submerged vegetation grows where the water is deepest, floating-leaved plants at higher elevations, and emergent species along the water's edge (Fig. 6.2). The depth to which submersed vegetation can grow is limited primarily by light penetration, which affects its photosynthesis. In coastal wetlands, both salinity and waterlogging influence plant species zonation (Pennings and Bertness 2001). The most salt-tolerant plants occur closest to tidal inputs or where salt water collects and evaporates, resulting in highly saline conditions. Species tolerant of flooding grow in the regularly flooded low intertidal zone, and species intolerant of flooding grow in the rarely flooded terrestrial border of the marsh. In other wetlands, temporal variation in hydrologic conditions throughout the system and frequent changes in flooding depth and duration may result not in zones, but in patches of different species depending on their tolerance to flooding and anoxia.

PLANT COMMUNITY DEVELOPMENT

The development of a wetland plant community is influenced by the conditions under which plants became established and by ensuing events, including the availability of viable seeds or other propagules, appropriate environmental conditions for germination and

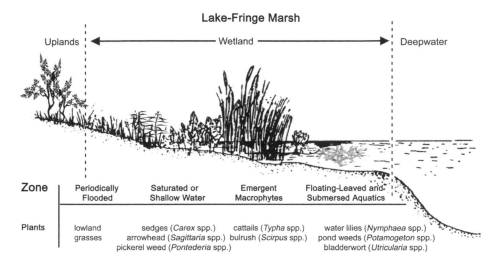

Lake-Fringe Marsh

Uplands ← — Wetland — → Deepwater

Zone	Periodically Flooded	Saturated or Shallow Water	Emergent Macrophytes	Floating-Leaved and Submersed Aquatics
Plants	lowland grasses	sedges (*Carex* spp.) arrowhead (*Sagittaria* spp.) pickerel weed (*Pontederia* spp.)	cattails (*Typha* spp.) bulrush (*Scirpus* spp.)	water lilies (*Nymphaea* spp.) pond weeds (*Potamogeton* spp.) bladderwort (*Utricularia* spp.)

FIGURE 6.2

Characteristic zonation of wetland plant species across a steep environmental gradient in a lake shoreline. After Mitsch and Gasselink (1993) with permission from John Wiley and Sons.

growth, and replacement of initial colonizers by other plants of the same or different species as new species colonize or site conditions change in response to abiotic and biotic factors. Changes in plant community composition are a result of both internal processes, such as competition between plants or the accumulation of sediment or peat (e.g., Moore and Bellamy 1974; Connell and Slatyer 1977; Connell et al. 1987), and external processes, such as climatic changes or disturbance (e.g., van der Valk 1981; Lugo 1997; Baldwin and Mendelssohn 1998; Battaglia et al. 1999). In wetlands, the most important external processes usually have to do with the hydrologic regime: changes in water depth, period of inundation, flow rate, and chemistry. Hydrologic conditions affect species composition, successional trends, primary productivity, and organic matter accumulation (e.g., Brinson et al. 1981; van der Valk 1987; Lugo et al. 1988).

The concept of succession, or the replacement of plant species in a sequence through time, has a long history in the study of plant communities and has changed somewhat over time. Originated by Clements (1916), succession involved three fundamental concepts in its classical use:

1. Vegetation occurs as recognizable groups of species, or community types;
2. Community change is stimulated by the biota (i.e., changes are facilitated and autogenic); and
3. Changes are linear (an orderly sequence) and are directed toward a mature stable climax ecosystem (Odum 1971).

Each of these concepts has since been rejected, at least in its simplistic form.

First, Gleason (1917) and others argued for an "individualistic" understanding of communities, in which each individual species was present due to its own unique set of adaptations to the environment. According to this view, one would rarely find distinct plant assemblages, but rather any sampling over space and time would reveal a continuum of overlapping sets of species, each responding in different ways to different environmental cues (Whittaker 1967; McIntosh 1980). Most ecologists today lean toward an individualistic view of plant communities, although we do recognize that some species depend on others (Callaway 1997).

Second, we now recognize that early colonists do not always stimulate transitions to later-succession species, but instead may have no effect or resist successional changes (Connell and Slayter 1977). In addition, much of the change in wetland communities is brought about by external drivers that affect hydrology, rather than by the plant community itself (e.g., van der Valk 1981; Wilcox and Simonin 1987; Reeder and Eisner 1994; Wilcox 1995).

Third, we now also recognize that the earth's climate is constantly changing, and thus there is no such thing as a permanent "climax ecosystem" for any site. As the earth has gone through warmer and cooler periods, the distributions of all habitat types have shifted across the globe. Wetlands, which are highly sensitive to variation in climate and hydrologic conditions, are ephemeral habitat types (Singer et al. 1996).

Today, we recognize that the composition of plant communities changes on a variety of time scales for a variety of reasons. As a result, the concept of ecological succession has broadened to mean any change over time in the species present in a community (Morin 1999). Below, we will first describe primary and secondary succession and then discuss the application of succession theory to wetlands.

Ecologists distinguish between primary and secondary succession. Primary succession occurs on sites where no plants have grown before, such as on new areas of wet soil formed at the deltaic mouth of a river, on a sand bar formed by sediment deposition in the curve of a river, or on a sand bar in a coastal lagoon formed by marine sediments transported into the estuary during a hurricane. Primary succession would also occur on unplanted constructed wetlands that are not placed on the sites of previous wetlands.

Secondary succession occurs when an existing plant community recovers from a disturbance. Wetlands experience a wide variety of natural disturbances that can kill vegetation. These include hurricanes, fire, deposition of thick layers of sediment in storms, deposition of thick mats of floating dead plant material (wrack), herbivory, and ice damage (Lugo 1997; Hardwick-Witman 1985; Conner et al. 1989; Ewel 1998; Pennings and Richards 1998; Morris et al. 2002; Ewanchuk and Berkness 2003). Wetlands also experience many artificial disturbances, such as draining and conversion to agriculture or other uses (Tiner 2003). The natural reestablishment of wetland vegetation on abandoned agricultural fields on river floodplains (Battaglia et al. 1995), or the recovery of wetland vegetation when drained marshes are reflooded (De Steven et al. in press), are also examples of secondary succession.

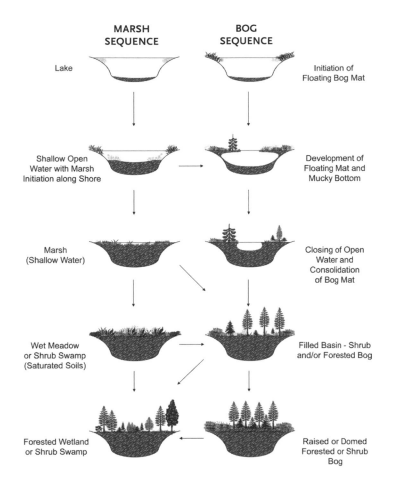

MARSH SEQUENCE

BOG SEQUENCE

Lake

Initiation of Floating Bog Mat

Shallow Open Water with Marsh Initiation along Shore

Development of Floating Mat and Mucky Bottom

Marsh (Shallow Water)

Closing of Open Water and Consolidation of Bog Mat

Wet Meadow or Shrub Swamp (Saturated Soils)

Filled Basin - Shrub and/or Forested Bog

Forested Wetland or Shrub Swamp

Raised or Domed Forested or Shrub Bog

FIGURE 6.3

Hydrarch succession a sequence of wetlands developing from the gradual filling in of lakes. Copyright © 1998 by R.W. Tiner. Reprinted by permission of Rutgers University Press.

ARE ALL WETLANDS UNDERGOING SUCCESSION TO TERRESTRIAL HABITATS? HYDRARCH SUCCESSION

The hydrarch model, an early view of wetland ecology, stated that wetlands were not particularly stable community types, but instead were transient stages in the successional development of a terrestrial forested climax community from a shallow lake (Fig. 6.3). According to this model, lakes gradually filled in as organic material from dying plants accumulated. This autogenic process, known as *terrestrialization,* began with open water and ended, perhaps centuries later, with upland vegetation (Lindeman 1941). The theory was that detritus would accumulate slowly at first through the decomposition of algae. When the lake became shallow enough to support the growth of rooted plants, the rate of organic deposition would increase, and eventually emergent plants would colonize. As peat continued to accumulate, shrubs and small trees would become established, adding further

Non-Ecotonal Wetlands

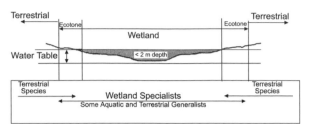

Ecotonal Wetlands

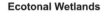

FIGURE 6.4
Wetlands located in ecotonal and
nonecotonal positions. After
Wissinger (1999) with permission of John Wiley and Sons.

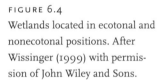
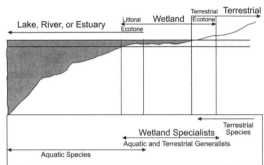

organic matter and drying the substrate through evapotranspiration. In time, a terrestrial forest would develop. It is important to note that the hydrarch model is autogenic: all changes are brought about by the plant community itself as opposed to external factors. Similar autogenic models have been proposed for other wetland systems, such as salt marshes and mangrove ecosystems. For example, some early ecologists felt that salt marshes were inherently transitional systems that would accumulate sediment and undergo succession into terrestrial plant communities (Penfound and Hathaway 1938).

The hydrarch succession model was initially attractive to ecologists because the strong zonation of plant species or assemblages in many wetlands gave the appearance of succession from wetland to terrestrial habitat. Many wetlands can be thought of as transitional systems, or ecotones, located between adjacent deepwater and terrestrial ecosystems (Fig. 6.4). As such, they are likely to both accumulate organic material from plant production and trap sediments in water runoff from the adjacent terrestrial environment. At the same time, wetlands that are located in such positions may also be influenced by allogenic forces that shift them toward more upland conditions, such as a lowering of the regional water table, or toward a more aquatic state, such as rising water levels. Thus, the simple fact that some terrestrial habitats occupy sites that previously were wetlands does not prove that the transition from wetland to terrestrial habitat occurred through autogenic processes.

Our current understanding of wetlands suggests that the hydrarch model (and its extensions to nonlake wetland types) is only partly correct, although autogenic processes are recognized as being very important in the successional development of peatlands (Moore and Bellamy 1974). It is correct that wetlands often accumulate organic matter and sediment over time, and this may lead to changes in the plant community. In most cases, however, the accumulation of organic matter is self-limiting, decreasing as the wetland becomes drier. As a result, autogenic wetland succession is likely to lead to different types of wetlands rather than to terrestrial habitats (Fig. 6.3). In addition, external changes in abiotic conditions that affect wetland hydrology (temperature, rainfall, sea level), and hence plant communities, appear to be more important to the long-term fate of most wetlands than do internal autogenic changes. Peatlands, which gain more control over their own hydrologic conditions by increasing water retention as soil organic matter accumulates, may be an exception (Moore and Bellamy 1974).

In the specific case of lakes, whether autogenic processes can lead from an open water body to a terrestrial climax forest has been debated (Heinselman 1963, 1975; van der Valk and Bliss 1971; Damman and French 1987). It is known that some upland forests occur on the sites of former lakes (Larsen 1982), but it is not clear that the successional process leading to their development was totally autogenic and not also influenced by allogenic changes that lowered the water table. The accumulation of peat occurs only under anoxic conditions. If oxygen is present, decomposition is enhanced, and peat does not accumulate as rapidly (Bridgham et al. 1991). Furthermore, when organic peats are drained, they oxidize and subside. As peat accumulates and approaches the water surface or the upper limit of the saturated zone, the rate of peat accretion becomes less than the rate of subsidence (Mitsch and Gosselink 2000). Thus, it is hard to see how an autogenic process of hydrarch succession can turn a wetland into a dry upland habitat without an outside force that changes the hydrologic conditions and lowers the water table. A more likely ultimate stage for autogenic succession might be a wet forest or wet prairie. For example, the vegetation in fifteen oxbow lakes in a river valley in Alberta, Canada, was shown to develop plant communities that progressed in a general sequence from submerged species, to floating-leaved and emergent communities, to a sedge meadow, and eventually to a wetland shrub and forest community (van der Valk and Bliss 1971) (Fig. 6.5).

The importance of internally driven processes in the successional development of northern peatlands should not be overlooked, however. In northern bog and fen complexes, changes in hydrologic conditions can be dramatically affected by biotic forces. In raised bogs, accumulated peat materials increase water retention and may result in a water table that is "perched" above the regional groundwater table (Moore and Bellamy 1974). In addition, water movement through shallow fens may be channeled by the peat, resulting in a patterned landscape of lower pools with mosses and herbaceous species and higher peat hummocks with ericaceous shrubs and stunted trees growing over *Sphagnum* mosses (Glaser et al. 1981, 1997; Siegel 1983; Siegel and Glaser 1987; Rochefort et al. 1990). Walker (1970) examined pollen profiles from British peatlands and found that the sequence of plant communities that developed had varied over time, with some reversals and skipped stages. A bog or wet forest was the most common endpoint in the sequence described.

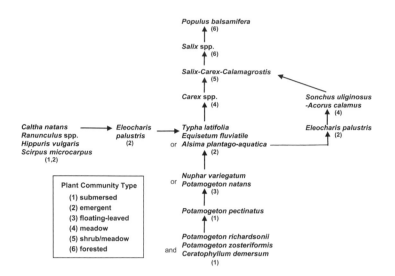

FIGURE 6.5

Diagram of the successional pattern in oxbow lakes of the Pembina River Valley, Alberta, Canada. Submerged macrophyte communities (at the left and bottom of the diagram) are replaced by emergent plant communities (in the center) and *Carex* (sedge) communities, which are ultimately replaced by *Salix* (willow) and *Populus balsamifera* (balsam popular) forests. Reproduced from van der Valk and Bliss 1971, with permission.

Thus, changes in these wetlands may be autogenic, but they are not necessarily directed toward a terrestrial climax.

In the case of salt marshes, the early view that these were in succession to terrestrial communities (Penfound and Hathaway 1938) has been replaced with the modern view that they are in relative equilibrium with sea level (Niering 1989; Davy 2000). During primary succession, salt marsh soils may develop and vegetation change for a number of decades (Olff et al. 1997). Similarly, constructed salt marshes typically require several decades before soil properties converge with those of natural marshes (Craft et al. 1999). Once the early decades of primary succession have passed, salt marsh soils continue to accumulate sediment from the water column and organic matter from dead roots. This building of soils, however, is counterbalanced by decomposition and compaction of soils. Moreover, deposition of sediments from the water column is a function of water depth and decreases as the marsh elevation increases relative to sea level (Morris et al. 2002). As a result, most salt marshes are in relative equilibrium with sea level. Exceptions occur when relative sea level is rapidly rising, in which case marshes may not be able to keep pace with sea level and will "drown" (Chmura et al. 1992), or when relative sea level is dropping, in which case marshes turn into terrestrial habitats (Hik et al. 1992).

Some wetlands maintain relatively stable plant communities despite severe changes in hydrology because the hydrologic changes are cyclical on a time scale that is too rapid for the vegetation to track. For example, tidal freshwater marshes experience daily changes in water level, tidal salt marshes may experience daily changes in both water level and salinity, and many depressional marshes and riverine forests are flooded seasonally. Such wetlands can be described as being in "dynamic equilibrium" with the abiotic forces, a condition that E. P. Odum (1971) called *pulse stability*. In the face of such hydrologic fluctuations, these wetlands maintain vegetation patterns quite different from those that would exist if either the wet or dry conditions were to persist for more extended periods. These natural hydrologic pulses move water and nutrients through the wetland ecosystems and enhance productivity. In addition, biotic events, such as seed dispersal or the movement of fish into river floodplains to spawn, are often timed to take advantage of these pulses (Junk et al. 1989; see Chapter 11).

REPLACEMENT OF SPECIES

The concept of ecological succession also deals with how one species replaces another in the community. Clements (1916) proposed that early colonizing species have a positive effect on species that establish later. For example, as early plants die and decompose, they might enhance the soil's fertility and improve the environment for later species. Connell and Slatyer (1977) suggested that early colonists might also have a negative effect, or no effect, on later species. They suggested that there are three basic types of interactions between early species and later ones: (1) facilitation, in which early species create a more favorable environment for the establishment of later species; (2) inhibition, in which early species actively inhibit the establishment of later ones; and (3) tolerance, in which there is no effect of early species on later ones. These three proposed mechanisms of interaction are points along a continuum of possible effects (Connell et al. 1987).

Succession in wetlands can occur through any of these mechanisms. Facilitation has commonly been documented in salt marshes, perhaps because of the severe physical stresses that plants experience in these conditions. In salt marshes of southern Spain, the cordgrass *Spartina maritima* aerates the sediment through radial oxygen loss, making conditions favorable for the establishment of *Arthrocnemum perenne,* a spreading prostrate plant (Castellanos et al. 1994). Similarly, facilitated succession of the shrub *Baccharis halimifolia* by *Spartina alterniflora* has been reported in salt marsh restoration projects in Louisiana (Egerova et al. 2003). In Rhode Island salt marshes undergoing secondary succession following disturbance by wrack (floating mats of dead plant material), early salt-tolerant colonists can facilitate the invasion of later salt-sensitive colonists because vegetative cover shades the soil and reduces salinities (Bertness and Ellison 1987; Bertness 1991a). Such facilitation occurs only if the elevation and disturbance size are conducive to salt buildup; otherwise, in less saline conditions, succession is purely a competitive process (Bertness and Shumway 1993; Shumway and Bertness 1994; Brewer et al. 1997). Facilitation may also occur on both marine and freshwater shorelines if tall vegetation protects smaller plants from wave stress (Wilson and Keddy 1986; Twolan-Strutt and Keddy 1996; Bruno 2000).

In many other cases, succession in wetlands is mostly a competitive process. Early establishing emergent or submerged plants with rapid growth may intercept light and keep it from reaching the substrate, thereby impeding the germination and seedling establishment of other species (Grace and Pugesek 1997; Grace 2001). Robust perennial plants such as cattails (*Typha* spp.) or reeds (*Phragmites* spp.) may outcompete other species in this manner. Species that are able to regenerate quickly in the spring from stored reserves in rhizomes or tubers are able to establish a vegetative cover before the shoots of other species appear (Grace 1987, 2001). Tolerance occurs when a new species successfully colonizes a site without either the facilitation or inhibition of other species. Although tolerance may occur most frequently, it is difficult to document unambiguously.

A final consideration is whether, through the process of ecological succession, wetlands reach a mature state, or whether allogenic forces tend to maintain constant change. In an influential but controversial paper that focused on ecosystem processes, E. P. Odum (1969) attempted to describe the maturation of ecosystems as a whole. Mitsch and Gosselink (2000) analyzed Odum's description of ecological succession as it applies to a range of wetland types. They concluded that wetlands have properties attributed by Odum to both "immature" and "mature" ecosystems. For example, nearly all of the nonforested wetlands had production to respiration ratios greater than one, and primary production tended to be very high compared with terrestrial ecosystems. These attributes, according to Odum, are characteristic of immature systems. However, detrital-based food webs in wetlands are characteristic of mature ecosystems. As described earlier, regular hydrologic cycles may maintain some wetlands at intermediate levels of development, and therefore the concept of pulse stability may describe wetland ecosystem succession better than the concept of developing and mature ecosystems (Cronk and Fennessy 2001). Finally, the fact that wetlands are so sensitive to changes in the hydrologic regime argues that the long-term succession of most types of wetlands will be determined largely by external forces such as changes in rainfall or sea level, rather than by the internal forces addressed by either Clements or Odum. Northern peatlands in which hydrologic conditions are strongly influenced by peat formation may be an exception although all wetlands are vulnerable to global climate change (see Chapter 12).

PLANT DISTRIBUTIONS IN WETLANDS

The distribution of plant species within most types of wetlands is driven by a combination of allogenic and autogenic factors (e.g., Grace and Wetzel 1981; Menges and Waller 1983; Wisheu and Keddy 1992). While there are no definitive models that fully describe the development of all wetland communities, the following concepts each help elucidate some of the processes and responses associated with plant distributions.

Plants all share a common requirement for a few basic resources: light, water, and mineral nutrients. Thus, most plants will grow fastest, and be most fecund, where these basic resources are in greatest supply. Grime (1979) proposed that competition, stress, and disturbance are the most important forces in structuring terrestrial herbaceous plant communities. In his C-S-R model, he grouped plants into three functional groups according to their life history traits and response to stress (which reduces growth rates) and disturbance (which removes vegetation or biomass).

1. *Competitors* have low reproduction and high growth rates. They are typical of undisturbed habitats with high resource availability. Species of cattail, *Typha*, could be viewed as competitors in freshwater marshes because they occupy the best habitats and competitively exclude other species from these habitats (Wisheu and Keddy 1992).

2. *Stress-tolerant* species have low reproduction and low growth rates, and generally occur in undisturbed, less productive areas where resource availability is low. Pickleweed *(Salicornia bigelovii)* could be viewed as a stress tolerator in salt marshes because it occupies areas with the highest soil salinities.

3. *Ruderal* species have high reproductive abilities, fast growth rates, and short life spans and commonly occur in disturbed, productive environments. They are not stress tolerant, and they tend to escape competition by dispersing (Grime 1977, 1979). Salt grass *(Distichlis spicata)* could be viewed as a ruderal species in salt marshes because it rapidly invades disturbed areas (Bertness and Ellison 1987).

Thus, based on the life history characteristics of a species, it is possible to predict where it will occur across gradients of stress and disturbance as well as predict what types of species will occur most frequently in certain habitats. Although Grime's model was initially proposed for terrestrial plant communities, it can be readily adapted to wetlands. For example, Menges and Waller (1983) adapted Grime's C-S-R model to show the relation of frequency of flooding and the physiological adaptations of plants to flooding in structuring an herbaceous wetland community (Fig. 6.6).

To Grime's C-S-R model, Kautsky (1988) added an additional category of *biomass storers,* which accumulate biomass in storage organs such as rhizomes or tubers. In this group of plants, vegetative regeneration dominates over sexual reproduction. These species are often found in conditions of low disturbance and high stress (such as low nutrient or light levels, or high salinity). Salt marsh cordgrass *(Spartina alterniflora),* which dominates many eastern North American salt marshes, is an example.

The common requirement of plants for a few basic resources leads to the concept of "inclusive" or overlapping niches, where many plants would potentially be able to grow

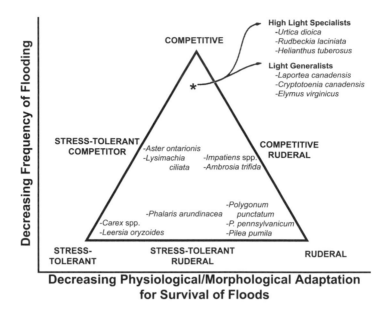

FIGURE 6.6

The C-S-R (Competitive—Stress-tolerant—Ruderal) triangle developed by Grime, adapted to show the relationship of frequency of flooding and degree of physical adaptations to flooding in a wetland. After Menges and Waller (1983).

well at the richer end of a gradient of soil fertility (Fig. 6.7). Species vary in their competitive abilities, however, with some being competitively superior and others subordinate. Wisheu and Keddy (1992) envisioned a trade-off between the ability of a species to interfere competitively with neighbors, and the ability to tolerate stressful conditions. Thus, the outcome of different competitive abilities and different tolerance limits is that species become differentially distributed along the resource and stress (or disturbance) gradient (Fig. 6.7). In this model, species that are poorer competitors will be excluded from the best end of the resource/stress gradient by one or more dominant species (Fig. 6.7b) but will survive in less suitable areas along the gradient according to their ability to tolerate stress or disturbance. At the peripheral end of the gradient, where stress or disturbance conditions are greatest, species may be excluded by competition with adjacent subordinate species that are better able to tolerate the adverse conditions (Fig. 6.7b). While this model might appear to account for species zonation patterns in wetlands, it can not be assumed without testing that competition and tolerance of stress or disturbance are the primary factors behind such species distributions. Work by Grace and Wetzel (1981) on cattails and by Bertness and colleagues (1992a) on salt marsh plants (see Vegetation Characteristics of Selected Wetlands below) provide excellent examples of experimental studies that supported the trade-off model.

Grime (1979) also observed that habitats with intermediate levels of biomass appeared to have the greatest number of plant species, and he postulated that there is a general

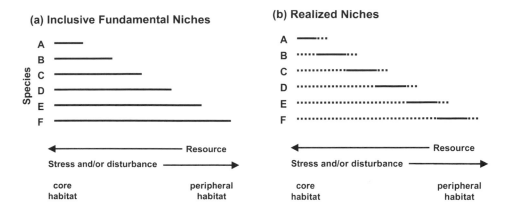

(a) Inclusive Fundamental Niches

(b) Realized Niches

FIGURE 6.7

Species distributions along a gradient (a) where they have inclusive niches and (b) where there are competitive hierarchies. Solid lines indicate areas along the fertility and stress gradient where species overlap, and dashed lines indicate the region from which a species is excluded. After Wisheu and Keddy (1992).

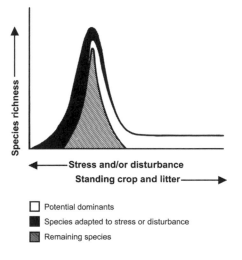

FIGURE 6.8

Species richness along a gradient of stress or disturbance versus standing crop. Note that x axis is reversed in direction from Fig. 6.7. From Keddy (2000) with permission of Cambridge University Press.

relationship in vegetation between species richness and standing crop (Fig. 6.8). He proposed that at one end of the gradient, species richness is low because of high levels of stress or disturbance; whereas, at the other end of the gradient, species richness is low because of dominance by a few strong competitors. Studies by Keddy and his associates on herbaceous emergent wetlands in North America show patterns that generally conform to this "hump-shaped" model (Day et al. 1988; Moore and Keddy 1989; Wisheu and Keddy 1989; Shipley et al. 1991). Species richness may be high or low at intermediate points along the community biomass gradient, but high diversity seldom occurs at either very high or very low biomass. Gough and colleagues (1994), working in brackish marshes on the Gulf Coast

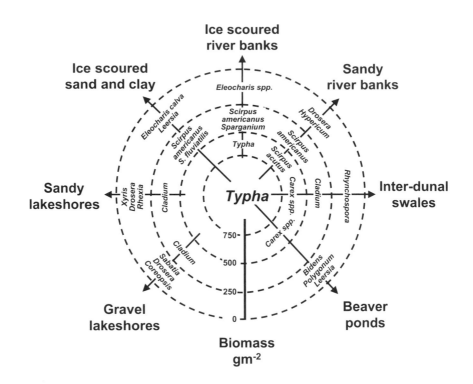

FIGURE 6.9

Centrifugal organization model for freshwater wetlands in eastern North America. The core habitat is dominated by robust leafy species and peripheral habitats that are stressed (e.g., by infertile sand, ice scouring, and beaver activity) are occupied by different species and communities. After Wisheu and Keddy (1992).

of the United States, found that flooding and salt stress set the potential number of species that could occur in an area (the rising side of the hump-shaped curve), while competition eliminated species from other areas (the decreasing side of the hump-shaped curve). Though this hump-shaped pattern has been reported frequently, it is by no means universal. For example, Moore and Keddy (1989) found no pattern when they examined species richness and biomass within fifteen different herbaceous wetlands.

CENTRIFUGAL ORGANIZATION MODEL

Wisheu and Keddy (1992) expanded the trade-off model by proposing that there are multiple environmental gradients in many wetlands. The more benign ends of each gradient may support similar species assemblages and are described as *core habitats*. The adverse ends of the various gradients, however, will support different species, each with unique adaptations to the particular adverse conditions involved. They termed this pattern *centrifugal organization* (Fig. 6.9). The central or core habitat would likely have low disturbance and high fertility, and be dominated by large leafy species. As described for freshwater wetlands in eastern North America, cattails (*Typha* spp.) might dominate the central habitat by reducing light levels for subordinate species (Wisheu and Keddy 1992).

Beyond this core habitat, different constraints such as low nutrient levels or disturbances create radiating axes along which different groups of species are arrayed. Across these gradients, it may be likely that plant biomass is greatest in the central habitat, but that species richness is highest in intermediate positions where competition is reduced and adverse conditions are not yet extreme. It should be noted, however, that numerous other environmental conditions in addition to soil fertility or disturbance affect wetland vegetation development (Fig 6.9). Gradients of anoxia in the soil associated with length and depth of inundation or gradients of salt concentrations in salt marsh soils are additional examples of conditions that structure the distribution of wetland plants (Bertness and Ellison 1987; Bertness 1991a, 1991b; Pennings and Bertness 2001).

Although evidence suggests that wetland communities can be arrayed in such a centrifugal pattern, objective tests are needed to determine that vegetation gradients do converge in core habitats. One prediction of this model would be that vegetation types with high biomass should be relatively similar to each other, whereas those at low biomass should be very different. Another prediction is that rare species will be restricted to peripheral habitats (Keddy 2000). Indeed, Moore and colleagues (1989) showed that many rare species were restricted to low biomass, infertile sites in North American wetlands. Another prediction is that eutrophication would result in shifts in plant species toward those of core habitats as small plants are replaced by large robust ones with larger canopies. Thus, eutrophication removes peripheral habitats and replaces them with core habitats, leading to an overall decrease in species diversity (Keddy 2000).

ASSEMBLY RULES

Another approach to classifying or organizing groups of wetland plant species is to focus not on plant communities, but on functional groups or guilds. The guild concept has several advantages over the generalized community concept:

1. It collapses the large number of species in a community into manageable subsets;
2. It defines guilds in terms of measurable functional properties; and
3. It enables prediction of what guilds will be found under specific environmental conditions.

The guild concept has been widely applied in the study of animal species, but it has been less used in plant ecology. Boutin and Keddy (1993) demonstrated the potential of this approach by classifying 43 species selected from a range of different wetland habitats across northeastern North America on the basis of 27 functional traits. These traits included:

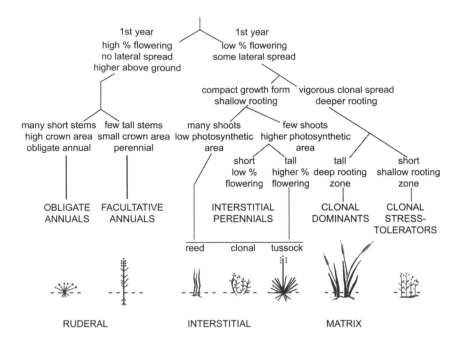

FIGURE 6.10

Wetland plants can be divided into functional groups, based on traits of life history and morphology. After Boutin and Keddy (1993).

1.   Relative growth rates;

2.   Height of juveniles, height of adults, and rate of shoot extension;

3.   Above- and belowground biomass allocation and photosynthetic area; and

4.   Morphological traits such as shortest and longest distance between aerial shoots.

An effort was made to choose traits that were likely to be associated with resource acquisition (Keddy 2000). A cluster analysis reduced the 43 species into 7 groups or guilds, within which the species were functionally similar (Fig. 6.10). These guilds ranged from fast-growing obligate or facultative annual species (ruderal), to perennials with a clumped growth form (interstitial), to clonal species with deeper roots or rhizomes that spread vegetatively (matrix species). Most of the guilds appeared to fall along a continuum of life histories and growth forms associated with different light regimes.

The traits of plants in these guilds can then be used to predict their presence in different wetland habitats. Keddy (1992b) described assembly and response rules by which an assemblage of plants can be predicted from (1) a list of potential species and their traits, and (2) the application of an environmental "filter." Filters are environmental conditions that eliminate plants from the species pool. Assembly rules predict which particular subset of traits (which guilds of plants) will be prevented from establishing under particular environmental conditions. Similarly, response rules can be used to predict changes in species composition as a result of changing environmental conditions that will eliminate some species and allow others with different traits to be added to the wetland ecosystem. Such knowledge of plant traits and environmental filters may be especially useful in restoring or constructing wetlands and selecting guilds of species that will succeed under the environmental conditions imposed.

ENVIRONMENTAL SIEVE MODEL

One of the major controls on the composition of any plant community is the ability of each species to become established, and to persist, under existing environmental conditions. The conditions that species require to germinate and become established may differ greatly from the conditions to which they are adapted when mature. The "regeneration niche" (Grubb 1977) focuses on seed longevity and the requirements for germination and seedling establishment, and is a critical aspect of wetland plant success. Many freshwater wetland plants require drawn down conditions for germination and establishment, although subsequent growth and reproduction may occur in a flooded environment. Similarly, many salt marsh plants require periods of low-salinity conditions for germination and establishment, although the growth of adults may occur under saline conditions (Zedler and Beare 1986; Callaway and Sabraw 1994). Many wetland plants are vegetatively spreading perennials with an indefinite life span, once they become established. In a survey of North American aquatic and wetland plants, only 14% were found to be annuals, and the remaining 86% were perennials (Kadlec and Wentz 1974). Thus, although the regeneration niche is critically important for annuals, it will be important only for initial establishment of perennials.

This situation is illustrated in the environmental sieve model proposed by van der Valk (1981) to predict wetland plant assemblages in prairie potholes under flooded or drawn down conditions. Water levels in these shallow depression wetlands commonly fluctuate; thus, the environmental filter is an allogenic change (the presence or absence of standing water). This qualitative model is based on three life history features of the species involved: life-span, propagule longevity, and plant establishment requirements. Wetland plants are separated into annuals (A), perennials with a limited life span (P), and vegetatively reproducing perennials that do not have a definite life span (V). The species are further divided into two groups according to longevity and availability of propagules (seeds or vegetative propagules). One group has long-lived propagules that persist in the wetland soils and can become established when the hydrologic conditions are right (seed bank or S species). The other group, dispersal-dependent species (D species) has short-lived propagules that can become established only if they reach the wetland during a period of suitable hydrologic conditions for germination. The plants in all these categories are further classified according to their germination and establishment requirements. Species

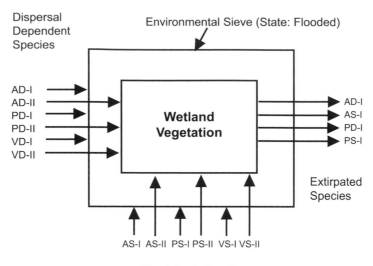

FIGURE 6.11

Environmental sieve model of wetland succession. The environment alternates between two states: drawn down and flooded (as shown). As a result, only those species with the proper life history features can become established, and other species, because of their life history characteristics, may be extirpated. When the wetland is drawn down, another set of species may become established, and the set shown passing through the sieve during flooded conditions will be extirpated. See text for explanation of the life history types. After van der Valk (1981).

that can become established only when there is no standing water are Type I; standing-water species that can become established under flooded conditions are Type II.

Combining these three classifications, there are twelve potential life history types (see Fig. 6.11). For example, in the vegetation of a prairie glacial marsh, cattail *(Typha x glauca)* is considered a VS-I species, a potentially long-lived perennial that spreads vegetatively and becomes established from seeds in the seed bank only during drawdowns (although *Typha* seeds may also be widely dispersed by wind). Common reed *(Phragmites australis)* is a VD-I plant, a vegetatively spreading perennial with seeds that also germinate on exposed soil during drawdowns, but that are not present in the seed bank. Beggartick *(Bidens cernua)* (AS-I) is a mudflat annual whose long-lived seeds are common in the seed bank and germinate during drawdowns, and waternymph *(Najas flexilis)* (AS-II) is a submerged annual whose seeds are present in the seed bank and germinate only when flooded (van der Valk 1981).

The environmental sieve (hydrologic state of the wetland) determines whether Type I or Type II species can become established (Fig. 6.11), and changing the sieve will favor species with certain life history types and eliminate others. Annuals are infrequent in wetlands that are flooded for multiple years, and AS-I species will be absent. D species are eliminated once the hydrologic conditions are unsuitable for their establishment, but

S species may survive in the seed bank, if not in the extant vegetation. V species, perennials with an indefinite life span, may persist for long periods of time and may require another disturbance such as destruction by muskrats (van der Valk and Davis 1979) or a drawdown followed by fire (Kirkman et al. 2000) to be extirpated from the wetland.

If succession is considered to be change in the species present in a community, the environmental sieve model may enable the prediction of allogenic succession in a wetland due either to normal changes in environmental conditions or unexpected perturbations. It is based on information that can be readily obtained from a study of the soil seed bank plus knowledge of basic life history traits. Its application has been primarily to freshwater marshes (van der Valk 1981). It is a qualitative model, since it only predicts which species will be present, not their abundance. In addition, the model ignores autogenic processes such as competition between species that may also greatly influence wetland community composition. Smith and Kadlec (1985) tested the model's ability to predict species composition in a Great Salt Lake marsh after fire and were satisfied with the qualitative results.

Additional environmental filters may be added to this general model as needed to understand or predict vegetation change in other wetland types. For example, Kirkman and associates (2000) proposed a successional sequence using hydrologic condition and fire as environmental sieves for forested depressional wetlands of the southeastern United States that frequently dry down. In their model, topographic position and soil texture are the primary drivers influencing the hydrologic regime. As length of the hydroperiod and depth of flooding decrease, the potential frequency of fire increases (Fig. 6.12). Drawdown must be long enough for germination and establishment of woody seedlings as well as for adequate growth to occur so that they can survive subsequent fire and/or deep inundation. During drawdown, fire acts as another environmental filter, however. In depressions with frequent fires that kill both seedlings and saplings, a grass-sedge marsh prevails. With fires of intermediate frequency in which only hardwoods are killed, a pond cypress *(Taxodium ascendens)* savanna results. Infrequent fires do not filter out the hardwoods, and a cypress-hardwood community occurs.

EFFECTS OF ABIOTIC AND BIOTIC DISTURBANCES

As noted earlier, disturbances may maintain the wetland plant community in a particular successional stage or reset successional processes to an earlier stage (Connell and Slatyer 1977). Infrequent catastrophic events, such as severe hurricanes, landslides, or extreme floods, may eliminate an entire community and so alter the habitat that different species become established. Lower-intensity disturbances, such as wind storms or fires, may cause a temporary disruption followed by secondary succession. In wetlands, hydrologic alterations are among the most common disturbances, occurring on both large and small scales and resulting from natural causes and human activities. At the large scale, a river may alter its course as a result of natural events or man-made occurrences. For example, the lower part of the Mississippi River has naturally changed course several times

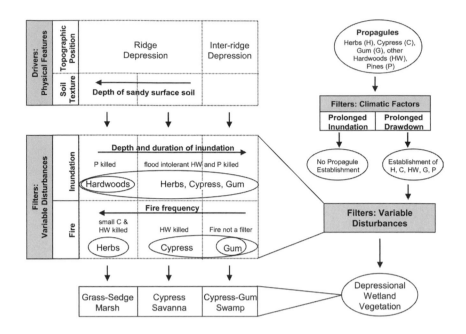

FIGURE 6.12

A conceptual model of ecosystem development in depressional wetlands of the southeastern United States. Drivers (stable physical features of the depression that control hydrologic and disturbance regimes) and filters (climatic and disturbance factors that control the establishment of species) are shown in gray boxes. Arrows from these boxes indicate the resulting environmental conditions or vegetation from each influencing factor. The propagules and establishing vegetation that emerge through the filters are shown in ovals. Resulting depressional wetland vegetation is indicated in the boxes at the bottom of the figure. After Kirkman and associates (2000).

in the last 6,000 to 8,000 years, forming new deltaic lobes at the mouth of the river in southern Louisiana. However, the total amount of freshwater and saltwater wetland area in the Louisiana coastal region is decreasing, due to natural land subsidence and human activities such as river levee construction, urban development, and oil and gas exploration (Gagliano et al. 1981; Salinas et al. 1986; Gagliano 1998). At a regional scale, the vegetation of prairie pothole wetlands is affected by natural climatic cycles. Communities shift from submerged and floating-leaved aquatic plants in wet years, to mudflat annuals and emergent perennials that establish in dry years (van der Valk 1981). In many parts of the United States, the hydrologic conditions of wetlands have been disrupted by the pumping of groundwater for agriculture or human consumption. Tiner (2003) suggests that regional groundwater withdrawal may pose the most insidious threat to geographically isolated wetlands or to wetlands that depend on groundwater as their main source of water.

At a smaller scale, disturbances commonly alter the natural hydrologic variations that are typical of particular wetlands. Beavers *(Castor canadensis)* affect the distribution of wetlands by impounding flowing waters. As a result, stream floodplain wetlands are converted from predominantly woody vegetation to open water and marshes (see Chapter 7; John-ston and Naiman 1990; Snodgrass 1997; Snodgrass and Meffe 1998). Many wetlands are ditched and drained for agriculture or other purposes, often resulting in direct habitat loss. It has been estimated that up to 97% of Carolina bays in South Carolina have been disturbed, either by agriculture (71%), logging (34%), or both (Bennett and Nelson 1991). The hydrologic regimes of coastal wetlands are often disturbed by building roads with in-adequate culverts through wetlands. Because water exchange through culverts is limited, both the tidal and the salinity regime in the wetland may be altered. Some of the responses in the wetland plant community that may occur as a result of hydrologic changes include:

1. An increase in numbers and dominance by invasive or exotic species;
2. A decrease in species richness;
3. A loss of species that are sensitive to disturbance;
4. Vegetation that is dominated by one species or one structural type; and
5. A decline in mutualistic interactions, such as with pollinators or mycorrhizae.

Other common disturbances to wetlands are the result of severe weather conditions. High energy floods scour stream beds, deposit sediment on the floodplain, and break and uproot plants. In cold climates, ice may scour lakeshores and salt marshes and open up areas for the establishment of new species (Morris et al. 2002; Ewanchuk and Bert-ness 2003). Hurricanes cause damage to coastal wetlands, depositing sediment in salt marshes and destroying trees in mangrove forests. In areas with infrequent hurricanes, mangroves grow larger than in areas where hurricanes are more frequent (Lugo 1997). Hurricanes that track inland may uproot or break trees in bottomland forests along river floodplains, resulting in canopy gaps and opportunities for recolonization by earlier suc-cessional species (Battaglia et al. 1999; Battaglia and Sharitz 2005, 2006). Under dry conditions, fire may be a disturbance that removes aboveground vegetation in wetlands. Fires in peatlands can remove hundreds of years of organic accumulation in a single burn and cause subsidence (Otte 1981). As previously noted (Kirkman et al. 2000), how-ever, fire may be a normal and essential part of the abiotic regime of wetlands that dry down on occasion.

Consumers also may have a substantial effect on wetland vegetation (see also Chapter 7), although usually less than 10% of macrophyte production is consumed live (Wetzel 1983; Cebrian 1999). In a comprehensive review of herbivory in freshwater wetlands, Lodge (1991) reported grazing reductions in root or shoot biomass of some plants as high as 100%, with crayfish and waterfowl being especially destructive grazers. Submersed and floating-leaved plants appear to be more susceptible to damage by invertebrate grazers emergent macrophytes, which are more vulnerable to vertebrate consumers.

Many wetland herbivores graze selectively, resulting in grazer-induced changes in the relative abundance of different plant species (Lodge 1991; Pennings and Bertness 2001). For example, crayfish reduce submerged macrophytes but have little effect on emergent plants. However, emergent species are more readily consumed by mammals (muskrats, nutria) and geese (Lodge 1991). Specialist herbivores such as beetles often attack plants that are relatively rare and may influence the distribution and abundance of their hosts without consuming much vegetation from the marsh as a whole (Hacker and Gaines 1997; Rand 1999). Geese strongly affect wetland plant species composition through a mixture of positive (disturbance, nutrient deposition) and negative (consumption) feedbacks (Jefferies 1988; Hik et al. 1992; Rowcliffe et al. 1998). Similarly, large mammals (livestock, feral horses) strongly affect salt marsh plant community composition (Pennings and Bertness 2001).

On occasion, consumers can have strong effects on wetland plant biomass. Haslam (1970) estimated that 80% of plants in a reed *(Phragmites communis)* marsh were destroyed by insect larvae. Similarly, there are reports of complete defoliation of water tupelo *(Nyssa aquatica)* by forest tent caterpillars *(Malacosoma disstria;* Conner and Day 1976), and of mangrove trees by various insects (Ellison and Farnsworth 2001). Littorine snails can sharply reduce plant biomass in salt marshes, and grapsid crabs can be important herbivores in subtropical salt marshes and mangroves (Smith et al. 1989; Bortolus and Iribarne 1999). Burrowing isopods can be important consumers of mangrove prop roots (Ellison and Farnsworth 1990). Nutria (Pennings and Bertness 2001) and muskrats (see Chapter 7) can literally "eat out" portions of emergent marsh.

PRIMARY PRODUCTIVITY

Just as the source of water and landscape position determine the type of wetland that develops and its hydrologic conditions (Fig. 6.1), they also are major determinants of wetland productivity. In general, "closed" wetlands that receive most of their water from precipitation, such as bogs, pocosins, and some seasonal or ephemeral wetlands, are oligotrophic (nutrient poor) and have low primary productivity. Increased inputs of groundwater and surface water enrich the nutrient and oxygen status and typically result in higher plant productivity in fens and marshes, some prairie potholes, Atlantic white cedar swamps, and southern deepwater swamps. Wetlands that receive pulses of nutrient-rich surface water, such as river floodplains, some lakeshore marshes, and tidal marshes, may be among the most productive. Generally, the more "open" a wetland is to water movement, the greater the plant productivity (Fig. 6.13). "Open" wetlands, especially tidal marshes, are often highly productive and may be among the most productive ecosystems in the world. In these wetlands, periodic inundation brings in oxygen and nutrient-rich sediments, and also flushes toxins from the system. Wetlands that receive nutrient subsidies, such as from agricultural runoff or sewage inputs, may also have higher productivity. However, other factors such as prolonged flooding and stagnant water may constrain wetland productivity.

There have been many studies of plant productivity in wetlands, and values reported vary greatly, depending on actual differences in the wetland ecosystems and also on the measurement techniques used (Table 6.1). In the examples that follow, we group wetlands

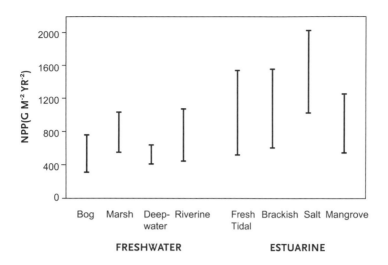

FIGURE 6.13

Generalized annual aboveground net primary productivity (ANPP) in various freshwater and estuarine wetlands. Redrawn from Craft (2001); data from references therein.

according to their major sources of water and report aboveground annual net primary productivity (ANPP) values from selected sites and studies. It should be noted that in some wetlands, such as bogs, much of the primary production is below ground; however, accurate measures of belowground biomass are difficult to obtain and are not given here.

Precipitation-dominated wetlands are usually poor in nutrients and have lower primary productivity than most other wetland types (Table 6.1). ANPP values for northern bogs typically range from 200 to 500 g m^{-2} yr^{-1}. *Sphagnum* mosses often dominate bogs, accounting for one-third to one-half of the total production (Grigal 1985), and other vegetation is usually stunted in growth. Other peatlands such as fens, which have considerably greater groundwater inputs, tend to be more nutrient rich and higher in productivity, especially forested fens (Reiners 1972; Szumigalski and Bayley 1996; Thormann and Bayley 1997). Bogs of the Appalachian Mountains, which are usually fens with some groundwater moving through them, also tend to be more productive than true northern bogs (Wieder et al. 1989). Little is known about the productivity of pocosins, probably because of the difficulty in sampling these dense evergreen bog ecosystems. Although bogs and fens accumulate peat that is rich in nutrients, most of the peat is below the rooting zone and thus unavailable to plants. Furthermore, most of the nutrients in the peat are in organic compounds and resistant to decomposition.

The productivity of many "geographically isolated" wetlands, such as Carolina bays, playas, vernal pools, and other ephemeral wetlands, has been poorly studied, if at all. Depression meadow Carolina bays with herbaceous vegetation have low ANPP (Schalles and Shure 1989), whereas forested bays might be a bit higher. Cypress domes are generally

TABLE 6.1. Examples of Annual Aboveground Net Primary Productivity
(ANPP, g m^{-2} yr^{-2}) of Selected Wetland Types

Wetland Type and Water Source	ANPP (g m^{-2} yr^{-2})	Location	Reference
Predominantly Precipitation			
Bogs			
open bog	264	Alberta, CA	Szumigalski and Bayley 1996
wooded bog	297	Alberta, CA	Szumigalski and Bayley 1996
wooded bog	390	Alberta, CA	Thormann and Bayley 1997
Carolina Bays			
depression meadow	211	South Carolina	Schalles and Shure 1989
Cypress Domes	969	Florida	Brown 1978
Greater Groundwater Component			
Prairie Potholes			
Scirpus fluviatilis	943	Iowa	van der Valk and Davis 1978b
Sparganium eurycarpum	1066	Iowa	van der Valk and Davis 1978b
Typha glauca	2297	Iowa	van der Valk and Davis 1978b
Carex atheroides	2858	Iowa	van der Valk and Davis 1978b
Fens			
northern fen (poor)	310	Alberta	Szumigalski and Bayley 1996
northern fen (rich)	360	Alberta	Szumigalski and Bayley 1996
forested fen	710	Minnesota	Reiners 1972
mountain bog (fen)	1045	West Virginia	Wieder et al. 1989
Atlantic White Cedar Swamp	1097	Virginia	Dabel and Day 1977
Greater Surface Water Component			
Southern Swamp Forests			
Acer-Nyssa	1050	Virginia	Dabel and Day 1977
mixed hardwood	831	Virginia	Dabel and Day 1977
Taxodium, nutrient poor	681	Georgia	Schlesinger 1978
Southern Floating Marsh	1960	Louisiana	Sasser and Gosselink 1984
Lake Shoreline Marshes			
Typha sp.	3450	Wisconsin	Klopatek 1974
Juncus effusus	1860	South Carolina	Boyd 1971
Tidal Freshwater Swamp			
Overstory	7442	Virginia	Fowler and Hershner 1989
Understory	4830	Virginia	Fowler and Hershner 1989
Tidal Freshwater Marshes			
tall reeds, grasses,	1500–	Eastern USA	Odum et al. 1984
Typha sp.	2000		

TABLE 6.1.   *(continued)*

Wetland Type and Water Source	ANPP (g m⁻² yr⁻²)	Location	Reference
fleshy-leaved macrophytes	700	Eastern USA	Odum et al. 1984
Riverine Wetlands			
Bottomland hardwood[a]	1374	Louisiana	Conner and Day 1976
Bottomland hardwood	1334	Kentucky	Mitsch et al. 1991
Bottomland hardwood	845	South Carolina	Giese et al. 2003
cypress-tupelo swamp[a]	1120	Louisiana	Conner and Day 1976
Impounded stagnant swamp	890	Louisiana	Connor et al. 1981
cypress swamp[b]	634	Kentucky	Mitsch et al. 1991
stagnant cypress swamp[c]	205	Kentucky	Mitsch et al. 1991
cypress strand (large trees)	896	Florida	Duever et al. 1984
cypress strand (small trees)	1542	Florida	Duever et al. 1984
Estuarine, Forested Wetlands			
mangrove, riverine	2458	Mexico	Day et al. 1987
mangrove, fringe	1607	Mexico	Day et al. 1987
mangrove, basin	399–695	Mexico	Day et al. 1996
Estuarine, Salt Marshes			
Spartina patens	4159	Louisiana	Hopkinson et al. 1980
Juncus roemerianus	3295	Louisiana	Hopkinson et al. 1980
Spartina alterniflora	1381	Louisiana	Hopkinson et al. 1980

[a]Sites separated from river by levees.
[b]Semi-permanently flooded, flowing water.
[c]Semi-permanently flooded, stagnant water.

connected to regional groundwater and thus have somewhat greater productivity than Carolina bays (Brown 1978). Similarly, prairie potholes, which are also considered to be "geographically isolated" wetlands, tend to be associated with groundwater and at times may support productive stands of emergent wetland macrophytes (van der Valk and Davis 1978b).

A wide range of ANPP values has been reported for freshwater swamp forests (Table 6.1). Atlantic white cedar *(Chamaecyparis thyoides)* stands in the Great Dismal Swamp are relatively productive and have higher ANPP than nearby maple-gum and hardwood forests (Dabel and Day 1977). In general, productivity tends to be higher in systems that have fluctuating water levels or moderately wet conditions where soil oxygen is not limiting year-round. This has been well-documented in studies of forested wetlands (e.g., Mitsch and Rust 1984; Megonigal et al. 1997) (Fig. 6.14). Bottomland hardwood stands in the Great Dismal Swamp have lower ANPP (Dabel and Day 1977) than is often reported in bottomland forests of river floodplains (e.g., Conner and Day 1976;

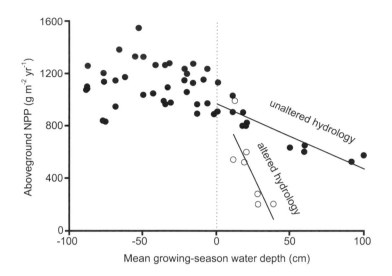

FIGURE 6.14

The relationship between aboveground net primary productivity and mean growing season water depth in bottomland forests of the southeastern United States. Sites with altered hydrologic conditions experienced increased flooding as a result of subsidence or impoundment. After Megonigal and colleagues (1997).

Mitsch et al. 1991). Growth of cypress trees (*Taxodium* spp.) is generally lower in sites with deep standing water and stagnant conditions (Mitsch and Ewel 1979; Conner and Day 1982), and also in sites that have been drained. In river floodplain forests, higher tree productivity has been correlated with higher annual river discharges and the input of nutrient-rich surface waters that provide a fertilizer effect (Mitsch et al. 1979; Brinson et al. 1981). Tidal freshwater swamps, which receive nutrients as a "tidal subsidy" as well as from adjacent overland runoff, may be particularly productive (Fowler and Hershner 1989).

Estimates of ANPP for emergent freshwater marshes typically range upward from 1,000 g m^{-2} yr^{-1}. Some of the highest values (up to 6,000 g m^{-2} yr^{-1}, which take into account belowground and aboveground production) come from artificially constructed fish ponds in the Czech Republic (Kvet and Husak 1978). Although ANPP values vary among marsh types and locations, many marshes have higher productivity than forested wetlands. Again, the source of water contributes to their productivity. Coastal floating marshes, common in Louisiana, receive nutrient inputs from groundwater. Tidal freshwater marshes are supplemented by tidal energy and surface water flows. Both of these types of marshes often have ANPP values falling in the range of 1,000 to greater than 2,000 g m^{-2} yr^{-1} (Sasser and Gosselink 1984; Odum et al. 1984). There are numerous factors in addition to nutrient inputs that are related to marsh productivity, including temperature, length of the growing season, and plant growth characteristics. Two of the dominant emergent macrophytes in many freshwater wetlands, cattails (*Typha* spp.) and reeds

(*Phragmites* spp.), are monocots with high photosynthetic efficiencies comparable to those calculated for intensely cultivated crops, such as sugar cane or corn (Mitsch and Gosselink 2000). These species, along with other tall perennial grasses and other monocots such as giant cutgrass *(Zizaniopsis millacea)* and maidencane *(Panicum hemitomon),* are generally more productive than broad-leaved herbaceous species.

Tidal salt marshes are highly productive with ANPP estimates ranging up to 8,000 g $m^{-2} yr^{-1}$ (Turner 1976). This high productivity occurs because salt marsh plants grow in full sunlight, with abundant water, often in fairly nutrient-rich sediments, and they experience a regular import of nutrients from estuarine tidal water. There is a wide divergence in ANPP values reported for salt marshes, however, caused by differences among sites in climate and tidal regime (Turner 1976) and by differences in methods used for measuring productivity. In Louisiana marshes, White and associates (1978) reported aboveground ANPP values of salt marsh cordgrass *(Spartina alterniflora)* ranging from 1473 to 2895 g $m^{-2} yr^{-1}$; values obtained by Hopkinson and associates (1980) using similar techniques were somewhat lower (Table 6.1). Aboveground productivity of *Spartina* is often higher along creek channels and in low marshes than in high marshes because of the increased exposure to tidal and freshwater flow (Mendelssohn and Morris 2000). Belowground production estimates vary widely, from 220 to 2,500 g $m^{-2} yr^{-1}$ adjacent to a tidal stream to 420 to 6,200 g $m^{-2} yr^{-1}$ on the marsh flat (Good et al. 1982). Constraints to vascular plant growth are imposed by soil anoxia, high salinity, and elevated levels of sulfide, which can be toxic (Mendelssohn and Morris 2000; see Chapter 4).

In addition to the primary production provided by angiosperms, algae in salt marsh and creek bank mud and in tidal creeks provide a substantial amount of primary production. Although the biomass of algae in the mud is small, production can be as high or higher than that of marsh macrophytes. Estimates of annual benthic microalgal production in salt marshes range from 10% to 60% of vascular plant productivity in the Atlantic and Gulf of Mexico coasts (Sullivan and Currin 2000) to 75% to 140% of vascular productivity in southern California (Zedler 1980).

Coastal mangrove forests range in productivity due to the variety of hydrologic conditions and landscape positions where they occur (Table 6.1). ANPP is commonly higher in riverine mangrove wetlands, likely because of greater nutrient loading and freshwater turnover in riverine sites (Day et al. 1987). Coastal fringe mangroves are somewhat lower in productivity; basin mangroves, which are in hydrologically isolated positions, have lower productivity yet, presumably because of increased soil salinity (Day et al. 1996). Mangrove productivity is often influenced by hurricanes in tropical areas as well as by salinity and soil fertility.

LIMITING NUTRIENTS IN WETLANDS

The relationships between nutrient availability, primary productivity, and plant species richness in wetlands are extremely important given the large changes that human beings are having on nutrient cycles worldwide (Vitousek 1994). At least two major questions arise:

1. What nutrient(s) limit plant growth and productivity in wetlands, and
2. How are wetlands affected by increased nutrient inputs, especially from anthropogenic sources?

In relatively undisturbed wetlands, comparative studies have shown that greater species diversity frequently is associated with somewhat lower nutrient status, and that the more species-rich wetlands typically have moderate productivity and standing crop (Bedford et al. 1999). Recent concern about effects of nutrient enrichment in wetlands has stemmed from widespread observations of declines in species diversity associated with nutrient increases, especially increases in nitrogen from atmospheric deposition or from agricultural or urban runoff waters. Numerous studies have reported changes in species composition, declines in overall plant species diversity, loss of rare and uncommon species, and replacement of native species by exotics when nutrient enrichment occurs (Ehrenfeld and Schneider 1991; Morris 1991; Bedford et al. 1999; Noe et al. 2001; Woo and Zedler 2002; Childers et al. 2003).

NITROGEN AND PHOSPHORUS LIMITATION

In terrestrial ecosystems, plant growth is often limited by low nitrogen availability (Schlesinger 1997), partly as a result of limited storage in soil and litter. In freshwater wetlands where organic matter and nitrogen accumulate in the soil, plant growth is often limited by phosphorus (Chiang et al. 2000) or co-limited by both (Shaver et al. 1998). Nitrogen:phosphorus (N:P) ratios in plant tissues and soils have been used to identify thresholds of nutrient limitation in wetlands. For example, concern about the decline in species richness in European herbaceous wetlands led to extensive studies of soil and plant tissue nutrient levels in these systems (Koerselman and Meuleman 1996; Verhoeven et al. 1990). These authors concluded that sites with plant N:P <14 were N limited, sites with N:P >16 were P limited, and sites with N:P between 14 and 16 were co-limited by N and P. These European wetlands have been highly manipulated, however, and do not represent natural situations, nor do they reflect the situation in forested sites.

In a comprehensive review of wetland studies from North America, Bedford and colleagues (1999) sought to determine the extent to which different types of freshwater temperate wetlands follow this model. Their survey included herbaceous and forested wetlands occurring on both peat and mineral soils, and focused on the relationship between increased nutrient supply and plant community composition and diversity. For all wetland types, a strong pattern that emerged from their review was that plants growing in marshes almost always have live tissue N:P less than 14, suggesting N limitation (Fig. 6.15). Marsh plants also tend to have higher N and P concentrations than plants in other wetland types. All other wetland types have some sites where plant live tissue N:P

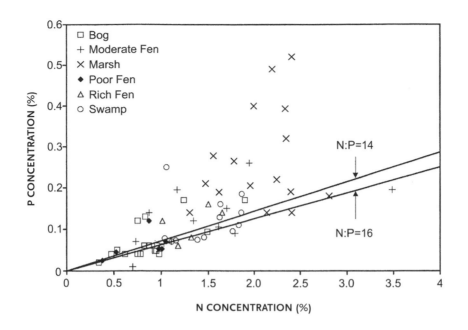

FIGURE 6.15

Phosphorus (P) and nitrogen (N) concentrations in live tissues of plants in temperate North American wetlands. After Bedford and associates (1999).

is less than 14 and some sites with N:P greater than 16, suggesting P limitation. Bogs and fens also have sites with plant tissue N:P between 14 and 16, suggesting co-limitation by both N and P.

Wetlands on mineral soils have significantly lower average soil N concentrations and N:P ratios than wetlands on peat substrates (Bedford et al. 1999), possibly because peat soils store comparatively large amounts of N in organic form, while mineral soils store comparatively large amounts of inorganic P. Significant portions of both of these soil nutrient pools may be relatively unavailable to plants, however. In a study of depressional wetlands of the southeastern United States, Craft and Chiang (2002) found that as much as 97% of total N was in recalcitrant organic forms, and up to 82% of soil P was bound to humic acids in the organic soils. Bedford and colleagues (1999) determined that if soil N:P ratios greater than 16 indicate P limitation, then the majority (70%) of temperate North American bogs and fens are P limited. If soil N:P ratios less than 14 indicate N limitation, the majority (61%) of temperate North American marshes and swamps are N limited. Using a different threshold for N and P limitation could, of course, affect these interpretations. For example, data from forested wetlands of the southeastern United States suggest that an N:P ratio above 12 in the litterfall indicates P limitation (Lockaby and Walbridge 1998). These generalizations about nutrient limitations should be treated with some caution, and it is likely that multiple nutrients are limiting in many wetlands.

Species richness in wetlands is obviously not related solely to nutrient availability, especially where the hydrologic regime can play a key role. However, the preponderance of evidence from ecosystems where humans have greatly enriched nutrient loading suggests a high potential for significant loss of plant species richness in wetlands with increasing eutrophication of the environment (Ehrenfeld and Schneider 1991; Bedford et al. 1999; Childers et al. 2003). The findings that plant communities in nutrient-rich wetland sites commonly have low species richness (e.g., Day et al. 1988; Shipley et al. 1991) further support this concern. Likewise, in a survey of Canadian wetlands ranging from low productivity wet meadows and riverine shorelines, to moderately productive fens and marshes, to high productivity cattail (*Typha* spp.) marshes, Moore and associates (1989) reported that infertile wetlands had a greater range of vegetation types, higher species richness, and many more rare species than did fertile wetlands.

EFFECTS OF NITROGEN AND PHOSPHORUS ENRICHMENT: THREE EXAMPLES

The best way to determine which nutrients are limiting in particular wetlands, or how nutrients affect species richness, is to manipulate nutrient availability and see what changes occur in the plant community. This can be done experimentally or may happen unintentionally as a result of human activity. There are numerous examples of the effects of increased N and P inputs on wetland productivity and/or species richness. Current rates of atmospheric nitrogen deposition in parts of Europe, for example, are great enough to alter the competitive relationships among plants and threaten wetland species adapted to infertile habitats (Morris 1991). Studies from ombrotrophic bogs in western Europe show that important peat-forming *Sphagnum* mosses are largely absent from bogs in areas where atmospheric deposition rates of nitrogen are high (Lee et al. 1986), and heathlands formerly dominated by shrubs have been converted to grasslands dominated by fast-growing nitrophilous grasses or grass-like species (Aerts and Berendse 1988). Increased productivity associated with higher fertility may be accompanied by increased rates of evapotranspiration, which can alter the hydrologic conditions in wetlands and may influence the direction of wetland community succession.

In the Everglades of southern Florida, plant communities shift along topographic gradients from deepwater sloughs to sawgrass *(Cladium jamaicense [C. mariscus ssp. jamaicense])* marshes to wet prairies to upland marl prairies (Gunderson 1994). Historically, low nutrient levels in the Everglades waters and peat substrates have been considered a primary factor in the persistence of the endemic Everglades flora (Davis 1991). Since the 1960s, agricultural runoff containing both P and N has resulted in a nutrient enrichment gradient in the northern part of the Everglades ecosystem (Koch and Reddy 1992; Craft et al. 1995). Coincident with increased nutrient loading, there has been a shift in Everglades plant communities. Native sawgrass and slough communities are being replaced by southern cattail *(Typha domingensis)* and broad-leaved cattail *(T. latifolia)*, especially in areas of high P enrichment. Sawgrass has high tissue N:P ratios, suggesting that this species has extremely low requirements for phosphorus and, consequently, may be able to use phosphorus under conditions of low availability (Daoust and Childers 1999). Experimental studies of N and P additions have shown that *Typha* has significantly higher growth rates and higher tissue concentrations of P under conditions of nutrient enrichment and increased water depth (Newman et al. 1996b). Thus, increased nutrient runoff from agricultural activities leads to enhanced growth and dominance (a form of exploitative competition) of cattail over sawgrass (Koch and Reddy 1992; Davis 1994; Newman et al. 1996b).

Coastal salt marshes are particularly vulnerable to eutrophication because estuaries concentrate nutrients from the entire upstream watershed (Valiela et al. 1992, 1997; Nixon 1995, 1997). Many experimental manipulations of nutrients have been conducted in salt marshes, with two general results. First, salt marsh plant communities are typically limited by N, not by P (Valiela and Teal 1974). Second, nitrogen enrichment often alters the competitive balance between different plant species, favoring tall plants like the low-marsh dominant *Spartina alterniflora* (cordgrass) and the high-marsh dominant *Phragmites australis* (reed), at the expense of shorter grasses and forbs (Levine et al. 1998; Emery et al. 2001, Pennings et al. 2002). A survey of marshes in Narragansett Bay, Rhode Island, compared sites with adjacent upland that was pristine (forested) or developed (forest had been cut down). Sites with developed uplands presumably received more nitrogen input from runoff. Developed sites had higher marsh plant biomass and were increasingly dominated by *S. alterniflora* and *P. australis* compared to sites without upland development, suggesting that localized coastal development might strongly alter salt marsh plant communities by affecting nutrient inputs to the marsh (Bertness et al. 2002).

CHARACTERISTICS OF SELECTED WETLANDS

Throughout the world, the types of plant communities that occur in wetlands are a result of climate, geomorphology and landscape position, soils (see Chapter 2), water source and chemistry, and numerous other environmental factors including disturbance. Wetlands are found on every continent except Antarctica and extend from the tropics to the tundra. Estimates of the extent of the world's wetlands generally range from around 7 to 9 million km², of which about 30% occur in tropical and 24.4% in subtropical regions, 11.6% in temperate areas, and 30% in boreal regions (Mitsch and Gosselink 2000). The classification and naming of wetland types is often confusing, as names have evolved over centuries in different parts of the world and often reflect regional or continental differences. Also, many wetland plant genera are globally ubiquitous (although they may be called by different common names in different regions), whereas other wetland plants are more locally constrained. The wetlands described here reflect a North American perspective and are chosen to be representative of the variety of wetland types rather than totally inclusive of the range of wetland plant communities that occur on this continent.

Northern bog and lake with ericaceous shrubs and conifer trees in northern Michigan. Courtesy of K. E. Francl.

Again, we have grouped them ecologically, according to major sources of water, with the understanding that sources and amount of water may vary considerably within a wetland type and that most wetlands receive water from more than one source.

WETLANDS WITH PREDOMINANTLY PRECIPITATION INPUTS

Northern Bogs

Bogs are freshwater wetlands that occur on acid peat deposits throughout much of the boreal zone of the world (Fig. 6.16). They are frequently part of a larger complex of peatlands that include fens, with readily apparent gradients of plant species distributions, biogeochemistry, and hydrology (Bridgham et al. 1996; see Fens and Related Peatlands below). Bogs are distinguished from fens, however, as they receive water and nutrients exclusively from precipitation (ombrogeneous). Precipitation inputs are greater than evapotranspiration losses, and slow decomposition of organic material under cold temperatures results in peat accumulation. Bog soils are organic, waterlogged, low in pH, and extremely low in available nutrients for plant growth (see Chapter 2). In addition, growing seasons are short. Thus, a specialized and unique flora occurs in this wetland habitat.

Mosses, primarily *Sphagnum*, are the most important peat-building plants in bogs. Bogs can be open *Sphagnum* moss peatlands, *Sphagnum*-sedge peatlands, *Sphagnum*-shrub peatlands, or bog forests; these types often form a mosaic across the landscape with other peatlands such as fens that are more influenced by groundwater. Plants often associated with *Sphagnum* in bogs include various sedges (*Carex* spp.), cottongrass *(Eriophorum vagi-natum)*, and a variety of ericaceous shrubs such as heather *(Calluna vulgaris)*, leatherleaf *(Chamaedaphne calyculata)*, cranberry and blueberry (species of *Vaccinium*), and Laborador tea *(Ledum groenlandicum)*. Trees such as spruce (*Picea* spp.) and larch or tamarack *(Larix larcina)* may occur in bogs, often stunted in growth to only a meter or two tall. In many northern peatlands, there is a considerable overlap of species along the hydrologic and chem-ical gradients from nutrient poor bogs to more mineral rich fens (see fens, below).

Vegetation development in many bogs may follow the model of hydrarch succession, or terrestrialization, at least to some degree (see Hydrarch Succession above). Through the buildup of soil organic matter, these peatlands have significant autogenic control over their development (Moore and Bellamy 1974). Primary production exceeds decomposi-tion of the peat substrates (Clymo et al. 1998), and the accumulation of peat affects hy-drologic conditions, chemistry, and plant community composition (Damman 1986; Bridgham et al. 1996; Bauer et al. 2003a). As peat builds up, it is often colonized by shrubs and then trees (see Fig. 6.3). Paleo-ecological evidence from several studies suggests a se-quence of plant associations from wet marshes to a *Sphagnum* bog or wet forest (Walker 1970). Other processes, such as paludification, when bogs exceed the basin boundaries and encroach on formerly dry land (e.g., Moore and Bellamy 1974; Bauer et al. 2003a; Yu et al. 2003), and fires (Kuhry 1994), complicate the patterns of bog successional devel-opment.

Sphagnum has the ability to acidify its environment, through the production of organic acids with high cation exchange capacity (Clymo and Hayward 1982). The acid environ-ment retards bacterial action and reduces decomposition rates, enabling peat accumula-tion. *Sphagnum* also maintains waterlogging in the substrate. Its compact growth habit and overlapping, rolled leaves form a wick that draws up water by capillarity. Many bog plants are adapted to waterlogged anaerobic environments by aerenchyma production, reduced oxygen consumption, and leakage of oxygen from the roots to the rhizosphere. Many bog plants also have adaptations to the low nutrient supply, such as evergreenness, sclerophylly (thickening of the plant epidermis to minimize grazing), uptake of amino acids as a nitrogen source, and high root biomass (Bridgham et al. 1996). In addition, carnivorous plants such as pitcher plants (*Sarracenia* spp.) and sundews (*Drosera* spp.) have the ability to trap and digest insects. Some bog plants, such as the sweet gale *(Myrica gale)* and alders (*Alnus* spp.) also carry out symbiotic bacterial nitrogen fixation in nod-ules on their roots.

Pocosins

Pocosins are evergreen shrub bogs (Fig. 6.17) restricted to the southeastern U.S. Atlantic Coastal Plain, chiefly in North Carolina. They occur on waterlogged, acid, nutrient-poor sandy or peaty soils (Bridgham and Richardson 1993; Richardson 2003) and are located primarily on flat topographic plateaus of the outer Coastal Plain (see Chapter 2). Their source of water is precipitation, and most of their water loss is through evapotranspiration

FIGURE 6.17

Short pocosin with ericaceous shrubs and pond pine *(Pinus serotina)* in eastern North Carolina.

during the summer and fall, although surface runoff also occurs, especially during winter and spring.

Evergreen shrub and tree species dominate in pocosins, and the composition and stature of the vegetation is related to depth of the peat and nutrient availability. On deep peat accumulations (>1 m), roots do not penetrate into the underlying mineral soils, and ombrotrophic shrub bogs develop (Otte 1981). Ericaceous shrubs in these communities, called *short pocosin,* include titi *(Cyrilla racemiflora),* fetterbush *(Lyonia lucida),* and honeycup *(Zenobia pulverulenta),* along with vines, particularly greenbriar *(Smilax* spp.). A sparse and often stunted canopy of pond pine *(Pinus serotina)* and loblolly bay *(Gordonia lasianthus)* may be present. Where organic substrates are shallower (approximately 50–100 cm), roots can penetrate into the underlying mineral soil, and the vegetation grows somewhat taller. Additional species in these tall pocosins may include red maple *(Acer rubrum),* black gum *(Nyssa sylvatica),* and sweetbay *(Magnolia virginiana).* Fire during drought may also be an important factor in pocosin community development. Shallow peat burns allow regeneration of pocosin species, although if the depth of the peat is reduced, roots of the recovering plants may be able to reach mineral soils. In an experimental study, Christenson and Wilbur (1995) reported dramatic post-fire shifts in species dominance that persisted after ten years.

Forestry, agriculture, and peat mining have had major impacts on pocosins in the 1960s and 1970s, and only approximately one-third of the original pocosins in North Carolina have remained relatively undisturbed (Richardson et al. 1981). It should be noted that pocosin vegetation also occurs in some Coastal Plain depressional wetlands (see Carolina bay section). These isolated depressional pocosins are coming under increased development

FIGURE 6.18
Carolina bay showing characteristic elliptical shape and zones of vegetation, Savannah River Site, South Carolina.

pressure since federal statutory authority over isolated wetlands was changed in 2001 (Richardson 2003; see Chapter 9).

Pocosins temporarily hold water, especially during winter and early spring, and then slowly release it to adjacent wetlands. Since they occur in close proximity to estuaries, this slow release of freshwater may stabilize the salinity of regional estuaries (Daniel 1981). Draining and development activities may greatly change these hydrologic outputs. Richardson and McCarthy (1994) reported that peat mining resulted in an increased runoff of approximately 30%. Furthermore, drainage and agricultural conversion have increased the turbidity and levels of phosphate, nitrate, and ammonia in adjacent estuaries (Sharitz and Gresham 1998).

Carolina Bays
Carolina bays are elliptical depressional wetlands (Fig. 6.18) that occur throughout the southeastern U.S. Atlantic Coastal Plain from New Jersey to northern Florida. On the Delmarva Peninsula, similar depressions are called *Delmarva bays*. These wetlands range in size from greater than 3,600 hectares to less than 1 hectare. Early estimates of their number were as high as 500,000 (Prouty 1952), although it is more likely that 10,000 to 20,000 currently exist (Richardson and Gibbons 1993). Carolina bays characteristically have no natural drainages into or from them, and overland water flows are minimal. Precipitation is their predominant source of water, and these shallow basins range from nearly permanently inundated to frequently dry, depending on their depth and local rainfall patterns. Most have highly variable hydroperiods (Sharitz 2003) and tend to be wetter in the winter and drier in the summer. Many small bays typically dry completely

during most summers and refill during fall and winter rains. Soils in the basins of Carolina bays range from highly organic to predominantly mineral, and most are underlain with sand and impervious clay layers that retard vertical water movement. This sandy clay hardpan is often assumed to limit interactions between surface and groundwater and result in a perched water table in the basin, although a few studies have shown some connection with shallow groundwater (Lide et al. 1995; Chmielewski 1996). The water in most bays is nutrient poor and acidic (pH range of 3.4 to 6.7) (Newman and Schalles 1990).

Plant communities in Carolina bays are influenced by soils and hydroperiod, and at least eleven vegetation types have been described (Schafale and Weakley 1990; Bennett and Nelson 1991). Pocosin communities, pond cypress *(Taxodium ascendens)* savannas, and pond cypress ponds are more common in bays on the lower Coastal Plain, which tend to have more organic soils. Herbaceous depression meadows are found on mineral soils in bays of the upper Coastal Plain, and nonalluvial swamps occur throughout. Various submersed and floating-leaved species such as bladderworts *(Utricularia* spp.), water lily *(Nymphaea odorata)*, and water shield *(Brasenia schreberi)* are often common in bay ponds. Depression meadows are dominated by graminoids, including grasses such as *Panicum, Leersia,* and *Dicanthelium;* sedges such as *Carex;* and rushes including *Juncus* and *Rhynchospora* as well as a variety of other herbaceous plants. Nonalluvial swamps may contain pond cypress as well as broad-leaved trees such as swamp tupelo *(Nyssa biflora)*, red maple *(Acer rubrum)*, and sweetgum *(Liquidambar styraciflua)*. Where pocosin vegetation occurs in bays, it is dominated by evergreen shrubs similar to that of the larger regional pocosins. Across this range of plant communities, Carolina bays have high plant species richness and contribute greatly to the regional biodiversity. The seed banks of some Carolina bays, especially depression meadows, are highly species rich (Kirkman and Sharitz 1994; Collins and Battaglia 2001; Mulhouse et al. 2005).

Rich zooplankton communities have been reported from Carolina bays (Mahoney et al. 1990), and a great variety of aquatic and semiaquatic insects live in these habitats (Taylor et al. 1999). These seasonal wetlands are critical breeding habitat for numerous species of amphibians, some of which are entirely dependent on these ecosystems (Gibbons and Semlitsch 1991) and may be found in huge numbers during the breeding season (Pechmann et al. 1991).

Many Carolina bays, especially the smaller ones, have been drained and converted to agriculture or other uses, and the great majority of those remaining have drainage ditches (Bennett and Nelson 1991). Since 2001, one of their most serious threats has come from a U.S. Supreme Court decision (see SWANCC decision in Chapter 9) which held that isolated nonnavigable waters are not protected under the Clean Water Act (Downing et al. 2003). As a result, many Carolina bays and other "geographically isolated wetlands" (Tiner 2003) are vulnerable to destruction unless other legal means of protection are developed (Sharitz 2003).

FIGURE 6.19
Cypress dome wetland with pond cypress *(Taxodium ascendens)* trees in Florida. Note that the tallest trees are in the center which is usually the deepest part of the wetland.

Cypress Domes

Cypress swamps found in nearly circular isolated depressions throughout the karst land-scape of Florida are called *cypress domes* due to the dome-like appearance of the tree canopy (Fig. 6.19). Trees are usually taller and grow faster in the center of the depressions than at the edge (Ewel and Wickenheiser 1988), although the reasons for this are not well under-stood. These depressions are formed by the dissolution of underlying limestone, and most are less than 10 hectares in size (Ewel 1998). Most of the water is received from precipi-tation, although surface inflows may also occur. Water may also move from these depres-sion ponds into shallow groundwater (Heimburg 1984). Pond cypress *(Taxodium ascen-dens)* and swamp tupelo *(Nyssa biflora)* are the dominant species, with slash pine *(Pinus elliottii)* co-dominant in partly drained cypress domes (Mitsch and Ewel 1979).

A major importance of these wetlands is in maintaining the regional biodiversity. Many are significant amphibian breeding grounds. In addition, since they hold water for long periods, cypress domes help prevent flooding of local areas and aid in groundwater dis-charge. Nearly all cypress domes in northern Florida have been harvested, although in many the trees have regenerated. The most detrimental human impact is caused by de-velopment and conversion to residential and commercial sites. Drainage of cypress domes also causes oxidation of the organic soils, land subsidence, and an increase in fire sus-ceptibility (Ewel 1998).

Prairie Potholes

One of the most important areas of freshwater wetlands in the world is the prairie pot-hole complex of North America (Mitsch and Gosselink 2000). These shallow depressional

FIGURE 6.20
Prairie pothole marsh wetland in the upper Midwest. From Tiner et al. (2002).

wetlands (Fig. 6.20) are found in Minnesota, Iowa, and the Dakotas in the United States, and in Alberta, Saskatchewan, and Manitoba in Canada. Although individual pothole marshes are usually small, they are regionally abundant. Between 4 and 10 million potholes are estimated to occur in Canada (Adams 1988), and about 2.3 million existed in the 1960s in North and South Dakota (Kantrud et al. 1989), although many had been drained by that time. Using assumptions from these estimates regarding abundance and size, van der Valk and Pederson (2003) suggested that these wetlands covered approximately 63,000 km^2 prior to drainage, a significant portion of the total inland area of the United States and Canada.

Precipitation is the primary source of water for prairie potholes. Annual precipitation can vary significantly from year to year, with periods of severe drought alternating with periods of above normal precipitation. Because of the small size of their catchments, changes in annual precipitation can result in major changes in annual water levels. Almost all prairie potholes also have some connection to groundwater (Winter 1989). They can be groundwater recharge sites, groundwater discharge sites, or groundwater flow-through wetlands. Because of these groundwater connections, prairie potholes are interlinked wetland complexes. In addition, during wet years when the basins fill, water may overflow on the surface from one basin to another. Such ephemeral surface-water connections may provide opportunity for seed dispersal or movement of aquatic animals among prairie potholes.

Herbaceous marshes containing robust perennial plants along with submersed species characterize prairie potholes throughout most of their range. Often, stands of emergent vegetation dominated primarily by one species such as cattail (*Typha*) will have high primary productivity (Table 6.1) (van der Valk and Davis 1978b). These marshes are among the richest in the world because of the fertile soils and warm summer climate. Natural changes in the composition and structure of the vegetation, however, are due to water-level changes caused by wet-dry cycles.

The vegetation of prairie potholes has been used as a model of predicting vegetation change associated with cyclic changes in hydrologic conditions (see Environmental Sieve Model). The periodic drawing down and refilling of these shallow basins results in changes in vegetation types and species that can be predicted from a knowledge of the seed bank, potential dispersal of plant propagules, and the conditions under which different species will germinate and become established (van der Valk 1981). The vegetation cycle results in four distinct stages: a dry marsh stage, a regenerating marsh stage, a degenerating marsh stage, and a lake stage (van der valk and Davis 1978b). During droughts when the substrate is exposed, perennial emergent species (e.g., *Typha*, *Scirpus*, *Sparganium eurycarpum*) and annual mud flat species (e.g., *Polygonum*, *Cyperus*, *Bidens cernua*) become established from the seed bank or from propagules dispersed into the basins. This dry marsh stage is followed by a wet marsh community when rainfall returns to normal and the basins refill. Under these conditions, the annual species that require exposed substrate for germination disappear, leaving the perennial emergents. Submersed species that can germinate under water (e.g., *Potamogeton*, *Najas flexilis*, *Myriophyllum sibiricum*) also appear. This wet marsh may persist for some years, but eventually the emergent vegetation begins to decline, perhaps due to the failure of some emergent species to continue to reproduce vegetatively (van der Valk and Davis 1978), or due to destruction by muskrats. This degenerating marsh may become a pond or shallow lake in which the dominant vegetation is primarily free-floating and submersed plants. This stage continues until drought again exposes the marsh bottom, allowing emergent and mud flat seeds to germinate. Details on animal response to changing pothole characteristics can be found in Chapter 7.

Prairie potholes are especially important ecologically and economically because they are the major waterfowl breeding area in North America. An estimated 50% to 80% of North America's game waterfowl species are produced in this region (Batt et al. 1989). Successful breeding requires availability of a variety of wetlands and wetland plants (for food and habitat) because no single wetland basin provides for all the reproductive needs of the birds through the breeding season (Swanson and Duebbert 1989). The existence of large numbers of small wetlands allows the birds to disperse across the landscape, thereby lowering their vulnerability to predation and diseases, and increasing the likelihood of successful reproduction and brood rearing (Kantrud et al. 1989).

About half the original prairie potholes in the Dakotas have been destroyed, mostly by agriculture, and more than 99% of Iowa's original marshes have been lost (Tiner 1984, 2003). Drainage of potholes significantly reduces their water-storage capacity, and destruction of natural vegetation buffers around remaining wetlands has significantly reduced valuable waterfowl nesting and rearing areas (Tiner 2003). Although prairie potholes are usually connected by groundwater flows during wet years, they are not connected to navigable waters, and thus their protection through federal regulations has been weakened as a result of the 2001 Supreme Court decision (see SWANCC decision in Chapter 9).

Other Ephemeral Wetlands

Many other types of wetlands have become established in poorly drained shallow depressions or on broad flats surrounded by upland. These wetlands often may dry during parts of the year, especially in summer when temperatures and evapotranspiration are high, and fill with water again following fall and winter rains or spring snowmelt in the North. Thus, their hydroperiods may fluctuate from wet to dry. Many of these depressional wetlands have been referred to as "isolated wetlands" because they do not appear to have well-defined surface water connections to other water bodies. Yet, many of these wetlands are hydrologically connected to other wetlands through groundwater flows or by infrequent surface spillovers. It has been suggested that "geographically isolated wetlands" may better describe these systems (Tiner 2003).

These wetlands may be naturally formed or be the result of human activities. In addition to the previously mentioned northern bogs, cypress domes, prairie potholes, and Carolina bays, other naturally occurring geographically isolated wetlands in North America include playas, vernal pools, sinkhole wetlands, salt flat lakes and wetlands, rainwater basin and sandhills wetlands, and other ponds. Tiner (2003) listed nearly thirty types of isolated wetlands in the United States, some of which are widely distributed and others which are specific to a particular geographic region. We describe here the ecological characteristics and importance of several of these wetlands. We also describe threats to these wetlands and their losses, where known. It should be noted that, in addition to the specific threats mentioned, many of these geographically isolated wetlands may no longer have legal protection, as discussed for Carolina bays and prairie potholes.

PLAYAS.   Playas are shallow recharge wetlands found in deserts and semiarid prairie areas of the southern Great Plains. They range in area from less than 1 hectare to greater than 250 hectares and average 6.3 hectares (Guthery and Bryant 1982). There are probably more than 30,000 of these small circular depressions, which are thought to result from a combination of dissolution of subsurface materials and wind action (Haukos and Smith 2003). Playas receive most of their water from rainfall and local runoff (including irrigation water), and it is rare for them to be connected to groundwater sources (Haukos and Smith 1994). These wetlands are usually dry in late winter, early spring, and late summer; multiple wet-dry cycles during a single growing season are common.

Compared to many other isolated wetlands, less is known about the ecology of playas. They are considered to be keystone ecosystems serving as biological refugia and critical sites of biodiversity in this semiarid and intensively agricultural region, however (Smith and Haukos 2002). More than 340 plant species have been recorded in playas (Haukos and Smith 1997), although most of these species are commonly found in other wetland

and terrestrial habitats. Due to the rapidly changing environmental conditions, the flora is dominated by annuals and short-lived perennials. In a survey of 224 playa wetlands, Smith and Haukos (2002) found that only 38% of plant species present in the early growing season were still present late in the season. Thus, the vegetation is influenced by the composition of the seed bank and the environmental conditions that regulate germination and seedling growth. In addition, the land surrounding most playas is cultivated, resulting in an increase in annual and exotic species (Smith and Haukos 2002).

Playas also support a broad array of bird species and are vital overwintering, migration, and breeding habitat for waterfowl in the region (Haukos and Smith 2003). They are recognized as important for invertebrates and amphibians as well. All flora and fauna occupying playas must be adapted to the fluctuating environmental conditions, and any alteration of the hydroperiod may have drastic effects on species persistence. Unfortunately, many playas have been affected by sedimentation as a result of cultivation and erosion of the surrounding landscape. This has caused a dramatic decrease in playa hydroperiod and altered floral and faunal communities (Haukos and Smith 1994). In addition, many playas also have been impacted by pit excavation, road construction, industrial and municipal wastewater, overgrazing, feedlot runoff, urban development, and deliberate filling (Haukos and Smith 2003).

VERNAL POOLS.   *Vernal pools,* broadly defined as ephemeral wetlands that form in permanent basins during the cooler part of the year but which dry during the summer months, are distributed throughout the world (Zedler 2003). These wetlands are largely collectors of rainfall and melt water, although groundwater inputs may occur in some. Depending on climate, geology, hydrology, and other factors, vernal pools may be dominated by trees and shrubs, by marsh and wet meadow species, by aquatic plants, or they may be devoid of vegetation (Tiner 2003). In the United States, vernal pools are particularly abundant on the Pacific Coast and in the glaciated landscapes of the North and Northeast. Although most vernal pools have been poorly studied, two types, west coast vernal pools and woodland vernal pools, have received greater attention because of their importance as habitats for rare plants and for amphibians.

West coast vernal pools, which occur in mound and swale topography, may be filled by winter rains characteristic of the region's Mediterranean climate, and then dry to extreme desiccating soil conditions during the summer (Zedler 2003). The isolated nature and unpredictable flooding of these wetlands promote endemism, thereby creating unique flora and fauna and making these vernal pools vital sites for the conservation of biodiversity (Tiner 2003). The flora of vernal pools in California contains numerous federally listed threatened and endangered species as well as state-endangered and rare species. The advantage of the ephemeral wetland habitat for these species is that it limits plant competition (Zedler 2003). The presence of standing water excludes or limits the growth of plants of the surrounding uplands, but likewise the drying excludes or limits species of permanent marshes. In the past, west coast vernal pools were used for grazing

FIGURE 6.21
Woodland vernal pool in January at the Savannah
River Site, South Carolina. Courtesy of D. E. Scott.

and other forms of agriculture. More recently, population growth and corresponding urbanization in California have greatly reduced the extent of these ecosystems, and the largest
remaining complexes are found in the open lands of military facilities.

Woodland vernal pools (Fig. 6.21) occur throughout forested regions of the United States.
These are seasonal ponds that are inundated during the wet season and typically dry out
almost every year. The flora may consist primarily of the surrounding forest trees and shrub
species as well as various grasses and herbs, depending in part on hydroperiod and canopy
openness, and vegetation characteristics are highly variable among these woodland pools
(Palik et al. 2001). Because predatory fish are not present, these seasonal wetlands can be
extremely productive sites for macroinvertebrate and amphibian reproduction, and several salamander species are entirely dependent on vernal pools for breeding (Gibbs 1993;
Semlitsch and Bodie 1998; Kenney and Burne 2000). While the vernal pool breeders require such habitats for reproduction and growth of larvae, adult salamanders and frogs
spend their lives in the surrounding woodland. Thus, the protection of vernal pools and
the surrounding forest is important for the conservation of biodiversity (Semlitsch and Bodie
1998; Kenney and Burne 2000). Unfortunately, since these pools are usually very small,
they are often destroyed by development activities.

SINKHOLE WETLANDS. These wetlands typically occur on karst landscapes where dissolution of the underlying limestone causes a slumping of the land surface. Cypress domes
of Florida are a well-known example (see earlier discussion), but sinkhole lakes and wetlands
occur in many other regions of the United States. Some receive groundwater discharge and

are connected to an intricate underground network of fissures and subterranean streams, while others are influenced primarily by precipitation and surface run-off. The vegetation varies geographically and in response to hydrologic conditions and other factors. Plant communities may be diverse and contain regionally and nationally rare species (Tiner 2003). Like other geographically isolated wetlands, they may be productive amphibian breeding grounds and feeding places for reptiles and other animals. One of the threats to sinkhole wetlands and their biota is groundwater withdrawal for irrigation or human consumption, which affects their drainage and may result in drying up of water sources (Tiner 2003).

SALT FLAT WETLANDS. In the Great Basin region and other arid regions of the western United States, salt flat lakes and wetlands are found at the ends of drainage systems. In northern areas where precipitation input equals or exceeds evapotranspiration, permanent lakes (such as the Great Salt Lake) occur, but in southern areas where evapotranspiration exceeds the input of precipitation, salt flats occur. These salt flats contain water for short periods in winter and spring, and become dry plains in summer. Both salt lakes and salt flats are important sources of food for migratory birds as well as for resident nesting species (Jehl 1994; Tiner 2003). Degradation of wet meadows may result from overgrazing, and groundwater withdrawal has adversely affected the hydrology of some of these wetlands (Tiner 2003)

RAINWATER BASIN AND SANDHILLS WETLANDS. In Nebraska, aeolian forces have created depressional wetlands in the Rainwater Basin in the south-central part of the state and in the Sandhills region of the northern and central areas. The Rainwater Basin wetlands depend on precipitation and overland runoff for their water supply (Frankforter 1996), and most are marshes, wet meadows, or ponds (Tiner 2003). Lakes and marshes in the Sandhills region are interconnected with the regional groundwater (LaBaugh 1986b; Winter 1986). Both Rainwater Basin and Sandhills wetlands have been identified as wetlands of international importance to waterfowl and other wildlife. Millions of waterfowl in the Central Flyway use these wetlands during spring migration (Gersib 1991); an abundance of aquatic invertebrates and fish provide a food source for these migratory birds. Agricultural activities, such as drainage and groundwater pumping, have been major causes of loss or degradation of these wetlands. At least 66% of the original area of Rainwater Basin wetlands has been lost (LaGrange 2001), as have more than 30% of the original Sandhills wetlands (Erickson and Leslie 1987).

WETLANDS THAT RECEIVE MORE GROUNDWATER INPUTS

Fens and Related Peatlands
Peatlands are wetland ecosystems that accumulate carbon because primary productivity exceeds decomposition, and dead organic material builds up as peat. Most of the global

peatland area is found in boreal and subarctic zones of the Northern Hemisphere (Gorham 1990), although peatlands also exist in southern locations (pocosins, southern Appalachian fens). The terminology applied to peatlands is often confusing. Throughout the world, many different names have been given to them, such as bog, fen, moor, mire, marsh, swamp, and heath. Bedford and Godwin (2003) compared several current definitions of fens and found differences that reflect both the scientific traditions and the region of the world from which they developed. There also are numerous classifications and descriptions of peatlands associated with their hydrologic and chemical characteristics, and their plant community composition (see Bridgham et al. 1996).

Peatlands are generally classified into ombrogenous (rain fed) and geogenous (receiving water from the regional water table or other outside sources). Ombrogenous peatlands vegetated largely with *Sphagnum* mosses and geogenous peatlands vegetated mostly with graminoid species (such as grasses, sedges, and rushes) are commonly called *bogs* and *fens,* respectively. Geogenous fens may be further divided into (1) limnogeneous peatlands developing along lakes and slow-flowing streams; (2) topogeneous peatlands developing in topographic depressions, with a portion of their water derived from the regional groundwater table; and (3) soligeneous peatlands that are affected by water from outside sources percolating through or over surface peat (Bridgham et al. 1996). It should be noted that there are numerous other classification schemes for these wetlands. There is also strong overlap among all these peatland categories in environmental conditions, such as soil or water pH, and in plant species. Thus, Bridgham and associates (1996) recommended that the term *peatland* be used for all these systems to reduce confusion. They suggested that the terms *bog* and *fen* be used only in a broad sense, with bogs referring to acidic, low alkalinity peatlands that are typically dominated by *Sphagnum* mosses, various species of ericaceous shrubs, and/or conifers such as spruces or pines. Similarly, fens should refer broadly to somewhat less acidic, more alkaline peatlands dominated by graminoid species, brown mosses, taller shrubs, and coniferous and/or deciduous trees (Bridgham et al. 1996). Bog and fen remain common in the peatland literature, however (e.g., Aerts et al 1999; Wheeler and Proctor 2000; Bauer et al. 2003a; Yu et al. 2003), and are used in this chapter (see Northern Bogs section).

The defining characteristic of all types of fens is the importance of groundwater inputs in determining their hydrology, chemistry, and vegetation (Bedford and Godwin 2003). Thus, fens occur where climate and the hydrologic and geologic setting sustains flows of mineral rich groundwater to the plant rooting zone. They may develop on slopes, in depressions, or on flats. The relatively constant supply of groundwater maintains saturated conditions most of the time, and the water chemistry reflects the mineralogy of the surrounding and underlying substrates. Fens may be slightly acidic (poor fens), circumneutral (rich fens), or strongly alkaline (extremely rich fens). In an extensive survey of North American fens, Bedford and Godwin (2003) reported pH values ranging from 3.5 to 8.4.

Peatland development is a dynamic process (e.g., Heinselman 1970; Kuhry 1994; Wheeler and Proctor 2000; Yu et al. 2001, 2003; Bauer et al. 2003a) that is controlled by

FIGURE 6.22
Fen peatland in Canada. Courtesy of K. E. Francl.

multiple autogenic and allogenic factors, as previously described for northern bogs. Climate, physiography, and peat accumulation all play a role. Terrestrialization (filling in of shallow lakes) and paludification (encroachment of bogs over formerly dry land) are the major processes in peatland development. The result is not a stable, uniform landscape, but rather a diverse mosaic of different landform types (Heinselman 1970), which leads to a mosaic of vegetation associations.

The vegetation of fens (Fig. 6.22) is generally dominated by bryophytes, sedges, grasses, dicotyledonous herbs, and coniferous trees. Vegetation of poor fens resembles that of bogs, with *Sphagnum* mosses and ericaceous shrubs. Rich fens, however, are dominated by sedges and brown mosses (mostly of the Amblestegiaceae), with many distinctive species of dicotyledonous herbs (Bedford and Godwin 2003). Tussock cottongrass *(Eriophorum vaginatum)*, sedges (genera of the Cyperaceae, especially *Carex*) and shrubs such as heather *(Calluna vulgaris)*, leatherleaf *(Chamaedaphne calyculata)*, Laborador tea *(Ledum groenlandicum)*, and cranberry and blueberry (*Vaccinium* spp.) may occur. In forested peatlands, trees such as spruce (*Picea* spp.) and tamarack or larch *(Larix laricina)* may be found, often in stunted condition. Individually and collectively, fens are among the most floristically diverse of all wetland types, supporting rare and uncommon bryophytes and vascular plant species (Bedford and Godwin 2003).

In a description of the Lake Agassiz peatlands of northern Minnesota, Heinselman (1970) described seven vegetation associations: (1) a rich swamp forest dominated by northern red cedar *(Thuja occidentalis)* with a shrub layer of alder *(Alnus incana)* and hummocks of *Sphagnum,* (2) a poor swamp forest dominated by tamarack with an understory of bog birch *(Betula pumila)* and *Sphagnum* hummocks, (3) a cedar string bog and fen complex with ridges of northern red cedar and treeless hollows of sedges (mostly *Carex* spp.) between them, (4) a larch string bog and fen complex in which tamarack dominated the ridges, (5) a black spruce *(Picea marina)* forest with a carpet of feathermoss *(Pleurozium)* and other mosses, (6) a *Sphagnum*-black spruce-leatherleaf bog forest of stunted black spruce and a heavy evergreen shrub layer over *Sphagnum* mosses, and (7) a *Sphagnum*-leatherleaf-laurel-spruce heath in which a low shrub layer including laurel *(Kalmia* spp.) and stunted spruce grew over a continuous blanket of *Sphagnum* mosses. These peatlands are typical of many of those in North America.

Southern mountain fens are uncommon wetlands located in the Appalachian highlands of the southern United States. Often colloquially called "bogs," these small wetlands (usually <1 ha in size) occur in headwater streams, on slopes intercepting the water table, in stream valleys no longer subject to flooding, and in isolated areas over resistant rock strata (Walbridge 1994). Most have organic soils. Typical plant communities include *Sphagnum* and other bryophytes, graminoids such as grasses, sedges *(Carex* spp.), rushes *(Juncus* spp.) and beakrushes *(Rhynchospora* spp.), an assortment of herbaceous species, shrubs, and trees such as red maple *(Acer rubrum)* and white pine *(Pinus strobus)*. There are probably fewer than five hundred of these mountain fen sites remaining (Moorhead and Rossell 1998), and many have been destroyed by grazing, logging, mining, or other development practices (Richardson and Gibbons 1993).

Peatlands are important wetland ecosystems for several reasons, including their vast extent across boreal regions. They are one of the largest "terrestrial" carbon reservoirs. Northern peatlands have accumulated about 400 to 500 Gt (1 Gt $= 10^{15}$ g) of carbon during the Holocene (Gorham 1991; Clymo et al. 1998; Roulet 2000; Vitt et al. 2000). Their extent, high-latitude location, and the large size of their carbon pool raise concerns that they may become significant sources for atmospheric carbon under a changing climate (Moore et al. 1998; Schindler 1998; see Chapter 12).

The Everglades

The Everglades (Fig. 6.23) is perhaps one of the most recognized wetlands in the world, its notoriety derived from the wealth of its biotic heritage as well as the magnitude of factors that threaten its resources (Gunderson and Loftus 1993). Occurring in the subtropical southern part of the Florida peninsula, the Everglades historically covered a vast area of about 1.2 million hectares; about half has now been drained for agriculture and development (Davis et al. 1994a). The bedrock substrate underlying most of the Everglades is limestone, of marine and freshwater origin, and the soil substrate is predominantly peat, formed during the last 5,000 years (Gleason and Stone 1994). It is the largest and most important freshwater subtropical peatland in North America (Koch and Reddy 1992).

Precipitation is the main route by which water enters the Everglades ecosystem (Duever et al. 1994). Thus, waters of the historic Everglades were probably very low in dissolved nitrogen and phosphorus (oligotrophic), but relatively high in calcium and

FIGURE 6.23
Everglades freshwater marsh and tree island complex in southern Florida. Courtesy of South Florida
Water Management District.

bicarbonate (Flora and Rosendahl 1982). Approximately 60% of the rain falls between
June and September, produced primarily by localized thunderstorms and, at times, tropical cyclones. The hydroperiod is quite variable, with water levels declining slowly during
the winter and droughts common during the dry spring months when evapotranspiration is high. Lake Okeechobee, to the north, is linked hydrologically with the Everglades
by groundwater connections and, before extensive levee construction, by overland flow
during high water periods. The topography of this region is very flat, and water moves
southward through the Everglades marshes at velocities ranging from approximately 0
to 1 cm/sec (Rosendahl and Rose 1982). This slow southerly flow of water inspired Marjorie
Stoneman Douglas (1947) to call the Everglades a "River of Grass."

The Everglades flora has temperate, tropical, and endemic taxa as a result of its climate and location. Major freshwater wetland plant communities include marshes and
wet prairies, forested communities (tree islands), and ponds and sloughs with little emergent vegetation (Gunderson 1994) (Fig. 6.23). These communities are arrayed in a mosaic influenced by hydrologic and substrate conditions.

Sawgrass *(Cladium jamaicense [C. mariscus ssp. jamaicense])* is the most common and
widespread species in the Everglades marshes. A robust, rhizomatous, perennial sedge
rather than a grass, as its name implies, sawgrass is well adapted to the low nutrient conditions as well as to flooding and also burning during droughts. Throughout much of the
Everglades, sawgrass marshes are interspersed with shallow sloughs that contain spikerush
(Eleocharis spp.) and floating-leaved aquatic plants such as water lily *(Nymphaea odorata)*,
yellow pond-lily *(Nuphar lutea)*, and submerged aquatics including bladderworts *(Utricularia* spp.). The submerged portions of most aquatic macrophytes in the Everglades are

covered with periphyton (a community of many species of microalgae, including calcareous species), which serve as a food web base, as well as oxygenating the water column and building calcite mud sediment (Browder et al. 1994; Gaiser et al. 2005a, 2005b). Periphyton standing crop is much greater in the Everglades than in other wetlands (Turner et al. 1999).

Wet prairies of graminoid species develop on peat or marl (limestone) substrates, and each soil type has distinct plant communities. Those on peat commonly are dominated by species of spikerush (*Eleocharis* spp.), beakrush (*Rhynchospora* spp.), or maidencane (*Panicum hemitomon*). Prairies on marl substrates are dominated by sawgrass and muhly grass (*Muhlenbergia* spp.). Tree islands are clumps of bayhead/swamp forest taller than the surrounding marsh. Canopy species include redbay (*Persea borbonia*) and sweetbay (*Magnolia virginiana*) as well as dahoon holly (*Ilex cassine*) and pond apple (*Annona glabra*), with a dense layer of shrubs underneath. Found throughout many parts of the Everglades marshes, these tree islands are often in the shape of an elongated teardrop with the long axis parallel to the main direction of flow.

The historic Everglades were hydrologically continuous. Major parts of the Everglades wetlands now have been drained for agriculture and urbanization, and the water flows in the remaining areas are fragmented by canals, large water conservation areas, and roads and drainage ditches and pipes. Today, only 0.62 million hectares of the original Everglades remain (Davis et al. 1994a), and these areas are threatened by a combination of drainage and altered hydroperiods caused by human development, and pollution from upstream agricultural activities. In particular, increased phosphorus loading from agricultural runoff in the northern parts of the remaining Everglades may be promoting an increase in cattail (*Typha domingensis*) and a decline in sawgrass in the sawgrass marshes. Increased nutrient loading may also be associated with a decline in the periphyton communities, which prosper in nutrient-poor waters (Newman et al. 1996b; Noe et al 2001; Childers et al. 2003; Gaiser et al. 2005a). Many exotic invasive plant species also threaten the plant communities of the Everglades. Among the most aggressive and difficult to control are melaleuca (*Melaleuca quinquenervia*), a pioneering Australian tree species; Brazilian peppertree (*Schinus terebinthifolius*); old world climbing fern (*Lygodium microphyllum*), which overtops and smothers Everglades tree islands; and torpedo grass (*Panicum repens*), which has replaced large areas of marsh plants in Lake Okeechobee (White 1994). Beginning in the late 1990s, a major restoration of the Everglades was initiated by the U.S. Army Corps of Engineers and the state of Florida to try to restore some of the hydrologic integrity of the Everglades (Comprehensive Everglades Restoration Plan 2000).

Atlantic White Cedar Swamps
These forests, dominated by *Chamaecyparis thyoides*, occur within a wide climatic range along the Atlantic and Gulf of Mexico coastline areas of the United States from Maine to Mississippi. Throughout their range, they are uncommon, however, having decreased

historically in area and in biological diversity (Laderman 1989). They are most abundant in the southeastern New Jersey Pine Barrens, in the Dismal Swamp of Virginia and North Carolina, and along several river systems in northwest Florida (Sheffield et al. 1998).

Atlantic white cedar swamps may occur in isolated basins, along lake shorelines, shoreward of coastal tidal marshes, on river floodplains, or on slopes (Laderman 1989). Hydrologic conditions can vary considerably among these forests, although flooding typically occurs in late winter and early spring, sometimes for extended periods. White cedar swamps occurring in basins, with precipitation as the major source of water, are usually oligotrophic. Those in other locations, however, may receive significant groundwater and are more nutrient rich (Laderman 1989). Most occur on peat soils of relatively low pH (2.5–6.7) (Day 1984; Whigham and Richardson 1988; Laderman 1989; Ehrenfeld and Schneider 1991). Under these conditions, *Chamaecyparis thyoides* may grow in dense, almost monospecific stands. Other canopy species commonly associated with Atlantic white cedar are red maple *(Acer rubrum)*, black gum *(Nyssa sylvatica)*, and sweetbay *(Magnolia virginiana)*, and pines such as loblolly *(Pinus taeda)*, white *(P. strobus)*, or pitch *(P. rigida)*.

Microsite conditions associated with seedling establishment and the regeneration niche (Grubb 1977) may affect successional processes in these forests. In most Atlantic white cedar wetlands, there is pronounced hummock-hollow microtopography, with hummock heights ranging from 70 to 100 or more centimeters (Ehrenfeld 1995a). These microtopographic features arise from woody debris around which sediments, organic matter, and dense mats of fine roots develop. It has been suggested that this microtopography, especially as it affects moisture availability, may be an important factor affecting seedling recruitment of *Chamaecyparis* (Ehrenfeld 1995a; Allison and Ehrenfeld 1999; Gengarelly and Lee 2005). Elevation above the water table influences soil moisture, pH, and redox potential. In several field studies, *Chamaecyparis* seedling recruitment has been found to be greatest at intermediate elevations on the hummocks (Ehrenfeld 1995b; Gengarelly and Lee 2005). Seedling establishment may be unsuccessful at the tops of hummocks and at low elevations in the hollows because of drought and prolonged flooding, respectively (Ehrenfeld 1995b). Thus, the autogenic process of hummock formation may aid forest regeneration.

Relatively open conditions are necessary for healthy growth of *Chamaecyparis* seedlings (Laderman 1989), and several studies have indicated poor seedling recruitment under the closed canopy in dense stands (Motzkin et al. 1993; Stoltzfus and Good 1998). This suggests that natural autogenic processes in which *Chamaecyparis* seedlings are replaced by more shade-tolerant species such as red maple may play a role in the decline of these forests. From age structure analyses and paleo-ecological investigations of an old-growth Atlantic white cedar swamp, Motzkin and associates (1993) determined that extensive *Chamaecyparis* establishment occurred during distinct episodes following disturbance events. Prior to European settlement, fires frequently destroyed existing Atlantic white cedar stands but allowed for subsequent regeneration from seed stored in the upper soil horizon or from surviving trees. Thus, allogenic factors associated with disturbances have

FIGURE 6.24

Southern deepwater swamp with baldcypress *(Taxodium distichum)* trees in Congaree National Park, South Carolina.

also been important in influencing the development of Atlantic white cedar swamps (Motzkin et al. 1993).

Much of the historic decrease in *Chamaecyparis thyoides* stands is attributable to selective logging for their valuable lumber, however, and to conversion to agricultural, industrial, or commercial uses (Motzkin et al. 1993). Up to 50% of the Atlantic white cedar area of North Carolina was cut between 1870 and 1890, for example (Frost 1987). Herbivory of seedlings and saplings by deer often has an impact on stand regeneration, and deer browse can destroy young stands (Laderman 1989). Swamps that have frequent, low-level disturbances such as suburban runoff and the presence of roads generally have few *Chamaecyparis* seedlings and lack soil conditions conducive to their growth (Ehrenfeld and Schneider 1991). It is likely, however, that adjacent land uses are more important than regional land-use patterns in affecting the runoff of sediments and contaminants into these swamps (Laidig and Zampella 1999).

WETLANDS THAT RECEIVE MORE SURFACE WATER INPUTS

Southern Deepwater Swamps

Deepwater swamps, primarily baldcypress-water tupelo *(Taxodium distichum–Nyssa aquatica)* forests (Fig. 6.24), are freshwater ecosystems that have standing water for most or all of the year (Penfound 1952). They are generally found along rivers and streams of the Atlantic Coastal Plain from Delaware to Florida, along the Gulf Coastal Plain to southeastern Texas, and up the Mississippi River to southern Illinois (Conner and Buford 1998). (Other southern deepwater swamps include cypress domes; see earlier section.) On river floodplains, these baldcypress-water tupelo swamps are found in meander scrolls created as the rivers change course (ridge and swale topography), oxbow lakes created as meanders become separated from the main river channel, and sloughs that are areas of ponded water in meander scrolls and backwater swamps (Brinson et al. 1981).

The major hydrologic inputs to these deepwater swamps are overflow from flooding rivers and runoff from surrounding uplands. In addition, larger and deeper topographic features may impound water from rainfall and may be connected with the regional groundwater. Even though deepwater swamps are commonly flooded, water levels may vary seasonally and annually. High water levels typically coincide with winter-spring rains and melting snow runoff. Low levels occur in the summer from high evapotranspiration and low rainfall (Wharton and Brinson 1979). During extreme droughts, even deepwater swamp forests may lack surface water for extended periods (Mancil 1969). Some peat development is characteristic of these deepwater ecosystems because of slow decomposition rates (Conner and Buford 1998). Since many deepwater swamps are found along the floodplains of rivers, their soils generally have adequate nutrients, and these forests are relatively productive (Table 6.1). However, anaerobic conditions associated with continuous flooding may limit the availability to plants of several nutrients and reduce their productivity (Wharton et al. 1982; Megonigal et al. 1997).

Southern deepwater swamps have unique plant communities that either depend on or adapt to the almost continuously wet conditions (Fig. 6.24). Dominant canopy species include baldcypress, water tupelo, and swamp tupelo *(Nyssa biflora)*. These species grow together or in pure stands. Other species that may occur include red maple *(Acer rubrum)*, black willow *(Salix nigra)*, swamp cottonwood *(Populus heterophylla)*, and green and pumpkin ash *(Fraxinus pennsylvanica* and *F. profunda)* in the overstory and buttonbush *(Cephalanthus occidentalis)*, water elm *(Planera aquatica)*, Carolina ash *(F. caroliniana)*, and Virginia sweetspire *(Itea virginica)* in the understory (Sharitz and Mitsch 1993).

Baldcypress wood is valuable for a variety of uses because of its durability and the ease with which it can be worked. The great majority of cypress swamps were logged during the late 1800s and early 1900s, and there has been a general decline in area of this forest type since then (Dahl et al. 1991). Establishment of these swamp species requires extended dry periods for germination and for seedlings to grow tall enough to survive future flooding (Johnson and Shropshire 1983; Wilhite and Toliver 1990). Growing season floods that submerge seedlings for extended periods will cause them to die (Mattoon 1916; Sharitz et al. 1990). In coastal areas, especially in Louisiana and Mississippi, eustatic sea level rise and land subsidence, coupled with coastal levee construction, are causing a significant increase in water levels in deepwater cypress swamps (Gosselink 1984). Most of this coastal area is experiencing an apparent water level rise of about 1 meter per century (Salinas et al. 1986). This inhibits the natural regeneration of baldcypress and limits opportunities for planting and long-term maintenance of coastal deepwater swamps. In addition, saltwater intrusion into these coastal wetland forests reduces their productivity and may cause mortality (Pezeshki et al. 1990; Conner 1994; Allen et al. 1996).

Riverine (Floodplain) Wetlands

Floodplain wetlands are riparian ecosystems in which the soil moisture is influenced by the adjacent river or stream. These wetlands may be narrow and relatively steep along small headwater streams in mountainous or hilly regions such as the U.S. Pacific Northwest, or broad and nearly flat as along the floodplains of large rivers of the southeastern Coastal Plain. Floodplain wetlands connect the river or stream with the adjacent upland. Thus, they receive water from over-bank flooding of the river or stream as well groundwater in some instances, and surface runoff and groundwater flows from the upland side. Local precipitation also contributes but is usually less important as a water or nutrient source. Typically, floodplain wetlands are long corridors that are functionally connected through the movement of water and materials such as nutrients and organic matter between upstream and downstream sites and between the adjacent upland and aquatic ecosystems (e.g., Vannote et al. 1980; Brinson et al. 1981; Johnson and Lowe 1985; Junk et al. 1989; see Chapter 11). Since they receive nutrient-rich waters, floodplain wetlands are often very productive (Table 6.1).

The greatest expanses of floodplain wetlands in the United States are in the South central, Southeast, and North central regions, along large river systems such as the Mississippi and its tributaries, the Atchafalaya (a major distributary of the Mississippi), Apalachicola, Tomigbee, and other rivers that drain into the Gulf of Mexico, and major rivers of the southern Atlantic Coastal Plain such as the Roanoke, Savannah, Altamaha, and others. Approximately 58% of the wetland forest area of the contiguous United States is in the southern regions, 22% in the North central, and 14% in the Northeast (Abernathy and Turner 1987), although large amounts of the original wetland forests have been cut (Dahl 1990). Climatic conditions and regional topography influence the stream and floodplain characteristics in different regions of the country. In the mesic climate of the Southeast, for example, precipitation exceeds evapotranspiration. Streams and rivers in this environment usually flow continuously and are seasonally pulsed. In upstream reaches of these southern rivers, gradients of slope may be steep to moderate and floodplains relatively narrow, but in the downstream reaches, slope gradients are flat and the floodplains are broad (Putnam et al. 1960; Wharton et al. 1982). In the Northeast, conditions are also mesic, and with the exception of headwater streams in areas such as the Appalachian Mountains, floodplains tend to be relatively wide (Cronk and Fennessy 2001). In the Northwest, evapotranspiration is equal to or slightly higher than precipitation. Streams in this region are often somewhat flashy, with temporally unpredictable peak flows. Stream gradients are steep upstream and more moderate downstream, and floodplain widths range from very narrow to relatively wide (Vannote et al. 1980). In the Southwest, however, the climate is arid, and evapotranspiration greatly exceeds precipitation. Streams in this environment tend to be very flashy, with temporally unpredictable floods and low mean flows. Along a single southwestern river, conditions may shift from wet to mesic to xeric. Their floodplains range from narrow to broad but are often dry downstream (Graf 1988).

FIGURE 6.25
Bottomland hardwood forest with large cherrybark oak *(Quercus pagoda)* and sweetgum *(Liquidambar styraciflua)* trees on a river floodplain in Congaree National Park, South Carolina.

Plant communities on floodplains are influenced by riverine processes such as timing, depth, and duration of over-bank flooding as well as by regional climate conditions. Since the majority of floodplain wetlands in the United States occur in the southern regions, we will give them greater emphasis. However, the vegetation of floodplains in other regions is briefly described.

Northeastern floodplain forests are usually hardwood. Species composition changes from east to west across the region and varies depending on specific site characteristics. Common dominant canopy species include maples such as red maple *(Acer rubrum)* and silver maple *(A. saccharinum)*, along with American elm *(Ulmus americana)*, American beech *(Fagus grandifolia)*, green ash *(Fraxinus pennsylvanica)*, sycamore *(Platanus occidentalis)*, and box elder *(A. negundo)*. Cottonwood *(Populus deltoides)* and willow (*Salix* spp.) are often found in low elevations (Lindsey et al. 1961; Dunn and Stearns 1987; Brinson 1990).

In the arid southwestern United States, riverine areas are often the only sites moist enough to provide suitable habitat for tree and shrub species. Typical trees of riparian zones are species of cottonwood, willow, and ash as well as the invasive Russian olive *(Elaeagnus angustifolia)* and saltcedar *(Tamarix ramisissima* and *T. chinensis)*. In the more montane and mesic areas of the West and Northwest, alder (*Alnus* spp.), cottonwood, and aspen (*Populus* spp.) occur as well spruce (*Picea* spp.) at higher elevations (Brinson 1990).

Southern river floodplains support vast bottomland hardwood forests (Fig. 6.25) that contain a diverse mixture of hardwood and conifer species (Kellison et al. 1998; Conner and

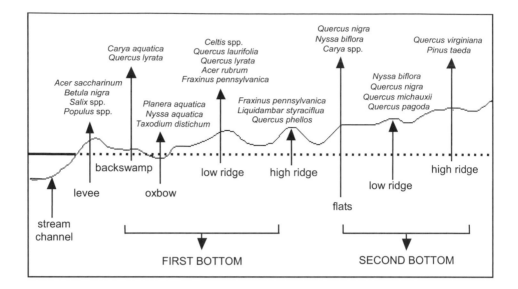

FIGURE 6.26

Idealized profile of a southern river floodplain showing the variation in topography and associated tree species. Soil texture ranges from very fine in the oxbow, fine on the flats, to coarse on the ridges. From Conner and Sharitz (2005), after Wharton and associates (1982).

Sharitz 2005). The most important condition determining species composition on these broad floodplains is the moisture gradient, or the gradient in anaerobic conditions (Wharton et al. 1982), which varies in time and space across the floodplain. These bottomland forests are extremely heterogeneous (Fig. 6.26), with very high species richness (Conner and Sharitz 2005). The lowest parts of the floodplain, such as oxbows formed from previous river channels that are nearly always flooded, support baldcypress-water tupelo *(Taxodium distichum—Nyssa aquatica)* swamps (discussed in the Southern Deepwater Swamps section). At slightly higher elevations, the soils usually are semipermanently saturated or inundated. Species such as overcup oak *(Quercus lyrata)* and water hickory *(Carya aquatica)* occur in back swamp depressions and willow, cottonwood, silver maple, and river birch *(Betula nigra)* are found on river levees. As elevations increase across these broad floodplains from lower areas (often called *first bottom*) to higher *(second bottom)* sites (Fig. 6.26), various mixtures of oaks, such as laurel *(Quercus laurifolia)*, willow *(Q. phellos)*, water *(Q. nigra)*, swamp chestnut *(Q. michauxii)*, and cherrybark *(Q. pagoda)* typically occur in association with other hardwoods such as green ash, sugarberry *(Celtis laevigata)*, and sweetgum *(Liquidambar styraciflua)*.

Successional patterns in the vegetation of southeastern river floodplain forests are poorly understood. Floodplain sites change over time due to deposition and erosion associated with floods, and small differences in elevation can result in great differences in site characteristics, including hydrologic conditions and soil anoxia. Primary succession occurs on new lands formed by deposition, such as sand bars adjacent to the river, and mud flats. Hodges (1997) describes likely successional patterns in poorly drained and better drained floodplain sites, beginning with species such as willow or cottonwood, and leading ultimately, through various other forest associations, to an elm-ash-sugarberry forest. Indeed, this forest association is the most common forest type in major floodplains of the Mississippi Valley and the Gulf Coastal Plain (Hodges 1997), but it is much less common in Atlantic Coastal Plain sites. Frequent hurricanes in the Atlantic region may allow less shade tolerant species such as sweetgum and red oaks, which can persist in the canopy for 200 years or longer, to be the dominant natural type (Sharitz et al. 1993; Allen and Sharitz 1999; Battaglia et al. 1999).

Southern floodplain forests have been extensively altered by timber harvesting and by farming. Native Americans and early European colonists cleared the rich bottomlands for crops (McCleery 1999). Throughout the 1800s, timber harvesting for domestic use and clearing for agriculture continued (King et al. 2005). In the 1900s, drainage and attempts to control water flow, first by private landowners and then by public agencies, especially the U.S. Army Corps of Engineers, allowed alluvial bottomland forests to be increasingly cleared. In recent years, there has been a modest attempt to reestablish hardwood forests on lands formerly used by agriculture (Allen and Kennedy 1989; King and Keeland 1999).

Several important ecological concepts have arisen from studies of the relationships of streams or rivers and their floodplains. Two of these, the river continuum concept and the flood pulse concept, are of special significance. The *river continuum concept* (Vannote et al. 1980) is focused mostly on the processing of organic material and productivity within the stream or river itself. It suggests that most organic matter introduced into streams from terrestrial sources (e.g., leaf litter) is in headwater regions where the stream is narrow and low in nutrients, and biodiversity is limited by low light and low temperatures. Invertebrate collectors and shredders in the stream reduce the organic matter in size as it travels downstream. In river midreaches, more light is available, phytoplankton thrive, and primary productivity in the stream increases. Invertebrate filter feeders process the fine organic matter from upstream, and coarse woody debris inputs from the floodplain increase food diversity and the variety of habitats. Biodiversity is highest in these midreach areas. Downstream as the river size increases, litter inputs from the floodplain are minor, and turbidity reduces primary productivity. Thus, there is a continuum of inputs of organic materials from the floodplain and of in-stream productivity and the processing of organic materials as well as a continuum of in-stream plankton communities and invertebrate consumers. In a similar concept, Johnson and Lowe (1985) define the *intrariparian continuum* as the continuum in the riparian corridor along a river's course. The characteristics of the floodplain communities along the river are determined by the geomorphic, hydrologic, and other physical processes that control the environment as the river develops from a small low-order stream to a larger high-order system.

The river continuum concept addresses mostly in-stream processes and does not adequately take into account the importance of floodplains to river systems, and vice versa. Furthermore, the river continuum concept was developed for low-order temperate streams and may not be generalizable to large temperate or tropical rivers with broad floodplains. The *flood pulse concept* (Junk et al 1989; see Chapter 11) proposes that the pulsing of the river discharge is the major force controlling the biota in the river floodplain, and that the river-floodplain exchange during periods of floodplain inundation is of enormous importance in determining the productivity of both the river and the adjacent riparian zone. Flood pulses deliver water and nutrients to sites across the floodplain, creating suitable conditions for biotic processes such as seed dispersal and seedling establishment (Schneider and Sharitz 1988; Jones and Sharitz 1998), occurrence of benthic invertebrates (Reese and Batzer, in review), and fish spawning (Lambou 1990). Furthermore, the floodplain provides nutrients, organic matter, and food to stream organisms as flood waters move back into the river (Knight and Bottorff 1984). The flood pulse concept may better describe the ecological situation in many of the vast southern floodplain forests, but both concepts provide valuable insights into the relationships between floodplains and their adjacent water bodies.

Freshwater Shoreline Wetlands

Lakeshore, or lacustrine, marshes are located around the world, along the edges of small and large lakes. Most of the world's lakes are small, with a high ratio of lacustrine marsh area to open water (Wetzel and Hough 1973). In the United States, many of the small isolated wetlands, such as prairie potholes, Carolina bays, and playas, act essentially as very small lakes and contain marshes dominated by herbaceous graminoids (grasses, sedges, rushes), other emergent wetland herbs, and floating leaved and submersed aquatics when periods of inundation are long enough to support these species (see earlier sections on these wetlands). Many of these small wetland marshes receive much of their water from precipitation and are relatively nutrient poor.

Along larger lakes with seiches (wind driven "tides"), such as the Great Lakes of the United States and Canada, wetlands occur in coastal lagoons behind natural barrier beaches or levees thrown up by wave action on the shore, or in the deltas of tributary rivers (Herdendorf 1987). Since shorelines have been stabilized along the Great Lakes, many of the remaining marshes are now managed and protected by artificial dikes (Herdendorf 1987; Wilcox and Whillans 1999). These wetlands receive much of their water as surface flows from the lakes themselves, in addition to surface runoff and groundwater from adjacent upland areas. Thus, they tend to be much more nutrient rich than most marshes in small lakes.

Plant species composition in lakeshore marshes varies greatly, but common species include graminoids such as reeds (*Phragmites*), cattails *(Typhn)*, wild rice *(Zizania aquatica)*, bur reed *(Sparganium eurycarpum)*, maidencane *(Panicum hemitomun)*, sedges (species of *Carex* and *Scirpus*), and spike rush (*Eleocharis*). Other typical herbaceous species are pickerelweed *(Pontederia cordata)*, arrowhead *(Sagittaria)*, and smartweed *(Poly-gonum)*, and floating-leaved or submersed species such as water lilies *(Nymphaea odor-ata)*, water shield *(Brasenia schreberi)*, water milfoil *(Myriophyllum* spp.), and pondweed *(Potamogeton)*. In these wetlands, plant communities typically show a zonation pattern according to depth, from wet meadows to more flooded marshes to aquatic beds (Glooschenko et al. 1993; Fig. 6.2).

Salt Marshes

Salt marshes occur along coastlines where wave action is moderate enough to allow the accumulation of sediments and growth of angiosperms (Chapman 1960). In the United States, salt marshes dominate the Atlantic and Gulf coasts but are rare on the Pacific Coast because of its steeply sloping shores and heavy wave action. Worldwide, salt marshes oc-cur at almost all latitudes but are largely replaced by mangroves (see Mangroves below) in the tropics. Salt marshes also occur at inland locations with salty, wet soils. Coastal salt marshes receive most of their water input from the ocean, with some contribution from precipitation and groundwater. The hydroperiod varies according to the nature of the lo-cal tidal regime, from large-amplitude tides driven primarily by the moon (e.g., the U.S. Atlantic Coast) to small-amplitude tides driven primarily by local weather conditions (e.g., the U.S. Gulf Coast). Soils vary from highly mineral to highly organic, depending on sed-iment input and decomposition rates, and development of soil is promoted by the marsh vegetation, which traps sediment and produces organic matter belowground. Salt marsh plant communities worldwide are dominated by a relatively small suite of plant species. Most common are plants from the genera *Spartina* and *Distichlis* (Poaceae), *Juncus* (Jun-caceae), *Arthrocnemum, Atriplex, Salicornia* and *Suaeda* (Chenopodiaceae), and *Limonium* (Plumbaginaceae). At any one geographic location, total plant diversity is low, typically ten to twenty species, with the dominant plants often arranged in striking zonation pat-terns parallel to the shoreline (Fig. 6.27).

Salt marsh plants must cope with the dual physical stresses of flooding and salinity (see Chapter 4). Flooding stress increases with decreasing elevation, but decreases again at creekbanks because of increased pore water exchange with tidal water. Salinity stress may be greatest at low marsh elevations or may rise to a peak in middle marsh elevations if evapotranspiration concentrates salts in the pore water (Pennings and Bertness 1999). In low-latitude salt marshes, unvegetated "salt pans" are a common feature of the high marsh landscape in areas where pore water salinities exceed levels that plants can tolerate. Within vegetated areas, plants respond to variation across the marsh in flooding and salinity with marked intraspecific variation in height, morphology, and palatability to herbivores (Va-liela et al. 1978; Seliskar 1985a, 1985b; Goranson et al. 2004; Richards et al. 2005).

Salt marsh plants are commonly arrayed in distinct zones parallel to the shoreline. These zonation patterns have been best studied in Rhode Island marshes, where they represent a simple trade-off between competitive ability and stress tolerance. Competi-tively superior plant species occupy the higher marsh zones, which are less stressful, and

FIGURE 6.27

Salt marsh along a tidal creek with saltmarsh cordgrass *(Spartina alterniflora)* at creek's edge on Sapelo Island, Georgia.

displace poor competitors to lower marsh elevations (Bertness and Ellison 1987; Bertness 1991a, 1991b; Bertness et al. 1992b; Bertness and Hacker 1994). The mechanisms producing zonation patterns in low-latitude salt marshes are more complex. In hotter climates, high evapotranspiration commonly leads to hypersaline conditions at intermediate marsh elevations (Pennings and Bertness 1999). Consequently, low-marsh zones may be occupied by species tolerant of flooding, intermediate marsh zones by species tolerant of high salinities, and the high marsh by competitive dominants (Pennings and Callaway 1992; Pennings et al. 2005).

Although competitive interactions determine the distribution patterns of the dominant plants in salt marshes, facilitative interactions may be important in mediating the distribution of many rarer species (Hacker and Bertness 1999). Many marsh plants leak oxygen from their rhizomes, increasing oxygen availability in the soil. Dense stands of marsh plants may reduce evaporation at the soil surface, thereby reducing salt accumulation and high salinities. In these ways, marsh plants may facilitate other individuals or species by reducing stress from flooding (Howes et al. 1981, 1986; Bertness 1991b) and salinity (Bertness and Hacker 1994; Callaway 1994; Hacker and Bertness 1995; Callaway and Pennings 2000). The importance of facilitative interactions appears to vary geographically as a function of climate and species composition (Bertness and Ewanchuck 2002; Pennings et al. 2003).

Invertebrates may also facilitate salt marsh plants by acting as ecosystem engineers (see Chapter 7), reducing physical stress or increasing nutrient availability. Because bivalves attach to each other and to plants, and deposit feces and pseudofeces on the marsh surface, they increase sediment stability and nutrient availability (Jordan and Valiela 1982; Bertness 1984; Dame 1996). Similarly, the burrowing activities of fiddler crabs increase oxygen and nutrient availability (Teal and Kanwisher 1961; Montague 1980, 1982; Bertness 1985; Bortolus and Iribarne 1999; see Chapter 7). Experiments have demonstrated that engineering by both bivalves and crabs can strongly increase marsh plant growth.

Depending on their geographic location, salt marshes are subject to a variety of natural disturbances. Ice can severely erode high-latitude marshes (Redfield 1972; Hardwick-Witman 1985). All salt marshes are subject to disturbance by floating mats of dead plant material (wrack), but this is particularly common at higher latitudes where all of the aboveground production dies back each winter (Hartman et al. 1983; Bertness and Ellison 1987; Pennings and Richards 1998). Other sources of disturbance in salt marshes include fire (Turner 1987; Taylor et al. 1994; Baldwin and Mendelssohn 1998b; Bortolus and Iribarne 1999), sedimentation (Rejmanek et al. 1988; Allison 1996), and herbivory (Lynch et al. 1947; Smith and Odum 1981; Jefferies 1988; Silliman and Bertness 2002).

Following disturbance, secondary succession in salt marshes occurs through some combination of facilitative and competitive interactions (Pennings and Bertness 2001). Disturbances that remove large amounts of vegetation at intermediate marsh elevations may lead to hypersaline soils (Iacobelli and Jefferies 1991; Bertness et al. 1992a). In this case, secondary succession is facilitated by highly salt-tolerant species that invade the disturbed areas first. Once the salt-tolerant species attain high cover and shade the soil, soil salinities return to normal levels and less salt-tolerant species invade (Bertness and Ellison 1987; Bertness 1991a; Bertness et al. 1992a). If disturbances are small, or occur at elevations that are not conducive to the development of hypersaline conditions, succession proceeds through purely competitive interactions (Bertness and Shumway 1993; Shumway and Bertness 1994; Brewer et al. 1997).

Salt marshes are highly productive systems, and there is a long history of ecosystem research in salt marshes that dates back to seminal work by Teal (1962). Most of the primary production enters the detrital food web (Cebrian 1999). The detrital food web has been best studied in the southeastern United States (Newell 1993, 1996, 2003; Silliman and Newell 2003). There, senescing leaves of cordgrass, *Spartina alterniflora,* undergo initial decay while attached to plant stems. Senescent leaves are heavily colonized by fungi, and fungal/leaf complexes are grazed by shredding invertebrates, especially snails and amphipods. Leaf fragments and invertebrate feces fall to the marsh surface, where further decomposition is primarily mediated by bacteria. The resultant detrital fragments comprise part of the diet of a wide variety of other marsh invertebrates (Pennings and Bertness 2001).

Although most primary production in salt marshes enters the detrital food web, the role of herbivores has historically been underestimated (Pennings and Bertness 2001). A wide variety of herbivores, including mammals (Ranwell 1961; Kiehl et al. 1996; Ford and Grace 1998), birds (Kerbes et al. 1990; Hik et al. 1992; Mulder and Ruess 1998), crabs (Bortolus and Iribarne 1999), snails (Silliman and Zieman 2001; Silliman and Newell 2003), insects (Foster 1984; Olmstead et al. 1997; Rand 1999; Finke and Denno 2004), and parasitic plants (Pennings and Callaway 1996) can have strong impacts on plant productivity and species composition. Herbivore pressure is greater, and the palatability of plants to herbivores lower, at low versus high latitudes (Pennings et al. 2001; Salgado and Pennings 2005; Pennings and Silliman 2005).

Salt marshes are important to humanity. They shelter coasts from erosion, filter nutrients and sediments from the water, and provide nursery and feeding grounds for many crustaceans and fishes. They have been fertile habitats for scientific study (Chapman 1960; Pomeroy and Wiegert 1981; Adam 1990; Pennings and Bertness 2001) and have contributed to general ecological theory regarding plant zonation, succession, and facilitation. Salt marshes have also proved vulnerable to anthropogenic impacts. The hydrology of many salt marshes has been altered by ditches, culverts, and dikes. Many salt marshes have been filled to allow coastal development. Finally, salt marshes are easily affected by eutrophication and pollution from coastal and up-river sources.

Tidal Freshwater Marshes

Tidal freshwater marshes occur along rivers upstream of salt marshes, in areas where water column salinities average less than 0.5 parts per thousand. Moving downstream, one encounters oligohaline (0.5–5 ppt), mesohaline (5–18 ppt), and finally salt (18–35 ppt) marshes. This sequence of habitat types occurs along an increasing gradient of sulfur and total dissolved salts, whose concentrations are several orders of magnitude higher in the ocean than in river water. For brevity, and because oligohaline and mesohaline marshes have not been extensively studied, we will focus on tidal freshwater marshes. Because tides propagate upstream farther than salt water does, tidal freshwater marshes experience a hydroperiod similar to that of salt marshes downstream but are flooded by river water rather than ocean water. Soils are more organic than those in downstream salt marshes. The plant community is dominated by a different suite of species, including species from the genera *Scirpus* (Cyperaceae), *Typha* (Typhaceae), and *Phragmites* and *Zizaniopsis* (Poaceae).

Historically, many tidal freshwater marshes along the southeastern coast of the United States were diked for rice cultivation. Although these agricultural efforts have now been abandoned, the systems often remain in a degraded state, with the abandoned dikes altering the hydrologic regime. Some diked areas are actively managed with an altered hydrologic regime intended to benefit waterfowl. Tidal freshwater marshes have received much less scientific attention than have salt marshes, and the best review remains that of W. E. Odum (1988).

Because tidal freshwater marshes occur at the low-salinity end of the estuary, the physical environment is much less harsh than in salt marshes. In particular, plants do not have to cope with high salinities or high concentrations of sulfides. As a consequence, the plant community is more diverse than that of salt marshes, extends to lower elevations

FIGURE 6.28
Mangrove wetland with red mangrove *(Rhizophora mangle)* trees in southern Florida.

in the intertidal zone, and may be more productive (Simpson et al. 1983; Odum 1988) although few rigorous comparisons have been made. Zonation patterns are much less distinct than in salt marshes, presumably because the strong gradients in salt and sulfide concentrations that help create different habitats in salt marshes are absent (Odum 1988).

Although plant zonation patterns are weak within tidal freshwater marshes, they are strong at the scale of the estuary, with a predictable turnover in species composition from tidal fresh to salt marshes (Wilson et al. 1996). These large-scale zonation patterns are caused by a trade-off between competitive ability and stress tolerance similar to the trade-off that creates zonation patterns within salt marshes (Crain et al. 2004). Competitively superior plants dominate the freshwater end of the estuarine gradient but can not survive in salt marshes. Plants that occur in salt marshes can tolerate the stressful conditions found there but are competitively excluded from the freshwater end of the salinity gradient (Crain et al. 2004).

Mangroves

Mangrove forests (Fig. 6.28), also known as *mangal*, are the tropical equivalent of salt marshes. They occur in the same locations—coastal areas with soft sediments and moderate wave action—but in geographic regions that lack hard freezes (Chapman 1976). Like salt marshes, mangroves receive most of their water input from the ocean, with the hydroperiod driven by the local tidal regime, and thus face the twin stresses of flooding and salinity. Mangrove forests differ from salt marshes in that, by definition, they are dominated by woody plants—trees and shrubs—rather than by grasses, rushes, and forbs. They are similar in that species diversity is low—at most 70 species worldwide, from about

19 families (Tomlinson 1986; Duke 1992). Species richness is high in the Indo-West Pacific and low in the eastern Pacific, Caribbean, and Atlantic (Ellison et al. 1999).

Less is known about mangrove plant communities than about salt marsh plant communities, in part because ecologists have paid more attention to salt marshes and in part because of the difficulties in experimentally manipulating trees. Nevertheless, many aspects of mangrove ecology appear to parallel those of salt marsh ecology. Like salt marsh plants, mangrove trees show striking variation in size and morphology across physical gradients, likely as a response to nutrient availability and physical stress (Lugo and Snedaker 1974; Feller 1995). Mangrove plants also display patterns of zonation across tidal elevation, but considerable overlap of zones often occurs, and few studies have experimentally addressed the causes of zonation (Chapman 1976; Smith 1992; Ellison and Farnsworth 2001). Finally, like salt marsh plants, mangrove plants participate in facultative mutualisms with wetland animals. Burrowing crabs improve soil quality in mangrove forests just as they do in salt marshes (Smith et al. 1991; Lee 1998). Massive sponges, which colonize exposed, submerged mangrove roots, benefit mangroves by providing nitrogen and protecting roots from attack by isopods (Ellison and Farnsworth 1990; Ellison et al. 1996). Mangrove roots, in turn, leak carbon which is incorporated into the sponges.

Mangroves are subject to both small and large-scale natural disturbances (Lugo and Snedaker 1974; Smith et al. 1994; Imbert et al. 1996; Swiadek 1997; Ellison and Farnsworth 2001). Tree-falls and lightning strikes create small gaps in the forest canopy. The wind and storm surge that accompany cyclonic storms can kill many trees over large areas. We do not have a general understanding of the process of secondary succession in mangrove forests. Because full recovery of disturbed forests may take decades, however, mangrove forests in areas subject to regular cyclonic storms may always be in early or intermediate stages of secondary succession rather than at equilibrium, "climax" stages.

Like salt marshes, mangrove plants are attacked by both terrestrial and marine herbivores. A variety of insects and mammals consume mangroves, affecting production, plant chemistry, and tree architecture (Farnsworth and Ellison 1991; Feller and Mathis 1997; Feller and McKee 1999; Ellison and Farnsworth 2001). In many parts of the world, grapsid crabs are important consumers of both live and detrital mangrove production, often keeping the forest floor almost completely clear of both leaf litter and understory vegetation (Snedaker and Lahmann 1988; Smith et al. 1989). Isopods attack subtidal, exposed mangrove roots, sharply slowing root growth (Ellison and Farnsworth 1990). Although herbivores affect the community ecology of mangrove forests, the majority of production nevertheless moves through the detrital food web (Twilley et al. 1992; Alongi 1996).

Like salt marshes, mangrove forests grade into freshwater, tidal systems upstream in estuaries. Although the geographical distribution of mangroves is limited by their intolerance to cold (MacMillan 1975), trees occur at higher latitudes in tidal freshwater than in tidal marine wetlands, suggesting that, in the absence of salt stress, mangrove trees are better able to deal with cold temperatures (Odum 1988).

Finally, also like salt marshes, mangrove forests are important to humanity (Ellison and Farnsworth 2001). They provide many of the same ecosystem services, sheltering coasts from erosion and severe storms, filtering nutrients and sediments, and providing nursery and feeding grounds for crustaceans and fishes. These services have received increasing attention in recent decades, as many mangrove forests have been lost to population growth, forestry, and aquaculture. Mangrove forests have not been studied as heavily as salt marshes but appear in most ecology textbooks because they provided one of the first and best tests of island biogeography theory (Simberloff and Wilson 1970; see Chapter 7).

ACKNOWLEDGMENT

Preparation of this chapter was supported by Financial Assistance Award Number DE-FC09-96SR18546 between the U.S. Department of Energy and the University of Georgia.

7

WETLAND ANIMAL ECOLOGY

Darold P. Batzer, Robert Cooper, and Scott A. Wissinger

The ecology of wetland animals has received much less research attention than the ecology of terrestrial, aquatic, or marine animals, particularly at the community and ecosystem level. As such, relatively little ecological theory has been developed in wetland systems, and the field of wetland animal ecology tends to adapt hypotheses generated in other ecosystems. This might make sense if wetlands were viewed as hybrids or ecotones between terrestrial and aquatic/marine ecosystems. However, wetlands are not simply transitional habitats, but have unique biotic characteristics unto themselves. Plant scientists have already come to this realization, and several wetland-specific paradigms have been developed to explain ecological patterns of wetland plants (see Chapter 6). Animal researchers are just beginning to develop such paradigms.

Because wetland animal ecologists still tend to rely on work in other ecosystems, it is probably useful to frame wetland animal ecology in relation to terrestrial, aquatic, and marine systems. In terms of energy base, wetlands appear to be hybrids of terrestrial and aquatic/marine habitats (Table 7.1). Terrestrial systems are trophically based on macrophytes (grasses, forbs, shrubs, trees), aquatic and marine systems are based mostly on algae, and wetland systems are based on both macrophytes and algae. In fact, in wetlands, animal communities above the waterline probably function much like terrestrial systems, and those below the waterline function like aquatic/marine systems. However, the "terrestrial" and "aquatic" communities of wetlands are intimately interconnected.

Wetlands are often described as highly diverse and productive ecosystems. However, depending on the wetland and the animal group, this may or may not be true, at least

TABLE 7.1. Ecological Characteristics of Terrestrial, Wetland, and
Aquatic/Marine Habitats

Ecological Factor	Terrestrial Forests, Grasslands	Wetland Marshes, Swamps, Seasonal Ponds	Aquatic/Marine Streams, Rivers, Lakes Near-shore Oceans
Trophic base of food webs	Macrophytes	Macrophytes, Algae	Algae
Invertebrates			
Diversity	High	Low	High
Productivity	High	Variable	High
Amphibians/reptiles			
Diversity	High	High	Low
Productivity	Variable	Variable	Low
Fish			
Diversity	—	Low	High
Productivity	—	High	High
Birds			
Diversity	High	High	Low
Productivity	High	High	Low
Mammals			
Diversity	High	Low	Low
Productivity	High	Variable	Variable

in relation to the diversity and productivity in terrestrial or aquatic/marine systems. For example, such a statement would often be erroneous for invertebrates (Table 7.1). Invertebrate diversity in wetlands is often much lower than in either terrestrial or aquatic/marine habitats, probably because of fluctuating abiotic conditions (Chapter 4). Invertebrates may be highly productive in some wetlands (seasonal ponds, marshes, tidal marshes), but in others (peatlands, swamps) productivity is typically low. In contrast, the herpetofauna (amphibians and reptiles) of wetlands is typically more diverse and productive than in either terrestrial or aquatic/marine habitats. Fish productivity in wetlands can be very high, but the diversity is typically quite low in comparison to aquatic or marine habitats. Bird diversity and production can be high in wetlands, but no more so than many terrestrial forests and meadows. While certain wetland mammals (beaver, nutria, and muskrats) are crucially important to wetland ecology, the overall diversity and productivity of mammals in wetlands is low. Overall, animal diversity and productivity in wetlands is not unusual and probably falls within the normal range of variation for ecosystems in general.

Recognizing that the ecological functions of animals in wetlands share features with the faunas of terrestrial and aquatic/marine habitats, we frame this chapter to focus

FIGURE 7.1
Mixed wetland habitats in Georgia's Okefenokee Swamp. The macrophytes in marshy areas and leaves and wood in forested areas are the most obvious energy sources for wetland animals.

on some broadly applicable principles but highlight unique aspects of wetlands. The roles of animals in food webs are probably their most important contribution to overall wetland ecosystem function, and so the initial section of this chapter focuses on animal trophic ecology. We then discuss variation in wetland animal communities, emphasizing how communities change both spatially and temporally. In the final section of the chapter, we narrow our focus and discuss the ecology of those animal populations that play especially important roles in wetland ecosystems or are of special interest to humans.

TROPHIC ECOLOGY

THE TROPHIC BASIS FOR ANIMAL PRODUCTION

A defining feature of many wetlands is the lush growth of plants such as emergent herbaceous vegetation in freshwater and estuarine marshes, and trees in freshwater swamps, mangrove swamps, and woodland ponds (Fig. 7.1). At first glance, it might seem obvious that the abundance of energy from these plants should provide the basis for wetland food webs. However, the true picture is much more complicated. Actually, an assortment of foods, including living macrophytes, detritus from macrophytes, algae, and microbes (bacteria, fungi), support populations of primary consumer animals. These foods can vary

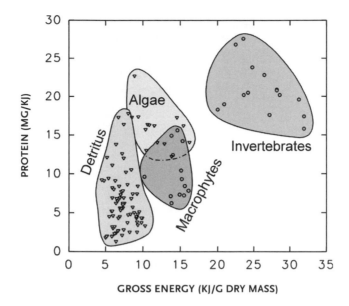

FIGURE 7.2

Relative qualities of detritus, living macrophyte tissue, and algae in terms of caloric and protein content. Figure was adapted from Bowen and associates (1995) with the permission of the senior author and the Ecological Society of America.

widely in nutritional quality (Fig. 7.2). The relative importance of each of these energy sources to overall wetland animal production fuels a continuing debate among wetland ecologists, and below we present and synthesize some diverse perspectives on this issue.

Macrophyte Herbivory

Wetland macrophytes are consumed by an assortment of herbivorous animals. In marshes, muskrats *(Ondatra zibethicus)* use emergent plants for food and to construct lodges and feeding platforms. In some cases, these rodents can consume a significant portion of the available plant biomass (Clark 2000, see below). Many species of waterfowl feed extensively on submersed aquatic plants or the seeds of emergent plants, and their grazing can impact plant-standing crops when ducks become locally abundant (Marklund et al. 2002). The explosive population increase of snow geese in the 1990s has led to the overgrazing of plant stands in tundra wetlands, possibly threatening ecosystem integrity (Kotanen and Jefferies 1997). In some estuaries, animals more commonly associated with uplands, such as hares (van der Wal et al. 1998), can be important herbivores on salt marsh plants. Also as in terrestrial habitats, insects can be important herbivores in wetlands. In salt marshes, an assortment of planthoppers feed on cordgrass *(Spartina)* and other emergent plants (Denno et al. 2002; Moon and Stiling 2002). Outbreaks of moth larvae can completely defoliate wetland trees (Goyer et al. 1990), and chrysomelid leaf beetles can consume most of the leaf production in some water lily beds (Wallace and O'Hop 1985).

Herbivorous insects (beetles and moths) are being used to biologically control invasive wetland plants (Malecki et al. 1993), which is clear evidence of the ecological importance of insect herbivores to wetlands (Blossey and Hunt-Joshi 2003). It is noteworthy that virtually all of the examples of herbivorous animals impacting macrophytes involve terrestrial animals, and that typically much of the herbivory is above the waterline. Few truly aquatic animals in wetlands seem adapted to feed on living macrophytes (Batzer and Wissinger 1996). So, in terms of macrophyte/herbivore interactions, wetland ecosystems probably function more like terrestrial forests or grasslands than like aquatic lakes or streams.

While macrophyte herbivory by terrestrial animals is clearly an important influence on wetland ecosystem function, only a handful of animal species consume living macrophytes in wetlands. Thus, the impact of herbivory is probably somewhat limited, except during population outbreaks. Even when herbivore densities are high, the vast majority of wetland plant production still is not consumed (Foote et al. 1988; Clark 2000; Marklund et al. 2002). Instead, most macrophyte tissue becomes detritus after the plants senesce.

Detritivory

If living macrophyte tissue is not the primary food base for animals in wetland food webs, the enormous influx of macrophyte detritus from annual senescence or autumn leaf fall would be a logical alternative. In fact, wetlands have been called *detritus-based ecosystems* (Odum and Heald 1975; Brinson et al. 1981). In terms of overall ecosystem function, that assessment is probably accurate because macrophyte detritus is clearly the major foundation for the microbial community (see Chapters 5 and 8). However, it has yet to be demonstrated that a substantial amount of the detrital energy cycling in the microbial loop is transformed into animal biomass. Detritus by itself is a relatively poor quality food source for animals (Fig. 7.2). Thus, the extent to which wetland animal production is based on macrophyte detritus remains an open question.

A profitable approach for assessing the relative importance of macrophyte detritus versus other sources of energy (e.g., algae) involves carbon stable isotope analysis. The carbon atom normally has an atomic weight of 12, but a small percentage ($<2\%$) of carbon atoms naturally has an atomic weight of 13. The $^{13}C/^{12}C$ ratio differs among various plants and animals because the isotopes are assimilated, metabolized, and excreted at different rates. Working under the assumption that an animal is what it eats, the carbon isotope ratio of a particular animal should mirror the ratio in its food, and this permits researchers to match animals to their food supply. This approach has advantages over simple gut analysis because it assesses not only food consumption but also assimilation into the animal's tissues. On the other hand, stable isotope analyses is complicated by difficulties in separating isotopic signatures among similar plants (and even seasonally within a single plant species), and by difficulties in relating the isotopic signature of a generalist feeding animal to its diverse food base.

Stable isotope studies have confirmed that some animals specifically adapted to consume macrophyte detritus, such as limnephilid caddisfly shredders, do in fact derive most of their carbon from detritus (Mihuc and Toetz 1994). Furthermore, community-wide analyses in California's Tijuana Estuary (Kwak and Zedler 1997) indicated that *Spartina* detritus was the primary source of carbon for fishes, although most invertebrates and a clapper rail depended directly or indirectly on macroalgae. Currin and associates (1995, 2003) and Stribling and Cornwell (1997) also found that *Spartina* detritus was an important food to animals (fish and invertebrates) in eastern U.S. tidal marshes, although they found that other macrophyte tissue, phytoplankton, and benthic algae were equally important. Wantzen and colleagues (2002a) concluded that much of the fish community in Brazil's Pantanal was based on macrophytes. In this tropical wetland, both herbivorous and detrivorous fishes were important, and the consumption of terrestrial insect herbivores by invertivore fish channeled additional macrophyte energy into the fish community. Other studies conclude that much of the animal production in wetlands is supported by foods other than macrophyte detritus (Neill and Cornwell 1992; Bunn and Boon 1993). On the floodplain of Venezuela's Orinoco River, for instance, 98% of the available carbon exists in the lush growth of wetland grasses, water hyacinth, and floodplain trees, but the carbon isotopic signatures of most fish and invertebrates matched planktonic and epiphytic algae rather than vascular plants (Hamilton et al. 1992; Lewis et al. 2001). Bouillon and colleagues (2002) found that most benthic invertebrates in an estuarine mangrove wetland were assimilating algae over mangrove-derived detritus, a noteworthy example because mangroves are the habitats where the axiom that wetlands are detritus-based systems was first developed (Odum and Heald 1975). France (1998) also found that fiddler crabs, important consumers in tropical mangrove wetlands and traditionally considered to be detritivores, were selecting foods other than vascular plant detritus.

A powerful research approach to assess the degree to which macrophyte detritus is supporting animal production in wetlands is to manipulate detrital supplies experimentally. In a Canadian study (Murkin et al. 1982), cattail cover was reduced by cutting to 0% (control), 30%, 50%, or 70% of the original standing stock, and the plant slash was removed. Initially in the spring, invertebrate biomass was lower in the cover reduction plots, suggesting a link between animal production and detrital reductions. However, as the season progressed, invertebrate biomass steadily increased in the removal plots until it exceeded the biomass in the control plot, suggesting that some other food source supported the invertebrate production. Waterfowl use of plots mirrored invertebrate population trends, and because these birds consume invertebrates, it was suggested the birds were responding to changes in invertebrate resource levels. In a subsequent study in Canada, Neckles and associates (1990) harvested and removed the emergent vegetation from one seasonal marsh at summer's end, while they left vegetation in a second marsh undisturbed. Despite the drastic decline in detritus availability in the manipulated marsh, invertebrate composition and abundance in the two habitats the next year remained remarkably similar. Animal production in these marshes did not appear to be detritus based. Similarly, in forested wetlands, logging is a manipulation that drastically affects detrital dynamics, with a reduction of leaf-fall inputs being a conspicuous loss. Although logging can alter animal community compositions, overall animal production in affected wetlands typically either remains similar or increases, instead of declining (Hutchens et al. 2004). In summary, experimental evidence that wetland animal production is based primarily on detritus is lacking.

To assess the trophic basis of animal production, we may need to readjust our thinking about wetlands. While accepting that the majority of energy cycling through wetlands passes through the detrital pool, it appears likely that much of the energy for wetland animals is being derived from other sources. Because macrophyte detritus is a poor-quality food relative to living macrophytes or algae both in terms of caloric and protein content (Fig. 7.2), relatively few wetland animals may be able to use macrophyte detritus as their primary food source despite its abundance. This might explain why many, if not most, detritivorous animals supplement their diets with algae (Mihuc 1997) and/or animal material (Wissinger et al. 2004b).

Before completing our discussion on the interactions of wetland animals and detritus, we should assess the impacts of animals on detrital decomposition. In streams, insect shredders are crucially important to detrital decomposition because they convert coarse particulate organic matter (e.g., leaves, wood) into smaller particles that can be utilized by other consumers (Table 7.2 describes some different functional feeding groups, including shredders). Although this concept has not been as well developed in wetland systems, similar scenarios may develop in some salt marshes and freshwater wetlands. Newell and Barlöcher (1993) estimated that when populations of the salt marsh periwinkle *(Littoraria irrorata)* were high, the snails could remove 2% to 3% of the available biomass of dead salt marsh cordgrass *Spartina* leaves from Georgia salt marshes daily. In a subsequent study in that ecosystem, Graca and associates (2000) found that an amphipod crustacean also consumed large amounts of decaying *Spartina* leaves, and their feeding stimulated fungal production on the remnant leaves. In a freshwater macrocosm experiment (Fazi and Rossi 2000), decay rates of alder leaves increased as densities of invertebrate shredders and scrapers increased. Oertli (1993) assessed leaf-litter processing and energy flow through macroinvertebrates in a woodland pond and attributed 11.2% of the breakdown of oak leaves to invertebrate shredders. Where shredding animals are abundant, they probably play important roles in decomposition. However, shredding organisms are rare in many wetlands, and degradation of detritus may instead occur through microbial and physical processes (Cuffney and Wallace 1987; Oertli 1993; Wissinger 1999; Batzer et al. 2005). Compared with the detailed knowledge about the relative roles of invertebrates, fungi, bacteria, and physical processes to litter decomposition in streams (e.g., Hieber and Gessner 2002), there is a surprising dearth of primary evidence from wetland ecosystems.

TABLE 7.2. Functional Feeding Groups (FFG)

FFG	Ingestion Method and Food Resource	Wetland Examples
Shredders	Shred living plants or plant detritus (leaves, wood)	Caddisfly larvae Muskrats
Collectors		
Gatherers	Collect small food items from surfaces	Midge larvae Dabbling ducks
Filterers	Collect small particles (algae, bacteria, protests, detritus) from water	Fingernail clams Mosquito larvae Spoonbill ducks
Scrapers	Scrape algae or biofilms from surfaces	Snails Frog tadpoles
Predators	Engulf animal prey	Dragonfly nymphs Salamanders Fish Herons
Piercers[a]	Suck fluids from plants or animals	Water bugs Plant bugs

[a]This category is not commonly used by researchers, and piercing predators (e.g., water bugs) are often lumped together with engulfing predators.

NOTE: Adapted from Cummins (1973).

Algal Herbivory

In the stable isotope studies discussed previously, the importance of algae to wetland food webs, relative to detritus, was a common theme. Stable isotope studies from an assortment of wetland types implicate algae as a particularly important energy base for food webs, including mangroves (France 1998; Bouillon et al. 2002), salt marshes (Currin et al. 1995, 2003; Kwak and Zedler 1997; Stribling and Cornwell 1997; Dittel et al. 2000; Herman et al. 2000), tidal mudflats (Melville and Connolly 2003), river floodplains (Hamilton et al. 1992; Lewis et al. 2001; Herwig et al. 2004), freshwater marshes (Neill and Cornwell 1992; Bunn and Boon 1993; Keough et al. 1998), and inland saline marshes (Hart and Lovvorn 2003). Most of these papers contain statements to the effect that the conventional wisdom of wetland food webs being based on macrophyte tissue needs to be reevaluated, and the importance of planktonic, benthic, and/or epiphytic algae needs to be more fully recognized.

Although this body of descriptive evidence points toward the importance of algae to animals in wetland food webs, few studies have evaluated relationships experimentally. However, those that have been conducted suggest a tight linkage between algae and wetland invertebrates. In an oligotrophic marsh in central Canada, separate studies by Campeau and associates (1994) and Gabor and colleagues (1994) both found that stimulating algal biomass through experimental nutrient enrichment increased invertebrate densities. Rader and Richardson (1994) found the same bottom-up "cascade" in the Florida Everglades, where nutrient enrichment from agriculture increased growth of algae and in turn invertebrates and small fish. Even in the absence of nutrient enrichment, a tight link between algae and invertebrates was suggested by studies in a permanent marsh in Manitoba (Hann 1991) and a seasonal marsh in California (Batzer and Resh 1991), where microcrustacean and/or midge grazers reduced algal biomass to very low levels. Because algae-consuming invertebrates are in turn consumed by predatory invertebrates, fish, and birds, the microscopic algae become a crucial foundation of wetland food webs.

One reason that algae might be overlooked in food web studies is that turnover rates are high, and standing crops are kept low by grazing; hence, algae are not as visually obvious to researchers as are macrophytes. The tendency of researchers to focus on resources that are abundant may be a flawed strategy when assessing food web interactions in wetlands because the abundance of a resource may simply suggest that few consumers eat that material. In contrast, those foods that support consumers are rapidly consumed and therefore might occur at low-standing stocks. (By analogy, if someone were trying to assess the diets of four-year-old children by what is left on their dinner plates, one might come to assume that they live primarily on vegetables.) While algal standing crops may be kept low by grazers at any one point in time, algae grow very rapidly, and this productivity may be sufficient to support much of the animal secondary production in wetlands (Lewis et al. 2001). Grazing can actually enhance productivity of algal periphyton in streams because only actively growing surface films remain (Lamberti and Resh 1983), but whether that relationship exists in wetlands has not been explored. Not all wetland algae, however, are palatable to consumers. While benthic, epiphytic, and planktonic algae are all believed to be important foods, floating beds of filamentous green algae (called *metaphyton*) are not consumed to any great extent (Neill and Cornwell 1992; Mihuc and Toetz 1994), which might explain why beds of metaphyton are able to develop in the first place. Hart and Lovvorn (2003) found that many organisms find amorphous detritus derived from algae to be a nutritious food but do not consume living algae.

It has been proposed that algae and detritus are not entirely separate entities in terms of carbon transfer to wetland animals (Wissinger 1999). Keough and associates (1998) suggest that algae can fix dissolved carbon derived from decomposing detritus, and so algae may serve as an indirect link between wetland detritus and animals.

Synthesis of the Trophic Basis for Wetland Animal Production
In Figure 7.3, we attempt to synthesize existing knowledge on the basis of wetland food webs. Living macrophytes are consumed by several herbivores, of which terrestrial animals such as muskrats, moth and beetle larvae, and waterfowl are particularly notable. However, most macrophyte tissue is not consumed and instead enters the detrital pool. Relatively few animals can directly consume plant detritus, probably because nutritionally this material is a poor-quality resource (Fig. 7.2). Most wetland detritus is probably

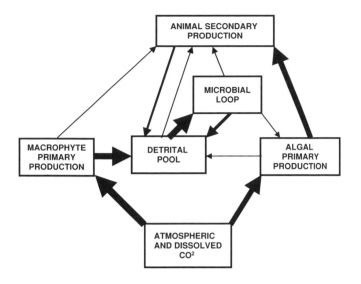

FIGURE 7.3
Schematic showing how animal secondary production in wetlands is based trophically on carbon from living macrophytes, detritus, and algae, with the link with algae being particularly strong.

consumed by the microbial community rather than animals. The extent to which the microbial community transfers energy from detritus to animals is not known. Rather than living or dead macrophytes, most evidence to date points toward algae as serving as the primary base of wetland food webs. Of course, exceptions to this general scheme will exist. For example, forested wetlands are shaded, and under restricted light conditions algal production will be reduced. Forested wetlands are probably detritus based, although algal production during leaf-off periods may still be important.

Why is it important to establish which energy sources are the foundation of food webs? If wetland food webs are based on living plants or detritus, it seems less likely that animal populations or communities will become food limited because of the enormous volume of these foods available in most wetlands. By contrast, if wetland trophic structure is algal based, food limitation is more likely to develop because the amount of algal biomass—especially the palatable planktonic, benthic, and epiphytic forms—available for wetland animal consumption is typically small (perhaps because animals compete intensively for this resource). Understanding the functional basis of wetland food webs will allow us to better predict consequences of habitat alterations.

PREDATION

The animal community in many wetlands is dominated by predators. Within the aquatic invertebrate community, predatory forms such as dragonflies, aquatic beetles, true bugs, and spiders abound, more so in wetlands than in aquatic habitats (e.g., lakes, rivers, or streams). Wetland reptiles, with the exception of some turtle species, are almost exclusively predaceous, and wetland fish (large or small) are mostly predaceous, typically on aquatic invertebrates or other fish. Adult and larval salamanders, and adult frogs and toads are all predators. While most frog larvae are considered algivores, predatory behavior by them is now known to be common (Petranka and Kennedy 1999). Among the birds, wading and shore birds prey on fish or invertebrates, and most songbirds in wetlands consume insects. Even those birds that are typically considered herbivores, such as dabbling ducks (mallards, teals), feed extensively on invertebrates when they require protein-rich food sources, especially while they are young ducklings, during feather molts, or when preparing for migration and nesting (Baldassarre and Bolen 1994).

Impacts of Predation

Predation can be a pervasive influence on wetland animal communities. In tidal mudflats and other temporary wetlands, such as drawndown impoundments, shorebirds (Order Charadriiformes) can form large flocks that have been shown via exclosure experiments to have a huge impact on benthic invertebrates. For example, Weber and Haig (1997) found that spring-migrating shorebirds reduced invertebrate abundance and biomass by about 50% but that impacts of predation varied spatially. Because shorebird flocks tend to feed in areas of highest invertebrate abundance, they proposed that a negative feedback loop existed that would tend to even out prey and predator distributions. However, they found only partial support for such a mechanism. Mercier and McNeil (1994) found a large temporal effect of the influence of shorebird predation on invertebrate numbers in overwintering habitats of Venezuela. Probably the largest effect of shorebird predation is exhibited by staging birds prior to migration, when concentrations in excess of one million birds have been observed (Wilson 1989).

Predation is also an important influence on birds themselves. Nest predation is the major cause of nest failure in most birds (Ricklefs 1969). Recent evidence implicates nest predation as a crucially important factor regulating certain waterfowl populations, especially in those associated with prairie potholes of North America, which are increasingly destroyed or fragmented from agricultural encroachment (Greenwood et al. 1995). Similarly, nest predation limits songbird populations (Sherry and Holmes 1995). In wetlands, nests built over water commonly are afforded increased protection from many nest predators compared with similar nests built over dry land. However, when a large area such as a river floodplain is inundated, some nest predators such as rat snakes and raccoons are capable of living an arboreal existence, and nest predation may actually increase in canopy nests at such times (Mullin et al. 2000). Birds such as Acadian Flycatchers (*Empidonax virescens*) may choose nest sites that minimize access by such predators (Wilson and Cooper 1998; Mullin and Cooper 2002).

Impacts of predation can ripple throughout wetland communities. After predaceous fish (bluegill, yellow perch, bullhead) became established in Lake Christina, a shallow waterfowl lake in Minnesota, water turbidity increased, submersed macrophyte beds declined, and benthic invertebrate populations became low (Hanson and Butler 1994a, 1994b). A wetland that historically had been a crucial feeding and staging area for migrating diving ducks no longer attracted significant bird numbers. In an effort to rehabilitate the habitat for waterfowl, fish were eliminated from the lake in 1987 using rotenone pesticide. In the first year after the fish kill, large cladocerans *(Daphnia)* became abundant, and phytoplankton populations declined (Hanson and Bulter 1994b). Water transparency increased and submersed macrophyte beds expanded, as did benthic macroinvertebrate populations. With the increased availability of plant and invertebrate foods, use by migrating ducks increased dramatically. In this wetland lake, both lower and higher trophic levels were being affected by fish predation.

In salt marshes of the southeastern United States, a snail grazer (the periwinkle, *Littoraria irrorata*) has the potential to virtually eliminate stands of cordgrass *(Spartina)*. However, Silliman and Bertness (2002) found that a trophic cascade operates in these marshes where predators (blue crabs, *Callinectes sapidus,* and diamondback terrapins, *Malaclemys terrapin*) limit populations of the periwinkles, preventing them from causing large-scale defoliation of the cordgrass. They suggest that some recent massive die-offs of cordgrass in the eastern United States might have developed because humans are overharvesting predatory blue crab, permitting periwinkle populations to explode. Batzer and Resh (1991) describe a similar trophic cascade in a California seasonal wetland. When densities of predatory beetle larvae were high, they found that predation kept densities of midge grazers low, and in the absence of grazers, biomass of algal periphyton accumulated. On the other hand, if beetle densities were low, midge populations exploded, and their grazing largely eliminated the algal periphyton. Once algae were gone, the midge populations crashed, presumably from lack of food.

Flocking shorebirds feeding in tidal mudflats have been shown to exert indirect trophic-level effects on invertebrates by either altering competition (Kent and Day 1983; Wilson 1989) or by feeding on predators of the invertebrates (Daborn et al. 1993). In the latter example, shorebirds fed on a grazing amphipod *(Corophium volutator),* which controlled the silicaceous benthic diatoms that were responsible in part for maintaining sediment cohesion. With the arrival of the migratory birds, grazing pressure on the diatoms decreased, and sediment strength increased.

Bottom-up Versus Top-down Control of Animal Populations

While every animal is influenced trophically from below by its food supply and most animals are concurrently influenced from above by predation, few studies have assessed the relative importance of each force or the interactions between bottom-up and top-down forces. Denno and colleagues (2002) used cage experiments with planthoppers in *Spartina* cordgrass stands to investigate the relative magnitude of two bottom-up forces, plant nutrition and plant structural complexity, and a top-down force, wolf-spider predation. They found that the relative influence of wolf-spider predation on planthoppers was greatest when plant condition was poor and plant thatch was present, typical of high marsh conditions. If the plants were nutritious and were lacking thatch, typical of low marsh

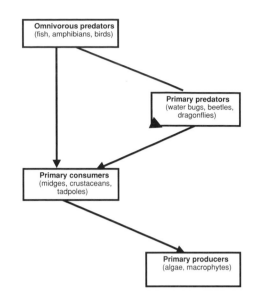

FIGURE 7.4

Direct and indirect pathways of predation in aquatic food webs of wetlands. Direct suppression of one trophic level by predation can result in an indirect enhancement of a second even lower trophic level, creating a trophic cascade. However, this indirect enhancement can be counterbalanced by any direct negative impacts of an omnivorous predator. The relative strengths of direct and indirect pathways of omnivory will determine the ultimate impact on a more basal species.

conditions, planthoppers were not limited by wolf-spider predation. The success of planthoppers in low marsh conditions was attributed to the insects' high growth rates, which permitted them to overwhelm any losses from predation, and mobility, which permitted them to evade capture in relatively open thatchless conditions.

Diehl (1992) also found that the structural complexity of aquatic plant stands affected the outcome of fish predation. He manipulated densities of predatory perch (*Perca fluviatilis*) in Swedish habitats with and without submersed vegetation and examined the responses of the invertebrate community. The perch were omnivorous, feeding both on predatory and nonpredatory invertebrates. Where submersed vegetation was present, perch foraging efficiency was reduced, and large predatory invertebrates were able to coexist with the fish (suggesting that habitat complexity should also be considered when modeling the effects of fish). No perch effect was evident on the populations of herbivorous and detritivorous invertebrates. However, Diehl attributed the lack of consumer response to the fact that when perch efficiency declined, the impacts of invertebrate predation probably increased. The effects of predation from fish and invertebrates counterbalanced. Because omnivorous predators (those that feed on more than one trophic level) can have both direct negative effects and indirect positive effects on lower trophic levels (Fig. 7.4), impacts on the overall food web can be complex.

Batzer (1998) found that chironomid midges in a New York marsh were also being affected by both top-down and bottom-up influences, although in this case, the bottom-up interaction from plants was nutritional rather than structural. Cage experiments were conducted where the density of large or small fish (bullheads or carp) was controlled and the biomass of cattail (*Typha*) litter was manipulated. Reducing small fish numbers and supplementing litter simultaneously enhanced densities of midges, although midge response to litter was less dramatic than the response to fish.

In wetland forests, the relative importance of top-down and bottom-up processes is not known. By comparison, in terrestrial forests, herbivorous insects are the major herbivores by biomass, and a trophic cascade involving insectivorous birds, herbivorous insects, and trees has been identified. Marquis and Whelan (1994) found increased numbers of caterpillars, increased leaf damage, and decreased productivity by saplings inside cages compared with exposed saplings, suggesting a top-down process. However, Forkner and Hunter (2000) mediated bird predation pressure in another exclosure study by manipulating nutrient levels, suggesting that the relative strength and expression of bottom-up versus top-down forces probably vary spatially in terrestrial forest systems. A similar situation probably exists for trophic relationships in floodplain forests, but spatial variation is likely complicated further by temporal variation in flooding. However, this is mere conjecture, since these sorts of trophic cascades have yet to be studied in floodplain forests. It seems likely that both top-down and bottom-up forces are operating in most habitats, but the mechanisms and outcomes of these interactions will vary spatially and temporally.

Predator/Permanence Models

In wetlands and lakes, predation is considered one of the most important forces shaping overall aquatic animal communities. The predator/permanence model developed by Wellborn and associates (1996) (modification shown in Fig. 7.5) proposes that animal communities are structured by two habitat transitions:

1. A permanence transition between temporary and permanent water habitats, and

2. A predator transition between habitats with and without fish.

Because the physical transition in permanence often covaries with the biotic transition in top predators (fish), it is difficult to infer the relative importance of the two conditions along predator-permanence gradients from comparative data alone. Habitat drying is a stress that many aquatic organisms can not tolerate, and thus temporary water habitats are inhabited only by organisms adapted to cope with desiccation (e.g., small invertebrates with rapid development; see Chapter 4). A wider range of organisms can successfully live in permanent water habitats. In permanent habitats (lakes and ponds), Wellborn and colleagues (1996) maintained that the presence or absence of predatory fish is the primary factor influencing animal communities. In permanent water habitats without fish (e.g., ponds geographically isolated from fish-bearing water, winterkill lakes), aquatic predators other than fish, such as large invertebrates or amphibians, are positioned at the top of aquatic food webs. In habitats with fish, populations of larger invertebrates and amphibians are reduced or eliminated by fish, and the invertebrate community becomes dominated by small-bodied, sessile forms that are less susceptible to fish predation.

Although the predator/permanence model is a valuable tool because it focuses attention on the importance of hydrology and fish predation, many wetlands do not fit

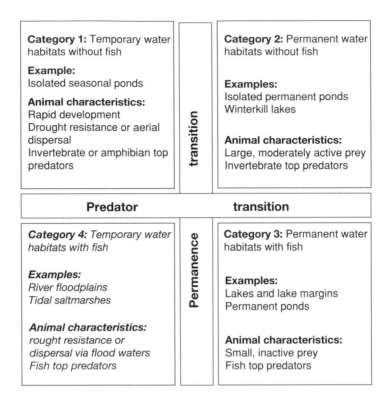

Category 1: Temporary water habitats without fish

Example:
Isolated seasonal ponds

Animal characteristics:
Rapid development
Drought resistance or aerial dispersal
Invertebrate or amphibian top predators

Category 2: Permanent water habitats without fish

Examples:
Isolated permanent ponds
Winterkill lakes

Animal characteristics:
Large, moderately active prey
Invertebrate top predators

transition

Predator　　　　　**transition**

Category 4: Temporary water habitats with fish

Examples:
River floodplains
Tidal saltmarshes

Animal characteristics:
rought resistance or dispersal via flood waters
Fish top predators

Category 3: Permanent water habitats with fish

Examples:
Lakes and lake margins
Permanent ponds

Animal characteristics:
Small, inactive prey
Fish top predators

Permanence

FIGURE 7.5

Permanence/predator gradients. Habitat Categories 1, 2, and 3 follow Wellborn and associates (1996), and Category 4 represents our modification of that model.

neatly into the three designated habitat categories designated by Wellborn and colleagues (1996):

1. Temporary water habitats;
2. Permanent water habitats without fish; and
3. Permanent water habitats with fish.

For example, some wetlands take on different characteristics over time. During a dry climatic cycle, a wetland might be a temporary habitat, but during a wet cycle, it may take on the character of a permanent water habitat without fish. Even if fish newly enter a wetland, it may take years before they become numerous enough to be functionally important and begin influencing overall community structure. Many wetlands actually fit into a fourth category (Fig. 7.5): temporary water habitats with fish (Kohler et al. 1999), of which floodplains or tidal marshes are good examples. These habitats are only temporarily inundated, but flood waters often contain fish. Presumably, animals inhabiting them must cope with both drying and fish predation. The permanence/predator model of Wellborn and colleagues (1996) also assumes that fish will exclude large active invertebrates via size-based prey selection because fish are bigger than the other aquatic animals. While this may be true in lakes, the fish in many wetlands are small bodied (small minnows, topminnows, pygmy varieties, immatures of larger taxa), and they often are of similar size to invertebrates. These small fish may not be able to exclude large invertebrates, and the two groups may coexist. For example, Georgia's Okefenokee Swamp teems with fish, but most are small species (Freeman and Freeman 1985); this wetland complex also supports a plethora of large-bodied invertebrate predators (Kratzer 2002). Zimmer and associates (2000) found that fathead minnows affected densities of most invertebrates in prairie wetlands but did not affect invertebrate size distributions, suggesting that size-based selection of prey was not occurring. The Wellborn model also does not address amphibian predation, which can be very important in wetlands. In high elevation fishless wetlands of Colorado, Wissinger and associates (1999a) found that invertebrate community structure was minimally influenced by physico-chemical variables, and instead, the presence or absence of predaceous salamanders exerted the most control on invertebrates. Perhaps expanding the predator/permanence paradigm (Fig. 7.5) to include amphibians will provide additional explanatory values.

COMMUNITY ECOLOGY
SECONDARY SUCCESSION

Succession is a change in community composition over time. Primary succession occurs after a new habitat is created, and a wetland example would be the slow conversion of a glacially created shallow lake into an herbaceous marsh, then a forested wetland, and ultimately an upland (see Chapters 3 and 6). Surprisingly, changes in animal communities along primary succession gradients have yet to be described. Secondary succession occurs after an established habitat is affected by fire, a weather event, or some other disturbance. For wetland animals, most research focus on succession has been on secondary processes that occur postdisturbance.

Drought Recovery
The response of animals in drought-affected wetlands of the North American Prairie (summarized in Murkin et al. 2000) is probably the best documented case of secondary succession for wetlands. (Details on plant responses can be found in the Chapter 6 section on prairie potholes.) In the prairie pothole region, wet and dry precipitation periods tend to cycle every few decades. During dry periods, water levels in wetlands can decline dramatically, and many prairie wetlands are dewatered, exposing the habitat bottom. This first stage of the wet-dry cycle is called the *dry marsh phase* (Fig. 7.6). As wetlands dry, aquatic animals must leave the wetlands, employ some sort of drought resistance strategy (see Chapter 4), or perish. Shore and wading birds will flock to drying wetlands to feed on newly exposed or stranded aquatic invertebrates and fish. Once the wetland dries, a dramatic botanical change occurs as seeds in the seed bank germinate and begin to grow (see Chapter 6). Certain birds

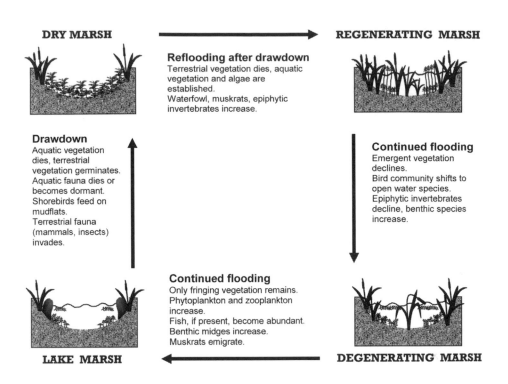

DRY MARSH ➡️ **REGENERATING MARSH**

Reflooding after drawdown
Terrestrial vegetation dies, aquatic vegetation and algae are established.
Waterfowl, muskrats, epiphytic invertebrates increase.

Drawdown
Aquatic vegetation dies, terrestrial vegetation germinates. Aquatic fauna dies or becomes dormant. Shorebirds feed on mudflats. Terrestrial fauna (mammals, insects) invades.

Continued flooding
Emergent vegetation declines.
Bird community shifts to open water species.
Epiphytic invertebrates decline, benthic species increase.

Continued flooding
Only fringing vegetation remains. Phytoplankton and zooplankton increase.
Fish, if present, become abundant. Benthic midges increase. Muskrats emigrate.

LAKE MARSH ⬅️ **DEGENERATING MARSH**

FIGURE 7.6

Successional trajectory of marsh habitats in response to periodic drying and prolonged reflooding in northern prairie marshes of central North America. Adapted from Murkin and Ross (1999), and portions reprinted with permission of John Wiley & Sons, Inc.

such as red-winged blackbirds find plant stands in dry marsh to be optimal nesting habitats (Murkin and Caldwell 2000), and the new growth of annual plants serves as food for an assortment of terrestrial herbivores (deer, insects).

Once sufficient rains return, wetlands refill, and the *regenerating marsh phase* begins (Fig. 7.6). Annual plants that germinated during the dry phase will die from flooding, whereas perennial emergent hydrophytes (sedges, reeds, cattails) expand. Submersed pondweeds that had disappeared in the dry phase become reestablished (see Chapter 6). Flooding forces the terrestrial fauna to vacate the wetland, but the wetland becomes recolonized by aquatic animals, emerging from dormancy or migrating back from surrounding wetlands. Aquatic invertebrate and amphibian populations can explode because an abundance of food and structure exists in the form of drowned annual plants and algae. Copious growth of algal food is stimulated by nutrients released from oxidized sediments and decaying vegetation (see Chapters 5 and 8). In the early stages of regeneration, invertebrate and amphibian populations will not yet be limited by predators (fish, large invertebrates), which are generally slower to reestablish. Dabbling ducks (mallards, teals) are especially attracted to the hemi-marsh conditions (roughly equal proportions of open water and plant cover) that develop during regeneration.

Regeneration usually lasts from three to five years. If flooding continues beyond that period, the *degenerating marsh phase* begins (Fig. 7.6). Stands of emergent plants will begin to thin as herbivores (muskrats, insects), disease, and the direct effects of prolonged flooding take their toll. Periods of unusually deep water that over-top emergent plants can magnify plant mortality. Minimal plant germination will occur under flooded conditions, so plants that die are not replaced, and the marsh begins to convert to a more open water condition. Aquatic invertebrates that live on plant surfaces (epiphytic forms) will decline with the loss of substrate, but invertebrates that live on mud substrates (benthic forms) may increase (Wrubleski 1999). Similarly, the avian community changes to one that prefers open water conditions (diving ducks, coots) (Murkin and Caldwell 2000). If fish occur, prolonged flooding will allow their populations to grow, and fish predation will begin shaping the overall animal community (see Fig. 7. 5). If emergent vegetation disappears from all but the fringes of the wetland, an extreme form of degeneration develops called the *lake marsh phase* (Fig. 7.6). The animal community of lake marsh will be dominated by a few species that thrive in open water (planktonic crustaceans, benthic midges, fish, piscivorous and planktivorous birds). Lake marsh will persist until another dry cycle dewaters the site, and then the cycle will repeat.

Because dabbling ducks, which are highly sought after by hunters, prosper during the earlier stages of the wet-dry cycle, many managers of wetlands use water control techniques to keep the wetlands in that condition. For example, moist-soil management is practiced on most wildlife management areas (Fredrickson and Taylor 1982). Moist-soil impoundments are dried and flooded yearly to stimulate growth of annual plants such as smartweed *(Polygonum)* and beggartick *(Bidens)* because these plants produce copious seed that is prime duck forage. Dense populations of aquatic invertebrates, especially midge larvae, develop in these newly flooded wetlands, and they are also highly desirable duck food. A second strategy used commonly to manage wetlands for waterfowl is called *semipermanent flooding*. This technique involves dewatering the wetland for a year or at least a summer season and then maintaining flooded conditions for the next three to five years. This kind of management maintains the wetland in the regenerating phase, which creates the hemi-marsh conditions preferred by many dabbling ducks, and it prevents the marsh from moving from regeneration into degeneration.

Conversion of Herbaceous Marsh to Forested Swamp

Some, but by no means all, herbaceous marshes will follow a successional trajectory toward becoming a forested wetland. This very slow process is difficult to track scientifically, and thus limited information is available on animal succession. However, clear differences in amphibian species composition exist between open and wooded wetlands. In a long-term comparative study in Michigan, species that dominated open habitat temporary wetlands such as toads *(Bufo americanus)*, treefrogs *(Hyla versicolor)*, green frogs *(Rana clumitans)*, leopard frogs *(Rana pipiens)*, and newts *(Notopthalmus viridescens)* have been replaced by wood frogs *(Rana sylvatica)*, and two ambystomatid salamanders *(Ambystoma maculatum* and *A. laterale*) as canopies have closed during forest succession (Skelly et al. 1999). The underlying mechanisms that control species shifts along canopy gradients are likely to be a combination of changes in dissolved oxygen, variation in food resources (both detrital and algal), and temperature (Werner and Glennemeier 1999; Skelly et al. 1999; Freidenburg and Skelly 2004).

More information about animal response to the conversion of marsh to swamp is available by studying the reverse process, the often rapid conversion of forested swamp into herbaceous wetland. A forested wetland can be converted naturally to an herbaceous state by fire, beaver activity, or other natural disturbances, but most documented instances of such change involve the human logging of forested wetlands. Removal of shade trees from wetlands opens up the forest floor to sunlight, which stimulates the growth of herbaceous plants and algae, and causes the formerly forested wetlands to take on the floristic characteristics of marshes (Perison et al. 1997; Gale et al. 1998) or wet meadows (Mitchell et al. 1995; Roy et al. 2000). Because the nature of the plant community influences the structure of the animal communities (Wigley and Roberts 1994), the former forested fauna dominated by salamanders, arboreal reptiles, and interior forest birds is replaced by a marsh or meadow fauna dominated by frogs, ground-dwelling reptiles, and edge- and meadow-nesting birds (Clawson et al. 1997; Hurst and Bourland 1996; Moorman and Guynn 2001; Phelps and Lancia 1995; Perison et al. 1997). There may be no overall decrease in animal species richness or diversity when a forested wetland is converted to an herbaceous wetland, but the nature of the animal community clearly changes. Presumably, if herbaceous wetlands undergo natural succession into forested wetlands, the animal community will also revert back into a typical forested fauna.

BIOGEOGRAPHY

Many wetlands occur almost as isolated habitat islands in an upland sea, and thus wetland researchers (e.g., Ebert and Balko 1987; Hall et al. 2004) have attempted to adapt tenets of the equilibrium theory of island biogeography (sensu MacArthur and Wilson 1967) to wetlands. MacArthur and Wilson (1967) postulated that for oceanic islands, an equilibrium develops between the immigration of new species and the extinction of those already present, and the equilibrium number of species is determined by (1) a distance effect (islands near a mainland source of species will be colonized by more species than those islands farther removed) and (2) an area effect (extinction rates on small islands will be greater than on larger islands) (Fig. 7.7). The issues of habitat size and isolation implicit in island biogeography seem likely to have application for isolated wetlands. However, some aspects of the theory will not apply to wetlands. Wetlands differ from islands in that there is seldom a single "mainland" source of species to colonize them. Further, many animals (birds, amphibians, insects) are transient residents of wetland habitats, moving between a specific wetland and other habitats to reproduce, develop, forage, seasonally migrate, or diapause.

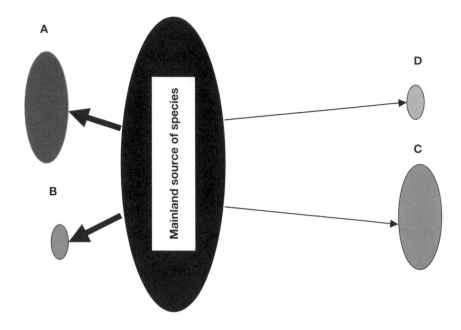

FIGURE 7.7

Adapting the equilibrium theory of island biogeography to isolated wetlands. The theory postulates that islands, and presumably isolated wetlands, close to a mainland source of species will be colonized by more species than islands farther removed from the mainland. Arrows represent this colonization and the width of the arrows the amount of colonization. The theory further postulates that extinction rates on small islands will be greater than on large islands. Thus, a large island in close proximity to the mainland will have numerous species (hence, the dark shading of island A), while a small island far removed from the mainland will have few species (hence, the light shading of island D). Islands B and C (medium shading) should have intermediary richness.

Metapopulation and metacommunity theory incorporates many of the same ideas about colonization and extinction in habitat patches, and so this theory also has appeal to some wetland researchers (Wissinger 1999; Semlitsch 2000; Cottenie et al. 2003; Kneitel and Miller 2003). A metapopulation is a set of small, spatially separated populations that are united together (Fig. 7.8). Even if an individual subpopulation becomes extinct, at least some of the subpopulations will survive, and colonists from the surviving patches will disperse back into extinct patches. Thus, a metapopulation persists in a balance of local extinction and colonization. A metacommunity simply consists of a set of metapopulations. In adapting metapopulation theory to management, Semlitsch (2000) maintains that for aquatic-breeding amphibians in wetlands, three crucial factors must be considered: (1) the number of individuals dispersing from individual wetlands; (2) the diversity of wetlands, especially in terms of hydroperiod; and (3) the probability of dispersal among adjacent wetlands or the recolonization of local populations.

Researchers have yet to test the whole of either island biogeography or metapopulation/metacommunity theory in wetland habitats. However, some portions of the theories

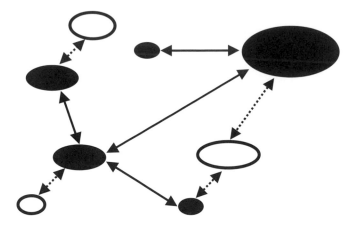

FIGURE 7.8

A metapopulation in isolated wetlands, with circles representing patches of wetland habitat. The filled circles indicate wetlands that are occupied by a species, and open circles represent temporarily vacant wetlands. Arrows indicate colonization pathways of the population. Theory suggests that vacant patches, where the population has gone extinct, will be eventually become recolonized by individuals from occupied patches.

have received attention, and below we review research on the importance of habitat isolation, habitat size, colonization, and extinction to wetland animal community development.

Habitat Isolation

Wilson, one of the original authors of the equilibrium theory of island biogeography, and Simberloff designed a direct test of the isolation aspect of the theory (Fig. 7.7) using wetland mangrove islands off the Florida coast. They first found all of the terrestrial animal species occurring on several small mangrove islands of varying distance from the mainland; this consisted of from 20 to 50 arboreal arthropods (spiders and insects) per island. Then they covered treatment islands with fumigation tents (the ones typically used for whole house pesticide treatments) and pumped in methyl bromide gas to kill all spiders and insects (only a few wood borers survived). Two control islands remained untreated. Recolonization of the defaunated wetland islands was then described. Simberloff and Wilson (1970) found that the islands nearest to the mainland were recolonized rapidly, and soon the species number reached an apparent equilibrium state (Fig. 7.9). The island farthest from the coast was colonized more slowly, and the equilibrium species number was lower than the other islands. The control islands maintained their normal species number, although community compositions varied over the study period. The results of this experiment supported the equilibrium theory of island biogeography in that equilibria seemed to develop and the equilibrium species number declined as habitats became more isolated from the source of colonists (Fig. 7.7). Natural disappearances also occurred on islands, even over the short study period, indicating that the extinction aspect of the theory was a frequent event.

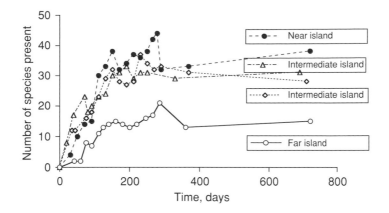

FIGURE 7.9

Postfumigation colonization curves for four small mangrove islands of varying proximities to the mainland sources of colonizers. Colonizers included an assortment of terrestrial insects and spiders. Proximity to the coast and community richness was related. The island nearest the coastline was colonized most rapidly, and the equilibrium species number was the greatest. The island farthest from the coast was colonized more slowly, and the equilibrium species number was lower. Figure was adapted from Simberloff and Wilson (1970) with the permission of the senior author and the Ecological Society of America.

For wetlands, habitat isolation can entail more than just a distance effect. Snodgrass and associates (1996) studied fish in isolated depressional wetlands of the southeastern United States. Despite lacking permanent surface connections to other water bodies and drying periodically, about 20% of the depressional wetlands supported fish. Apparently, these habitats can be colonized or recolonized by fish during periods of unusually high water. They found that fish occurred most frequently in depressional wetlands in close proximity to other aquatic habitats, but that proximity alone did not explain fish assemblage structure. The elevation difference between isolated wetlands and other water bodies was also important. If a significant elevation gradient existed between an isolated wetland and a nearby water body, fish movement was apparently inhibited. Snodgrass and associates (1996) maintained that connectivity, rather than simple proximity, was the factor most likely to influence movements of fish from source populations into isolated depressional wetlands. Baber and colleagues (2002) studied fish distributions in temporary wetlands of Florida, and they reiterated that the connectivity of isolated temporary wetlands with permanent water bodies played an importance role in community development. Gray and colleagues (2004) found that interwetland landscape complexity (mostly agricultural influences) can affect amphibian community composition in playa wetlands of the U.S. southern high plains.

As wetlands become increasingly isolated from each other due to habitat destruction and fragmentation, many animals populations will be threatened (Semlitsch 2000). A lack of certain species of amphibians (Lehtinen et al. 1999; Hamer et al. 2002), turtles

(Joyal et al. 2001), fish (Lafferty et al. 1999), and butterflies (Wettstein and Schmid 1999) has been associated with greater habitat isolation. However, wetland birds (Calme and Desrochers 2000), toads (Bradford et al. 2003), and insects (Brose 2003), which all have well-developed dispersal capabilities, were found to occupy even the most remote wetlands, indicating that not all wetland animal distributions are limited by habitat isolation.

Habitat Size

In ecology, it is generally accepted that a larger habitat will support more species than a smaller habitat (Fig. 7.7), given that other factors are equal. For example, wetland complexes that arise from beaver activity tend to include more types of habitats and subhabitats (open ponds, marshes, flooded forests, shrub swamps, abandoned wet meadows), and may contain more species than a comparably sized wetland of one type (Naiman et al. 1988). However, it is common for wetland researchers to find the relationship between animal species richness and wetland size to be rather weak, whether for birds (Calme and Desrochers 2000), amphibians (Kolozsvary and Swihart 1999; Snodgrass et al. 2000; Eason and Fauth 2001; but see Lehtinen and Galatowitsch 2001), or invertebrates (Schneider and Frost 1996; Wissinger et al. 1999a; Brose 2003; Batzer et al. 2004; Hall et al. 2004). However, for aquatic animals, both habitat size and water permanence may affect richness, and because size and permanence can be covariates (larger habitats are often more permanent; Wissinger et al. 1999a), isolating the influence of size will be complicated. Because the link between water permanence and species richness can be quite strong (Jeffries 1994; Schneider and Frost 1996; Kolozsvary and Swihart 1999; Wissinger et al. 1999a; Snodgrass et al. 2000; Eason and Fauth 2001; Batzer et al. 2004), some scientists have suggested that water permanence might be a useful replacement for habitat size when adapting island biogeography theory to wetlands (Ebert and Balko 1987; Brooks 2000). However, Hall and associates (2004) maintained that the ephemeral nature of many wetlands might preclude the development of an equilibrium between colonization and extinction, making it inappropriate to apply island biogeographic theory to temporary wetlands. Clearly, any attempt to associate faunal richness with wetland size must factor out the effects of permanence (and vice versa) before the analysis is clean. Muddying the waters further is the additional relationship between water permanence and predation (Fig. 7.5), which can either increase (by predator mediated coexistence) or decrease (by elimination of vulnerable species) taxa richness depending on interaction strengths.

The nature of wetland organisms might also contribute to a weak relationship between faunal richness and habitat size. A primary reason that habitat size is believed to affect diversity is that a larger habitat contains a wider range of microhabitats (Fig. 7.7), and this heterogeneity provides opportunities for a wider variety of organisms, especially specialists. However, wetlands are highly variable systems, and any specific set of microhabitat conditions might develop only sporadically. It would be risky for an animal to specialize on a narrow range of environmental conditions. Rather, being a generalist, capable of coping with whatever conditions develop, might be the more prudent strategy (Batzer et al. 2004). Habitat generalists can probably persist in a variety of habitats, large and small, and thus habitat size becomes less important.

Because of the weak relationship between wetland size and faunal richness, and the fact that some wetland animals actually prefer small, ephemeral wetlands, Snodgrass and colleagues (2000) challenged the notion that discussions concerning wetland conservation or destruction should rely heavily on habitat size. Instead, they advocate focusing on conserving a diversity of wetland sizes and hydroperiods across landscapes.

Colonization of Wetlands

Many wetland animals are noted for their colonizing abilities. Insects and birds, the two most diverse animal groups in wetlands, probably achieve their dominance because flight enables them to find or escape from constantly changing wetland environments. When a previously dry wetland floods, insects and waterfowl arrive within days or even hours. Mosquitoes, midges, dragonflies, and beetles are often observed depositing eggs in wetlands as they become inundated (Streever et al. 1996; Brown et al. 1997; Mitsch et al. 1998; Wrubleski 1999; Keiper and Walton 2000). Waterfowl find newly flooded seasonal ponds to be especially valuable sites for foraging and nesting. However, despite the evidence for rapid colonization by many winged wetland taxa, few studies have actually quantified dispersal rates and gene flow for rapidly colonizing species (Bohonak and Jenkins 2004).

Sometimes, aerial colonization involves predictable, cyclic movements between habitats. It is well known that most wetlands birds migrate between habitats to breed and to overwinter. In addition, many insects migrate between permanent and temporary wetlands, and some possess a life history syndrome that involves wing dimorphism (Wissinger 1997; Langellotto and Denno 2001; see also Chapter 4). Long-winged adults of some beetles and water bugs overwinter in permanent habitats and then migrate to colonize refilled temporary habitats in spring. Depending on the duration of the wet phase, one or more flightless short-winged, but highly fecund, generations are completed in those temporary habitats. As habitats dry, a dispersing generation of long-winged, but sexually immature, individuals develops that returns to permanent waters. This flight polymorphism not only facilitates dispersal but also allows for the rapid establishment of large populations in temporary habitats (Batzer and Wissinger 1996). Wing dimorphism is also prevalent in terrestrial planthoppers that inhabit coastal wetlands and research has revealed that (1) energetic trade-offs exist between reproduction and dispersal; (2) dispersal patterns are density dependent; (3) habitat heterogeneity helps maintain polymorphisms; and (4) life history strategies are affected by disturbance regimes (Denno and Roderick 1990, 1992; Langellotto and Denno 2001).

Even flightless wetland taxa arrive at newly inundated wetlands in remarkably short order. Petranka and associates (2003) found that seven amphibian species colonized some newly created wetlands during the initial wet cycle. Fish, which one would assume would have difficulty accessing isolated habitats, were found within a few years to have colonized isolated beaver ponds created by damming seepage of closed peatlands (Ray et al. 2004). Despite being extirpated by periodic drought, fish (Snodgrass et al. 1996; Zimmer et al. 2000) and amphibians (Bradford et al. 2003) often are broadly distributed across complexes of isolated wetlands, indicating that habitat recolonization is rapid.

Small zooplankton and mites are assumed to disperse passively—either by wind, rain, or on animal vectors (Wiggins et al. 1980; Williams 1987). This assumption has been fostered by the widespread and cosmopolitan distributions of many zooplankton species, although Jenkins and Underwood (1998) note the scant evidence for zooplankton dispersal rates by wind or water. While there is considerable potential for internal and external bird and mammal transport of fish, amphibians, and invertebrates, and wind dispersal of resistant stages of small invertebrates, few studies have actually quantified colonization rates (Bilton et al. 2001; Okamura and Freeland 2002; Figuerola and Green 2002; Cáceres and Soluk 2002). One exception is for parasitic water mites that disperse while attached to their insect hosts (Bohonak et al. 2004). A second example is for fairy shrimp whose diapausing eggs can survive passage through the guts of salamanders that migrate to temporary wetlands to feed on these large, nutritious prey (Whiteman et al. 1996). Fairy shrimp dispersal rates estimated from genetic differences among populations are nearly identical to the colonization rates inferred from inter-habitat movements of salamanders (Bohonak and Whiteman 1996).

Three techniques have been used to quantify dispersal of wetland animals. The first is to use traps to estimate rates and distances of dispersal (e.g., Delettre and Morvan 2000). Lundkvist and colleagues (2002) used traps that mimic the reflectance spectra of wetland breeding habitats to estimate the movements of adult diving beetles and found that beetles that inhabit temporary waters were more mobile than those typically found in permanent wetlands. The use of stable isotopes is a second technique likely to become important for understanding animal dispersal (Hobson 1999). Caudill (2003) enriched natal habitats with a ^{15}N isotope and found that there was considerable movement of a mayfly among different ponds within a beaver wetland complex. Finally, dispersal rates can be inferred from estimates of gene flow (Bohonak and Roderick 2001). This technique relies on several critical assumptions (e.g., long-term equilibrium of drift and gene flow), and direct measurement of individual movements will always be an important benchmark for genetically inferred dispersal rates (Bohonak and Jenkins 2004). All of these methods will become increasingly important as ecologists pursue a landscape-level, metacommunity (Fig. 7.8) understanding of ecological systems.

Many wetland animals that live in temporary wetlands (invertebrates, amphibians, fish) have desiccation-tolerant stages to complement other dispersal and colonization strategies (adaptations of animals for desiccation resistance are described in Chapter 4). One advantage of desiccation resistance is that it guarantees rapid establishment after refilling. Like plant seed banks, the "egg banks" of certain invertebrates can be long lived, and many species can deposit broods with individuals that hatch during different subsequent wet-dry cycles (Adams 1984; Dodson 1987; De Stasio 1989; Taylor et al. 1990; Brendonck 1996; Cáceres 1997; Havel et al. 2000; Medland and Taylor 2001). The multiple generations that are stored in egg banks ensure that a diverse community of animals will be quickly established after drying events (Brock et al. 2003). The zooplankton community in refilling basins will not necessarily reflect the community composition before the previous drying event because of different dormancy periods and diapause strategies (Brock et al. 2003; Brendonck and De Meester 2003).

One strategy useful to assess the proportional contributions of persistence through desiccation resistance and recolonization is to compare the animals that emerge from experimentally rehydrated sediments with the communities observed when the basins refill (persistence + aerial colonization). Using this technique, Wissinger and Gallagher (1999) found that desiccation tolerance played a more important role in the reassembly of communities after an extended drought in temporary habitats (63–71% of all colonizers) than in an adjacent permanent wetland (38% of all colonizers). Similarly, Dietz-Brantley and associates (2002) found that aestivating invertebrates made up a significant component of colonization in Carolina bay wetlands. Anderson and Smith (2004) found that only 30% of all colonists in temporary playa wetlands of Texas originated from aestivating stages. The relative importance of desiccation tolerance may depend on the harshness of drying, and Anderson and colleagues (1999) predict that colonization from aestivating organisms should be least important in arid regions where substrates become inhospitable to most organisms.

Wetland invertebrates are excellent candidates for the study of dispersal, gene flow, and local adaptation for a variety of reasons including (1) the relatively discrete boundaries of wetland habitats; (2) the relative ease with which they can be sampled; (3) relatively large populations and short generation times that facilitate the estimation of population-level parameters; and (4) the frequent elimination, creation, or restoration of habitats by humans that offer opportunities to study colonization events.

Biogeographic Effects on Species Extinction

Animal extinctions, even at a local scale, are difficult to document because long-term study is typically required (see Semlitsch et al. 1996), and thus little empirical evidence on extinction events for wetland animals exists. Lafferty and colleagues (1999) used historical data on the distributions of the now endangered tidewater goby *(Eucyclobius newberryi)* from a series of isolated coastal wetlands in California to assess the relationship between habitat size and extinction. They found that, consistent with island biogeography theory, extirpation rates of this fish were greater in small than large wetlands and surmised that small wetlands were more sensitive to drought. For wetland fish, drought is frequently the mechanism for local extinction (Snodgrass et al. 1996; Baber et al. 2002). While invertebrates are also susceptible to drought, Jeffries (1994) found that invertebrate survival, even in drought-affected ponds, was ultimately dependent more on biotic processes such as predation or reproductive success than habitat drying. In Chapter 4, Mendelssohn and Batzer propose that most wetland animals are well adapted to drought and for them, routine drying is not a significant constraint. Extinctions probably occur when an unusual condition develops in a wetland habitat, and not from natural environmental variation.

HABITAT HETEROGENEITY

Embedded in the concept that larger habitats will support more species is the idea that larger habitats will contain a broad range of subhabitats, offering opportunities for more species. Also, larger habitats are more likely to feature the natural processes, especially natural disturbances, which maintain a diversity of subhabitats and the species they contain.

Edge Effects

It has been long recognized that edges, or ecotones, the boundaries between habitats or subhabitats, are sites of increased species diversity because they tend to contain species that occupy each of the adjacent habitats as well as the actual edge (Leopold 1933; Yahner 1988). Wetland-upland boundaries would seem to be a particularly good example of this increased species diversity, especially in instances where the transition zone between the two habitats is large (Kilgo et al. 1998). Thus, a target of management prescriptions by early wildlife biologists often included a mosaic of juxtaposed habitats with an optimal amount of edge (Leopold 1933).

More recently, it has been recognized that there are also negative effects associated with certain types of edge (Gates and Gysel 1978; Paton 1994). For example, bird nests can have decreased survival in smaller forest fragments (Wilcove 1985) or in landscapes with more fragmentation of forest habitats (Robinson et al. 1995). The cause is generally believed to be increased numbers of and/or vulnerability to a variety of nest predators attracted to edge situations. In some landscapes, increased fragmentation also makes remaining fragments more vulnerable to brood parasites such as the Brown-headed Cowbird *(Molothrus ater)* (Robinson et al. 1995). Also, increased desiccation that can occur along the edges of forests has been shown to decrease the abundance of litter-dwelling arthropods (Burke and Nol 1998).

However, the notion of decreased productivity along forest habitat–open habitat edges does not necessarily hold for all habitats or taxa. For example, juxtaposition of wetlands with certain types of uplands appears to be a necessary feature in the life history of many species of aquatic herpetofauna (Gibbons 2003). Many species of forest-dwelling amphibians require nearby wetlands for breeding (Semlitsch 1998, 2000). Conversely, some aquatic organisms such as turtles require a safe adjacent upland habitat in which to lay their eggs or to hibernate (Buhlmann 1995; Burke and Gibbons 1995). In some cases, wetland-upland boundaries may be travel routes for predators, but this is poorly documented. And it is likely that watercourses can serve as pathways for some predators and brood parasites to access otherwise intact forests, but evidence is again lacking.

Evidence of negative effects of edges on avian nest success in wetland ecosystems, mainly bottomland hardwood forests, is equivocal. Saracco and Collazo (1999) found approximately 90% of artificial nests placed near ecotones between bottomland forest and agriculture were depredated, compared with about 55% along forest-river edges. Moorman and associates (2002) reported that Hooded Warbler *(Wilsonia citrina)* nest success was unaffected by distance to edge in a bottomland forest, but that likelihood of nest parasitism was greater near clearcut edge. Twedt and colleagues (2001) found that timber harvest negatively affected nest success in tree-nesting birds in bottomland forests. However, nest success of a variety of bottomland forest songbird species was unaffected by creation of openings in a companion study. Nest success in that study was more likely related to flooding patterns, which provide protection for nests and may affect predator behavior (Wood 1999). Also, edge effects at the local scale are likely to be mediated by factors operating at larger spatial scales, such as degree of fragmentation in a landscape; thus, edge effects on nest success are variable (Rodewald 2002).

Gap Dynamics

Habitat heterogeneity in general and edges in particular are created by natural disturbances such as fire, floods, extreme weather events, and insect outbreaks, and by human activities such as agriculture, logging, and urbanization. On a smaller scale, in forested wetlands, gap-phase dynamics is an ongoing natural process. In general, these processes maintain a diversity of subhabitats within an overall habitat type or ecosystem (e.g., a variety of successional stages and species dominance patterns within a bottomland hardwood forest), and are key processes for maintaining biodiversity in the system. However, disturbances have a spatial and temporal scale, and effects on a system or level will depend on those scales (Pickett et al. 1989).

In forested wetlands, canopy disturbance is a major factor affecting forest structure and composition, and can in turn affect animal community structure (Moorman and Guynn 2001). Tree-fall gaps represent a distinct microhabitat that differs from the understory of the surrounding forest in vegetation structure, plant species composition, and microclimatic conditions. If gaps are large enough, species associated with early successional habitats will occupy them (Moorman and Guynn 2001). Arthropods, in particular, seem to respond positively to gaps (Blake and Hoppes 1986), although more work is needed on this topic, especially in bottomland forests. For example, insect abundance and distribution were influenced by flooding as well as by canopy disturbance in an Arkansas bottomland forest (Gorham et al. 2002). Blake and Hoppes (1986) captured more birds in gaps compared with the adjacent forest understory in an upland woodlot. Kilgo and associates (1999) captured more birds during fall migration in the largest (40-m radius) artificial gaps than in gaps of smaller size in a bottomland forest. Using the same study sites, Menzel and colleagues (2002) found more bat activity in forest gaps and Carolina bay wetlands than in forested habitats, probably because these habitats provided an open area in which to forage. However, several researchers have found decreased abundance of salamanders in bottomland forest gaps (Cromer et al. 2002) or in clearcuts (Clawson et al. 1997; Perison et al. 1997) compared with the forest interior. Differences were likely due in part to increased temperatures in forest openings, but clearcuts also contained less litter, an important habitat component for salamanders.

Hemi-marsh Concept

The realization that freshwater marsh habitats that contained a roughly equal mixture of open water and emergent plant cover (or hemi-marsh) are most productive for waterfowl has long been a tenet for managing marshes for wildlife (Weller 1978). Whether caused by natural succession (Fig. 7.6; Murkin et al. 2000), fire (De Szalay and Resh 1997), or mechanical mowing (Murkin et al. 1982; Batzer and Resh 1991; De Szalay and Resh 1997), waterfowl and invertebrate use of marshes tends to peak under heterogenous hemi-marsh conditions. Numerous ecological mechanisms probably contribute to this response. Hemi-marshes typically develop soon after drought events or other disturbances and are thus in the early regenerating stage of succession (Fig. 7.6). Assorted foods for animals are present, including seeds from annual plants, detritus, algae, and invertebrates. The interspersed plant stands provide substrates for invertebrates, nesting sites for birds, and protective cover from predation for many animals. Open water patches provide habitat for fish and foraging waterfowl (Murkin and Caldwell 2000) and are attractive to aerially colonizing insects (Batzer and Resh 1991; De Szalay and Resh 1997). The edge habitat between plant and open water patches may provide additional animal habitat (Murkin et al. 1992)

FOCAL WETLAND ANIMALS

While all animal species will contribute to the functioning of wetland ecosystems, some play particularly crucial roles. Names attributed to these species include "keystone species" or "ecosystem engineers." Each has a significant impact on numerous other species in a system through predation, buttressing food webs, or physically modifying habitat structure. Some other species may not play such crucial roles in wetland ecosystems but are sensitive to ecological changes and may serve as indicators or bellwethers of environmental impacts. Next, we discuss the ecology of what we consider some of the most important animal species or groups in wetlands, acknowledging that numerous deserving animals do not appear in our list.

BEAVERS

The beaver is a large rodent indigenous to much of North America *(C. canadensis)* and parts of Europe and Asia *(C. fiber)*. Beavers play a unique role in wetland ecology because, other than man, they are the only organisms capable of creating wetlands (Muller-Schwarze and Sun 2003). The beaver is often cited as the archetypical example of an ecosystem engineer. Jones and associates (1994) defined *ecosystem engineers* as organisms that directly or indirectly modulate the availability of resources to other species by causing physical state changes in biotic or abiotic materials. The ecological importance of the beaver stems largely from habitat modifications resulting from their dam-building activities.

The construction of a beaver dam initiates a sequence of events (Naiman et al. 1988; Hammerson 1994). The area behind the dam becomes flooded, and a channel or smaller wetland area is converted into a pond. Any upland trees or shrubs in the pond area die as soils around their roots become anoxic. Shoreline forests are also modified because beavers cut riparian trees or shrubs for food and building material. With the loss of trees, the pond canopy opens. The open water pond is then invaded by aquatic plants (pond weeds, lily pads). This "beaver pond" condition can persist for many years. Eventually, however, the beaver colony will die out from disease, or the colony will move from the area as food resources become limited. After abandonment, the dam will erode and breach, and the pond will drain. The plant seed bank in the exposed sediments will sprout, and a wet meadow habitat will develop. Slowly, trees and shrubs will reinvade, and the habitat will eventually revert back to its former forested state.

During this sequence, an assortment of important hydrologic, biogeochemical, and ecological processes are affected (Naiman et al. 1988; Naiman et al. 1994). After dam construction, the overall precipitation storage capacity of the habitat will increase due to the pond, and the variability in discharge and the current velocity of the stream will decline. The water table in the affected area may become elevated. Sediments being carried downstream will settle in the pond, and downstream turbidity may decrease. Oxygen dynamics will change, and hypoxic or anoxic conditions may develop in the pond area as plants killed by flooding decay. As mentioned earlier, a formerly upland plant community will be replaced by a wetland flora. In addition, planktonic algae may become more prevalent in the wetland pond than they were in the precursor stream channel. The stream invertebrate community will be replaced by a wetland fauna, and the functional nature (see Table 7.2) of this community will change. A community previously dominated by collector-filterers that filter food from flowing water and scrapers that graze on rock surfaces will be replaced by a community dominated by collector-gatherers that gather particles from surfaces and by invertebrate predators. Rolauffs and colleagues (2001) found that the dam itself supports a unique invertebrate fauna. Although the original stream channels generally support many more aquatic invertebrates than a wetland pond on a per m² basis, the much larger wetted area of the beaver pond will produce a greater total biomass of these animals. A stream herpetofauna dominated by salamanders and snakes may be replaced by a pond fauna dominated by frogs, turtles, and lizards (Metts et al. 2001). Flow-dependent lotic fishes will be replaced by lentic fishes, and early colonizing small-bodied fish will be replaced by larger-bodied predators as the ponds age (Snodgrass and Meffe 1998; Collen and Gibson 2001). Even after the dam is abandoned and the pond drains, there is a characteristic fish fauna associated with heavily vegetated channels that flow through wet meadows (Snodgrass and Meffe 1998). Finally, an assortment of birds, particularly waterfowl, find beaver ponds to be prime foraging, roosting, and brood-rearing sites (McCall et al. 1994).

The recovery of the beaver from the severe population depression that occurred during the fur-trapping era has had important consequences for landscape ecology (Muller-Schwarze and Sun 2003). Naiman and associates (1994) reported that 13% of the land in a 300 km² area of northern Minnesota was converted into new beaver meadows and ponds from 1927 to 1988. However, over a similar period in South Carolina, Snodgrass (1997) reported only 0.5% of the overall landscape was influenced by beavers. Beaver-created habitats can significantly alter the patch dynamics of landscapes (Wright et al. 2004), although the importance of beavers may vary regionally.

MUSKRATS

The muskrat is another aquatic rodent found throughout North America, and in much of Europe and Asia where it has been introduced by man. Fully grown, they measure about 60 centimeters in length and weigh about 1.5 kilograms. Muskrats are chiefly herbivores, eating various wetland plants, especially cattails *(Typha)* and bulrushes *(Scirpus)* (Clark 2000); they also use the leaves and stems to construct houses. Because their herbivorous behavior can affect wetland succession, the muskrat, like the beaver, has been touted as an ecosystem engineer.

In a classic book on muskrat population ecology, Errington (1963) describes how muskrat numbers undergo cyclic population fluctuations induced by social and physiological factors interacting with predation and disease. Errington suggested that when muskrat populations become high, they can decimate stands of emergent wetland plants in events called *eat-outs*. In fact, muskrats have long been considered a primary factor in the development of "lake marsh" conditions (Fig. 7.5), and this role in marsh succession contributes to the ecosystem engineer moniker. However, Clark (2000) maintains that little empirical evidence exists to demonstrate that muskrat herbivory can eliminate stands of cattails or reeds. In a study at Delta Marsh, Canada, he estimated how much of the total standing crop of emergent vegetation was removed by muskrats through cutting, consumption, and wastage. He found that at most 11% and as little as 1% of the plant standing biomass was removed by muskrats, even where populations were high. Clark concluded that muskrats may contribute to declines of emergent vegetation but suggests that the term *eat-out* overstates their importance. He further notes that where eat-outs have been reported, the events often coincide with high water events and speculated that declines of emergent vegetation might have been mostly related to undesirable hydrologic conditions for the plants. Muskrats in general do poorly when water fluctuations are extreme (Virgl and Messier 1996), perhaps because their food supply is inhibited.

Even if muskrats are not ecosystem engineers, they are still very important to marsh ecology. Connors and associates (2000) found that muskrat activity (feeding, burrowing, house formation) increased nitrogen mineralization and nitrification rates, and thus influenced wetland soil nitrogen dynamics. They anticipated that muskrats would increase floristic diversity by thinning monoculture stands of cattail, but their study did not support that hypothesis. De Szalay and Cassidy (2001) found that the open water halo surrounding muskrat lodges supported an invertebrate community that was different from the community in intact plant stands. An important role of muskrats may be in creating more spatially complex stands of emergent plants, providing opportunities for a greater variety of animals. Muskrats may also influence litter decomposition. Freshly cut plant material has different nutritional qualities than postsenescent detritus (van der Valk and Davis 1978b), and cut material is generally concentrated around muskrat houses; both factors produce unique conditions for decomposition (Clark 2000). Besides creating the hemi-marsh conditions that waterfowl prefer (see earlier), the houses that muskrats build are commonly used as waterfowl nesting platforms. Not all ecological impacts of muskrats are positive. In Eurasia, where the muskrat is an exotic invader, they may alter the structure of indigenous plant communities (Smirnov and Tretyakov 1998).

COLONIAL WADING BIRDS

Of all bird orders, arguably the one with the greatest percentage of species adapted to wetland habitats is the Ciconiiformes, or wading birds (Sprunt et al. 1978). The order consists of the herons, egrets, and bitterns (Family Ardeidae); ibises and spoonbills (Family Threskiornithidae); storks (Family Ciconiidae); and flamingoes (Family Phoenicicopteridae). Other than spoonbills and flamingoes, whose bills are adapted for filter feeding in shallow water, wading birds are well adapted to feed in both terrestrial and shallow water habitats. Their legs are long and unfeathered, with long, unwebbed toes that provide a solid footing in a variety of substrates. Their bills are long and pointed, allowing them to feed on a variety of prey, from fish, crabs, and other aquatic prey to small mammals and large insects in pastures. For the most part, though, wading birds, as the name implies, are tied to water in some way.

Of the various ways that wading birds are tied to water and wetlands, perhaps none is more intriguing, or has been the subject of more theoretical discussions in the literature, than their propensity for forming breeding colonies. Also known as *heronries* or *rookeries,* wading bird colonies can vary in size from a few breeding pairs of a single species to thousands of pairs of multiple species. Nests are usually placed in small trees or shrubs, often with many nests per tree. Colony sites are often traditional, in that they are used year after year, although they tend to slowly migrate as nesting substrate is gradually lost in portions of the colony. Thus, between the increased number of large birds in a particular area, and the fixed location of the colony over time, the colony site is both conspicuous to potential predators and is likely to result in a depletion of prey in the immediate area around the colony. What, then, is the advantage for these birds to nesting colonially?

First, although the colony site is conspicuous to predators, it often has several features that make it resistant to widespread nest depredation. The exact colony location is critical. Often, the colony is located on an island surrounded by deep water, thus discouraging many terrestrial mammalian predators. In the southeastern United States, the presence of alligators enhances protection against significant nest predators such as raccoons *(Procyon lotor).* The alligators benefit from the occasional nestling that loses its balance and falls into the water, but the advantage to the birds far outweighs these losses. With many nesting pairs, there are also many eyes to watch for predators, thus discouraging other predators such as crows.

Second, although food can become locally depleted near the colony, the colony can actually serve as a means of transferring information about food location. According to the information center hypothesis, birds in the colony can learn about location of food from birds arriving at the colony with food (Ward and Zahavi 1973). Information transfer would be especially important for species that feed on clumped prey that are locally abundant, such as fish schools, but are unpredictable in space and time. For example, Great Blue Herons *(Ardea herodius)* breeding in colonies were most likely to depart in the direction from which successfully foraging individuals returned to the colony with food (Krebs 1974). Because wading birds often forage in groups as well, the departing bird is more likely to find an exact location where it can successfully capture its patchily distributed prey.

Another important consequence of many large birds nesting in one location is the local increase in nutrient availability. Studies conducted at communal roosting and nesting assemblages indicate substantially enhanced local nutrient availability as the result of the deposition of excreta (Hutchinson 1950; Onuf et al. 1977; Oliver and Legovic 1988). In addition, Bildstein and colleagues (1992) found that the mass of nutrients imported to a South Carolina estuary by White Ibis *(Eudocimus albus)* from nearby freshwater feeding sites was substantial when compared with those from atmospheric sources and could vary considerably among years.

Because of the importance of conserving wading bird colony sites, many fish and wildlife agencies maintain a wading bird rookery atlas, which includes the species composition and location of the rookeries. In addition, a North American Waterbird Conservation Plan, a continent-wide conservation plan for wading birds and other colonial waterbirds, has been developed (Kushlan et al. 2002). The focuses of this plan include determining the status of waterbird populations, monitoring population numbers and demographics, identifying key factors in maintaining waterbird populations, and identifying and conserving important bird areas such as rookery sites. Other specific issues involving wading birds include contaminants and damage to aquaculture facilities by fish-eating species (Kushlan and Hafner 2000). As with other large-scale conservation efforts, the success of colonial waterbird conservation will depend on an ecosystem approach to management with the participation of many partners.

ENVIRONMENTALLY SENSITIVE BIRDS

The term *environmental indicator* can have several meanings. For example, an organism can be an indicator of the negative effects of some sort of perturbation, such as a pollutant. Or, an organism can be so closely associated with a particular habitat that, should that habitat be reduced in size or otherwise perturbed severely enough, that organism can be measured and can serve as a metric of the degree of perturbation of that system.

Birds have been and continue to be important indicators of both kinds of perturbations (Furness and Greenwood 1993; Kushlan 1993; Novak et al. in press). A classic example of an indicator of a pollutant otherwise unseen is the response of upper trophiclevel birds to organochlorine insecticides such as DDT (dichloro-diphenyl- trichloromethane). These highly persistent pesticides, used for control of mosquitoes and other insect pests, tend to magnify in concentrations at higher trophic levels. In addition to immediate mortality in high doses, fish-eating birds such as herons and egrets, Brown Pelicans *(Pelecanus occidentalis),* Ospreys *(Pandion haliaetus),* and Bald Eagles *(Haliaeetus leucocephalus),* and other raptors such as Peregrine Falcons *(Falco peregrinus),* which feed on shorebirds and waterfowl, exhibited thinning of their eggshells to the point where the eggs were crushed during incubation. Not surprisingly, each of the above species was federally listed as threatened or endangered at some point. Since the restriction of the use of DDT in the United States in the 1960s and 1970s, raptor populations have rebounded.

Similarly, waterbirds can serve as monitors of a variety of other pollutants, including heavy metals, radionuclides, acidification, oil, and air pollution (Furness and Greenwood 1993). For example, waterbirds exhibited massive reproductive failures in response to elevated levels of contaminants, especially selenium, in agricultural wastewater ponds and the Kesterson Reservoir in the San Joaquin Valley, California (Ohlendorf et al. 1989). When unhatched eggs of species such as American Avocets *(Recurvirostra americana)* and Black-necked Stilts *(Himantopus mexicanus)* were investigated, the embryos frequently exhibited bizarre deformities caused by elevated selenium levels. Again, as higher trophic level organisms, waterbirds contained magnified levels of contaminants that could have otherwise gone undetected.

In addition to being indicators of the negative effects of pollutants, birds are sometimes so intimately tied to a particular habitat type or ecosystem that they can therefore serve as an indicator of the integrity of that system. By integrity, we mean a system that contains all of its native biodiversity and the ecological processes that maintain that biodiversity. For example, throughout most of the United States, Clapper Rails *(Rallus longirostris)* are found only in salt and brackish marshes and mangroves (Eddleman and Conway 1998). Therefore, if these habitats decline in quality or quantity, we would expect to see a negative response by Clapper Rails, as noted by Novak and associates (in press). They found decreased eggshell integrity and increased DNA strand breakage in populations exposed to polychlorinated biphenyls and metals.

In fact, virtually every major ecosystem type has at least one bird species that is closely associated with that ecosystem, and therefore, those species should serve as effective indicators of the health of their respective ecosystems. For example, Ormerod and Tyler (1993 and citations therein) described the relationship between aspects of Dipper *(Cinclus cinclus)* breeding ecology and stream quality. Similarly, the Louisiana Waterthrush *(Seiurus motacilla)* can serve the same function in streams of the eastern United States (Brooks et al. 1998). Although aquatic invertebrates are the most widely used indicators of stream water quality, they may not reflect conditions within larger scales. For example, landscape scale perturbations that fragment forests may have no effect on water quality but can lead to increased nest predation and parasitism levels. It is likely that bioindicators that combine birds and invertebrates will be superior to either alone (Brown and Batzer 2001).

In forested wetlands, the Prothonotary Warbler *(Protonotaria citrea)*, a cavity-nesting songbird of the southeastern United States, has been shown to be sensitive to certain perturbations that affect ecosystem integrity (Wood 1999). Nest success was not affected by timber harvests that removed trees in patterns designed to mimic natural disturbances such as wind or ice storms or prolonged flooding. However, nest success was related to interannual variation in hydrology. In years when plots were partially flooded, water provided some protection from nest predators to nests built over inundated areas. Dry years, or years of prolonged flooding, had decreased nest success. This same relationship was found experimentally by Hoover (2003). Similarly, productivity by Wood Ducks *(Aix sponsa)* in South Carolina bottomland forests was related to wetland hydrologic conditions (Kennamer 2001). Thus, perturbations that affect the natural hydrology of large river floodplains are likely to be manifested in decreased productivity of these species.

Although there are many other examples of birds as potentially effective indicators of wetland ecosystem integrity, exact metrics have not been developed for the most part. For example, potentially appropriate metrics of integrity might include the following characteristics of colonial waterbird populations: genotoxicity, mixed function oxidases, metallothionein induction, tissue concentration of contaminants, eggshell quality, other physiological responses, histopathology and teratology, growth, behavior, reproductive performance, mortality, presence/absence, distribution, and population indices (Kushlan 1993). If a population fails to show an effect using one metric, does it mean that there is no effect, or that the wrong metric was used? Clearly, use of several metrics (and indicator species) is desirable, and development of useful metrics relating avian indicator species to their ecosystems would seem to continue to be a fruitful area of research.

WETLAND FISH

After hydrology, some argue that the presence or absence of fish is the most important factor influencing the ecology of aquatic animal communities in wetlands (Wellborn et al. 1996; Zimmer et al. 2002; Fig. 7.5). Fish are top-predators in many wetlands, and thus when present, they can dramatically affect the structure of lower trophic levels. When many people think about fish in wetlands, large individuals come to mind. However, while several large-bodied species inhabit wetlands, in terms of ecological function, it is probably small individuals (larval forms or diminutive species) that are most important. In salt marshes, large fish are mostly restricted to tidal creek channels, while the bulk of a salt marsh expanse is dominated by small species such as *Fundulus* (Kneib 1997b; West and Zedler 2000), gobies (Laffaille et al. 2000; Thomas and Connolly 2001), or assorted immatures (Mathieson et al. 2000; Thomas and Connolly 2001). In tidal freshwater systems, a similar pattern develops (Castellanos and Rozas 2001). In isolated depressional wetlands that support fish (many are fishless), the fish community is dominated by small species such as small sunfishes, small minnows, sticklebacks, mosquitofish, or topminnows (Snodgrass et al. 1996; Zimmer et al. 2002). Even in river floodplains, where large fish are commonly observed, empirical sampling indicates that most fish in floodplains are small (Ross and Baker 1983; Lewis et al. 2001).

Despite their size, these small fish can exert a significant influence on wetland ecology. A small wetland fish species that has been demonstrated to be very important ecologically is the fathead minnow *(Pimephales promelas)*. Fatheads are widely distributed in prairie wetlands across north central North America. Zimmer and colleagues (2002) found that fathead minnows had numerous ecosystem impacts on prairie wetlands, including suppressing salamander and invertebrate numbers and increasing algal chlorophyll *a* concentrations, presumably via a trophic cascade from planktivore reductions (Fig. 7.4). Zimmer and colleagues (2000) and Tangen and associates (2003) found that the presence or absence of fathead minnows had more influence on the invertebrate community structure in prairie wetlands than did water chemistry, peripheral agricultural practices, or past drainage history.

To assess predatory impacts of fish in some New York marshes (Batzer 1998; Batzer et al. 2000), enclosure/exclosure experiments were used to manipulate densities of adult and larval fish (carp and brown bullheads). Although the large adult fish did not have a detectable impact on small fish or invertebrates, larval fish had a dramatic impact on densities of bottom dwelling midges (Batzer 1998). The impacts of fish on invertebrate prey living in beds of submersed pondweeds were less obvious, however. While mud substrates supported midges almost exclusively, a wide assortment of invertebrates inhabited plant surfaces, including numerous predatory forms (damselflies, water bugs). Batzer and associates (2000) found that although fish were clearly consuming midges, experimental exclusion of fish unexpectedly harmed rather than benefited the midges. They concluded that fish were also consuming invertebrates that were predators and competitors of midges, and these indirect beneficial effects of fish on midges were more than compensating for any negative direct effects. Because most wetland fish are omnivorous (feed on more than one trophic level), assessing their impacts on food webs can be complex (Fig. 7. 4).

The importance of indirect effects of fish predation has been more thoroughly examined in salt marshes with the killifish *Fundulus heteroclitus*. Kneib and Stiven (1982) manipulated densities and size classes (small, medium, and large) of *F. heteroclitus* in large marsh enclosures and found that small surface dwelling invertebrates were suppressed by small fish, but were enhanced by larger fish (>7 cm). They hypothesized that small fish fed directly on the small invertebrates, but larger fish were instead consuming a secondary predator, the grass shrimp *(Palaemonetes pugio)*. The suppression of grass shrimp densities indirectly benefited surface dwelling invertebrates. Subsequent work by Posey and Hines (1991) further suggested that top-down control of grass shrimp by *F. heteroclitus* has a range of effects because the grass shrimp also fed on predatory anemones, and thus responses of basal species in the food webs were variable. When predatory fish are common in wetlands, they probably have important impacts on food web dynamics, but the end result of impacts may at times be difficult to predict without careful experimentation.

While we have focused on the impacts of small fish, large fish should not be overlooked. Besides being the source of larval progeny, an important ecological influence of large bodied fish is through bioperturbation. The common carp *(Cyprinus carpio)* is a large Eurasian minnow that is now established in wetlands throughout the world. The bottom-feeding behavior of large adult carp is believed to affect water-column and benthic ecological processes. Several studies have tested that hypothesis by manipulating adult carp densities or biomass, and these studies suggest that carp activity increases water turbidity (King et al. 1997; Lougheed et al. 1998; Angeler et al. 2002; Schrage and Downing 2004), total phosphorous and nitrogen levels (Angeler et al. 2002), and sediment oxygen demand and particle settlement rates (Robertson et al. 1997). Combined with their trophic impacts on invertebrates (Batzer 1998; Lougheed et al. 2004; Schrage and Downing 2004) and indirectly on phytoplankton, carp may be keystone organisms in many wetlands.

AMERICAN ALLIGATORS

The American alligator *(Alligator mississippiensis)* is a large crocodilian endemic to the southeastern United States from eastern North Carolina to eastern Texas. Adults typically reach a length of 4.0 to 4.5 meters but have been reported as long as 6 meters, weighing in excess of 1000 pounds. They primarily inhabit freshwater swamps and marshes but are also associated with rivers, lakes, and smaller bodies of water. They are a classic example of a keystone species, partly because they are apex predators in most of the systems they inhabit, but mainly because their behavior includes creation of deeper open water areas, or alligator holes, that retain water when the marsh or floodplain is dry (Meffe and Carroll 1997). Holes are often connected via one or a series of tunnels or dens, which they also excavate (McIlhenny 1935).

Alligators have a reciprocal relationship with wetlands—they depend on them, but some wetlands, especially the southern Florida Everglades, are shaped by them in return. Alligators use their mouths, tail, and webbed hind feet to dig and thrash out a small hole about the size of their body, which is gradually enlarged. The material thrown out around the holes forms a raised berm high enough to support trees and other woody vegetation in an otherwise treeless environment. The trees support a number of biota that would not otherwise be present. Similarly, cattails, arrowleaf, and other emergent vegetation grow around the margins of the hole, and floating leaved plants become established in the open water. Holes can take on different structures and contain different plant species depending on surrounding vegetation (Palmer and Mazzotti 2004). Alligator holes thus increase spatial heterogeneity, influence plant community composition and structure, and increase biological diversity.

The area of open water is kept free of thick mats of plants by the activity of the alligators. Many small aquatic organisms, such as grass shrimp, water fleas, and mosquitofish, spend their lives within a single alligator hole. The holes also aggregate populations of fish and shellfish, turtles, and other herpetofauna, attracting other predators such as raccoons, mink, and wading birds.

Alligators also build their nests on raised areas such as stream banks so as to keep them out of the water during times of flooding. These nest mounds, which are made from sticks, leaves, small branches, and mud, provide relatively dry refugia for terrestrial animals during such times. Several turtle species, especially the Florida red-bellied turtle *(Chrysemys nelsoni),* routinely use the base of alligator nests to deposit and incubate their own eggs (Goodwin and Marion 1977; Deitz and Jackson 1979). Over time, the nests also decompose to form peat. Peat fires, long in duration but cooler and slower moving than catastrophic wildfires, are common in the Everglades and are an important process in that ecosystem.

The importance of alligator holes as sites of concentrated biological activity becomes critical during dry seasons. The hole itself retains water and is a place where the alligator can wait out the dry period until the winter rains. During droughts, the holes are refugia for many aquatic organisms, offering resilience for populations over broad spatial scales. Alligator holes become critical foraging sites for wading birds such as herons and egrets, which would likely be unable to find adequate food in the marsh otherwise. Until the 1960s, the Everglades provided the primary nesting area for wading bird populations in the southeastern United States. Since then, only 5% to 10% of the populations that once nested there continue to use the area (Ogden 1978, 1994), likely due to alterations to hydrology (i.e., less wet season habitat) caused by development. Thus, alligator holes are likely to become even more critical for wading birds and other wetland biota on a year-round basis, justifying the claim that the alligator is the keeper of the Everglades.

AMPHIBIANS

Wetland amphibians consist of two main groups: (1) frogs and toads (or anurans) and (2) salamanders. Both groups rely on wetlands for reproduction. On maturation, some amphibian adults (bullfrogs, sirens) remain in wetlands, while others (ambystomatid salamanders, treefrogs) live terrestrially, only returning to the wetlands to breed. A small number of salamanders exhibit flexible life histories in which larvae either metamorphose into terrestrial, "metamorphic" adults or retain a larval morphology and remain aquatic as "paedomorphic" adults (Whiteman 1994).

Most anuran larvae consume algae or detritus, and competition for these resources can develop (Werner 1992). Some anuran larvae will prey on small invertebrates or eggs and larvae of other amphibians, suggesting that functional roles of anuran larvae in food webs may be complex (Petranka and Kennedy 1999). Despite the belief that many tadpoles are important primary consumers, the degree to which they affect detrital breakdown or algal standing stocks and productivity in wetlands is largely unknown.

Salamander larvae are carnivorous and have multiple trophic roles in wetland food webs including (1) reciprocal predator-prey interactions with large invertebrate predators such as dytiscid beetles and dragonfly nymphs (i.e., they prey on and are preyed on by these invertebrates; Morin 1981, 1983a; Wissinger et al. 1999a; Yurewicz 2004); (2) competition with invertebrate predators for shared prey (Caldwell et al. 1980; Wilbur and Fauth 1990); and (3) when there are more than one species, interacting simultaneously as competitors, intraguild predators, and cannibals (Morin 1983b; Yurewicz 2004; Whiteman and Wissinger 2004). In some cases, salamander larvae increase invertebrate and/or anuran diversity via predator-mediated coexistence (e.g., Morin et al. 1983; Fauth 1999), whereas elsewhere they eliminate vulnerable prey species (e.g., Morin 1983a; Wissinger et al. 1999b). In fishless permanent wetlands with paedomorphs, salamander populations may contain many different cohorts, and smaller conspecifics may be cannibalized (Whiteman and Wissinger 2004). Although salamanders maybe the top aquatic predators in many temporary wetlands, few studies consider their potential to exert top-down control on food webs (Blaustein et al. 1996).

Hydroperiod (degree of water permanence) variation influences amphibian distribution, and the presence or absence of fish, often a covariate of hydroperiod, is perhaps the most important determinant of amphibian community composition in wetlands (Skelly et al. 1999). Within a genus, different anuran species can replace each other along permanence gradients, and the predator-permanence model of Wellborn and associates (1996), discussed earlier (Fig. 7.5), was in part developed to explain these replacements. Several evolutionary/ecological trade-offs underlie replacements. One trade-off is between the high activity and growth rates that facilitate timely metamorphosis in temporary habitats and the relatively low activity, risk-sensitive foraging behaviors that facilitate coexistence with predators (salamanders in long-duration temporary habitats and fish in permanent habitats). Such trade-offs may explain the replacement of chorus frogs *(Pseudacris triseriata)* or *Hyla gratiosa* treefrogs in vernal wetlands by spring peepers *(Triseriata crucifer)* or *Hyla cinerea* treefrogs in permanent or semipermanent habitats with salamander or fish predators (Skelly 1995, 1997; Leips et al. 2000). A second trade-off involves predator-avoidance strategies. For example, green frog larvae *(Rana clamitans)* are better at avoiding dragonfly predators than bullfrog larvae in temporary habitats, but the reverse is true for the avoidance of fish predators in permanent ponds (bullfrog larvae are unpalatable to fish; Werner and McPeek 1994; Peacor and Werner 1997; Eklov 2000). Many anuran larvae exhibit phenotypic plasticity in behaviors, morphology, and physiology, depending on the density and types of predators and competitors present (McCollum and Van Buskirk 1996; McCollum and Leimberger 1997; Van Buskirk 2000; Relyea and Werner 2000; Relyea 2001). This plasticity is common in wetlands where inter-annual variation in hydroperiod creates temporal variability in the presence or absence of predators and competitors.

The worldwide decline and disappearance of amphibians has focused attention on these animals and led to a flurry of experimental research and monitoring of amphibian distribution and abundance (Pechmann et al. 1991; Alford and Richards 1999; Houlahan et al. 2000; Alford et al. 2001; Collins and Storfer 2003). A number of conservation issues associated with the amphibian decline focus on wetland species. Despite government protections, wetlands—especially small, isolated, temporary habitats—continue to decline. Many amphibians breeding in these habitats can not maintain viable populations in permanent habitats with fish. Indeed, conservation of amphibian biodiversity is one of the strongest and best-documented reasons for protecting small, isolated wetlands (Semlitsch and Bodie 1998; Semlitsch 2000). A second issue is related to the rapid increase in constructed wetlands to mitigate for encroachment on small natural wetlands. The most important flaw in the design of constructed wetlands is that they are too deep and too permanent compared with the natural wetlands they are designed to replace (Mitsch and Wilson 1996). Because of the strong negative effects of fish predators (and aggressive permanent-habitat amphibians such as bullfrogs), pond-like mitigation wetlands will have different species compositions than the destroyed natural habitats (Adams 2000; Snodgrass et al. 2000). Ambystomatid salamanders should be particularly vulnerable to details of hydroperiod in mitigation wetlands—fish are likely to be present if they are too permanent, and there will be insufficient time for larval development if they are too ephemeral (Semlitsch 1987; Kats et al. 1988; Rowe and Dunson 1995; Skelly et al. 1999; Snodgrass et al. 2000; Pechmann et al. 2001; Egan and Paton 2004). Even when mitigation habitats are well designed, adult amphibians often home toward the locations of natal habitats, suggesting the need for active management strategies including translocation and inoculation (Lehtinen and Galatowitsch 2001; Marsh and Trenham 2001).

Other wetland amphibian conservation issues are related to landscape position and biphasic life cycles (aquatic larvae and terrestrial adults). Wetland laws rarely protect terrestrial buffer zones, migration corridors, or surrounding terrestrial habitats, all of which are important for the viability of breeding amphibian populations (Dodd and Cade 1997; Taylor and Scott 1997; Semlitsch 1998; Knutson et al. 1999; Lehtinen et al. 1999; Mazerolle 2001; Houlahan and Findley 2003). For example, the presence of canopied forests reduces dehydration during emigration from breeding sites for many species (Rothhermel and Semlitsch 2002). Next, the population dynamics of species that breed in isolated, depressional habitats are likely to be influenced by metapopulation processes (Fig. 7.9). Spatial distribution of breeding and adult terrestrial habitats at the landscape level may be a more appropriate unit for conservation than an individual wetland (Marsh and Trenham 2001; Trenham et al. 2003). Wetland complexes with a variety of hydroperiods, basin sizes, and canopy covers embedded in a diverse terrestrial matrix are likely to support the highest diversity of wetland amphibians (Pechmann et al. 1989; Knutson et al. 1999; Skelly et al. 1999; Snodgrass et al. 2000).

FIDDLER CRABS

The fiddler crab (*Uca* spp.) is a smallish species (usually <5 cm in length) that has long been a curiosity because males have one oversized claw (that to some resembles a fiddle) used primarily in altercations with other males or to attract females. However, fiddler crabs are one of the ecologically most important animals in salt marshes throughout the world. They can become quite numerous, the larvae are important foods for fish, and the adults are consumed by a host of salt marsh birds (Grimes et al. 1989). To protect themselves from predators and provide refugia during high tides, fiddler crabs excavate long burrows in salt marsh substrates. The bioturbation caused by burrowing is perhaps the most important impact of fiddler crabs on salt marsh ecology.

In a South Carolina salt marsh, McCraith and associates (2003) found that fiddler crab burrow density ranged from 40 to 300/m², and sediment-reworking rates ranged between 4,400 and 57,000 cm³/m²/yr. Their burrowing mixed the upper layers (8 to 15 cm) of the sediment. This "roto-tilling" and the resultant aeration undoubtedly affects sediment composition and biogeochemical cycles in salt marsh systems. Bioturbation from fiddler crabs can decrease sulfate reduction and increase concentrations of total iron and Fe(III) (Gribsholt et al. 2003). Fe(III) respiration comprised virtually all of the carbon oxidation in bioperturbed sediments, whereas sulfate reduction was the dominant respiration process in undisturbed sediments (Kostka et al. 2002). However, the impacts of roots from emergent plants such as *Spartina* probably still exceed impacts of fiddler crab burrowing on the overall sediment biogeochemistry in salt marshes (Gribsholt et al. 2003). Nonetheless, fiddler crabs probably merit consideration as ecosystem engineers.

MIDGES

Midges (Diptera: Chironomidae) are small, nondescript flies whose worm-like larvae live in virtually every freshwater wetland. Although noncharismatic, a compelling case can be made that these insects are among the most ecologically important animals in freshwater wetlands. While most animal groups in wetlands are not particularly diverse (Table 7.1), the same can not be said of the chironomid midges. In many if not most wetlands, midges will comprise a large portion of the total animal species richness. For example, researchers have collected 54 midge species from a depressional wetland in South Carolina (Leeper and Taylor 1998), 62 species from a Canadian lakeshore marsh (Wrubleski and Rosenberg 1990), 48 species from a rich fen in Canada (Rosenberg et al. 1988), and 51 species from the Florida Everglades (King and Richardson 2002). Midges are notoriously difficult to identify to species, and thus their diversity is probably underestimated in most habitats.

Besides being diverse, midges can reach extremely high population densities. In most wetlands, midges are among the most abundant invertebrates, and densities of more than 10,000 larvae/m² are common (Batzer et al. 1997; Wrubleski 1999). The genus *Chironomus* has fairly large larvae, and when they are abundant, the standing stock biomass can be large (Wrubleski 2005). Midges tend to develop rapidly, and in many habitats, midge species have multiple generations per year. Thus, standing stocks at any particular time may vastly underestimate annual midge production.

It is commonly said that invertebrates in wetlands are the primary link between plant primary production and higher trophic levels (Batzer and Wissinger 1996). This statement may be especially true for midges. Midges are important consumers of plant material, consuming algae and macrophyte detritus (Batzer and Resh 1991; Campeau et al. 1994; Batzer 1998). Midges are then consumed by a wide array of wetland predators. Important invertebrate predators of midges in wetlands include dragonflies, beetles, and leeches (Rasmussen and Downing 1988; Batzer and Resh 1991). In a study of a New York marsh, virtually every fish examined, regardless of species, was found to have midge larvae in its guts (Batzer et al. 2000). Many adult ducks consume invertebrates when they need protein to prepare for reproduction or migration, and midges are the mostly commonly consumed taxon (Murkin and Batt 1987; Batzer et al. 1993). Newly hatched ducklings also require invertebrate foods, and these inept predators find midge adults emerging from pupae at the water's surface to be easy prey (Chura 1961). Swallows similarly scoop up midges as they emerge. Midges in general seem almost defenseless to predation, and the key to their success is to reproductively overwhelm the effects of predation. The result is that a large portion of the energy flowing through food webs of freshwater wetlands may be funneled through midges.

In addition to their ecological importance, midges appear to be among the few wetland invertebrates useful for environmental bioassessment. Most invertebrate species in wetlands are ecological generalists, adapted to cope with a range of environmental conditions (Batzer et al. 2004); this tolerance probably makes them poorly suited as environmental indicator species. However, many midges are more specialized, perhaps because the diverse nature of the group forces more niche differentiation. King and Richardson (2002) found that the absence of specific midge species indicated habitat impairment in the Florida Everglades. Mouthpart deformities of midges are also a useful indicator of sublethal effects of pollutants (Dermott 1991).

CADDISFLIES

Larval caddisflies (Trichoptera) live in a wide range of wetland habitats (Wiggins 1973, 1996). The tiny microcaddisflies (Hydroptilidae) and several families of large-bodied case makers (Lepistomatidae, Leptoceridae, Molannidae, and Sericostomatidae) are lentic generalists, occurring in both permanent wetlands and the littoral zone of lakes and ponds. In contrast, temporary-habitat species of net-tube makers (Polycentropidae), northern case makers (Limnephilidae), and giant case makers (Phryganeidae) are wetland specialists with life cycles tailored to the intermittent surface water that typifies many wetlands. Species compositions shift from permanent to semipermanent to temporary wetlands (Wissinger et al. 2003), and this shift in part reflects the absence of desiccation tolerant stages or strategies in permanent habitat species. Species replacements are also the result of trade-offs between traits that facilitate timely emergence from drying habitats (e.g., high activity rates) and traits that facilitate coexistence with permanent-habitat predators (risk-sensitive, low activity rates; Wissinger et al. 1999a, 2003).

Limnephilids in particular possess a suite of life cycle adaptations for life in temporary wetlands including (1) rapid larval growth timed to the seasonal presence of surface water; (2) adult diapause in adjacent terrestrial habitats when wetlands are dry; (3) the deposition of desiccation-tolerant egg masses in dry wetland basins; and (4) larval emergence from protective egg masses only after wetland basins refill (Wiggins 1973; Wiggins et al. 1980;

Richardson and Mackay 1984; Wissinger et al. 2003). *Ironoquia plattensis* has the unique trait of crawling from drying basins into adjacent uplands habitats to pupate (Whiles et al. 1999). Because of the importance of the terrestrial adult diapause stage, many wetland caddisflies are probably sensitive to changes in land use in adjacent terrestrial habitats, suggesting the need for protecting terrestrial buffer zones around wetlands.

Limnephilid caddisflies are thought to be *the* most important detritivores in many wetlands (Wissinger 1999). The onset of larval development in many limnephilids is triggered by autumn refilling of basins and coincides with the pulse of detritus from terrestrial leaf fall and the senescence of wetland plants. The diets of many limnephilids are dominated by detritus (Berte and Pritchard 1986; Mihuc and Toetz 1994; Whiles et al. 1999; Wissinger et al. 2003), but compared with stream-inhabiting caddisflies (e.g., Jacobsen and Friberg 1995; Graca et al. 2001), the effects on detritus decomposition in wetlands has been poorly documented (Barlocher et al. 1978; Mackay and Wiggins 1979). Detritus is often a nutritionally incomplete food source (Fig. 7.2), and many detritivorous caddisflies supplement their diets with animal material (Winterbourn 1971; Anderson 1976; Mackay and Wiggins 1979; Berté and Pritchard 1986; Giller and Sangpradub 1993; Wissinger et al. 2004b), including that derived from cannibalism (Wissinger et al. 2006). This protein supplement should accelerate growth and enable escape from rapidly drying habitats.

A distinctive feature of most wetland caddisfly larvae is a portable case fashioned from silk and plant or mineral matter. Several explanations for the evolution of case building are of particular relevance to wetland habitats. Cases protect caddisfly larvae from predators such as fish, salamanders, and invertebrates (Otto and Svensson 1980; Johansson and Johansson 1992; Wissinger et al. 2004a, 2006). Cases also enhance oxygen exchange; wetland species will undulate their abdomen to create currents through the case (Wiggins 1973, 1996; Williams et al. 1987). Finally, cases can reduce the vulnerability of larvae and/or pupae to desiccation and/or freezing (Otto 1983; Zamora-Munoz and Svensson 1996).

Despite having protective cases, wetland caddisfly larvae are eaten by many predators (Johansson and Nilsson 1992; Wissinger et al. 1999a, 2006). Because caddisflies feed heavily on detritus and periphyton, and often comprise much of the invertebrate biomass in wetlands, they are probably important links between primary production and higher trophic levels (Whiles et al. 1999). Moreover, adults provide food for fish, frogs, and insectivorous birds. There is a clear need for experimental research to complement comparative and anecdotal evidence for the trophic importance of caddisflies in wetlands both as primary consumers of detritus and algae and as important conduits of secondary production up through wetland webs.

Invertebrates are widely used for stream bioassessment programs, and three insect orders, the Ephemeroptera, Plecoptera, and Trichoptera (collectively referred to as the EPT taxa), are considered environmentally most sensitive (Karr and Chu 1999). Because wetland caddisflies are strongly influenced by water quality (oxygen), hydroperiod, and riparian conditions, and are also so important ecologically, they are probably a group that merits more research attention for wetland bioassessment (Wilcox et al. 2002).

8

WETLAND ECOSYSTEM PROCESSES

Robert G. Wetzel

WETLANDS AS ECOSYSTEMS

When we speak of wetlands, we are generally referring to the land-water interface of lakes, reservoirs, and rivers. As is noted throughout this book, great significant is often given to the boundaries of wetlands, usually for socioeconomic rather than scientific reasons. The shoreline of a lake or river, or the boundary of a wetland, is a dynamic physical boundary between the land and the water. In reality, many wetlands occur in areas of low physical elevational gradients where the physical shoreline of a lake or river and the functional boundary of the wetland are diffuse and always changing.

The gentle, small slopes along most water margins are conducive to sedimentation as flow from upland areas slows and the transport energy dissipates. Particles of dead organic matter then settle and accumulate. Rates of transpiration by emergent and floating macrophytes are often extremely high and result in water losses to the atmosphere that are greater than evaporation from an equivalent area of water (Wetzel 1999a). Water losses by aquatic plant evapotranspiration can be sufficiently large to appreciably reduce water levels of fresh waters and surrounding terrestrial areas. Thus, the water within wetlands is highly dynamic on many scales—temporally on daily, weekly, and seasonal scales, and spatially within the sediments, accumulated detritus, and plant stands. The shoreline is not only physically variable and diffuse, but functionally the changing water content is enormously important to the microbiota within the sediments and the plants and animals growing in these regions.

By definition, the water table of wetlands is near, at, or above the hydrosoil (sediment) surface. These changing hydrologic conditions are primary drivers of nutrient fluxes in the sediments and all aspects of the plant biology—physiology, growth, and productivity. Because of the very nature of low elevational gradients within wetlands, there is a tendency for these regions of the whole ecosystem to retain organic matter either produced there by wetland plants or organic matter imported to these regions from upland areas. Small differences in topography in such a shallow environment create highly variable habitat conditions. Those varying physical habitats result in a great diversity of organisms.

These wetland organisms exist in a functionally coupled way that allows for unusually high growth and productivity, among the highest in the biosphere. It is important that we examine *why* the metabolism and productivity of these wetland plants are so great. That high collective metabolic capacity frequently functions as a huge sieve that can control facets of the biogeochemical and energetic fluxes as water moves through them to the lake or river waters adjacent to them.

GENERATION AND RETENTION OF HIGH AMOUNTS OF ORGANIC MATTER

As noted earlier, the physical attributes of low slope and reduced flows as energy is dispersed laterally in wetlands are compounded simply by the high surface area of many large plants in and on the water. The physical resistance of these surfaces, and the dense microflora growing on these surfaces (discussed later), induce retention and sedimentation of imported particles of organic matter. The accumulated organic matter and associated nutrients promotes two basic features of wetland ecosystems, namely, an anoxic, reducing habitat of vigorously growing microbial communities on and within the sediments and organic debris, and very actively growing aquatic plants that are adapted to these growth conditions.

LARGER AQUATIC PLANTS

Aquatic macrophytes can be distinguished on the basis of morphology and physiology (Fig. 8.1). Emergent and floating-leaved but rooted aquatic plants are erect from an extensive rhizome/foot base and are physiologically similar to terrestrial plants. Because rooting tissues grow in water-saturated anaerobic sediments, oxygen must be obtained for respiration from aerial organs (see review of Wetzel 2001). Oxygen, carbon dioxide, and other gases move within and through interconnecting aerenchymatous and intercellular cortical gas spaces of shoots and roots.

Submersed aquatic plants (Fig. 8.1) face the additional problems of markedly reduced rates of diffusion of gases in water (10,000 times slower than in air) and reduced availability of light. Leaves are only a few cells in thickness, and photosynthetic pigments are concentrated in epidermal tissue. Leaves tend to be much more divided, with greater surface-to-volume ratios, than are leaves of other aquatic or terrestrial plants. This morphology maximizes exposure of cellular surfaces to reduced light, gas, and nutrient availability under water.

Vegetative clonal reproduction is a major mechanism for population growth and dispersal among aquatic plants. Sexual reproduction and genetic recombination has been retained, but it is commonly subordinate to vegetative reproduction. Vegetative clonal growth occurs by fragmentation and dispersal of aboveground tissues; winter buds (turions); and horizontal expansion by rhizomes, tubers, corms, and bulbs. Many of the most effectively competitive aquatic plants combine continuous clonal growth with production of seeds for long-distance dispersal. Aerial flowering dominates among aquatic plants, even submersed plants, with most pollination by insect or wind vectors.

Most aquatic macrophytes are perennial with multiple cohorts or continuous replacement, growth, and senescence. In many cases, cohort longevity is in the range of 30 to 40 days (cf. reviews of Wetzel 1990, 2001). As a result of continuous partial mortality and populations with high turnover of leaves, much of the annual production does not survive to be measured as seasonal maximum biomass. Roots and rhizomes of submersed macrophytes make up a lesser portion (1–40%) of total plant biomass than is the case for floating-leaved (30–70%) or emergent (30–95%) macrophytes.

The productivity of wetland plants is extraordinary (Fig. 8.2). On a unit-area basis, the net primary productivity of aquatic macrophytes is among the highest of any community in the biosphere (reviewed in Wetzel 2001).

1. Emergent macrophyte productivity ranges from 1,000 to as much as 10,000 g ash-free dry mass (AFDM) m^{-2} yr^{-1}.

2. Freely floating macrophyte productivity ranges from 300 to 5,000 g AFDM m^{-2} yr^{-1}.

3. Floating-leaved rooted macrophyte productivity is more modest, ranging from 100 to 500 g AFDM m^{-2} yr^{-1}.

4. Submersed macrophyte productivity is variable ranging from as little as 5 to as much as 1,500 g AFDM m^{-2} yr^{-1}.

Nearly all of the macrophyte productivities far exceed those of phytoplankton (25–200 g AFDM or 50–450 g C m^{-2} yr^{-1}). Seasonal variations in aquatic macrophyte productivity are great. In the temperate zone, productivity of aquatic macrophytes is directly related to changes in sunlight and temperatures. Some submersed plants persist under ice cover, although net productivity is low or zero. In the tropics, growth is often nearly continuous.

PERIPHYTON AS A CRITICAL METABOLIC COMPONENT OF AQUATIC ECOSYSTEMS

Periphyton commonly refers to microbial communities attached to and living on substrata (Fig. 8.3). These substrata surfaces may be living plants or animals, organic detrital

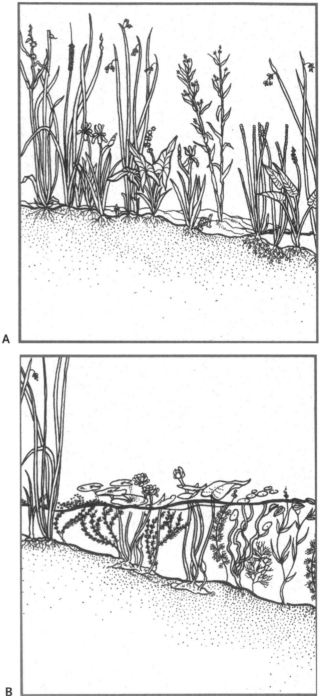

FIGURE 8.1
Growth forms of aquatic macrophytes: (A) emergent, (B) floating-leaved but rooted, and (C) submersed growth forms of aquatic macrophytes. Drawings from *Through the Looking Glass: A Field Guide to Aquatic Plants*, courtesy of the Wisconsin Department of Natural Resources and the University of Wisconsin Extension Service.

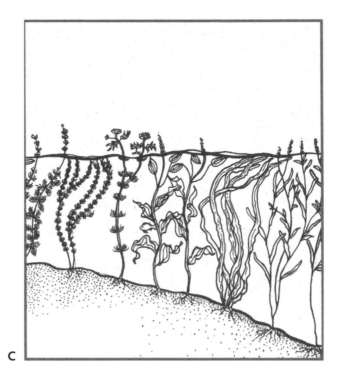

C

materials in various stages of decomposition, or nonliving. Although the etymological history of the word *periphyton* is complex (cf. review of Wetzel 2001), the important characteristic of periphyton is that it consists of a complex community of active, inactive, and senescent heterotrophic and autotrophic microorganisms, inorganic and dead organic particles, and extracellular mucilaginous materials, largely mucopolysaccharides. Three important relationships of periphyton communities within wetland ecosystems should be recognized.

Relationship 1

Microbial periphyton in natural aquatic ecosystems is commonly perceived as a combination of algal autotrophs and heterotrophic microbes. Many periphytic communities, particularly in groundwater, are totally heterotrophic in complete darkness and utilize imported organic substrates. In most surface-water wetland ecosystems, however, periphytic communities are combined mixtures of autotrophic algae/cyanobacteria and heterotrophic bacteria, viruses, fungi, and protists.

Relationship 2

The physical structure of periphyton communities is such that gaseous and ionic exchanges with the surrounding aqueous environment occur at rates orders of magnitude slower than those that occur in the surrounding water. As a result, much of the metabolism within the

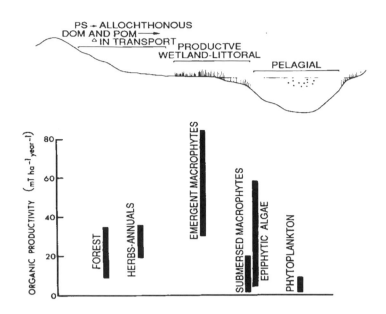

FIGURE 8.2

The lake ecosystem showing the drainage basin with terrestrial photosynthesis (PS) of organic matter, movement of nutrients and dissolved (DOM), and particulate (POM) organic matter in surface water and groundwater flows toward the lake basin, and chemical and biotic alteration of these materials en route, particularly as they pass through the highly productive and metabolically active wetland-littoral zone of the lake or river per se (net organic productivity in metric tons per hectare per year). Modified from Wetzel (1990.)

periphyton community is coupled mutualistically (Wetzel 1993, 1996). Because of this intimate physiological interdependence, internal nutrient and energetic recycling within the relatively closed community is intense. Metabolism, growth, and productivity within periphyton communities rely heavily on internal recycling and conservation of resources—the result is an unusually high efficiency of utilization and retention of captured external resources and a very high productivity (Wetzel 1990).

Relationship 3

The fate of the nutrients and organic energy of periphyton communities within aquatic communities is highly diverse spatially and temporally. Most of the organic matter produced by algae/cyanobacteria of periphyton is degraded to CO_2 microbially by bacteria and protists within the periphytic community. Many of the nutrients released during decomposition are actively sequestered and retained by the viable components of the periphyton community. The fate of available living or dead organic matter of the periphytic communities that is not utilized and respired microbially is very complex, and often depends on the changing chemical and physical conditions of the supporting macrophyte substrata. Although most of the organic production is heterotrophically metabolized by

EPIPHYTIC - ON PLANT SURFACES
EPIPELIC - ON BENTHIC SUBSTRATA

FIGURE 8.3
Locations of epipelic and epiphytic growth forms of periphyton. Drawing from *Through the Looking Glass: A Field Guide to Aquatic Plants,* courtesy of the Wisconsin Department of Natural Resources and the University of Wisconsin Extension Service.

microbes and relatively little of the periphytic production passes to higher trophic levels, the impacts of higher trophic levels on the periphytic development and its ecosystem roles can be significant at certain times.

Important ecological aspects of these primary questions are where the periphytic communities grow and the type of substrata to which they attach. Surface waters are a series of spatial and temporal gradients. Physically streams and river ecosystems are elevational gradients both longitudinally along their length and laterally within the drainage basin and especially their floodplains (Wetzel 1989). The aqueous portions of those gradients oscillate seasonally with hydrologic and other environmental variations. Similarly, the wetland and littoral regions surrounding lakes and ponds exist as complex gradients from upland wetlands, to littoral zones of changing aquatic vegetation along a depth gradient, to aphotic surfaces in deeper waters. Substrata heterogeneity is great and extends over a range from relatively inert rock, to dead particulate organic matter, to highly dynamic living plant and animal surfaces.

ORGANIC MATTER INPUTS FROM TERRESTRIAL SOURCES

The wetland-littoral complex produces major sources of organic matter in most freshwater ecosystems. This source can be augmented by terrestrial vegetation. In wetlands surrounding lakes or in wetlands of river floodplains, the loading of organic matter as particulate terrestrial vegetation directly to the water is usually small in comparison to the continual inputs of dissolved organic matter. In wetlands adjacent to woodland streams, leaf-fall from terrestrial vegetation can constitute a major seasonal input of particulate and dissolved organic matter. In larger rivers, external dissolved and particulate organic matter is derived largely from the floodplain wetlands and groundwaters from adjacent terrestrial sources.

Most of the particulate organic matter is decomposed within the land-water interface wetlands and littoral regions. Losses result from a combination of decomposition of plant organic matter with evasion of respiratory CO_2 and methane to the atmosphere, fragmentation of particulate organic matter by turbulence and macroinvertebrates, and export losses of dissolved and fine particulate organic matter. Fragmentation of coarse particulate organic matter by feeding activities of immature macroinvertebrates can increase markedly rates of microbial degradation. Much greater amounts of CO_2 are released from benthic respiration than the amount of oxygen consumed, which emphasizes the prevalence of anaerobic metabolism utilizing alternative electron acceptors (nitrate, ferrous iron, sulfate, organic compounds) rather than oxygen. Export of organic matter is predominantly as dissolved organic matter of relatively recalcitrant chemical compounds, often associated with origins from lignin and cellulose structural tissues of higher plants and various bacterial degradation products.

HYDROLOGIC COUPLINGS OF ORGANIC MATTER

The physical and biotic structure and resulting metabolism of a wetland ecosystem are strongly coupled to the hydrology and resulting chemical loadings from its drainage basin. Rivers and lakes interact with adjacent surficial and shallow groundwater flows, which change continuously in response to a combination of local and regional rainfall. Plant evapotranspiration by nearshore littoral and wetland vegetation can cause highly dynamic, bidirectional seepage conditions over various periods of time. These water loss processes alter nearshore recharge from shallow groundwater sources as well as hydrosoil water storage and fluctuations in water levels.

Hydrology is a primary driver underlying high wetland productivity. Hydrologic budgets attempt to quantify the inputs (precipitation, stream flow, overland flow, and groundwater discharge) and outflows (surface evaporation, evapotranspiration, surface outflows, groundwater recharge) of water in wetland ecosystems (LaBaugh 1986a; Wetzel 1999a; Mitsch and Gosselink 2000; see Chapter 2). Groundwater discharge or upwelling (movement of subsurface waters to surface waters) and recharge or downwelling (movement of surface waters into the subsurface zone) in wetlands are important components of the hydrologic cycle because nutrients and dissolved organic matter can be transported to biota or be exported.

Wetland groundwater models are typically constructed to predict net movement of water over large temporal and spatial scales in wetlands. However, many complex small-scale temporal and spatial variations occur at the macrophyte root-zone scale (e.g., Mann and Wetzel 2000a, 2000b). These variations and unpredictable small-scale reversals in groundwater recharge and discharge are often neglected in studies that examine deeper groundwater interactions (>1 m depth). These small-scale reversals of vertical exchange in the wetland can function independently of the deeper groundwater, and they are certainly of major importance to the biota inhabiting the shallow sediments and sediment surfaces (e.g., Kahn and Wetzel 1999).

Temporal shifts in subsurface water recharge zones are commonly coupled to rainfall (e.g., Winter 1981; Mann and Wetzel 2000b). These subsurface flow variations are potentially important to the biota of the ecosystem. For example, significant differences occur in nutrients and dissolved organic matter concentrations between surface and subsurface waters. When transport flows are toward shallow sediment sites, they can be critical for utilization by wetland biota.

High productivity of emergent littoral and wetland vegetation can rapidly increase rates of sedimentation of partially decomposed organic matter. The resulting decreases in wetland and lake basin volume, expanding habitat, and emergent vegetation can result in gradual transitions to conditions where evapotranspiration losses of water exceed collective water inputs. As a result of these aquatic plant and microbial biologically mediated water losses, gradually increasing water losses greater than inputs set forth a progressively accelerating transition of some shallow lakes to form wetlands to eventually to form terrestrial ecosystems (Wetzel 1979, 1999a; Glime et al. 1982).

FLUXES OF ORGANIC MATTER AND ENERGY IN AQUATIC ECOSYSTEMS

Evaluation of the rates of energy fixation by primary producers in terrestrial and aquatic communities, and the rates of transfer of this energy to higher trophic levels, are foundations of trophic dynamic analyses. In the pelagic zone of lakes, trophic structure and energy fluxes are based almost solely on particulate organic matter (POM) (Lindeman 1942; Hutchinson 1959). Flows of energy within the trophic structures are focused on predation by ingestion of particles of organic matter. Many particulate filtering and predatory organisms consume variable amounts of particulate detritus (dead POM) that clearly dominates over living POM (e.g., Saunders 1972; Wetzel 1995).

As the metabolism of community components was analyzed with increasing accuracy, however, a number of pathways and rates of transfer of organic carbon demonstrated many inconsistencies that could not be explained within the conventional food web paradigms. Total annual budgets of carbon fluxes in lakes and especially rivers demonstrated the overriding importance of dissolved organic matter (DOM) derived from terrestrial and wetland-littoral-floodplain production of higher plants and periphyton (Wetzel 2002). Much of the heterotrophic respiration of organic matter occurs in sediments, particularly in shallower waters of high aquatic plant productivity, with net evasions of CO_2 to the atmosphere in quantities many times in excess of the rates of carbon fixation by the phytoplankton. Organic matter from upland sources (allochthonous) and wetland-littoral aquatic plants and associated periphyton is always the primary source of organic carbon and energy to

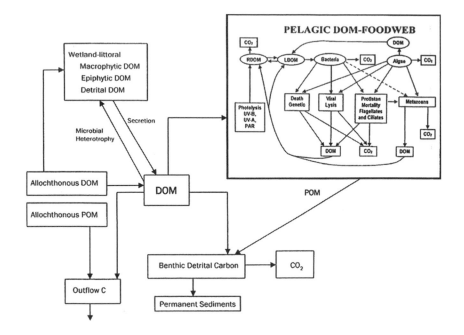

FIGURE 8.4

Detrital structure and primary fluxes of dissolve organic carbon in lake ecosystems. The food web structure of predominantly pelagic components (box) reflects the importance of the microbiota, the microbial loop, and physical processes by which most other organic matter inputs are metabolized heterotrophically or degraded by physical processes directly to CO_2. DOM = dissolved organic matter, LDOM = labile DOM, RDOM = recalcitrant DOM, POM = particulate organic matter.

river ecosystems and can and often constitutes the dominant input of organic carbon to lake and reservoir ecosystems.

Metabolism of particulate detritus (nonliving POM) and particularly dissolved organic matter from many pelagic, littoral, and allochthonous sources dominate both material and energy fluxes (Fig. 8.4). Loading and fluxes of DOM from allochthonous and littoral sources are critical because of their chemical differences from those produced by algal photosynthesis. Important is the crucial role that microbial communities attached to particulate detritus has in altering organic compounds released during senescence and subsequent decomposition.

A further important distinction, emphasized in Figure 8.4, is that ingestion of living particulate organic matter, while significant at times, is not the predominant cause of mortality of organisms (Wetzel 1995, 2001). Nonpredatory death and metabolism of nonliving POM by prokaryotic and protistan heterotrophs dominate in all aquatic ecosystems. In any discussion about quantities of organic matter and relative rates of its use, the annual time period is the only meaningful interval in comparative quantitative analyses of material and energy fluxes at population, community, and ecosystem levels (Wetzel 1995). Essentially, all inland water ecosystems are microbially based heterotrophic ecosystems. Heterotrophic utilization, largely

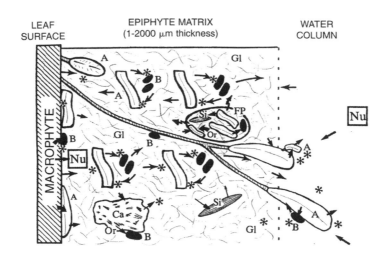

LEAF SURFACE   EPIPHYTE MATRIX (1-2000 μm thickness)   WATER COLUMN

FIGURE 8.5

Diagram of the supply of nutrients (Nu, such as organic and inorganic forms of carbon, phosphorus, and nitrogen) to benthic algae and other microbes within a periphyton matrix on a substratum, in this case a submersed macrophyte leaf. Arrows indicate routes of nutrient cycling from the substratum and the water column, which represent the major external sources of nutrient supply to the periphytic matrix. A = algae, B = bacteria, Gl = microbially derived glycocalyx, Ca = calcium carbonate, Si = siliceous frustules of dead diatoms, Or = organic debris, * = excreted enzymes, FP = fecal pellets. Reprinted from Burkholder (1996), with permission from Elsevier.

of DOM, within lake and stream ecosystems greatly exceeds autochthonous autotrophic production. The carbon budgets of many different types of surface waters have been examined in some detail (e.g., Wetzel and Otsuki 1974; Cole et al. 1994). No inland water ecosystem has yet been found that does not release greater quantities of respired CO_2 to the atmosphere than carbon is fixed photosynthetically within the water body.

ATTACHED MICROBIAL COMMUNITY METABOLISM AND INTERACTIONS

STRUCTURE AND COUPLINGS AMONG PERIPHYTIC ORGANISMS

Periphyton develops as a three-dimensional community enmeshed with hydrated glycocalyx and other mucopolysaccharide materials that are secreted by bacteria and algae. Detrital particles and precipitated calcium carbonate crystals accumulate within the glycocalyx materials and encourage adsorption of nutrients (P, NH_4, and others) and various organic substances (Fig. 8.5). Nutrients may be assimilated as inorganic ions or from organic compounds with excreted enzymes such as phosphatases utilized and released by leaching, excretions, secretions, or cell lysis of the microbes (Burkholder 1996). Epiphytic microfauna can release enzymes and nutrients during feeding and excretion, as in fecal pellets, with still viable algae and bacteria that have become nutrient enriched during passage through the animals as well as waste products and detrital particles.

Periphyton communities contain other nutrient-sequestering or -releasing materials. Microbial photosynthesis within the periphyton can induce massive precipitation of calcium carbonate in moderately hard waters. Additionally, siliceous frustules of dead diatoms, organic debris of dead microbes and protists, and the hydrated glycocalyx/mucopolysaccharides all form adsorptive surfaces. Moribund microflora and fauna are also attacked by fungi and result in some nutrient recycling and potential release by diffusion. Some bacteria and algae are directly attached to the substratum and can obtain or release important nutrients or gases from the living or moribund substratum. Many of the microbes of periphyton are loosely attached within the overstory matrix, and some have stalks or other attachment structures to the substratum (Fig. 8.5).

Microbes embedded within the polysaccharide matrix are relatively isolated from the surrounding water medium. As a result, diffusion dependence can be an inhibiting process for resource renewal and acquisition. The polysaccharide matrix is potentially permeated by microchannels that may act as conduits in which diffusion of organic and inorganic nutrients is faster than through the polysaccharide matrix (Lock 1993; Costerton et al. 1994, 1995; De Beer et al. 1994; Wimpenny and Colasanti 1997). The size of the microchannels varies greatly, often in the range of 5 to 50 μm, and they permeate the matrix in dendritic, likely fractal patterns (see Fig. 19-6 of Wetzel 2001). The development of the polysaccharide matrix as well as the size of the microchannels is influenced by external factors. For example, microchannel size increased in the presence of high dissolved organic matter and when exposed to ultraviolet irradiance of high sunlight (Wetzel et al. 1997; unpublished). Fluxes of nutrient ions or dissolved gases among microbial components within the periphyton or to and from the overlying water would be faster in the liquid of the microchannels than through the polysaccharide matrix itself.

Photosynthetic products of algae, such as oxygen or soluble organic substrates, released intercellularly, can be used by bacteria, or they may diffuse into the channels and to the overlying water. Reciprocally, bacteria secrete organic micronutrients, such as vitamins, CO_2, and enzymes, intercellularly that may persist in the polysaccharide matrix for some time before being assimilated by algae or other microbes or before diffusing from the matrix. Extracellular enzymes, either bound to membranes or released, may hydrolyze dissolved organic matter or nutrients from other microbes, especially algae, or from DOM or particulate organic matter adsorbed from the overlying water. These hydrolyzed products can then be assimilated by microbes, adsorbed by the polysaccharide matrix, or diffused into the microchannels or overlying water. Fluxes among the different components are part concentration–mediated, but such gradients are fluctuating because of changes in metabolism (e.g., availability of light for photosynthesis). Nutrient net flux and direction depends on the differences between concentrations of the bulk water and matrix, which can change rapidly with differences in metabolism and environmental conditions (e.g., light, water movements) (Riber and Wetzel 1987). When the concentrations of nutrients of both the periphyton and the overlying water are low, the net flux will be small or even zero.

Photosynthesis clearly dominates metabolism among algae and cyanobacteria, and most species are obligate photoautotrophs. The products of photosynthesis (ATP and organic carbon compounds) provide chemical energy and organic compounds needed for cellular synthesis. Without adequate light, cells usually die after storage compounds are used, or they enter a metabolically inactive state until light becomes available. A number of algae exhibit heterotrophy (chemoorganotrophy). In this process, dissolved organic compounds are assimilated under aerobic conditions (aerobic dissimilation) as a source of carbon and energy both in the dark and in the light (e.g., Tuchman 1996; Wetzel 2001). A few algae are mixotrophic and assimilate CO_2 in small amounts simultaneously with organic compounds both in the light and especially in darkness. The capacity to utilize organic substrates requires specific enzymes and dissimilatory pathways that many algae do not possess. At naturally occurring substrate concentrations, the low affinity of algae for simple organic substrates renders heterotrophy a relatively inefficient process in comparison to photoautotrophy. Moreover, algae can not compete effectively with bacteria for available substrates (e.g., McKinley and Wetzel 1979).

Rates of heterotrophic growth within dense periphyton communities, however, have been poorly studied. If abundant concentrations of organic carbon substrates are available, light-independent biochemical reactions of the Calvin cycle may be blocked and ATP utilized to transport extracellular organic substrates into the chloroplast, or into the cell in cyanobacteria. True photoheterotrophy involves photosynthetic production of ATP and reducing power needed for assimilation of the organic substrates. Photoheterotrophy could potentially augment photoautotrophy among algal and cyanobacterial communities of periphyton (Tuchman 1996). Exogenous dissolved organic substrates are certainly more concentrated within periphytic communities than is the case among phytoplankton. Steep environmental gradients, particularly of light (e.g., Losee and Wetzel 1983; Kühl and Jørgensen 1992), within the attached communities could enhance photoheterotrophic utilization of organic substrates released by active, senescing, and moribund microbiota.

PRODUCTIVITY OF PERIPHYTON COMMUNITIES: GROWTH REGULATION AND HABITAT VARIABLES

Growth and productivity of periphyton communities are regulated by two dominant processes: (1) resource availability and (2) predation by higher animal ingestion. Resources regulating growth include external resources in the surrounding water medium, such as light and nutrients; internal resources, such as nutrients that are obtained from the abiotic or living substrata to which the periphyton communities are attached; and internal recycling within periphyton among algae and associated microbiota. The community responses to these variables are summarized in Table 8.1.

TABLE 8.1   Summary of Common Responses of Epilithic, Epipelic, and Epiphytic Autotrophic
Microbiota to Dominant Physical, Chemical, and Biotic Resource Parameters

Environmental Parameter	Epilithic	Epipelic	Epiphytic
Physical			
Water movement	High in rivers and upper littoral areas; molar abrasion high	High → low in depth gradient; decreasing with depth	High exchange in water column; low exchange within dense submersed macrophtye stands
Substrata	Stable at low-to-moderate water velocities	Unstable; subject to frequent disturbance	Stable in position but changing with growth and senescence; often increasing seasonally
Temperature	Often marked seasonal and diurnal fluctuations	Decreasing with increasing depth; higher and variable in epilimnion, low and more stable in metalimnion	Commonly high in shallow areas and changing widely seasonally
Light			
Quantity	Steep seasonal changes, especially Low in canopied streams; steep exponential declines with depth	High → low in depth gradient; rapid decrease within sediments	Moderate to high; decreasing with depth but often increasing seasonally as submersed macrophytes develop upward into water column
Quality	Selective attenuation by water column	Steep selective attenuation of red and blue spectra within periphyton and within sediments	Selective attenuation in water column and by pigments within periphyton communities
Habitat available	Moderate; sorting by wave action and flowing water; sets particle size and surface area	Low, essentially two-dimensional	High, particularly among submersed macrophytes; projection into water column, three-dimensional

Chemical-biotic	Usually oxic; low nutrients	Reducing but diurnally oxic; high nutrients	Oxic, with diurnal variations
General conditions	Usually oxic; low nutrients	Reducing but diurnally oxic; high nutrients	Oxic, with diurnal variations
Inorganic nutrients			
Phosphorus	Low, often restrictive	Very high from interstitial waters	Low, variable; some from macrophyte
Nitrogen	Low, often restrictive	Very high from interstitial waters	Low, variable; some from macrophyte
CO_2 (HCO_3^-)	Usually adequate to high	Very high from sediment metabolism	Low to high; much internal recycling
Others	Usually adequate	High	Low; likely much internal recycling
Organic substrates/nutrients			
Organic micronutrients	Low, but variable with season in lakes and floodplain inundation in rivers	Very high from sediment metabolism	Low, high microbial competition, much internal recycling
Heterotrophy	Algal heterotrophy low or absent; bacterial heterotrophy low to moderate	Algal heterotrophy potentially moderate, likely low, bacterial heterotrophy very high	Algal heterotrophy low; bacterial heterotrophy high
Primary productivity	Low to moderate	Low	High
Symbiotic/mutualistic interactions among microbes and substrata	Low	Moderate to high	High to very high

NOTE: Modified from Wetzel (2001).

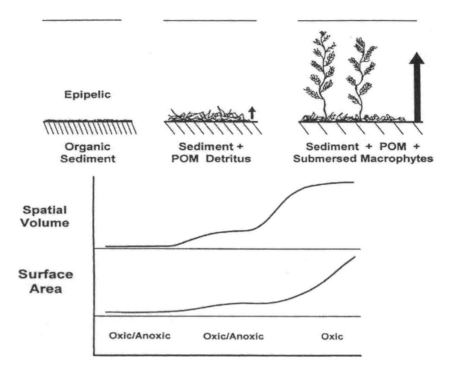

FIGURE 8.6

Transition of substrata surface area for colonization and growth of periphyton communities from a predominantly two-dimensional spatial habitat through increasing surface area of particulate organic matter (POM) detritus to a fully three-dimensional spatial habitat of surface area of submersed aquatic plants projecting up into a water column. Reprinted from Wetzel (2001), with permission from Elsevier.

Habitat availability markedly affects the composite productivity of periphytic communities. Sediment habitats, for example, are approximately two-dimensional and provide much less surface area and have much lower periphyton productivity than a three-dimensional habitat, such as the finely divided leaves of submersed macrophytes (Fig. 8.6). The epiphytic communities have manifold greater productivity as the spatial volume of the habitat projects upward into the water column and enhanced light field (e.g., Allen 1971).

As nutrient availability increases in the surrounding water, particularly of phosphorus and nitrogen, shifts in species composition and increases in growth and biomass of attached algae occur on substrata. Within a specific range of water turbulence and current velocities, the boundary layer thickness between the periphyton communities and the overlying water is reduced with increasing current velocities (e.g., Riber and Wetzel

1987; Losee and Wetzel 1993). Enhanced nutrient exchange with the overlying water occurs as a result. However, there is a strong tendency for water movements to move around the macrophytes, and as a result, the boundary layers at the periphyton surfaces are very large. Under these conditions, turbulence is greatly reduced, and transport-exchange of gases and ions between periphyton and the surrounding water is largely relegated to diffusion processes (Riber and Wetzel 1987; Sand-Jensen and Mebus 1996). Physical instability can occur as periphyton communities develop and increase in thickness. Portions of the community may then slough off and enter into the detrital POM pool of the sediments.

Many microbiota of periphyton communities are apparent habitat generalists, although some species have distinct specialized substrata preferences (Burkholder 1996). Although many substrata preferences are nonobligate ectosymbioses, others are more biochemically mutualistic endosymbioses with host plants, fungi, or animals. In some cases, small concentrations of poorly characterized substances, released from the substrata, are utilized by the periphyton.

Physical properties of the substratum influence success of attachment and retention, particularly in relation to water movements and susceptibility to detachment, sloughing, and dislodgement. Periphyton development is often concentrated in crevices, depressions, and other protected areas of nonliving or living substrata (Burkholder and Wetzel 1989; Characklis and Wilderer 1989; Burkholder 1996; Wetzel 2001). As a new substratum is formed, such as a new macrophyte leaf, new particulate detritus, or a scoured rock surface, it is colonized initially by weak physical attraction between the substratum and hydrophobic areas of microbial, largely bacterial, cells. This initial weak bonding is quickly strengthened by secretion of adhesive glycocalyx and mucopolysaccharides that anchor the organisms to the surface.

It is very difficult to quantify the influence of chemical dynamics within periphyton communities on different growth and competition of organisms within the complex matrix. For example, phosphate ions can be metabolized by active microbes but are also adsorbed to inorganic (e.g., $CaCO^{-3}$) and organic particulate matter within the periphyton community and matrix (Moeller et al. 1988; Burkholder et al. 1990). In addition to the water column as a nutrient or organic source for attached microbes, the underlying substrata can be effective in supplying nutrients, allelopathic substances, or other essential or inhibitory compounds (Burkholder and Wetzel 1990; Borchardt 1996; Gross 1999; Ervin and Wetzel 2003).

Because of the rapidity with which nutrients and other metabolically important compounds are moving within the periphyton community on small spatial scales (micrometers), very few studies have really examined flux and exchange rates among intact communities. Cells are in close juxtaposition, often in direct contact. As a result, fluxes of products occur rapidly with intense rates of exchange and recycling. Methodologies to quantify such fluxes require tracing methods at cellular levels with short time intervals. Some of the better methods involve track light microscope and track scanning electron microscope autoradiography (e.g., Pip and Robinson 1982a, 1982b; Moeller et al. 1988;

Paul and Duthie 1988; Burkholder et al. 1990). All of these techniques have limitations and are demanding, but they do offer one of the best means to evaluate pathways at the cellular levels.

At the community level *within* periphyton communities, microsensors based on electrochemistry have permitted quantitative evaluations of fluxes and distributions of ions and gases at spatial and temporal scales essential to understand the complexity of these communities. As biological reactions precede the electrochemical reactions, micro-biosensors, involving many different types of ion, polarization, and redox reactions (Kühl and Revsbech, 2001), can follow changes in concentrations of gases (O_2, H_2, N_2O, H_2S, and CO_2) and ions (pH, NO_2^-, NO_3^-, NH_4^+, Ca^{2+}, S^-). These properties can be evaluated at rapid time scales appropriate to the metabolically induced changes within the periphyton and across boundaries of the periphyton.

Epifluorescent microscopy and confocal epifluorescent microscopy allow evaluation of quantitative changes in specific enzymes by use of highly specific substrates and dyes. For example, leucine-aminopeptidase activities within periphyton communities were moderated by the algal-bacterial coupling with changes in internal pH (Francoeur and Wetzel 2003). Periphytic aminopeptidase activities had pH optima much higher (pH > 9.5) than found in other organisms and were stimulated by the periphytic algal photosynthesis. Regulation of phosphatase, glucosidase, and xylosidases in periphyton was strongly regulated by rapid internal changes of pH, oxygen, light-mediated photosynthesis, and dissolved organic matter, particularly phenolic humic substances (Espeland and Wetzel 2001a, 2001b; Espeland et al. 2001, 2002).

Fiber-optical microprobes collect and direct light signals between the sensor fiber tip and the opto-electronic measuring system and analyze light intensities, spectral compositions, or fluorescence from the immediate surroundings of the probe tip. Physico-chemical variables can be measured via optical changes in fluorescence or absorption of an indicator dye or compound that reacts at the sensor tip. Not only can these optical fiber electrodes be used to determine spectral optics within periphyton communities under different environmental conditions (Kühl and Jørgensen 1992), the microprobes can be additionally coupled with the diffusion and flux dynamics of specific fluorescent enzymatic substrates and dyes penetrating into and moving about within the periphyton matricies. Such techniques can allow direct evaluations of changes in enzymatic activities for very specific enzymes.

RECYCLING: THE KEY TO NUTRIENT FLUXES AND MAXIMIZING PRODUCTIVITY OF PERIPHYTON

Macrogradients

Any discussion of the carbon and nutrient retention and cycling in wetlands made up of macrophyte and periphyton communities is fraught with problems of extreme spatial and temporal heterogeneity. Most periphyton communities are associated with land-water interface regions of wetland habitats grading into littoral regions of ponds, lakes, and river floodplains—all shallow environments that receive sufficient sunlight to support photosynthesis. As mentioned earlier, heterotrophic periphyton in darkness is important and widespread, but the mutualistic metabolic coupling between microproducers and microbial heterotrophs forms a much more productive and responsive community.

Periphyton communities develop at all land-water interface areas. Spatially, however, the periphytic development is extremely variable, not only in relation to the two- versus three-dimensional development of substrata discussed earlier, but also in regard to topographical variations in elevation. Most land-water habitats are in depression areas where elevational gradients are small and extend horizontally for large distances, often far exceeding the size of the water body itself. Many of these habitats, particularly in the tropics, experience wide seasonal variations in water level with long periods (months) of alternating inundation and dewatering or even desiccation. These oscillating fluctuations occur at the microlevel of the periphyton communities as well. For example, in shallow wetland areas of only a few centimeters, daily cycles of evapotranspiration can cause shifts of water level of two centimeters or more and induce significant shifts in area of inundated periphyton (e.g., Ward 1998). Some of the hydrologic losses can be recovered during nighttime periods or precipitation events. These small changes in depth of only a few millimeters can induce significant metabolic effects by exposure of periphyton communities to marked variations in ultraviolet light, ion and nutrient concentrations, pH, dissolved gases, and other constituents on a diurnal basis (Kahn and Wetzel 1999).

Within the zones of sufficient light to support periphytic photosynthesis, substrata variability is great but can be organized into several general zones in regard to potential nutrient availability from the substrata (Wetzel 1996, 2001).

ZONE 1. Saturated hydrosoils and pools among emergent macrophytes of wetlands contain massive amounts of macrophyte detritus and particulate organic matter. Despite translocation and conservation of large amounts of nutrients to the rooting tissues during the active growth cycle, the decomposing detritus releases large amounts of soluble organic matter and nutrients, particularly organic phosphorus and nitrogen (Wetzel 1999b; Reddy et al. 2004). Because many of the emergent plants are perennials with multiple population cohort turnovers, the supply of detritus and nutrient release are more or less constant and readily and efficiently utilized by periphyton communities associated with this detrital and sediment mass. Nutrient utilization from the sediments has been contrasted to that obtained from the overlying water with nutrient-diffusing artificial substrata (Fairchild et al. 1985; Carrick and Lowe 1988; Pringle 1990). Although these methods have problems (e.g., contaminating organic materials from the diffusing media), there was clear indication that the nutrients do diffuse from the substrata to the attached communities, as was demonstrated from living macrophyte tissues experimentally (Moeller et al. 1988).

ZONE 2. Submersed macrophytes commonly possess morphology of thin, finely divided and reticulated leaves. The increased surface area of leaves enhances interception of light and exchange of gases and ions with the surrounding water. Of course, this increased surface area results in markedly increased surface area for microbial colonization. For example, leaf surface area available for colonization by epiphytic microbiota on a submersed linear-leaved macrophyte *(Scirpus subterminalis)* averaged 24 m^2 m^{-2} of the bottom in a moderately developed littoral zone of a lake in Michigan (Burkholder and Wetzel 1989). These extensive surfaces project highly diverse microhabitats with attached periphyton communities upward into littoral environments of relatively abundant light and dissolved gases as well as nutrients diffusing from the high decomposition of interstitial waters of detritus and sediments. There is clear evidence that even though low amounts of nutrients are released from submersed macrophytes, these sources constitute important inputs to periphyton and are very efficiently utilized in the adhering structured community (Harlin 1973; Moeller et al. 1988; Burkholder 1996). The significance of the substratum nutrient source is more important in oligotrophic waters and decreases under eutrophic conditions as the nutrient availability in the surrounding water becomes very high.

Nutrient acquisition by periphyton from the substrata and retention internally for recycling is not only limited to phosphorus and nitrogen. For example, silica requirements of attached diatoms and certain chrysophytes can be met in part from both inorganic substrata and from supporting macrophytes (e.g., *Equisetum*) that have high silica content in their tissues (e.g., Jørgensen 1957). In this case, the attached diatoms have a great competitive advantage over planktonic diatoms that often experience reduction of silica concentrations in the water to limiting levels.

During senescence of macrophytes, appreciable nutrient content is translocated to rooting tissues, particularly among herbaceous perennials that dominate among aquatic plants. Some senescence and degradation of leaf tissues, however, results in the loss of cellular integrity and leaching of nutrients and dissolved organic compounds from the leaves. These compounds, particularly labile amino acids, were readily utilized and sequestered by the periphytic microflora (Bicudo et al. 1998).

ZONE 3. The high nutrient availability of the interstitial waters of sediments encourages the prolific development of benthic periphyton as long as light is sufficient. Many of the epipelic algae and cyanobacteria are adapted to very low irradiances, and active net photosynthesis is common at less than 10 μmol m^{-2}s^{-1} (e.g., Carlton and Wetzel 1987, 1988). Because organic sediments are especially susceptible to disturbance and burial by water movements and animals that would alter light availability, many of the algal species migrate, often in rhythmic fashion, to compensate for light attenuation by and within the sediment (cf. Round 1981). Mineral nutrients (Fe, Si, and trace elements) can leach from rock along facies where solubilities may be greater than from other rock surfaces. Microaggregations of periphyton in these crevice areas indicate acquisition of the minerals as well as protection from abrasion (Krejci and Lowe 1986).

ZONE 4. Aggregations of periphyton communities will develop in open water in many quiescent areas of standing water within wetlands that persist for moderate periods of time. These metaphyton communities are neither strictly attached to substrata nor truly suspended in the water. Metaphyton often fragments from dense epiphytic or epipelic periphyton communities, clump, and are loosely attached in dense microbial accumulations in littoral areas. The metabolism of metaphyton can be extremely active, with high photosynthetic rates and intense internal nutrient recycling and retention. For example, in hard waters, metaphyton can induce massive precipitation of $CaCO_3$ with coprecipitation of phosphate. This photosynthetically induced mechanism (Otsuki and Wetzel 1972) of phosphate sequestering by metaphyton, for example, is a major mechanism for maintenance of oligotrophic conditions by phosphorus limitation in the massive Everglades wetlands of Florida.

Microgradients

The microbial community develops successively on surfaces in a typical logarithmic sigmoid growth curve until the thickness of the periphyton becomes unstable and portions of the most recent community development slough off (Wetzel 1993). Thickness of the community is dictated largely by water movements—in more turbulent water (rivers, wave-swept areas), the tendency is toward more dense, compressed communities than is the case in the loosely attached communities of quiescent waters. The latter can extend to a few centimeters, but most of the loosely attached periphyton communities are in the range of 1 to 2 millimeters.

Nutrients, gases, and organic compounds diffuse into the microbial communities of periphyton from the surrounding ambient medium or from the inert, living, or dead substratum on which the periphyton is growing, as briefly summarized earlier. The rates of diffusion along these gradients into the periphyton are of course mediated by differences in concentrations, which are in part altered by metabolism of the organisms, sorptive sinks, and inorganic/organic chemical reactions that alter solubilities. Once these compounds enter the periphyton from external exogenous sources in the water and from the substratum to which the community is affixed, many of these gases and compounds are vigorously recycled internally. The periphyton matrix is permeated by microchannels that can alter and increase diffusion rates, but the periphyton is relatively impervious to throughflow (cf. Riber and Wetzel 1987; Wetzel et al. 1997). Most communities are composed of a tight integration of living and dead algal and bacterial cells, particulate detritus, and inorganic particles bound within an organic matrix of largely extracellularly released polysaccharide secretions (e.g., Lange 1976; Lock et al. 1984; Lock 1993; Costerton et al. 1995). Periphyton communities in which diatoms dominate tend to be more porous and contain more extensive microchannels than is the case where cyanobacteria dominate. Stalked, nonmucilaginous diatom and filamentous green algae may increase the porosity of the communities, but very little is known of variations in diffusion rates within the communities under differing biodiversity.

Bacteria and algae/cyanobacteria in periphyton are directly coupled metabolically. For example, simultaneous measurements of rates of photosynthesis and of bacterial productivity by protein synthesis showed that when photosynthesis was inhibited, bacterial productivity and growth was immediately suppressed (Neely and Wetzel 1995; Espeland et al. 2001). This type of mutualism is likely related to the production of oxygen and labile dissolved organic substrates released by the algae and utilized by the bacteria. In like fashion, phosphorus uptake kinetics of periphyton were found to be acutely limited by boundary-layer mass transfer and a power function of flow velocity of the overlying water (Riber and Wetzel 1987). Kinetic calculations based on turnover measurements indicated that internal recycling of phosphorus and recycling from the boundary layer, rather than external uptake, accounted for most of the phosphate turnover within intact periphyton. Under optimal conditions, it was estimated that the turnover time of phosphorus was so rapid that phosphorus was recycled between algae and bacteria every 15 seconds. Denitrification rates by denitrifying bacteria within epiphytic as well as epipelic periphyton can be high in the dark and on senescent macrophyte tissues but are inhibited by oxygen produced by periphytic algae or the living macrophyte tissues (Risgaard-Petersen et al. 1994; Eriksson and Weisner 1996).

Similarly, CO_2, specific growth factors (e.g., vitamins), and other products produced by bacteria can influence growth and metabolism of algae/cyanobacteria (Wetzel 1993, 1996). Steep gradients exist within these attached microbial communities that 1) require rapid, intensive recycling of carbon, phosphorus, nitrogen, and other nutrients among producers, particulate and dissolved detritus, and bacteria and protists; 2) augment internal recycling and losses with small external inputs of carbon and nutrients from the overlying water or from the supporting substrata; and 3) encourage maximum conservation of nutrients.

As the density and thickness of periphyton communities increase successionally, the rates of diffusion and penetration of gases and nutrients into the community decrease. Simultaneously, the intensity of internal nutrient recycling increases to the point where the community is maximizing efficiencies of utilization and retention with recycling of the essential resources (Wetzel 1993, 1996).

MODULATION OF PERIPHYTON BY LIGHT AVAILABILITY

Periphyton communities are known to be able to adapt to both extremely high and extremely low light availability. Under both circumstances, primary accommodation to the light extremes is by modification of pigments. Under high light, particularly of ultraviolet (UV) irradiance, both slowly reversible and irreversible, nonphotochemical damage occurs to proteins within the reaction center affecting photosystem II (Falkowski and Raven 1997). High-energy photons of UV can ionize molecules and result in irreversible damage to photochemical processes as well as damage absorptive components, such as thymidines, of DNA. Carotenoids, such as β-carotene, and nonessential, aromatic amino acids offer some protection, and damage to DNA can be partially repaired during dark periods. Even when adapted to high light intensities, periphyton and metaphyton light saturate at relatively low intensities (100–400 μmol m^{-2} s^{-1}; Hill 1996). Algal productivity and photosynthetic oxygen production within the periphyton can be significantly reduced by exposure to modestly enhanced UV irradiance (Kahn and Wetzel 1999). Bacterial productivity coupled to rates of algal photosynthesis, as discussed earlier, was reduced as a result. Some evidence (Bothwell et al. 1993; Francoeur and Lowe 1998) suggests that long-term adaptation by periphytic diatoms in streams can reverse initially inhibitory effects of UV on growth after several weeks of species succession.

Often, in shaded environments (deep habitats, tree canopies, emergent and other aquatic plants, turbid waters), algae/cyanobacteria of periphyton are shade adapted with marked increases of light-absorbing pigments, particularly chlorophylls. Usually the lower light limits are in the range of 5 to 10 μmol m^{-2} s^{-1} (Wetzel et al. 1984; Lorenz et al. 1991). The habitats at which such light limitations occur are highly variable—from a few centimeters to over a hundred meters of depth in lakes, and within a few hundred micrometers within periphyton communities.

Light attenuation in relation to photosynthetic productivity of periphyton should be examined at two spatial scales—changes with depth in the water column before reaching the periphyton and at a microscale within the periphyton complex. The alterations of light with increasing depth are complex and have been treated in great detail in Kirk (1994), Wetzel (2001), and Helbling and Zagarese (2003). The depth at which light is attenuated to approximately 0.1% of surface insolation, the approximate compensation point of lowest irradiance where sufficient ATP (adenosine triphosphate) can be generated photosynthetically to compensate for respiratory losses, varies greatly.

In shallow lakes and ponds, complex competitive interactions of macrophytes, attached microbiota, and phytoplankton occur. This subject has received intensive study in the past two decades with some attempts to design reasonable paradigms, wholly frustrated by the extreme natural spatial and temporal variability (see reviews in Scheffer 1998 and Wetzel 2001). Light penetration to much of the sediment surface of these shallow waters can support invasion and growth of macrophytes over much of the basins. Submersed macrophyte dominance prevails when nutrient concentrations of the water are low with a high N:P ratio (>>10:1). As nitrogen and phosphorus concentrations increase, transitions occur in the submersed aquatic plant communities and the periphyton associated with them. Submersed macrophyte dominance can be maintained by mechanisms (e.g., abiogenic turbidity, especially clays; sequestering of nutrients by macrophytes; and large zooplankton herbivory) that suppress the development of profuse phytoplankton communities. A shift to phytoplankton-dominated conditions, where submersed macrophytes are suppressed or eliminated by shading, can result from prolific development of algae or cyanobacteria adapted to competition for light as nutrient levels increase. The phytoplankton increase biogenic turbidity, reduce light for submersed macrophytes, and reduce the grazing pressure (because of food particle size) of large zooplankton on phytoplankton. Losses of the submersed macrophyte three-dimensional habitat result in a collapse of the largest of periphyton habitats and a marked reduction of wetland and littoral productivity.

Attenuation of light at the microcommunity level within periphyton communities is now reasonably well studied, but generalizations are difficult owing to the extreme heterogeneity. Light is attenuated very rapidly within periphyton communities, but spatial variability is high. Light gaps occur, and variable light attenuation occurs among cell aggregations, calcium carbonate crystals, pigmented cell aggregations, and dead diatom frustules, some of which act as light conduits (Losee and Wetzel 1983). Different species dominating the epiphytic community can also influence the nature of cellular structure and relative penetration of light into the communities as a whole (Dodds 1992). Photosynthetic pigments of algae and cyanobacteria attenuate light selectively in the red and particularly the blue portions of the spectrum (Losee and Wetzel 1983; Jørgensen and Des Marais 1988). Other components (bacteria, carbonates, dead diatoms) are not light selective. Back-scattering of light within periphyton likely increases the efficiency of light utilization.

MODULATION OF MACROPHYTES AND PERIPHYTON BY MORTALITY AND LOSSES: WHAT DO THEY MEAN TO HIGHER TROPHIC LEVELS?

Growth dynamics and productivity of periphyton can not be effectively analyzed in relation to their roles in the ecosystem without an appreciation and quantification of mortality losses and rates of turnover. Great emphasis has been given to periphyton as a food supply for animals and movement of carbon, nutrients, and energy within the food web. A number of processes contribute to mortality, losses, and interference competition, including predatory mortality, largely by grazing invertebrates and fishes; natural physiological senescence, death (often genetically programmed death), population turnover; diseases, and viral mortality; and physical disturbances from water movements and substrata instabilities (reviewed in Wetzel 2001; see also Bott 1996; Lamberti 1996;Peterson 1996; Steinman 1996).

Heavy grazing of periphyton by animals (insect larvae, crayfish, and certain fishes) can result in reductions of periphyton biomass and productivity. In some cases, moderate grazing of periphyton stimulates microbial growth rates by means of improved light availability within the periphyton communities and perhaps enhanced nutrient availability from the water as well as from the feeding activities of the animals. Supporting evidence for the latter, however, is poor. Although most periphyton communities are not grazed by animals, attached microbial-grazer interactions and mortality vary with herbivore type, nutrient and light availability for compensatory growth, and disturbance frequency. There is some evidence that grazing mortality of periphyton is greater in streams than in standing waters; grazing mortality of periphyton in wetlands is likely a very small percentage of the total production.

Most of the aquatic plant and periphyton production cycles without ingestion by animals. Losses of natural plant and periphyton communities by natural senescence and cellular death constitute a major fate of production. A significant portion of death is genetically programmed, and estimates indicate at least 30% and often greater than 50% of microbial cellular death is viral in origins (Wetzel 1995, 2001). Utilization by protists such as sessile flagellates and ciliates is very poorly known as they feed within the periphytic matrix and microchannels. Utilization of released dissolved organic substrates from cells is largely metabolized to CO_2, much of which is recycled and utilized, along with organic and inorganic nutrients, within the periphyton. Most of the macrophyte and periphyton production enters the pool of detrital organic matter in wetlands of both lake and river ecosystems and is rapidly metabolized to dissolved organic compounds, CO_2, and methane. Nutrients are often recycled in an efficient community mutualism.

Disturbance to the substrata and surrounding habitats of periphyton communities occur over a large spectrum from severe physical disruption of substrata, such as during river flooding, to much more gradual but nonetheless severe shifts in water level, water depth, and associated physical and chemical factors. Although much study has been directed to disturbances of substrata and periphyton in streams, much greater periphyton productivity and ecosystem constituents occur in quiescent habitats (floodplains, littoral areas, and other wetlands). Very little is known about disturbance events, periodicities, and hydrology in these environments in relation to periphyton development, growth, productivity, and trophic interactions.

DEFENSIVE MECHANISMS AND ALLELOCHEMICAL "COMMUNICATION" WITHIN WETLANDS

Selection pressure from competition among wetland plants has led to the development of numerous competitive adaptations. Submersed, verticillate macrophytes such as *Hydrilla*, *Elodea*, and *Myriophyllum* are capable of rapid shoot elongation and sloughing of shaded leaves in response to reduced light intensity (Grace and Wetzel 1978; Barko and Smart 1981; Ervin and Wetzel 2002), adaptations that concentrate photosynthetic tissues within the photic zone of water bodies. High rates of aboveground production provide a competitive advantage through shading of nearby competitor species (e.g., *Typha latifolia*, *Juncus effuses*, and *Hydrilla verticillata* [Grace and Wetzel 1982; Van et al. 1998; Ervin and Wetzel 2002). Vegetative growth strategies often rely on vegetative clonal growth with reduction of sexual reproduction (Grace 1993). Many of these clonal methods of propagation also function in perenniation or supplemental resource exploitation (e.g., adventitious root formation and autofragmentation in *Myriophyllum*; Smith et al. 2002).

Wetland and aquatic macrophytes not only compete with other macrophytes, but also face competition from attached epiphytic microbial communities for both light and nutrients. There is some indication that various allelopathic interactions exist between macrophytes and epiphytic microbial communities; only in a few cases is the chemical evidence compelling (cf. reviews of Gross 1999 and Ervin and Wetzel 2003).

Aggressive chemical mechanisms function effectively as well. For example, certain invasive species can release chemical compounds that have allelopathic effects on selected species of the indigenous plant community (Hierro and Callaway 2004). The native species may not have had previous exposure to, and sufficient time to develop defensive mechanisms to cope with, the allelochemical compounds and rapidly give way to the invasive species.

HERBIVORY

Various toxic metabolites (phenolic compounds, terpenoids, alkaloids) are well known to deter herbivory on aquatic plants (Ervin and Wetzel 2003). Some hormonal sesquiterpenoid and glucosinolate compounds function both as antiherbivore defenses as well as allelopathic agents in suppressing growth of competitive plants (e.g., Toong et al. 1988; Bede et al. 1999a, 1999b; Bede and Tobe 2000; Siemens et al. 2002). Sulfur-containing compounds (trithianes) are known among aquatic plants and macroalgae (Characeae) that have both antimicrobial and antiherbivore properties (Wium-Andersen 1987; Gross 1999). Some elegant studies have isolated specific polyphenolic and lignan compounds from specific aquatic plants that confer antiherbivory properties against the crayfish (Wilson et al. 1999b; Kubanek et al. 2000). Glucosinolate compounds are produced by watercress *(Nasturtium officinale)* that function in both allelopathic and antiherbivory properties (Newman 1991; Newman et al. 1992, 1996a).

Such studies support the hypotheses of Lodge (1991) and Newman (1991) that aquatic and wetland macrophytes may be well defended chemically against herbivory. Evidence suggests that phenolic compounds are more likely responsible for herbivory deterrence than are alkaloids. Plant damage, as via herbivore feeding activities, can result in immediate induction of phenolic production and suppression of feeding by a variety of invertebrate herbivores.

Less toxic chemical defenses are more widespread among plant species than are more narrowly distributed highly toxic compounds. Herbivores can adapt to novel, more toxic chemical defenses of plants by becoming specialists. Alternatively, herbivores can become generalists but at the cost of reduced feeding success on any particular plant species (Cornell and Hawkins 2003). The limited literature on phytochemical defense mechanisms among aquatic plant and wetland communities provide support for a co-evolutionary model. Herbivory responses are sufficiently distinct, however, to indicate diffuse coevolution. Microorganisms may select for plant defense compounds. As plant species diversify, novel defense chemicals will become widespread. The tendency then would be for herbivores to adapt to it and eventually develop mechanisms to disable such compounds.

POTENTIAL EFFECTS OF GLOBAL CHANGES IN CLIMATE
AND RELATED ENVIRONMENTAL CONDITIONS
ON ECOSYSTEM PROCESSES

A number of environmental parameters have been discussed in relation to influences on the productivity and microbial interactions of periphyton communities. Changes in environmental conditions as a result of anthropogenic impacts will translate to the growth and productivity of periphyton communities, their fate, and organisms that utilize periphyton. Several examples will illustrate the potential.

Aquatic bacteria, fungi, and detritivore invertebrates of many waters utilize organic carbon inputs from periphyton communities growing on detrital leaves and related organic materials from riparian trees and wetland/littoral aquatic plants. This energy is further transferred to other components of the food web, including fish. If the chemical composition of this particulate detritus is altered, periphytic growth and development may be altered as well.

Increases in atmospheric CO_2 are occurring at a steady rate and are anticipated to double by about 2065 to almost 720 parts per million. Experimental studies evaluated CO_2–induced changes in chemical composition of particulate detritus, and dissolved organic matter leaching from it, as well as the corresponding effects on attached bacteria, fungi, and detritivorous insect larvae utilizing these materials. Detritus of leaves grown on elevated CO_2 had higher concentrations of lignin and phenolic compounds and much higher C:N ratios than in detritus grown at ambient (360 ppm) CO_2 (Tuchman et al. 2002, 2003a, 2003b). Periphytic bacterial and fungal growth was suppressed and of altered quality. Detritivorous insect larvae feeding on these materials from plants grown on enriched CO_2 consumed less, assimilated less, and grew appreciably less with increased mortality and delayed larval development. Growth of fish feeding on these invertebrates was also appreciably reduced. Rates of decomposition of the particulate organic matter were also markedly reduced.

Coincident with and coupled to increases in the CO_2 concentrations in the atmosphere are increases in temperatures. Despite variations in the model predictions, an increase in mean temperature of between 1 and 3°C will occur in the present century, with perhaps a greater warming in the central parts of continents. Summer precipitation is anticipated to decrease appreciably, with marked increases in evapotranspiration, in some continental regions and increase in others. River flows are anticipated to fluctuate to a much greater extent relative to base flow on an annual basis than was the case previously. Altered hydrology and river flows, altered precipitation regimes (e.g., less frequent but more intense precipitation events), altered time of snowmelt events, and others will alter habitat quality of floodplains, littoral areas, and wetlands (e.g., Poiani and Johnson 1991; Grimm 1993; Poiani et al. 1996). Obviously, these hydrologic alterations will greatly modify habitat for periphyton development and productivity both spatially and chemically as alterations in concentration and ionic strength occur.

Reduction of ozone in the stratosphere, in part as a result of reactions with chlorofluorohydrocarbon compounds use in refrigeration and propellant devices, has resulted in large increases in the amounts of UV-B and, to a lesser extent, UV-A reaching the surface of the Earth (Kerr and McElroy 1993; Blumthaler and Webb 2003). The increases vary with atmospheric conditions but are in the range of 1% per decade near the equator and greater than 13% per decade at latitudes greater than 45°. The increased ultraviolet irradiance can lead to accelerated photolytic degradation of dissolved organic matter in water both by direct photolysis to CO_2 as well as alteration of complex macromolecules to simple substrates readily utilizable by bacteria (reviewed in Wetzel 2003). Reduction in the photoprotective capacities of dissolved organic matter in natural waters results in physiological and genetic injury to microbes, particularly many algae, or forces shifts in resource allocation to production of protective UV-absorbing compounds, such as mycosprorine-like amino acids or radical scavenging compounds. Small changes in dissolved organic matter of natural waters can cause marked reductions in productivity of periphyton (e.g., Kahn and Wetzel 1999), changes in species biodiversity, and alterations of energy transfers to higher trophic levels feeding on the periphyton (Bothwell et al. 1993).

9
UNITED STATES WETLAND REGULATION AND POLICY

D. Eric Somerville and Bruce A. Pruitt

Wetland regulation and policy in the United States is dictated by an amalgam of statute, regulation, judicial decisions, administrative policy, and public sentiment that has changed many times over the decades and continues to evolve even today. The relative rigor of wetland regulation has been likened to a clock pendulum that swings with the prevailing sympathies of the American populace and can change dramatically with changes in presidential administration or congressional majority. In the earliest days of the American colonies, wetlands and marshes in the eastern United States were considered wild places or wastelands that had to be tamed in order for the new nation to grow. Even the capitol city, Washington, D.C. is built on a vast wetland complex at the mouth of the Potomac River that was drained and filled to facilitate building the nation's seat of government. Such descriptive monikers as the Great Dismal Swamp on the North Carolina–Virginia border and Tate's Hell Swamp in northwestern Florida provide lasting evidence of the opinions of America's earliest colonists.

Never has a concerted effort to drain, dike, levee, fill, or otherwise alter wetlands on a national scale been undertaken so efficiently and so effectively than that which was facilitated by the U.S. government in the nineteenth and early twentieth centuries (Mitsch and Gosselink 2000). Stream and river channelization and efforts to drain even some of the largest wetlands in the country were enthusiastically endorsed and funded by the U.S. Congress. In addition, as the United States became an industrial center, point source discharges of industrial and municipal waste had so fouled the nation's waterways by the middle of the twentieth century that many were unsafe to swim in, and little aquatic life was able to prosper. The depths to which aquatic resources in the United States had fallen was exemplified by the Cuyahoga River in Ohio, which was able to catch fire and burn in 1969 due to the level of industrial pollution in its waters.

However, by the 1960s, the public's attitudes toward the environment, including wetlands and other aquatic resources, had begun to change and ultimately led to a number of federal statutes intended to regulate activities with potentially adverse impacts on the nation's natural resources. Together, the laws passed by Congress from approximately 1965 to 1985 remain the foundation for most environmental regulation in the United States. However, the implementation of these statutes and the programs they authorized continues to evolve, due largely to new judicial interpretations but influenced also by the prevailing public and congressional sentiment of the times.

This chapter traces the evolution of contemporary federal wetland regulation and policy in the United States. While the emphasis is on national legislation, initiatives, and policies, it is incumbent on the reader to also recognize that many states have adopted local regulatory policies or programs that in many cases provide even greater protection of wetland resources. The chapter will conclude with a brief discussion of wetland functional assessment and its role in the regulatory process. While there have been numerous functional assessment methodologies proposed in the United States over the last 25 years, our focus will be on the hydrogeomorphic approach to wetland functional assessment, which was developed in the 1990s and was subsequently endorsed by six of the federal agencies primarily responsible for regulating, managing, or impacting wetland resources in the United States.

WETLAND DEFINITIONS

There have been numerous wetland definitions in the United States, due in part to the diversity of wetland types and the varied landscapes in which they are found. Regional differences in climate, precipitation, geology, and land cover have led to the formation of a wide variety of wetland types in the United States (Tiner 1995), each often typified by unique vegetative communities. Wetland definitions have also been heavily influenced by the intent and application of the definition, and by the interests, expertise, or responsibility of the individual or agency proposing the definition. Shaler (1890) wrote perhaps one of the first definitions found in a U.S. government document when he defined *swamp* as:

> [A]ll areas . . . in which the natural declivity is insufficient, when the forest cover is removed, to reduce the soil to the measure of dryness necessary for agriculture. Whenever any form of engineering is necessary to secure this desiccation, the area is classified as swamp.

Agricultural issues were paramount to the establishment and expansion of the early colonies, and these same interests dominated the economic strength of the nation in the late nineteenth century, especially in the southern and midwestern portions of the country. Shaler's definition reflected this importance in its reference to the ability and profitability of land to support germination, growth, and productivity of agriculture.

The term *wetland* was not even in common use until the middle of the twentieth century (Mitsch and Gosselink 2000). The U.S. Fish and Wildlife Service (USFWS) has been monitoring trends affecting the extent of the nation's wetland resources since the early 1950s. The USFWS developed a wetland classification system related to the production of wetland-dependent plants and animals, and Shaw and Fredine (1956) officially defined *wetlands* for the USFWS:

> [Wetlands are] low lands covered with shallow and sometimes temporary or intermittent waters. They are referred to by such names as marshes, swamps, bogs, wet meadows, potholes, sloughs, and river-overflow lands. Shallow lakes and ponds, usually with emergent vegetation as a conspicuous feature, are included in the definition, but the permanent waters of streams, reservoirs, and deep lakes are not included. Neither are water areas that are so temporary as to have little or no effect on the development of moist-soil vegetation. Usually these temporary areas are of no appreciable value to the species of wildlife considered in this report.

Although this definition is related to critical habitat of wetland-dependent wildlife, three important attributes of wetlands are implicit in the definition: hydrology, hydric soils, and an expression of hydrophytic vegetation ("development of moist-soil vegetation").

The USFWS established the National Wetlands Inventory in 1974 to "develop and provide resource managers with information on the location, extent, and types of wetlands and deepwater habitats" (USFWS 2002). For much of the remainder of the decade, the National Wetlands Inventory concentrated on selected priority areas of the country, such as the Pacific, Atlantic, and Gulf coastal regions, and the prairie potholes region of the Upper Midwest. However, by the late 1970s, the USFWS and Congress recognized that completing a comprehensive inventory of the nation's wetlands would not only benefit resource managers and land planners, but would also require a long-term commitment of resources and proper funding (USFWS 2002).

Congress provided more explicit goals and objectives for the National Wetlands Inventory in the 1986 Emergency Wetlands Resources Act, which required the USFWS to conduct status and trend studies of the nation's wetlands and report the findings to Congress each decade. The USFWS amended its wetland classification in the late 1970s and utilizes this classification to compile the status and trends reports. The current official USFWS wetland definition, developed to support its classification system, which was itself developed to support the National Wetlands Inventory, expresses more explicitly the attributes of wetland hydrology, hydric soils, and hydrophytic vegetation (Cowardin et al. 1979):

> Wetlands are lands transitional between terrestrial and aquatic systems where the water table is usually at or near the surface or the land is covered by shallow water. For the purposes of this classification, wetlands must have one or more of the following three attributes: (1) at least periodically, the land supports predominantly hydrophytes; (2) the substrate is predominantly undrained hydric soil; and (3) the substrate is nonsoil and is saturated with water or covered by shallow water at some time during the growing season of each year."

Other federal agencies have also developed definitions for wetlands, each based on the respective agency's congressional mandates, regulatory responsibilities, and policies. The 1972 Federal Water Pollution Control Act, and the subsequent 1977 amendments to that act, which became commonly referred to as the Clean Water Act (CWA), gave the U.S. Army Corps of Engineers (USACE) and the U.S. Environmental Protection Agency (USEPA) congressional authority to regulate activities proposing to place dredged or fill material in waters of the United States. Subsequently, in 1977, wetlands subject to federal jurisdiction under the CWA were formally defined as:

> Those areas that are inundated or saturated by surface or ground water at a frequency and duration sufficient to support, and that under normal circumstances do support, a prevalence of vegetation typically adapted for life in saturated soil conditions. Wetlands generally include swamps, marshes, bogs, and similar areas. (42 FR 37, 125–26, 37128–29)

Subsequently, in response to growing concern about the adverse impacts to the nation's wetlands as a result of agricultural interests, the U.S. Department of Agriculture (USDA) included the "Swampbuster" provisions in the 1985 Food Security Act. The current USDA definition of wetlands includes several of the same provisions, and in some cases the same language, as the USACE 1977 definition:

> [The term] wetland, except when such term is a part of the term "converted wetland," means land that (1) has predominance of hydric soils; (2) is inundated or saturated by surface or groundwater at a frequency and duration sufficient to support a prevalence of hydrophytic vegetation typically adapted for life in saturated soil conditions; and (3) under normal circumstances does support a prevalence of such vegetation, except that this term does not include lands in Alaska identified as having a high potential for agricultural development and a predominance of permafrost soils. (7 CFR 12.2[a])

In response to congressional debate during the President George H. W. Bush administration in the early 1990s concerning the delineation of federally jurisdictional wetlands, the USEPA asked the National Research Council (NRC) to conduct a study related to the scientific rationale for wetland delineation. NRC convened a 17-member committee, the

Committee on Characterization of Wetlands, which included representatives of universities, industry, environmental organizations, and legal professions, to review existing protocols and methods related to the determination of federal jurisdictional wetland boundaries. The committee acknowledged three definitions of wetlands in the United States at the time of their study: the 1977 USACE definition, the 1979 USFWS definition, and the 1985 USDA definition. However, the committee developed its own reference definition of wetlands to guide its research on determination methods (NRC 1995):

> A wetland is an ecosystem that depends on constant or recurrent, shallow inundation, or saturation at or near the surface of the substrate. The minimum essential characteristics of a wetland are recurrent, sustained inundation, or saturation at or near the surface and the presence of physical, chemical, and features of wetlands are hydric soils and hydrophytic vegetation. These features will be present except where specific physiochemical, biotic, or anthropogenic factors have removed them or prevented their development.

Despite that the above referenced definitions include both regulatory and nonregulatory definitions of wetlands, their common attributes include explicit reference to wetland hydrology, hydric soils, and the presence of vegetation specifically adapted to survive in saturated soils.

As described in subsequent sections of this chapter, the degree of federal oversight of activities in wetlands and other waters of the United States and the geographic extent of areas subject to this oversight has alternately expanded and contracted since the early twentieth century as a result of statute, policy, and judicial decisions. The general expansion of federal jurisdiction since the early 1970s has not been without its detractors and advocates both inside and outside of government, and the scope of federal jurisdiction in the United States continues to evolve over three decades after the Clean Water Act became law.

FEDERAL JURISDICTION OF WETLANDS
EARLY REGULATION AND POLICY: NINETEENTH CENTURY

Federal oversight of wetlands has changed dramatically since the first federal regulations affecting wetlands in the United States were passed by Congress in the mid-nineteenth century. Since that time, a litany of federal statute has been passed that has affected federal regulation and oversight of wetlands and other waters of the United States. (Table 9.1). Contemporary federal wetland regulation and policy bears little resemblance in most cases to these early pieces of legislation. Mitsch and Gosselink (2000) observe that in many cases, federal and state legislation and policy accepted and even encouraged the drainage and "reclamation" of wetlands prior to the 1970s.

One of the earliest federal acts authorizing such activities was an 1849 statute that granted the State of Louisiana "those swamp and overflowed lands, which may be or are found

TABLE 9.1   Timeline of Major U.S. Federal Statutes, Regulations, and Policy
Initiatives Affecting Wetlands

2002	National Wetland Mitigation Action Plan
1993	Clean Water Action Plan
1990	Memorandum of Agreement between USEPA and Department of the Army concerning mitigation under the CWA Section 404(b)(1) Guidelines
1989	North American Wetlands Conservation Act
1988	"No Net Loss" Policy
1985	Food Security Act ("Swampbuster" provisions)
1977	Clean Water Act
	Executive Order 11988: Floodplain Management
	Executive Order 11990: Protection of Wetlands
1972	Federal Water Pollution Control Act
	Coastal Zone Management Act
1969	National Environmental Policy Act
1967	Fish and Wildlife Coordination Act
1948	Water Pollution Control Act
1899	Rivers and Harbors Act

unfit for cultivation" (Chapter 87, An Act to Aid the State of Louisiana in Draining Swamp Lands Therein, 9 Stat. 352 (1849); cited in NRC 1995). This statute was intended to authorize and aid the construction of levees and drains necessary to "reclaim" the wetlands and make them suitable for agriculture. This statute also became the precursor for a broader piece of legislation called the Swamp Land Act of 1850, which similarly ceded federal wetlands to the states of Arkansas, Alabama, California, Florida, Illinois, Indiana, Iowa, Michigan, Mississippi, Missouri, Ohio, and Wisconsin in order to permit their reclamation for agriculture. Ultimately, 64 million acres were transferred under the act. However, the vague description of lands suitable for transfer in the wording of the statute—"wet and unfit for cultivation"—led to significant dispute, and by 1888, almost 200 cases of swamp land litigation reached the U.S. Supreme Court (Gates 1968, cited in NRC 1995).

The judicial branch of government has had a long history of interpreting, and in some cases revising, federal regulation and policy concerning the waters of the United States. Many of the earliest efforts to regulate activities in waters of the United States stemmed from the federal government's authority to regulate interstate and foreign commerce, as provided in Article I, Section 8 of the U.S. Constitution (a.k.a. Commerce Clause). Shortly after the Constitution was ratified, the U.S. Congress began enacting legislation aimed at regulating and further developing the nation's navigable waters to protect and expand their role in trade and commerce (Downing et al. 2003). However, Article III, Section 2 of the Constitution gives the federal court system jurisdiction over admiralty and maritime cases. Thus, while Congress developed legislation to regulate activities in navigable waters pursuant to the Commerce Clause, the federal courts were simultaneously asserting jurisdiction in admiralty and maritime cases in those same federalized waters (Downing et al. 2003).

One of the earliest Supreme Court cases to have pivotal ramifications on the regulation of waters in the United States was Gibbons v. Ogden, 22 U.S. 1 (1824), in which the Court ruled that the Commerce Clause of the U.S. Constitution did in fact give Congress the authority to control the navigable waters of the United States. Subsequent Supreme Court cases in the late nineteenth and early twentieth centuries began to define the scope and extent of "navigable waters" over which congressional authority extended. By 1921, Supreme Court decisions had defined the scope of congressional jurisdiction to include nontidal waters that were presently used, susceptible to use, or that had ever been capable of use to transport interstate waterborne commerce at any time in history even if the water body was no longer "navigable in fact."

EARLY TWENTIETH-CENTURY REGULATION AND POLICY: 1900–1970

Rivers and Harbors Act of 1899

Again, with the Commerce Clause as its fundamental authority, Congress authorized the USACE to maintain maritime navigation by regulating dredging and filling of navigable waters under Section 10 of the Rivers and Harbors Act of 1899 (RHA). The jurisdiction of RHA Section 10 extended no further than the traditional navigable waters of the United States, as previously defined by the Supreme Court in The Steamer Daniel Ball, 77 U.S. (10 Wall.) 557 (1871):

> Those rivers . . . are navigable in fact when they are used, or are susceptible of being used, in their ordinary condition, as highways for commerce, over which trade and travel are or may be conducted in the customary modes of trade and travel on water. And they constitute navigable waters of the United States within the meaning of the acts of Congress in contradistinction from the navigable waters of the states, when they form in their ordinary condition by themselves, or by uniting with other waters, a continued highway over which commerce is or may be carried on with other states or foreign countries in the customary modes in which commerce is conducted by water.

However, Section 13 of the RHA, commonly referred to as the Refuse Act, applied a different standard to the scope of the USACE's jurisdiction to implement the provisions of this Section. The Refuse Act prohibited the discharge or deposition of "any refuse matter of any kind or description whatever other than that flowing from streets and sewers passing therefrom in a liquid state" (33 U.S.C § 407). Of particular interest considering the ensuing century's aquatic resources legislation and litigation, Section 13 defined the jurisdiction of the USACE in implementing the provisions of the Refuse Act as "any tributary of any navigable water from which the same (i.e., pollutants) shall float or be washed into such navigable water" (33 U.S.C § 407). Thus, there were two inconsistent definitions within the RHA to delineate the jurisdiction of the USACE to implement the provisions thereof. Section 10 was restricted to those waters that were "navigable in fact," while Section 13 covered activities well outside these limits, extending to all tributaries from which pollutants could be discharged into navigable waters.

Early efforts to utilize the authority of the Refuse Act to address activities having potentially negative effects on water quality were not generally supported by the U.S. Department of Justice or by the Army Judge Advocate General's Office (Downing et al. 2003). However, in 1970, President Richard M. Nixon signed Executive Order 11574, establishing a large-scale permit program to be administered under the provisions of the Refuse Act that required sources of industrial pollution to be authorized prior to their discharge into navigable waters. Implementation of this permit program was hindered though by the lack of regulatory standards or criteria with which proposed permits could be evaluated or conditioned (Downing et al. 2003). Two years after President Nixon signed Executive Order 11574, Congress would attempt to address this disparate scope of regulatory jurisdiction during development of the nation's first comprehensive piece of legislation addressing all types of water pollution.

Evolution of Public Opinion

Public and scientific opinion, and even that of selected federal agencies, concerning wetlands and water quality had been slowly shifting for decades leading up to Executive Order 11574 in 1970. Public and private acquisition of wetlands for conservation and management of migratory waterfowl began in the late nineteenth century and led to the "duck stamp" program in 1934, whereby federal licenses were sold to waterfowl hunters over age sixteen in the United States. Funds generated by the sale of Federal Migratory Bird Hunting and Conservation Stamps (i.e., duck stamps) continue even today to be used by the USFWS to purchase or lease wetland habitat for the National Wildlife Refuge System. Concurrent with the federal duck stamp program, private conservation groups (e.g., Ducks Unlimited in 1937) organized and began raising public awareness and resources to protect wetlands and other aquatic habitat critical to migratory waterfowl.

State legislatures on both coasts of the United States were soon confronted with the issue of continued filling of coastal wetlands brought to their attention by concerned citizens. In the late 1950s, citizens of Westport, Connecticut, became alarmed at proposals to fill a salt marsh on Sherwood Island State Park. Although their lobbying efforts failed to save the marsh, it did lead to passage of a Connecticut state law that authorized the Water Resources Commission to regulate dredging "in order to safeguard wildlife habitat, improve navigation and prevent shoreline erosion" (Vileisis 1997). Nearly concurrent with these efforts in Connecticut, a citizens group in California called "Save the San Francisco Bay Association" began lobbying against plans by the City of Berkeley to fill approximately 2,000 acres of wetlands adjacent to the San Francisco Bay. The California state legislature created the San Francisco Bay Conservation Study Commission in 1964 and ultimately enacted a permanent regulatory program to oversee all proposals to fill portions of the bay (Vileisis 1997).

Popular books on the fate of chemicals in the environment and on wetlands and the impacts of anthropogenic activities thereon further raised the public's awareness and concern for the state of the nation's aquatic resources. Rachel Carson's seminal work, *Silent Spring* (1962), documented the ramifications of pesticides in the environment and is widely regarded as a catalyst for the public's outcry in favor of regulations to safeguard environmental quality in the United States. William Niering's *The Life of the Marsh* (1966) and John and Mildred Teal's *Life and Death of a Saltmarsh* (1969) described how these sensitive ecosystems function and the impacts they had incurred as a result of pollution and development.

Despite the public's growing concern for the environment and its interest in wetlands in particular, federal regulation and policy continued to be largely in favor of draining wetlands for agricultural development, flood protection, or other ambitions. The Watershed Protection and Flood Prevention Act of 1954 authorized the USDA Soil Conservation Service (SCS) to plan and execute "works of improvement for the conservation and proper utilization of land," including soil conservation, flood prevention, or water utilization. The SCS embarked on an ambitious "stream improvement" program whereby streams were channelized (i.e., deepened and straightened) to facilitate water movement in the channels and thereby reduce flooding on adjacent floodplains. By 1971, the SCS had channelized 6,000 miles of streams (Vileisis 1997), but the U.S. House of Representatives Subcommittee on Conservation and Natural Resources called for oversight hearings on stream channelization in June of that year. Assistant Secretary of the Interior Nathaniel P. Reed told the subcommittee that if the SCS completed the 1000-plus projects planned at the time in the southern United States, up to 300,000 acres of forested wetlands would be lost (Vileisis 1997). Nonetheless, agricultural interests prevailed, and Congress failed to approve a one-year moratorium on stream channelization. Opponents of the program were forced to turn to the court system to end the practice.

A SALIENT DECADE FOR FEDERAL ENVIRONMENTAL REGULATION: 1967–1977

The U.S. Congress passed the Fish and Wildlife Coordination Act (FWCA) in 1967, which was the first of many federal environmental laws passed in the ensuing decade that collectively remain the foundation of federal environmental regulation and policy in the United States. The FWCA required that any federal agency or any other public or private entity seeking federal authorization or license to impound, divert, or modify any stream or other body of water for any purpose, including navigation or drainage, must first consult with the USFWS and the state agency responsible for administration of wildlife resources in that state to identify "means and measures that should be adopted to prevent the loss of or damage to such wildlife resources" (16 U.S.C § 662[b]).

Two years later, the National Environmental Policy Act (NEPA) of 1969 (amended in 1975) instructed all federal agencies to evaluate and consider environmental impacts of proposed major federal actions. NEPA expanded consultation requirements for federal agencies and other entities receiving federal funding by requiring that every recommendation or report on major federal actions, including proposed legislation, assess the environmental impact of the proposed action (42 U.S.C. § 102[C]). Furthermore, NEPA required consultation with any federal agency having legal jurisdiction or special expertise with respect to any environmental impact as well as input from applicable federal, state, and local agencies authorized to develop and enforce environmental standards in the jurisdiction where environmental impacts were anticipated.

On July 9, 1970, President Richard M. Nixon presented the U.S. Congress with a plan to reorganize parts of the federal government and form the U.S. Environmental Protection Agency (USEPA). President Nixon proposed consolidating some of the responsibilities held at that time by many disparate government entities, including but not limited to the Interior Department; the Department of Health, Education, and Welfare; the Food and Drug Administration; the Agriculture Department; the Atomic Energy Commission; and the Council on Environmental Quality into a new agency devoted to environmental protection, regulation, enforcement, and research in the United States. Following hearings in the U.S. House of Representatives and the U.S. Senate during the summer of 1970, the USEPA officially came into existence on December 2, 1970 (USEPA 1992a).

In 1972, Congress enacted the Coastal Zone Management Act (CZMA) in recognition of the detriment to coastal zone resources that over development was causing. The CZMA codified a national policy intended "to preserve, protect, develop, and where possible, to restore or enhance, the resources of the Nation's coastal zone" (16 U.S.C § 1452[1]). The CZMA further encouraged states to develop coastal management programs to protect natural resources, "including wetlands, floodplains, estuaries, beaches, dunes, barrier islands, coral reefs, and fish and wildlife and their habitat, within the coastal zone" (16 U.S.C § 1452[2][A]).

In 1977, President Jimmy Carter signed Executive Order 11988: Floodplain Management, which established a number of programmatic policies directed at avoiding the short-term and long-term adverse impacts associated with modification and occupancy of floodplains. Executive Order 11988 directed federal agencies to evaluate the potential effects of any of its actions, including regulatory (permitting) actions, on the "natural and beneficial values" of floodplains (42 CFR 26951). The same year, President Carter also signed Executive Order 11990: Protection of Wetlands, which directed federal agencies to "minimize the destruction, loss or degradation of wetlands, and to preserve and enhance the natural and beneficial values of wetlands" while carrying out the agencies' responsibilities. While this directive effectively eliminated direct federal incentives for the conversion of wetlands to nonwetlands, it did not apply to federal regulatory programs affecting the activities of private parties on nonfederal property (42 CFR 26961).

Clean Water Act

The original 1948 Water Pollution Control Act (Ch. 758; P.L. 845) "authorized the Surgeon General of the Public Health Service, in cooperation with other federal, state and local entities, to prepare comprehensive programs for eliminating or reducing the pollution of interstate waters and tributaries and improving the sanitary condition of surface and underground waters" (USFWS 2003). This act underwent significant congressional amendment in 1961, 1966, and 1970. By the time Congress again amended the act in 1972, the Federal Water Pollution Control Act (FWPCA) had become the preeminent water pollution control legislation in the United States with the stated goal to "restore and maintain the chemical, physical, and biological integrity of the Nation's waters" (33 U.S.C § 1251[a]).

Even though the 1972 FWPCA was intended as comprehensive water pollution control legislation, Congress extended the jurisdiction of the new law only to "navigable waters of the United States," consistent with Section 10 of the RHA. There was no direct reference to "wetlands" or "tributaries" anywhere in the 1972 FWPCA, despite language defining the jurisdictional reach of Section 13 of the RHA (discussed earlier) as well as the direct reference to "wetlands" in the CZMA of 1972. In addition, the same language defining the limits of the FWPCA's jurisdiction was utilized throughout the act, including sections of the law addressing point source discharges of industrial and sewage pollution, discharges of dredged or fill material, water quality standards, and oil spill prevention and clean up.

In fact, Congress intentionally failed to explicitly define the term *navigable waters* in the FWPCA, in part to avoid any unnecessarily limited interpretation of such language (Downing et al. 2003). Instead, the FWPCA defined "navigable waters" as the "waters of the United States, including the territorial seas" (33 U.S.C § 1362[7]). No further clarification or definition for "waters of the United States" was provided. However, the intended jurisdiction of the FWPCA is alluded to in committee reports, such as the U.S. Congress House of Representatives Report, which noted that the "Committee fully intends the term 'navigable waters' to be given the broadest possible constitutional interpretation" (H.R. Rep. No. 92–911, at 131 [1972]; cited in Downing et al. 2003). This general language was also adopted by the U.S. Senate and included in the Senate report (S. Rep. No. 92–1236, at 144 [1972]).

Consequently, the USACE was left to issue regulations to specifically define the extent of its jurisdiction pursuant to the FWPCA Section 404, and the USACE did so consistent with the limited geographic scope under which it had traditionally regulated activities under Section 10 of the RHA (see *The Steamer Daniel Ball* [1871]). A national environmental advocacy group, the Natural Resources Defense Council (NRDC), challenged the USACE in federal court over the narrow interpretation of its congressional mandate to regulate the discharge of dredged or fill material into "navigable waters." In NRDC v. Callaway, 392 F. Supp. 685 (D.D.C. 1975), the U.S. District Court for the District of Columbia agreed with the NRDC and found that the provisions of the FWPCA, intended as they were by Congress to cover "the waters of the United States, including the territorial seas," were not limited to waters that passed the traditional tests of navigability.

Following the *NRDC v. Callaway* decision, and a previous court decision broadening the formally recognized jurisdiction of the FWPCA Section 404 program to include man-made conveyances (United States v. Holland, 373 F. Supp. 665, 673 [M.D.Fla. 1974]), the USACE redefined "navigable waters" in its implementing regulations in 1975 and included specific reference to "wetlands" and "tributaries" (40 FR 31320:31324). Concurrently, Congress was debating the desired scope of Section 404 of the FWPCA in light of the *NRDC v. Callaway* decision.

Ultimately, Congress reauthorized and amended the FWPCA in 1977 as the Clean Water Act (CWA), and the term "navigable waters" was replaced with "waters of the United States." The USACE implementing regulations were finalized in 1977, at which time the USACE also adopted the new terminology (42 FR 37122:37127) consistent with the recent CWA amendments (Downing et al. 2003), which is further defined at 33 CFR 328.3(a) (Box 9.1).

The new CWA Section 404 permitting program that regulated the discharge of dredged or fill material into waters of the United States quickly became the target of parties opposed to government infringement on private property rights. In 1985, United States v. Riverside Bayview Homes, 474 U.S. 121 (1985), became the first case specifically addressing the CWA Section 404 program to be heard by the U.S. Supreme Court. Citing its 1977 regulations defining "waters of the United States" to include all navigable waters and non-navigable tributaries to those waters as well as wetlands adjacent to both navigable and nonnavigable waters, the USACE had denied a CWA Section 404 permit to a developer wishing to fill marshes near Lake St. Clair in Michigan. The developer took the USACE to district court, charging that it did not have the authority to require authorization to regulate dredge and fill activities in wetlands. While the developer won in the lower court, the U.S. Supreme Court reviewed the legislative history of the 1972 FWPCA and concluded that adjacent wetlands are a fundamental component of the overall hydrologic cycle and therefore play an important role in the protection of water quality of other waters of the United States (Wood 2004). The Supreme Court unanimously overruled the lower court, concluding that the USACE had acted reasonably in interpreting the CWA to require permits for the discharge of dredged or fill material into wetlands adjacent to the "waters of the United States." The *Riverside Bayview Homes* decision firmly established the authority of the USACE to regulate the discharge of dredged or fill material into wetlands adjacent to other waters of the United States and still forms the pivotal basis for that authority 20 years later.

The 1977 CWA added additional provisions to the Section 404 program intended in part to address the massive influx of permit applications from parties seeking authorization from the USACE. The vastly expanded jurisdiction of the CWA Section 404 regulatory program relative to the RHA Section 10 program had created a severe

For the purpose of this regulation these terms are defined as follows:

(a) The term waters of the United States means

   (1) All waters which are currently used, or were used in the past, or may be susceptible to use in interstate or foreign commerce, including all waters which are subject to the ebb and flow of the tide;

   (2) All interstate waters including interstate wetlands;

   (3) All other waters such as intrastate lakes, rivers, streams (including intermittent streams), mudflats, sandflats, wetlands, sloughs, prairie potholes, wet meadows, playa lakes, or natural ponds, the use, degradation or destruction of which could affect interstate or foreign commerce including any such waters:

      (i) Which are or could be used by interstate or foreign travelers for recreational or other purposes; or

      (ii) From which fish or shellfish are or could be taken and sold in interstate or foreign commerce; or

      (iii) Which are used or could be used for industrial purpose by industries in interstate commerce;

   (4) All impoundments of waters otherwise defined as waters of the United States under the definition;

   (5) Tributaries of waters identified in paragraphs (a) (1) through (4) of this section;

   (6) The territorial seas;

   (7) Wetlands adjacent to waters (other than waters that are themselves wetlands) identified in paragraphs (a) (1) through (6) of this section.

   (8) Waters of the United States do not include prior converted cropland. Notwithstanding the determination of an area's status as prior converted cropland by any other Federal agency, for the purposes of the Clean Water Act, the final authority regarding Clean Water Act jurisdiction remains with EPA.

imbalance of resources and personnel in the USACE dedicated to reviewing and processing these permits in a timely, efficient, and effective manner. Under the new CWA Section 404(f), Congress granted statutory exemptions for normal farming, silviculture, and ranching activities, including plowing; seeding; cultivating; minor drainage; harvesting for the production of food, fiber, and forest products; construction of farm or stock ponds; irrigation ditches; farm roads; forest roads; or temporary roads (33 U.S.C § 1344[f]).

Congress also authorized the USACE to issue general permits on a state, regional, or nationwide basis for any category of similar activities having only minimal adverse environmental effects when performed separately or cumulatively (33 U.S.C § 1344[e][1]). The Nationwide Permit program soon became used to authorize approximately 90,000 small projects every year that would have otherwise required individual permits complete with public comment periods, a NEPA document, and an individual analysis under the CWA 404(b)(1) Guidelines (Wood 2004). Despite its honorable intent, the Nationwide Permit program would become a lightening rod for environmental groups protesting the manner in which the USACE administered the CWA Section 404 program, and the USACE itself would modify and reduce the scale of projects capable of being permitted by a nationwide general permit many times in the following decades.

CWA 404(b)(1) Guidelines

While the USACE was charged by Congress to implement the regulatory program created by Section 404 of the CWA, the USEPA was tasked with administering the entire CWA and also maintained an oversight role for Section 404. In fact, the guidelines for reviewing applications for the discharge of dredged or fill material were established in regulations instituted by USEPA in conjunction with the USACE. These guidelines, commonly referred to as the CWA Section 404(b)(1) Guidelines (40 CFR 230), were first promulgated in 1975 and revised in 1980.

The stated purpose of the guidelines borrowed language from the CWA itself: "'to restore and maintain the chemical, physical, and biological integrity' of the waters of the United States through the control of discharges of dredged or fill material" (40 CFR 230.1[a]). The guidelines further established that the degradation or destruction of special aquatic sites, which include sanctuaries and refuges, wetlands, mud flats, vegetated shallows, coral reefs, and stream riffle and pool complexes, "may represent an irreversible loss of valuable aquatic resources" (40 CFR 230.1[d]). The guidelines set out general procedures to be followed during the evaluation of proposals to discharge dredged or fill material (40 CFR 230.5), outlined specific restrictions on those discharges (40 CFR 230.10), and described the factual determinations that must be documented regarding the short-term and long-term effects of proposed discharges (40 CFR 230.11, 230.12; Subparts C, D, E, and F).

One of the fundamental precepts in the guidelines is that no discharge of dredged or fill material may be permitted if practicable alternatives exist that would have fewer adverse impacts on the aquatic environment, as long as the alternative does not cause other significant adverse environmental impacts (i.e., significant impacts to nonaquatic ecosystems) (40 CFR 230.10[a]). The guidelines also clarify that practicable alternatives include, but are not limited to, activities that avoid discharges of dredged or fill material into aquatic sites altogether (40 CFR 230.10[a][1][i]) or placement of discharges of dredged or fill material in other locations (i.e., other jurisdictional waters) (40 CFR 2301.10[a][1][ii]). Furthermore, Subpart H of the guidelines provides specific examples of activities to minimize the adverse effects of discharges of dredged or fill material into waters of the United States, including actions considering the location of the discharge (40 CFR 230.70), the material to be discharged (40 CFR 230.71), control of the material after it has been discharged (40 CFR 230.72), the manner in which the material is discharged (40 CFR 230.73), and other similar considerations.

Although not included in the 1975 version of the guidelines, the discussion on impact minimization in the 1980 version of the guidelines included reference to "habitat development and restoration techniques," which could be used "to minimize adverse impacts and to compensate for destroyed habitat" (40 CFR 230.75[d]). Collectively, efforts to avoid, minimize, and then mitigate for impacts to jurisdictional waters of the United States as a result of authorized discharges of dredged or fill material would become the cornerstone of the CWA Section 404 program, and the third part of this triad, referred to commonly as compensatory mitigation, would capture the interest of researchers, policy makers, and environmental groups for decades.

REGULATION AND POLICY SINCE THE CLEAN WATER ACT

Food Security Act of 1985 (Swampbuster)

Since passage of the Clean Water Act in 1977, there have been no federal statutes passed by Congress that had greater implications for wetlands regulation and conservation on a national scale than the Food Security Act (FSA) of 1985. The Wetland Conservation provision included in the FSA, commonly referred to as Swampbuster, formally established wetland conservation rules for agricultural lands included in USDA farm programs.

Swampbuster denied farmers federal commodity price supports, crop insurance, and federal loans if they drained, filled, or otherwise converted a wetland for agricultural use after December 23, 1985. Wetlands converted prior to this date became known as "prior converted" croplands and were not subject to the Swampbuster provisions so long as the cropland did not meet the USDA definition of wetland hydrology (i.e., ponded water on the surface for greater than fourteen consecutive days) and the land had produced at least one agricultural commodity during the five years preceding 1985.

Once a site has been designated as prior converted, it is also not subject to regulatory requirements of the CWA Section 404 program. However, if no agricultural commodity is planted for more than five consecutive years and wetland characteristics return (i.e., wetland hydrology, hydric soils, and hydrophytic vegetation), the cropland is considered abandoned and becomes a wetland subject to the Swampbuster provisions and the CWA Section 404 regulatory requirements. The FSA also defined *farmed wetlands* as areas that had been drained, dredged, filled, leveled, or otherwise manipulated for agricultural use before December 23, 1985, but which maintained wetland hydrology characteristics despite that they were nonetheless dry enough in some years to permit crops or hay to be produced. Maintenance of existing drainage structures in farmed wetlands (e.g., ditches) was permitted, but they could not be expanded or enhanced beyond their original configuration or efficacy. Land-clearing activities were prohibited from farmed wetlands, and they were subject to the same abandonment provisions as prior converted cropland.

"No Net Loss" (1988)

In response to a perceived inconsistency in the manner that various federal agencies were addressing wetlands conservation and regulatory programs and a lack of cooperation among those agencies themselves, the USEPA convened a National Wetlands Policy Forum in 1987. The forum provided an opportunity for a cross section of representatives from federal and state agencies; nongovernment organizations; academia; and business, farming, and industry interests to discuss a broad range of issues related to wetlands.

Despite the diverse interests represented on the forum, its final report included opinions reached by consensus to establish goals and policies for the nation's remaining wetland resources. Accordingly, the forum's report stated a fundamental objective (Conservation Foundation 1988):

> . . . to achieve no overall net loss of the nation's remaining wetlands base and to create and restore wetlands, where feasible, to increase the quantity and quality of the nation's wetland resource. . . .

Presidential candidate George H. W. Bush adopted the forum's recommendation in February 1989 at a symposium sponsored by the waterfowl conservation group Ducks Unlimited, and he formally endorsed the "no net loss" concept during his first budget address to Congress as the newly elected president of the United States in 1990. Consequently, there was a renewed incentive for federal agencies to work together in order to achieve a unified federal policy to promote wetland conservation and restoration. The existing regulatory policy of promoting compensatory mitigation as a means to compensate for the impacts to wetlands authorized by the CWA Section 404 program again became a national focus. The "no net loss" ambition was also supported by President G. H. W. Bush's successor, President W. J. Clinton.

Compensatory Mitigation

In its 1986 Consolidated Rule (33 CFR 320.4[r]), the USACE adopted the 1978 definition of mitigation provided by the Council on Environmental Quality (CEQ), which included avoiding impacts, minimizing impacts, rectifying impacts, reducing impacts over time, and compensating for impacts (40 CFR 1508.20). Formed by Congress as part of NEPA in 1969, CEQ coordinates federal environmental policies and initiatives and serves as a mediator in agency disputes over the adequacy of environmental impact assessments. Thus, the 1986 USACE mitigation policy applicable to all CWA Section 404 permit actions essentially reiterated both CEQ and the 1980 version of the CWA Section 404(b)(1) Guidelines: avoidance, minimization, and compensation.

In 1990, the USACE and USEPA signed a Memorandum of Agreement (MOA) concerning the determination of mitigation under the CWA Section 404(b)(1) Guidelines. The "Mitigation MOA" articulated the policy and procedures to be used during the permit review process to determine the type and level of compensatory mitigation necessary to compensate for unavoidable adverse impacts of authorized discharges of dredged or fill material into jurisdictional waters of the United States. The MOA reiterated that compensatory mitigation was a requirement of the CWA Section 404 program for unavoidable adverse impacts to all waters of the United States, including streams, rivers, and lakes, but also that efforts to first avoid and minimize those impacts consistent with the CWA Section 404(b)(1) Guidelines were paramount. Furthermore, the MOA stressed that the determination of what level of mitigation constitutes appropriate and practicable was based solely on the functions and values of the aquatic resource to be impacted.

In response to a number of reports critical of various facets and emerging trends concerning compensatory mitigation in the CWA Section 404 program (e.g., Kusler and Kentula 1990; Jackson 1990; GAO 2001; NRC 2001), the George W. Bush administration released the National Wetlands Mitigation Action Plan (Action Plan) on December 26, 2002. The Action Plan affirmed the administration's commitment to the "no net loss" policy first adopted in 1990 and set forth "a series of actions to improve the ecological performance and results of wetlands compensatory mitigation under the CWA and related programs." These actions included clarification of mitigation guidance and performance standards; improving mitigation accountability, data collection, and availability; and development of new or revised policy and technical standards to encourage mitigation planning in broader, watershed contexts.

Subsequently, the USACE and USEPA issued a joint memorandum to the field providing guidance on compensatory mitigation as part of the implementation of the Action Plan. The guidance provided a checklist to assist permit applicants compiling compensatory mitigation plans by ensuring that they include the information necessary for agency personnel to rapidly and effectively assess the likelihood of the proposal's success and, concomitantly, the proposal's consistency with the 1990 Mitigation MOA and the CWA Section 404(b)(1) Guidelines. In addition, the USACE issued a unilateral memorandum to the field on October 29, 2003, that outlined "model operational guidelines for creating or restoring wetlands that are ecologically self sustaining." The USACE memorandum was intended to provide additional technical support to help permit applicants select appropriate mitigation sites and compile compensatory mitigation plans containing the basic requirements for success. The guidance also specifically addressed ten recommendations for operational guidelines for wetland restoration included in the NRC's critique of CWA Section 404 mitigation, which itself included both technical and programmatic guidelines (NRC 2001) (Box 9.2).

REVISIONS TO THE JURISDICTIONAL LIMITS OF "WATERS OF THE UNITED STATES"

Judicial decisions of wetlands case law had profound implications on wetland regulation in the United States in the 1990s by affecting the very definitions of "fill material," "discharge of fill material," and even "waters of the United States."

Case law and agency regulations extending as far back as 1983, some of which originated from activities that actually took place on the ground in the late 1970s, had effectively expanded the scope of CWA Section 404 to include mechanized land clearing. In Avoyelles Sportsmen's League v. Marsh, 715 F.2d 897, 924 n.43 (5th Cir. 1983), a case that involved mechanized land clearing and disking (i.e., shallow plowing) in forested jurisdictional wetlands, the U.S. Court of Appeals for the Fifth Circuit upheld a lower court's ruling that the movement and redeposit of dredged or fill material in waters of the United States may reasonably be considered an "addition" of a pollutant and therefore subject to the regulatory requirements of CWA Section 404 despite that no actual addition of material had occurred.

In 1986, the USACE issued a regulation formally defining the "discharge of dredged material" as any addition of dredged material into the waters of the United States, except for *de minimis* or incidental soil movement occurring during normal dredging operations

(51 FR 41:206, 232). However, in response to a lawsuit filed in North Carolina, North Carolina Wildlife Federation v. Tulloch (C90-713-CIV-5-BO [E.D.N.C.]), the USACE, in conjunction with the USEPA, revised the definition in 1993 to remove the *de minimis* exception. The so-called Tulloch rule instead defined the "discharge of dredged material" to include:

> ... without limitation, any addition or redeposit of dredged materials, including excavated materials, into waters of the United States which is incidental to any activity ... including mechanized land clearing, ditching, channelization, or other excavation, which has or would have the effect of destroying or degrading any area of waters of the United States. (33 CFR 323.2[d][1])

However, the American Mining Congress filed a lawsuit challenging the new agency definition of "discharge of dredged material," and in 1997, the U.S. District Court of the District of Columbia declared that the rule was invalid and outside of the USACE and USEPA statutory authority (American Mining Congress v. U.S. Army Corps of Engineers, 93–1754 SSH). The lower court's decision was upheld in 1998 by the U.S. Court of Appeals for the District of Columbia (National Mining Association v. U.S. Army Corps of Engineers, 145 F.3d 1399 [D.C. Cir. 1998]). Thus, the agencies' brief expansion of CWA Section 404 regulatory jurisdiction to include "incidental fallback" of dredged material during activities for which the primary purpose was to excavate material from jurisdictional waters of the United States and not to otherwise raise the bottom elevation of those waters for the purpose of making them nonjurisdictional had been curtailed. However, as outlined in the agencies' final revisions to the regulatory definition of "discharge of dredged material" (64 FR 89:25120), other activities involving the redeposit of dredged material in locations away from the point at which it was excavated remained under the purview of the CWA Section 404 if those redeposits involved discharges greater than only incidental fallback (e.g., side-casting material excavated from a ditch into adjacent jurisdictional wetlands or other waters of the United States).

Isolated Waters

As described previously in this chapter, the rather ill-defined scope of jurisdiction written into the CWA by Congress has led to an evolution of regulatory oversight concerning wetlands and other waters. This evolution has in large part been fueled by over three decades of wetlands case law that has consistently challenged the federal agencies' interpretation and administration of the CWA–sometimes arguing that it was too broad, and other times petitioning that it was too narrow. In the late 1990s and early 2000s, a number of judicial decisions significantly altered the jurisdiction of the federal government to regulate activities affecting the nation's aquatic resources by altering the effective definition of "waters of the United States" subject to regulation under the CWA.

The USACE implementing regulations of 1977 included not only a definition for *wetlands*, as noted previously in this chapter, but also a broader definition for "waters of the United States," of which wetlands were a part (Table 9.1). In the preamble of a 1986 reissuance of the definition of waters falling under the jurisdiction of the CWA, the USACE and USEPA included specific examples of the types of links to interstate commerce that could serve to establish jurisdiction over intrastate waters not part of the tributary system or adjacent wetlands. These examples included use of waters (or wetlands) by migratory birds protected by international treaties or that cross state lines, use of waters by endangered species, or use of waters to irrigate crops sold in commerce (51 FR 41217 [1986]; 53 FR 20765 [1988]). The USACE stated elsewhere in the preamble that these examples and the reissuance of the definition were not intended to alter the scope of jurisdictional waters in any way, but rather clarified the scope of existing jurisdictional regulations (cited in Stevens, J. Dissenting Opinion SWANCC v. USACE, 531 U.S. 159 [2001]). Nonetheless, these examples collectively became known as "The Migratory Bird Rule."

In 1980, the USACE asserted jurisdiction over man-made, seasonally wet depressions (i.e., pits) on a California salt mine by claiming that the pits provided habitat for migratory birds, which provided a connection to interstate commerce, and by default, USACE jurisdiction. The respondent, Leslie Salt Company, protested that the depressions were not under the regulatory jurisdiction of CWA Section 404 and took the USACE to court. While a lower court found in favor of Leslie Salt Company, the Court of Appeals for the Ninth District reversed the district court's decision, finding that (1) there was no distinction in the USACE regulations between natural and man-made waters; (2) there was no impediment to regulatory jurisdiction created as a result of seasonal versus year-round ponding of water; and (3) that the Commerce Clause of the U.S. Constitution was "broad enough to extend the Corps' jurisdiction to local waters which may provide habitat to migratory birds and endangered species" (Leslie Salt Co. v. U.S., 896 F.2d 354 [9th Cir. 1990]) (cited in Downing et al. 2003). The Court of Appeals had effectively reinforced a perceived connection between isolated waters and interstate commerce based on migratory birds— a connection suggested by the USACE and USEPA in 1986.

While the isolated, nonnavigable, intrastate waters at issue in *Leslie Salt Co. v. U.S.* had a documented history of use by migratory birds (55 different species), a subsequent case challenging the agencies' authority to regulate isolated waters based on migratory birds had no such record. In Hoffman Homes v. Administrator, 961 F.2d 1310 (7th Cir. 1992), the Seventh District Court of Appeals overturned a USEPA chief judicial officer who had levied a monetary penalty against Hoffman Homes for filling an isolated, intrastate wetland that was suitable habitat for migratory birds but for which there was no documented history of such use. The Seventh District decision was based in part on the fact that the *potential* use of a wetland by migratory birds was insufficient to invoke Congress' power under the Commerce Clause (Downing et al. 2003). However, the government requested a rehearing, and the same court of appeals reached essentially the opposite conclusion. In Hoffman Homes v. Administrator, 999 F.2d 256 (7th Cir. 1993), the court noted that the definition of "waters of the United States" included reference to "all other waters" for which the "degradation or destruction . . . could affect interstate or foreign commerce" (33 CFR 328.3). The court also noted that millions of dollars were spent annually in the United States by persons traveling to other states to hunt, trap, or observe migratory waterfowl, and therefore the cumulative loss of habitat used by such wildlife presented a potential detriment to interstate commerce.

In an appeal of yet another case involving isolated wetlands, this one a criminal conviction in Maryland, the Court of Appeals for the Fourth Circuit threw out the portion of the agencies' definition of "waters of the United States" that included "other waters" for which jurisdiction was based solely on the fact that their degradation *could* affect interstate commerce (U.S. v. Wilson, 133 F.3d 251 [4th Cir. 1997]). The decision effectively invalidated the agencies' regulation of activities affecting isolated, intrastate wetlands or waters in the states of Maryland, Virginia, North Carolina, South Carolina, and West Virginia for which no documented connection with interstate commerce existed. The USEPA and USACE released guidance in May 1998 that clarified that the agencies would "continue to assert CWA jurisdiction over any and all isolated water bodies, including isolated wetlands, based on the CWA statute itself, where (1) either agency can establish an actual link between that water body and interstate or foreign commerce and (2) individually and/or in the aggregate, the use, degradation or destruction of isolated waters with such a link would have a substantial effect on interstate or foreign commerce" (USEPA and USDOA 1998).

Perhaps no other single wetland regulatory or judicial decision has elicited greater attention in recent years than Solid Waste Agency of Northern Cook County (SWANCC) v. USACE, 531 U.S. 159 (2001). In a narrowly split decision (5–4), the U.S. Supreme Court called into question the authority of the USACE to require CWA Section 404 permits for the discharge of dredged or fill material into isolated, nonnavigable, and intrastate waters. However, the Court's decision questioned not only the USACE's regulatory authority under CWA Section 404, but also the incorporation of such water bodies into the CWA regulatory definition of "waters of the United States." As a result, the implications of the Court's decision in *SWANCC v. USACE* was not limited to the CWA Section 404 program, but also included ramifications for all provisions of the CWA, including the National Pollution Discharge Elimination System (Section 402), the oil spill and prevention program (Section 311), water-quality standards (Section 303), and water-quality certification (Section 401), and continues to be debated in courts around the country.

A consortium of suburban Chicago municipalities had selected an abandoned sand and gravel pit as the site for a solid waste disposal site. The USACE originally declined to take jurisdiction over the isolated, nonnavigable, and entirely intrastate waters on the site, in part because they lacked hydrophytic vegetation. However, the USACE later reversed its decision and opted to exert jurisdiction over the site citing that over 121 species of migratory birds, at least some of which cross state lines, had been observed there. Despite that SWANCC had been issued all other requisite state and local permits, the

USACE refused to authorize the project under CWA Section 404. SWANCC challenged the USACE jurisdiction over the site and the merits of its refusal to issue the Section 404 permit. The district court ruled in favor of the USACE, and SWANCC appealed to the Seventh District Court of Appeals (SWANCC v. USACE, 191 F.3d 845 [7th Cir. 1999]). The court of appeals also ruled in favor of the USACE, citing its own earlier decision in *Hoffman Homes v. Administrator* (1993).

On January 9, 2001, the U.S. Supreme Court ruled by a narrow majority that the Migratory Bird Rule exceeded the authority granted to the USACE under CWA Section 404 (531 U.S. 159 [2001]). Further, the Court opined that Congress had intended for CWA jurisdiction to be somehow related to its power to regulate commerce related to navigation, as evidenced by Congress' reference to navigable waters. Writing for the majority, Justice W. H. Rehnquist stated, "We cannot agree that Congress' separate definitional use of the phrase 'waters of the United States' constitutes a basis for reading term 'navigable waters' out of the statute" (*Id.* at 683).

In a strongly worded dissenting opinion, joined by Justices Souter, Ginsburg, and Breyer, Supreme Court Justice John Paul Stevens criticized the Court's majority opinion by stating that it:

> . . . rests on two equally untenable premises: (1) that when Congress passed the 1972 CWA, it did not intend to "exert anything more than its commerce power over navigation"; and (2) that in 1972 Congress drew the boundary defining the Corps' jurisdiction at the odd line on which the Court today settles.

Criticizing the majority's deference to the traditional rights of states to determine land and water use, the dissenting opinion further noted that:

> The destruction of migratory bird habitat, like so many other environmental problems, is an action in which the benefits (e.g., a new landfill) are disproportionately local, while many of the costs (e.g., fewer migratory birds) are widely dispersed and often borne by citizens living in other States. In such situations, . . . federal regulation is both appropriate and necessary (Stevens, J., Dissenting Opinion SWANCC v. USACE, 531 U.S. 159 [2001]).

The USEPA and USACE issued joint guidance on January 19, 2001, clarifying the scope of regulatory jurisdiction following the Supreme Court's decision (Guzy and Andersen 2001). The agencies noted that while the Supreme Court invalidated the assertion of jurisdiction over the abandoned sand and gravel pits at issue in *SWANCC v. USACE* based solely on the Migratory Bird Rule, it did not entirely strike down even the provision of the agencies' definition of "waters of the United States" that the Migratory Bird Rule was intended to clarify, nor did it address the scope of the nation's waters that it believed Congress did in fact intend to regulate under the CWA. Nevertheless, the agencies' guidance stated that isolated, nonnavigable, intrastate waters whose only connection to interstate commerce was their use of habitat by migratory birds were no longer to be considered waters of the United States.

Many environmental and natural resources advocacy groups voiced opposition to the Supreme Court's decision and warned of potentially dire consequences. Ducks Unlimited warned that the *SWANCC* decision could have significant consequences for breeding waterfowl in North America (Petrie et al. 2001), and the Association of State Wetland Managers reported that the SWANCC decision could potentially remove federal regulatory oversight from as much as 30% to 60% of the nation's wetlands (Kusler, n.d.).

The practical implications of the *SWANCC* decision are still being determined. Numerous cases concerning the precise scope of federal jurisdiction have come before federal district and appellate courts since the *SWANCC* decision. These cases have not been limited to ponds, depressions, and other waters lacking a definitive surface water connection to other waters. Rather, numerous cases have challenged the federal regulatory jurisdiction over activities in or ostensibly affecting the tributary (i.e., stream) system itself. Judicial decisions in these cases have been as incongruous as the sentiment of the Supreme Court Justices themselves in *SWANCC v. USACE*. Numerous cases have found that the *SWANCC* decision did not alter the regulatory jurisdiction of tributaries to navigable waters (Table 9.2, "affirming" section), while other courts have reached very different conclusions (Table 9.2, "challenging" section). Similarly, some courts have held that man-made conveyances (e.g., ditches) remain jurisdictional if they are connected to natural tributaries (e.g., Headwaters v. Talent Irrigation District, 243 F.3d 526 [9th Cir. 2001]), while other courts have taken opposing positions on the matter (e.g., U.S. v. Newdunn, 195 F. Supp. 2d 751 [E.D. Va. 2002]).

At least sixteen states currently have programs in place for regulating activities in isolated wetlands, including Florida, Maine, Maryland, Massachusetts, Michigan, Minnesota, New Hampshire, New Jersey, New York, Ohio, Oregon, Pennsylvania, Rhode Island, Vermont, Virginia, and Wisconsin. In addition, there have been efforts in these and other states to expand or initiate wetlands protection legislation (e.g., the proposed South Carolina Isolated Wetlands Act of 2004). At least six states imposed new restrictions on altering isolated wetlands following the *SWANCC* decision, but most have failed in the attempt or are facing court challenges (Watson 2001). The U.S. government continues to argue in court briefs that the *SWANCC* decision affected only isolated, nonnavigable, and intrastate waters. Nonetheless, the debate continues as scientists, regulatory agencies, the courts, and the regulated public continue to debate the implications of the *SWANCC* decision on the scope of federal jurisdiction and the definition of "waters of the United States."

WETLAND DELINEATION

Given the convoluted and often contentious history of defining the scope of federal jurisdiction over wetlands and other waters of the United States, it should come as no surprise that the act of actually delineating the boundaries of wetlands in the field has also had an

TABLE 9.2   Post-SWANCC Case Law Affirming and Challenging the Regulatory
Jurisdiction of Nonnavigable Tributaries to Navigable Waters

Affirming	Summary of Decision
Headwaters v. Talent Irrigation District, 243 F.3d 526 (9th Cir. 2001)	"Even tributaries that flow intermittently are 'waters of the United States'"
U.S. v. Interstate General Company, 152 F. Supp. 2d 843 (D. Md. 2001)	Rejected arguments that SWANCC removed jurisdiction over nonnavigable tributaries.
U.S. v. Krilich, 393 F3d. 784 (4th Cir. 2002)	SWANCC did not alter regulations interpreting "waters of the United States," except for 33 CFR 328.3(a)(3) ~ migratory birds.
Community Assoc. for Restoration of the Environment v. Henry Bosma Dairy, 305 F.3d 953 (9th Cir. 2002)	A drain that flowed into a canal that flows to a river is jurisdictional.
Idaho Rural Council v. Bosma, 143 F. Supp. 2d 1169 (D. Idaho 2001)	"[W]aters of the United States include waters that are tributary to navigable waters."
Aiello v. Town of Brookhaven, 136 F. Supp. 2d 81 (E.D. NY 2001)	A nonnavigable pond and creek that were determined to be tributaries of navigable waters are therefore "waters of the United States" themselves.
U.S. v. Lamplight Equestrian Center, No. 00 C 6486, 2002 WL 360652 at 8 (ND Ill. 2002)	"Even where the distance from the tributary to the navigable water is significant, the quality of the tributary is still vital to the quality of the navigable waters."
U.S. v. Budday, 138 F. Supp. 2d 1282 (D. Mont. 2001)	Water quality of tributaries, despite that they may be distant from navigable water streams, is still vital to the quality of those navigable waters.
U.S. v. Rueth Development Company, 189 F. Supp. 2d 874 (N.D. Ind. 2001)	Jurisdiction remains over wetlands adjacent to a nonnavigable (man-made) waterway that flows into a navigable water.

Challenging	Summary of Decision
Rice v. Harken Exploration Company, 250 F.3d 264 (5th Cir. 2001)	A body of water is subject to CWA jurisdiction only if the body of water is itself navigable or adjacent to an open body of navigable water.
U.S. v. Rapanos, 190 F. Supp. 2d 1011 (E.D. Mich. 2002)	Wetlands not directly adjacent to navigable waters are not federally jurisdictional under the Oil Pollution Act of 1990 (33 U.S.C. 2701 et seq.; 104 Stat. 484).

TABLE 9.2   (continued)

Challenging	Summary of Decision
U.S. v. Needham, No. 6:01-CV-01897, 2002 WL 1162790 (W.D. La. 2002)	A nonnavigable drainage ditch that was also not adjacent to an open body of navigable water is not federally jurisdictional under the Oil Pollution Act of 1990 (33 U.S.C. 2701 et seq.; 104 Stat. 484).
U.S. v. Newdunn, 195 F. Supp. 2d 751 (E.D. Va. 2002)	Wetlands and tributaries not contiguous or adjacent to navigable waters are outside CWA jurisdiction.
U.S. v. RGM Corporation, 222 F. Supp. 2d 780 (E.D. Va. 2002)	Wetlands on property that is not contiguous with a navigable river can not be considered adjacent to that navigable river and are therefore nonjurisdictional.

NOTE: From 68 FR 10:1997 (Advanced Notice of Proposed Rulemaking on the Clean Water Act Regulatory Definition of "Waters of the United States").

argumentative history since passage of the 1977 CWA. Despite that the USACE included wetlands in its definition of "waters of the United States" in the USACE 1977 implementing regulations (33 CFR 328.3[a]), no federal agency had a standardized, documented protocol for delineating wetlands in the field until nearly a decade later (Table 9.3).

In 1980, the USEPA issued interim guidance on identifying wetlands in the field, which it updated and expanded in 1983 (NRC 1995). A revised draft was prepared in 1985 and subjected to both internal and external review. The USEPA wetland delineation manual was then modified based on these reviews and published in 1988 (NRC 1995). Meanwhile, the USACE Waterways Experiment Station had been working on a wetland delineation manual since 1978. Preliminary versions of the USACE manual were tested in the field, and the final manual was published in 1987 (Environmental Laboratory 1987).

Shortly thereafter, the USACE joined with the USEPA, USDA, and the USFWS to integrate the various methods proposed to delineate wetlands and develop a joint manual. The result of this effort was the 1989 *Federal Manual for Identifying and Delineating Jurisdictional Wetlands* (Federal Interagency Committee for Wetland Delineation 1989). However, the 1989 manual was immediately targeted by farming interests (i.e., Farm Bureau), the oil and gas industry, and other politically influential groups who complained that the new manual grossly expanded the acreage of wetlands that would now fall under the federal government's regulatory jurisdiction (Vileisis 1997). Soon, private property advocates also voiced opposition to the 1989 manual, and letters protesting the manual as a violation of private property rights flooded the USACE, USEPA, and the White House (Vileisis 1997).

The George H. W. Bush administration published a proposed modification of the 1989 manual in 1991 (56 FR 40466) that was reportedly influenced in large part by the White

TABLE 9.3   Timeline of Significant Wetland Classification, Delineation,
and Functional Assessment Initiatives in the United States

2002	National Academy of Sciences, "Compensating for wetland losses under the Clean Water Act" (NRC 2001)
1995	National Academy of Sciences, "Wetlands: characteristics and boundaries" (NRC 1995)
	Smith et al., "An approach for assessing wetland functions using hydrogeomorphic classification, reference wetlands, and functional indices"
1993	Brinson (1993), "A hydrogeomorphic classification for wetlands"
1991	Revisions to the 1989 Federal Interagency Manual (never adopted)
1989	Federal Manual for Identifying and Delineating Jurisdictional Wetlands (FICWD 1989)
1988	National list of plant species that occur in wetlands (USFWS) (Reed 1988)
1987	Corps of Engineers Wetland Delineation Manual (USACE) (Environmental Laboratory 1987)
	Adamus et al. (1991), "Wetland Evaluation Technique (WET)"
1985	Wetland Manual (USEPA)
1979	Classification of wetlands and deep water habitats of the United States (USFWS) (Cowardin et al. 1979)
1977	Clean Water Act amendments
	"Wetlands" included as component of "waters of the U.S." in USACE regulations

House, the Office of Management and Budget, and Vice President Dan Quayle's Council on Competitiveness (Vileisis 1997). The proposed 1991 revisions were immediately vilified by the scientific community and environmental advocacy groups nationwide, and the 1991 manual was never proposed for final adoption.

In 1993, President William J. Clinton placed the USDA Natural Resources Conservation Service in charge of making wetland delineations on agricultural lands in the United States for both the CWA and the Swampbuster provisions of the 1985 FSA. President Clinton also formally adopted the 1987 USACE wetland delineation manual for all nonagricultural lands nationwide, consistent with recent recommendations of the National Academy of Sciences (Vileisis 1997). As of 2005, the 1987 manual remains the official wetland delineation method of the four federal agencies with administrative, oversight, or advisory roles in the CWA Section 404 program: USACE, USEPA, USFWS, and USDA.

Subsequently, in 1994, the Department of Agriculture, Department of Interior, USACE, and USEPA entered into a Memorandum of Agreement (MOA) concerning the delineation of wetlands for purposes of Section 404 of the CWA and the FSA. The MOA was developed to streamline the wetland delineation process on agricultural lands, to promote consistency between the CWA and the FSA, and to provide predictability and simplification for USDA program participants. The 1996 and 2002 FSA amendments changed the wetland conservation provisions, producing inconsistency between them and the CWA, and making the 1994 MOA obsolete and illegal for NRCS to follow. Consequently, the USDA withdrew from the MOA on January 18, 2005, and the USACE also withdrew on January 24, 2005. On February 25, 2005, the USDA and USACE issued new Joint Guidance on conducting wetland determinations for the FSA and CWA that included the following provisions (USDA NRCS 2005):

1. The NRCS will conduct wetland determinations for the purpose of implementing the Swampbuster provisions of the FSA, and in providing other financial and technical assistance authorized by law;

2. The USACE will conduct wetland determinations for CWA purposes;

3. Both agencies will inform landowners that their wetland determinations may not apply to the other agency's wetland programs;

4. The NRCS may not disclose confidential information regarding personal information of an agricultural commodity producer, such as objectives or decisions, conservation compliance determinations, natural resources inventories, or environmental assessments to agencies outside of the USDA. This includes wetland delineations and labels. If a wetland determination made by the NRCS is needed for CWA purposes, the NRCS may encourage the producer to provide a copy directly to the USACE, or the USACE will request a copy from the landowner, but the NRCS will not provide it to the USACE;

5. The USACE and NRCS will coordinate as much as possible on wetland determinations and violations that involve both agencies' jurisdiction, to maximize consistency and minimize delay and inconvenience for the landowner; and

6. The guidance encourages interagency coordination on training, wetland delineation procedures, and developing local operating agreements to improve service to the public.

Thus, while both the USACE and the NRCS play important roles in the delineation of wetlands in the field, the respective outcomes of each agency's investigation may not fully apply to the other agency's programs, regulations, or mandates. Generally, however, this potentially confusing situation is restricted to agricultural lands, and wetlands on all nonagricultural lands in the United States are delineated in the field according to the procedures included in the USACE's 1987 manual.

WETLAND FUNCTIONS AND VALUES

The principle tenet of compensatory mitigation, as implied in the CWA Section 404(b)(1) Guidelines and stated quite clearly in the subsequent 1990 Mitigation Memorandum of

Agreement between the USACE and the USEPA, is that mitigation projects will replace the functions lost or impaired at the impacted sites. The National Wetlands Policy Forum that introduced the "no net loss" policy supported by every U.S. presidential administration since 1988 also recognized the need to develop technical guidance for functional replacement of wetlands (Conservation Foundation 1988). However, depending on the specific resource being impacted, this is not always a readily attainable goal (NRC 2001). Furthermore, there has historically been little consensus among wetland scientists and the regulatory community regarding the best mechanisms to measure wetland function or even how to define "wetland functions."

The need for functional assessment in the regulatory program is firmly rooted in the USACE implementing regulations (33 CFR 320) and the CWA Section 404(b)(1) Guidelines (40 CFR 230). The USACE regulations observe that "most wetlands constitute a productive and valuable public resource" (33 CFR 320[b][1]) and further state that no permit to discharge dredged or fill material into wetlands will be granted unless the USACE public interest review concludes that the benefits of the proposed wetland alteration outweigh the damage to the wetlands resource (33 CFR 320[b][4]). However, the evaluation of permit applications to discharge dredged or fill material into wetlands or other jurisdictional waters of the United States must adhere to the CWA Section 404(b)(1) Guidelines, which requires that the permitting authority (typically the USACE, but the CWA includes a provision under Section 404[g] allowing states to petition the USEPA to administer its own individual and permit program) document the potential short-term and long-term effects of a proposed discharge of dredged or fill material on the physical, chemical, and biological components of the aquatic environment (40 CFR 230.11). The CWA Section 404(b)(1) Guidelines further require that the permitting authority "determine the nature and degree of effect that the proposed discharge will have, both individually and cumulatively, on the structure and function of the aquatic ecosystem and organisms" (40 CFR 230.11[e]).

Wetlands have been referred to as providing both functions and values. In fact, many wetland practitioners have used the phrase "functional values," which may actually be considered a misnomer despite that it appears in both federal and state policy documents. Adamus and associates (1991) defined *wetland functions* as " physical, chemical, and biological processes or attributes of wetlands that are vital to the integrity of the wetland system." In fact, many functions result from an interaction of more than one process. Examples of wetland functions include the temporary storage of surface water, maintenance of characteristic subsurface hydrology, nutrient cycling, removal and sequestration of elements and compounds, retention of particulates, exportation of organic carbon, maintenance of characteristic plant communities, and maintenance of habitat for wildlife (Ainslie et al. 1999).

In contrast, "wetland values" are the goods and services perceived as beneficial or valuable to society that emanate directly or indirectly from wetland functions. Examples of wetland values include shoreline and stream bank erosion control; creation of natural products for human use (e.g., bottomland hardwood timber); water-quality improvement;

recreation; flood protection; commercial and sport hunting, fishing, and trapping; and maintaining biodiversity and open space (USEPA 1992b).

The functions and values performed or provided by wetlands should be treated separately. However, the boundary between a wetland function and a wetland value is not always discrete, and some of the processes occurring in wetlands or as a result of wetlands could be perceived as both a function and a value. In the strictest sense, wetland functions occur regardless of society's perceived benefits, goods, or services derived from them. However, there is a direct relationship between the "functional health" of a wetland and the benefits or goods it is capable of providing. For example, riverine wetlands that have not been hydrologically decoupled from overbank flood events from the adjacent stream due to channelization may export organic carbon—a function. In turn, labile organic carbon exported to the stream supports aquatic macroinvertebrates, which provide food for fish and thereby supports sport fishing—a potential value. Furthermore, "while wetland functions are natural processes . . . that continue regardless of their perceived value to humans, the value people place on those functions in many cases is the primary factor determining whether a wetland remains intact or is converted for some other use" (National Audubon Society 1993).

FUNCTIONAL ASSESSMENT METHODS

Several functional assessment methods have been introduced over the past two decades (see reviews by Lonard et al. 1981; Lonard and Clairain 1985; Bartoldus 1999). The applicability of the methods ranges from specific types of wetlands (Larson 1976; Adamus et al. 1990; Lipsky 1997) to general usage across different wetland types and physiographic provinces (Hollands and Magee 1985; Adamus et al. 1987; Brinson et al. 1995). Of these, the Wetland Evaluation Technique (WET) (Adamus et al. 1987, 1991) and the hydrogeomorphic approach to wetland functional assessment (HGM) (Brinson et al. 1994; Smith 1994) have probably been used and tested more extensively in the United States than most other methods.

WETLAND EVALUATION TECHNIQUE

In response to an effort initiated in 1981 by the USACE to identify or develop a technique to assess wetland functions and values for regulatory and planning needs, a wetland functional assessment procedure developed by the Federal Highways Administration (Adamus 1983; Adamus and Stockwell 1983) was selected as the basis from which to develop a wetland functional assessment method to meet the time and resources constraints of the CWA Section 404 regulatory program (USACE Waterways Experiment Station 1988). The objective of WET was to assess most recognized wetland functions and values while also being rapid, reproducible, and applicable in a variety of wetland types (USACE Waterways Experiment Station 1988).

WET assesses eleven functions and values (Adamus et al. 1987): groundwater recharge, groundwater discharge, floodflow alteration, sediment stabilization, sediment/toxicant retention, nutrient removal/transformation, production export, wildlife diversity/abundance, aquatic diversity/abundance, recreation, and uniqueness/heritage. Each of the above referenced functions and values is evaluated in terms of effectiveness/opportunity, social significance, and habitat suitability. A series of interpretive keys are utilized to assign probability ratings of high, moderate, or low to each function and value within each category.

Despite that WET has probably been used to assess every type of wetland throughout the United States, its critics have cited an inability to account for regional variability in wetland ecosystems (Novitzki et al. 1995), its lack of basis on defined local reference conditions, and its lack of resolution. A wetland assessment area not rated as high or low is assigned a moderate rating by default, and consequently, many wetland assessment areas are assigned a moderate rating. While the principal author of WET hoped that regional versions of the assessment technique would be developed to help account for regional differences in wetland structure and function, and also that five different assessment levels would be created to aid resolution (Adamus 1988, cited in Novitzki et al. 1995), none of these efforts materialized.

HYDROGEOMORPHIC APPROACH TO WETLAND FUNCTIONAL ASSESSMENT

HGM Classification

The hydrogeomorphic (HGM) approach to wetland functional assessment is presently being used, tested, refined, and regionalized in a variety of wetland settings throughout the United States. The HGM assessment method was preceded by the hydrogeomorphic classification system (Brinson 1993). The incredible diversity and variability of wetland ecosystems across the United States is a result of differences in climate, soil properties, physiography, biogeographic distributions, and numerous other "background" factors. Wetlands classification is an important precursor to functional assessment because classification reduces natural variability between wetland types and helps identify key functions potentially performed by similar wetlands. In addition, classification simplifies model development and helps reduce the level of effort for data acquisition, reduction, and interpretation.

The HGM classification is based on the geomorphic setting, primary water source, and hydrodynamics of the wetland (Brinson 1993). Hydrologic and geomorphic factors control how wetlands function, and the clarification of this relationship is among the fundamental strengths of the HGM classification (Brinson 1993). Geomorphic setting refers to the landscape position of the wetland, which will affect in large part how water enters the wetland and the energy it may exert on the structure and function of the wetland. Brinson (1993) recognized different geomorphic positions related not only to landscape position, but also to the position and orientation of the wetland to hydrologic inputs and outputs. Hydrodynamics in wetlands include both direction and magnitude components. Direction of flow is a function of both the nature of the wetland with respect to the water source and outlet and may also be affected by the influence of lunar tides. In general, riverine wetlands exhibit linear, unidirectional flow regimes, whereas fringe (e.g., tidal) systems exhibit bidirectional flow regimes. Magnitude or velocity of flow is related to the kinetics of water source, the slope and roughness of the wetland, and the nature of the outlet. Smith and associates (1995) defined seven hydrogeomorphic wetland classes based largely on geomorphic setting: riverine, depressional, slope, mineral soil flats, organic soil flats, estuarine fringe, and lacustrine fringe.

To illustrate the components of the HGM classification and their influence on wetland structure and function, groundwater slope wetlands are described here. Groundwater slope wetlands occur at topographic changes in slope, such as where groundwater intersects the land surface at or immediately above a footslope (i.e. the junction of a hillside and a valley bottom). However, slope wetlands may also occur where a relatively impermeable buried soil horizon retards soil water infiltration and instead redirects the flow of shallow groundwater preferentially down gradient until it intersects a backslope. Groundwater contributions to slope wetlands may also occur as a result of the upward movement of water due to potentiometric head differential or, in glaciated regions, where a shallow perched aquifer develops in a permeable surface horizon overlying a subsurface horizon of lower permeability. In any case, the relative capacity of hydrologic inputs to slope wetlands to physically affect the structure of the wetland is limited to the influence of long-term saturation on soil development and plant growth. That is, most slope wetlands are not characterized by the same soil deposition and redistribution processes that typify wetlands in alluvial floodplains.

Application of the HGM classification system at the regional scale requires the development and testing of subclasses. For example, Pruitt (2001) characterized four subclasses of riverine wetlands found in valley settings within the Piedmont physiographic region of Georgia: depression riverine, beaver riverine, coarse mineral slope, and fine mineral slope. Once wetlands in a given region are classified, HGM functional assessment models may be developed to target those classes or subclasses of wetlands that are of interest. However, not all regional wetland classes fit neatly into the seven basic HGM classes (e.g., Alaskan black spruce bogs, Florida Keys salt ponds). Despite the relative rigor of the HGM classification, Brinson and colleagues (1995) note that scale and the "continuous nature of water sources between extremes in wetland class" can make classification sometimes difficult.

HGM Functional Assessment

The hydrogeomorphic approach to wetland functional assessment emerged as a promising new method for the evaluation of wetland functions in the mid 1990s (Smith 1994). Although the assessment approach was developed with the intention of providing a tool for regulatory programs, there is nothing inherent to the procedure that limits its use to regulatory applications (Brinson et al. 1994).

HGM functional assessments are guided by regional HGM guidebooks developed for a specific ecoregion or physiography. Initially, an interdisciplinary assessment team identifies reference wetlands and reference conditions and establishes the reference domain. The reference domain includes all wetlands within a defined geographic or physiographic area that belong to a regional wetland subclass. Identification of reference wetlands within the reference domain is critically important to establish the range of natural variability existing within a regional wetland subclass and provides in situ data for scaling the level of function for other wetlands within the reference domain. It is imperative that reference wetlands include specific wetland sites that span the degree of disturbance or condition present within the regional subclass and reference domain. That is, reference wetlands should be representative of a variety of attributes and conditions caused by both natural and anthropogenic influences and thereby include wetlands ranging from poor quality on one end of the scale, to what would be considered reference standard conditions on the high end. Reference standard conditions represent the highest, sustainable level of functionality across the complete suite of functions applicable to the specific regional wetland subclass. In turn, the highest, sustainable level of function is also assumed to be achievable only by wetlands subjected to the least amount of anthropogenic disturbance or alteration. The USACE has compiled a comprehensive series of modules detailing the steps in development of regional HGM guidebooks (Smith 2001; Smith and Wakeley 2001; Wakeley and Smith 2001; Clairain 2002).

Similar to the U.S. Fish and Wildlife Service's Habitat Evaluation Procedure (USFWS 1980), HGM functional assessments estimate the functional capacity or the degree, magnitude, or level at which a wetland performs a function. The functional capacity is based on either a quantitative direct measure of a specific physical, chemical, or biological process or a qualitative indirect estimate of the physical wetland characteristics that affect that process or function. Generally, for instance, flood frequency in riverine wetland classes can be measured directly from stream gage data, if available, or estimated indirectly by either field indicators or remote sensing tools (e.g., historic aerial photography, drift or wrack lines, drainage patterns in wetlands, silt lines on tree trunks). A subindex ranging from 0 to 1.0 is assigned each variable based on departure from reference standard conditions, literature values, best professional judgment, or a combination of them. For example, assuming that reference standard conditions for riverine wetlands in a given reference domain are characterized by annual flooding (i.e., a recurrence interval of 1 year), the subindex for flood frequency may range from 1.0 for an annual recurrence interval to 0.10 for a 10- to 25-year recurrence interval.

Subindex scores based on site-specific conditions determine the functional capacity index (FCI) for each wetland function within the wetland assessment area. The FCI therefore reflects the ability of a wetland to perform a function relative to all wetlands from a regional wetland subclass in a reference domain. The functional indices in HGM are based on mathematical assessment models that define the relationship between wetland properties, the surrounding landscape, and the wetland functional capacity. For example, the

FCI for the function *temporarily store surface water* in a regional guidebook for western Kentucky (Ainslie et. al. 1999) is:

$$FCI = [(Vfreq \times Vstore)^{1/2} \times (Vslope + Vrough)/2]^{1/2}$$

where

$$FCI = \text{Functional Capacity Index,}$$
$$V = \text{variable,}$$
$$freq = \text{flood frequency,}$$
$$store = \text{floodplain storage volume,}$$
$$slope = \text{floodplain slope, and}$$
$$rough = \text{floodplain roughness.}$$

In this model, variables that are multiplied are considered dependent on each other, and independent variables are summed. In order to normalize the result of the model on a scale from 0 to 1.0, the arithmetic and geometric means of the products and sums, respectively, are calculated.

The HGM approach to wetland functional assessment is well suited to meet the requirements of the CWA Section 404 wetland regulatory program. By conducting several HGM functional assessments at a site-specific scale, federal jurisdictional wetlands of high functionality can be avoided or impacts can be minimized. If impacts to federal jurisdictional wetlands are unavoidable, HGM functional assessments can be used to evaluate pre- and post-project conditions as well as mitigation conditions (wetland impacts and compensatory mitigation, respectively). Mitigation project targets and success criteria can be identified by assessing the mitigation site potential relative to reference conditions for wetlands in the same regional subclass and reference domain. The mitigation project target is then based on the highest, sustainable level of function that can be expected at the mitigation site given its disturbance history, surrounding land use, connectivity, and other environmental conditions.

In 1997, the USACE in conjunction with USEPA, USFWS, USDA, and the Federal Highways Administration announced a National Action Plan to Implement the Hydrogeomorphic Approach to Assessing Wetland Functions, 62 FR 119:33607–33620. The stated goal of the National Action Plan was to support the development of 25 to 30 regional HGM guidebooks sufficient to address 80% of the CWA Section 404 permit workload requiring wetland functional assessments.

Several regional guidebooks have been developed and tested in various parts of the United States since 1997. These efforts have included a cross section of different physiographic provinces and wetland classes present nationwide (Table 9.4). While the development of regional guidebooks continues, the federal support for these projects declined in the early 2000s relative to earlier efforts. Nonetheless, various consortia of federal, state, and local government agencies, advocacy groups, and nonprofit organizations continue to develop regional guidebooks throughout the country (Table 9.5).

Arkansas	Forested Wetlands in the Delta Region of Arkansas, Lower Mississippi River Alluvial Valley
Atlantic and Gulf Coastal Plain	Wet Pine Flats on Mineral Soils in the Atlantic and Gulf Coastal Plains
Florida	Low-Gradient, Blackwater Riverine Wetlands in Peninsular Florida
Florida	Depressional Wetlands in Peninsular Florida
Florida (Everglades)	Flats Wetlands in the Everglades
Gulf of Mexico	Northwest Gulf of Mexico Tidal Fringe Wetlands
Kentucky	Low Gradient, Riverine Wetlands in Western Kentucky
Nebraska	Rainwater Basin Depressional Wetlands in Nebraska
Northern Rocky Mountains	Intermontane Prairie Pothole Wetlands in the Northern Rocky Mountains
	Riverine Floodplains in the Northern Rocky Mountains
Oregon	Willamette Valley Ecoregion, Riverine Impounding and Slope/Flat Subclasses
Tennessee	Low-Gradient Riverine Wetlands in Western Tennessee
Yazoo River Basin	Selected Regional Wetland Subclasses, Yazoo Basin, Lower Mississippi River Alluvial Valley

SUMMARY

The history of federal regulation of activities in or affecting wetlands in the United States has been marked by often contentious debate in the halls of Congress, the court system, and among the American populace since Congress first exerted its authority under the Commerce Clause of the U.S. Constitution to regulate activities in the nation's waterways. Contemporary regulations and federal policies affecting wetlands and other jurisdictional waters of the United States are built on a complex assemblage of statutes, judiciary decisions, and agency policies and mandates that spans almost 200 years. The Clean Water Act of 1977 (as amended) provides the basis for modern wetland regulation in the United States, despite that the term *wetland* does not appear anywhere in the statute. Until the U.S. Congress affirmatively amends the Clean Water Act or enacts additional legislation to comprehensively define the scope of jurisdictional waters of the United States and address the federal government's role in the regulation of activities affecting those waters, the future of regulatory oversight in these environs is likely to continue to evolve. However, the competing interests and often intense lobbying by parties on both sides of the debate make such congressional action unlikely in the near future.

As a result, it may fall on state or local governments to clarify the often ambiguous regulatory environment concerning wetlands and other waters. As described this chapter, individual states and even communities within states have been at the forefront of wetlands

TABLE 9.5   Regional Guidebooks Under Development for Assessing Wetland
Functions Using Either they Hydogeomorphic Approach or Concepts Embodied Therein

Alaska	Precipitation-driven Wetlands on Discontinuous Permafrost in Interior Alaska.
	Slope/Flat Wetland Complexes in the Cook Inlet Basin Ecoregion, Alaska
	Riverine and River Proximal Slope Wetlands in Coastal Southeast and Southcentral Alaska
	Tidal Fringe Wetlands in Alaska
Central Appalachian Mountains	Wetlands of the Ridge and Valley Province of the Central Appalachian Mountains
Georgia	Riverine Wetlands in the Piedmont Physiographic Region
Idaho	Low-gradient, Broad Basin, Groundwater Fed Slope with Spring Fed Riverine Inclusion
Mississippi	Headwater Riverine Wetlands in the Mississippi Coastal Plain
Kansas	Wooded and Herbaceous Riverine Wetlands in Kansas
Nebraska, South Dakota	Depressions Nebraska Sandhills in Nebraska and South Dakota
New Jersey	Tidal Fringe Wetlands in the New Jersey Meadowlands
South Carolina	Headwater Riverine Wetlands in the South Carolina Coastal Plain
Tennessee	Depressions and Mineral Flats on the Highland Rim in Tennessee

protection in the past, and many states continue to take steps to safeguard aquatic environments from the increasing pressures of development, agriculture, and infrastructure improvements independent of, or in response to, federal legislative or judicial actions.

The role of wetland functional assessment in the regulatory arena is similarly replete with sometimes opposing viewpoints. Compilation of a single wetland assessment methodology suitable for use in all wetland types and regions of the United States that is also universally endorsed by federal and state natural resources agencies and the regulated public has proven elusive, as evidenced by the myriad of functional assessment methodologies proposed to date. The hydrogeomorphic approach to wetland functional assessment was built on the foundation provided by some of these earlier methods and clarified the utility of wetland classification as a precursor to wetland assessment. Wetland functional assessment, and indeed wetland science in general, is a fairly recent area of study, and HGM utilizes recent advances in the understanding of how wetlands function to emphasize the critical role of landscape setting and hydrodynamics as fundamental components affecting the function of different wetland types. Only time will tell whether HGM will continue to evolve, grade into revised subsequent assessment methods, or be effectively disregarded for an altogether different approach to wetland functional assessment.

10

WETLAND RESTORATION

Joy B. Zedler

Restoration is the process of assisting the recovery of an ecosystem that has been degraded, damaged, or destroyed (Society for Ecological Restoration 2002). It is a broad arena, with some projects as small as the excavation of a 10-m² depression intended to hold water briefly in spring (a vernal pool) and others measuring in the thousands of km². Some restoration needs are as simple as ceasing the drainage of water, while others are fraught with difficulty. Some goals can be accomplished on site; others require consideration of entire watersheds, river basins, or other distant locations (e.g., wintering grounds of wetland birds). Some projects are strictly about habitat conservation, while others involve economic and cultural concerns. Among the world's most challenging wetland restoration projects is restoring the Mesopotamian wetlands (Fig. 10.1) to a functional ecosystem that not only supports biodiversity but also entices a culture of exiled Marsh Arabs to return to southern Iraq, where they can resume their wetland-based livelihoods. The "Eden Again" project (ITAP 2003) might seem overly ambitious, but its long-term goals are inspiring a generation of ecological restorationists.

It is often difficult to imagine how many unknowns and uncertainties there are in attempting to reassemble nature. A nursery rhyme (Box 10.1) might help set the stage for this discussion of ecosystem restoration because attempts to reassemble Humpty Dumpty have many parallels in wetland restoration. The difficulties do not mean that restoration work should be delayed until there are clear guidelines and predictable outcomes. Much can be gained in the process of attempting restoration. There is an excellent model for learning while doing, namely, adaptive management (cf. Thom 2000 for coastal wetland

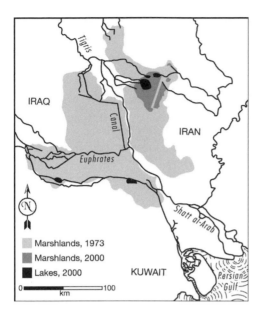

FIGURE 10.1
Location of Iraqi marshlands in 1973 before extensive water diversions and drainage and in 2000 after severe degradation. From ITAP (2003), with permission. Changes include huge canals built to drain the wetlands, replacement of wetlands by irrigated agriculture and oil fields, formation of thick salt crusts in former wetland basins, diversion of water in the Tigres and Euphrates rivers by upstream dams, and loss of waterbirds and extinction of an otter. Only one area (near the Iran border) retained significant wetland biota.

applications), which we have tailored to focus on experimental testing of alternative restoration approaches in phased modules, with knowledge gained in early modules used to design later modules and experiments (*adaptive restoration;* Zedler and Callaway 2003). Adaptive restoration is an efficient way to fill knowledge gaps, as both the science of restoration ecology and the practice of ecological restoration are simultaneously advanced. Restorationists can fulfill the urgent needs of wetland restoration while learning how to do so more effectively; they can restore the many ecosystem services that wetlands provide, including aesthetic features that benefit people of all ages. The first step, however, is acknowledging what key information is not known. Once unknowns are identified, projects can be designed to obtain that information.

How does the restoration of an ecosystem progress? Hands-on experience, accounts in the literature, and several areas of ecological theory can help predict the general course of wetland restoration. There is no cookbook for wetland restoration, nor is there a simple trajectory that describes how restored sites will develop. Nor is this chapter a "how-to" guide. Instead, it is a discussion of the restoration process with examples concerning starting points, institutions that foster wetland restoration, alternative goals, strategic placement of wetland restoration projects within watersheds, site-based tactics, surprises, ways to evaluate progress and outcomes, long-term stewardship, and adaptive restoration. I draw extensively on my firsthand experiences in the United States with California estuarine restoration and Wisconsin freshwater wetlands. Wherever local guidebooks are available (e.g., Thompson and Luthin 2004 for restoring Wisconsin wetlands on private lands), readers are urged to consult such resources for specific approaches in specific locations. Because surprises are common, an adaptive approach can help identify cause-effect relationships and make future restorations more predictable.

BOX 10.1 A NURSERY RHYME UPDATED. . . .

Humpty Dumpty fell off a wall; Humpty Dumpty had a great fall; all the king's horses and all the king's men couldn't put Humpty together again. But *why* couldn't this egg-shaped character be restored? Was it impossible? Or did the king's "restorationists" have the right target and use the wrong approach, or did they aim for the wrong target?

Imagine their plight after Humpty had broken into a dozen pieces, his innards had decomposed and his shell had blown away, leaving no trace. Imagine further that the wall had fallen apart and passers-by had scavenged the building blocks. Once the blocks were gone, rainstorms quickly eroded the soil behind the wall, forming a gully beneath Humpty's former perch. If you had been responsible, how would you have proceeded?

The king's men were unable to find any descriptions of either the egg-shaped character or the wall in their historical condition, so they looked for other structures and wall-sitters to use as a reference system. They found a picket fence with a mourning dove nest in a branch just over the wall. "Aha," they said, "perhaps this is what used to be here—a fence, a bush, a nest, and an egg." They bought some boards and built a section of fence over the gully and planted several shrubs. They told the king they were confident that, in time, the fence would provide a trellis for the shrubs, the shrubs would grow strong and lush, and a branch would attract a bird to nest and produce a new Humpty. The king was pleased and considered the matter closed. Shortly afterward, the restoration project received an environmental award.

But it was not the end of the story. Five years later, a princess walked along the path. She saw the gully, the section of fence (in disrepair), and the remnants of dead shrub plantings with nursery labels still intact. The gully was a mass of weeds and brambles. "What an interesting site," she said. "I can see that effort was spent here trying to accomplish something, perhaps slowing erosion. Unfortunately, it doesn't look like anyone considered the source of the problem, which is upstream of the site, or used native species plantings that might stabilize an eroding site, or replanted what didn't survive." She approached the king, who had a file on Humpty Dumpty's "successful recovery" but no record of any erosion control project. She convinced him to let her Restoration Ecology class use the site and its watershed to experiment with plantings of several native species to reduce erosion.

While not everyone lived happily ever after, a process of "learning while restoring" was set in motion so that future gully-restorers were able to see which species grew well. Furthermore, the entire kingdom benefited from the experiment because the field experiments showed that shrubs grew poorly, so money and time were no longer wasted on planting shrubs.

The moral of this story is that *restoration should be treated as an uncertainty* because (1) targets for restoration are often unclear, (2) it is easy to promise "successful recovery" but difficult to reproduce a fully functional system, (3) projects are often declared successful in order to please the client or close the books, (4) assessment is rarely sufficient to detect long-term effectiveness or to undertake corrective measures, and

(5) the solutions to restoration problems often involve processes that occur off site. It is thus recommended that restoration be considered within landscape contexts; that experiments take the place of trial-and-error approaches, in order to determine which restoration measures are most effective; and that the understanding of outcomes in early experiments be applied to later restoration efforts.

CATASTROPHIC VERSUS CHRONIC DEGRADATION

The desire to restore an ecosystem can follow a wide variety of degradation processes, some resulting from sudden events, others from slow, cumulative changes. In southwestern Spain, a dike that confined zinc mine wastes broke in 1998, releasing tons of toxic sediments to the nearby river, which in turn carried the materials to the highly prized Donaña Marshlands, which are a national park. Because the causes of degradation were clear and the impacts were immediately recognized as undesirable, it was obvious that some form of restoration was needed. Planning for the "Doñana 2005" project began immediately, and funds were obtained to implement several restoration actions (Martinez et al. 1999). Knowing the cause-effect relationships between the event and the damage to downstream ecosystems was helpful in figuring out what to do and how to do it. As in Box 10.1, there were still many difficulties, but the planning was more readily focused than where the degradation process is slow and multiple disturbances contribute to the undesirable outcome. The following example of chronic degradation of water quality in streams and downstream wetlands illustrates a more complicated process, in which experimentation was needed to identify cause-effect relationships.

Prior to degradation, landscapes in the U.S. Midwest had fully vegetated rolling hills with well-developed soils that infiltrated rainfall and dissolved nutrients. Thus, surface runoff to streams was usually clear and cool, and the aquatic habitats could support high biodiversity of algae, invertebrates, fish, and riparian plants. When a bison herd wallowed among the grasses, turbid runoff would have followed the next rainfall, but the stream and its biota would have recovered from the pulse of sediment, and the disturbed grassland would have healed itself through vegetative expansion and seedling recruitment.

Once humans populated the landscape, their cultivated fields and urban areas began to disturb and compact the soil, contribute nutrients, and shed more water, which then can move loose sediment to the stream, along with nutrients leached from soils along the way. Run-off from urban areas and from fields with exposed soil becomes warm, and it stays warm in streams that lack shade trees. Alien species accompany humans, and

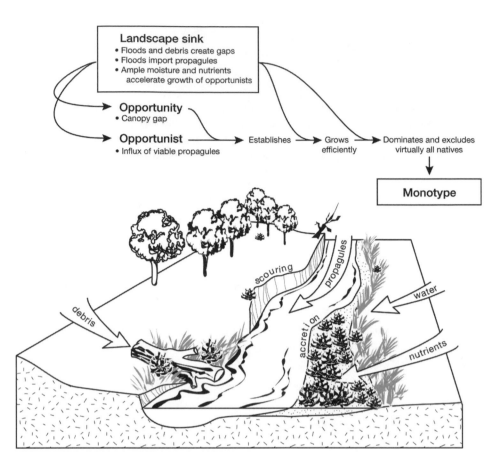

FIGURE 10.2

Wetland invasions are readily explained by their position as landscape sinks, which provide many opportunities for invasion and propagules of many opportunists to invade. From Zedler and Kercher (2004), with permission from Taylor & Francis Inc.

many have propagules that float downstream into wetlands where flows slow and particles and materials dissolved in the abundant runoff become trapped. As a result, most wetlands are mildly to severely degraded. Very few can be considered pristine.

What are the impacts of chronic degradation in midwestern U.S. landscapes? Because water flows downhill, low places and their associated wetlands function as "landscape sinks." The more disturbance to the upland, the more potential for materials to flow into wetlands, which accumulate the impacts of disturbances from entire watersheds. The opportunities provided by excess inflows of everything plants need to thrive are matched by the availability of opportunists that rise to the occasion (Fig. 10.2). Thus, wetlands are not only readily degraded in human-occupied landscapes, they are also easily invaded by aggressive plants. Aggressive, competitive invaders further degrade wetlands by displacing natives and forming monotypes (Fig. 10.2).

Degradation that occurs slowly over long time periods might be due to many causes, which are hard to pinpoint. For example, increased surface runoff can be followed by the invasion of aggressive plants and the displacement of natives, without a clear understanding of which attribute of runoff (excess water, nutrients, sediments, toxic materials?) is at fault or which shift occurs first (demise of natives allowing invaders to establish, or establishment of invaders that outcompete natives?). Because the cause-effect relationships need to be clear in order to identify restoration actions, research becomes necessary.

Kercher and Zedler (2004) revealed the processes by which one invasive wetland plant, reed canary grass *(Phalaris arundinacea)*, forms monotypic vegetation that displaces a diverse wet prairie. Using 140 mesocosms (tubs of 1.1-m² area and 0.9-m depth), they compared the expansion of reed canary grass and the demise of the resident vegetation across 27 treatments (3 levels of flooding $\times$ 3 levels of nutrient addition $\times$ 3 sediment applications) plus additional untreated controls. Flooding killed some resident species, opening the canopy and providing sufficient light for the reed canary grass seedlings (4/mesocosm) to flourish (Kercher and Zedler 2004; Lindig-Cisneros and Zedler 2002a). With an influx of nutrients and topsoil, including rhizomal subsidies from parent plants (Maurer and Zedler 2002), the invader outgrew the other resident species via vegetative expansion. In one growing season, three of the treatments formed monotypes; in 2 years, 11 treatments (55 mesocosms) supported monotypes (Kercher, unpubl. data).

The treatments that led to monotypes in the mesocosms were designed to mimic stormwater inflows—namely, an influx of excess water, nutrients, and nutrient-rich sediments. What is unique in this experiment is the ability to identify interactions among those factors. While flooding, nutrients, and topsoil influxes can stimulate reed canary grass invasions independently, the combination shows synergistic effects, doubling the effect that would be expected from adding the individual disturbances together! Storm water is not a single factor but a soup that nourishes opportunistic invaders, such as reed canary grass. Thus, restoration of downstream wetlands must tackle three upstream problems simultaneously—the discharge of excess water, the application of excess nutrients to fields and lawns, and the disturbance of soils.

In addition to the problems that result from their sink position, wetlands across the globe experience deliberate filling, renegade dumping, water withdrawals and diversions, damming, dredging, channelization, drainage, and contamination. Severe disturbances produce highly degraded wetlands, with little visible sign of their predisturbance condition. If their hydric soils have been oxidized through decomposition or burned off during peat fires (as in central Wisconsin's Buena Vista Marsh), the only evidence of their former wetland status might be historical records and aerial photos (Fig. 10.3).

While catastrophic and chronic degradation of natural wetlands is a common stimulus for restoration efforts, not all wetlands are remnants of historical wetlands. Some have formed in places that were never historically wet (e.g., upslope of road berms that trap water, depressions left by gravel pits, or constructed stormwater retention basins). Like

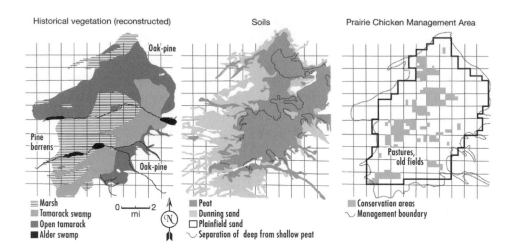

Historical vegetation (reconstructed)   Soils   Prairie Chicken Management Area

Oak-pine

Pine barrens

Oak-pine

Pastures, old fields

≡ Marsh   0 ——— 2   ■ Peat   ■ Conservation areas
■ Tamarack swamp   mi   ■ Dunning sand   ⌣ Management boundary
■ Open tamarack   (N)   □ Plainfield sand
■ Alder swamp   ⌣ Separation of deep from shallow peat

FIGURE 10.3

The wetlands that once dominated Buena Vista Marsh in central Wisconsin were not apparent from soils after drainage for agriculture and subsequent peat fires. The history of the site was determined from land survey records (cf. Zedler 1966).

altered natural wetlands, many of these novel ecosystems are dominated by alien species and could be enhanced to increase their conservation value.

Degraded wetlands thus form a spectrum (Table 10.1), that is, a two-dimensional array including those with long histories as wetlands and those created by humans, with each category ranging from mildly to severely disturbed. To describe the spectrum further, disturbance could be quantified according to the wetland's similarity with regional reference systems (Brinson 1993). Some degraded sites would retain elements of their historical hydrologic conditions, soils, and biota, while the most disturbed might not even be wet. For a specific site, calculating its similarity with suitable reference sites before, during, and after restoration, would help to identify unknowns and suggest alternative approaches that could be tested in experimental plots. Once under way, changes in similarity could be used to track progress (cf. later section on assessment).

ENABLING RESTORATION EFFORTS

The potential for restoring a wetland to some more desirable condition entices many people to take action, individually or aided by an institution that facilitates wetland restoration efforts. A farmer might decide to attract wildlife and reduce losses incurred by frequent flooding by ceasing to cultivate the low spots on the farm. Another might need governmental assistance to fill ditches, break drain tiles, remove accreted sediments, and replant native vegetation. If the task is large, other mechanisms might be brought into play. For example, the desire of citizens and agency personnel to set aside a marginal farm and restore Patrick Marsh was fulfilled when Wisconsin officials identified it as a potential mitigation site, and

Degradation History	On-site Efforts That Might Be Needed			
	Minimal	Moderate	Substantial	Complete
Mildly degraded: Small canopy gaps caused by vehicles or human trampling	Prevent further damage; wait for self recovery; watch site	Replant; remove invasives if needed	Probably not necessary	Not necessary
Moderately degraded: Large areas with loss of soil and vegetation (e.g., peat fire, landslide, bulldozer scrape)	Amend soil; wait and see if native plants recover	Amend soil; replant with seeds of native plants	Amend soil; replant with seeds and transplants; control invasives	Probably not necessary
Severely degraded: Site receives inflows of agricultural runoff and supports an invasive monotype	Mow or graze to encourage native plant reestablishment (a common practice in Europe); allow dominant invader to persist	Herbicide to kill the invasive; seed with native plant species	Herbicide to kill the invasive; plant a native cover crop; spray with more specific herbicide repeatedly	Bulldoze and remove topsoil and rhizomes; replant with native species
Obliterated: Drained and filled site functions as an upland	Minimal effort would not restore the wetland	Halt drainage; aim for wet conditions only in very wet seasons or years	Remove fill; reexpose wetland soil; aim for seed bank regeneration	Remove fill; decompact soil; amend soil; adjust topography; replant with seeds and transplants

NOTE: Cf. Zedler (1999). While moderate actions might have sufficient effect in mildly degraded sites, more substantial efforts will be needed in severely degraded sites. Examples of increasing effort are indicated.

the Department of Transportation paid for improvements as compensation for filling other wetlands during highway construction. Citizens can be powerful in initiating restoration projects and finding money to support them. Sometimes, citizens form nonprofit organizations to give their efforts credence and exert pressure on local government. This process and a determined couple, Jim and Barbara Peugh, led the City of San Diego to acquire (for about $3 million) an 8-hectare arm of Mission Bay, California, which would otherwise have been filled to support condominiums. Once the land was acquired, the local activists helped set restoration goals, design changes to the often-stagnant lagoon, wrote proposals for funding, and helped implement the funded projects. Citizens, nongovernmental organizations, and agencies can create restoration visions, but where do they find the money?

In the United States, funds are available for landowners who wish to volunteer land for restoration. At the federal level, the U.S. Fish and Wildlife Service (USFWS) can pay for restoration and creation of wetlands and adjacent upland habitat under its "Partners for Wildlife Program." This program has been very popular in Wisconsin, where individual landowners have returned water and adjacent upland habitat to 4,500 sites on 4,737 hectares of the agricultural landscape (Thompson and Luthin 2004). Across the nation, farmers can take advantage of additional programs that are part of the U.S. Farm Bill, for example, the Wetland Reserve Program, Conservation Reserve Program, and Conservation Reserve Enhancement Program. These voluntary programs encourage farmers to work with the U.S. Department of Agriculture Natural Resources Conservation Service and Farm Service Administration to design and restore former wetlands. For example, the Wetland Reserves Program establishes individual projects that last ten or thirty years or include permanent easements (with more financial assistance for longer agreements). For landowners within the nation's coastal areas, the National Oceanic and Atmospheric Administration's Coastal Habitat Program encourages restoration of wetlands along ocean and estuarine shores and along the Great Lakes. In addition, a number of nongovernmental organizations engage in wetland creation and restoration, both nationally and internationally (e.g., The Nature Conservancy (www.tnc.org) and Ducks Unlimited [Tori et al. 2002]) as well as locally (e.g., the Wisconsin Waterfowl Association and community nature centers). These sources of assistance enable volunteers to propose lands for wetland restoration. In addition, considerable restoration in the United States takes place as a result of governmental mandates.

Other funds become available through the process of compensatory mitigation (NRC 2001). Under the U.S. Clean Water Act, the discharge of materials to wetlands (e.g., filling) is regulated by the U.S. Army Corps of Engineers. If a highway department needs to fill a wetland to build or widen a highway, the damages to the wetland must be mitigated, either by avoiding, minimizing, or compensating for losses. Rerouting the highway could avoid the damage, but alternative routes might not be possible. Reducing the width or constructing a bridge instead of a lengthy roadbed could minimize damage, but some fill is still unavoidable. Compensation is then required, often at a ratio of restored:filled that is greater than 1, depending on the quality of the filled site (NRC 2001). How well does this mandatory program work?

NOTE: From NRC (2001).

1. Consider the hydrogeomorphic and ecological landscape and climate.

2. Adopt a dynamic landscape perspective.

3. Restore or develop naturally variable hydrologic conditions.

4. Whenever possible, choose wetland restoration over creation.

5. Avoid overengineered structures in the wetland's design.

6. Pay particular attention to appropriate planting elevation, depth, soil type, and seasonal timing.

7. Provide appropriately heterogeneous topography.

8. Pay attention to subsurface conditions, including soil and sediment geochemistry and physics, groundwater quantity and quality, and infaunal communities.

9. Consider complications associated with wetland creation or restoration in serious degraded or disturbed sites.

10. Conduct early monitoring as part of adaptive management.

Compensatory mitigation actions have restored and created thousands of wetlands across the nation, although with mixed results (NRC 2001). Some permits have required compensatory actions, but the work was never done, or if implemented, the sites have not met criteria in the permits. Based on the few available studies of permit compliance, Turner and associates (2001) projected that for every 100 hectares that are permitted to be filled, 178 hectares of mitigated wetland would be required as compensation, but only 134 hectares would actually get "built." Of the 134 hectares built, 77 to 104 hectares would develop as required, complying with permit requirements. However, only 16 to 19 hectares would pass more stringent ecological requirements for functional equivalency with reference wetlands. Thus, the "net increase" of 178 hectares is not likely a net gain in area but instead a net loss in both area and function. The record reviewed by Turner and associates (2001), though far from a complete census of mitigation efforts nationwide, strongly suggests that mitigation efforts fail to compensate for lost wetlands. More broadly, there is concern that the mitigation process has resulted in a reduction in the diversity of wetland ecosystem types as well (Bedford 1996). The National Research Council (2001) reviewed 25 reports on restored and reference wetlands and made several recommendations for improving the compensatory mitigation program (Box 10.2), some of which are now being incorporated into the regulatory program.

Whether wetlands are restored voluntarily or in response to mandates, it is important to understand the overall effect of restoration on landscapes. The kinds of projects that are easiest to undertake (pond creation) do not necessarily replace the biota or functions that are lost with drainage or filling, even if the site lost was highly degraded. In Indiana, for example, most of the wetlands that have lost area through the permitting process are forested ecosystems, while most of the compensatory wetlands are shallow-water herbaceous wetlands (Robb 2002). To retain the full range of wetland functions and the maximum capacity to support biodiversity, decision makers need to track changes in area of each historical wetland type as well as their positions in watersheds. Are wetlands shifting from forested to herbaceous, from a few large to many small, from variable to stable water levels, from wet meadows to ponds, from urban to rural areas? The historical databases are often too general to answer such questions.

Historically, most mitigation efforts were undertaken by the developers who filled or drained nearby wetlands, and permits tended to call for on-site compensation. The NRC (2001) evaluation concentrated on such efforts, as the literature did not yet include evaluations of two alternatives that have since gained popularity. Mitigation banks and in-lieu-fee programs offer alternatives to on-site, permittee-conducted mitigation projects. Banks are wetlands that are restored "up front," with credits (areas of restored wetland) sold to those who need to mitigate damages to wetlands. Large banks occur off site but can be placed in suitable sites that meet regional wetland restoration needs (NRC 2001). In-lieu-fees can also provide flexibility in project location and design, as mitigators pay a fee to a responsible party and the money is used to implement projects that are coordinated over a region (NRC 2001). Fees might be used to fulfill an ambitious watershed-based plan that involves preserving some wetlands (although this results in a net loss of acreage) and enhancing and restoring others. While both mitigation banks and in-lieu-fees allow strategic planning to occur at watershed scales, thereby improving chances of restoring wetlands in landscape locations where the intended functions are likely to be sustainable, neither is free of problems. Some argue that water-quality improvement functions are needed more in urban areas, where wetlands are being lost most rapidly, than at mitigation bank sites; others argue that in-lieu-fees accrue too slowly, relative to the pace of wetland destruction, such that functions are not sustained. Time and future investigators will tell how well these newer alternatives assist the United States in meeting its national goal of no net loss in wetland area and function.

Many restoration efforts are site based, following the initiatives of individual activist or community groups. A highly motivated couple recently took on the challenge of restoring Iraqi wetlands that were deliberately drained about 15 years ago. Dr. Azzam Alwash, who grew up among these 20,000 km² of wetlands, and his American wife, Dr. Suzie Alwash, worked from their California home to obtain funding for a wetland restoration strategy. With seed money from the State Department (via the Iraq Foundation), they hired Dr. Michelle Stevens to convene a Technical Advisory Panel, who subsequently identified key components of a restoration strategy (Box 10.3, Box 10.4, Fig. 10.4). Azzam then returned to his homeland, where he facilitated restoration by seeking funding and negotiating renewed water flows from upstream reservoirs. The enormity of the challenge in Iraq exceeds that of restoring the Everglades, which was also catalyzed by an individual, Marjory Stoneman Douglas (1978). Perhaps the efforts in Iraq will come to fruition like Douglas's work, which ultimately grew into a multibillion-dollar federal-state program. One thing is clear—the efforts of one or two people can make a real difference.

The technical advisory panel envisioned alternatives that would avoid the largest problems, initiate restoration where it would be most feasible, and suggest both off-site and on-site activities that would be needed to begin wetland restoration. Despite all the constraints, two attributes offered unusual opportunities. First, the dominant and most desired reed *(Phragmites australis)* is an aggressive species that is easy to establish. Second, the Marsh Arabs who tended the reeds for building fences and shelters (including meeting rooms that match images carved over 5,000 years ago) were likely to return from exile and resume their tending of reed marshes, which involves harvesting and planting stems to vegetate shallow waters, later harvesting new stems to build up mounds and construct shelters for use while fishing. Still, there were many unknowns, and the panel endorsed adaptive restoration approaches, with early restoration modules designed to test ideas that could then be applied in later modules.

RESTORE WHAT?

WHICH WETLAND TYPE?

A range of restoration targets is possible (Hobbs and Norton 1996), and suggestions for wetland restoration goals are likely to come from divergent sources (Ehrenfeld 2000). While the stakeholders might have very specific objectives in mind, nearly everyone has a visual image of what they would like to see in a particular place. The esthetic appeal of wetlands is often sufficient cause for rallying support for restoration efforts. In North America, the photography and text of Littlehales and Niering (1991) captured images of the finest examples of freshwater marshes, coastal wetlands, swamps and riparian wetlands, and peatlands that the continent has to offer. Yet, the diversity of landscape settings and wetland types exceeds what can be pictured in one book. How many kinds of wetlands are there on a single continent or in a single country?

For the United States, Cowardin and colleagues (1979) identified nearly 200 wetland types within five "systems" (marine, estuarine, riverine, lacustrine, and palustrine), "subsystems" (based on intertidal position, water depth and flow), and "classes" (based on substrate types

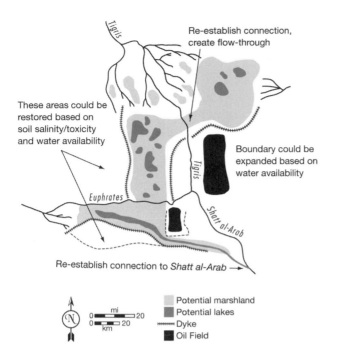

Re-establish connection,
create flow-through

These areas could be
restored based on
soil salinity/toxicity
and water availability

Boundary could be
expanded based on
water availability

Tigris

Euphrates

Tigris

Shatt al-Arab

Re-establish connection to *Shatt al-Arab* →

mi
0 — 20
0 — 20
km

Potential marshland
Potential lakes
Dyke
Oil Field

FIGURE 10.4
Sketches intended for
discussions of restoration
options with stakeholder
groups. Site-specific restoration plans can be developed
once stakeholder priorities are
known and physical con-
straints (soil salinity and
toxicity, water availability) are
understood. The draft
concepts cover three areas: A.
the Central Marsh, B.
Hawizeh Marsh, and C.
Hammar Marsh. From ITAP
(2003), with permission.

and vegetation features). This classification forms the basis of the USFWS National Wetland Inventory (NWI), an inventory and mapping project of wetlands that remain, in relation to potentially restorable wetlands (often determined from maps of hydric soils).

Brinson (1993) classified U.S. wetlands by their geomorphic (topographic) setting, water
source and transport (precipitation, groundwater, or surface flows), and hydrodynamics
(direction of flow and strength of movement). A wetland can occur in a depression, form
part of a peatland, extend along a river, or occur at the fringe of a water body. It can be
fed only by rainfall, primarily by groundwater, primarily by surface flows, or a combination. Water flows can be unidirectional or bidirectional, as in tidal marshes, with quiet
water (ponds) or forceful flows (rocky and cobble beaches). As Bedford (1996) concluded:
"What emerges from this elegantly simple conceptual scheme is a very large number of
potential hydrogeomorphic classes of wetlands."

In setting targets for a restoration site, planners need to consider first its topographic setting, water source, and hydrodynamics. Potential functions of the restored ecosystem
should be predictable, in part, from these abiotic features. For example, a peat mound formed
by groundwater seepage can discharge water and support high plant diversity, while a
lakeshore wetland can stabilize sediments, and a depressional wetland fed by surface water
can improve water quality. Different types of wetland support unique communities of plant
and animal species and have unique functional capacities, such as rates of water and sediment retention, nutrient sequestration, denitrification, and primary productivity. Thus, Brinson's "hydrogeomorphic classification" provides a useful basis for wetland restoration, by
recognizing strong relationships between wetland setting and function. Attempts to restore

the structure (species composition) and functions of one type of wetland in the hydrogeomorphic setting of another type of wetland would be a waste of time and money.

WHICH WATERSHED POSITION?

Historical inventories of wetland types, sizes, and locations provide valuable information for setting restoration goals. It would seem prudent to establish restoration priorities with a broad spatial and temporal view. Bedford (1996) recommended that "wetland profiles" be developed within landscapes, on the scale of major drainages (areas of about 1800 km²). Profiles would characterize the hydrogeologic and climatic settings within each landscape, identify the wetland types that have been lost or modified, and catalog types and relative abundances of wetland types that remain, noting those with special heritage/biodiversity value (Bedford 1996).

Johnson (2004) recently undertook the task of profiling wetlands in Summit County, Colorado, which has many steep-sloped watersheds that are not highly modified, as well as lower-elevation, flatter lands that are disturbed by roads and developments. In order to characterize the area of each wetland type and to make comparisons of wetland profiles among landscape units, he first explored and defined up to three "process domains" that corresponded to high-, medium-, or low-elevation proportions of the watershed (some watersheds had only one or two domains). Then, he calculated areas of each wetland type using Brinson's hydrogeomorphic classification. Understandably, high- and low-elevation "ecoregions" contrasted strongly in their wetland profiles—the high-elevation ecoregion had more area in slope wetlands than riverine wetlands, and the low-ecoregion had the reverse. Thus, profiles were similar within but different between ecoregions defined as process domains, in keeping with Bedford's (1996) expectations. Johnson then compared profiles for reference and modified landscapes to see if humans have altered wetland profiles. As permit records have shown elsewhere (e.g., Robb 2002), humans have increased depressional wetlands at the expense of riverine wetlands—but only for the high-elevation ecoregion in Summit County; at mid elevation, riverine wetlands covered more area and slope wetlands less area than in reference landscape units, and in low lands, fringe wetlands and irrigated meadows increased, while riverine wetlands decreased. The general point is that human-modified landscapes have different profiles from the reference landscape, and the wetlands that remain today have different relative area than in historical times. Further analyses of these data would show whether or not the numbers and sizes of wetlands differ among ecoregions and with human modifications as well as whether connectivity among wetlands and streams is consistent across space and time.

Defining a target for entire watershed restoration (area x type of wetland) requires more effort than plotting data on remaining wetlands. The extra work of classifying and cataloging wetlands within reference landscapes should be worth the effort, as results can help with both goal setting for wetland restoration and with prioritization of projects. Then, planners can tackle the many issues associated with restoring individual sites.

Wetland ecosystems function to support biodiversity, improve water quality, and abate flooding, among other things. In the United States, these three general functions are valued enough to justify spending billions of dollars to restore and sustain them, and we now call them ecosystem services. Calling biodiversity support an ecosystem service is a general way of saying that wetlands support many species that people use. In fact, a major U.S. effort to buy and restore wetlands grew out of hunters' and fishers' appreciation of game and fish, both of which were declining during the 1930s drought (dust bowl years; Zedler et al. 1998). Later, the Clean Water Act grew to include wetland protection in recognition of the nutrient- and contaminant-removal services of wetlands. And after the 1993 flooding of the Mississippi River Valley, many scientists suggested that the calamitous loss of floodplain property would not have occurred if wetlands had been able to retain their flood-abatement service. For example, Hey and Philippi (1995) calculated that restoring 5.3 million hectares of wetlands within the Mississippi River Valley could have prevented most of the damage caused by the 1993 flood.

Is it realistic to include all three functions in the objectives for a single wetland restoration site? Most wetlands perform all three services to some degree, but it is probably rare for a single wetland to perform all of them well. In part, this is because of the constraints that landscape position impose on wetlands, and in part because of negative relationships among the three services. In today's highly modified landscapes, which often have more runoff, more mobile sediments, and more nutrient release than natural landscapes, a wetland restored to improve water quality would need to be placed where it would receive "dirty" water. While water-cleansing functions could be maximized by restoring wetlands with shallow, slow-flowing water, the inflowing sediments and nutrients would settle out and be buried or processed through assimilation or, in the case of nitrogen, undergo denitrification. The shallow water that would maximize these processes (Crumpton 2001) would not maximize flood storage. Nor would assimilation of nutrients by plants foster species-rich vegetation; instead, aggressive, invasive species would grow best, crowding out natives and lowering overall diversity. Wetlands designed to store significant volumes of floodwater would likewise be too deep and have hydroperiods that are too flashy (rapid shifts from low to high inundation) to maximize diversity. It is not surprising that "working wetlands" designed for water-quality improvement or flood abatement are dominated by only a few species, typically one or two invasive plants.

WHICH GOAL FOR A SPECIFIC SITE?

Many wetland restoration efforts begin with a site that is in obvious disrepair and for which there are many restoration options. The spectrum of restoration goals ranges from exact duplication of some prior condition to a facsimile of a nearby reference site to a novel state that is more compatible with current environmental conditions, which are not likely to be the same as when the wetland developed. In laying out options, planners encounter various problems in their search for restoration models, as in Box 10.1: (1) records of pre-existing conditions are lacking or incomplete (cf. Egan and Howell 2001); (2) historical conditions were not static, so there is no strong rationale for an exact match between the restoration and the ecosystem at the time it was damaged (Pickett and Parker 1994); (3) nearby sites might not be suitable references due to confounding variables, such as different hydrologic conditions; (4) the natural conditions that allowed the wetland to develop its unique characters may no longer exist; (5) the functions that the former wetland performed are not at all obvious; and (6) current stakeholders might have very different ideas about what they want, what they are willing to fund, and what they are willing to manage in perpetuity. Wisconsinites like to hunt, and landowners tend to favor ponds that attract waterfowl, while coastal Californians are especially concerned about the impacts of urbanization, and their concerns focus on protection of rare habitats and endangered species. The process of setting site-specific objectives will benefit from involving the relevant stakeholders and considering conditions beyond the immediate site and time frame (Hobbs 2004).

Despite the mentioned difficulties, reference sites are of great utility in restoration. For example, the Ayuquila River in southern Jalisco, Mexico, has lost most of its riparian forest in the broad valleys where people and agricultural activities are concentrated. Until Anastasia Allen (2004) began sampling potential reference sites, there was no clear target for restoration efforts that were planned by the local university campus (University of Guadalajara–Autlán). Local ecologists knew where to find several small woodland remnants, but there were no quantitative data on how many species were present, nor which woody species had been abundant, formed the tree canopy, and could reproduce now that upstream dams caused flooding in the dry season instead of the wet season. After sampling small forest remnants, she linked the ecological features of twelve sites to geomorphologic conditions and identified at least one that could serve as a restoration target for each type of stream reach, for example, broad, asymmetrical, and steep-sided valleys.

IDENTIFYING FEASIBLE GOALS
WHAT KINDS OF WETLANDS ARE READILY RESTORED?

Because the conditions of degraded wetlands (Table 10.1) and restoration efforts both form a spectrum, it is difficult to generalize about the ease of restoration. A site that is little degraded should be easy to restore to a level of structure and function present in suitable reference sites, relative to a highly degraded site. Nevertheless, there seems to be consensus among wetland restorers that cattail-dominated emergent marshes and cattail-lined ponds are easy wetlands to restore (NRC 2001). Ponds and other shallow-water wetlands are easy to create, and they are popular with landowners. They are clearly wetlands, so they fulfill the mitigation requirement of providing an ecosystem that meets regulatory standards (wetland hydrology, soils, and vegetation). But ponds are not always what has been lost in a region (S. Eggers, U.S. Army Corps of Engineers, unpubl. data), nor are they always desirable landscape features. In Indiana, shallow-water systems are the primarily target for mitigation projects, even though forested wetland is typically what is being lost (Robb 2002). In Oregon, wetlands with permanent standing water are not common natural landscape features, since dry summers lead to drawdowns. The creation of ponds with permanent standing water fostered invasions by alien bullfrogs *(Rana catesebeiana),* facilitated by nonnative fish that prey on native invertebrates that would otherwise eat the bullfrog tadpoles (Adams et al. 2003). The result is an "invasional meltdown" (Simberloff and Von Holle 1999). Ponds and open water systems have a place in wetland restoration, but one wetland type does not fulfill all restoration needs.

WHAT KINDS OF WETLANDS ARE DIFFICULT TO RESTORE?

Any wetland that requires long time periods to grow dominant features will be difficult to restore in the short term. Forested wetlands, especially those dominated by slow-growing species, are obvious examples (Mitsch and Wilson 1996). Peatlands also fit this description, as mosses and other organic substrates need to accumulate; this process is very slow, and restoration efforts are too young to estimate the time frames needed to mimic reference sites (Gorham and Rochefort 2003).

Species-rich wetlands are challenging because a few colonizers, native pioneers or native and exotic invasives, tend to establish and dominate sites that begin as disturbed, open areas. Other species will likely be limited by propagule dispersal, growing conditions, or dependencies on other species that are not yet sufficiently abundant (e.g., nurse plants, hosts, overstory species that provide shade, etc.). Wetlands that are species rich, such as fens, are typically low in nutrients, while many restoration sites are nutrient-rich former agricultural lands. Nutrient-poor restoration sites, such as excavations that expose subsoil, are likely to be missing other vital attributes, such as water-retaining organic matter in the soil. Where dispersal constraints limit the arrival of propagules, plantings and introductions can compensate, but costs rise, especially for rare species.

Wetlands that support rare species are not easily restored to full diversity levels (Zedler 1998). If the rare species do become established, they might not persist if their many requirements on- and off-site are lacking. An attempt to reestablish an endangered hemiparasitic annual plant to a San Diego Bay salt marsh restoration site encountered several difficulties. In the first reintroduction site, native pollinators appeared to be limiting, so a larger range of planting sites was chosen (Parsons and Zedler 1997). In later research, exotic annual grasses were shown to interfere with the hemiparasite's need to attach its haustoria onto perennial plants that can supply enough resources for growth to maturity (Fellows and Zedler 2005). In contrast to these constraints on a rare plant, the dominant of the high salt marsh, *Salicornia subterminalis,* was readily reestablished at Tijuana Estuary by transplanting mature plants with their sod (personal observation).

Temporarily inundated or saturated wetlands are challenging because a small error in depth or substrate type or drainage potential can produce a site that is as dry as upland or as wet as a permanently saturated site. Also, it is unclear if species that occupy temporary wetlands do so because of the average moisture conditions or in response to extreme water levels (either maxima or minima). For some animals, it is likely a threshold response—if a vernal pool is wet for two weeks, then some fairy shrimp can complete their life cycle; if it is wet for a shorter period, the population will not persist, and if it is wet for longer period, predators might colonize and consume these large, slow-swimming invertebrates. On average, a two-to-four week inundation period might sustain the species. In other cases, wetness extremes might determine species persistence. For example, a depression dominated by upland plants might become dominated by wetland plants during a series of unusually wet years, during which redox conditions become stressful to all but a subset of the plant community. Once wetland perennials are well established, many would likely persist during subsequent dry years, at least in the lower elevations of the site. The area that is dominated by wetland plants expands and shrinks in response to rising and falling water levels (Kantrud et al. 1989). When Dr. Richard Novitzki (pers. com.) attempted to restore temporary wetlands in Oregon, he was unlucky in trying to do so during a three-year drought. It might take a decade to experience the extremes that would allow establishment of native wetland plants. In this case, the difficulty of providing a naturally occurring type of wetland, instead of a pond, had financial implications as well because the effort was part of a mitigation bank, and the site was required to support obligate wetland species (those that are typically restricted to wetlands), not just facultative species (which also grow in uplands; see Reed 1988; Tiner 1999). Regulators were reluctant to certify the bank because hydrologic conditions (water quantity and quality) were not yet demonstrated by the presence of obligate plants.

Sedge meadows are difficult to restore where there are inadequate groundwater flows. The Wisconsin Department of Transportation attempted to restore sedge meadows in two sites, one with sufficient groundwater discharge and one without. Hydrologists used isotopic analyses to determine where each site received most of its water; one received 74% of the surface water (top 15 cm) and 100% of its subsurface water (15–100 cm depth) from groundwater. The other received none of its surface water and only 22% to 64% of its subsurface supply from groundwater, that is, rainfall supplied most of its water; hence, it was more subject to drought (Hunt 1996). Groundwater-fed wetlands are difficult to restore where today's groundwater supplies differ from historical levels in both quantity and quality. Around Madison, Wisconsin, city wells have lowered groundwater levels, and agricultural activities have added nitrates and other contaminants to the water.

In regions subject to acid rain, soil and water have become acidified, and restoration of alkaline wetlands and their calciphilic vegetation is difficult. In the Netherlands, for example, diverse fens and fen meadows and other valued wetland types are being degraded by acidification and eutrophication (Klotzli and Grootjans 2001). Groundwater drawdown leads to oxidation of peat, which releases nutrients (internal eutrophication). Nutrients also arrive via surface water flows and aerial deposition of nitrogen. Under the altered conditions, grasses become dominant, and sedges and herbs decline (van der Hoek and

Braakhekke 1998). Plugging drainage ditches and stripping turf might counter the effects of groundwater drawdown (van der Koek and Braakhekke 1998), but if the soil is still acidic, calciphiles will be difficult to reintroduce, even following liming (van Duren et al. 1997). Given that many kinds of wetlands are difficult to restore and that even the "easier" wetlands are hard to restore to full diversity and function, there is a clear need for predictive power—the ability to say, with accuracy, what outcomes will result when specific restoration measures are taken in specific places.

HOW THEORY CAN HELP

Although we are still a long way from providing the specific predictions that are needed, a rich body of ecological theory offers much advice for restorationists. Suppose that restoration is proposed for a place with no data on historical species composition or ecosystem function (as in Box 10.1); can we proceed with planning based on ecological principles and restoration experiences elsewhere? I think we can.

The riparian forests along southwestern Mexico's Ayuquila River have been replaced by corn fields, trampled by free-ranging cattle and deprived of their normal wet-season flooding by an upstream dam (Allen 2004). While the subtropical deciduous forests of the region's steep hillsides are still intact, the river floodplains are nearly devoid of natural vegetation. In this setting, Dr. Luis Manuel Martínez began to envision what the valley bottoms might have looked like historically and what they might become if trees could be reintroduced. When a sugar factory caused a molasses spill into the river, damaging the downstream fishery and leading local citizens to demand mitigation, funds became available to initiate restoration work. Dr. Martínez initiated a water-quality monitoring program and suggested that University of Wisconsin (UW) colleagues, myself included, help develop plans for riparian forest restoration. Ecological theory provided guidance in answer several questions (Table 10.2):

1. Which Targets are Appropriate?

Ecosystem theory helps us characterize the attributes of suitable targets, since it is widely recognized that ecosystems are dynamic and open (Pickett and Parker 1994). Thus, the effort to restore Ayuquila River forests should not aim for a static system but one that can change over time in response to chronic shifts in environmental conditions (e.g., climate change) as well as catastrophic events, such as floods. In addition, the target should not be developed in isolation from its dynamic landscape, since ecosystems—and especially riparian ecosystems—are open entities (Pickett and Parker 1994). It follows that information on potential reference sites should come from multiple forest remnants and sites that have large trees that might indicate an ability to persist even under highly altered conditions, such as the reversal of hydroperiods from wet-season flooding to dry-season flooding.

Theory on diversity and function (Loreau et al. 2001) predicts that introducing many species will enhance functioning, but so will the introduction of those species that are known to be "overachievers." Diversity theory was tested recently in an intertidal restoration site, where the marsh-plain species pool consists of 8 halophytes that are readily planted (excluding a parasitic plant). Several colleagues showed that, relative to monotypes and unplanted plots, the planting of 6-species assemblages (vs. 3, 1, or 0) increased canopy complexity (Keer and Zedler 2002), increased biomass above- and belowground, and increased the amount of nitrogen stored by the system (Callaway et al. 2003). In addition, this study documented the importance of one species, *Salicornia virginica*, as having disproportionate influence on productivity; however, the diversity effect was present even where this species was absent (Callaway et al. 2003). Theory was thus supported by the field test—restoration planning needs to consider both species number and composition.

While growing 6 to 8 halophytes for introduction into restoration sites is feasible, much greater effort would be needed to reproduce species-rich communities, such as tropical forests. In considering which species to aim for in restoring riparian forest along the Ayuquila River, Allen's (2004) sample of 60 plots (5 per site, 6,000 m² total) found 77 woody plant species—too many to recommend for immediate reintroduction, especially since propagation methods are unknown. Aiming for restoration sites that are species rich and inclusive of desirable species is thus warranted. Allen (2004) narrowed the field by prioritizing species on the basis of their ability to grow to tree size (i.e., found as trees in reference sites) and on their ethnobotanical value. The latter attribute recognizes the need to use more than ecological theory to predict restoration outcomes; she reasoned that planting species valued by local people would bring more support to the restoration program in the form of volunteers to plant trees and willingness to allow fencing of restoration plots to exclude cattle.

Where ecosystem services other than biodiversity support are critical, such as nutrient removal to improve water quality, it is necessary to consider internal feedbacks that might operate (Suding et al. 2003). For example, a wetland designed to remove nitrogen from corn fields as water flows toward the river would likely change in response to the nutrient influx it was designed to treat. Eutrophication theory predicts that species diversity is not sustainable in nutrient-rich wetlands (Bedford et al. 1999). This is certainly true for agricultural wetlands invaded by reed canary grass (Galatowitsch et al. 1999, 2000; Green and Galatowitsch 2001; Kercher and Zedler 2004). Although productivity is enhanced by nutrient enrichment, plant diversity is not sustainable. Thus, for wetlands, restoration of the nutrient-removal (water-quality-improvement) and biodiversity-support functions are not compatible goals. If species-rich wetlands are the restoration target, then they should be placed upstream of nutrient influxes or downstream of treatment wetlands that can improve water quality (Zedler 2003). It is not yet clear if diverse riparian forests that might be restored along the Ayuquila River would be subject to eutrophic conditions, and if so, whether they would persist or convert to a few aggressive species.

2. Where Should Restoration Begin?

When an entire watershed needs attention, or a complex of former wetlands becomes available for restoration, restoration efforts might need to be prioritized and phased in over time. A geographic information system can be very useful for identifying and comparing

TABLE 10.2   Questions That Arise During the Restoration Process, Associated
Issues, and Relevant Theory

Basic Questions for Restoration Projects	Associated Unknowns and Issues	Relevant Ecological Theory
1. What should the goal be?	Which restoration targets are suitable for the landscape?	1. Theory on dynamic, open nature of ecosystems
	How many and which species should be reintroduced to achieve desired ecosystem functions?	2. Diversity-function theory
	Can one site maximize both biodiversity and ecosystem services?	3. Eutrophication theory
2. Where should restoration begin within the watershed?	Which former wetlands have the fewest constraints? Where is degradation reversible?	4. Theory on reversibility and alternative states
	Should we restore a few large or many small wetlands?	5. Island biogeography theory
3. Can abiotic conditions be alleviated?	What physical conditions would support the most species and functions?	6. Topographic heterogeneity theory
	What physical preparations are needed?	7. Succession theory
	Which microhabitats will support the desired species?	8. Niche theory
4. How should the biota be manipulated?	Which functional groups are needed; which should be introduced and when?	9. Succession theory
	How should we prepare the wetland for desired species?	10. Assembly theory, regeneration niche, interspecific interactions
	Is it feasible to control unwanted invaders?	11. Invasibility and competition theory
	Will the system respond to bottom-up or top-down manipulations?	12. Food web dynamics
	Which propagules should be sought? Does genotype matter?	13. Locally adapted ecotypes, extended phenotypes
5. How should the wetland ecosystem be sustained?	Will the restored system persist?	14. Resilience theory

NOTE: See text and Box 10.5 for predictions from each theory on how the ecosystem will develop.

potentially restorable wetlands. With maps that depict alternatives, strategic planning of wetland restoration projects becomes possible at the landscape scale. In the United States, where hydric soils have been mapped and digitized, one can superimpose the most current wetland inventory and subtract areas that are still wetlands to identify potentially restorable wetlands. One criterion for prioritizing wetland restoration sites is their potential for performing critical landscape functions, such as nutrient removal, discussed earlier.

Additional criteria are suggested by theory on reversibility and alternative states. Suding and associates (2003) focused on the restorability of environmental conditions, the restorability the biota, and internal feedbacks among the biota and the environment that might prevent an altered system from returning to its historical state. Their predictions are relevant to the Ayuquila River example, as the restored forest will need to be able to perpetuate itself under highly altered hydroperiods because upstream dams and withdrawal of water for irrigation are likely to be permanent. Although information is inadequate for predicting the species and assemblages that could best sustain themselves, one can predict that some plantings will fail to grow to reproductive maturity or to recruit offspring under altered conditions. Hence, Allen (2004) used data on current recruitment to prioritize species for reestablishment in restoration sites; those that were present as seedlings and saplings were obviously able to reproduce under altered hydroperiods.

Island biogeography (Simberloff et al. 1999) predicts that large sites are likely to include a wide array of habitats and support many species, through increased dispersal to the site and decreased extirpation once established in the site. A general rule of thumb for a phased project would be to start at a site that has potential to become large and then expand it over time, learning which species and assemblages persist. Still, a few large wetlands will not necessarily replace many small ones, especially when restoring pools that are needed by amphibians (Semlitsch and Bodie 2003) or fens that are characteristic of some hilly landscapes (Bedford and Godwin 2003).

3. Can Abiotic Constraints be Alleviated?

Most wetland restoration projects involve some manipulation of abiotic conditions to achieve goals, but which of many options are most needed? Basic factors, such as water-level regimes and topography, can be manipulated in a thousand ways, but we rarely know exactly which features are critical to the desired ecosystem state. Theory on topographic heterogeneity (allowing habitat segregation; Larkin et al. 2006), succession (the progression of changes on newly exposed and disturbed sites), and niches (including safe sites for seed germination) can help guide the initial manipulations of restoration sites. In restoring sedge meadows, for example (Figs. 10.5, 10.6), one might sculpt the surface to create mounds and depressions and introduce sediments, organic matter, and nutrients to accelerate soil formation, thus creating environmental gradients so that desired species can find suitable conditions somewhere within the site.

The restoration of floodplain forest along the Ayuquila River offers an opportunity to test the need for varied topography and soil amendments as well as to identify the

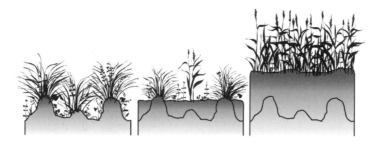

FIGURE 10.5

Tussock sedge meadows fill in with sediments and create opportunities for reed canary grass to invade and form monotypes. From Werner and Zedler (2002), with permission from Taylor & Francis Inc.

FIGURE 10.6

Michelle Peach (UW–Madison, pers. com.) attempted to reproduce tussocks by creating mounds; however, the dry summer led tops to become dominated by cottonwood seedlings, while cattails filled in the bottoms, which were at the level of groundwater. Photo by M. Peach.

regeneration niche of each tree species. Planting experiments could vary many alternatives, and since the project is being guided by faculty at the University of Guadalajara–Autlán, the experiments could be monitored by students who want research experience.

4. How Can the Biota be Manipulated?

Species can be enticed, introduced, or controlled. Plants, animals, and microorganisms can be manipulated to guide the wetland along a desired pathway and to accelerate the

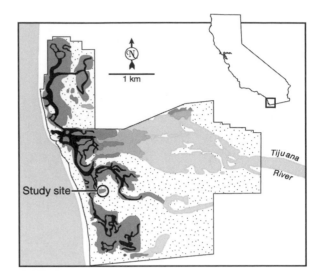

FIGURE 10.7

Tijuana Estuary's Model Marsh resisted both natural succession and efforts to assist revegetation. Hypersaline soil surfaces developed during low tides, and sediments accreted on seedling transplants during floods.

development process, but ecological communities are too complex to imagine exactly how to achieve a specific composition. Predictions from succession (Parker 1997) and assembly theory (Keddy 1999) should be helpful. For example, a large excavated tidal marsh in Tijuana Estuary (Fig. 10.7) immediately became hypersaline and laden with floodborne sediments; even the most broadly tolerant species, perennial pickleweed *(Salicornia virginica)*, could not establish itself in the first three years (Zedler et al. 2003). An understanding of the desired species' regeneration niches (Grubb 1977) became essential, and experimentation with organic matter addition (Trnka and Zedler 2000), plant spacing (based on ideas of MacMahon 1998), and topographic heterogeneity demonstrated the value of adding organic matter as kelp compost (O'Brien and Zedler, in press). On the marsh plain, kelp compost significantly increased soil organic matter (by 17% at 0–5-cm depth), total Kjeldahl nitrogen (by 45% at 5–8 cm), and inorganic nitrogen (by 35% at 5–8 cm), and decreased surface bulk density (by 16% at 0–5 cm) over control plots; transplant survivorship and growth improved as a consequence. In cordgrass plots, *Spartina foliosa* plants grew 11 centimeters taller and 47% denser than in controls (O'Brien and Zedler, in press). Planting marsh plain halophytes in tight clusters also improved transplant survivorship (by 18%) but not growth. Surprisingly, tidal creek networks increased the survivorship of only two of the five halophytes that were transplanted onto the marsh plain. The adaptive approach allowed us to learn how to accelerate revegetation during the restoration process.

Mycorrhizae appear to be widespread in wetlands, although the functions they carry out for upland plants (assistance with phosphorus uptake) are not likely to be as important in landscape sinks. Cooke and Lefor (1998) found mycorrhizae on all 89 species they investigated in freshwater wetlands of Connecticut. Bauer and associates (2003b) found mycorrhizae on many species and in various hydrologic conditions of three freshwater marshes in Indiana. Likewise, Turner and Friese (1998) and Turner and colleagues (2000) found mycorrhizae associated with several plant species in Ohio fens. In monotypic stands of white cedar *(Chamaecyparis thyoides)* swamps of New Jersey, Cantelmo and Ehrenfeld (1999) found mycorrhizae to be more abundant on the tops of hummocks than in the more anaerobic bases. The functional role of mycorrhizae in freshwater wetlands needs to be determined (Turner and Friese 1998; Bauer et al. 2003b). Although upland restoration projects (especially prairies) often involve additions of mycorrhizae, there is not yet a rationale for doing so in wetlands.

Species' establishment requirements will be uncertain in many wetlands, and experimental manipulations will be needed to learn while planting restoration sites. Allen (2004) selected 15 species for early reestablishment based on their potential utility to local people and their potential to establish under the river's much-altered hydroperiod. Thus, a small subset of the species pool (77 woody species) was suggested as a starting point. Restoration planners can now design experiments to test alternative soil preparation, species assemblages, plant spacing, and the like.

Species differ greatly in their establishment requirements (cf. Middleton 1999, Appendix 2, which gives germination requirements for hundreds of species). Some plants require open land (e.g., willows), while others will only establish under nurse plants or following the establishment of matrix-forming dominants (such as tussock sedges). For British grasslands, Pywell and colleagues (2003) were able to characterize the performance of 58 species in restoration experiments. Grasses outperformed forbs (as in a Wisconsin wetland restoration experiment; Veltman 2002). Of the 38 traits that Pywell and colleagues compared, those that conferred "restorability" were colonization ability, ruderality, germination rate, and autumn germination for year-1 establishment, while traits that conferred persistence were competitive ability, vegetative growth, and viable seed banks. Their advice for retaining higher species richness was to work in areas with low-fertility soil, then add more species several years after restoration, and to lower soil fertility. In landscape sinks, however, it is difficult to prevent soils from becoming eutrophic.

Genotype also matters, at least in salt marsh restoration, where it has been tested and evaluated in detail (Seliskar et al. 2002). In 1989, a 0.2-hectare tidal marsh plain was excavated near the University of Delaware–Lewes. Seliskar and colleagues planted replicate patches of smooth cordgrass, *Spartina alterniflora,* from Delaware, Massachusetts, and Georgia. Five years later, the patches differed significantly in above- and belowground biomass, root and rhizome distribution, height, density, and carbohydrate reserves (Seliskar et al. 2002). Furthermore, ecosystem attributes (edaphic respiration and chlorophyll concentration, plus larval fish abundance in pit traps) differed between patches. In salt marshes and other ecosystems, "extended phenotypes" operate; the entire community of organisms is influenced by the matrix species' genotype (Whitham et al. 2003).

Invasive species cause substantial problems in wetland restoration sites and will need attention repeatedly (D'Antonio and Meyerson 2002; Zedler and Kercher 2004). Of the

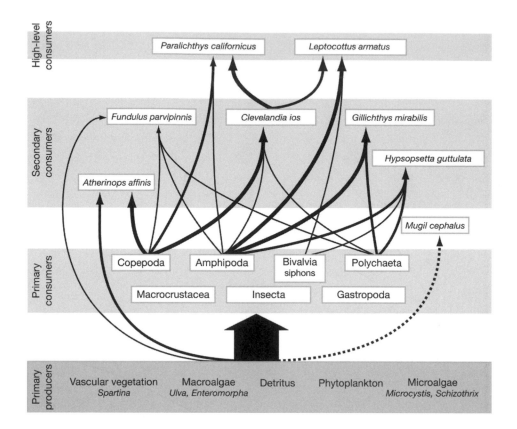

High-level consumers

Secondary consumers

Primary consumers

Primary producers

Paralichthys californicus

Leptocottus armatus

Fundulus parvipinnis

Clevelandia ios

Gillichthys mirabilis

Hypsopsetta guttulata

Atherinops affinis

Mugil cephalus

Copepoda

Amphipoda

Bivalvia siphons

Polychaeta

Macrocrustacea

Insecta

Gastropoda

Vascular vegetation
Spartina

Macroalgae
Ulva, Enteromorpha

Detritus

Phytoplankton

Microalgae
Microcystis, Schizothrix

FIGURE 10.8

Wetland food webs are typically complex and difficult to describe; this one developed from stable isotope studies followed by analysis of fish gut contents. From West and associates (2003), with permission from Springer Science and Business Media. Kluwer Academic Publishers, *Env. Biol. Fishes* 67:297–309, figure 7).

thirty-three plant species considered most invasive on a global scale, eight are wetland species: *Arundo donax, Polygonum cuspidatum (= Fallopia japonica = Reynoutria japonica), Lythrum salicaria, Melaleuca quinquenervia, Mimosa pigra, Schinus terebinthifolius, Spartina anglica,* and *Tamarix ramosissima* (GISD 2004). Most of these species were deliberately introduced, not knowing that they would later become invasive.

Ideally, invasions by exotic or overly aggressive species will be prevented initially by planting cover crops that rapidly usurp light and root space, but when invaders establish, rapid responses will be needed, involving herbicides or hand removal or other means. Such work can benefit from the predictions of invasibility theory. Where resource availability exceeds uptake, exotic species can invade most easily (Davis et al. 2000), and restoration sites are notably invasible due to disturbances that create canopy gaps (enhancing light), release nutrients, and provide water. The greatest problem in Wisconsin wetlands and wetland restoration sites is the invasion of reed canary grass, and there is no sure cure. Current research concerns a comprehensive approach, using herbicides

BOX 10.5 PRINCIPLES THAT FOLLOW FROM THEORY AND TESTS IN RESTORATION SETTINGS

NOTE: From Zedler (2005).

SUITABLE TARGETS

Target ecosystems are dynamic and open, rather than static and closed.

Suitable reference data should come from multiple sites and long time periods that include modal and extreme conditions.

DIVERSITY-FUNCTION

Establishing species-rich assemblages should speed ecosystem development and shorten restoration time.

Introducing "high-performing species" should accelerate the development of functions such as productivity.

EUTROPHICATION

Nutrient influxes to wetlands reduce plant species richness while increasing productivity; hence, biodiversity and high productivity are not necessarily compatible goals.

Restoration of wetlands in strategic landscape positions can improve conditions downstream.

Topsoil removal can reverse nutrient loading.

REVERSIBILITY OF DEGRADATION

Simply removing the stress that caused degradation might not suffice to recover the ecosystem.

Increased effort will not necessarily reverse degradation.

Recovery is severely constrained where the stress can not be removed.

ISLAND BIOGEOGRAPHY

Large restoration sites should attract and sustain more species.

Restoring many small sites has validity for some ecosystems.

Restoration sites that are near existing habitat blocks should attract and sustain more species than isolated sites.

NICHE

The restoration of fully functional ecosystems requires the manipulation of sites to include the variety of habitats that comprise desired species' niches.

(Continued)

BOX 10.5 (CONTINUED)

SUCCESSION

More degraded sites require more site preparation.

Potential early dominants of a restoration site should be predictable from key attributes of species in the regional pool, while actual establishment might be limited by site conditions at the time of species' introductions.

Some early dominants can persist indefinitely.

Succession can be jump-started by introducing woody plants.

Animal activities influence restoration, especially via dispersal.

Slowing or reversing succession requires considerable effort and continual stewardship.

TOPOGRAPHIC HETEROGENEITY

The addition of topographic heterogeneity to a restoration site should enhance both species richness and functional diversity.

ASSEMBLY FACILITATION COMPETITION

Conditions that support mature plants can differ substantially from those that stimulate germination and establishment (the regeneration niche)

Plants benefit from facilitators in stressful restoration sites.

Tipping the competitive balance toward desired species and away from opportunists is challenging.

INVASIBILITY

Invasive species are a significant threat to the restoration of native vegetation.

FOOD WEB DYNAMICS

Both bottom-up and top-down controls can influence restoration progress.

EXTENDED PHENOTYPES

Locally adapted genotypes are suitable for mildly degraded sites; while highly degraded sites might require alternative genotypes of key species—or novel combinations of more tolerant species.

RESILIENCE

Ecosystems that naturally experience environmental extremes should have high resilience.

Restored vegetation gains resilience when multiple, broadly tolerant species and multiple functional groups are present.

specific to grasses, planting of grass-free seed mixes, long-term maintenance with spot herbicide treatment until the invader has dropped to a few small patches, then reintroduction of native grasses (M. Healy and J. Zedler, UW, work in progress).

An understanding of food webs can also be key to wetland restoration, since one needs to know if it is sufficient to introduce nutrients to enhance plant growth (a type of "bottom-up control") or if species at the top of the food chain should be manipulated ("top-down controls"). In the latter case, predictions might follow from trophic cascades (a predator reduces the abundance of its prey and thereby increases the abundance of the prey's prey) or size-selective predation (the food species of the preferred size of prey would increase (Fig. 10.8). Rarely do we know how food webs function in restoration sites, although a few studies compare food sources of various trophic levels in restored and natural wetlands using stable isotopes (Rothe and Gleixner 2004).

5. How Might the Wetland Ecosystem Be Sustained?

All restoration sites need some maintenance in response to invasive species, disturbances, pulsed events, and climate change. Hence, restorationists need some idea of how well the wetland will resist change or recover following change. Resilience theory predicts that an ecosystem will recover when both external properties (e.g., dispersal, migration) and internal traits (e.g., seed banks, resprouting capability) allow. For example, bald cypress (*Taxodium distichum*) forests in southern Illinois require flooding for seed dispersal and drawdowns for seed germination (Middleton 1999). Remnant riparian forests along the Ayuquila River are subject to flooding (Allen 2004), but the resilience of the vegetation to artificial flood regimes (inundation and debris deposition outside the rainy season) is yet to be explored. Without sufficient background information, restorationists will need to extrapolate from reference systems that are known to withstand flooding in order to predict the species and assemblages that will be resilient.

GENERAL PREDICTABILITY

While ecological theory can not yet provide specific predictions of how to restore wetlands, several principles are offered as general guidance (Box 10.5; Zedler 2000).

COMBINING THEORY TO DESIGN MULTIFUNCTIONAL WETLANDS

Wetlands are valued for their many ecosystem services, but there is considerable debate over the degree to which restored wetlands provide those functions (NRC 2001). To design wetlands with multiple services well, theory suggests that several features are required. First, to sustain multispecies assemblages of microorganisms, plants, and animals, the wetland should have high habitat and topographic heterogeneity (Cantelmo and Ehrenfeld 1999; Larkin et al., 2006). To slow water flows, the wetland should have features that increase friction and trap water in depressions, and have organic soils to absorb water and pervious substrate to allow infiltration. When shallow pockets of standing water warm up, more rapid growth of microorganisms would use up the dissolved oxygen, and the resulting anoxic conditions should facilitate nitrogen removal through bacterially mediated denitrification (conversion of nitrate to harmless N_2 gas). And to improve water quality, the wetland should have relatively deep depressions for sediments to settle out and trap phosphorus that is adsorbed onto soil particles. Theoretically, the ability to sustain multiple functions would have its basis in high topographic variability, but sedimentation would tend to flatten the topography. If a biological process could sustain topographic variability, this problem would be solved. An ecosystem engineer (Jones et al. 1994) is called for.

Is there a reference wetland with the mentioned qualities? The Upper Midwest's sedge meadows might be such a system. The dominant sedge, *Carex stricta,* builds tussocks that allow the plant to keep its growing points above shallow water while creating a variety of microsites for other plants, arthropods, small mammals, and microorganisms (Fig. 10.5). A tussock meadow might support 10 to 11 plant species per 30-centimeter-tall tussock (Werner and Zedler 2002) and 60 or more per site (in 30 1-m^2 plots; Kercher and Zedler 2004). Regrettably, few tussock meadows remain. Those that escaped cultivation have borne the brunt of runoff from adjacent fields. Obliterated by sediments, the smooth, bare land surface attracts weeds. When enriched with nutrients, the invasive plants spread across the meadows, leaving few other species in their tracks (Fig. 10.5).

If there is an "ideal multifunctional wetland," it would probably not be sustainable in today's overused watersheds. Excess flooding and nutrients would degrade the wetland and reduce biodiversity. Hence, planners need to consider options in seeking to restore wetland functions where hydrologic conditions are substantially modified. At least three alternatives are available. (1) Seek the best landscape positions for restoring fully functional ecosystems, employing a broad-based landscape strategy. (2) Identify and repair the problems upstream in order to enhance chances of fulfilling restoration objectives downstream. (3) Identify the constraints of an impaired watershed and aim for a target that is appropriate for current conditions, as in Box 10.1.

RESTORING FUNCTIONS AT THE WATERSHED SCALE

A landscape perspective is critical to restoration (Aronson and Le Floc'h 1996). Because wetlands are "landscape sinks," their restoration is subject to constraints and opportunities imposed by current land uses within the upstream portion of the watershed. A wetland in a watershed that is mostly agricultural, and where former wetlands have been tiled and ditched, will probably receive water, sediments, nutrients, and contaminants in excess of historical (predrainage) levels. A watershed strategy might begin by restoring key upstream wetlands to improve wetlands farther downstream. The aim to restore all three wetland functions (biodiversity support, water-quality improvement, and flood abatement) in the watershed could involve different types of wetlands, each in an appropriate position (Fig. 10.9).

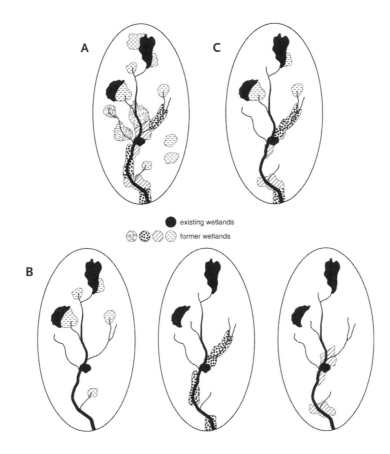

FIGURE 10.9

A watershed plan for the strategic placement of wetland restoration projects would likely require restoration of different types of ecosystems to achieve three major wetland services, namely, biodiversity support (A), water-quality improvement (B), and flood abatement (C). Redrawn from Zedler (2003) by Kandis Elliot.

Locating Wetlands to Restore Biodiversity

Wisconsin's Department of Natural Resources began this process for the Milwaukee River Basin (Fig. 10.10; WDNR 2002). First, the potentially restorable wetlands were defined as areas with hydric soil that are not now wetland. These formed the first GIS (geographic information system) layer. Next, existing habitats were mapped from open-space categories (grassland, forest, etc.) in the Wisconsin Land Use GIS. Finally, conditions surrounding each potentially restorable wetland (a neighborhood analysis) were examined to determine the percent increase in combined habitat area that would occur if it a wetland adjacent to an existing habitat area were restored. An additional GIS layer mapped the potentially restorable wetlands that could increase habitat size the most, for example, greater than 50% increase in habitat block area. This innovative approach led to a series of user-friendly maps that should be of great use to landscape restoration planners. Using one criterion—the potential to increase the area of existing habitat blocks—might not maximize potential to

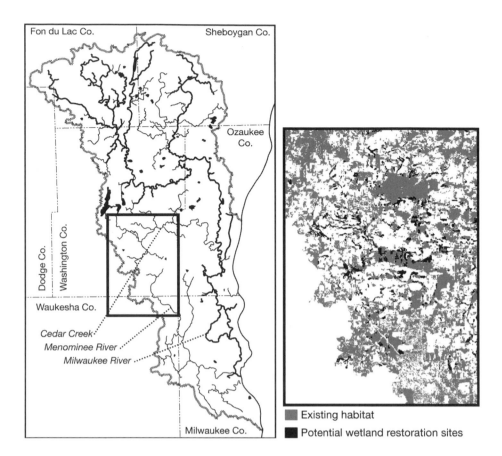

Existing habitat

Potential wetland restoration sites

FIGURE 10.10

The Milwaukee River Basin is the focus of planning efforts, wherein the potentially restorable wetlands can be prioritized for their ability to create large habitat blocks. From WDNR (2002).

support biodiversity, however. Once a map shows the potentially restorable wetlands that can most increase the area of habitat blocks, biologists can consider which habitat blocks might have features that are suitable for desired species. For example, in Minnesota's riparian wetlands, fish and amphibians need open water of large and small area, respectively, while birds correlate more strongly with forest and wetland area (Mensing et al. 1998).

Locating Wetlands to Improve Water Quality

A second innovative approach to the strategic location of wetland restoration projects within landscapes has been undertaken by Crumpton (2001) for a large watershed in Iowa, where over 80% of historical wetlands have been drained for agriculture (Dahl 1990), and where notable quantities of nitrate are discharged to the Mississippi River. In order to curb nitrate discharges, the Natural Resources Conservation Service developed a Conservation Enhancement Reserve Program (CREP) that drew on a series of scientific studies of how best to trap nitrates using restored wetlands. Crumpton played multiple roles

in developing the science through experimentation with mesocosms to determine optimal wetland attributes (water depth, nitrate concentrations in inflowing water, loading
rates, and residence time) for maximum denitrification and by using simulation models
to determine the landscape position where a wetland would remove the most nitrate. The
result was a prescription for locating wetland restoration projects and for designing the
wetland so that size and water depth were optimal (Box 10.6). These prescriptions transferred directly to selection criteria for applications made by landowners who wish to en-
roll their drained wetlands into the CREP. At a much larger scale, Mitsch and associates
(2001) calculated that nitrogen loadings to the Gulf of Mexico could be abated by restoring 2.0 to 5.3 million hectares of wetland and 7.7 to 19.4 million hectares of bottomland
hardwood forest within the 300-million-hectare Mississippi River Basin.

Locating Wetlands to Abate Flooding
In a third approach, McAllister and associates (2000) developed a flood attenuation index, which allowed them to suggest restoration priorities among 119 landscape subunits
within a 274,540 km² portion of the U.S. prairie pothole region. Similarly, Richardson
and Gatti (1999) ranked the need to restore subunits of a southern Wisconsin landscape
by calculating the potential of drained wetland basins to trap sediments, if the basins were
restored.

Various recommendations have been developed for placing wetlands in locations
that will abate flooding. Following the catastrophic flooding of the Mississippi River,
Hey and Philippi (1995) calculated that flooding would be abated in the Upper

Mississippi River by restoring 5.3 million hectares of wetlands in the basin. Later, Hey and colleagues (2002) identified six optimal sites for water-storage wetlands that would reduce flooding in the Upper Mississippi Basin. Their recommendation is to allow wetlands to drain until just before peak flood flow. Then, using water-control structures, outflows would be plugged and water retained in large wetland systems upstream of the Mississippi River. In some cases, levees might need to be constructed to provide the necessary water-storage capacity, but the authors' models indicate that wetlands in key landscape positions can be used to abate flooding, as defined by reducing peak water depth.

The mentioned examples suggest ways to locate wetland restoration projects within large landscapes for individual purposes; however, none offers a strategy for positioning wetland restoration projects to serve *multiple* purposes. One study, however, employed all three functions in a landscape strategy for protecting existing wetlands, rather than restoring former wetlands. Cedfeldt and colleagues (2000) rated wetlands by type, location, and perceived function in order to select a subset of wetlands (out of >1,000) as having high priority for conservation. It would be feasible to adopt a similar approach for prioritizing former wetlands that should be restored in order to regain all lost functions within watersheds.

A landscape strategy for wetland restoration would aim to sustain all major functions of wetlands within watersheds. It would also aim to retain some semblance of the wetland profile that once occurred, such that historical types of ecosystems would be represented in approximately the same proportions. The princess in Box 10.1 did not address questions such as, is this the best place to test plantings of different species, and is this the region's most serious erosion problem? Like many restoration projects, her planning began where there was an opportunity to restore a degraded place. In larger programs, such as Farm Bill initiatives and public funding, regional planning becomes essential. The larger the program and the more widely distributed the restoration work, the more important it is to coordinate site selection with larger restoration goals. In the next decade, I expect the strategic placement of restoration projects within watersheds to move from the realm of modeling into practice. To do so will require additional research (Box 10.7).

SITE-BASED TACTICS

While a landscape strategy is critical for efficient recovery of all wetland services within watersheds, it is not prudent to wait for such strategies before undertaking restoration of sites where landowners and land stewards are motivated to begin work. Even if a restored wetland can not achieve its full potential, as will be the case where the water supply is low-quality runoff or nutrient-rich groundwater, restoration can proceed, and restorationists can learn how to maximize gains under various constraints.

The hydrologic conditions, soil, topography, vegetation, fauna, and microbial communities of a degraded wetland might all need to be manipulated to achieve a planned outcome.

Following are examples of actions that can be employed, with testing alternatives that assess cause-effect patterns within an adaptive restoration framework being the preferred option.

RESTORING HYDROLOGIC CONDITIONS

Nothing is more basic to a wetland ecosystem than its hydrologic conditions (Poff et al. 1997; Keddy 1999, 2000; Mitsch and Gosselink 2000). Most wetlands have experienced some form of hydrologic alteration (Box 10.8).

The catchall term *hydrologic conditions* includes hydroperiod (inundation regime), flow rates, water volumes, and water quality. Because each of these factors is variable with time, and because "natural" conditions are poorly described, it is difficult to specify a single condition that would constitute "restoration." Restorationists typically aim for one or two key attributes of the hydrologic conditions that characterize a specific wetland type (cf. Amon et al. 2002), such as a high water in spring and a summer drawdown for a midwestern sedge meadow, or continuous flooding for an emergent marsh.

Eertman and associates (2002) report that tidal flow was the "engine" for restoration of a salt marsh following the accidental breaching of a dike that was built to provide arable land. Given access to tidal flows, the agricultural fields were quickly converted to mudflat, which then became vegetated with halophytes, colonized by mudflat macrofauna, and utilized by waterbirds. Although tidal restoration was not planned, researchers capitalized on the event and learned that tidal flows continued to cause

BOX 10.8 HYDROLOGIC DEGRADATION AND RESTORATION

Hydrologic conditions have been greatly altered and must undergo various corrections to restore wetlands. Hydrologic degradation has been caused by

Drainage for agriculture, mosquito abatement, or urban development

Reduced hydroperiod due to dams, culverts, levees, locks, and dikes

Prolonged hydroperiod through reservoir discharge, impoundment

Salinity changes, either lowered or increased

Shift in water source, usually via groundwater decline and surface water increase

Change in timing of hydroperiod (often due to diversions from reservoirs)

Sedimentation that raises topography relative to the water table

Restoration of hydrologic conditions involves

Flood releases from reservoirs

Removal of structures

Construction of new structures

Dredging to change elevation and/or improve water flow

---

geomorphological changes over a ten-year period. Likewise, Warren and colleagues (2002) found that differences in tidal flooding explained slow-to-fast rates of salt marsh recovery in Connecticut.

Galatowitsch and van der Valk (1996a) evaluated hydrologic conditions in 62 prairie potholes that had been drained for agricultural use and then restored; approximately 60% were as wet or wetter than planned; 20% were considered hydrologic failures. Experience at the Kankakee wetlands in Indiana shows that restoring hydrologic conditions is complicated, especially where groundwater is important to the water budget (Bledsoe and Shear 2000; Sidle et al. 2000).

In a Lake Erie wetland, Wilcox and Whillans (1999) describe how the loss of a barrier beach and increased hydroperiod were overcome by installing a dike with a water-control structure. Artificially lowering water levels allowed the marsh to regenerate from the seed bank in one growing season. While the use of engineered structures, which require maintenance in perpetuity, is not highly recommended (NRC 2001), they are often essential in highly modified landscapes. For example, the Nature Conservancy's "Emiquon" project aims to convert a 3000-hectare corn field along the Illinois River to wetland. The site is ditched to allow drainage and separated from the river by a major levee. Pumps are used to move water collected by the drainage ditches into the adjacent river. However, the river level is managed by the U.S. Army Corps of Engineers without regard for wetland restoration needs. Hence, water levels are higher than historically, and simply breaching the levee would fill the restoration site with deep water. Unless the entire river were restored to its historical hydroperiod, the levee must remain in place, and water-level control, including pumping, will likely be needed.

For riverine wetlands, restoring flood flows is not simply a matter of reintroducing water, but at the right time, for the right duration, and with the right degree of force (Middleton 1999). A highly publicized flood restoration in Arizona's Grand Canyon occurred as an experiment in 1996, but the single, moderate-intensity flood pulse did not replicate the frequency or magnitude of natural events (Stevens et al. 2001).

Along the Kissimmee River, a long-duration flood pulse is needed to restore hydrologic conditions to some of the 16,000 hectares of floodplain wetlands that were cut off from their water supply following channelization (Toth et al. 2002). In this well-known Florida case, a 9-meter deep, 75-meter-wide channel replaced the natural river meander, purportedly to control flooding. Prior to channelization, the broad floodplain was inundated 25% to 50% of the time, thereby supporting willows *(Salix caroliniana)*, buttonbush *(Cephalanthus occidentalis)*, and emergent herbaceous vegetation. Fishes found refuge among the vegetation, and an abundance of birds made use of the heterogeneous habitats, especially those that formed as the waters receded and concentrated fish and invertebrates in drying pools (Toth et al. 2002). The channel failed to control flooding of adjacent lands, and it destroyed wetlands and habitat for many species of wildlife. Restoration of the river's prolonged hydroperiod involves complex hydrologic modeling and coordination of multiple stakeholders up and down the river. The first phase of restoration, involving removal of water-control structures, was completed in 2001, and 24 kilometers of river were reconnected (Whalen et al. 2002).

RESTORING SOIL

Wetland soils develop where water or saturated conditions occur, and they carry out a host of processes that are critical to wetlands, many of which are beneficial to society. For example, the ability of soil particles to trap phosphorus helps wetlands cleanse throughflowing water, thereby improving the quality of groundwater that is used for drinking or recreation. Carol Johnston developed a long list of functions for the NRC (2001; Box 10.9).

The presence of water wholly transforms soil structure and function (cf. Richardson and Veprasek 2001). When water moves into soil, the ability of oxygen to diffuse into the soil drops precipitously because oxygen is 1/10,000th as soluble in water as in air. In addition, microorganisms increase their activity with moisture, especially where organic matter collects, as it does in "landscape sinks" (Figs. 10.2, 10.11). Low diffusion and high use of oxygen rapidly produces anoxic conditions, under which hydric soils develop. With anoxia, organic matter accumulates because microbial decomposition is slower (less efficient) than in aerobic soils. With anoxia, sulfur becomes reduced to hydrogen sulfur, emitting the characteristic rotten egg smell, and decomposition of carbon-containing

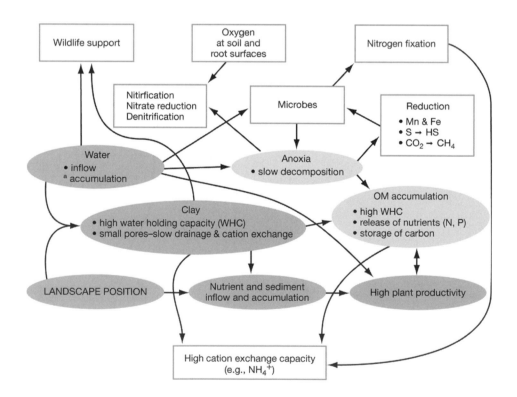

FIGURE 10.11

The fact that wetlands form in landscape sinks differentiates their soils from uplands and leads to specific soil chemistry. Nutrient removal functions derive from anaerobic conditions.

compounds leads to the formation of methane with its marsh-gas smell. Also, and critically important for society, a variety of bacteria reduce nitrates (that contaminate drinking water) to harmless nitrogen gas. Phosphorus can become more soluble under anoxic conditions, depending on the soil pH and redox potential.

The drainage of water also transforms the structure and functioning of the wetland. Many marshes have been diked and drained in order to use the land for pasture or crop production. Drainage aerates the soil, increases decomposition, and allows sediments to compact and subside. In drained salt marsh soils, the high sulfur content leads to additional problems. Acid sulfate soils develop when pyrite (FeS_2) becomes oxidized. Soil pH drops to levels that are toxic to both plants and animals. Under drained conditions, nitrogen and phosphorus are stored in precipitates with iron and aluminum, and ammonium is protected from bacterial nitrification, so nitrates do not form or leach away. Portnoy and Giblin (1997) recognized many unknowns in the proposed restoration of tidal flows to diked wetlands and proceeded to test the effect of adding seawater. They hypothesized that the buffering capacity of seawater would raise pH, that ammonium and phosphorus would be mobilized, and that toxic sulfides would not develop, due to precipitation of sulfur by abundant iron. Their microcosm experiment (using 15-cm-diameter cores, rewetted in the greenhouse) supported all hypotheses, with increased pH, increased nitrogen, and phosphorus mineralization, and no concern about sulfide toxicity.

The degree to which wetland soils can be degraded is illustrated by events during and following wetland drainage. In Israel's Hula Valley, an extensive drainage ditch network designed to augment agricultural land had multiple impacts on the site and waters downstream (Hambright and Zohary 1999; Box 10.10). These problems did not exist when the 45- to 75-km^2 area had saturated soils and supported a shallow lake and papyrus swamps rich with wildlife. Can the critical wetland services (dust control, water storage, nutrient retention) be restored?

Restoration of historical water regimes would rapidly reverse some patterns (e.g., peat would no longer produce dust), but not others (subsided lands would remain lower than predrainage). Some effects of water on soil are quick; some are delayed, and many are long lasting. Upland soils that become inundated become anoxic within hours to days; peat forms over decades to centuries, and once formed, hydric soils persist indefinitely. The soils of former wetlands leave their marks on the landscape long after ditching and drainage dry out sites and eliminate wetland biota.

Soil chemistry (pH, nutrient levels, mineral composition) is critical to plant growth, and restored wetlands will not necessarily match the conditions in reference sites; furthermore, scales of sampling chemical profiles might affect the determination of equivalency between restored and natural wetlands (Hunt et al. 1997, 1999). Handa and Jefferies (2000) tested nutrient additions, peat mulch and nutrients plus mulch, in Hudson Bay revegetation trials where Lesser Snow Geese had eliminated all plants and caused soils to compact and become hypersaline. Reestablishment of *Puccinellia phyrganoides* plugs was enhanced where soils were improved and geese were fenced out of the research plots (Handa and Jefferies 2000).

Some wetland restoration sites lack soil (e.g., gravel pits) or have soil that has been degraded through land filling (adding contaminants, concrete, broken glass, etc.), peat oxidation (from aeration or fires), eutrophication, or salinization (Whisenant 1999). Soil amendments can be useful in changing the nutrient status (by adding a source of carbon to tie up nitrogen; adding fertilizers to supply missing nutrients) or organic content to improve moisture conditions. Kelp compost works well in restoring vegetation to hypersaline soils of tidal marshes, although reasons are poorly understood (Callaway 2001; O'Brien and Zedler, in press). At the opposite extreme, soils that are artificially rich in nutrients might require removal to restore native vegetation. For example, rock-plowed soils in the Everglades are artificially rich in nutrients; removal of the entire surface soil facilitates regrowth of native wet prairie species (Dalrymple et al. 2003).

RESTORING TOPOGRAPHY

Elevation and topographic heterogeneity are key attributes that determine the frequency, depth, and duration of inundation. On gradual slopes, a difference in elevation as small as 10 centimeters can shift vegetation from one assemblage to another (Zedler et al. 1999; Bledsoe and Shear 2000). In undulating topography, even slight depressions can impound water long enough to eliminate vegetation or ensure its growth, depending on the rainfall and flooding regimes. Restoring sites to their historical elevations and topographic variability thus requires a high degree of precision if the restoration target is exacting.

In Louisiana, a state with over 3.5 million hectares of wetlands, coastal marshes are subsiding at alarming rates, following river diversions, construction of canals, and accelerated rates of sea level rise (Turner 1997, 2001). With deeper inundation, vegetation dies, and valuable shellfish and finfish habitats are lost. One method of countering marsh loss is terracing, in which sediments are formed into ridges that are arranged to reduce the distance over which wind can move water (fetch). With less fetch, there is less erosion. Once in place, terraces are transplanted for stabilization and sediment trapping (Rozas and Minello 2001). Another method is to trap sediments using discarded Christmas trees, also employed in Great Lakes wetland restoration (Wilcox and Whillans 1999). The boldest approach is to redivert flows from the Mississippi River across subsiding marshlands. This involves installing costly water-control structures in the existing levee system. DeLaune and associates (2003) assessed the effects of the 1991 Caernarvon diversion and found substantial accretion in Breton Sound estuary, concluding that subsidence can be slowed or even reversed by river diversion.

Variable topography can enhance species richness and ecosystem functions (Larkin et al., 2006). Ecosystem engineers, such as tussock sedges and hummock-forming cedars, can be reintroduced to appropriate restoration sites to provide a variety of microsites for microorganisms, other plants, and many arthropods and small mammals; however, the results will not be instantaneous. Methods for accelerating the development of tussocks, hummocks, depressions, and the like are needed. In some cases, it might be as simple as leaving a wetland construction site unsmoothed.

In many places, the presence of shallow depressions of different depth and size affords migratory birds a dependable source of food over a prolonged period of time. In the upper midwestern United States, the shallowest potholes thaw first and produce invertebrates early in the spring when the earliest migrating ducks need resting and feeding stopovers en route to their nesting grounds farther north. On the Kissimmee River floodplain, fish and invertebrates are concentrated first in shallow pools and then in deeper pools as floodwaters recede; birds are quick to take advantage of concentrated foods (Toth et al. 2002; Fig. 10.12). As discussed earlier, it is possible that topographic heterogeneity is likely a key to wetland multifunctionality; high surface area and varied microsites of mounds and ridges support high biodiversity.

RESTORING VEGETATION

Plants form the matrix of a wetland, fuel the food web, stabilize and aerate wetland soil, create nesting habitat, and make wetlands esthetically pleasing. A few natural wetlands lack vascular plants (e.g., saline mudflats, hot springs), most support at least a few species, and a few are refuges for dozens to hundreds of plant species (e.g., fens;

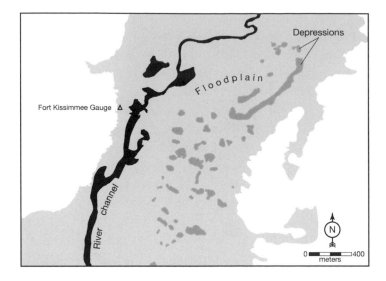

FIGURE 10.12

Toth and associates (2002) depict the Kissimmee River floodplain as a topographically heterogeneous landscape with depressions that retain water after floodwaters subside. Redrawn by Kandis Elliot.

Bedford et al. 1999). Restoring water to former prairie potholes has not produced the full complement of wetland species, as many species are poorly dispersed and unable to establish (Galatowitsch and van der Valk 1996b; Middleton 1999; Seabloom and van der Valk 2003).

Seed bank analyses, which are typically conducted under a limited suite of temperature, light, and moisture conditions, are useful in comparing restored and natural wetlands (Galatowitsch and van der Valk 1996b), although they do not always indicate what will actually grow in a restored wetland (Brown 1998). Seeds can accumulate at restoration sites via wind, water, and animal dispersal, and it is prudent to check seed banks before spending large sums on plantings. For example, it is unnecessary to plant *Salicornia virginica* to southern California salt marshes, if seed sources are nearby—this species establishes readily in tidal systems, and plants develop at appropriate elevations (pers. obs.); however, all the other native species need to be introduced to ensure their widespread establishment (Lindig-Cisneros and Zedler 2002b).

In some cases, seed banks are dominated by weedy species, such as clonal grasses or long-lived trees; hence, it is prudent to allow germination, apply control measures, and then plant natives. At the University of Wisconsin Arboretum, we herbicided *Phalaris arundinacea* twice to remove adult and regenerating sprouts and seedlings, then burned to remove the dead thatch before sowing seed. Native plants dominated in year one, but *P. arundinacea* resumed dominance in year two (J. Wilcox 2004, see below).

Plantings can follow many protocols, such as sowing seeds, growing seedlings in pots and transplanting when young or older, salvaging prior to site contouring and replanting, digging plants from donor sites and transplanting, introducing cuttings (e.g., *Salix* poles), planting mixtures or monotypes, planting in clusters or grids, and spacing tightly or sparsely. Because there are so many possibilities and because each site and time of planting will affect outcomes, it might be helpful to test alternatives until reliable approaches are developed and predictability improves.

Prairie potholes that are rewetted following long periods of drainage for agriculture typically have fewer species and different proportions of sedge meadow and submersed aquatic plants (Galatowitsch and van der Valk 1996b). Introducing seeds or transplants is not a sure solution. For example, some *Carex* seeds are difficult to germinate (van der Valk et al. 1999), and saline restoration sites can be too harsh for transplants to establish (Zedler et al. 2003). Brown and Bedford (1997) report that transplanting soil is an effective technique for establishing diverse vegetation in New York; however, importing soil to reestablish sedge meadow in Wisconsin had only short-term benefits (Hey and Philippi 1999).

The relationships between plant species richness, hydrologic regimes, soils and nutrient levels are not well known, but there is wide agreement that low-nutrient soils allow more species to coexist because no one species becomes productive enough to crowd out the others (Grootjans et al. 1996; Bedford et al. 1999). In central Europe, species-rich meadows lose diversity when drained (via moisture loss and internal eutrophication; Koerselman et al. 1993). Mowing can prevent aggressive plants from outcompeting subordinates, and this is a common management practice (e.g., Grootjans et al. 1996). In New York State, Drexler and Bedford (2002) linked the loss of diversity to nutrient flows into a species-rich fen; aggressive species formed monotypic stands in response to nutrients that arrived by surface flows in one area and via groundwater in another.

Less clear is how species-rich vegetation affects ecosystem function. The southern California salt marsh study discussed earlier showed that species-rich assemblages enhanced biomass, nitrogen crop, canopy layering, and recruitment (Fig. 10.12). While different relationships between diversity and function might be characteristic of other wetland types, one pattern seems to hold for multiple wetland types, namely that restored examples are less diverse than reference wetlands. In the Kissimmee River floodplain, seed banks were judged inadequate to restore the full diversity of plants following reintroduction of river flows (Wetzel et al. 2001). In prairie potholes, the species found where hydrologic conditions were restored were a subset of those found in reference potholes, presumably because dispersal was limiting and no planting was done (Seabloom and van der Valk 2003).

RESTORING FAUNA

Restoring populations of animals—especially fish and birds—is a typical goal for wetlands. For small streams, rare clams and mussels join fish, crayfishes, dragonflies and damselflies, and amphibian species as a priority (Richter et al. 1997), and in saline wetlands, habitat for shrimp and crabs is a high priority for restoration (Able and Hagan 2000; Jivoff and Able 2003). The most diverse and numerous animals (nematodes, oligochaete

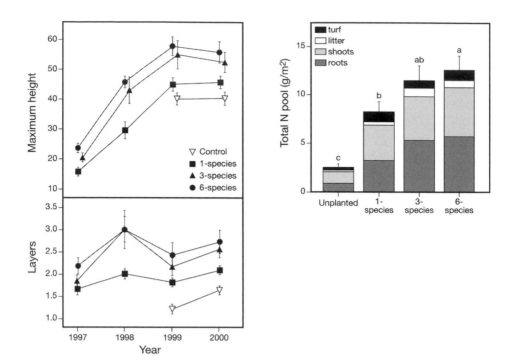

FIGURE 10.13

Transplanting 6 halophytes to a salt marsh plain enhanced canopy complexity, aboveground biomass, and nitrogen crop compared with plantings with 0, 1, or 3 species. Cf. Keer and Zedler (2002) and Callaway and colleagues (2003).

and polychaete worms, most insect groups) are often ignored, even though they play extremely important roles in food chains and in decomposition. Minello and colleagues (1994) report on the importance of including sufficient "edge" between creeks and the marsh plain, as many fish feed at the plant-water border. Salt marshes in Galveston Bay have been modified to increase the length of creek-marsh edge in a replicated experiment that allowed researchers to pinpoint cause and effect. Birds tend to be more diverse and numerous early in tidal wetland restoration, where vegetation has not yet covered their mudflat feeding areas (Eertman et al. 2002; Warren et al. 2002).

If you build the habitat, the desired animals might come, but generalists are more likely to show up and flourish than specialists. In prairie wetlands, bird use was similar for restored and natural sites (Ratti et al. 2001), as was the case after restoring drained wetlands in New York (Brown and Smith 1998). In contrast, Delphey and Dinsmore (1993) found fewer nesting birds in recently restored prairie potholes. Also, attempts to restore habitat for the endangered light-footed clapper rail *(Rallus longirostris levipes)* in San Diego Bay did not achieve that goal (Zedler 1998; Fig. 10.13).

Being able to attract the desired animals to a restoration site requires knowledge of their specific habitat requirements, including dispersal corridors. We have shown that tidal creeks are critical to growth of fish in southern California tidal marshes. Based on data for fish feeding on the marsh surface (where they obtain six times as much food as in creeks), as well as experiments testing fish metabolism at different temperatures and activity rates, Madon and associates (2001) predicted that fish would grow substantially more when they have access to the salt marsh via tidal creeks. It is not yet clear if tidal creek networks are essential to birds that feed on fish. When the habitat seems appropriate but the desired animals still do not come, reintroductions might be called for.

Of great importance to wetland animals is the condition of the adjacent landscape. Clapper rails need a high-tide refuge, and they are sometimes hit by cars when the only "habitat" they can find during the highest tides of the year is a parking lot or street. Belding's Savannah sparrows use tall subshrubs in the transition from salt marsh to upland to perch and sing (mate attraction), and they forage in uplands, especially during the nonnesting season. Many amphibians need to move from pond to pond and are greatly influenced by interwetland distances (Knutson et al. 1999; Semlitsch and Bodie 2003). And cover that attracts predators might have negative impacts on wetland species. At Tijuana Estuary, researchers are not allowed to use tall stakes to mark plots because native raptors might use them as perches, enhancing risks for nesting clapper rails or Savannah sparrows. Local birders can be excellent sources of information useful to restoration.

RESTORING MICROBIAL COMMUNITIES

Microorganisms are ubiquitous, but which ones make use of restored versus natural wetlands is entirely unknown. A few studies in wetlands have investigated mycorrhizae and microbial activities, but most research on microbial organisms has focused on algae, especially cyanobacteria, diatoms, and a few species of green algae. Algae are especially important for their nitrogen-fixing capability (by some cyanobacteria), high productivity, and high palatability for wetland consumers (see Chapters 7 and 8). How these important organisms develop in restoration sites has received much less attention.

The roles of some microorganisms have been evaluated in restoration sites. Langis and associates (1991) reported that benthic nitrogen fixation was low in a fully vegetated restoration site in San Diego Bay, California, as well as in the nearby reference site. However, researchers in North Carolina suggest that microbial mats are critical sources of nitrogen in newly restored marshes (Currin et al. 1996; Piehler et al. 1998). Currin and colleagues (1996) reasoned that the low plant cover and coarse sediments of the restored marsh were responsible for enhanced nitrogen-fixation rates five- to tenfold greater than those in the reference site. Piehler and colleagues (1998) found evidence for differential nitrogen-fixation rates for marshes of one and six years since restoration. The one-year-old marsh was consistently higher in nitrogenase activity (an indicator of nitrogen-fixation) and chlorophyll (an indicator of productivity). Because nitrogen supplies (from inorganic nitrogen and decomposing organic matter) were limiting to cordgrass growth in restored sites, the benthic microbial assemblages were seen as key suppliers of nitrogen (Piehler et al. 1998).

Thus, microbial organisms might accelerate salt marsh restoration. Whether or not there are situations where microbial organisms would need to be manipulated to achieve restoration is unstudied. The presence of microbial organisms is universal in wet sites, but composition and functions might differ in restored and natural communities.

Some changes in microbial organisms can serve as indicators of restoration progress. The Everglades is an oligotrophic ecosystem with extremely low levels of phosphorus. Where fertilizers flow in from adjacent pastures, fields, and urban areas, periphyton (including algae, bacteria, and microfauna) increases and serves as an early indicator of eutrophication. Thus, reduced microbial biomass would indicate ecosystem recovery following the removal of phosphorus by treatment wetlands (Noe et al. 2001).

Restoration planning involves matching the manipulations of hydrologic conditions, soils, topography, vegetation, and animals to desired targets. Hence, an important early step is to admit which is not known, that is, what predictions are uncertain. Once various approaches to restoration have been identified, I recommend establishing field experiments to test the effectiveness of alternative restoration actions—"adaptive restoration" (Zedler and Callaway 2003).

EXPERIMENTAL APPROACHES FOR RESTORING
INVASIVE MONOTYPES TO SPECIES-RICH VEGETATION

The multiple traits that make species invasive traits (such as clonal growth) allow them to establish and spread, but their presence in landscape sinks seems to explain their ability to form monotyes (Zedler and Kercher 2004). One invasive clonal grass, *Phalaris arundinacea,* follows the pathways of agricultural and urban runoff. In Wisconsin, it is so widespread a dominant that it can be mapped from satellite imagery. A survey for the southern part of the state shows that it dominates over 40,000 hectares with greater than or equal to 80% cover in over 15% of the wetland area considered (Bernthal and Willis 2004). While the species is regarded as native, a number of introductions for forage and streambank erosion control have most certainly contaminated the gene pool. Wetlands next to pastures and streams that are dominated by reed canary grass are easily invaded by the seeds, rhizome fragments, floating branches, or clonally subsidized tillers of this aggressive plant. As its cover increases, native species are excluded, and the outcome is a monotype.

How might restoration of a reed canary grass monotype be undertaken, in order to reinstate species-rich vegetation in Lower Greene Prairie (UW–Madison Arboretum)? Because we do not know which species can replace reed canary grass or when to sow their seeds, we divided the area into eight plots; four were left in reed canary grass and four were treated with herbicide (glyphosate) to kill adults in August 2001. Herbicide was applied again in 2002 to kill seedlings and resprouting clones. The dead stems and litter in treated plots were burned in late fall of 2002, and seeds of thirty-three native species were sown to half of the three treatment plots in mid December 2002, just before frost. The following March, the other half was sown with stratified seeds.

Establishment and growth were followed through the 2003 growing season, during which time reed canary grass regrew from the seed bank and by resprouting from rhizomes that survived two herbicide treatments. Obviously, reed canary grass is resilient to control measures. The adaptive restoration approach, however, is suggesting which species can establish most readily, which microsites are most vulnerable to reed canary grass reinvasion, and which seeding treatments are most effective (J. Wilcox, UW–Madison, pers. com.).

Experiences with reed canary grass indicate the need for comprehensive, long-term maintenance of invasive species in wetlands. Monotypes can be treated with repeated applications of glyphosate, but regrowth is likely where there is a continual influx of plant resources and propagules. A newer herbicide that attacks grasses preferentially shows promise for follow-up control after cover crops of native forbs are beginning to establish. Sethoxydim appears to allow growth of graminoids (e.g., *Carex, Scirpus*) and forbs, while nearly eliminating fruiting of reed canary grass and cutting its biomass in half (C. A. Annen, Michler and Brown, pers. com.). Hence, repeated treatment of patches is possible, and once the invasive grass has been checked, experimental reintroductions of native grasses could proceed. The timing of application, however, can make a difference to herbicide effectiveness. Field experiments suggest that systemic poisons such as these are best applied in late summer, when plants are moving reserves belowground (C. Reinhardt and S. Galatowitsch, U. Minnesota, pers. com.).

Still, the fact that landscape sinks are vulnerable to invasions means that excess runoff and nutrient and sediment inflows need to be dealt with upstream. Very likely, a combination of watershed improvements and a long-term, comprehensive program of weed control will be needed. Even then, the more species-rich native vegetation might not resemble that prior to invasion. To determine which species to reestablish in wetlands that are dominated by invasive monotypes, the adaptive restoration approach is highly recommended.

SURPRISES AND THEIR LESSONS

Even the best-planned restoration projects are subject to unexpected events. Klotzli and Grootjans (2001) report on 40 years of experience in restoring wetlands in the Netherlands and conclude that unpredictable events should be expected. The following examples (like the hypothetical ones in Box 10.1) suggest problems that could be prevented in future projects.

Excavation of a Filled Wetland Uncovered Toxic Materials

In a mitigation site along San Diego Bay, the California Highway Department was surprised to find an urban dump containing toxic refuse (lead paint) under the fill they were excavating as compensation for widening Interstate Highway 5. The project could not proceed until the site was overexcavated and toxic materials moved off site to an appropriate toxic-waste facility, greatly increasing project cost.

Lesson: Characterize soil cores in known fill sites.

Excavation Encountered a Hard Pan at Tijuana Estuary

As bulldozer operators excavated the Tidal Linkage in 1997, they encountered a hard pan at the elevation of the proposed salt marsh plain. Consultants used a power auger to bore holes for planting cordgrass (as blocks of salvaged sod). Most of the transplants died after a few years, with no clear understanding of the effect of the hard pan. When we learned about the hard pan, we implemented our experimental plantings on the other side of the channel by breaking up the hard pan and adding fine sediment that was salvaged from an adjacent sewage lagoon.

Lesson: Characterize subsoil during site assessment.

Excavation Encountered Indian Relics

When bulldozers at Tijuana Estuary removed the 2 meters of alluvium that covered a historical salt marsh, they revealed pot shards and charcoal that were evidence of former human habitation. A standard exploration was required to determine if the site was a significant archeological site or not. Project construction ceased for a month while sample pits were excavated and soils sieved to look for relics. When the survey determined that the site was not significant anthropologically, the project proceeded, but there was no contingency plan for moving the site if the outcome had been different.

Lesson: Anticipate potential for anthropological significance.

Erosion Shifted Habitat Type

In San Diego Bay, the 9-hectare Marisma de Nación was excavated to precise elevations and then experienced excessive erosion. Because most of the site was designed to grow cordgrass (*Spartina foliosa*) for clapper rail nesting, most of the topography was excavated below elevations typical of the marsh plain. When the site's one large meandering channel was opened to tidal flushing from San Diego Bay, tidal water tended to flow over the surface of the marsh instead of up the channel. Within a few years, sheet flows eroded away the transplanted cordgrass near the tidal inlet (Haltiner et al. 1997).

Lesson: Aim for geomorphological features that mimic natural contours.

Gog-Li-Hi-Te Marsh Accreted Excess Sediment

At Gog-Li-Hi-Te marsh in Puget Sound, Simenstad and Thom (1996) measured excessive sedimentation in tidal creeks and on the marsh plain, a consequence of placing the mitigation site upstream in a sediment-laden river. Channels became shallower and vegetation shifted toward more brackish species, although young salmon were found in the creeks and were making use of invertebrate foods in the restored site (Shreffler et al. 1992).

Lesson: Characterize potential for sediment influx during site assessment.

Massive Mortality of Seedling Transplants Followed
Flooding and Sedimentation at Tijuana Estuary.

We expected high survivorship of seedlings in Tijuana Estuary's 8-hectare restoration site; however, the large marsh plain became extremely hypersaline, with soil paste salinity greater than 10% shortly after the marsh plain was flooded with tidewater. Hot, dry southern California air evaporated tidal water as it spread over the large marsh plain, leaving salts behind. Seedlings could not cope with the combination of hypersaline soils that stressed roots and sediment coatings that stressed leaves (Zedler et al. 2003). In retrospect, a large, dark-colored (more organic) marsh plain would heat up during daytime low tides much more than a narrow marsh plain with light-colored substrate (Zedler et al. 2003).

Lesson: Be cautious in extrapolating experiences from small to large restoration sites.

Coots Trampled Transplanted Seedlings While Feasting on an Algal Bloom at Tijuana Estuary

The excavation of the Tidal Linkage was designed to connect two tidal channels and expand salt marsh habitat for endangered birds. Cutting a channel into the sewage lagoon no doubt liberated nutrient-rich sediments, which likely mobilized nitrogen and phosphorus, catalyzing a bloom of *Enteromorpha* and Ulva. During high tides, the algae floated onto the marsh plain where we had carefully planted 90 seedlings in each of our 190 2-by-2-meter experimental plots. The algae were entrained by the seedlings, smothering some and attracting coots to others. Coot trampling damaged seedlings, requiring transplantation to reestablish the experimental design (cf. Callaway et al. 2003).

Lesson: Anticipate interference from herbivores, even if herbivory is not an issue in mature marsh vegetation.

A Native Scale Insect Irrupted

In San Diego Bay, a native scale insect, *Haliaspis spartina,* irrupted in restored cordgrass stands, but not in natural stands (Boyer and Zedler 1996). While we reasoned that the short stature of restored cordgrass canopies precluded use by the scale insect's natural predator (a beetle, *Coleomegilla fuscilabris*), the effect of the predator has not been tested. Surprisingly, the effect of the herbivorous scale was reduced by nitrogen additions, which apparently strengthened plant resistance (Boyer and Zedler 1996).

Lesson: Anticipate prey outbreaks where restored habitat can not support natural predators.

A Riparian Restoration Project in a San Diego Regional Park Lost Its Water Source

When a San Diego River project complied with mitigation requirements, the California Department of Transportation was freed of liability for providing riparian habitat for endangered least Bell's vireos (Kus 1998). The next year, a major flood shifted river flows to a different channel, cutting off flows to the mitigation site. Without river inflows, the site dried out, costly transplanted trees died, and upland shrubs invaded the site. This $10-million project has little future because (1) the dam diverted water away from an older, deeper channel of the San Diego River, so there is no easy way to recapture flows; (2) the former diversion dam is on private property, outside the bounds of the regional park's jurisdiction; and (3) there is no longer a funding obligation because the mitigation project complied with its five-year contract.

Lessons: Ensure natural flood pulses can be sustained; purchase lands that house critical structures (e.g., the diversion dam); extend mitigation responsibility beyond five years.

A Restored Sedge Meadow Converted to Cattails in Madison, Wisconsin

In one of the first efforts to import soil in order to establish a species-rich wetland, the Wisconsin Highway Department restored several native sedge meadow species as part of its highway mitigation program (Ashworth 1997). Hey and Philippi (1999) used this site as one of their four "cases for wetland restoration" because the soil importation effort was innovative at the time. Shortly after the project complied with its five-year criteria, however, a flood inundated the site, and cattails replaced the desired vegetation.

Lessons: Design sites to withstand flooding; consider flood regimes in setting mitigation compliance time periods.

There will always be surprises, and diverse experiences such as those mentioned can help future restorationists develop preventative measures. In addition, I recommend a thorough monitoring program to assist in explaining unexpected events.

EVALUATING PROGRESS AND OUTCOMES

How does a wetland restoration site develop? Starting conditions are rarely documented in detail, and thorough evaluations of changes postrestoration are likewise rare due to time and cost. Prior to restoration, each objective should be matched with one or more measures that will indicate progress and, ultimately, achievement of the desired outcomes. Not only does such an exercise assist planning monitoring, it helps to clarify objectives. When faced with the need to specify what will be measured, when and how, goals as vague as "achieve success" become meaningless. The need to conduct monitoring should be included in project plans and budgets from the beginning.

Zedler and Callaway (2000) reviewed the assessment approaches reported in 26 papers about coastal projects that involved excavating uplands (14 papers), using dredge material (10), or removing dikes (5). Most of the projects were less than 5 hectares in area; most had short-term monitoring of less than 4 years, many involved only a single assessment, and most evaluated only 1 or 2 attributes of the restored ecosystem. Sediments and soils were evaluated in 14 papers, plants in 10, topography in 3, and birds in 2. For soils, organic matter content and texture were typically evaluated. For plants, cover, density, and/or biomass were measured, sometimes adding species number, plant height, and total stem length (as a surrogate biomass). For invertebrates, birds, and fish, composition and density were assessed, sometimes with gut analysis of fish. The evaluation of Gog-Li-Hi-Te by Simenstad and Thom (1996) provided the most thorough record of ecosystem development—16 functional attributes were assessed over a 7-year period; only a few showed trajectories toward functional equivalence with reference systems.

Where a research funding complements a monitoring contract, more attributes can be evaluated and better understanding of shortcomings developed. My collaborators documented changes in many attributes of a San Diego Bay mitigation site over a ten-year period. The restored salt marsh was intended to compensate for the loss of nesting habitat for the endan-

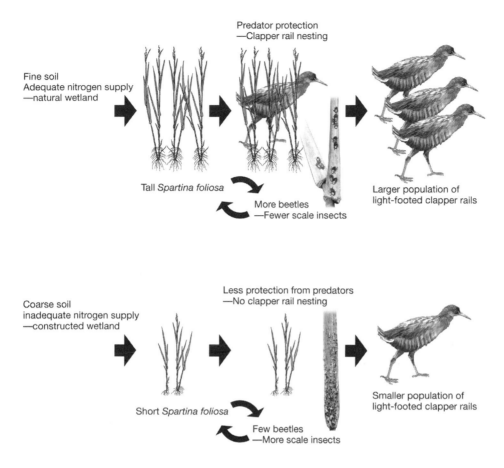

Fine soil
Adequate nitrogen supply
—natural wetland

Predator protection
—Clapper rail nesting

Tall *Spartina foliosa*

More beetles
—Fewer scale insects

Larger population of
light-footed clapper rails

Coarse soil
inadequate nitrogen supply
—constructed wetland

Less protection from predators
—No clapper rail nesting

Short *Spartina foliosa*

Few beetles
—More scale insects

Smaller population of
light-footed clapper rails

FIGURE 10.14

Relationships between soil, plant canopy architecture marsh insects, and clapper rails became clear in attempts to create nesting habitat for an endangered bird in San Diego Bay marshes. Cf. Zedler and Powell (1993). Cordgrass = *Spartina foliosa;* beetles = *Coleomegilla fucilabris,* scale insects = *Heliaspis spartina;* clapper rails = *Rallus longirostris levipes.* Note that small-scale experiments (2 x 2-m plots) indicated that cordgrass would grow tall enough for clapper rails, but when fertilization was undertaken at the large scale (20 x 20-m plots), cordgrass was outcompeted by an annual halophyte, *Salicornia bigelovii;* at the same time, sediments accreted, and cordgrass declined overall. Illustration compiled by Kandis Elliot.

gered light-footed clapper rail *(Rallus longirostris levipes),* which was known to build most of its nests within the tallest areas of cordgrass *(Spartina foliosa).* Knowledge of the bird's habitat requirements proved crucial to evaluating restoration effectiveness, and attempts to create habitat that the birds would use was critical to developing some of that knowledge.

In California salt marshes, cordgrass grows tallest next to tidal creeks and bays (Zedler et al. 1999) (Fig. 10.14). Although the mitigation site was designed to provide large areas of "edge" between tidal channels and cordgrass marsh islands, the smaller creeks and rivulets of natural marshes were not included. And, in order to maximize the area of cordgrass, most of the topography was graded low enough to support this "creek-edge" vegetation, with relatively steep, narrow slopes at the margins for marsh plain and high marsh vegetation. In natural marshes, these adjacent habitat types provide important support functions for rails when the tides inundate the cordgrass. The birds time their nesting to avoid the highest water levels in the cordgrass, but they move to higher elevations during high tides and floods, and they require cover in the high marsh and marsh-upland transition in order to avoid predators. The need for a high-water refuge is greatest during January and February. Storms that coincide with high spring tides that occur during the daytime increase predation risk for clapper rails that try to move inland to escape high water.

Marsh construction began in an area of fill that was excavated to create channels surrounding 8 islands. A second 8-hectare area was excavated from sandy dredge spoil that was designed with a deep, wide meandering channel through the center (Haltiner et al. 1997). The islands were completed in 1984; the second area was completed in February 1990. Most of the assessment occurred in the island site because rails were observed there, and human access was restricted to reduce disturbance and allow nesting. Despite these measures, clapper rails never nested in that site nor in any other constructed cordgrass marsh in San Diego Bay. Comparison of where clapper rails did and did not nest (Zedler 1993) helped explain why none of the constructed marshes attracted nesting. Nests were found where cordgrass produced at least 100 stems per square meter, with at least 60 that were taller than 60 centimeters and 30 that were taller than 90 centimeters (in late summer). Constructed marshes tended to have high stem densities but short plants. Years of experimentation with nitrogen addition convinced us that plants could be forced to grow tall but that nitrogen subsidies would be needed indefinitely in order to sustain tall plants (Lindig-Cisneros et al. 2003). The sandy soils of filled sites were simply too coarse to retain nitrogen, and belowground biomass did not accumulate sufficient reserves for internal recycling. Furthermore, nitrogen fixation rates were too low to supply enough nitrogen for tall plant growth (Langis et al. 1991).

We summarized ten years of monitoring data to show the long-term pattern of marsh development (Figs. 10.14, 10.15) and concluded that the site would not likely support nesting habitat because of its coarse soil (Zedler and Callaway 1999). We relativized the data from the marsh islands to that of the reference site (the specific habitat that was supposed to be replaced through mitigation) to remove the effect of interannual variability in plant growth. The resulting trajectories allowed us to predict that soil nitrogen might match that of the reference site after more than 40 years, that soil organic matter would be equivalent in about 22 years, but that cordgrass would never match the densities and height distributions of nesting habitat, in part because the accretion of sediments was tending to elevate cordgrass habitat to marsh-plain elevations, where succulents, not cordgrass, grow best. The 25-year comparisons of Craft and associates (1999, 2003) for salt marsh

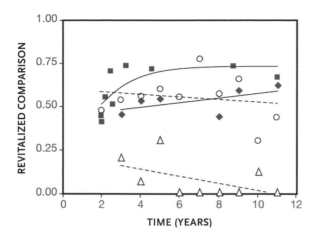

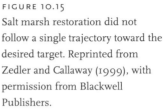

FIGURE 10.15
Salt marsh restoration did not
follow a single trajectory toward the
desired target. Reprinted from
Zedler and Callaway (1999), with
permission from Blackwell
Publishers.

soil in North Carolina corroborate our findings. Although cordgrass *(S. alterniflora)* height
is of less concern in their region, they documented slow development of soil, especially
the accumulation of soil nitrogen and organic matter.

The ecological goals of a project suggest appropriate attributes to assess. Those that are
especially useful in salt marsh restoration are soil total Kjeldahl nitrogen (TKN = organic nitrogen plus ammonium), soil organic matter, soil texture, soil salinity, plant canopy architecture (e.g., height histograms for *S. foliosa* intended for bird nesting; layering for salt marsh
plain vegetation); vegetation cover from low-elevation remote sensing imagery; abundances
of invertebrates that serve as foods for target animal species; fish species richness and abundance, size distributions of fish within specific habitat types (e.g., tidal creek orders), fish gut
contents to document food use, and nesting and production of fledglings by target bird species.

Tracking the development of restored or constructed marshes requires consistent and long-
term assessment of multiple attributes and their simultaneous evaluation in appropriate reference sites. Understanding the results requires coordinated experimentation (such as nitrogen addition) and observational research (comparison of areas with and without nests).
While systematic data collection allows long-term comparisons, it is unlikely that cause-effect mechanisms can be pinpointed without the ability to explore ecosystem functioning beyond the requirements of mitigation permits. Funding from a variety of federal, state, and
nongovernmental sources (NOAA Coastal Ocean Program, USFWS Biological Resources Division, California Department of Transportation, California Sea Grant Program, Earth Island
Institute) made it possible to conduct research along with monitoring at San Diego Bay.

Most projects will not have the luxury of researchers who are willing to share in fundrais-
ing for monitoring and study. Rapid assessment tools will likely be used in place of detailed measures of community structure and ecosystem functioning. For regions where
the basic research has been done, a selection of indicators might suffice to characterize
ecosystem development.

Few ecosystems are entirely self-sustaining in our modern world. Most are subject to direct use, such as oceans that are overfished; bays, estuaries, and lakes that are polluted by point-source and nonpoint-source discharges; swamps that are cut for timber; and meadows that are mowed for hay. Obviously, such ecosystems need careful management to retain the resources that people value. But even places that are free of human intrusion feel the impacts of the earth's more than 6 billion people. Because wetlands typically occur in the sinks of the landscape, they lose resiliency when upstream disturbances release excess water, sediments, nutrients, acids, and other contaminants, plus floating propagules from alien species. In addition, wetlands receive influxes of nitrogen and acid rain from the air, along with wind-blown dust and propagules. Furthermore, the species that depend on wetlands are affected by events nearby and in distant locations. Shorebirds that migrate from North to South America or from Europe to Africa can experience population declines well outside their breeding range. Can any wetland persist in perpetuity without stewardship? Probably not. Nor can a restored wetland be expected to persist indefinitely once a 5-, 10-, or even 20-year monitoring period has passed. Since "natural wetlands" are still being invaded by alien species, it is easy to predict that restored wetlands will experience similar challenges and be even more susceptible to major shifts in structure and functioning, as illustrated by the surprises already experienced (see above).

The problems that plague natural wetlands (see earlier section on starting points) will also threaten the viability and persistence of restored wetlands. Sedimentation, erosion, or subsidence might shift elevations and alter topographic heterogeneity; invasive species might become increasingly dominant; and extreme events, such as catastrophic floods or droughts, earthquakes, windthrows, debris deposition, or disease epidemics, might eliminate key habitats or species. It seems likely that recently restored wetlands would have fewer attributes that confer resilience than natural wetlands (Box 10.11).

The NRC (2001) panel on compensatory mitigation called for mitigation sites to be transferred to a land-stewarding organization for long-term observation, identification of problems, and implementation of corrective measures as needed. Given the potential for surprises along the restoration path, it is prudent to set aside funding for investigation of causes and implementation of mid-course corrections. Setting up the restoration within an adaptive restoration framework can facilitate identification of cause-effect mechanisms and implementation of corrective measures.

ADAPTIVE RESTORATION: AN APPROACH THAT SIMULTANEOUSLY ADVANCES ECOLOGY AND ACCOMPLISHES RESTORATION

Adaptive restoration begins by recognizing what we do not know about restoring a specific site (Zedler and Callaway 2003). The unknowns might be what targets are appropriate, how to achieve desired targets, or how to monitor the site to determine when targets are met.

Seed and rhizome banks for regrowth of diverse native vegetation

Organic soils as a reserve for moisture and nutrients

Topographic heterogeneity at multiple vertical and spatial scales

High species diversity and redundancy of plant and animal guilds so that the functions of lost species can be replaced by those that remain

Large trees or shrubs that can ameliorate environmental stresses, such as wind

Large habitat patch size that can attract animals, some of which might bring in native propagules

Stakeholders (those with a vested interest in the site) need to come together to identify critical gaps in knowledge and prioritize the "need to know" for each restoration project or for specific regions. For restoration to be adaptive, the decision-making structure must include scientists who can best explain how the knowledge can be obtained and what research can be incorporated into the restoration project, and funds need to be available for strategic research and monitoring (not just data gathering).

Procedural guidelines (Box 10.12) can be followed, but like the restoration process itself, the adaptive restoration approach can be tailored to the stakeholder group, the restoration situation, and the resources available. For example, stakeholders can identify a central goal, and practitioners can suggest an array of techniques to achieve it, but once field plots assigned to different implementation treatments begin to differentiate, the outcomes will suggest how to proceed in subsequent phases. The approach that proves most effective in phase one can be employed in phase two, with additional experiments to develop further refinement. If progress is not sufficient in any of the treatments, it might be necessary to alter the goals to suit the site or to alter the site further to suit the goal.

At Tijuana Estuary, adaptive restoration is being used to restore up to 200 hectares of coastal wetlands in sequential modules so that information obtained in early modules is used to inform later modules. The first site was the nearly 0.7-hectare Tidal Linkage, implemented in 1997. Questions that had high priority and were answerable at the small site were, How should the marsh plain be planted? Which native species would colonize on their own, and which need to be planted? While considering experimental designs that would answer these questions, we realized that we could simultaneously address an area of scientific controversy by asking, Will planting species-rich assemblages jump start ecosystem functioning?

BOX 10.12 GUIDELINES FOR RESTORING DEGRADED WETLANDS USING AN ADAPTIVE RESTORATION APPROACH

1. Select the restoration site.

2. Assemble the adaptive restoration team to examine the site and background materials (landscape position, surrounding land use, water sources, water quality, size of site, constraints on modification, historical data on "natural" condition, potential reference sites in the region, etc.).

3. Consider alternative restoration goals, and select one or more as the general project goal. A general goal might be to vegetate the site with native species and attract wildlife. Other goals might be to slow flood waters or improve water quality.

4. Identify unknowns about how to achieve the goal. These might be based on the attributes of a topographically variable site (e.g., same plantings in different habitat types) or alternative techniques that might be used on a homogeneous site (seeding vs. plantings), or both.

5. Consider additional unknowns that could be explored at this site. The science of ecology offers many theories that suggest how site conditions affect ecosystem development.

6. Brainstorm, posing many alternative restoration experiments that could be done.

7. Through an iterative process that involves arguments for and against alternatives, select the design that aims to achieve the most that the site might support.

8. Draw an adaptive restoration site plan.

9. Record how the adaptive restoration design was developed, what sampling will be done and by whom, when data will be provided and to whom, and who will make decisions regarding mid-course corrections.

10. If funds are not available, write proposals pitched for the specific funding source. The problem is obtaining funding that can begin when the work needs to be done on the site. Coordinating planning, funding, and personnel is extremely difficult. Hence, adaptive approaches are most likely to be feasible where there are salaried personnel in charge, background funding for implementation, and some capacity for data collection. Once the site is built, it is easier to obtain funding for the related research, but the field sampling needs to begin at the time of project completion.

11. Identify appropriate outlets for published results and who will take the lead on each aspect of the study.

12. Implement the plans, with scientists directing treatment application and changes as needed.

13. Reconvene the adaptive management team at intervals to discuss results of the research and monitoring. Decide how long to run the experiment before the

(Continued)

BOX 10.12 (CONTINUED)

initial evaluation of outcomes. Determine trade-offs between achieving the most desirable target and implementing the most efficient approach in future restorations. Decide which approach should be applied to treatments plots that were unsatisfactory.

14. Summarize and interpret data; draft news articles and scientific manuscripts; circulate manuscripts for "in-house" review; revise further until ready to submit to peer-reviewed journals.

15. Evaluate the costs and benefits of performing the restoration adaptively. Would a traditional "trial-and-error" approach likely have been cheaper and less effective?

16. Promote the use of the findings in future manipulations of the site and in future restoration projects—this is the critical step that makes restoration adaptive.

17. For large sites that can restore subareas in phases, adaptive restoration "comes into its own." The site can be divided into modules, with experiments in the first module producing guidance for use in implementing subsequent modules. Each new module will tackle a new question, involve a new experiment, and produce results for the next module. By the time the last modules are ready for restoration, it is conceivable that outcomes might be accurately predicted.

We established 87 2-by-2-meter experimental plots in 5 blocks along the marsh plain (Fig. 10.15). We left 3 plots per block unplanted to test for volunteer colonization. We then tested the effect of planting each of the 8 common halophytes alone and in randomly drawn assemblages of 3 species and 6 species. We chose 4 response variables: the recruitment of seedlings, the rate of development of complex canopies, the accumulation of biomass, and the accumulation of nitrogen. We found that 1 species should not be planted because it invades too aggressively on its own; 2 species can recruit readily from seed and could be introduced as small numbers of adults; and the remaining 5 species need to be planted, in order to be present (Lindig-Cisneros and Zedler 2002b). We also found that diversity matters to ecosystem function; that is, planting more species provides more complex canopies (Keer and Zedler 2002) and accelerates the rate of biomass and nitrogen accumulation (N is a limiting nutrient in this system; Callaway et al. 2003). It was not simply a "sampling artifact" of including the most productive species because the richness effect appeared even in the absence of the community dominant. We concluded that both species richness and composition affect the functioning of this ecosystem.

The approach became increasingly adaptive when the second restoration site was planted according to findings from the first. The aggressive invader was not planted, and the five species that required planting were chosen for further experimental plantings.

We asked, How densely should seedlings be planted to improve survivorship and accelerate the development of dense canopies? Another question concerned the need for soil amendments to improve seedling establishment and vegetative spread to accelerate the development of plant cover (O'Brien and Zedler, in press).

The second site (the 8-ha Model Marsh) was amenable to testing alternative ways to configure sites and to answer a question of interest to both scientists and managers: How does the inclusion of topographic complexity (excavation of tidal creek networks) accelerate development of ecosystem function? Six areas were graded flat and smooth, and then tidal creek networks were excavated in three of the six. Response variables concerned both the vegetation and the food web. We use fish feeding (i.e., gut contents) on the marsh plain to indicate algal and invertebrate food availability (West et al. 2003). This ambitious restoration program cost $3.1 million to implement. Construction experienced inevitable delays, as did the funding of research proposals. Then, when the site was excavated and planted with several thousand seedlings, hypersalinity and unpredicted sedimentation killed most of the plantings (Zedler et al. 2003). At that point, the research also had become adaptive, as the experiment had to be redesigned within the constraints of the numbers of seedlings of each species that remained. The combination of a large site with horizontal heterogeneity (provided by different cluster densities) and vertical heterogeneity (provided by creeks) allows us to explore the responses of both vegetation and food webs and, based on preliminary findings, to recommend the inclusion of tidal creeks in future restoration designs.

There is no cookbook for restoration, but there is a general recipe for adaptive restoration (Box 10.12). While not every project can involve a university research community, as at Tijuana Estuary and other National Estuarine Research Reserves, project proponents, implementers, and monitors must be willing to change actions in response to knowledge gained on site and in similar restoration contexts. Likewise, researchers need to present their findings in formats that are user friendly (e.g., our Handbook for Southern California salt marshes; Zedler 2001). Rather than expecting one recipe to suit all projects, users can learn from ongoing adaptive restoration projects and tailor approaches to suit local needs.

ACKNOWLEDGMENTS

Funding from Earth Island Institute, the National Science Foundation (DEB 0212005 to J. Zedler, J. Callaway and S. Madon), California Sea Grant, NOAA Coastal Ocean Program, and NOAA National Estuarine Research Reserves supported the research at Tijuana Estuary. Funding for research on reed canary grass in freshwater wetlands came from USEPA-STAR grant number R-82801001-0 (with R. Lathrop and K. Potter) and USGS Eastern Region State Partnership Program grant (with E. Kirsch). I thank R. Sharitz for inviting this contribution and D. Larkin, M. Kentula and S. Galatowitsch for substantial help with the text. I am indebted to dozens of students and colleagues who have collaborated on wetland restoration research and to Suzanne van Drunick and the National Research Council (2001) panel for their review of compensatory mitigation.

11

FLOOD PULSING AND THE DEVELOPMENT AND MAINTENANCE OF BIODIVERSITY IN FLOODPLAINS

Wolfgang J. Junk and Karl Matthias Wantzen

In the first article of the Ramsar Convention, *wetlands* is defined as "areas of marsh, fen, peatland or water, whether natural or artificial, permanent or temporary, with water that is static or flowing, fresh, brackish or salt, including areas of marine water the depth of which at low tide does not exceed six meters" (Navid 1989). This definition encompasses coastal and shallow marine areas (including coral reefs) as well as river courses and temporary lakes (Hails 1996). It was first adopted to embrace all the wetland habitats of migratory waterbirds but is now widely accepted for wetlands in general.

The large number of different wetland types scattered over all continents and the large habitat diversity inside individual wetlands results in a large species diversity. Twenty-five percent of the earth's total vertebrate biodiversity resides in inland waters and wetlands (Stiassny 1999). About 20% of the total biodiversity in India occurs in inland water habitats (Gopal 1997). Wetlands such as the Pantanal of Mato Grosso in Brazil, the Okavango Delta in Africa, Keoladeo National Park in India, the Wadden Sea in Germany, the Danube Delta in Romania, and Kakadu National Park in Australia are renowned for an abundance of waterfowl.

With respect to their hydrologic regime, wetlands can be divided into systems with rather stable water levels, such as bogs, fens, mires, and the littoral zones of many lakes, and systems with strongly fluctuating water levels that oscillate between a terrestrial and an aquatic phase, such as intertidal wetlands, river floodplains, internal river deltas, and ephemeral and perennial wetlands embedded in these habitats. In systems with a pulsing hydrologic regime, which are the subject of this chapter, ecological conditions are very complex because the change between terrestrial and aquatic phases dramatically modifies the environment, and organisms have developed a variety of adaptations to cope with these changes. Some authors consider wetlands as ecotones where aquatic and terrestrial species meet (Hansen and di Castri 1992; Naiman and Decamps 1990). Others consider wetlands as unique ecosystems with specific characteristics (periodically or permanently waterlogged anoxic soils, adapted plants and animals) (Junk 1980; Odum 1981; Mitsch and Gosselink 2000).

In comparison to other ecosystems, wetlands are extremely valuable in terms of ecosystem goods, services, biodiversity, and cultural considerations. The average value of wetlands (US\$ 14,785 ha^{-1} yr^{-1}) is higher than the value of rivers (US\$ 8,498 ha^{-1} yr^{-1}), forests (US\$ 969 ha^{-1} yr^{-1}), or grasslands (US\$ 232 ha^{-1} yr^{-1}) (Constanza et al. 1997). Yet wetlands are highly threatened ecosystems. The impacts of anthropogenic activities cascade down entire catchments to the rivers and associated wetlands. European countries, the United States, most Asian countries, and Australia have destroyed or modified most of their wetlands through land reclamation, water extraction, water pollution, and the like. The floodplains of most rivers are influenced by reservoirs, dikes, and channel modification, which alter the flood regimes and interrupt longitudinal and lateral connectivity. Increases in the human population and increasing globalization of commerce accelerate the need for water, hydroelectric power, agriculture, and areas for settlement, including regions of Africa and South America that up to now have been minimally affected (Junk 2002). These modifications affect biodiversity, as has already been shown for temperate region wetlands and for charismatic species of the tropics. However, compared with what is known about terrestrial ecosystems, a paucity of information exists for wetlands (Gopal and Junk 2000).

In this chapter, we will characterize flood-pulsing wetlands in terms of their hydrology, describe adaptations of plants and animals that transition between terrestrial and aquatic conditions, evaluate the importance of wetlands for development and maintenance of biodiversity at landscape scales, and discuss the impact of human modifications of the flood pulse on species diversity.

CHARACTERIZATION OF FLOOD-PULSING SYSTEMS

Floodplains are "areas that are periodically inundated by the lateral overflow of rivers or lakes, and/or by direct precipitation or groundwater; the resulting physicochemical environment causes the biota to respond by morphological, anatomical, physiological, phenological and/or ethological adaptations and produces characteristic community structures" (Junk et al. 1989). This definition comprises narrow fringing floodplains along the headwaters, extended floodplains along the middle and lower courses of lowland rivers, and immense deltas of large rivers, such as the Amazon River, the Ganges and Bramaputra rivers, the Mekong River, and the Mississippi River. It also includes depressions that are periodically flooded by rainwater, such as the Roraima and Rupununi savannas in Brazil and Suriname (Junk 1993), pans and vleis in South Africa (Silberbauer and King 1991), and many Australian wetlands (Kingsford et al. 1999). Some rivers form large internal deltas that become periodically flooded, for

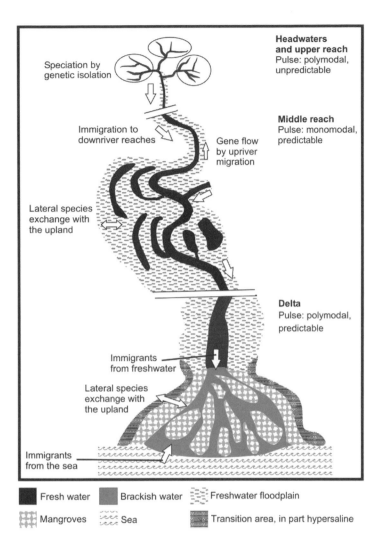

FIGURE 11.1

Flood pulsing, speciation, and species exchange in large river floodplain systems. Note that boundaries between the different areas are fluent with large transition zones. Modified from Junk and Wantzen 2004.

example, the Pantanal at the upper Paraguay River, the inner Niger River Delta, the Okavango Delta, and Lake Eyre in Australia, each of which is renowned for supporting a diversity of wildlife.

Near the coast, water quality changes from fresh to brackish, and finally to seawater in intertidal marine systems, such as salt marshes, mangrove forests, mud flats, sandy beaches, and rocky shores. The fluent hydrologic and hydrochemical transition between the ecosystems is accompanied by a fluent transition between the associated fauna and flora. In addition to a specific tide-adapted flora and fauna, intertidal ecosystems harbor an assortment of terrestrial, freshwater, and marine organisms (Fig. 11.1).

TABLE 11.1   Major Types of Flood Pulses, Origin of Water, and
Types of Rivers Affected

Type of Flood Pulse	Origin of Water	Types of Rivers
Monomodal predictable	Dry and rainy season	Large tropical rivers
	Snow melt	Large middle- and high-latitude rivers
Monomodal unpredictable	Unpredictable multiannual heavy rains	Rivers in arid regions
Polymodal predictable	Tidal influence	Rivers in the tidal zone
Polymodal unpredictable	Heavy local rainfall	Low-order Rivers worldwide
	Heavy regional rainfall and snow melt	Large rivers in temperate regions

NOTE: From Junk (in press).

Conceptional considerations linking intertidal systems with pulsing freshwater systems are just beginning to emerge. These systems are therefore treated only cursorily in this chapter.

HYDROLOGY

In all floodplains, hydrology is the major driving force. Amplitude, duration, shape, frequency, timing, and predictability are all important characteristics of the flood pulse. A classification of river floodplains with respect to pulse frequency and predictability is given in Table 11.1. Many large tropical rivers exhibit a monomodal, predictable flood pulse corresponding to dry and rainy seasons. In high latitudes, melting snow in spring and early summer largely determines flood regimes. Small rivers are influenced by local or regional rainfall events and can have unpredictable pulses of short duration. Near the coast, the flood pulse is influenced by the tide (Fig. 11.1). Amplitude and duration of flooding varies among floodplain types, and also varies within the floodplain, depending on local relief. When water rises to the bankfull level, the flow pulse reconnects all within-bank habitats and resources and has a homogenizing effect on previously isolated patches (Puckridge et al. 1998; Arscott et al. 2001). In semiarid and arid regions, pulses become erratic and may occur only every few years resulting in multiannual "boom and bust periods" for aquatic organisms (Kingsford et al. 1999).

The large variety of flood pulses, and the even larger range of response of plants and animals to pulses, makes generalization difficult. However, some general trends have been observed. Flood-adapted organisms profit from the "benefits" of flooding such as nutrient enrichment, organic matter accumulation, or breeding sites, while nonadapted species will suffer significant losses from flooding.

With increasing distance from the equator, the timing of flooding becomes increasingly important because plants and animals become influenced by seasons. Floods in summer are most influential because organisms are physiologically active. In winter, when most plants and animals are resting, floods may have less impact (nonadapted trees suffer less mortality during winter flood events than those during summer floods (Junk et al. 1989). But unpredictable flooding or drought in areas where predictable flood pulses are normal is also deleterious for even flood-adapted biota.

In terms of duration, short and frequent flooding has effects different from those of a single long-lasting flood. Short floods may trigger reproduction or break dormancy of organisms, but these floods may be too brief for development to be completed. Carp *(Carassius carpo)* and pike *(Esox lucius)* often begin spawning in floodplains of the Rhine after summer floods; however, because of river regulation, their offspring rarely have sufficient time to develop (Wantzen, pers. obs.). Amplitude is important, especially to plants, because deep flooding stresses emergent macrophytes and seedlings much more than shallow flooding. The predictability of floods permits plants and animals to develop adaptations to wet and dry periods, and enables more efficient use of the benefits provided by the flood pulse. A slowly rising and falling water level allows aquatic and terrestrial animals to escape, whereas flash floods drown many terrestrial invertebrates and increase the risk to aquatic animals of stranding.

The hydraulic energy of flowing water continually modifies the floodplain. It sets back plant communities through erosion, accelerates and modifies succession through sediment deposition, and increases habitat diversity by creating heterogeneous sediment patches. In reaches that receive large amounts of coarse bed load from upstream regions, the river flows frequently modify the floodplain through braiding and create areas of porous interstitial habitat of great importance to certain fauna (Arscott et al. 2001). In temperate regions, downwelling areas, where river water enters the sediment, are preferred spawning grounds for salmon and trout. During the subterranean passage, organic material is filtered, but the water becomes loaded with dissolved nitrogen and phosphorous that favor the growth of algae and terrestrial plants in upwelling areas (Stanford et al. 1994; Stanford 1998). As rivers grow in size, the particle sizes of sediments and the rates of geomorphological change in the floodplain tend to decrease (Minshall 1988). A similar trend occurs with increasing distance from the parent river to the outer zone of a floodplain. The importance of the interstitial areas for metazoans decreases as particle size of the sediment and oxygen content decreases. However, changes in the redox potential lead to complex chemical reactions within the sediments, including nutrient loading of pore water.

The sediment loads and particle sizes suspended in floodplain water decline with increasing distance from the parent river, and serially connected floodplain lakes can act as refining sediment traps (Marchese et al. 2002; Wantzen et al. 2005). Areas in the Pantanal of Mato Grosso that are far removed from large rivers show little recent turnover of inorganic sediments. Apart from recent depositions in the coalescent fans of the

Pantanal's Taquari River (Hamilton et al. 1998) and São Lourenço River, which result from anthropogenic erosion in the catchments, the majority of the larger geomorphological features were caused by Pleistocene river activities (Colinvaux et al. 2001).

The origin of the water also affects species diversity via chemical composition of water and sediments. Rivers with nutrient-rich water and an abundance of fertile sediment have highly productive floodplains, whereas rainwater-fed floodplains are more oligotrophic. However, water chemistry can change considerably as retention time in the floodplain increases because of the uptake and release of chemical substances by plants and animals and exchange with sediments (Furch and Junk 1997; Kern and Darwich 1997; Weber 1997; Kreibich and Kern 2003). The impact of water chemistry on biodiversity varies for different groups. High fertility is often related to a reduced plant biodiversity because highly productive species outcompete less productive species. However, in pulsing systems, the flood pulse affects interspecific competition through mortality from drought and flood stress. Low-fertility floodplains are often species rich, but some plant and animal groups might be excluded, for example, mollusks and many aquatic macrophyte species in acidic and nutrient-poor Amazonian blackwater river floodplains.

CONNECTIVITY

The species composition of floodplain lakes and species exchange with the parent river depend on the connectivity, that is, the time and extent of connection between the floodplain lakes and the parent river. The term *connectivity* has been transferred by Amoros and Roux (1988) from landscape ecology to limnology. Connectivity levels vary from a permanent connection to a short-term connection during extreme floods (Ward et al. 1999; Wantzen and Junk 2000; Junk and Wantzen 2004; Wantzen et al. 2005). With decreasing connectivity, the impact of the river on the floodplain lake diminishes, and the lake develops its own limnological characteristics.

Maintaining connectivity between floodplain water bodies and permanent rivers or lakes is especially crucial for certain larger aquatic animals. Some fish, decapod crustacea, turtles, and manatees would become extinct in areas during years of extreme drought if they did not have access to permanent water bodies such as large rivers and lakes. The biodiversity of many groups corresponds to the biodiversity in the parent rivers or lakes. Floodplains that receive their water from rivers with few fish species will also be species-poor in fish. The aquatic flora and fauna of floodplains without connections to permanent water, and fed only by rainwater or melting snow, must be able to survive dry periods in resting stages or immigrate via land or air.

For the Austrian Danube River floodplain near Regelsbrunn, Tockner and associates (1999) have shown that species number and community structure of many aquatic organisms change depending on the connectivity level, but in different ways. In general, the diversity of fishes and mollusks decreases with decreasing connectivity. Macrozoobenthos, dragonflies, and aquatic macrophytes are most diverse at intermediate levels of connectivity. Amphibians are most diverse in lakes with low connectivity.

The quality of connectivity changes when the floodplain lakes, at very high water levels, change from water storage systems to water transport systems, that is, from lentic to lotic systems (*limnophase* and *potamophase,* sensu Neiff 1990). Strong flow pulses during the potamophase can clean floodplain lakes of organic matter that accumulated during extended isolation and set back aquatic plant communities (Wantzen et al. 2005). For example, annual aquatic macrophytes form floating communities in Amazonian floodplain lakes with low connectivity. Water levels of isolated lakes fluctuate minimally, and floating aquatic macrophyte communities persist and become increasingly colonized by palustric nonfloating plants. Organic matter accumulates, and floating islands are formed that finally become colonized by shrubs and trees, covering large parts of the lakes. The end of this autogenic succession would be a swamp forest. However, flow pulses during extreme flood events can clean lakes of this vegetation, restarting autogenic succession (Junk and Piedade 1997).

The succession of animal and plant species is defined by a tight interplay of abiotic forces, such as river current and sediment deposition (allogenous succession), and by biotic forces, for example, by competition between species (autogenous succession), which complement each other at variable ratios along the longitudinal and transversal axes of river-floodplain systems. Generally, upstream regions are regularly set back by erosion, with little biotic interference on the colonization conditions of plants or animals (except in areas with beavers). In the lower sections with extended floodplains, flood pulse–driven succession may be overlain with plant-succession and "flushing" of deposited organic matter (as described earlier), plant-mediated channel blockage (Wantzen et al. 2005), and, in dry-wet-seasonal floodplains, with plant-mediated fire cycles (Nunes da Cunha and Junk 2004).

In tidal wetlands such as wadden areas and mangroves, hydrologic processes are also driven by an interplay of erosion, deposition, and the biogenic retention and production of sediments. Additionally, the intensity of this interplay is determined by the distance of a certain point in the floodplain from the parent ocean or river, and tidal channels also enhance the exchange of water and dissolved and suspended matter between the aquatic and the terrestrial parent systems. Regular flood events are in both cases overlain by stochastic disturbance due to rain storms and torrential floods; however, intense drought events are much rarer in marine floodplains. The main differences between freshwater and marine floodplain systems are the periodicity of flooding, the relative homogeneity of the marine habitat over long distances compared with the changing environment along river courses, and differing water chemistries.

DEFINITION AND CLASSIFICATION OF WETLAND ORGANISMS

As organisms may spend their whole life cycle in wetlands or only parts of it, defining what constitutes a "wetland species" is rather difficult. Plants can be classified as terrestrial species

TABLE 11.2   Habitat Requirements and Migratory Status of
Bird Species of the Pantanal

	Number of Species			
	Aquatic, Wetland Dependent	Terrestrial, Wetland Dependent	Terrestrial, Wetland Independent	Total
Breeding	43–47	33–39	220–275	297–361
Nearctic migrants	13	1	6	20
Austral migrants wintering	4	1	6	11
Other austral migrants	5	2	37	44
Nomadic	11	0	2	13

NOTE: From Junk and colleagues (in press).

that can not tolerate flooding or soil saturation during the growing season, aquatic species that can not tolerate dewatering, or wetland species that can tolerate both conditions (NRC 1995). Studies on the biodiversity of wetland plants normally restrict species to one of these categories. There are, however, many definitions of aquatic and wetland plants (e.g., Penfound 1952; Sculthorpe 1967; Tiner 1991; Barrett et al. 1993; Cook 1996; Mitsch and Gosselink 2000). A broad definition characterizes the wetland flora as plants "growing in water or on a substrate that is at least periodically deficient in oxygen as a result of excessive water content" (Cowardin et al. 1979). Studies of wetland animals concentrate mostly on aquatic species, an approach that is certainly too narrow to describe the biodiversity in wetlands, and specifically in floodplains.

Flood-pulsing systems have a special status among wetlands because of the Aquatic Terrestrial Transition Zone (ATTZ), which oscillates between a pronounced terrestrial phase and a pronounced aquatic phase. During high water, floodplains are colonized mostly by aquatic and palustric species. There are, however, also many terrestrial species that can tolerate short periodic flooding, such as many upland tree species. Other terrestrial species colonize nonflooded habitats inside the floodplain, for example, terrestrial birds and insects that live in the canopy of floodplain forests. During the low-water period, the ATTZ of floodplains becomes dry and is colonized by terrestrial plant and animal species that may or may not be wetland specific. These terrestrial species are integral parts of the wetlands because they contribute considerably to bioelement cycles, food webs, primary and secondary production, community structure, and biodiversity.

Gopal and Junk (2000) account for these issues and define *wetland species* as "all those plants, animals and microorganisms that live in a wetland permanently or periodically (including migrants from adjacent or distant habitats), or depend directly or indirectly on the wetland habitat or on another organism living in the wetland." To be useful in practice, this comprehensive definition requires a division into the subcategories shown in Box 11.1.

This broader view and classification of species living in wetlands allows further subdivision using adaptations and life history traits driven by specific environmental variables. An important parameter for environmental analyses is the complexity of biotic reactions to the environmental conditions of a specific wetland. It permits criteria for comparing biodiversity between wetlands to be formulated and hypotheses on the role of wetlands for speciation of organisms to be developed. A broad definition of wetland biodiversity is also essential for framing management of biodiversity in a landscape perspective. Table 11.2 presents an example of how this classification can be used for birds of the Pantanal. Of the 390 confirmed bird species of the Pantanal, only 104 are considered to be wetland dependent, and none is endemic. About 73% of the bird species also occur in nonwetland habitats, but several of them, such as the Hyacinth Macaw *(Anodorhynchus hyacinthinus)* and the Golden-collared Macaw *(Ara auricollis),* today have their largest populations inside the Pantanal because of better protection. Another 75 species are migrants, and 13 species are nomadic (Junk et al., in press). This emphasizes the overregional importance of large wetlands for the maintenance of biodiversity. For higher plants, the situation is similar. To date, 1,903 species of higher plants in the Pantanal have been described (Pott and Pott 2000). Of this total, 247 species are categorized as aquatic macrophytes and 1,656 species as terrestrial. Of the terrestrial species, 756 species are woody plants, and most of these colonize nonflooded or briefly flooded habitats inside the Pantanal (Junk et al., in press).

STRATEGIES TO SURVIVE FLOODING AND DROUGHT

Species living in the ATTZ must either tolerate alternating flooding and drought or move periodically to permanent water bodies or permanent terrestrial habitats. In moist tropical and temperate regions, floodplains are typically covered by flood-tolerant forests. In semiarid regions, drought stress during dry periods is important, and forest cover becomes sparse. Tree species with broad ecological tolerances immigrate from surrounding uplands and may relegate obligate wetland species to low-lying areas, such as the margins of lakes and river channels. Open areas become colonized by terrestrial plants that have a flood-tolerant seed bank in the sediment. In semiarid and arid temporary wetlands that are fed by rainwater only, these species often exhibit a high tolerance to increased salinity.

When the water recedes from the ATTZ, mobile aquatic animals move to the main river channel or to permanent water bodies. If those animals are trapped in drying pools, most will die, but some species have an impressive tolerance to stagnation and drying. Accessory air-breathing organs allow some fish species to survive under very low oxygen conditions including *Callichthys callichthys* (Callichthyidae), *Plecostomus plecostomus* (Loricariidae), and some Cichlidae in South America (Junk et al. 1983); *Misgurnus fossilis* (Cobitidae) in Europe; some members of the Channidae, Anabantidae, and Clariidae in Africa and Asia; and the lung fish *Neoceratodus forsteri* in Australia. Other aquatic animals, such as pulmonates of the Family Ampullariidae; some bivalve species; the lung fish *Protopterus* (Africa); the synbranchids *Amphipnous cuchia* (India), *Monopterus albus* (East Asia), *Synbranchus afer* (Africa), and *S. marmoratus* (South America); and the eggs of annual Cyprinodontidae, can all survive in dry sediments of ephemeral waterbodies. Frogs in semiarid and arid regions aestivate during the dry season and have numerous adaptations in reproductive strategy and larval development for unpredictable floods (Main et al. 1959; Bentley 1966).

Aquatic macrophytes and zooplankton can produce a drought-tolerant seed and egg bank. In temporary wetlands of Australia, 73 aquatic macrophyte species and 67 zooplankton species have been recorded germinating or hatching from sediments that had been dry for many years (Brock et al. 2003). These persistent seed and egg banks are not completely exhausted by a single or even successive wetting events and are crucial for the ecological resilience of episodic, intermittent, and semipermanent wetlands. They also represent a defensive mechanism against seed predators. Wild rice *(Oryza perenis)* grows on the lowest-lying areas of the Amazon floodplain, which can not be colonized by trees or more competitive perennial grasses. These areas are exposed only during periods of very low water, which occur every few years. Wild rice seed production is very high in the first year because seed-feeding insects are rare. However, in consecutive years of low water level, the number of ripe seeds actually declines sharply because of an increased insect attack. Years with relatively high levels interrupt rice growth but also reduce insect populations. (Junk, pers. obs.).

Periodicity in resource availability, primarily food, habitat, and breeding places, forces organisms to develop life history traits for changing environmental conditions. In the tropics, most fish species spawn with the onset of rising water, when food availability and shelter for the juveniles is high (Winemiller 1991). In the Amazon River floodplain, migrating species, such as *Prochilodus*, accumulate large amounts of fat for gonadal development and spawning migrations during high water periods but virtually starve during low-water periods (Junk 1985).

Short-term and unpredictable flooding or strongly variable discharge increases the risk of desiccation for aquatic organisms and requires more flexible reproduction strategies. These strategies are not only influenced by environmental factors such as flood pulses and seasonal change but also by food and habitat availability. Studies of fish in southeastern Australian streams with highly variable discharge patterns indicate that spawning is triggered mostly by increasing day length and rising temperature, suggesting evolutionary affinities in some species to groups of northern, warm-water origin (McDowall 1981; Humphries et al. 1999; Low Flow Recruitment Hypothesis). In southern Queensland, *Melanotaenia splendida fluviatilis* spawns prior to floods (Milton and Arthington 1984) in densely vegetated in-channel habitats of creeks, which ensures recruitment of eggs and larvae during the period of greatest environmental stability. More advanced–stage juveniles then disperse during months of higher stream discharge and intermittent flooding (Milton and Arthington 1985). *Melanotaenia splendida splendida* in the Black-Alice River system of northern Queensland spawns both prior to and during flood periods. Beumer (1979) concluded that this reduced the risk of desiccation because a 14- to 20-day delay in upstream spawning migration ensures that spawning does not occur until the wet season has commenced and water levels are more stable. Other species, such as *Craterocephalus marjoriae, C. strecusmuscarum*, and *C. fluviatilis* (Milton and Arthington 1983), also have extended breeding seasons. The golden perch *(Macquaria australasica)* resorb their gonads if suitable conditions do not develop.

In Amazonia, herbivorous manatees *(Trichechus inunguis)* reproduce during the high-water period when aquatic macrophytes are most available. In contrast, piscivorous river dolphins *(Inia geoffrensis, Sotalia fluviatilis)* and egrets reproduce during low-water periods when fish are most concentrated. For the large river turtles *(Podocnemis* spp.), the availability of breeding places is crucial. These turtles bury their eggs during low-water periods in exposed sand banks of the river channel (Junk and da Silva 1997). Floodplain birds exhibit a diversity of life history traits to varying habitat, breeding conditions, and food availability. Colonial ground breeders, such as terns and skimmers, nest during the low-water period on exposed sandbars in the river channel, but jacanas *(Jacana jacana)* nest during the high-water period on aquatic macrophytes (Petermann 1997). In large floodplain systems, some bird species are known to migrate internally. For instance, the sand-colored nighthawk *(Chordeiles rupestris)* breeds on sandbars, and if their local habitats flood, they migrate to portions of the Amazonian river system that still have low water levels (Sick 1967).

The flood pulse varies not only in annual but also in multiannual intervals because of the impact of climatic anomalies, such as the El Niño and La Niña Southern Oscillation. The impact of these variations can affect the populations and distributions of long-lived plants and animals. For example, in recent years, farmers have reported the spread of the tree *Vochysia divergens* into pastures of the Pantanal of Mato Grosso. An analysis of the age structure of the stands indicates that wildfires during a multiyear dry period in 1960s limited the distribution of this tree to the wetter areas. With the subsequent multiyear wet period, which still exits today, the tree is spreading (Nunes da Cunha and Junk 2004). We anticipate another reduction in the population during the next long-term dry period as wildfires become more prevalent. In the central Amazon River floodplain, a multiyear period of floods at the beginning of the 1970s led to the death of shrubs and trees in the lowest lying parts of the floodplain because their root systems were submersed for five consecutive years. Recolonization of this area by trees will only become possible during a long-term period of low floods that permits establishment of new seedlings (Junk 1989).

In intertidal habitats, frequent predictable and short terrestrial and aquatic phases have led to the development of highly specialized plant and animal species such as mangroves (Kathiresan and Bingham 2001). Processes similar to those that occur in freshwater floodplains annually occur here twice daily. The mangrove trees have a number of adaptations to desiccation (in a hot and saline environment), a lack of oxygen in the soils, and an unstable environment, such as xeromorphic leaves, salt glands, buttress roots, pneumatophores, and large, viviparous seeds. The tree stems and roots form a biogenic hard substrate for a large number of epiphytic algae and vertebrate and invertebrate colonizers. The capacity of some organisms to process tannin-rich mangrove leaves is an important adaptation in these habitats. For Grapsidae and Ocypodidae, the most abundant and diverse families of brachyuran crabs, these leaves represent their principal food source. Assimilation efficiency varies considerably depending on the plant species, the stage of decomposition, and the crab species, and can exceed 80% (Emmerson and McGwynne 1992). Large numbers of crabs lead to quick turnover of mangrove detritus. *Ucides cordatus* consumed 81% of the litter of a *Rhizophora mangle*–dominated mixed forest stand in northern Brazil (Nordhaus 2004). In the tropics, freshwater crabs are also known to consume leaf litter; however, they occur in much lower numbers and recycle only a very small fraction of the leaf litter. In temperate freshwater systems, maximum rates of 75% of consumed leaf litter have been reported for streams (Cummins et al. 1989). However, in floodplains, invertebrate shredders seem less important (Neiff and De Neiff 1990; Capello et al. 2004; Wantzen and Wagner, 2006).

SPECIATION AND EXTINCTION: THE IMPACT OF PALEOCLIMATIC HISTORY ON SPECIES DIVERSITY

Most floodplain lakes have a very shallow morphometry and are therefore strongly affected by changes in precipitation patterns. These patterns affect species abundance and overall community structure considerably, but may not affect which species occur because fauna and flora are adapted to today's variation in hydrology. As already stated, during strong El Niño years, precipitation in the Amazon River basin is low, and floods in the Amazon River floodplain are of short duration (Schöngart et al. 2004). The rain forest suffers drought stress and becomes susceptible to fire. Populations of aquatic or wet-adapted plant and animal species decline. When the climate becomes wet again, wet-adapted species recover, and instead the populations of drought-adapted species are affected negatively. In the case of long-lived plants and animals, recovery can last decades.

When short-term oscillations develop into a long-term trend, some species become locally extinct, while new species immigrate into the area. An analysis of about 1,000 studies on species distributions in Europe indicates that anthropogenic global warming has already affected species diversity and that many cold-adapted species have moved northwards or, in mountains, to higher altitudes (Leuschner and Schipka 2004). In addition to small climatic oscillations over years or decades, larger low-frequency oscillations over centuries and millennia also occur. Studies on hydroclimatic variability in the western United States indicate that four heavy drought events have occurred over the past three millennia (Woodhouse 2004). The impact of these events on wetland species diversity is not known; however, we can assume large site-specific differences depending on geographic position, wetland size, and connectivity with large permanent water bodies.

During the ice ages, climatic changes were dramatic: large parts of northern Europe, Asia, and North America were covered by ice. In Europe, glaciers covered England, Scandinavia, and the Baltic Sea and advanced to about 53°N. In central North America, glaciers advanced to about 40°N. The sea level was about 130 meters lower than today, which increased the gradient of the rivers and exposed large parts of the continental shelves. The climate was drier, the total discharge of most rivers was smaller, and the discharge pattern was dominated by snow melt. River floodplains were flooded in spring and early summer, dry during late summer, and deeply frozen in winter. When possible, warm-adapted species moved southward. Species that did not find suitable habitats became extinct. The preponderance of rheophilic fish species in large North American and European rivers (Dettmers et al. 2001; Galat and Zweimüller 2001) might be the result of ice ages hindering the development of a species-rich floodplain fish fauna. When the climate again warmed, species moved northward to colonize the new habitats. Aquatic and wetland species often disperse along river corridors such as the Mississippi River in North America. Here, extinction rates were comparatively small (Moyle and Herbold 1987).

In other regions, species could not escape the climatic and hydrologic changes and became extinct, for example, in many river systems along the northern Pacific coast. Recolonization began mostly by air (e.g., flying aquatic insects; transport of propagules of algae, zooplankton, and aquatic macrophytes by the wind or aquatic birds) or by water (e.g., anadromous trout and salmon that moved northward along the coastline). The 14 subspecies of coastal cutthroat trout *(Oncorhynchus clarki)* occupy a wide range of habitats from California to Alaska, including highly mobile populations that migrate between inland waters, estuarine waters, and coastal seawaters. The species is considered one of the earliest pioneers to reoccupy inland areas of the Pacific coast after glaciation (North-cote 1997) and is a good example of radiation of a species in newly emerging river flood-plain systems. In Europe, where southward migrations were hindered by high mountains (Alps, Pyrenees, Carpathian Mountains), extinction rates were high, and species diversity of less-mobile species is now low because the postglacial time period has been too short for speciation.

It is generally assumed that during the ice ages, the climate in the tropics was drier and about 5°C cooler. However, there is some controversy about impacts at a regional scale. Some authors (summarized in Haffer and Prance 2001; Van der Hammen and Hooghiem-stra 2000) suggest a fractionation of the Amazonian rain forest into small forest islands and strips along river corridors that provided enough water and an invasion of savanna vegetation. Others refute major climate changes and maintain that savanna did not re-place Amazonian lowland forests (Colinvaux et al. 2001). However, there is no doubt that the Amazon River and its tributaries eroded their valleys deeply because of the higher de-clivity as a consequence of lower sea level, and as a result, floodplains were probably much smaller than today (Irion et al. 1997, 1999). Nonetheless, there were always floodplains available, and the vast catchment area of the Amazon River buffered regional differences in precipitation.

Highly flood-adapted plant and animal species always found suitable habitats in Ama-zonia and expanded their ranges in postglacial times, when the rising sea levels dammed back the rivers about 2,500 kilometers inside the continent and increased the floodplain area. Therefore, the number of adaptations to the flood pulse, the number of flood-adapted species, and the number of endemic floodplain species is very high. We estimate that there are about 1,000 flood-adapted tree species in the Amazon basin, as compared with about 100 species in North American bottomland hardwood forests and only 50 species in Euro-pean floodplain forests. The number of fish species in Amazonia may reach 4,000 (Schäfer 1998), of which 50% are thought to occur in the large river floodplains and the other 50% in the headwaters. The biodiversity of the avifauna of the entire Amazonian floodplain sys-tem can not be evaluated yet, but studies show large species numbers and numerous en-demic species. On Marchantaria Island, a small island at the Amazon near Manaus, Peter-mann (1997) recorded 204 bird species and described many adaptations to the flood pulse with respect to feeding, breeding, habitat selection, and migration pattern.

An analysis of habitat preferences of Amazonian woody plants suggests that drought and fire stress also affect distributions. The central Amazon floodplain yearly receives 2,100 millimeters of precipitation, and all the tree species there are flood tolerant. Of the 224 tree species found in 4 hectares of the Amazon River floodplain in the Mamirauá Reserve, 103 species occur only in the upper part, which is subjected to a mean flood amplitude of less than 3 meters and a mean flood duration of less than 45 days. Ninety-four species are re-stricted to deeper-lying areas and tolerate mean annual flood periods of up to 230 days and mean flood heights of up to 8 meters. Only 27 species occur across the entire gradient, and only 38 species also occur in adjacent nonflooded habitats (Wittmann et al. 2002).

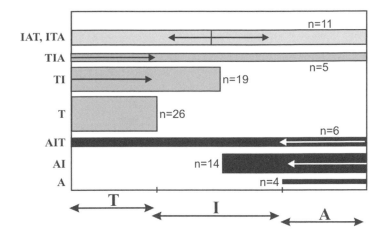

Distribution of 85 tree species in the Pantanal of Poconé according to their preference along the flood gradient. T = terrestrial habitats normally not subjected to inundation; I = habitats inundated during short periods (<2 months); and A = habitats with a pronounced aquatic phase (up to 6 months). Arrows indicate the assumed direction of expansion of the species from the center of maximum density. Figure according to Nunes da Cunha and Junk (1999).

Drier conditions in the savanna belt south of the Amazon rain forest probably also had considerable impacts on wetlands. It is believed that the Pantanal of Mato Grosso was mostly cool and dry during the last glacial period. From 8,000 to 3,500 BP it became warm and wet, from 3,500 to 1,500 it was warm and dry, and only since 1,500 to the present was it again warm and wet (Iriondo and Garcia 1993; Stevaux 2000). Aquatic and wetland species immigrated from the surrounding savanna (Cerrado biome), the northern Amazon biome, and the southern Chaco biome. There are very few endemic species in the wetland because of the relatively short period of this wetland's existence, and because flood pulses hinder speciation by forcing species to be mobile, enhancing genetic exchange. The Pantanal supports 756 woody plant species. Of 85 analyzed species, 18 are restricted to periodically flooded habitats, 45 to permanently dry habitats, and the remaining 22 occur over the entire flood gradient (Fig. 11.2). The situation is similar for the Okavango Delta, a large inland delta in southern Africa. The Okavango Delta is also situated in an area with low precipitation (650 mm vs. 1200 mm in the Pantanal), and the area also changed in extent because of wet and dry periods during past glacial and interglacial periods. There are very few endemic species in the area. Of 223 shrubs and trees of the Okavango Delta, only 17 are considered aquatic or semiaquatic (Ramberg et al., in press).

Paleo-climate has also strongly affected intertidal systems through changes in sea level, temperature, sediment load, and freshwater inflow (Yulianto et al. 2004). However, effects on distribution and species composition could be compensated in part because of connectivity along coastlines. The mangrove biodiversity anomaly, which shows a maximum number of species in the Indo-West Pacific and a minimum number in the Caribbean and western Atlantic, is explained by the vicariance hypothesis. This hypothesis asserts that mangrove taxa evolved around the Tethys Sea during the late Cretaceous Period, and that regional species diversity resulted from in situ diversification after continental drift. Patterns of nestedness at the community and species levels point toward three independent regions of diversification: southeast Asia, the Caribbean and eastern Pacific, and the Indian Ocean region (Ellison et al. 1999). Genetic studies by Dodd and associates (1998), however, show significant differentiation between mangroves in eastern and western Atlantic provinces, and they conclude that it is unlikely that the Atlantic mangroves dispersed from the Tethys via the Pacific.

SPECIES EXCHANGE BETWEEN FLOODPLAINS AND PERMANENT WATER BODIES

The flood pulse triggers active species exchange between permanent aquatic habitats and the ATTZ. When the water rises, aquatic organisms are swept in (Boedeltje et al. 2004) or immigrate from permanent aquatic habitats. When the water recedes, aquatic species move back or build drought-resistant resting stages in the ATTZ. The species pool varies according to geographic region. On a global scale, terrestrial species numbers increase from higher to lower latitudes. For aquatic organisms, this same increase does not necessarily occur. Some groups seem most diverse in temperate regions. Patrick (1966), studying Peruvian streams near Tingo Maria in the foothills of the Andes, found that species numbers of algae, protozoa, and insects were similar or even lower than in comparable streams in temperate regions and related this finding to a limited number of available niches. Data indicate that diversity in some aquatic groups, such as Odonata, decapod Crustacea, and fish is greater in the tropics, while for Trichoptera and Chironomidae it is similar. For Plecoptera and Ephemeroptera, the tropics appear less diverse than temperate regions (Fittkau 1973, 1982), although data from the tropics are limited.

Welcomme (1985) found a positive correlation between the number of fish species and the size of the river, expressed by basin area or some correlate such as the length of the main channel or stream order. Therefore, the species pool of potential immigrants to the floodplain increases with the size of the parent river. There are 263 fish species listed for the entire Pantanal (Britski et al. 1999). This number is higher than that of other large floodplains, such as the Okavango Delta, for which only 71 species are reported (Table 11.3). This is probably not a result of the larger size of the Pantanal (160,000 km² vs. 20,000 km² of the Okavango Delta) but instead because of the lower number of fish species in the Okavango/Sambezi River system (134) than the Paraná/Paraguay River system (355). Both floodplains are species poor in comparison to the Amazon River floodplain. While the exact number of fish species in the Amazon River floodplain system is unknown, Goulding and colleagues (1988) estimate that

Pantanal		Okavango	
Families	*Species*	*Families*	*Species*
Potamotrygonidae	3	Mormyridae	6
Pristigasteridae	1	Cyprinidae	17
Gasteropelecidae	1	Distichodontidae	3
Cynodonitidae	1	Hepsetidae	1
Crenuchidae	3	Claroteidae	1
Parodontidae	2	Amphiliidae	2
Hemiodontidae	3	Schilbeidae	1
Prochilodontidae	1	Clariidae	6
Curimatidae	8	Mochokidae	6
Anostomidae	10	Anabantidae	2
Lebiasinidae	1	Mastacembelidae	1
Characidae	76	Characidae	4
Cichlidae	16	Cichlidae	18
Poeciliidae	1	Poeciliidae	3
Erythrinidae	3		
Rhamphichthyidae	2		
Gymnotidae	1		
Sternopygidae	4		
Hypopomidae	3		
Apteronotidae	2		
Doradidae	8		
Auchenipteridae	8		
Ageneiosidae	3		
Pimelodidae	24		
Aspredinidae	3		
Cetopsidae	1		
Trichomycteridae	8		
Scoloplacidae	1		
Callichthyidae	13		
Loricariidae	36		
Rivulidae	9		
Belonidae	2		
Sciaenidae	2		
Synbranchidae	1		
Achiridae	1		
Lepidosirenidae	1		
Total	263		71

NOTE: Data from Junk and colleagues (in press) and Ramberg and associates (in press).

about 700 fish species occur in the lower reach of the Negro River, excluding the tributaries. For the middle Amazon River floodplain around Manaus, a similar number could probably be assumed. The high diversity in that area was shown by Bayley (1983), who collected more than 226 fish species in a small lake (Lago Camaleão). During high-water events, most of the species utilize the extensive floodplain forest at least periodically for food and shelter (Saint-Paul et al. 2000).

What attracts species to immigrate from permanent aquatic and terrestrial habitats into the ATTZ? During floods, the ATTZ offers aquatic organisms many habitats such as open water areas of varying depths, macrophyte beds, and floodplain forests, each providing shelter and a variety of food sources. Fish can exploit detritus, phytoplankton and periphytic algae, aquatic and terrestrial herbaceous plants, fruits and seeds from the floodplain forest, zooplankton, epiphytic aquatic invertebrates, terrestrial invertebrates, and the like. Neotropical floodplain fish show significant dietary changes, and stable istotope ratios differ between flood and dry periods (Wantzen et al. 2002). In temperate regions, higher temperatures on floodplains during spring and summer attract warm-adapted species and trigger spawning. Alternatively, cold-adapted species such as young salmon and trout use floodplain habitats during winter.

In lowland floodplains, strong daily oscillations in the oxygen level of the water with higher temperatures can be limiting for aquatic immigrants. Floodplain lakes of the Amazon River are often anoxic from 3 to 5 meters downwards and have very low oxygen concentrations during the night even in the upper water layer. Rheophilic species only visit floodplain areas near the main channel, where oxygen levels remain high (Junk et al. 1983).

Fish have developed different strategies to make use of the different resources provided by the floodplain. Welcomme and Halls (2001) differentiate between floodplain-specific species ("black fish"), riverine species ("white fish"), and species of intermediate status ("gray fish"). Black fish are adapted to very low oxygen concentrations and often exhibit parental care (nesting, egg fanning, oral manipulation). Resistance to low oxygen concentration is also widespread in gray fish and many white fish because they live in the floodplain during at least certain life stages. Many white fish and some gray fish migrate in large groups for spawning: experiments indicate that migration is triggered by the flood pulse (Junk et al. 1997). In the Amazon River, few species live permanently in the river channel (e.g., some large catfish). Black and gray fish that are forced by low water levels to retreat to permanent floodplain lakes and river channels return to the ATTZ with the first floods, as do juveniles and adults of many white fish. Of 101 fish species in the Miranda River in the Pantanal floodplain, 43% are black, 15% are white, and 42% are gray (Resende and Palmeira 1999). Willink and associates (2000) concluded that with the elimination of the northern Pantanal wetlands, for example, by the construction of a riverine transport system, areas with high fish species diversity, including species of high economic value, would be destroyed, and 40% to 60% of the species could be eliminated.

TABLE 11.4   Mammal Orders and Number of Families and Species in the
Pantanal and the Okavango Delta

Orders	Families (Species)	
	Pantanal	Okavango
Didelphimorpha	1 (7)	
Xenarthra	2 (6)	
Insectivora		1 (5)
Macroscelidea		1 (1)
Chiroptera	6 (37)	7 (26)
Primates	2 (4)	2 (3)
Pholidota		1 (1)
Lagomorpha		1 (1)
Rodentia	10 (16)	7 (30)
Carnivora	4 (17)	7 (34)
Tubulidentata		1 (1)
Proboscidea		1 (1)
Perissodactyla	1 (1)	2 (2)
Artiodactyla	2 (6)	4 (22)
Total	28 (94)	35 (127)

NOTE: From Junk and colleagues (in press) and Ramberg and associates (in press).

SPECIES EXCHANGE BETWEEN FLOODPLAINS
AND TERRESTRIAL HABITATS

Terrestrial species migrate into the floodplain for many of the same reasons as aquatic species. When dry, the ATTZ provides a large area with an abundance of food that is otherwise not exploited. The value of floodplains is reduced by brief dry periods and unpredictable, flash flood pulses that limit the use of food resources, inhibit completion of important parts of the life cycle (e.g., the development of soil-living invertebrate larvae), and increase flood-induced mortality. In temperate regions, the timing of the flood pulse with the season has implications for terrestrial immigrants. Dry periods in summer favor colonization by terrestrial species. There are also terrestrial species that permanently live in the floodplain because they find suitable conditions even during flooded period (e.g., many birds, canopy-dwelling insects).

Species exchange also depends on the available species pool and the mobility of the species. Therefore, biogeographic conditions have a strong influence on the species composition of periodic immigrants. A comparison of the Pantanal with the Okavango Delta shows that the number of mammal species is about 25% higher in the Okavango Delta and that there are large differences in the community composition. Twice as many Rodentia and Carnivora and nearly four times as many Artiodactyla live in the Okavango Delta, while bats are more diverse in the Pantanal (Table 11.4).

Mammalian diversity is affected by resource availability and in turn affects resources for other species (Sinclair et al. 2003). The large number of mammal species in the Okavango Delta (Mbaiwa 2003) might be the result of the extended wet season because the local rainy season is followed by a second surge of water coming down the Okavango River catchment (Anderson et al. 2003). This leads to an extended and predictable period of food availability in comparison to the surrounding savanna. Furthermore, the delta provides water during the dry season. Here, at least 30% of the mammal species have an extended breeding season. Many mammals migrate back to the uplands at the beginning of the rainy season, but during the critical dry season, the floodplains increase their survival rate and the overall carrying capacity of the surrounding savannas (Ramberg et al., in press). In South America, however, mammalian migrations between uplands and floodplains are much less developed.

In seasonal floodplains, a large diversity of terrestrial predators follow terrestrial herbivores and feed also on aquatic animals trapped in remnant pools. Carrion-feeders such as vultures, crows, marabous, hyenas, silphid beetles, and ants play a major role in the recycling of dead fishes and the carcasses of other animals. On the other hand, rising water level also drives terrestrial organisms out of the floodplain and makes them easy prey, for example, army ants patrol along the rising ATTZ to capture invertebrates (Adis et al. 2001), and snakes (*Bothrops* spp.) prey on small terrestrial mammals and lizards as they leave terrestrial refuges.

Studies in Amazonia, the Pantanal, and some European rivers show that most terrestrial invertebrates immigrate from nonflooded habitats, although some develop from resting stages (Adis and Junk 2002). Diversity of most terrestrial invertebrate groups in the Amazon River floodplain, for example, Symphyla, Archeognata (Adis et al. 1996; Adis and Sturm 1987), spiders (Höfer 1997), springtails (Gauer 1997), ants, termites (Martius 1997), and oribatid mites (Franklin et al. 1997), is lower than in adjacent nonflooded habitats. It could be argued that low species diversity decreases interspecific competition for food and habitat, but there is little evidence that resources are limiting during low-water periods. For some groups (e.g., tiger beetles and pseudoscorpions), species numbers in the floodplain are nearly as high as in the neighboring upland (Adis and Mahnert 1990; Zerm et al. 2001).

Termites are important consumers of organic material and can be bioengineers in shallowly flooded tropical floodplains (Pantanal, Okavango Delta, and parts of the Tonle Sap floodplain) because they build earthen mounds that rise above the maximum water level. These earthen mounds are important refuges for terrestrial animals during flooded periods. In the deeply flooded Amazon River floodplain, however, soil-living termites are lacking, and instead only tree-living species are found (Martius 1997).

Terrestrial invertebrates of large Amazonian river floodplains exhibit a number of morphological, physiological, phenological, and ethological adaptations to periodic flooding. The dry sediment is used by soil-living animals for oviposition and as larval habitat. Most species are univoltine, whereas their relatives in the nonflooded upland are multivoltine.

Migration, gonadal development, and aestivation are triggered by floods or flood-induced local climatic changes (Adis 1997; Adis and Messner 1997; Adis and Junk 2002).

In comparison, terrestrial invertebrates of European floodplain invertebrates have few adaptations. Most species use a "flood avoidance strategy" by escaping to nonflooded areas or a "risk strategy" where high losses during floods are compensated by high reproduction rates during terrestrial periods (Adis and Junk 2002). These general survival strategies do not prevent animals from developing more specialized strategies, for example, using the different food items provided by the river at different times of the year, as shown for shore-living terrestrial animals along the Tagliamento River (Tockner et al. 2000; Paetzold and Tockner 2005). Frequent unpredictable flash floods in the Tagliamento River, however, set narrow limits to the efficiency of these strategies.

The term *connectivity*, as used to describe the level of connection between floodplain lakes and the parent river, can also be applied to describe the relationship between terrestrial floodplain habitats and permanently dry uplands. Lateral connectivity decreases with increasing distance and also with obstacles that hinder migration or dispersal of terrestrial organisms, such as river channels. The exchange of organisms between floodplain areas and the upland is certainly more intensive in adjacent areas than between the upland and an island in the middle of a large river. Based on the Flood Pulse Concept, we predict a decrease in the diversity of terrestrial plant and animal species with decreasing connectivity, although this hypothesis has yet to be tested.

There is continual pressure by terrestrial plants and animals to colonize floodplains because once the stress from flooding is overcome, species deal with less interspecific competition and can exploit better nutrient conditions and water supplies (Fig. 11.1). Within the floodplain, flood pulse–induced habitat changes favor genotypic and phenotypic plasticity that are prerequisites for speciation and species diversity. According to West-Eberhard (1989), phenotypic plasticity can accelerate speciation by directional selection of already well-adapted phenotypes. Henderson and associates (1998) also postulated that the demand of a habitat for plasticity could well accelerate macroevolution via genetic assimilation and therefore suggested that the Amazon floodplain has been important for macroevolution. Floodplains in general may considerably increase intraspecific genetic variability, although to what extent this contributes to speciation is unknown. Ecophysiological studies on the Amazonian tree species *Himatanthus sucuuba*, which occurs both in the upland and the floodplain, show that trees growing in the floodplain are better adapted to flood stress than those growing in the upland (Ferreira 2002). Periodic fragmentation of forest communities by river activity and high habitat diversity are considered key processes for enhancing species diversity of trees in paleo-floodplains in the Sub-Andean area of the Amazon (Salo et al. 1986; Räsänen et al. 1987; Salo 1990). Population variation in the growth response to water-level fluctuations has also been reported for marsh plants (Lessmann et al. 1997).

However, because longitudinal and lateral connectivity favors genetic exchange between uplands and floodplains, it may hinder speciation. Of the 26 known species in the millipede genus *Pycnotropis,* three species are restricted to Amazonian floodplain forests (Vohland 1999). Large catchment areas harbor different *Pycnotropis* species. In the Amazon River floodplain downriver of Iquitos, only *Pycnotropis tida* occurs. Genetic studies have shown that near Manaus, this species invades plantations and disturbed areas of the uplands (Vohland and Adis 1999). Upland individuals are multivoltine, but floodplain specimens are univoltine. Genetic data suggest ongoing genetic differentiation, but successful interbreeding indicates that genetic separation of the populations has not yet reached the species level (Bachmann et al. 1998). Similarly, specimens of floodplain populations of the insect *Neomachilellus scandens* (Meinertellidae) are morphologically identical to specimens from upland populations but are adapted to the flood pulse by having a univoltine life cycle, while upland specimens are multivoltine. Populations exhibit considerable genetic differences, but interbreeding experiments have not been conducted (Wolf and Adis 1992). For three leguminaceous shrubs colonizing the Amazon River floodplain from Iquitos to Manaus, electrophoretic studies give the first indications of the impact of unidirectional gene flow in plants and show that homozygosity is favored in populations with a high extinction probability (Hill et al. 1978). Finally, Henderson and colleagues (1998) postulate that the large overall species diversity in the main stem floodplain is not because of in situ evolution, but might be the result of a slow trickle of species from the headwaters (Fig. 11.1).

SPECIES EXCHANGE BETWEEN DIFFERENT FLOODPLAINS

Many floodplain plant and animal species occur over large portions of a river catchment because the flood pulse stimulates mobility and dispersal of organisms. Limiting factors for dispersal are geographic barriers (waterfalls), chemical barriers (water and sediment quality), and differences in the character of the flood pulse. Human-made barriers include dams and reservoirs that interrupt longitudinal connectivity, dikes that limit lateral connectivity, and water pollution that makes areas inhabitable. In Amazonian rivers, rapids and waterfalls at the edges of the Central Brazilian and Guiana Shields limit up-river distribution of many fish, turtles, dolphins, and manatees. In the black water tributaries of the Amazon River, low pH and low nutrient content are chemical barriers for some fish (Goulding et al. 1988), mollusks, and many aquatic macrophytes (Junk et al. 1997).

Species exchange between floodplains of different catchment areas can occur actively by air or land by birds, flying insects, migrating mammals, amphibians, and reptiles or passively via transport by wind or migrating animals. Aquatic birds are particularly important to biotic wetland connectivity because they can cover large distances by aerial migration. Of the 390 bird species recorded in the Pantanal, 75 species are migrants, and 13 are nomadic (Table 11.2). Intertropical migrants move between different wetlands according to water and food availability or habitat availability for breeding and molting. These migrants periodically increase the total numbers, biomass, and the species diversity of birds dramatically. At the Great Salt Lake of Utah, up to 1.5 million Horned Grebes

(Podiceps auritus) aggregate to molt. Most aquatic birds of the Northern Hemisphere breed in high latitudes and then migrate south to wintering grounds. Many European and Asian species move to Africa; many Asian species move to India and some even to Australia. European populations of the Common Crane *(Grus grus)* spend the winter in southern Spain, North Africa, and Sudan; Asian populations migrate to northern India and China. The White Stork *(Ciconia ciconia)* spends the winter in the savannas south of the Sahara Desert, extending down to South Africa. North American species, for example, Osprey *(Pandion haliaetus),* Greater and Lesser Yellowlegs *(Tringa melanoleuca, T. flavipes),* Upland Sandpiper *(Batramia longicauda),* and other shorebirds, spend the winter in South America. Migrations of wetland birds of the Southern Hemisphere are much less spectacular and are almost exclusively restricted to between the southern neotropics and temperate regions barely reaching southernmost Brazil. One of the few exceptions might be the poorly understood migration pattern of the Snail Kite *(Rostrhamus sociabilis).*

Migrating waterbirds in semiarid and arid areas are adept at detecting ephemeral wetlands. Lake Eyre, a large ephemeral lake in the arid zone of Australia, only floods every few years. During the 1990 flood, about 300,000 waterbirds including 135,000 shorebirds were recorded from the lake (Kingsford and Porter 1993), and with the associated Cooper Creek floodplain and nearby lakes, habitat for more than a million waterbirds of approximately 75 species was provided. Many species bred because food resources were abundant. Breeding events of the magnitude of 1990 probably occur about once every 10 years (Kingsford et al. 1999). Banding data indicate that most Australian waterbird species are capable of flights exceeding 1000 kilometers (Blaker et al. 1984). In Africa, observations from isolated pans in Namibia suggest that birds follow rain fronts and descend onto pans as they fill (Simmons et al. 1998). However, after a boom period, populations often crash.

Interwetland dispersal of aquatic invertebrates and plants by endozoochory (in guts) and ectozoochory (on feathers and feet) of migratory waterbirds is a frequent process and may at least in part explain the wide geographical ranges of many aquatic macrophytes, algae, and plankton species (Santamaria 2002). Pulsing systems benefit from the introduction of propagules by birds because periodic intense droughts reduce species numbers. Efficiency of dispersal decreases with distance, but is to a certain extent compensated by the large number of migrating waterbirds (Clausen et al. 2002; Figuerola and Green 2002; Green et al. 2002). Studies on aquatic macrophytes suggest that broadly distributed species have higher genetic variation than species with restricted distributions (Crawford et al. 1997). The genetic differentiation among neighboring populations in pond-dwelling organisms may be the result of effective monopolization of resources by founder populations, yielding a strong buffer effect against newly invading genotypes (De Meester et al. 2002).

Coesel and associates (1988) explained the split of the desmid algae in South America into an east-Andean and west-Andean flora because the Andes can not be crossed by many waterfowl. There is, however, a high similarity of desmid algae in water bodies and wetlands in the north–south direction along waterfowl flyways; this observation points toward a north–south dispersal of the desmids by birds. One flyway follows the inter-Andean valleys, and another follows the Caribbean coastline, where algal transport is interrupted because the algae can not survive in saline water. Species distribution also occurs in the reverse south–north direction, as shown by Löffler (1968). About 20% of the nonmalacostracan crustaceans of tropical high-Andean lakes, including the genera *Boeckella* and *Pseudoboeckella*, also occur on the southern tip of the continent. This suggests that the high Andes acts as a climatic highway for cold-adapted species extending from the Antarctic to Venezuela and also emphasizes the importance of migrating waterfowl. Amezaga and colleagues (2002) recommend that species-oriented conservation programs for waterbirds consider their role in the dispersal of other aquatic organisms and that they operate at a migratory flyway level.

SPECIES EXCHANGE BETWEEN INTERTIDAL WETLANDS AND OTHER HABITATS

In intertidal wetlands, the total number of species of terrestrial plants and animal groups is lower than in pulsing freshwater ecosystems because in addition to flood and drought stress, flora and fauna are subjected to heavy osmotic stress. The vascular flora of the Indian Sunderban comprises only about 100 species (34 families and 57 genera), including 30 tree species and 32 shrubs (Debnath and Naskar 1999). Thirty-six species are considered "true mangroves" and the remaining as "mangrove associates."

The situation is similar for mammals, amphibians, and reptiles. In the Sunderban, there are only 49 species of mammals, 8 species of amphibians, and 59 species of reptiles (Gopal and Chauhan, in press), which is considerably less than in the Pantanal or Okavango Delta. Complete data sets on terrestrial insect diversity in all types of pulsing systems are lacking. However, the diversity is probably much lower in intertidal systems than in freshwater floodplains because the soil and canopy faunas are poorly developed, and these groups represent the bulk of insect diversity in freshwater floodplains. Most soil-living insects can not tolerate frequent floods and high salinity. Their functions in intertidal litter decomposition are filled by mangrove-specific animals such as crabs. The relatively low number of tree species in mangroves and extreme microclimatic conditions limit the canopy fauna to highly specialized species and a few visitors.

On the other hand, the number of fish species in intertidal wetlands is comparatively high. These highly mobile animals can enter marine floodplains when conditions are appropriate. In the Sunderbans, 53 pelagic fish species, 124 demersal brackish and marine species (Sarker 1989), and 31 freshwater species (Sanyal 1999) are described. In the mangroves of Vietnam, 260 fish species have been recorded (Hong and San 1993). Total biodiversity is increased considerably by representatives of invertebrate groups that occur predominantly or exclusively in the marine environment, such as tintinnids, radiolarians, foraminiferans, sponges, hydroids, anemones, ascidians, polychaetes, tanaids, and barnacles. Crustaceans (240 species) and mollusks (143 species) make up a large part of the macroinvertebrate species diversity of the Sunderban (Gopal and Chauhan, in press).

Mangals are also the home of "manglicolous fungi," a specialized fungal group with more than 120 species worldwide (listed by Hyde 1990).

Intertidal wetlands also support many bird species. On the Bangladesh side of the Sunderban, 315 bird species have been recorded (Hussain and Acharya 1994), approximately 95 of which are waterfowl (Scott 1989). Intertidal wetlands are important breeding, feeding, molting, and stopover sites for migrating birds. Almost 100,000 Common Shelducks *(Tadorna tadorna)* molt in the German Wadden Sea. Approximately 100 of the more than 300 bird species recorded from the Indian side of the Sunderban undertake migrations (Chaudhuri and Choudhury 1994). Seventy-seven bird species have been recorded in the Pacific mangroves of Colombia, of which 43% are permanent residents, 22% are regular visitors, and 18% are temporary winter residents.

ALTERING THE FLOOD PULSE: IMPACTS ON BIODIVERSITY

There is no doubt among scientists that long-term changes of the flood pulse will severely affect community structure, community distribution, and species diversity, but few studies have quantified these changes. Furthermore, alterations of the flood pulse are often correlated with other changes, and it becomes difficult to isolate the impacts of individual factors. For instance, the construction of a large reservoir modifies the flood pulse downriver, but it also diminishes sediment loads, accelerates erosion of the river channel, modifies water quality, increases phytoplankton and zooplankton densities, and interrupts longitudinal connectivity. Therefore, before giving examples, we would like to first classify the major types of change and describe the expected general impacts on flora and fauna as predicted by the Flood Pulse Concept.

Construction of reservoirs for hydroelectric power generation, irrigation, or flood control and construction of lateral dikes for flood protection cause major changes in flood pulses. Dams with a short water retention time have a minimal effect on the flood pulse as the water flows through them in a nearly natural hydrologic pattern. Their impact on species diversity is mainly derived by the interruption of longitudinal connectivity, which can affect migrating aquatic species such as salmon in temperate regions and migrating characids, carp, and catfish in the tropics. Small and medium hydropower plants are planned for the upper sections of nearly all tributaries to the Pantanal, which will cut off the breeding sites for some economically very important catfish and characid fish species such as *Pseudoplatystoma fasciatum, P. corruscans,* and *Salminus maxillosus (cachara, pintado, dourado).*

Larger reservoirs reduce the flood amplitude and introduce the risk that water might be released during periods that do not mirror the natural flood regime. This happens in the Cuiabá River in Mato Grosso, where a large reservoir controls the water flow of the Manso River, its main tributary. A water release from the Manso Dam during the 2001 dry season washed away the majority of skimmer nestlings of the Cuiabá River. During the past few years, low water levels have been about 0.5 meters higher, while normal floods have been lower than before the dam was built. Breeding success of shorebirds such as terns has been low probably because vegetation-free sandbars used as nesting places have been lost. In contrast, the number of shallow water bodies has increased, which favors the survival of aquatic macrophytes such as water hyacinth. The dissolved oxygen concentration in these habitats has been reduced. Fish-eating birds no longer frequent these areas because of the low visibility of prey and their own vulnerability to predators. Based on long-term observations in other regions of the Pantanal (Wantzen et al. 2005), we anticipate that dense floating macrophyte islands will develop, and organic detritus will accumulate. Lower and shorter floods will also modify plant cover by favoring terrestrial species. Fires will become more frequent in these areas because of drier conditions and will quickly eliminate flood-resistant, but fire-intolerant, tree species such as *Vochysia divergens* (Nunes da Cunha and Junk 2004). On the other hand, this reservoir is not large enough to control extreme floods, which might be catastrophic for wildlife populations and cattle that can not cope with unpredictable, extreme flood events.

Very large reservoirs or a combination of numerous locks, dams, levees, and water diversions can profoundly modify not only the amplitude of the flood pulse, but also its duration, shape, and timing. This has far-reaching consequences for fauna and flora. The importance of the timing of the flood pulse with respect to the seasons in temperate regions has been shown by Ahn and associates (2004) for the Illinois River. Over the past 100 years, the hydrologic regime changed from a rather predictable pulsing system with a flood peak in spring and a low-water period in summer to a system with unnaturally rapid fluctuations year-round. With natural flood pulses, moist-soil plants grew on the extensive mud flats that were exposed during summer and reached maturity before the next flood. These plants produced seeds and tubers for waterfowl during their fall and spring migrations, and habitat and food for aquatic invertebrates and fish during the subsequent flood. Under current erratic flood conditions, moist-soil plants are flooded during the vegetative period, decreasing productivity. The Decurrent False Aster *(Boltonia decurrens)*, a federally listed threatened species in the United States (USFWS 1988) that is endemic to the Illinois River, may become extinct.

In semiarid and arid regions, water retention and diversion might be catastrophic for many organisms. Erratic high floods provide important flood pulses for ephemeral wetlands and are of vital importance not only for the specific wetlands, but also at a continental scale for migrating waterbirds, as shown for Cooper Creek in Australia (Kingsford et al. 1999).

The importance of the shape of floods is also evident with poplars (*Populus* spp.). Poplars require a pronounced flood disturbance because seeds germinate only on vegetation-free sediment banks. Further, seedlings can establish only when the groundwater level drops slowly so the tap-root can maintain contact with groundwater. A lack of disturbance by current or rapidly falling water levels will inhibit natural recruitment of poplar stands (Rood and Mahoney 1990). But controlled pulsing can also be an important management tool, for example, to increase food production for waterfowl in North American floodplains (Fredrickson and Taylor 1982).

While dams mainly influence longitudinal connectivity and hydrologic characteristics, dikes which were built for flood protection influence the lateral connectivity between river and floodplain or between floodplain and the hinterlands. For centuries, low dikes along the Rhine River protected parts of the floodplain against minor floods during summer to provide pasture for domestic animals (so-called summer dikes), but these dikes did not inhibit major floods. The impact of these dikes on biodiversity is difficult to isolate because the floodplain forests that naturally covered most of these areas were removed to establish pastures. Consequences of these dikes, however, included the accelerated deposition of fine sediments on the floodplain, the flattening of the soil surface, a decrease in habitat diversity (Nienhuis and Leuven 2001), and an increased invasion of terrestrial herbaceous species. The impacts of high dikes for flood protection are more obvious. They isolate the floodplain from the main channel and completely modify vegetative cover and the associated fauna. Bottomland hardwood forest communities will disappear within a few decades because conditions for natural recruitment are eliminated.

Besides river floodplains, human alterations of pulses into tidal wetlands have also had important impacts on biodiversity. In Europe, many intertidal wetlands have been eliminated by land reclamation or modified by flood protection measures. Mangrove wetlands worldwide are threatened by timber harvest, overexploitation of fishery resources, construction of fish and shrimp culture ponds and paddy fields, land reclamation for civil construction, water pollution and solid waste disposal, and salinity change. Human exploitation of mangrove forests, especially conversion to paddy fields, has accounted for the reclamation of about 7,000 km² of the Sunderban since the advent of British administration in the eighteenth century. Key species such as the Javan rhinoceros *(Rhinoceros sondaicus)*, water buffalo *(Bubalus bubalis)*, swamp deer *(Cervus duvauceli)*, gaur *(Bos frontalis)*, and hog deer *(Axis porcinus)* have disappeared locally during the last century. Others such as the Bengal tiger *(Panthera tigris)* and the Ganges River dolphin *(Platanista gangetica)* now occur only in protected reserves, wildlife sanctuaries, and national parks (Gopal and Chauhan, in press). The functional relationships among the different ecosystems that make up the coastal regions require *integrated coastal zone management* (ICZM). This term describes a continuous and dynamic process uniting government and the community, science and management, and sectoral and public interest in preparing and implementing an integrated plan for the protection and development of coastal systems and resources (GESAMP 1996). ICZM includes the establishment of protected areas, sustainable management of natural resources, and restoration/rehabilitation measures (Macintosh and Ashton 2002).

A major threat to intertidal systems is the predicted rise in the sea level caused by the anthropogenic increase in "greenhouse gases." The rise in the sea level does not change the flood pulse but shifts the intertidal belt farther inland and may cause backflooding in estuary systems, as predicted for Australian coastal wetlands (Eliot et al. 1999). To what extent intertidal systems can shift is an open question and will be site specific. Many coastlines are not geomorphologically suitable or are already occupied by humans. Additional stress factors to coastal wetlands include increasing temperature, changes in the hydrologic regime (rainfall, evapotranspiration, runoff, salinity), and increasing tropical storm intensity. Because mangroves are highly specialized and already live close to their tolerance limits, they might be particularly sensitive to minor variations in hydrologic or tidal regimes (Davis et al. 1994b; Kjerfve and Macintosh 1997).

CONCLUSIONS

Flood-pulsing wetlands (freshwater and intertidal floodplain systems) are ecosystems characterized by a pronounced change between terrestrial and aquatic phases. They receive their water from rivers, lakes, rainfall, melting snow, groundwater, or, in the case of intertidal systems, from the sea. Connectivity with permanent aquatic habitats is of fundamental importance to biodiversity because of species exchange. Floodplains isolated from permanent water bodies will have a lower species richness and lack many aquatic species.

Depending on the local hydrologic regime, flood pulses vary in amplitude, duration, frequency, shape, timing, and predictability. Changes in elevation of a few decimeters or meters can considerably modify the impact of the flood pulse and increase habitat diversity. Hydromorphic processes can permanently modify wetland surfaces, affect sediment consistency and heterogeneity, and through erosion and sediment deposition set back biotic community development (Junk et al. 1989).

Floodplains harbor a set of species uniquely adapted to a change between terrestrial and aquatic conditions. Predictable pulsing over long time periods favors the development of adaptations. Thus, human-induced changes in the flood pulse can profoundly affect species distributions within floodplains and cause reductions in abundance or even species extinctions (Ahn et al. 2004). Floodplains are also important to numerous species from connected terrestrial, freshwater, and marine ecosystems. Although species diversity is often high (Gopal and Junk 2000), the number of endemic species in most floodplains is low because flood pulsing facilitates the dislocation of organisms and hinders speciation by genetic isolation. Long-distance transport of propagules of aquatic organisms, such as algae, zooplankton, and aquatic macrophytes by aquatic birds among otherwise isolated wetlands may explain the wide distributions of these organisms (Santamaria 2002). On the other hand, permanent changes in environmental conditions require morphological and physiological plasticity, which are prerequisites for speciation and species diversity (West-Eberhard 1989; Henderson et al. 1998). For instance, geographic separation of populations of trees in paleo-floodplains by dislocation of river courses might lead to speciation (Salo et al. 1986). Flood-pulsing systems are very sensitive to hydrologic changes, which can lead to extinction of highly adapted species. Because of the large size of their parent rivers, large tropical river floodplains (e.g., the Amazon River floodplain) are more resilient to hydrologic changes, and they harbor numerous highly specialized species.

The large number of species in flood-pulsing systems, including terrestrial, aquatic, and floodplain species, imparts a special importance to the systems for the maintenance of biodiversity at a landscape scale. Many terrestrial species that are endangered in habitats outside the floodplains maintain healthy populations within the wetlands. All large floodplains are periodically visited by immigrants from adjacent terrestrial and aquatic ecosystems, or from other wetlands, to feed, use water, reproduce, and the like. The elimination of floodplains or major changes in the flood pulse would not only harm floodplain-specific species, but could also strongly impact populations of migratory species, reducing the carrying capacity of the entire landscape for these species and for the human beings. Populations of migrating birds could even be affected at intercontinental scales.

ACKNOWLEDGMENT

We greatly acknowledge the correction of the English by the editor Dr. Darold Batzer.

12

CONSEQUENCES FOR WETLANDS OF A CHANGING GLOBAL ENVIRONMENT

Mark Brinson

One of the major components of global climate change is water balance. Few ecosystems are so dependent on water as wetlands, and thus vulnerable to changes in water sources and evapotranspiration. As a general rule, wetlands will diminish under drier conditions because water inputs will be reduced, while the opposite is true for climates that become wetter. We need only compare an arid state like Arizona, with less than 1% wetland coverage, with Florida and Louisiana, with greater than 33% coverage (Fretwell et al. 1996), to see a correspondence between climate and wetland abundance.

We also know that climate, and especially temperature, has changed dramatically over the history of the earth in the absence of human activity. Much detailed information about climate changes since the Wisconsin glacial maximum (~18,000 years ago) comes from the vegetation record in pollen profiles in lake and wetland sediments. A number of studies allow us to reconstruct both temperature and atmospheric composition of gases from glacial ice cores many millennia earlier (Alley 2000). Good records of CO_2 concentrations capture the recent record of human activity from preindustrial CO_2 levels of 280 ppm (parts per million) to the present level of 380 ppm. Corresponding estimates of water temperatures show past fluctuations within a 4°C range until the end of the Little Ice Age (ca. 1500–1850 AD), after which some of the highest temperatures have been recorded (Fig. 12.1), with the 1990s being the warmest decade and 1998 the warmest year (Mann et al. 1999). We can conclude from this history that climate change is normal but that the recent trend in human-induced warming is likely to continue into the foreseeable future. Because of various degrees of uncertainty, much of the information in this chapter is necessarily speculative.

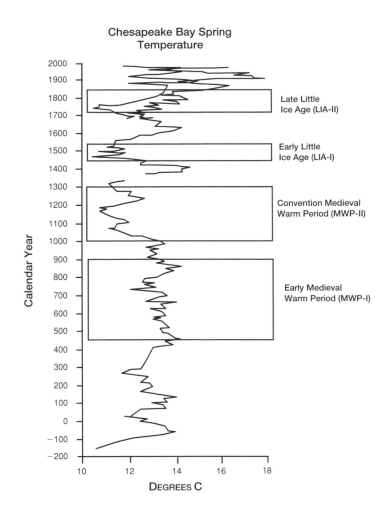

FIGURE 12.1

Spring temperatures of the Chesapeake Bay. After Cronin and associates (2003).

The history of converting wetlands to other uses is very short by comparison, and that of wetland protection is even shorter. Given that the United States, for example, has converted approximately 50% of its pre-Colonial wetlands to other land uses (in the lower 48 states), it is doubtful if global change would cause either a gain or loss of wetlands of that magnitude in so little time. This fact simply points to the necessity of evaluating more critically how we will manage the remaining 50%. The fact that similar losses have occurred throughout the world makes more urgent an understanding between direct human alterations of wetlands through draining and diking, and the more indirect ones related to climate change (Brinson and Malvarez 2002; Junk 2002). The issue becomes even more complicated when one realizes that wetlands may alternatively serve as sinks for atmospheric CO_2, thus ameliorating climate change, and as sources of methane, thus contributing to atmospheric warming.

All of these issues take place within a geopolitical framework that ranges from no-net-loss policies at national and regional scales in the United States to international agreements that deal with climate change (van Dam et al. 2002), of which wetlands are only one part (Box 12.1). When wetlands are viewed as potential sinks for atmospheric CO_2, their capacity is small relative to the short-term potential of other land uses to sequester this greenhouse gas. On the other hand, wetland soils contain a disproportionate stock of organic carbon (Table 12.1) (Schlesinger 1977). This means that unless wetlands are managed to maintain those stocks, they could contribute substantially to the already accelerating rate of atmospheric CO_2 accumulation.

This chapter begins with the assumptions used for establishing the scenarios for climate change, with increasing temperature as a given, but change in water balance being much less predictable. The effects of increasing temperature on biota are examined next along with altered water balance and increasing CO_2 concentrations. In some cases, very different conclusions can be drawn depending on whether species populations or ecosystems are being considered. Recognition of wetland types, which vary in the relative importance of water sources, is used as a way to examine scenarios in response to global change. How species redistribute themselves along changing moisture and temperature gradients will depend on dispersal powers and geographic barriers, some of which are the result of human activities. In contrast, the dispersal of invasive species is testimony that human activities have lowered geographic barriers. Finally, a number of management issues relate to climate change. Some fall into the category of how wetlands can play a

TABLE 12.1   Estimated Stocks of Detrital Organic Carbon

Ecosystem Type	Mean Total Profile Detritus (kg C m^{-2})	World Area (ha $\times$ 10^8)	Total World Detritus (Mg C $\times$ 10^9)
Tropical forest	10.4	24.5	255
Temperate forest	11.8	12.0	142
Boreal forest	14.9	12.0	179
Woodland and shrub	6.9	8.5	59
Tropical savanna	3.7	15.0	56
Temperate grassland	19.2	9.0	173
Tundra and alpine	21.6	8.0	173
Desert scrub	5.6	18.0	101
Extreme desert, rock, ice	0.1	24.0	3
Cultivated	12.7	14.0	178
Swamp and marsh	68.6	2.0	137
Total		147	1,456

NOTE: Highest-standing stocks are found in wetlands (swamp and marsh) and zones containing extensive peatlands (e.g., boreal forest and tundra). Despite the low areal coverage of swamp and marsh, global-standing stocks are the same order of magnitude as some of the largest biomes. From Schlesinger (1977).

role in ameliorating change, while others are simply ways of mitigating the effects of climate change on wetlands.

ASSUMPTIONS

Global change in its broadest sense includes not only warming and changes in precipitation, but also human-induced changes in the direct alteration of wetlands through drainage, eutrophication, altered land use, and increased frequency of fire. This occurs against a backdrop of historical variations in climate such as the Little Ice Age and Milankovitch cycles, the latter corresponding to glacial and interglacial episodes over the past 800,000 years (Sturman and Tapper 1996). These patterns obviously were not human induced. For the purposes of this discussion, we focus mainly on global climate warming and associated changes in precipitation, forced largely by changes since the beginning of the Industrial Revolution.

We must rely on general circulation models (i.e., mathematical models of climate predictions; IPCC 1995) as the basis for making predictions about climate change. The geographic scale of these models is rather crude (yet improving), so climate change for wetlands in any particular region can not be predicted in detail. While temperature predictions are always positive (but rates of change may differ by latitude), water balance is not so easily predicted because it depends on both precipitation and temperature, the latter influencing evapotranspiration.

Reliance on annual average temperatures can be misleading, however, because of potential changes in the nature of temperature variation. For example, average annual minimum temperatures have increased at twice the rate of maximum temperatures (IPCC 1995). This can occur with warmer nights and no change in daytime temperatures or with warmer temperatures during one season and not another. Species that are sensitive to frost (mangroves) may respond to winter temperatures more than changes in annual average temperatures would suggest (Lugo and Patterson Zucca 1977). Responses in species composition and productivity have already been reported for arid temperate grassland communities (Alward et al. 1999).

It could be argued that wetlands will be affected by these changes to a greater extent than upland ecosystems (Kusler and Burkett 1999; Burkett and Kusler 2000). First, wetland biota are especially sensitive to small changes in the proximity of the soil surface and the water surface or water table. The difference between wetland plant species being classified as "obligate" or "facultative" can be a matter of only a few centimeters of average water table or water depth (see Chapter 6). Second, wetlands have been fragmented by dams, highways, dikes, roads, drainages, and other changes, thus restricting the capacity of wetland species to migrate to their "preferred" climate in another area. For coastal wetlands, dikes, roadways, and other land use impediments often block them from migrating landward in response to rising sea level. Finally, wetlands have already been stressed by human activities due to changes in hydrology, eutrophication, pollution by toxicants, and other alterations. These stressors may cause local extinctions, not to mention reduction in the total genetic pool due to declining areas of favorable habitat. Additional changes due to altered temperatures and water balance may further contribute to deterioration of wetland area and condition.

Extreme events exacerbate the unpredictability of climate change effects. The frequency, tracks, duration, and intensity of tropical storms and hurricanes may change (Michener et al. 1997). Warmer sea surface temperatures, for example, may increase the frequency of hurricanes and cause them to travel to higher latitudes. Coastal marshes and mangroves are particularly affected, which may have conflicting outcomes. On one hand, the rate of soil accretion may increase from storm-generated sediment supplies, thus offsetting potential effects from accelerating rates of rising sea level (Cahoon et al. 1995). On the other hand, wind effects from hurricanes can cause tree loss in both mangroves and freshwater forested wetlands, possibly reducing their capacity to stabilize sediments during these episodes.

With increasing global temperatures, and associated increases in storms and floods, there has been concern over the spread of infectious diseases. Some, such as malaria, yellow fever, and dengue, depend on mosquito vectors, with the popular belief that the diseases are associated mainly with wetland conditions. Dengue and yellow fever were common from the seventeenth century onwards in the United States, with yellow fever killing tens of thousands of people as far north as New York in 1878 (Reiter 1996). Temperature and favorable habitat for vectors of arboviruses may be a necessary but not sufficient condition for disease prevalence in human populations. Public health practices and lifestyles have a greater influence on the spread of these diseases than the temperature tolerance of their vectors (Marshall 1997). Increased incidence of West Nile virus in recent years (Bourgeade and Marchou 2003) is apparently unrelated to changes in temperature.

Finally, wetlands may play a role in the "missing carbon"* in the global carbon cycle. This involves the redistribution of organic carbon on land whereby erosion, sediment transport, and sediment deposition occurs within terrestrial ecosystems (Stallard 1998). Agricultural fields, roadways, grazed areas, landslides, wind erosion, and fire-flood events are erosion sources. Depositional environments in wetlands are riverine wetlands on floodplains, lacustrine fringe wetlands on margins and of lakes and reservoirs, and other wetland areas positioned to accumulate sediments. Earlier models assumed that this terrestrially derived carbon would eventually be deposited in the ocean and estuaries. Stallard (1998) estimates that burial of organic carbon in terrestrial sites approaches 10^{15} g C yr^{-1}. Because data to make these estimates can not be derived from remote sensing, as is the case for mobilization due to land use changes, the role of wetlands has not been fully recognized.

These assumptions are at once simplistic and potentially conflicting. This is due in part to the low spatial resolution of general circulation models (GCM) and in part to uncertainty of the relative importance of feedbacks and interactions of CO_2, temperature, and precipitation. For the purpose of this chapter, we will assume that increased CO_2 may result in short-term increases in plant net primary production but that these effects may not be long lasting. Extremes in temperature (i.e., frost, nighttime temperatures, seasonality, etc.) tend to be more influential in affecting species composition than changes in annual averages. Despite all of these subtleties, we can assume that drier conditions will lead to reduced wetland abundance, and wetter conditions will have the opposite effect.

EFFECTS ON CARBON BALANCE

The influence of higher concentrations of atmospheric CO_2 is most commonly measured by doubling the CO_2 levels in the laboratory and in the field. For example, marshes on the Chesapeake Bay, where some of the earliest relevant studies took place, showed quite striking increases in photosynthesis with raised CO_2 levels (Arp et al. 1993). Work in the Arctic tundra initially showed a spike in photosynthesis, but this effect was short lived as increases in rates of respiration effectively cancelled out the initial sequestering (Oechel et al. 1993). These Arctic study sites continue to experience a net source to the atmosphere, and further warming could increase emissions even more (Oechel et al. 2000).

Responses of plants to CO_2 enrichment are further masked by human-caused enrichment by nitrogen and phosphorus in wetlands and contributing aquatic ecosystems. Strong competitors such as *Typha* tend to flourish when excessive nutrients are available. When low fertility sites, such as bogs and some lake shorelines, are exposed to nutrient enrichment, they favor weedy, aggressive species that can outcompete the native dominant species

* Missing carbon is the difference between the estimated sources (fossil fuel burning, land clearing, concrete production, etc.) and the increase in atmospheric CO_2.

as well as those that are rare and endangered (Wisheu and Keddy 1992). In these situations, CO_2 enrichment may contribute to loss of sensitive species and thus reduce local plant biodiversity. On the other hand, concurrent increases in temperature could have exactly the opposite effect on interspecific competition if water stress increases, thus favoring C-4 species under conditions that would otherwise favor C-3 species under CO_2-rich exposure. These trends are further complicated by shifts in allocation of growth between aboveground and belowground parts (Drake et al. 1996). It is difficult to predict the simultaneous effects of CO_2 enrichment and a drying climate, especially if the latter causes changes in species composition and accelerates the rate of soil organic matter oxidation.

Interest in decomposition of soil organic matter is especially relevant in wetlands because organic carbon accumulation under anoxic conditions is induced by waterlogged soils. Peatlands have received special attention because of the large amounts of carbon that they have accumulated over millennia (Table 12.1). Bridgham and associates (1995) identified three local controls on decomposition of soil organic matter and concurrent nutrient release: temperature that affects microbial metabolism, water table position that regulates the anoxic-oxic soil boundary, and the quality of organic matter that varies in nutrient concentration. As it turns out, all three are important, and they interact in ways that require that all be considered simultaneously. For a 10°C rise in temperature in laboratory experiments, methanogenesis resulted in a 28-fold increase over the first meter in depth of bog peat, a 16-fold increase for surface bog peat, and only a 2-fold increase for beaver meadow soil. Emissions of methane were reduced with deeper water tables because the unsaturated and oxic surface stratum provides an opportunity for methane to be oxidized before it escapes to the atmosphere. These results emphasize the importance of not treating organic matter as a single pool, but one that can differ by wetland type, soil depth, and hydroperiod. Dalva and colleagues (2001) predicted from the GCM 2xCO$_2$ model (i.e., doubling the CO_2 concentration) that higher temperatures and drier conditions for eastern Canada would result in approximately doubling of CH_4 and CO_2 emissions during the growing season. Ombrotrophic bogs in cool temperate zones have been shown to emit significant quantities of CO_2 during the nongrowing season, indicating that existing models developed to predict temperature-dependent exchanges may be insensitive and inaccurate at lower temperatures (Roehm and Nigel 2003).

Seasonally and perennially frozen soils in the boreal and arctic zones encompass one of the largest stores of terrestrial organic carbon globally (Gorham 1991). Significant warming in the past century has already caused a change in structure of the plant community from tundra tussock to shrub cover type (Oechel et al. 2000). Warming of these regions has increased the active zone in permafrost (i.e., lowered the permafrost table) with two alternative results. On one hand, thawing promotes drainage, and soil organic matter is exposed to increased rates of decomposition, with corresponding releases of CO_2 and methane to the atmosphere. The specific mechanism appears to be stimulation of soil respiration of organic carbon deep in the soil due to elimination of permafrost and increased drainage (Goulden et al. 1998). Potentially better growth conditions for shrubs do not necessarily offset this source of CO_2. In fact, denser vegetation has an insulating effect that serves to maintain permafrost. Alternatively, where soils become more water-logged due to thawing, CO_2 sequestering increases. Under more anoxic conditions, methane emissions increase at the expense of CO_2 (Smith et al. 2004). Since methane is a much stronger greenhouse gas than CO_2, the net effect is most likely a positive feedback of increasing the atmospheric concentrations of both gases.

If all of the arctic and boreal soil carbon were released by climatic warming, the concentration of atmosphere CO_2 could increase as much as 50%. For arctic tundra, there are recent indications of acclimation to warmer temperatures and thus lower net CO_2 losses (Oechel et al. 2000). However, these sites are still a net source to the atmosphere, and further warming could increase emissions (Oechel et al. 1993). The contribution of peat bogs in the boreal zone (50–70°N latitude) to atmospheric methane is estimated at 60% of global total.

Additional feedbacks may contribute as well. Fire is an important albeit infrequent natural phenomenon in the boreal zones (Van Cleve et al. 1991). Higher frequency and intensity of fires are expected to accompany drier conditions. It is not the combustion of vegetation, which constitutes only 1.5% of the total carbon pool, but the burning of accumulated peat that contributes the lion's share of emissions. Peat fires would stimulate a positive feedback of further atmospheric warming (Gorham 1991). Other processes that may affect high latitude peatlands arc (1) increased plant production in response to CO_2 enrichment that may be neutralized by faster rates of decomposition, (2) increased nutrient availability due to enhanced decomposition that could increase plant production, and (3) lowering of the water table that could affect the emissions of methane to the atmosphere (Bridgham et al. 1995).

Regardless of the details for each of the mechanisms of carbon release and sequestering, Net Ecosystem Exchange (NEE) is the ultimate test of the effectiveness of wetlands to sequester or emit carbon (see Chapter 5). In contrast to net photosynthesis, net primary production, and community respiration, NEE represents the positive or negative flux (or steady state, when NEE = 0) of carbon between the atmosphere and the ecosystem in question. (By convention, a positive NEE represents sequestration, while negative NEE represents emission to the atmosphere.) Much of the work on NEE is being conducted in major biomes of terrestrial ecosystems that provide a basis for extrapolation over large geographic regions. In contrast to relatively homogeneous uplands, wetlands are highly heterogeneous in hydrologic regimes, size, and vegetation cover. Eddy diffusion flux towers, which are the preferred method for making these measurements (Falge et al. 2002), require intensive and continuous data collection over long periods of time to integrate daily, seasonal, and interannual sources of variation. It is unlikely that studies will soon provide equivalent estimates of NEE for an array of wetlands over such broad geographic areas.

EFFECTS ON SPECIES COMPOSITION AND REDISTRIBUTION

Wetland species are not necessarily optimally adapted to their habitat, but are simply better competitors than more purely terrestrial and aquatic species. They are habitat specialists

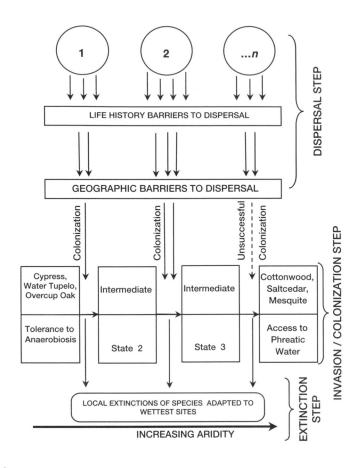

FIGURE 12.2

Conceptual model of factors contributing to changes in species composition of riverine forest undergoing increasing aridity in the warm-temperate region. Centers of dispersal (1, 2,... *n* at top) are potential sources of species that may migrate during climate change. Life history barriers to dispersal are plant and animal traits. Geographic barriers to dispersal are physical impediments. The paired rectangular boxes represent four of many possible states, ranging from a continuously saturated wetland (left side) to arid riparian community (right side). Shifts in species from one state to another during climate warming and drying occurs by the addition of species (invasion/colonization step) and by the extirpation of species (extinction step). Adapted from Michener and associates (1997). Also see Davis and colleagues (2005).

that can survive nowhere else on the landscape. One of the major values of wetlands is their contribution to biodiversity and wildlife in most landscapes (Brinson and Verhoeven 1999; Bedford et al. 2001). This is expected to change because of warming, altered water balance, and the influence of CO_2 concentrations on photosynthetic mechanisms.

Using the existing distribution of species along moisture and temperature continua as a conceptual model (Euliss et al. 2004), one scenario is to assume that plant and animal species in freshwater wetlands would gradually redistribute their populations to higher (once cooler) latitudes and equivalent moisture regimes (Grimm 1993). Following this logic, wetland communities would actually shift from their present geographic location to warmer and drier (or wetter) climates (Michener et al. 1997). Ash-elm-silver maple forests of the Upper Midwest would be replaced by cypress-tupelo swamps that are currently limited to lower latitudes. Tundra wetlands in the arctic permafrost region would be replaced by black spruce forests currently growing in discontinuous permafrost areas of the taiga. In each case, migration and colonization by wetland plants and animals could be predicted by adding species that migrate from their once more favorable climatic conditions elsewhere and the removal of species that become locally extinct because of changing environmental conditions. Species that survive the changed conditions locally would be those that have broadly adaptive traits suited to the new environment. An understanding of these traits may allow predictions of survival under future environmental conditions (Keddy 1992a, 1992b).

If all species had instantaneous dispersal powers in response to climate change, and enough was known about tolerances of individual species, it might be possible to predict species responses with great accuracy. However, climate change may be one of the easier variables to resolve. Many confounding, nonlinear factors come into play. These variables can be evaluated by considering three steps or bottlenecks, illustrated in Figure 12.2, for species in an area undergoing increasing aridity. The dispersal step may be limited by traits of the species themselves. Those that would otherwise rapidly disperse may then be limited by formidable geographic barriers induced by climate change. For species that can overcome these barriers, colonization would take place at the location along the moisture continuum that is favorable for their establishment. Finally, for those species unable to disperse, the extinction step may come into play as the local climate becomes too dry (or warm) to support them. Extinction may occur due to competitive exclusion by other resident or newly arrived species, to water stress from a drying conditions, or to other factors, including disease, herbivory, predation, and lack of pollinators.

This concept of bottlenecks to species dispersal and colonization is in sharp contrast, however, to observations of the response by recently introduced, nonnative species that rapidly expand their distribution (e.g., *Lythrum salicaria* L. and *Typha x glauca* Godr.) (Fig. 12.3). Galatowitsch and colleagues (1999) attribute these expansions to hydrologic alterations and increases in salinity, respectively, rather than effects from climate change. Further, the proliferation of exotic species may be favored also by nutrient loading as suggested by phosphorus enrichment in the Everglades (Childers et al. 2003). *Phragmites australis* has proliferated at the landward edge of salt marshes in part due to nitrogen enrichment of groundwater (Bertness et al. 2002; Silliman and Bertness 2004). Given the combination of factors that lead to successful colonization and local extinctions, the tendency is toward increasing dominance by the invasive species. There is little doubt that strongly invasive exotic species will play a large role in community composition of wetlands undergoing abiotic changes from climate change.

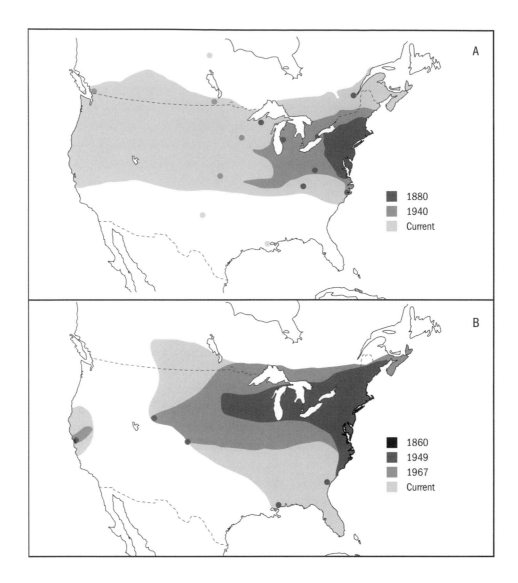

FIGURE 12.3

Changes in the distribution of (A) *Lythrum salicaria* and (B) *Typha x glauca* (and *T. angustifolia*) in North America. From Galatowitsch and associates (1999).

Dispersal rates can not be predicted entirely from life history characteristics, however. Rapid latitudinal changes in the ranges of tree species during the time of continental glacial retreat (over the past 16,000 to 10,000 years) can not be explained strictly by their dispersal capacity (Clark et al. 1998; Powell and Zimmermann 2004). Rare, long-distance mechanisms that may contribute to such rates include dispersal by birds and mammals, transport by tornados and other storms, and movement by water along riparian corridors. For upland plant communities of eastern North America, the rate of change in species composition due to global warming has been predicted to increase at two to five times the rate experienced in the past 18,000 years since the glacial maximum (Overpeck et al. 1991).

For aquatic invertebrates and fish, the predicted warming of water by 4°C would be equivalent to a northward latitudinal shift of about 680 kilometers (Sweeney et al. 1992). In streams and adjacent riverine wetlands, aquatic invertebrates would mature more quickly, and organic matter would be consumed at higher rates. The habitat for trout species in the Rocky Mountain region of North America is predicted to decline by 7% to 16% with an increase in only 1°C air temperature, and 42% to 54% with a 3°C increase (Keleher and Rahel 1996; Rahel et al. 1996). Some of this effect on habitat may be offset by warming of very cold surface waters at high latitudes, such as ice-covered streams in Alaska (Poff et al. 2002), assuming species dispersal is not restricted by geographic barriers.

During the latest glacial retreat, fish moved northward in the Mississippi River basin in apparent response to warming conditions (Briggs 1986). Few other waterways are so well connected across climatic gradients, however. Migration corridors for some streams, for example, are oriented longitudinally, which should restrict migratory pathways for species of aquatic insects that can not disperse over land. And even for those species capable of dispersing along stream channels, formidable barriers now exist in the form of dams and deteriorated water quality. Even for migratory bird populations, which presumably have few dispersal barriers, climate change presents some formidable challenges. Potential effects to waterfowl populations of the Mississippi Flyway are anticipated to be negative (Fig. 12.4), as recognized for the prairie pothole region (PPR) (Box 12.2). On the other hand, migratory bird species could be conceptualized as quite adaptable to climate change, given the fact that their populations have endured several continental glacial maxima in what must be but a short period of their evolutionary history. Thus, it is important to point out that changes in wetlands due to climate change will probably never be as pernicious as the recent activities of society in filling and draining them.

Geographic barriers for some wetland species may be so formidable that they are unlikely to be overcome in the time frame projected for climate change. For example, the flora of alpine wetlands, restricted to the highest peaks in the continental United States, is particularly vulnerable because an increase in temperature will eliminate species that require cold thermal regimes (Halpin 1997).

In other cases, geographic relocation may be constrained by human activity, not the least of which involves the draining and filling of wetlands. Simulations of a wetland model by Johnson and associates (2005) predicted that the most productive habitat for breeding waterfowl would shift under a drier climate from the historic center of the PPR (Dakotas and southeastern Saskatchewan) to the eastern and northern fringes, respectively, areas where most wetlands have been drained or are currently less productive. Again, this argues for the protection and restoration of remaining wetlands as insurance for a future of climate warming.

Finally, CO_2 enrichment itself has the potential to alter species composition in some wetlands types, independently of hydrologic or temperature changes. For example, higher CO_2

BOX 12.2 PREDICTIONS FOR WATERFOWL IN THE NORTHERN GREAT PLAINS OF NORTH AMERICA

The prairie region of the northern United States and southern Canada is vital to the Mississippi Flyway for breeding waterfowl, especially ducks. These populations have been carefully managed by controlling their harvest after it was realized that populations could be decimated with uncontrolled hunting (Sorenson et al. 1998). Populations also undergo large fluctuations naturally due to multiyear climatic cycles of above- and below-average precipitation, characterized as a "boom or bust" cycle. Breeding waterfowl populations and the number of ponds in the prairie pothole region are strongly related to the Palmer Drought Severity Index for May during 1955 to 1996 (Sorenson et al. 1998). Three climate scenarios were tested to project effects of climate change: equilibrium doubled CO_2 and transient climate change scenarios for 2020 and 2050. The results of these simulations (Fig. 12.4) all predict large decreases in both pond numbers and size of populations. These results can not be extrapolated to other regions where drying and drought years may be less frequent and severe.

Sorenson and associates (1998) point out a mitigating factor whereby migrating pairs may overfly the prairie pothole regions during drought years, and move on to boreal forest and tundra regions, thus adjusting somewhat to reduced habitat availability. Although the breeding success of these pairs is projected to be lower, warmer temperatures are likely to alter the wetlands of boreal and tundra regions as described earlier. Further, dabbling ducks are predicted to respond more opportunistically than other species during wet years (Viljugrein et al. 2005). Much of the uncertainty for these scenarios lies in the potentially limited capacity of waterfowl populations to recover from low numbers during drought years in what historically has been a boom or bust cycle.

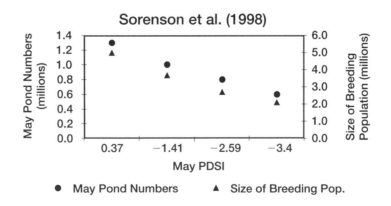

FIGURE 12.4

Simulated relationship between the Palmer Drought Severity Index (PDSI) for May and the number of ponds and duck breeding populations in the prairie pothole region of the United States. The May PDSI of 0.37 is an average for 1955 to 1996. Data from that period were used to predict the other three PDSI scenarios. Adapted from Sorensen and colleagues (1998).

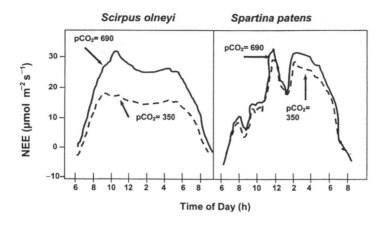

FIGURE 12.5

Net Ecosystem Exchange (NEE) for a C-3 species *(Scirpus olneyi)* and a C-4 species *(Spartina patens)*. Normal and elevated CO_2 concentrations were 350 and 690 ppm, respectively. From Drake (1992). Reproduced with permission from the *Australian Journal of Botany*, published by CSIRO Publishing, Melbourne, Australia. Copyright CSIRO.

concentrations favored C-3 species, in comparison with their C-4 counterparts (Fig. 12.5) in marshes on the Chesapeake Bay. This resulted in an actual decrease in biomass of the C-4 component with 4 years of high CO_2 exposure (Arp et al. 1993; Drake 1992). There are many other variables in addition to CO_2 uptake, however, that should be taken into account including water use efficiency, insect grazing, and soil microbial activity (Thompson and Drake 1994). Therefore, broad generalization of the effect of CO_2 enrichment on wetland communities is not currently feasible (Marsh 1999).

EFFECTS ON WETLAND TYPES

We have just examined some of the direct effects of changes in temperature and CO_2 on species, and possible implications for community change. The situation for the warming of permafrost areas is much more complicated because the physical environment has cascading effects that have not been completely resolved. However, given that hydrology is a major control over wetland processes and structure, hydrologically distinct wetland types will be examined for possible patterns in response to climate change.

Dominant sources of water to wetlands are precipitation, surface flows (overland, overbank, or tidal), and groundwater discharge (see Chapter 3). With a change in net input of water (i.e., the site becomes wetter or drier), one can expect different scenarios depending on wetland type. Under wetter conditions (i.e., net increase in water content), newly formed wetlands would appear, and existing wetlands would expand in size and experience longer duration and depth of flooding. This latter condition may cause shifts in relative species abundance such that submerged and floating wetland species adapted to deeper water would increase abundance relative to emergent species. As a general rule, however, wetland area will expand in response to wetter conditions, all other factors equal, as suggested by the comparison between Arizona and Florida at the beginning of the chapter.

Of greater relevance to climate change is a negative site water balance and the extent to which different wetland types are vulnerable to decreasing size, change in state,* or total loss of wetland identity. (Wetlands controlled mostly by changing sea level will be treated separately.) As a general rule, wetlands dependent on precipitation are highly vulnerable to a drying climate while those dependent on regional groundwater flow systems will be the least vulnerable (Winter 2000). Precipitation-dependent wetlands, such as mineral or organic soil flats, are already at the "dry end" of the spectrum in hydroperiod. They occur in flat landscapes with poor soil drainage, such the coastal plain regions of the eastern United States and northern Alaska. Whereas mineral soil flats would simply change into uplands with drying, the final disposition of organic soil flats (e.g., precipitation-dependent peatlands) would be more complex (Fig. 12.6a). For deep peat deposits, lowered water tables would lead to increased organic matter oxidation and resulting subsidence to a point where the water table would achieve a newly stabilized range of fluctuation. Depending on surrounding topography, groundwater discharge may actually increase as the wetland surface subsides, thus reducing the rate of subsidence over time (Turner 2004). One of the consequences for acidic peat bogs would be the loss of locally rare species such as orchids and insectivorous plants. For histic epipedons, the shallow, organic-rich deposits may disappear altogether resulting in either a mineral soil flat or, more likely, upland conditions. Sites that are replaced by uplands would no longer support biogeochemical cycles characteristic of wetlands (Chapter 5). Isolated depressional wetlands that rely on precipitation, such as the vernal pools of California, are particularly vulnerable, especially in face of the declining numbers caused by increasing human intervention (King et al. 1996).

Hydroperiods driven by surface water include those adjacent to rivers and lakes. A reduction in frequency or magnitude of high flows that inundate riverine floodplains would dry them, further isolate them from stream channels (Fig. 12.6b), and replace wetland plant species with ones less tolerant to flooding (Johnson et al. 1976; Auble et al. 1994).

Aquatic communities that depend on riparian floodplains for protection from predators and seasonal export of organic matter (Sparks et al. 1990; Bayley 1995) would suffer if the floodplains become disconnected because of reduced flood frequencies. Floodplain wetlands dependent on a snowmelt hydrology may be particularly vulnerable to change because peak flows from early season snowmelt may disappear or become greatly reduced (Rood and Mahoney 1990). Analogues of this effect are seen below reservoirs that store flood flows and thus "shave" downstream flood peaks, transforming floodplain forests to

---

*A *change in state* is the transformation from one ecosystem class to another (Hayden et al. 1991). Broadly interpreted, upland could become wetlands and vice versa, irregularly flooded tidal marshes could become regularly flooded or even subtidal, and so forth.

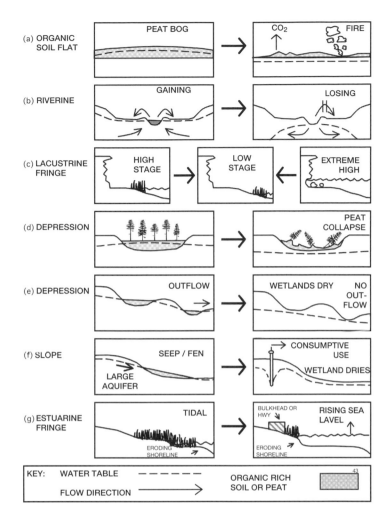

FIGURE 12.6
Anticipated effects of a drying climate on wetland classes. Change occurs as indicated by the direction of the arrows between panels.

species with less flood tolerance. Riverine wetlands would likely become reduced in size, and the proportion of floodplain that is wetland would diminish (Kroes and Brinson 2004). In extreme cases, streams may undergo a transformation from gaining to losing streams (Fig. 12.6b). Largest changes are predicted for snow-dominated basins of mid to high latitudes (Nijssen et al. 2001).

Lake fringe wetlands also tend to be driven by surface water, responding to both seasonal and interannual variations in lake water levels (Fig. 12.6c). Multiannual cycles cause the position of these types of wetlands to migrate back and forth across shallow shorelines (Keough et al. 1999). Their susceptibility to climate change will depend largely on local shoreline morphology. For example, deepening of water under a wetter climate could eliminate some wetlands, especially where the shoreline becomes too steep, or the wave energy too high, to allow plants to establish. Lower water levels would require that plants become established lakeward, but this could happen only if protective barrier beaches form along the shoreline (Kowalski and Wilcox 1999). This is of particular importance for the Great Lakes, where a drying climate will result in a decline in levels with implications for migratory shorebirds, amphibians, and other wetland-dependent species (Chao 1999; Kling et al. 2003).

Groundwater is the principal water supply for many other wetlands. Under a wetter climate regime, rising water tables will create new or expanding wetland areas and make existing wetlands even wetter. For drying, the opposite is predicted and is projected to result not only in reductions of the number of wetlands in the prairie pothole region (Fig. 12.6e), but to reduce breeding waterfowl populations (Box 12.2). Drawdown of water tables can have irreversible consequences. In the northern Tampa Bay area of Florida, peat-based cypress domes have dried due to drawdown for consumptive use (Fig. 12.6d). In other cases, peat oxidation and irreversible subsidence have been accompanied by more destructive fires, invasion of weedy upland plants, and abnormally high tree-fall (Rochow 1994). For riverine wetlands that rely on groundwater as their dominant source in arid climates of the western United States, riparian cottonwood forests have died as a result of groundwater pumping (Scott et al. 1999). These human-induced changes, however, typically occur more abruptly than those expected from a drying climate. Further, because many groundwater-supplied wetlands are supported by large aquifers, the rate at which they are affected by climate change may be slower than those supplied by precipitation and surface water (Winter 2000). Slope wetlands such as fens exemplify this situation (Fig. 12.6f).

Coastal wetlands are influenced by variables that are absent or less influential in interior, freshwater wetlands. First is the relatively smaller effect of changing moisture balance due largely to the relatively inexhaustible supply of water from the ocean. Consequently, coastal wetlands do not have the same degree of drying or wetting that would affect inland wetlands due to climate change. Further, the salinity of most coastal wetlands strongly selects for dominance by halophytes, thus constraining species richness and reducing options for changes in plant species composition. With sea level and salinity as major controls, changes in temperature and precipitation are less likely to be expressed.

Some climate change scenarios predict an increase in the intensity of tropical storms and hurricanes. The interaction of storms with sea level and salinity could have amplifying effects (Michener et al. 1997) superimposed on a host of other stressors and impacts due to local and direct human effects, including eutrophication, changes in hydrology, exposure to toxic chemicals, changes in community composition from overharvesting, and the introduction of new species (Poff et al. 2002). For example, one of the largest coastal wetlands in the United States, the Mississippi Delta, continues to undergo change, albeit somewhat lower than the 0.9% per year loss of emergent habitat that occurred from 1956 to 1978 (Turner 1997). Coastal marshes are particularly sensitive to hydrologic

CONTROVERSY OVER WETLAND LOSS IN THE MISSISSIPPI DELTA

Coastal wetland loss in the northern Gulf of Mexico has been attributed to a number of factors, including rising sea level that drowns plants, subsidence from autocompaction of the deep sediments (with concomitant sediment starvation), oil and gas withdrawal, hydrologic and salinity changes, introduction of pollutants, and effects of pests such as muskrat "eat-outs" (Turner 1997). In an attempt to sort out the most likely causes, Turner (1997) examined four possibilities: the network of dredged canals and spoil banks, a decline in sediment delivery, construction of navigation and flood protection levees on the Mississippi River, and salinity changes. Based on his analysis, he identified the construction of dredged canals as the principal cause, thus rejecting the other three, while proposing a paradigm shift that recognizes plant activity as central to interacting with physical forces to maintain wetland condition. One could draw the conclusion from his analysis that restoration practices that depend on enhancing sediment supply may not be successful. Day and colleagues (2000) reanalyzed some of the same data and concluded that multiple factors were responsible for wetland loss. The debate continued with a lively exchange of views and rebuttals published in the Technical Notes and Comments section in *Estuaries* 24 (4), August (2001). In this debate, the relative importance of rising sea level takes a back seat in importance to causes resulting from anthropogenic alterations.

The stakes are very high in this debate because billions of dollars are being spent on restoration in the Mississippi Delta. While there is general agreement that canals are a key factor in wetland loss, it does not mean that large-scale diversion of river water and sediments should be rejected as an important strategy for wetland restoration. As with other major restoration protects, such as the Everglades, getting the science right is a necessary but not sufficient step to successful restoration. This chapter and Chapter 10 (restoration) emphasize that the response of society to global change is fraught with uncertainty.

alterations, in part because the vegetation can survive only within a relatively narrow tidal range. In some cases, this amounts to only a few decimeters change in depth for salt marshes in microtidal regions (McKee and Patrick 1988). Consequently, subsidence of marsh surfaces following hydrologic modification from tide gates, weirs, and dikes makes it unlikely that these now-collapsed surfaces can be effectively restored given that sea level is changing in the opposite direction. For large tidal areas such as the Mississippi Delta, multiple factors have led to the degradation of the wetlands (Guntenspergen and Vairin 1998), leading to disagreements on causes and remedies (Box 12.3).

Accelerated rates of rising sea level can drown plants and convert marshes to open water unless vertical sediment accretion is sufficient to compensate. River sediment delivery to coastal regions has decreased considerably with the proliferation of river impoundments. In fact, subsidence of land may even exceed the sea level effect, as is the case

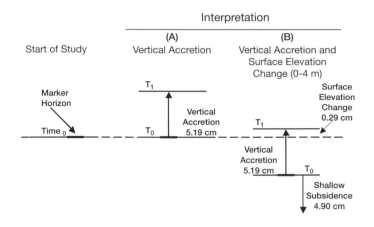

FIGURE 12.7

Interpretation of data derived from measuring sediment accumulation (accretion) and shallow subsidence in coastal wetlands. Vertical accretion (A) measures only sediment accumulation above a marker horizon. This could be misinterpreted as a rise in elevation that could offset rising sea level of equal proportion. However, when shallow subsidence is taken into account (B), the elevation change is much smaller. From Cahoon and associates (1995).

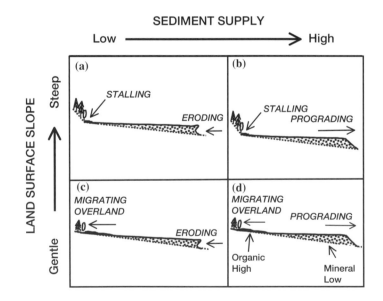

FIGURE 12.8

Four combinations showing the influence of slope and sediment supply on the capacity of tidal marshes to maintain surface area exposed to rising sea level. From Brinson and colleagues (1995a).

for parts of the Mississippi Delta where autocompression of Pleistocene deposits may be tenfold greater than the eustatic (true) rise in sea level, the latter due mostly to thermal expansion of the ocean and partially by glacial melting (Gornitz et al. 1982). This compression is compounded by the fact that sediment discharge to the Delta has decreased by 50% since 1860 due largely to dams on contributing drainages (Kesel 1989). Further, sea level does not rise at a constant annual rate, but rather can produce short-term rises in excess of 1 centimeter per year over multiyear periods even though the long-term trend is much lower (Stumpf and Haines 1998). Rising sea level is not an issue in high northern latitudes, however. In the northern coast of Canada, parts of Alaska, and Scandinavian countries, relative sea level is actually falling because of continental rebound in response to the melting of continental glaciers.

Effects of higher temperatures can not be completely discounted as influencing coastal marshes, however. Mangroves are expected to migrate to higher latitudes as the incidence of frost is reduced. This may result in dramatic structural changes as marshy grasslands are replaced by forests. Mangrove forests are predicted to survive where freezes occur less than once every 8 years; at a frequency of once every 12 years, mangroves are predicted to replace salt marsh (Chen and Twilley 1998). At higher latitudes, changes in temperature may cause shifts in species composition. The distribution of *Juncus gerardi* Loisel. from Maritime Provinces of Canada to Virginia and *J. roemerianus* from southern Maryland to Florida are examples of species that would likely change their range distribution.

Despite the varied effects of temperature and subsidence, rising sea level is the principal force affecting coastal wetlands. However, there are two components to the force: vertical and horizontal. Most work has focused on the vertical component, whereby the capacity of wetland surfaces to keep up with rising sea level is determined by the capacity of sediment accretion to match the rate of rising sea level. At the lower end, too little sediment supply simply results in the drowning and elimination of plants as described earlier. At the other extreme, high levels of sediment accumulation become self-limiting as the elevation of the soil surface begins to exceed the reach of tides that transport the sediments. In practice, these vertical processes are simultaneously measured with a sediment elevation table that detects both the absolute change in sediment elevation and the accumulation of sediment by the burial of a sediment marker (Fig. 12.7). If subsidence is not taken into account, rates of sediment accumulation by themselves will not provide the information needed to determine whether the wetland surface is keeping pace with rates of rising sea level (Cahoon et al. 1995). For this analysis, both the rate of shallow (or deep) subsidence and the rate of sediment accretion are needed.

Even where wetlands are locally drowning, however, rising sea level does not necessarily result in a net loss of wetland area. For this, the horizontal component must be taken into account (Titus 1986). Rising sea level may interact with coastal landscapes in at least four ways, depending on the steepness of the landward slope and the sediment supply to the wetland surface (Fig. 12.8). If the wetland edge is eroding (or subsiding and effectively becoming subtidal), wetland area can be maintained at steady state by conversion of the adjacent land to wetlands through landward migration (transgression). If landward migration is stalled because the slope is steep, corresponding losses to open water will occur. Gains in wetlands can also occur where sedimentary regimes develop over time, in response to protection from erosion, as documented by Redfield (1972) for Barnstable Marsh in Massachusetts.

MANAGEMENT AND POLICY OPTIONS

For the past quarter of a century, wetland conservation and management have been well institutionalized in the United States (Kusler 1992) and worldwide (Finlayson and van der Valk 1995). The functions and values of wetlands have been well established (NRC 1995, 2002), and restoration of degraded wetlands is a routine regulatory requirement in the United States (NRC 2001) and many other parts of the industrialized world. With this framework of protection and restoration, society is well positioned to develop strategies for dealing with changes due to a changing climate. The first strategy is to develop a "management plan" to maintain the attributes and services that will be threatened because of changing global climate. The other is to consider how wetlands may serve as a partial solution to ameliorate climate change due to their capacity to sequester atmospheric CO_2.

PREPARATION FOR CHANGE

As general circulation models become more sophisticated and reliable, regions that will become wetter or drier can be predicted with greater confidence. In regions exposed to wetter conditions, a focus on protecting additional wetland area might be regarded as compensation for the huge alterations that have occurred since precolonial times in the United States. Additional wetland establishment is most likely in transitional areas of existing upland-wetland boundaries. However, poorly drained flats that were not wetlands because of formerly arid conditions may also be transformed into wetlands. Expansion of wetlands, particularly where land use has been established for agriculture and resident land uses, can cause socioeconomic displacement. In agricultural areas, the likely response may be to facilitate drainage to protect traditional crop cultivation. Shifting to crops such as paddy rice that are tolerant of both flooding and warmer temperatures may maintain some wetland biogeochemical processes but have little importance in maintaining native plant and animal species. Because of likely disruptions of agriculture in a changing climate (IPCC 1995, 2001), the tendency for society to maintain crop production will outweigh, with few exceptions, incentives to enhance biodiversity associated with expanding area of wetlands. On one hand, expanding wetland area may interfere with traditional societal infrastructure, similar to problems caused by beaver impoundments (Naiman et al. 1988). On the other hand, current regulatory practices of wetland protection and preservation may now serve as a type of flood insurance for a future with a wetter climate.

In a drying climate, an array of options for maintaining biodiversity ranges from proactive to passive. For wetlands that rely solely on precipitation as a water source, such as mineral or organic soil flats, little can be done to ameliorate the effects of drying, except by minimizing other contributing human activities. The oxidation of organic soils is particularly pernicious because of the proposed positive feedback to atmospheric warming due to accelerated emissions of greenhouse gases. Locally rare species that may face extinction could be transplanted for the purposes of establishing sustainable populations in regions that will support equivalent wetland types and climate in the future. The endemism now found in precipitation-driven wetlands, such as the vernal pools of California (Zedler 1987), will become more tenuous as available habitat diminishes.

Wetlands that rely on surface water sources adjacent to rivers and lakes often contain widely distributed species because populations are well connected by aquatic corridors. The consequences of drying are fairly predictable (Fig. 12.6). However, the additional pressure to store and divert water for human activities from these same sources will directly contribute to loss of wetlands. The scarce wetlands in arid climates are often at risk because of direct competition with irrigated agriculture (Brinson and Malvarez 2002). Long growing seasons and fertile soils of many arid climates lack only sufficient water for high crop yield. Governmental and private entities should anticipate where future scarcities are likely and put into action solutions to address this problem.

Lacustrine wetlands, in theory, should migrate away from current shorelines as lake levels fall, and should reestablish in shallow areas protected by waves. The amount of time for coastal wetlands to adjust to a range of lower levels of large lakes is difficult to predict (Keough et al. 1999). The location of future habitats, however, should be predictable from detailed information on shoreline geomorphology and sediment dynamics. Lacustrine fringe wetlands currently exposed to multiyear fluctuations in lake levels, such as those experienced by the Laurentian Great Lakes, should allow the testing of predictive models.

Groundwater-dependent wetlands, such as fens, seeps, and some depressions, are often isolated, and thus their biota are vulnerable to local extinctions. The lag time of reduced flows to groundwater wetlands would buffer effects of climate change relative to other wetland types (Winter 2000). The combination of reduced water tables and lower precipitation can result in elimination of wetland status altogether, especially for those that are small and shallow or located in arid climates to begin with. However, drier conditions will likely increase human demand for groundwater, a source of competition that could magnify climatic effects (Frederick and Gleick 1999).

In short, inland wetlands in a drying climate will become smaller and rarer, thus leading to predictable loss of capacity to support species, and particularly endemics that are dependent on wetlands for part or all of their life cycle. The main strategy available is to protect those that remain and, to the extent possible, restore and repopulate sites that provide appropriate habitat (Bedford et al. 2001). The necessity of proliferating vulnerable species in climates undergoing wetting as a result of climate change has not been seriously evaluated.

Sea level–controlled coastal wetlands differ from inland ones by the certainty that they must move landward along low slopes to maintain their size (Fig. 12.6g). Sediment supplies are also essential. The management approach in either case is relatively straightforward. For landward movement, requirements for migration can be predicted from topographic information. Societal impediments can be severe in countries that increasingly and selectively populate the seacoast with residents and vacationers, as in the United States. Sediment supplies may be reduced further under drying trends if sediment-trapping impoundments proliferate to supply domestic and agricultural consumption from rivers with diminishing flows. While the flora of sea level–controlled wetlands is not particularly species rich, animal species diversity is normally quite high. The strong connection between coastal wetlands and nearby estuarine and marine fisheries is well established and may provide additional incentives to protect coastal wetlands and the adjacent lands that they will occupy in the future.

Other issues can be anticipated that are not directly associated with global climate change but will nevertheless be exacerbated with a drying climate (Brinson et al., in press). The presence of barriers to migration (both natural and human caused, such as dams and dikes) will have intensified effects where species are forced from their current habitats due to changes in temperature and hydroperiod. Removal of these barriers may become a favored restoration option, although intentionally moving species may be preferable. Changes in frequency and seasonality of fire may have effects on wetlands that have not even been considered or are difficult to predict. Reductions in water flows, leading to less capacity to dilute sources of pollution, could have secondary effects on aquatic biota (Poff et al. 2002).

MANAGEMENT FOR CARBON SEQUESTERING

The first principle of managing carbon sequestering may be to "do no harm." One application of the precautionary principle (Gollier et al. 2000) would be to place greater emphasis on protecting carbon that is already stored in organic-rich wetlands soils. Enhanced drainage and an increased frequency of fire are likely the current causes of large and potentially controllable emissions from peatlands. During periods of drought, peatlands are particularly susceptible to fire that burns deep into peat and, within a short time, transports the equivalent of thousands of years of carbon sequestering back to the atmosphere, a situation that is exacerbated by the greater fire frequency from human presence. The most extreme cases of subsidence (and thus CO_2 emissions) in peatlands result from drainage for agriculture, exemplified by East Anglian Fenlands in the United Kingdom and the Everglades (USA) and San Joaquin Delta in the United States (Lugo et al. 1990). In wetlands where fire is frequent and critical for maintaining biodiversity, such as wet savannas on mineral soils (Walker and Peet 1983), there is little capacity to augment the already low levels of organic matter.

A second principle may be that a global problem of climate change must be matched with a global strategy to ameliorate its effects. International treaties and agreements (Box 12.1) should appropriately incorporate wetlands as a factor in influencing the global climate change. As such, wetlands would be perceived as a resource of international importance and, at the same time, serve as an umbrella to protecting other ecosystem functions and values.

Consistent with the "do no harm" principle are other "low risk" management strategies such as the no-net-loss policy in the United States (Conservation Foundation 1988). Such a policy justifies protection measures locally that may have far-reaching worldwide effects. This requires the dual approaches of reducing the rate of wetland alteration while at the same time using restoration and enhancement to offset losses. Restoration is not a panacea, however, because of long time lags necessary to sequester atmospheric CO_2.

Manipulation of water levels to reduce the zone of methanogenesis may be one way of reducing emission of a major greenhouse gas. Major sources of methane from wetlands are widely dispersed globally, with about equal levels coming from wetlands in the tropics, subtropics, and boreal/arctic zones (Aselmann and Crutzen 1989). Methanogenesis in remote areas, such as those of high latitudes, can not be reduced by water table manipulation because of the high costs of doing so over large, inaccessible areas.

While measures to reduce the frequency of surface fires may be more feasible, the amount of biomass of affected aboveground parts is small relative to soil organic matter (Schlesinger 1977). Further, when fires inevitably occur, the lower frequency may be neutralized by ones that combust more fuel per fire and thus result in the same amount of greenhouse gas emissions over the long term. Scenarios such as this need to be conceptualized and modeled to determine what strategies are feasible and useful. Finally, management strategies that address only carbon sequestering, or limiting gaseous carbon emissions, may have unanticipated effects on other functions and values of wetlands.

SUMMARY

Global climate change in temperature, moisture, CO_2 enrichment, and rising sea level is expected to have profound effects on the distribution of wetlands and dependent biota. Some anticipated effects are highly speculative, while others that appear to be common sense have not been adequately tested. Where climates become wetter, some gain in wetland area is expected, although measures to protect social infrastructure, especially agriculture, will likely control expansion. Where climates become drier (Table 12.2), increasing competition for domestic use and irrigated agriculture will exacerbate the otherwise inevitable shrinkage of wetland area. Within remaining wetland areas, changes in species composition are expected from an increase in temperature and CO_2 enrichment. Warmer temperatures are expected to cause shifts in species distributions, provided that dispersal barriers do not restrict movement to areas of favorable habitat. Aquatic organisms in cold climates and at high altitudes will face especially formidable barriers because they have nowhere to go in some cases. Boreal and arctic peatlands in permafrost regions are potentially vast sources of additional CO_2 and methane, and thus will release greater quantities of greenhouse gases for further atmospheric

TABLE 12.2   Summary of Patterns of Response and Management Options by
Wetland Type Under Warmer and Drier Conditions

Wetland Type	Response to a Warming and Drying Climate	Major Alteration or Problem	Management Options
Permafrost peatlands	Improved drainage oxidizes peat and facilitates fire	Further emission of greenhouse gases	Fire control; options limited
Riverine floodplain	Reduced ground-water discharge and overbank sources	Floodplain species changes; deteriorating water quality	Reduce competing withdrawals; generate flood pulses below impoundments
Depression and slope	Reduction in size and number	Loss of wetland-dependent species	Transplant species to newly favorable climate
Estuarine fringe (tidal)	Accelerated rate of rising sea level	Migration landward is blocked	Remove barriers and limit human encroachment
Lacustrine fringe	Shoreline recession	Change in location of favorable habitat	Predict and protect location of favorable habitat
Mineral soil flats	Loss of wetland attributes	Switch from wetland to upland status	None

warming and climate change. Tidal wetlands will be less influenced by changes in temperature and moisture and more by the influence of accelerating rates of rising sea level. If tropical storms and hurricanes increase in frequency and intensity, both tidal wetlands and others near the coast will be influenced by disturbances in addition to stressors induced by human activities.

The uncertainty of the geographic effects of wetter or drier climates makes it difficult to form strategies for compensatory action with confidence. For example, wetlands that depend on precipitation as a dominant water source will be among the first to disappear with a drying climate, and little can be done to maintain them. At the other extreme are wetlands fed by groundwater from large aquifers, but they may be in direct competition with increased societal demands for the same water resources in a drying climate. Protection of the distribution and condition of present-day wetlands is a minimal strategy toward preparing for the maintenance of future wetlands values in the face of climate change. Some species may actually have to be transplanted to other geographic regions to prevent their extinction. At the opposite extreme, invasive species, now problematic in some regions, are expected to expand under a changing climate. Managing wetlands toward additional carbon sequestering is a strategy to combat the additional emissions of CO_2 and methane from areas of melting permafrost, increased peat fires, and lowered water tables under a drying climate.

ACKNOWLEDGMENTS

The preparation of this paper was supported, in part, by a grant to the Virginia Coast Reserve–Long Term Ecological Research program supported in part by Grants No. DEB-0080381 from the National Science Foundation. I thank Jon Kusler for the leadership he has provided in drawing attention to the influence of climate change on wetlands through the many workshops and symposia that he has organized on the topic and for his advice on an earlier version of this chapter. Glenn Guntenspergen kindly provided many helpful suggestions on this chapter.

LITERATURE CITED

Abernathy, V., and R. E. Turner. 1987. U.S. forested wetlands: 1940–1980. *BioScience* 37: 721–27.

Able, K. W., and S. M. Hagan. 2000. Effects of common reed *(Phragmites australis)* invasion on marsh surface macrofauna: Response of fishes and decapod crustaceans. *Estuaries* 23: 633–46.

Acosta, C. A. and S. A. Perry. 2001. Impact of hydropattern disturbance on crayfish population dynamics in the seasonal wetlands of Everglades National Park. *Aquatic Conservation* 11(1):45–47.

Acosta, C. A., and S. A. Perry. 2002. Spatio-temporal variation in crayfish production in disturbed marl prairie marshes of the Florida Everglades. *Journal of Freshwater Ecology* 17: 641–50.

Adam, P. 1990. *Saltmarsh ecology*. Cambridge: Cambridge University Press.

Adams, A. 1984. Crytobiosis in Chironomidae (Diptera)—two decades on. *Antenna* 8: 58–61.

Adams, G. D. 1988. Wetlands of the prairies of Canada. In *Wetlands of Canada*, 155–98. Ecological Land Classification Series, No. 24. National Wetlands Working Group. Ottowa, Ontario: Environment Canada; and Montreal, Quebec, Canada: Polyscience Publications Inc.

Adams, J. J. 2000. Pond permanence and the effects of exotic vertebrates on anurans. *Ecological Applications* 10: 559–68.

Adams, M. J., C. A. Pearl, and R. B. Bury. 2003. Indirect facilitation of an anuran invasion by non-native fishes. *Ecology Letters* 6: 343–51.

Adamus, P. R. 1983. *A method for wetland functional assessment.* Vol. 2: *FHWA Assessment Method.* FHWA-IP-82-24. Washington, D.C.: U.S. Department of Transportation, Federal Highways Administration, 138 pp.

———. 1988. The FHWA/Adamus (WET) method for wetland functional assessment. In *Management use and value of wetlands*. Vol. 2: *The ecology and management of wetlands,* eds. D. D. Hook, W. H. McKee, Jr., H. K. Smith, J. Gregory, V. G. Burrell, Jr., M. R. DeVoe, R. E. Sojka, et al., 128–33. Portland, OR: Timber Press.

Adamus, P. R., R. D. Smith, and T. Muir. 1990. *Manual for assessment of bottomland hardwood functions*. EPA 600/3-90/053. Vicksburg, MS: Army Engineer Waterways Experiment Station.

Adamus, P. R., and L. T. Stockwell. 1983. *A method for wetland functional assessment: Volume I, Critical review and evaluation concepts.* Federal Highway Agency FHWA-IP-82-23, Washington, D.C.: U.S. Department of Transportation.

Adamus, P. R., L. T. Stockwell, E. J. Clairain, M. E. Morrow, L. P. Rozas, and D. R. Smith. 1987. *Wetland Evaluation Technique (WET), Volume II: Methodology.* NTIS No. 189968, U.S. Army Engineer Waterways Experiment Station, Vicksburg, MS.

———. 1991. *Wetland Evaluation Technique (WET), Volume I: Literature review and evaluation rationale.* Technical Report WRP-DE-2. Vicksburg, MS: U.S. Army Engineer Waterways Experiment Station.

Adis, H., and V. Mahnert. 1990. On the species composition of Pseudoscorpiones from Amazonian dryland and inundation forests in Brazil. *Revue Suisse Zool* 97: 49–53.

Adis, J. 1997. Terrestrial invertebrates: Survival strategies, group spectrum, dominance and activity patterns. In *The Central Amazon floodplain. Ecology of a pulsing system,* ed. W. J. Junk, 299–317. *Ecological Studies* 126. Berlin, Germany: Springer.

Adis, J., J. W. de Morais, and U. Scheller. 1996. On abundance, phenology and natural history of Symphala from a mixedwater inundation forest in Central Amazonia, Brazil. *Acta Myriapodologica, Mém. Mus. Natn. Hist. Nat.,* 169: 607–16.

Adis, J., and W. J. Junk. 2002. Terrestrial invertebrates inhabiting lowland river floodplains of Central Amazonia and Central Europe: A review. *Freshwater Biology* 47: 711–31.

Adis, J., M. Marques, and K. M. Wantzen. 2001. First observations on the survival strategies of terricolous arthropods in the northern Pantanal wetland of Brazil—scientific note. *Andrias* 15: 127–28.

Adis, J., and B. Messner. 1997. Adaptations to life under water: Tiger beetles and millipedes. In *The Central Amazon floodplain. Ecology of a pulsing system,* ed. W. J. Junk, 319–30. *Ecological Studies* 126. Berlin, Germany: Springer.

Adis, J., U. Scheller, J. W. deMorai, c. Rochus, and J. M. G. Rodriguez. 1997. Symphyla from Amazonia non-flooded forests and their adaptations to inundation forests. *Entomologica Scandinavica Supplement* 15: 307–17.

Adis, J., and H. Sturm. 1987. On the natural history and ecology of Meinertellidae (Archaeognatha, Insecta) from dryland and inundation forests of Central Amazonia. *Amazoniana* 10: 197–218.

Aerts, R. and F. Berendse. 1988. The effect of increased nutrient availability on vegetation dynamics in wet heathlands. *Vegetatio* 76: 639.

Aerts, R., J. T. A. Verhoeven, and D. F. Whigham. 1999. Plant-mediated controls on nutrient cycling in temperate fens and bogs. *Ecology* 80: 2170–181.

Ahn, C., D. C. White, and R. E. Sparks. 2004. Moist-soil plants as ecohydrology indicators for recovering the flood pulse in the Illinois River. *Restoration Ecology* 12: 207–13.

Ainslie, W. B., S. D. Smith, B. A. Pruitt, T. H. Roberts, E. J. Sparks, L. West, G. L. Godshalk, and M. V. Miller. 1999. *A regional guidebook for assessing the functions of low gradient, riverine wetlands in western Kentucky.* Technical Report WRP-DE-17. Vicksburg, MS: U.S. Army Engineer Waterways Experiment Station.

Aldridge, K. T., and G. G. Ganf. 2003. Modification of sediment redox potential by three contrasting macrophytes: Implications for phosphorus adsorption/desorption. *Marine and Freshwater Research* 54: 87–94.

Alford, R. A., P. M. Dixon, and J. H. K. Pechmann. 2001. Global amphibian population declines. *Nature* 414: 449–500.

Alford, R. A., and S. J. Richards. 1999. Global amphibian declines: A problem in applied ecology. *Annual Review of Ecology and Systematics* 30: 133–65.

Allen, A. E. 2004. Determining reference sites and priority species for riparian restoration, Ayuquila River, west central Mexico. Master's thesis, University of Wisconsin, Madison.

Allen, B. P., and R. R. Sharitz. 1999. Post-hurricane vegetation dynamics in old-growth forests of the Congaree Swamp National Monument. In *On the Frontiers of Conservation,* 306–12. Hancock, MI: George Wright Society Bulletin.

Allen, H. L. 1971. Primary productivity, chemo-organotrophy, and nutritional interactions of epiphytic algae and bacteria on macrophytes in the littoral of a lake. *Ecological Monographs* 41: 97–127.

Allen, J. A., and H. E. Kennedy. 1989. *Bottomland hardwood reforestation in the lower Mississippi valley.* Stoneville, MS: U.S.D.A. Forest Service Experiment Station.

Allen, J. A., S. R. Pezeshki, and J. L. Chambers. 1996. Interaction of flooding and salinity stress on baldcypress *(Taxodium distichum). Tree Physiology* 16: 307–13.

Alley, R. B. 2000. The two-mile time machine. Princeton, NJ: Princeton University Press.

Allison, S. K. 1996. Recruitment and establishment of salt marsh plants following disturbance by flooding. *American Midland Naturalist* 136: 232–47.

Allison, S. K., and J. G. Ehrenfeld. 1999. The influence of microhabitat variation on seedling recruitment of *Chamaecyparis thyoides* and *Acer rubrum. Wetlands* 19: 383–93.

Alongi, D. M. 1996. The dynamics of benthic nutrient pools and fluxes in tropical mangrove forests. *Journal of Marine Research* 54: 123–48.

Alongi, D. M., and A. Sasekumar. 1992. Benthic communities. In *Tropical mangrove ecosystems,* eds. A. I. Robertson and D. M. Alongi, 137–71. Washington, D.C.: American Geophysical Union.

Alward, R. D., J. K. Detling, and D. G. Milchunas. 1999. Grassland vegetation changes and nocturnal global warming. *Science* 283: 229–31.

Amezaga, J. M., L. Santamaria, and A. J. Green. 2002. Biotic wetland connectivity—Supporting a new approach for wetland policy. *Acta Oecologica* 23: 213–22.

Amon, J. P., C. A. Thompson, Q. J. Carpenter, and J. Miner. 2002. Temperate zone fens of the glaciated midwestern USA. *Wetlands* 22: 301–17.

Amoros, C., and A. L. Roux. 1988. Interaction between water bodies within the floodplains of large rivers: Function and development of connectivity. *Münstersche Geographische Arbeiten* 29: 125–30.

Anderson, C. R., B. L. Peckarsky, and S. A. Wissinger. 1999. Tinajas of Southeatern Utah: invertebrate reproductive strategies and the habitat templet. In *Invertebrates in freshwater wetlands of North America: Ecology and management*, eds. D. P. Batzer, R. D. Rader, and S. A. Wissinger, 791–810. New York: John Wiley and Sons.

Anderson, J. A. R. 1983. The tropical peatswamps of western Malaysia. In *Mires: Swamps, bogs, fens, and moors. Part B. Ecosystems of the world 4B*, ed. A. J. P. Gore, 181–99. Amsterdam: Elsevier.

Anderson, J. T., and L. M. Smith. 2004. Persistence and colonization strategies of playa wetland invertebrates. *Hydrobiologia* 513: 77–86.

Anderson, L., T. Gumbricht, D. Hughes, D. Kniveton, S. Ringrose, H. Savenije, M. Todd, J. Wilk, and P. Wolski. 2003. Water flow dynamics in the Okavango River Basin and Delta: A prerequisite for the ecosystems of the Delta. *Physics and Chemistry of the Earth*, Parts A/B/C, 28: 1165–72.

Anderson, N. H. 1976. Carnivory by an aquatic detritivore, *Clistorina magnifica* (Trichoptera Limnephilidae). *Ecology* 57: 1081–85.

Angeler, D. G., M. Alvarez-Cobelas, S. Sanchez-Carrillo, and M. A. Rodrigo. 2002. Assessment of exotic fish impacts on water quality and zooplankton in a degrade semi-arid floodplain wetland. *Aquatic Sciences* 64: 76–86.

Armstrong, J., F. Afreen-Zobayed, and W. Armstrong. 1996. *Phragmites* die-back: Sulphide- and acetic acid-induced bud and root death, lignifications, and blockages within aeration and vascular systems. *New Phytology* 134: 601–6.

Armstrong, J., and Armstrong, W. 2001. An overview of the effects of phytotoxins on *Phragmites australis* in relation to die-back. *Aquatic Botany* 69: 251–68.

Armstrong, W. 1982. Waterlogged soils. In *Environment and plant ecology*, 2d ed., ed. J. R. Etherington, 290–330. Chichester, U.K.: John Wiley and Sons.

Aronson, J., and E. Le Floc'h. 1996. Vital landscape attributes: Missing tools for restoration ecology. *Restoration Ecology* 4: 377–87.

Arp, W. J., B. G. Drake, W. T. Pockman, P. S. Curtis, and D. F. Whigham. 1993. Interactions between C-3 and C-4 salt-marsh plant species during 4 years of exposure to elevated atmospheric CO_2. *Vegetatio* 104: 133–43.

Arscott, D. B., K. Tockner, and J. V. Ward. 2001. Thermal heterogeneity along a braided floodplain river (Tagliamento River, northeastern Italy). *Canadian Journal of Fisheries and Aquatic Sciences* 58: 2359–73.

Aselmann, I., and P. J. Crutzen. 1989. Global distribution of natural freshwater wetlands and rice paddies, their net primary productivity, seasonality and possible methane emissions. *Journal of Atmospheric Chemistry* 8: 307–58.

Ashworth, S. M. 1997. Comparison between restored and reference sedge meadow wetlands in south-central Wisconsin. *Wetlands* 17: 518–27.

Atkinson, M. R., G. P. Findlay, A. B. Hope, M. G. Pitman, and K. R. West. 1967. Salt regulation in the mangroves *Rhizophora mucronata* Lam. and *Aegialitis annulata*. *Royal British and Australian Journal of Biological Sciences* 20: 589–99.

Atkinson, T. C. 1998. Techniques for measuring subsurface flow on hillslopes. In *Hillsope hydrology*, ed. M. J. Kirby, 73–120. John Wiley and Sons, Chichester.

Atlas, R. M., and R. Bartha. 1993. *Microbial ecology*, 3d ed. Redwood City, CA: Benjamin/Cummins.

Auble, G. T., J. M. Friedman, and M. L. Scott. 1994. Relating riparian vegetation to present and future streamflows. *Ecological Applications* 4: 544–54.

Augenfield, J.M. 1963. Effects of oxygen deprivation on aquatic midge larvae under natural and laboratory conditions. *Physiology and Zoology* 40: 149–58.

Aust, W.M., and R. Lea. 1992. Comparative effects of aerial and ground logging on soil properties in a tupelo-cypress wetland. *Forest Ecology and Management* 50: 57–73.

Austin, B. 1990. *Methods in aquatic bacteriology.* Chichester, U.K.: John Wiley and Sons.

Azam, F., T. Fenchel, J.G. Field, J.S. Gray, L.A. Meyer-Reil, and F. Thingstad. 1983. The ecological role of microbes in the sea. *Marine Ecology Progress Series* 10: 257–63.

Azous, A.L., and R.R. Horner, eds. 2001. *Wetlands and urbanization: Implications for the future.* Boca Raton, FL: Lewis Publishers.

Baakza, A., A.K. Vala, B.P. Dave, and H.C. Dube. 2004. A comparative study of siderophore production by fungi from marine and freshwater habitats. *Journal of Experimental Marine Biology and Ecology* 311: 1–9.

Baber, M.J., D.L. Childers, K.J. Babbitt, and D.H. Anderson. 2002. Controls on fish distribution and abundance in temporary wetlands. *Canadian Journal of Fisheries and Aquatic Sciences* 59: 1441–50.

Bachmann, L., J. Tomiuk, J. Adis, and K. Vohland. 1998. Genetic differentiation of the millipede *Pycnotropis epiclysmus* inhabiting seasonally inundated and non-flooded Amazonian forests. *Journal of Zoological Systematics and Evolutionary* 36: 65–75.

Bailey, P.C., P.I. Boon, D.W. Blinn, and W.D. Williams. In press. Salinisation as an ecological perturbation to rivers, streams and wetlands of arid and semi-arid zones. In *The role of disturbance in rivers of the world's dry regions*, ed. R. Kingsford, ch. 11. Cambridge, U.K.: Cambridge University Press.

Baker, T.T. III, G. Lockaby, W.H. Conner, C.E. Meier, J.A. Stanturf, and M.K. Burke. 2001. Leaf litter decomposition and nutrient dynamics in four southern forested floodplain communities. *Soil Science Society of America Journal* 65: 1334–47.

Baldassarre, G.A., and E.G. Bolen. 1994. *Waterfowl ecology and management.* New York: John Wiley and Sons, Inc.

Baldwin, A.H., M.S. Egnotovich, and E. Clarke. 2001. Hydrologic change and vegetation of tidal freshwater marshes: Field, greenhouse, and seedbank experiments. *Wetlands* 21: 519–31.

Baldwin, A.H. and I.A. Mendelsohn. 1998. Effects of salinity and water level on coastal marshes: An experimental test of disturbance as a catalyst for vegetation change. *Aquatic Botany* 61: 255–68.

Baldwin, D.S. 1999. Dissolved organic matter and phosphorus leached from fresh and 'terrestrially' aged river red gum leaves: implications for assessing river-floodplain interactions. *Freshwater Biology* 41: 675–85.

Baldwin, D.S., and A.M. Mitchell. 2000. The effects of drying and re-flooding on the sediment and soil nutrient dynamics of lowland river-floodplain systems: A synthesis. *Regulated Rivers: Research and Management* 16: 457–67.

Baldwin, D.S., A.M. Mitchell, and G.N. Rees. 2000. The effects of in situ drying on sediment-phosphate interactions in sediments from an old wetland. *Hydrobiologia* 431: 3–12.

Balla, S.A., and J.A. Davis. 1993. Wetlands of the Swan Coastal Plain. *Managing Perth's wetlands to conserve the aquatic fauna*, vol. 5. Perth, Australia: Water Authority of Western Australia.

Barbour, M. G., J. H. Burk, W. D. Pitts, F. S. Gilliam, and M. W. Schwartz. 1998. *Terrestrial plant ecology,* 3d ed. New York: Addison Wesley Longman, Inc.

Bardecki, M. 1984. What value wetlands? *Journal of Soil and Water Conservation* 39: 166–69.

Barko, J. W., and R. M. Smart. 1981. Comparative influences of light and temperature on the growth and metabolism of selected submersed freshwater macrophytes. *Ecological Monographs* 51: 219–35.

Barlocher, F., R. J. Mackay, and G. B. Wiggins. 1978. Detritus processing in a temporary vernal pond in southern Ontario. *Archiv fur Hydrobiologie* 81:269–95.

Barras, S. C., and J. A. Kadlec. 2000. Abiotic predictors of avian botulism outbreaks in Utah. *Wildlife Society Bulletin* 28: 724–29.

Barrett, S. C. H., C. G. Eckert, and B. C. Husband. 1993. Evolutionary processes in aquatic plant populations. *Aquatic Botany* 44: 105–45.

Bartoldus, C. C. 1999. *A comprehensive review of wetland assessment procedures: A guide for wetland practitioners.* St. Michaels, MD: Environmental Concern, Inc., 196 pp.

Batt, B. D. J., M. G. Anderson, and F. D. Caldwell. 1989. The use of prairie potholes by North American ducks. In *Northern Prairie Wetlands,* ed. A. G. van der Valk, 204–207. Ames, IA: Iowa State University Press.

Battaglia, L. L., J. R. Keough, and D. W. Prichett. 1995. Early secondary succession in a southeastern U.S. alluvial floodplain. *Journal of Vegetation Science* 6: 769–76.

Battaglia, L. L. and R. R. Sharitz. 2006. Responses of floodplain forest species to spatially condensed gradients: A test of the flood-shade tolerance tradeoff hypothesis. *Oecologia* 147: 108–118.

Battaglia, L. L. and R. R. Sharitz. 2005. Effects of natural disturbance on bottomland hardwood regeneration. In *Ecology and management of bottomland hardwood systems: The state of our understanding,* eds. L. H. Fredrickson, S. L. King, and R. M. Kaminski, 121–136. Gaylord Memorial Laboratory Special Publication No. 10. Puxico, MO: University of Missouri-Columbia.

Battaglia, L. L., R. R. Sharitz, and P. R. Minchin. 1999. Heterogeneity of hurricane disturbance and regeneration patterns in an old-growth bottomland hardwood community. *Canadian Journal of Forest Research* 29: 144–156.

Battle, J. M., and S. W. Golladay. 2001. Hydroperiod influence on breakdown of leaf litter in cypress-gum wetlands. *American Midland Naturalist* 146: 128–45.

Batzer, D. P. 1998. Trophic interactions among detritus, benthic midges, and predatory fish in a freshwater marsh. *Ecology* 79: 1688–98.

Batzer, D. P., F. de Szalay, V. H. Resh. 1997. Opportunistic response of a benthic midge (diptera: Chironomidae) to management of California seasonal wetlands. *Environmental Entomology* 26: 215–222.

Batzer, D. P., S. E. Dietz-Brantley, B. E. Taylor, and A. E. DeBiase. 2005. Macroinvertebrate communities in forested depressional wetlands of South Carolina and Minnesota: Evaluating regional differences. *Journal of the North American Benthological Society* 24: 403–14.

Batzer, D. P., C. R. Jackson, and M. Mosner. 2000. Influences of riparian logging on plants and invertebrates in small, depressional wetlands of Georgia, U.S.A. *Hydrobiologia* 441: 123–32.

Batzer, D. P., M. McGee, V. H. Resh, and R. R. Smith. 1993. Characteristics of invertebrates consumed by mallards and prey response to wetland flooding schedules. *Wetlands* 13: 41–49.

Batzer, D. P., B. J. Palik, and R. Buech. 2004. Relationships between environmental characteristics and macroinvertebrate communities in seasonal woodland ponds of Minnesota. *Journal of the North American Benthological Society* 23: 50–68.

Batzer, D. P., and V. H. Resh. 1991. Trophic interactions among a beetle predator, a chironomid grazer, and periphyton in a seasonal wetland. *Oikos* 60: 251–57.

Batzer, D. P., and S. A. Wissinger. 1996. Ecology of insect communities in nontidal wetlands. *Annual Review of Entomology* 41: 75–100.

Bauer, I. E., L. D. Gignac, and D. H. Vitt. 2003a. Development of a peatland complex in boreal western Canada: Lateral site expansion and local variability in vegetation succession and long-term peat accumulation. *Canadian Journal of Botany* 81: 833–47.

Bauer C. R., C. H. Kellogg, S. D. Bridgham, and G. A. Lamberti. 2003b. Mycorrhizal colonization across hydrologic gradients in restored and reference freshwater wetlands. *Wetlands* 23: 961–68.

Bayley, P. B. 1983. Central Amazon fish populations: Biomass, and some dynamic characteristics. Ph.D. diss., Dalhousie University, Halifax, Canada.

———. 1995. Understanding large river-floodplain ecosystems. *BioScience* 45: 153–58.

Beckett, P. M., W. Armstrong, and J. Armstrong. 2001. Mathematical modelling of methane transport by *Phragmites:* The potential for diffusion within the roots and rhizosphere. *Aquatic Botany* 69: 293–312.

Bede, J. C., W. G. Goodman, and S. S. Tobe. 1999a. Developmental distribution of insect juvenile hormone III in the sedge, *Cyperus iria* L. Phytochemistry 52:1269–1274.

———. 1999b. Production of insect juvenile hormone III and its precursors in cell suspension cultures of the sedge, *Cyperus iria* L. *Plant Cell Reports* 19: 20–25.

Bede, J. C., and S. S. Tobe. 2000. Activity of insect juvenile hormone III: Seed germination and seedling growth studies. *Chemoecology* 10: 89–97.

Bedford, B. L. 1996. The need to define hydrologic equivalence at the landscape scale for freshwater wetland mitigation. *Ecological Applications* 6: 57–68.

Bedford, B. L., and K. S. Godwin. 2003. Fens of the United States: Distribution, characteristics, and scientific connection versus legal isolation. *Wetlands* 23: 608–29.

Bedford, B. L., D. J. Leopold, and J. Gibbs. 2001. Wetland ecosystems. In *Encyclopedia of Biodiversity*, ed. S. A. Levin, 5: 781–804. New York: Academic Press.

Bedford, B. L., M. R. Walbridge, and A. Aldous. 1999. Patterns in nutrient availability and plant diversity of temperate North American wetlands. *Ecology* 80: 2151–69.

Bell, D. T., F. L. Johnson, and A. R. Gilmote. 1978. Dynamics of litter fall, decomposition and incorporation in the streamside forest ecosystem. *Oikos* 30: 76–82.

Benbow, M. E., and R. W. Merritt. 2004. Road-salt toxicity of select Michigan wetland macroinvertebrates under different testing conditions. *Wetlands* 24: 68–76.

Bennett, S. H., and J. B. Nelson 1991. *Distribution and status of Carolina bays in South Carolina*. Nongame and Heritage Trust Publication No. 1. Columbia, SC: SC Wildlife and Marine Resources Department.

Benson, D. H., and J. Howell. 1990. Sydney's vegetation 1788–1988: Utilization, degradation and rehabilitation. *Proceedings of the Ecological Society of Australia* 16: 115–27.

Bentley, P. J. 1966. Adaptations of amphibia to arid environments. *Science* 152: 619–23.

Bernthal, T. W., and K. G. Willis. 2004. *Using Landsat imagery to map invasive reed canary grass* (Phalaris arundinacea): *A landscape level wetland monitoring methodology.* Wisconsin Department of Natural Resources.

Berté, S. B., and G. Pritchard. 1986. The life histories of *Limnephilus externus* Hagen, *Anabolia bimaculata* (Walker) and *Nemotaulius hostilis* (Hagen) (Trichoptera, Limnephilidae) in a pond in southern Alberta, Canada. *Canadian Journal of Zoology* 64: 2348–56.

Bertness, M. D. 1984. Ribbed mussels and *Spartina alterniflora* production in a New England salt marsh. *Ecology* 65: 1794–1807.

———. 1985. Fiddler crab regulation of *Spartina alterniflora* production on a New England salt marsh. *Ecology* 66: 1042–55.

———. 1991a. Interspecific interactions among high marsh perennials in a New England salt marsh. *Ecology* 72: 125–37.

———. 1991b. Zonation of *Spartina patens* and *Spartina alterniflora* in a New England salt marsh. *Ecology* 72: 138–48.

Bertness, M. D., and A. M. Ellison. 1987. Determinants of pattern in a New England salt marsh plant community. *Ecological Monographs* 57: 129–47.

Bertness, M. D., and P. J. Ewanchuck. 2002. Latitudinal and climate-driven variation in the strength and nature of biological interactions in New England salt marshes. *Oecologia* 132: 392–401.

Bertness, M. D., P. J. Ewanchuk, and B. R. Silliman. 2002. Anthropogenic modification of New England salt marsh landscapes. *Proceedings of the National Academy of Sciences USA* 99: 1395–98.

Bertness, M. D., L. Gough, and S. W. Shumway. 1992a. Salt tolerances and the distribution of fugitive salt marsh plants. *Ecology* 73: 1842–51.

Bertness, M. D., and S. D. Hacker. 1994. Physical stress and positive associations among marsh plants. *The American Naturalist* 144: 363–72.

Bertness, M. D., and S. W. Shumway. 1993. Competition and facilitation in marsh plants. *The American Naturalist* 142: 718–24.

Bertness, M. D., K. Wikler, and T. Chatkupt. 1992b. Flood tolerance and the distribution of *Iva frutescens* across New England salt marshes. *Oecologia* 91: 171–78.

Betson, R. P. 1964. What is watershed runoff? *Journal of Geophysical Research* 69: 1541–52.

Beumer, J. P. 1979. Reproductive cycles of two Australian freshwater fishes: The spangled perch *Therapon unicolor* and the east Queensland rainbowfish *Nematocentris splendida. Journal of Fish Biology* 15: 111–34.

Bicudo, D. C., A. K. Ward, and R. G. Wetzel. 1998. Fluxes of dissolved organic carbon within attached aquatic microbiota. *Verhandlungen Internationale Vereinigung Limnologie* 26: 1608–13.

Bildstein, K. L., E. Blood, and P. Frederick. 1992. The relative importance of biotic and abiotic vectors in nutrient transport. *Estuaries* 15: 147–57.

Bilton, D. T., J. R. Freeland, and B. Okamura. 2001. Dispersal in freshwater invertebrates. *Annual Review of Ecology and Systematics* 32: 159–81.

Birch, H. F. 1958. Effect of soil drying on humus decomposition and nitrogen availability. *Plant and Soil* 10: 9–31.

Birch, H. F., and M. T. Friend. 1956. Humus decomposition in East African soils. *Nature* 178: 500–501.

Bird, F. L., P. I. Boon, and P. D. Nichols. 2000. Physiochemical and microbial properties of burrows of the deposit-feeding thalassinidean ghost shrimp *Biffarius arenosus* (Decapoda: Callianassidae). *Estuarine, Coastal and Shelf Science* 51: 279–91.

Blackburn, T. H. 1983. The microbial nitrogen cycle. In *Microbial geochemistry*, ed. W. E. Krumbein, 63–89. Oxford, U.K.: Blackwell Scientific.

Blake, J. G., and W. G. Hoppes. 1986. Influence of resource abundance on use of tree-fall gaps by birds in an isolated woodlet. *Auk* 103: 328–40.

Blaker, M., S. J. Davies, and P. N. Reilly. 1984. *The atlas of Australian birds*. Melbourne, Australia: Royal Ornithologists Union, Melbourne University Press.

Blanch, S. J., G. G. Ganf, and K. F. Walker. 1999a. Growth and resource allocation in response to flooding in the emergent sedge *Bolboschoenus medianus*. *Aquatic Botany* 63: 145–60.

———. 1999b. Tolerance of riverine plants to flooding and exposure indicated by water regime. *Regulated Rivers: Research and Management* 15: 43–62.

Blaustein, L., J. Friedman, and T. Fahima. 1996. Larval *Salamandra* drive temporary pool community dynamics: Evidence from an artificial pool experiment. *Oikos* 76: 392–402.

Bledsoe, B. P., and T. H. Shear. 2000. Vegetation along hydrologic and edaphic gradients in a North Carolina coastal plain creek bottom and implications for restoration. *Wetlands* 20: 126–47.

Bliss, C. M., and N. B. Comerford. 2002. Forest harvesting influence on water table dynamics in a Florida flat woods landscape. *Soil Science Society of America Journal* 66: 1344–49.

Blodau, C., and T. R. Moore. 2003. Experimental response of peatland carbon dynamics to a water table fluctuation. *Aquatic Sciences* 65: 47–62.

Blom, C. W. P. M., and L. A. C. J. Voesenek. 1996. Flooding: The survival strategies of plants. *Trends in Ecology and Evolution* 11: 290–95.

Blossey, B., and T. R. Hunt-Joshi. 2003. Belowground herbivory by insects: Influence on plants and aboveground herbivores. *Annual Review of Entomology* 48: 521–547.

Blumthaler, M., and A. R. Webb. 2003. UVR climatology. In *UV Effects in Aquatic Organisms and Ecosystems,* Comprehensive Series in Photochemical and Photobiological Sciences, eds. E. W. Helbling and H. Zagarese, 21–58. Cambridge: European Society of Photobiology.

Bodelier, P. L. E., and H. J. Laanbroek. 2004. Nitrogen as a regulatory factor in methane oxidation in soils and sediments. *FEMS Microbiology Ecology* 47: 265–77.

Boedeltje, G., J. P. Bakker, A. Ten Brinke, J. M. van Groenendael, and M. Soesbergen. 2004. Dispersal phenology of hydrochorous plants in relation to discharge, seed release time and buoyancy of seeds: The flood pulse concept supported. *Journal of Ecology* 92: 786–96.

Bohn, H. L. 1971. Redox potentials. *Soil Science* 112: 39–45.

Bohn, H. L., B. L. McNeal, and G. A. O'Connor. 1985. *Soil Chemistry,* 2d ed. New York: John Wiley & Sons.

Bohonak, A. J., and D. G. Jenkins. 2004. Ecological and evolutionary signficance of dispersal by freshwater invertebrates. *Ecology Letters* 6: 783–96.

Bohonak, A. J., and G. K. Roderick. 2001. Dispersal of invertebrates among temporary ponds: Are genetic estimates accurate? *Israel Journal of Zoology* 47: 367–386.

Bohonak, A. J., B. P. Smith, and M. Thornton. 2004. Distributional, morphological, and genetic consequences of dispersal for temporary pond water mites. *Freshwater Biology* 49: 170–80.

Bohonak, A. J., and H. H. Whiteman. 1999. Dispersal of the fairy shrimp *Branchinecta coloradensis* (Anostraca): Effects of hydroperiod and salamanders. *Limnology and Oceanography* 44: 487–93.

Boix, D., J. Sala, R. Moreno-Amich. 2001. The faunal composition of Espolla Pond (NE Iberian Peninsula): The neglected biodiversity of temporary waters. *Wetlands* 21: 577–92.

Bolen, E. G., L. M. Smith, H. L. Schramm Jr. 1989. Playa lakes: Prairie wetlands of the southern high plains. *Bioscience* 39: 615–23.

Boon, P. I. 1991a. Bacterial assemblages in rivers and billabongs of southeastern Australia. *Microbial Ecology* 22: 27–52.

————. 1991b. Enzyme activities in billabongs of southeastern Australia. In *Microbial enzymes in aquatic environments*, ed. R. J. Chrost, 286–97. New York: Springer-Verlag.

————. 2000a. Bacterial biodiversity. In *Biodiversity in wetlands: Assessment, function and conservation*, eds. B. Gopal, W. J. Junk, and J. A., Davis, 1: 281–310. Leiden, The Netherlands: Backhuys.

————. 2000b. Carbon cycling in Australian wetlands: The importance of methane. *Verhandlungen Internationale Vereinigung für Theoretische und Angewandte Limnologie* 27: 37–50.

Boon, P. I., and K. Lee. 1997. Methane oxidation in sediments of a floodplain wetland in southeastern Australia. *Letters in Applied Microbiology* 25: 138–42.

Boon, P. I., A. Mitchell, and K. Lee. 1997. Effects of wetting and drying on methane emissions from ephemeral floodplain wetlands in south-eastern Australia. *Hydrobiologia* 357: 73–87.

Boon, P. I., D. J. W. Moriarty, and P. G. Saffigna. 1986. Nitrate metabolism in sediments from seagrass *(Zostera capricorni)* beds of Moreton Bay, Australia. *Marine Biology* 91: 268–76.

Boon, P. I., and R. J. Shiel. 1990. Grazing on bacteria by zooplankton in Australian billabongs. *Australian Journal of Marine and Freshwater Research* 41: 247–57.

Boon, P. I., and B. K. Sorrell. 1991. Biogeochemistry of billabong sediments. I. The effect of macrophytes. *Freshwater Biology* 26: 209–26.

————. 1995. Methane fluxes from an Australian floodplain wetland: The importance of emergent macrophytes. *Journal of the North American Benthological Society* 14: 582–98.

Boon, P. I., P. Virtue, and P. D. Nichols. 1996. Microbial consortia in wetland sediments: A biomarker analysis of the effects of hydrological regime, vegetation and season on benthic microbes. *Marine and Freshwater Research* 47: 27–41.

Boopathy, R. 2003. Anaerobic degradation of no. 2 diesel fuel in the wetland sediments of Barataria-Terrebonne estuary under various electron acceptor conditions. *Bioresource Technology* 86: 171–75.

Booth, D. B., D. Hartley, and R. Jackson. 2002. Forest cover, impervious-surface area, and the mitigation of stormwater impacts. *Journal of the American Water Resources Association* 38: 835–45.

Borchardt, M. A. 1996. Nutrients. In *Algal ecology: Benthic algae in freshwater ecosystems*, eds. R. J. Stevenson, M. Bothwell, and R. Lowe, 183–227. New York: Academic Press.

Bortolus, A., and O. Iribarne. 1999. Effects of the SW Atlantic burrowing crab *Chasmagnathus granulata* on a *Spartina* salt marsh. *Marine Ecology Progress Series* 178: 79–88.

Bostrom, B., J. M. Andersen, S. Fleicher, and M. Janson. 1988. Exchange of phosphorus across the sediment-water interface. *Hydrobiologia* 170: 229–44.

Bothwell, M. L., D. Sherbot, A. C. Roberge, and R. J. Daley. 1993. Influence of natural ultraviolet radiation on lotic periphytic diatom community growth, biomass accrual, and species composition: Short-term versus long-term effects. *Journal of Phycology* 29: 24–35.

Bott, T. L. 1996. Algae in microscopic food webs. In *Algal ecology: Benthic algae in freshwater ecosystems*, eds. R. J. Stevenson, M. Bothwell, and R. Lowe, 573–608. New York: Academic Press.

Bouillon, S., A. V. Raman, P. Dauby, and F. DeHairs. 2002. Carbon and nitrogen stable isotope ratios of subtidal benthic invertebrates in an estuarine mangrove ecosystem (Andhra Pradesh, India). *Estuarine Coastal and Shelf Science* 54: 901–13.

Boulton, A. J. 1991. Eucalypt leaf decomposition in an intermittent stream in south-eastern Australia. *Hydrobiologia* 211: 123–36.

Boulton, A. J., and P. I. Boon. 1991. A review of methodology used to measure leaf litter decomposition in lotic environments: Time to turn over an old leaf? *Australian Journal of Marine and Freshwater Research* 42: 1–43.

Boulton, A. J., and M. A. Brock. 1999. *Australian freshwater ecology*. Adelaide, Australia: Gleneagles Publishing.

Boulton, A. J., S. Findlay, P. Marmonier, E. H. Stanley, and H. M. Valett. 1998. The functional significance of the hyporheic zone in streams and rivers. *Annual Review of Ecology and Systematics* 29: 59–81.

Boulton, A. J., and P. J. Suter. 1986. Ecology of temporary streams—An Australian perspective. In *Limnology in Australia*, eds. P. De Deckker and W. D. Williams, 313–27. Melbourne, Australia: CSIRO Publishing.

Bourgeade, A., and B. Marchou. 2003. Yellow fever, Dengue, Japanese encephalitis and West Nile virus infection: Four major arbovirus diseases. *Medecine et Maladies Infectieuses* 33: 385–95.

Boutin, C., and P. A. Keddy. 1993. A functional classification of wetland plants. *Journal of Vegetation Science* 4: 591–600.

Bowen, S. H., E. V. Lutz, and M. O. Ahlgren. 1995. Dietary protein and energy as determinants of food quality—Trophic strategies compared. *Ecology* 76: 899–907.

Boyd, C. E. 1971. The dynamics of dry matter and chemical substances in a *Juncus effusus* population. *American Midland Naturalist* 86: 28–45.

Boyer, K. E., and J. B. Zedler. 1996. Damage to cordgrass by scale insects in a constructed salt marsh: Effects of nitrogen additions. *Estuaries* 19: 1–12.

Braccia, A., and D. P. Batzer. 2001. Invertebrates associated with woody debris in a southeastern U.S. forested floodplain wetland. *Wetlands* 21: 18–31.

Bradford, D. F., A. C. Neale, M. S. Nash, D. W. Sada, and J. R. Jaeger. 2003. Habitat patch occupancy by toads *(Bufo punctatus)* in a naturally fragmented desert landscape. *Ecology* 84: 1012–23.

Bradley, P. M., and J. T. Morris. 1991a. The influence of salinity on the kinetics of NH_4+ uptake in *Spartina alterniflora*. *Oecologia* 85: 375–80.

————. 1991b. Relative importance of ion exclusion, secretion, and accumulation in *Spartina alterniflora* Loisel. *Journal of Experimental Botany* 42: 1525–32.

Breckle, S. W. 2002. Salinity, halophytes and salt affected natural ecosystems. In *Salinity: Environment—Plants—Molecules*, eds. A. Lauchli and U. Luttge, 53–77. Dordrecht, Netherlands: Kluwer Academic Publishers.

Brendonck, L. 1996. Diapause, quiescence, hatching requirements: What we can learn from large freshwater branchiopods (Crustacea:Branciopoda: Anostraca, Notostraca, Conchostraca). *Hydrobiologia* 320: 85–97.

Brendonck, L., and L. De Meester 2003. Egg banks in freshwater zooplankton: Evolutionary and ecological archives in the sediment. *Hydrobiologia* 491: 65–84.

Brendonck, L., and W. D. Williams. 2000. Biodiversity of wetlands of dry regions (drylands). In *Biodiversity in wetlands: Assessment, function and conservation,* eds. B. Gopal, W. J. Junk, and J. A. Davis, 1: 181–94. Leiden, The Netherlands: Backhuys.

Brewer, J. S., J. M. Levine, and M. D. Bertness. 1997. Effects of biomass removal and elevation on species richness in a New England salt marsh. *Oikos* 80: 333–41.

Bridgham, S. D., S. P. Faulkner, and C. J. Richardson. 1991. Steel rod oxidation as a hydrologic indicator in wetland soils. *Journal of Soil Scientists Society of America* 55: 856–62.

Bridgham, S. D., C. A. Johnston, J. Pastor, and K. Updegraff. 1995. Potential feedbacks of northern wetlands on climate change—An outline of an approach to predict climate-change impact. *BioScience* 45: 262–74.

Bridgham, S. D., J. Pastor, J. A. Janssens, C. Chapin, and T. J. Malterer. 1996. Multiple limiting gradients in peatlands: A call for a new paradigm. *Wetlands* 16: 45–65.

Bridgham, S. D. and C. J. Richardson. 1993. Hydrology and nutrient gradients in North Carolina peatlands. *Wetlands* 13: 207–218.

Briggs, S. V., and M. T. Maher. 1983. Litter fall and leaf decomposition in a river red gum (*Eucalyptus camaldulensis*) swamp. *Australian Journal of Botany* 31: 307–16.

Briggs, S. V., M. T. Maher, and S. M. Carpenter. 1985. Limnological studies of waterfowl habitat in south-western New South Wales. I. Water chemistry. *Australian Journal of Marine and Freshwater Research* 36: 59–67.

Briggs, S. V., and S. A. Thornton. 1999. Management of water regime in River Red Gum *Eucalyptus camaldulensis* wetlands for waterbird breeding. *Australian Zoologist* 31: 187–97.

Brinson, M. M. 1977. Decomposition and nutrient exchange of litter in an alluvial swamp forest. *Ecology* 58: 601–9.

———. 1990. Riverine forests. In *Forested wetlands ecosystems of the world,* eds. A. E. Lugo, M. M. Brinson, and S. Brown, 87–141. Amsterdam: Elsevier Science.

———. 1993a. *A hydrogeomorphic classification for wetlands.* Wetlands Research Program Technical Report WRP-DE-4. Vicksburg, MS: U.S. Army Corps of Engineers Waterways Experiment Station.

———. 1993b. Changes in the functioning of wetlands along environmental gradients. *Wetlands* 13: 65–74.

Brinson, M. M., B. E. Bedford, B. Middleton, and J. Verhoeven. In press. Temperate freshwater wetlands: Response to gradients in moisture regime, human alterations, and economic status. In *Environmental future of aquatic ecosystems,* ed. N. Polunin. Cambridge, U.K.: Cambridge University Press.

Brinson, M. M., F. R. Hauer, L. C. Lee, W. L. Nutter, R. D., Rheinhardt, R. D. Smith, and D. Whigham. 1995b. *A guidebook for application of hydrogeomorphic assessments to riverine wetlands.* Technical Report WRP-DE-11. Vicksburg, MS: Army Engineer Waterways Experiment Station.

Brinson, M. M., W. Kruczynski, L. C. Lee, W. L. Nutter, R. D. Smith, and D. L. Whigham. 1994. Developing an approach for assessing the functions of wetlands. In *Global wetlands: Old world and new,* ed. W. J. Mitsch, 615–24. Amsterdam: Elsevier Science B.V.

Brinson, M. M., A. E. Lugo, and S. Brown. 1981a. Primary productivity, decomposition and consumer activity in freshwater wetlands. *Annual Review of Ecology and Systematics* 12: 123–61.

Brinson, M. M., and A. I. Malvarez. 2002. Temperate freshwater wetlands: Types, status and threats. *Environmental Conservation* 29: 115–33.

Brinson, M. M., and R. D. Rheinhardt. 1998. Wetland functions and relations to societal values. In *Southern forested wetlands: Ecology and management,* eds. M. G. Messina and W. H. Connor, 29–48. Boca Raton, FL: Lewis Publishers.

Brinson, M. M., and J. Verhoeven. 1999. Riparian forests. In *Maintaining biodiversity in forested ecosystems,* ed. M. L. Hunter, ch. 8, 265–99. Cambridge, England: Cambridge University Press.

Britski, H. A., K. Z. de S. de Silimon, and B. S. Lopes. 1999. Peixes do Pantanal: Manual de identificação. EMBRAPA, Serviço de Produção de Informção – SPI, Brasília, DF, Brazil.

Britto, D. T., A. E. Thomas, J. Ruth, A. E. S. Lapi, and H. J. Kronzucker. 2004. Cellular and whole-plant chloride dynamics in barley: Insights into chloride-nitrogen interactions and salinity responses. *Planta* 218: 615–22.

Britton, R. H., and A. J. Crivelli. 1993. Wetlands of southern Europe and North Africa: Mediterranean wetlands. In *Wetlands of the world,* eds. D. F. Whigham, D. Dykyjova, and S. Hejny, 1: 129–94. Dordrecht, Germany: Kluwer Academic.

Brix, H., B. K. Sorrell, and H. H. Schierup. 1996. Gas fluxes achieved by in situ convective flow in *Phragmites australis. Aquatic Botany* 54: 151–63.

Brock, M. A., D. L. Nielsen, R. J. Shiel, J. D. Green, and J. D. Langley. 2003. Drought and aquatic community resilience: The role of eggs and seeds in sediments of temporary wetlands. *Freshwater Biology* 48: 1207–18.

Brooks, R. P., T. J. O'Connell, D. H. Wardrop, and L. E. Jackson. 1998. Towards a regional index of biological integrity: The example of forested riparian ecosystems. *Environmental Monitoring and Assessment* 51: 131–43.

Brooks, R. T. 2000. Annual and seasonal variation and the effects of hydroperiod on benthic macroinvertebrates of season forest ("vernal") ponds in central Massachussetts, USA. *Wetlands* 20: 77–715.

Brose, U. 2003. Island biogeography of temporary wetland carabid beetle communities. *Journal of Biogeography* 30: 879–88.

Browder, J. A., P. J. Gleason, and D. R. Swift. 1994. Periphyton in the Everglades: Spatial variation, environmental correlates and ecological implications. In *Everglades: The ecosystem and its restoration,* eds. S. M. Davis and J. C. Ogden, 379–418. Boca Raton, FL: St. Lucie Press.

Brown, S. C. 1998. Remnant seed banks and vegetation as predictors of restored marsh vegetation. *Canadian Journal of Botany* 76: 620–29.

Brown, S. C., and D. P. Batzer. 2001. Birds, plants, and macroinvertebrates as indicators of restoration success in New York marshes. In *Bioassessment and management of North American freshwater wetlands,* eds. R. B. Rader, D. P. Batzer, and S. A. Wissinger, 237–248. New York: John Wiley and Sons.

Brown, S.C., and B.L. Bedford. 1997. Restoration of wetland vegetation with transplanted wetland soil: An experimental study. *Wetlands* 17: 424–37.

Brown, S.C., and C.R. Smith. 1998. Breeding season bird use of recently restored versus natural wetlands in New York. *Journal of Wildlife Management* 62: 1480–91.

Brown, S.C., K. Smith, and D. Batzer. 1997. Macroinvertebrate responses to wetland restoration in northern New York. *Environmental Entomology* 26: 1016–24.

Brown, S.L. 1978. A comparison of cypress ecosystems in the landscape of Florida. Ph.D. diss., University of Florida, Gainesville.

Bruno, J.F. 2000. Facilitation of cobble beach plant communities through habitat modification by *Spartina alterniflora*. *Ecology* 81: 1179–92.

Buchan, A., S.Y. Newell, M. Butler, E.J. Biers, J.T. Hollibaugh, and M.A. Moran. 2003. Dynamics of bacterial and fungal communities on decaying salt marsh grass. *Applied and Environmental Microbiology* 69: 6, 676-6, 687.

Buck, J.D. 1979. The plate count in aquatic microbiology. In *Native aquatic bacteria: Enumeration, activity and ecology,* eds. J.W. Costerson and R.R. Colwell, 19–28. Philadelphia: ASTM Press.

Buesing, N., and M.O. Gessner. 2002. Comparison of detachment procedures for direct counts of bacteria associated with sediment particles, plant litter and epiphytic biofilms. *Aquatic Microbial Ecology* 27: 29–36.

Buhlmann, K.A. 1995. Habitat use, terrestrial movements, and conservation of the turtle, *Deirochelys reticularia*, in Virginia. *Journal of Herpetology* 29: 173–81.

Bullock, A., and M. Acreman. 2003. The role of wetlands in the hydrological cycle. *Hydrology and Earth System Sciences* 7: 358–89.

Bunn, S.E. 1986. Origin and fate of organic matter in Australian upland streams. In *Limnology in Australia,* eds. P. De Deckker and W.D. Williams, 277–91. Melbourne, Australia: CSIRO Publishing.

Bunn, S.E., and P.I. Boon. 1993. What sources of organic carbon drive food webs in billabongs? A study based on stable isotope analysis. *Oecologia* 96: 85–94.

Buol, S.W., and R.A. Rebertus. 1988. Soil formation under hydromorphic conditions. In *The ecology and management of wetlands, vol. 1. Ecology of wetlands,* eds. D.D. Hook et al., 1: 253–68. London and Sydney: Croom Helm.

Burdick, D.M., and I.A. Mendelssohn. 1990. Relationship between anatomical and metabolic responses to soil waterlogging in the coastal grass *Spartina patens*. *Journal of Experimental Botany* 41: 223–28.

Burke, D.M., and E. Nol. 1998. Influence of food abundance, nest-site habitat, and forest fragmentation on breeding ovenbirds. *Auk* 115: 96–104.

Burke, V.J., and J.W. Gibbons. 1995. Terrestrial buffer zones and wetland conservation: A case study of freshwater turtles in a Carolina Bay. *Conservation Biology* 9:1365–69.

Burkett, V., and J. Kusler. 2000. Climate change: Potential impacts and interactions in wetlands of the Untied States. *Journal of the American Water Resources Association* 36: 313–20.

Burkholder, J.M. 1996. Interactions of benthic algae with their substrata. In *Algal ecology: Benthic algae in freshwater ecosystems,* eds. R.J. Stevenson, M. Bothwell, and R. Lowe, 253–97. New York: Academic Press.

Burkholder, J. M., and R. G. Wetzel. 1989. Epiphytic microalgae on a natural substratum in a hardwater lake: Seasonal dynamics of community structure, biomass and ATP content. *Archiv für Hydrobiologie/Supplement* 83: 1–56.

————. 1990. Alkaline phosphatase and algal biomass on natural and artificial plants in an oligotrophic lake: Re-evaluation of the role of macrophytes as a phosphorus source for epiphytes. *Limnology and Oceanography* 35: 736–47.

Burkholder, J. M., R. G. Wetzel, and K. L. Klomparens. 1990. A direct comparison of phosphate uptake by adnate and loosely attached microalgae within an intact biofilm matrix. *Applied and Environmental Microbiology* 56: 2882–90.

Cáceres, C. E. 1997. Temporal variation, dormancy, and coexistence: A field test of the storage effect. *Proceedings of National Academy of Science, USA.* 94: 9171–75.

Cáceres, C. E., and D. A. Soluk. 2002. Blowing in the wind: A field test of overland dispersal and colonization by aquatic invertebrates. *Oecologia* 131: 402–8.

Cahoon, D. R., D. J. Reed, and J. W. Day, Jr. 1995. Estimating shallow subsidence in microtidal marshes of the southeastern United States: Kaye and Barghoorn revisited. *Marine Geology* 128: 1–9.

Calder, I. R. 1977. A model of transpiration and interception loss from a spruce forest in Plynlimon, central Wales. *Journal of Hydrology* 33: 247–65.

————. 1978. Transpiration observations from a spruce forest and comparisons with predictions from an evaporation model. *Journal of Hydrology* 38: 33–47.

Caldwell, J. P., J. H. Thorp, and T. O. Jervey. 1980. Predator-prey relationship among larval dragonflies, salamanders, and frogs. *Oecologia* 46: 285–89.

Callaway, J. C. 2001. Hydrology and substrate. In *Handbook for Restoring Tidal Wetlands,* ed. J. B. Zedler, 89–118. Boca Raton, FL: CRC Press.

Callaway, J. C., G. Sullivan, and J. B. Zedler. 2003. Species-rich plantings increase biomass and nitrogen accumulation in a wetland restoration experiment. *Ecological Applications* 13: 1626–39.

Callaway, R. M. 1994. Facilitative and interfering effects of *Arthrocnemum subterminale* on winter annuals. Ecology 75:681–686.

Callaway, R. M. 1997. Positive interactions in plant communities and the individualistic-continuum concept. Oecologia 112:143–149.

Callaway, R. M., and S. C. Pennings. 2000. Facilitation may buffer competitive effects: Indirect and diffuse interactions among salt marsh plants. *The American Naturalist* 156: 416–24.

Callaway, R. M., and C. S. Sabraw. 1994. Effects of variable precipitation on the structure and diversity of a California salt marsh community. *Journal of Vegetation Science* 5: 433–38.

Calme, S., and A. Desrochers. 2000. Biogeographic aspects of the distribution of bird species breeding in Quebec's peatlands. *Journal of Biogeography* 27: 725–32.

Campeau, S., H. R. Murkin, and R. D. Titman. 1994. Relative importance algae and emergent plant litter to freshwater marsh invertebrates. *Canadian Journal of Fisheries and Aquatic Sciences* 51: 681–92.

Cantelmo, A. J., and J. G. Ehrenfeld. 1999. Effects of microtopography on mycorrhizal infection in Atlantic white cedar (*Chamaecyparis thyoides* [L.] Mills.). *Mycorrhiza* 8: 175–80.

Capello, S., M. R. Marchese, and I. Ezcurra de Drago. 2004. Decomposition and invertebrate colonization of *Salix humboldtiana* leaf litter on the Middle Paraná River floodplain. *Amazoniana* XVIII: 125–43.

Capone, D. G., and R. R. Kiene. 1988. Comparison of microbial dynamics in marine and freshwater sediments: Contrasts in anaerobic carbon metabolism. *Limnology and Oceanography* 33: 725–49.

Carlton, R. G., and R. G. Wetzel. 1987. Distributions and fates of oxygen in periphyton communities. *Canadian Journal of Botany* 65: 1031–37.

———. 1988. Phosphorus flux from lake sediments: Effect of epipelic algal photosynthesis. *Limnology and Oceanography* 33: 562–70.

Carrick, H. J., and R. L. Lowe. 1988. Response of Lake Michigan benthic algae to an in situ enrichment with Si, N, and P. *Canadian Journal of Fisheries and Aquatic Sciences* 45: 271–79.

Carter, V. 1986. An overview of the hydrologic concerns related to wetlands in the United States. *Canadian Journal of Botany* 64: 364–74.

Castellanos, D. L., and L. P. Rozas. 2001. Nekton use of submerged aquatic vegetation, marsh, and shallow unvegetated bottom in the Atchafalaya River Delta, a Louisiana tidal freshwater ecosystem. *Estuaries* 24: 184–97.

Castellanos, E. M., M. E. Figueroa, and A. J. Davy. 1994. Nucleation and facilitation in saltmarsh succession: Interactions between *Spartina maritima* and *Arthrocnemun perenne*. *Journal of Ecology* 82: 239–48.

Catallo, W. J., J. T. Blankenmeyer, R. P. Gambrell, J. H. Pardue, and K. R. Reddy. 1999. Workshop I synopsis: Biogeochemical processes. In *Ecotoxicology and risk assessment for wetlands*, eds. M. A. Lewis, F. L. Mayer, R. L. Powell, M. K. Nelson, S. J. Klaine, M. G. Henry, and G. W. Dickson, 26–67. Pensacola, FL: SETAC Press.

Caudill, C. C. 2003. Measuring dispersal in a metapopulation using stable isotope enrichment: High rates of sex-biased dispersal between patches in mayfly metapopulation. *Oikos* 101: 624–30.

Cavalieri, A. J., and A. H. C. Huang. 1981. Accumulation of proline and glycinebetaine in *Spartina alterniflora* Loisel. in response to NaCl and nitrogen in the marsh. *Oecologia* 49: 224–28.

Cebrian, J. 1999. Patterns in the fate of production in plant communities. *The American Naturalist* 154: 449–68.

Cedfeldt, P. T., M. C. Watzin, B. D. Richardson. 2000. Using GIS to identify functionally significant wetlands in the northeastern United States. *Environmental Management* 26: 13–24.

Chabbi, A., K. L. McKee, and I. A. Mendelssohn. 2000. Fate of oxygen losses from *Typha domingensis* (Typhaceae) and *Cladium jamaicense* (Cyperaceae) and consequences for root metabolism. *American Journal of Botany* 87: 1081–90.

Chambers, R. M., T. J. Mozdzer, and J. C. Ambrose. 1998. Effects of salinity and sulfide on the distribution of *Phragmites australis* and *Spartina alterniflora* in a tidal saltmarsh. *Aquatic Botany* 62: 161–69.

Chanton, J. P., and J. W. H. Dacey. 1991. Effects of vegetation on methane flux, reservoirs, and carbon isotopic composition. In *Trace gas emissions by plants*, eds. T. D. Sharkey, E. A. Holland, and H. A. Mooney, 65–72. San Diego: Academic Press.

Chao, P. 1999. Great Lakes water resources: Climate change impacts analysis with transient GCM scenarios. *Journal of the American Water Resources Association* 35: 1499–1507.

Chapman, V. J. 1960. *Salt marshes and salt deserts of the world.* London: Leonard Hill Limited.

———. 1976. *Mangrove vegetation.* Vaduz, Liechtenstein: J. Cramer.

Characklis, W. G., and P. A. Wilderer, eds. 1989. *Structure and function of biofilms.* Chichester, U.K.: John Wiley & Sons.

Chaudhuri, A. B., and A. Choudhury. 1994. *Mangroves of the Sundarbans, Volume 1: India.* Gland, Switzerland: World Conservation Union.

Chen, R., and R. R. Twilley. 1998. A gap dynamic model of mangrove forest development along gradients of soil salinity and nutrient resources. *Journal of Ecology* 86: 1–15.

Chen, R. L., and J. W. Barko. 1988. Effects of freshwater macrophytes on sediment chemistry. *Journal of Freshwater Ecology* 4: 279–87.

Chiang, C., C. B. Craft, D. Rogers, and C. J. Richardson. 2000. Effects of four years of N and P additions on Everglades plant communities. *Aquatic Botany* 68: 61–78.

Childers, D. L., R. F. Doren, R. Jones, G. B. Noe, M. Rugge, and L. J. Scinto. 2003. Decadal change in vegetation and soil phosphorus pattern across the Everglades landscape. *Journal of Environmental Quality* 32: 344–62.

Chmielewski, R. M. 1996. Hydrologic analysis of Carolina bay wetlands at the Savannah River Site, South Carolina. Master's thesis, University of Wisconsin, Milwaukee.

Chmura, G. L., R. Costanza, and E. C. Kosters. 1992. Modelling coastal marsh stability in response to sea level rise: A case study in coastal Louisiana, USA. *Ecological Modelling* 64: 47–64.

Christensen, N. L. and R. B. Wilbur. 1995. Short- and long-term effects of fire on vegetation and biogeochemical processes in southeastern evergreen shrub bogs (pocosins) (abstract only). In *Fire in wetlands: A management perspective,* eds. S. I. Cerulean and R. T. Engstrom, 30. Tallahassee, FL: Proceedings of the Tall Timbers Fire Ecology Conference, No. 19. Tall Timbers Research Station.

Chrost, R. J. 1991. Environmental control of the synthesis and activity of aquatic microbial ectoenzymes. In *Microbial enzymes in aquatic systems,* ed. R. J. Chrost, 29–50. New York: Brock/Springer-Verlag.

Chura, N. J. 1961. Food availability and preferences of juvenile mallards. *Transactions of the North American Wildlife Conference* 26: 121–34.

Clairain, E. J. 2002. *Hydrogeomorphic approach to assessing wetland functions: Guidelines for developing regional guidebooks.* Chapter 1, Introduction and Overview of the Hydrogeomorphic Approach. ERDC/EL TR-02-3. Vicksburg, MS: U.S. Army Engineer Research and Development Center.

Clark, J. S., C. Fastie, G. Hurtt, S. T. Jackson, C. Johnson, G. A. King, M. Lewis, et al. 1998. Reid's paradox of rapid plant migration. *Bioscience* 48: 13–24.

Clark, W. R. 2000. Ecology of muskrats in prairie wetlands. In *Prairie wetland ecology,* eds. H. R. Murkin, A. G. van der Valk, and W. R. Clark, 249–86. Ames, IA: Iowa State University Press.

Clausen, P., B. A. Nolet, A. D. Fox, and M. Klaassen. 2002. Long-distance endozoochorous dispersal of submerged macrophyte seeds by migratory waterbirds in northern—A critical review of possibilities and *limitations. Acta Oecologica* 23: 191–203.

Clawson, R. G., B. G. Lockaby, and R. H. Jones. 1997. Amphibian responses to helicopter harvesting in forested floodplains of low order, blackwater streams. *Forest Ecology and Management* 90: 225–35.

Clements, F. E. 1916. *Plant succession. Publication 242. Carnegie Institute of Washington.*

Clymo, R. S., and P. M. Hayward. 1982. The ecology of *Sphagnum.* In *Bryophyte ecology,* ed. A. J. E. Smith, 229–89. London: Chapman and Hall.

Clymo, R. S., J. Turnen, and K. Tolonen. 1998. Carbon accumulation in peatland. *Oikos* 81: 368–88.

Coesel, P. F. M., S. R. Duque, and G. Arango. 1988. Distributional patterns in some neotropical desmid species (Algae, Chlorophyta) in relation to migratory bird routes. *Revista Hydrobiologia Tropical* 21: 197–205.

Cole, J. J., N. F. Caraco, G. W. Kling, and T. K. Kratz. 1994. Carbon dioxide supersaturation in the surface waters of lakes. *Science* 265: 1568–70.

Colinvaux, P. A., G. Irion, M. E. Räsänen, M. B. Bush, and J. A. Nunes de Mello. 2001. A paradigm to be discarded: Geological and paleoecological data falsify the Haffer & Prance refuge hypothesis of Amazonian speciation. *Amazoniana* 16: 609–46.

Collen, P., and R. J. Gibson. 2001. The general ecology of beavers (*Castor* spp.), as related to their influence on stream ecosystems and riparian habitats, and the subsequent effects on fish–A review. *Reviews in Fish Biology and Fisheries* 10: 439–61.

Collins, B. S., and L. L. Battaglia. 2001. Hydrology effects on propagule bank expression and vegetation in six Carolina bays. *Community Ecology* 2: 21–33.

Collins, J. P., and A. Storfer 2003. Global amphibian declines: Sorting the hypotheses. *Diversity and Distributions* 9: 89–98.

Colmer, T. D. 2003. Long-distance transport of gases in plants: A perspective on internal aeration and radial oxygen loss from roots. *Plant Cell and Environment* 26: 17–36.

Comprehensive Everglades Restoration Plan. 2000. Water Resources Development Act (WRDA). Public Law 106–541, Title VI, Section 601.

Connell, J. H., I. R. Noble, and R. O. Slatyer. 1987. On the mechanisms producing successional change. *Oikos* 50: 136–37.

Connell, J. H., and R. O. Slatyer. 1977. Mechanisms of succession in natural communities and their role in community stability and organization. *The American Naturalist* 111: 1119–44.

Conner, W. H. 1994. The effect of salinity and waterlogging on growth and survival of baldcypress and Chinese tallow seedlings. *Journal of Coastal Research* 10: 1045–49.

Conner, W. H., and M. A. Buford. 1998. Southern deepwater swamps. In *Southern forested wetlands: Ecology and management,* eds. M. G. Messina and W. H. Conner, 261–87. Boca Raton, FL: Lewis Publishers.

Conner, W. H., and J. W. Day, Jr. 1976. Productivity and composition of a bald cypress-water tupelo site and a bottomland hardwood site in a Louisiana swamp. *American Journal of Botany* 63: 1354–64.

———. 1982. The ecology of forested wetlands in the southeastern United States. In *Wetland: Ecology and management,* eds. B. Gopal, R. E. Turner, R. G. Wetzel, and D. F. Whigham, 69–87. Jaipur, India: National Institute of Ecology and International Scientific Publications.

Conner, W. H., J. W. Day, Jr., R. H. Baumann, and J. Randall. 1989. Influence of hurricanes on coastal ecosystems along the northern Gulf of Mexico. *Wetlands Ecology and Management* 1: 45–56.

Connor, W. H., J. G. Gosselink, and R. T. Parrondo. 1981. Comparison of the vegetation of three Louisiana swamp sites with different flooding regimes. *American Journal of Botany* 68: 320–31.

Conner, W. H., and R. R. Sharitz. 2005. Forest communities of bottomlands. In *Ecology and management of bottomland hardwood systems: The state of our understanding*, eds. L. H. Fredrickson, S. L. King, and R. M. Kaminski, 93–120. Gaylord Memorial Laboratory Special Publication No. 10. Puxico, MO: University of Missouri–Columbia.

Connors, L. M., E. Kiviat, P. M. Groffman, and R. S. Ostfeld. 2000. Muskrat (*Odontra zibethicus*) disturbance to vegetation and potential net nitrogen mineralization and nitrification rates in a freshwater tidal marsh. *American Midland Naturalist* 143: 53–63.

Conrad, R. 2002. Control of microbial methane production in wetland rice fields. *Nutrient Cycling in Agroecosystems* 64: 59–69.

Conservation Foundation. 1988. *Protecting America's wetlands: An action agenda*. Washington, D.C.: The Conservation Foundation.

Constanza, R., R. d'Arge, R. de Groot, S. Farber, M. Grasso, B. Hannon, K. Limburg, S. Naeem, R. V. O'Neill, J. Paruelo, R. G. Raskin, P. Sutton, and M. van den Belt. 1997. The value of the world's ecosystem services and natural capital. *Nature* 387: 253–60.

Cook, C. D. K. 1996. *Aquatic and wetlands plants of India*. Oxford, U.K.: Oxford University Press.

Cooke, J. C., and M. W. Lefor. 1998. The mycorrhizal status of selected plant species from Connecticut wetlands and transition zones. *Restoration Ecology* 6: 214–22.

Cornell, H. V., and B. A. Hawkins. 2003. Herbivore responses to plant secondary compounds: A test of phytochemical coevolution theory. *American Naturalist* 161: 507–22.

Costerton, J. W., Z. Lewandowski, D. De Beer, D. Caldwell, D. Korber, and G. James. 1994. Biofilms, the customized microniche. *Journal of Bacteriology* 176: 2137–42.

Costerton, J. W., Z. Lewandowski, D. E. Caldwell, D. R. Korber, and H. M. Lappin-Scott. 1995. Microbial biofilms. *Annual Review of Microbiology* 49: 711–45.

Cottenie K, E. Michels, N. Nuytten, and L. DeMeester. 2003. Zooplankton metacommunity structure: Regional vs. local processes in highly interconnected ponds. *Ecology* 84: 991–1000.

Cowan, S. T. 1962. The microbial species—A macromyth? In *Microbial classification*, eds. G. C. Ainsworth and P. H. A. Sneath, 433–55. Cambridge, U.K.: Cambridge University Press.

Cowardin, L. M., V. Carter, F. C. Golet, and E. T. LaRoe. 1979. *Classification of wetlands and deepwater habitats of the United States*. FWS/OBS-79/31. Washington, D.C.: U.S. Fish and Wildlife Service.

Craft, C. B. 2001. Biology of wetland soils. In *Wetland soils: Their genesis, hydrology, landscape and separation into hydric and nonhydric soils*, eds. J. L. Richardson and M. J. Vepraskas, 107–35. Boca Raton, FL: CRC Press.

Craft, C. B., and C. Chiang. 2002. Forms and amounts of soil nitrogen and phosphorus across a longleaf pine-depressional wetland landscape. *Soil Science Society of America Journal* 66: 1713–21.

Craft, C., P. Megonigal, S. Broome, J. Stevenson, R. Freese, J. Cornell, L. Zheng, and J. Sacco. 2003. The pace of ecosystem development of constructed *Spartina alterniflora* marshes. *Ecological Applications* 13: 1417–32.

Craft, C., J. Reader, J. N. Sacco, and S. Broome. 1999. Twenty-five years of ecosystem development of constructed Spartina alterniflora (Loisel) marshes. *Ecological Applications* 9: 1405–19.

Craft, C. B., J. Vymazal, and C. J. Richardson. 1995. Response of Everglades plant communities to nitrogen and phosphorus additions. *Wetlands* 15: 258–71.

Crain, C. M., B. R. Silliman, S. L. Bertness, and M. D. Bertness. 2004. Physical and biotic drivers of plant distribution across estuarine salinity gradients. *Ecology* 85: 2539–49.

Cramer, G. R., A. Lauchli, and V. S. Polito. 1985. Displacement of Ca2+ by Na+ from the plasmalemma of root cells. *Plant Physiology* 79: 207–11.

Crawford, D. J., E. Landolt, D. H. Les, and E. Tepe. 1997. Allozyme variation and the taxonomy of *Wolffiella*. *Aquatic Botany* 58: 43–54.

Crawford, R. M. M. 1992. Oxygen availability as an ecological limit to plant distribution. *Advances in Ecological Research* 23: 93–185.

Crome, F. H. J. 1986. Australian waterfowl do not necessarily breed on a rising water level. *Australian Wildlife Research* 13: 461–80.

———. 1988. To drain or not to drain? Intermittent swamp drainage and waterbird breeding. *Emu* 88: 243–48.

Cromer, R. B., J. D. Lanham, and H. G. Hanlin. 2002. Herpetofaunal response to gap and skidder-rut wetland creation in a southern bottomland hardwood forest. *Forest Science* 48: 407–16.

Cronin, T. M., G. S. Dwyer, T. Kamiya, S. Schwede, and D. A. Willard. 2003. Medieval Warm Period, Little Ice Age, and 20th century temperature variability from Chesapeake Bay. *Global and Planetary Change* 36: 17–29.

Cronk, J. K., and M. S. Fennessy. 2001. *Wetland plants. Biology and ecology*. Boca Raton, FL: Lewis Publishers.

Crownover, S. H., N. B. Comerford, and D. G. Neary. 1995. Water flow patterns in cypress/pine flat woods landscapes. *Soil Science Society of America Journal* 59: 1199–1206.

Crumpton, W. G. 2001. Using wetlands for water quality improvement in agricultural watersheds: The importance of a watershed scale approach. *Water Science and Technology* 44: 559–64.

Cuffney, T. F., and J. B. Wallace. 1987. Leaf litter processing in coastal plain streams and floodplains of southeastern Georgia, U.S.A. *Archiv für Hydrobiologie, Supplement* 76: 1–24.

Cummins, K. W. 1973. Trophic relations of aquatic insects. *Annual Review of Entomology* 18: 183–206.

Cummins, K. W., M. A. Wilzbach, D. M. Gates, J. B. Perry, and W. B. Taliaferro. 1989. Shredders and riparian vegetation. *BioScience* 39: 24–30.

Currin, C. A., S. B. Joye, and H. W. Paerl. 1996. Diel rates of N-2-fixation and denitrification in a transplanted *Spartina alterniflora* marsh: Implications for N-flux dynamics. *Estuary and Coastal Shelf Sciences* 42: 597–616.

Currin, C. A., S. Y. Newell, and H. W. Paerl. 1995. The role of standing *Spartina alterniflora* and benthic microalgae in salt-marsh food webs—Considerations based on multiple stable-isotope analysis. *Marine Ecology—Progress Series* 121: 99–116.

Currin, C. A., S. C. Wainright, K. W. Able, M. P. Weinstein, and C. M. Fuller. 2003. Determination of food web support and trophic position of the mummichog, *Fundulus heteroclitus*, in New Jersey smooth cordgrass (*Spartina alterniflora*), common reed (*Phragmites australis*) and restored salt marshes. *Estuaries* 26: 485–510.

D'Angelo, E. M., and K. R. Reddy. 1999. Regulators of heterotrophic microbial potentials in wetland soils. *Soil Biology and Biochemistry* 31: 815–30.

Dabel, C. V., and F. P. Day, Jr. 1977. Structural composition of four plant communities in the Great Dismal Swamp, Virginia. *Torrey Botanical Club Bulletin* 104: 352–60.

Daborn, G. R., C. L. Amos, M. Brylinsky, H. Christian, G. Drapiau, R. W. Fass, J. Grant, et al. 1993. An ecological cascade effect: Migratory birds affect stability of intertidal sediments. *Limnology and Oceanography* 38: 225–231.

Dacey, J. W. H. 1981. Pressurized ventilation in the yellow waterlily. *Ecology* 62: 1137–47.

Dahl, T. E. 1990. *Wetlands losses in the United States 1780s to 1980s.* Washington, D.C.: U.S. Department of the Interior, Fish and Wildlife Service (also www.fws.gov/wetlands/bha/SandT/SandTReport.html).

————. 2000. *Status and trends of wetlands in the conterminous United States: 1986–1997.* Washington, D.C.: U.S. Department of Interior, Fish and Wildlife Service.

Dahl, T. E., C. E. Johnson, and W. E. Frayer. 1991. *Status and trends of wetland in the conterminous United States, mid 1970s to mid 1980s.* Washington, D.C.: U.S. Fish and Wildlife Service.

Dalrymple, G. H., R. F. Doren, N. K. O'Hare, M. R. Norland, and T. V. Armentano. 2003. Plant colonization after complete and partial removal of disturbed soils for wetland restoration of former agricultural fields in Everglades National Park. *Wetlands* 23: 1015–29.

Dalva, M., T. R. Moore, P. Arp, and T. A. Clair. 2001. Methane and soil and plant community respiration from wetlands, Kejimkujik National Park, Nova Scotia: Measurements, predictions, and climatic change. *Journal of Geophysical Research-Atmospheres* 106: 2955–62.

Daly, H. V, J. T. Doyen, and A. H. Purcell III. 1998. *Introduction to insect biology and diversity,* 2d ed. New York: Oxford University Press.

Dame, R. F. 1996. *Ecology of marine bivalves: An ecosystem approach.* Boca Raton, FL: CRC Press.

Dame, R. F., and D. M. Allen. 1996. Between estuaries and the sea. *Journal of Experimental Marine Biology and Ecology* 200: 169–85.

Damman, A. W. H. 1986. Hydrology, development, and biogeochemistry of ombrogenous peat bogs with special reference to nutrient relocation in a western Newfoundland bog. *Canadian Journal of Botany* 64: 384–94.

Damman, A. W. H., and T. W. French. 1987. *The ecology of peat bogs of the glaciated northeastern United States: A community profile.* Washington, D.C.: U.S. Department of Interior, U.S. Fish and Wildlife Service, 100 pp.

Daniel. C. C. III. 1981. Hydrology, geology, and soils of pocosins: A comparison of natural and altered systems. In *Pocosin wetlands,* ed. C. J. Richardson, 66–108. Stroudsburg, PA: Hutchinson Ross Publishing.

D'Antonio, C., and L. A. Meyerson. 2002. Exotic plant species as problems and solutions in ecological restoration: A synthesis. *Restoration Ecology* 10: 703–13.

Daoust, R. J., and D. L. Childers. 1999. Controls on emergent macrophyte composition, abundance, and productivity in freshwater Everglades wetland communities. *Wetlands* 19: 262–75.

David, P. G. 1996. Changes in plant communities relative to hydrologic conditions in the Florida Everglades. *Wetlands* 16: 15–23.

Davis, M. A., J. P. Grime, and K. Thompson. 2000. Fluctuating resources in plant communities: A general theory of invasibility. *Journal of Ecology* 88: 528–34.

Davis, M. B., R. G. Shaw, and J. R. Etterson. 2005. Evolutionary responses to changing climate. *Ecology* 86: 1704–14.

Davis, S. M. 1991. Growth, decomposition, and nutrient retention of *Cladium jamaicense* Crantz and *Typha domingensis* Pers. in the Florida Everglades. *Aquatic Botany* 40: 203–24.

———. 1994. Phosphorus inputs and vegetation sensitivity in the Everglades. In *Everglades: The ecosystem and its restoration,* eds. S. M. Davis and J. C. Ogden, 357–78. Delray Beach, FL: St. Lucie Press.

Davis, S. M., L. H. Gunderson, W. A. Park, J. R. Richardson, and J. E. Mattson. 1994. Landscape dimension, composition, and function in a changing Everglades ecosystem. In *Everglades: The ecosystem and its restoration,* eds. S. M. Davis and J. C. Ogden, 419–44. Boca Raton, FL: St. Lucie Press.

Davy, A. J. 2000. Development and structure of salt marshes: Community patterns in time and space. In *Concepts and controversies in tidal marsh ecology,* eds. M. P. Weinstein and D. A. Kreeger, 137–56. Dordrecht, The Netherlands: Kluwer Academic Publishers.

Day, F .P. Jr. 1982. Litter decomposition rates in the seasonally flooded Great Dismal Swamp. *Ecology* 63: 670–78.

———. 1983. Effects of flooding on leaf litter decomposition in microcosms. *Oecologia* 56: 180–84.

———. 1984. Biomass and litter accumulation in the Great Dismal Swamp. In *Cypress swamps,* eds. K. C. Ewel and H. T. Odum, 386–92. Gainesville, FL: University Presses of Florida.

Day, J., G. Shaffer, L. Britsch, D. Reed, S. Hawes, and D. Cahoon. 2000. Pattern and processes of land loss in the Mississippi Delta: A spatial and temporal analysis of wetland habitat change. *Estuaries* 23: 425–38.

Day, J. W., Jr., W. H. Conner, F. Ley-Lou, R. H. Day, and A. M. Navarro. 1987. The productivity and composition of mangrove forests, Laguna de Términos, Mexico. *Aquatic Botany* 27: 267–84.

Day, J. W., Jr., C. Coronado-Molina, F. R. Vera-Herrera, R. Twilley, V. H. Rivera-Monroy, H. Alvarez-Guillen, R. Day, and W. Conner. 1996. A 7-year record of above-ground net primary production in a southeastern Mexican mangrove forest. *Aquatic Botany* 55: 39–60.

Day, R. T., P. A. Keddy, J. McNeill, and T. J. Carleton. 1988. Fertility and disturbance gradients: A summary model for riverine marsh vegetation. *Ecology* 69: 1044–54.

De Beer, D., P. Stoodley, F. Roe, and Z. Lewandowski. 1994. Effects of biofilm structures on oxygen distribution and mass transport. *Biotechnology and Bioengineering* 43: 1131–38.

De Datta, S. K. 1981. *Principles and practices of rice production.* New York: John Wiley and Sons.

De Groot, J. C., and C. V. Van Wijck. 1993. The impact of desiccation of a freshwater marsh (Garines Nord, Camargue, France) on sediment-water-vegetation intercations. Part 1. Sediment chemistry. *Hydrobiologia* 252: 83–94.

De Meester, L., A. Gómez, B. Okamura, and K. Schwenk. 2002. The monopolization hypothesis and the dispersal-gene flow paradox in aquatic organisms. *Acta Oecologia* 23: 121–35.

De Stasio, B. T. 1989. The seed bank of a freshwater crustacean: Copepodology for the plant ecologist. *Ecology* 70: 1377–89.

De Steven, D., R. R. Sharitz, J. H. Singer, and C. D. Barton. In press. Testing a passive revegetation approach for restoring Coastal Plain depression wetlands. *Restoration Ecology.*

De Szalay, F. A., and W. Cassidy. 2001. Effects of muskrat *(Ondatra zibethicus)* lodge construction on invertebrate communities in a Great Lakes coastal wetland. *American Midland Naturalist* 146: 300–310.

De Szalay, F. A., and V. H. Resh. 1997. Responses of wetland invertebrates and plants important in waterfowl diets to burning and mowing of emergent vegetation. *Wetlands* 17: 149–56.

Debnath, H. S., and K. R. Naskar. 1999. A comparative study on the magroves and associated flora in the Ganga delta (Sunarbans) and Bay Islands (Andaman and Nicobar). In *Sundarbans magal,* eds. D. N. Guha Bakshi, P. Sanyal, and K. R. Naskar, 277–92. Calcutta, India: Naya Prokash.

Deitz, D. C., and R. Jackson. 1979. Use of American alligator nests by nesting turtle. *Journal of Herpetology* 13: 510–12.

DeLaune, R. C., A. Jugsujinda, G. W. Peterson, and W. H. Patrick. 2003. Impact of Mississippi River freshwater reintroduction on enhancing marsh accretionary processes in a Louisiana estuary. *Estuary and Coastal Shelf Science* 58: 653–62.

DeLaune, R. D., and W. H. Patrick, Jr. 1990. Nitrogen cycling in Louisiana Gulf Coast brackish marshes. *Hydrobiologia* 199: 73–79.

DeLaune, R. D. and C. J. Smith. 1985. Release of nutrients and metals following oxidation of freshwater and saline sediment. *Journal of Environmental Quality* 14: 164–68.

Delettre, Y. R., and N. Morvan 2000. Dispersal of adult aquatic Chironomidae (Diptera) in agricultural landscapes. *Freshwater Biology* 84: 299–411.

Delphey, P. J., and J. J. Dinsmore. 1993. Breeding bird communities of recently restored and natural prairie potholes. *Wetlands* 13: 200–206.

Denno, R. F., C. Gratton, M. A. Peterson, G. A. Langellotto, D. L. Fincke, and A. F. Huberty. 2002. Bottom-up forces mediate natural-enemy impact in a phytophagous insect community. *Ecology* 83: 1443–58.

Denno, R. F., and G. K. Roderick. 1990. Population biology of planthoppers. *Annual Review of Entomology* 35: 4489–520.

———. 1992. Density-related dispersal in planthoppers: Effects of interspecific crowding. *Ecology* 73: 1323–34.

Dermott, R. M. 1991. Deformities in larval *Procladius* spp. and dominant Chironomini from the St. Clair River. *Hydrobiologia* 219: 171–85.

Dettmers, J. M., D. H. Wahl, D. A. Soluk, and S. Gutreuter. 2001. Life in the fast lane: Fish and foodweb structure in the main channel of large rivers. *Journal of the North American Benthological Society* 20: 255–65.

Devai, I., and R. D. DeLaune. 1995. Evidence for phosphine production and emission from Louisiana and Florida marsh soils. *Organic Geochemistry* 23: 277–79.

Devai, I., L Felfoldy, I. Wittner, and S. Plosz. 1988. Detection of phosphine: New aspects of the phosphorus cycle in the hydrosphere. *Nature* 333: 343–45.

Diehl, S. 1992. Fish predation and benthic community structure: The role of omnivory and habitat complexity. *Ecology* 73: 1646–61.

Dietz-Brantley, S. E., B. E. Taylor, D. P. Batzer, and A. E. DeBiase. 2002. Invertebrates that aestivate in dry basins of Carolina bay wetlands. *Wetlands* 22: 767–75.

Dingman, S. L. 1994. *Physical hydrology.* Upper Saddle River, NJ: Prentice Hall.

Dittel, A. I., C. E. Epifanio, S. M. Schwalm, M. S. Fantle, and M. L. Fogel. 2000. Carbon and nitrogen sources for juvenile blue crabs *Callinectes sapidus* in coastal wetlands. *Marine Ecology—Progress Series* 194: 103–12.

Dodd, C. K., and B. S. Cade 1997. Movement patterns and the conservation of amphibians breeding in small, temporary ponds. *Conservation Biology* 12: 331–39.

Dodd, R. S., Z. A. Rafii, F. Fromard, and F. Blasco. 1998. Evolutionary diversity among Atlantic cast mangroves. *Acta Oecologica* 19: 323–30.

Dodds, W. K. 1992. A modified fiber-optic microprobe to measure spherical integrated photosynthetic photon flux density: Characterization of periphyton photosynthesis-irradiance patterns. *Limnology and Oceanography* 37: 871–78.

Dodson, S. I. 1987. Animal assemblages in temporary desert rock pools: Aspects of the ecology of *Dasyhelea sublettei* (Diptera: Ceratopogonidae). *Journal of the North American Benthological Society* 6: 65–71.

Dolman, A. J., J. B. Stewart, and J. D. Cooper. 1988. Predicting forest transpiration from climatological data. *Agricultural and Forest Meteorology* 42: 337–53.

Douglas, M. S. 1947. *The Everglades: River of grass.* Miami, FL: Hurricane House.

———. 1978. *The Everglades: River of grass.* Miami, FL: Banyan Books.

Downing, D. M., C. Winer, and L. D. Wood. 2003. Navigating through Clean Water Act jurisdiction: A legal review. *Wetlands* 23: 475–93.

Drake, B. G. 1992. A field study of the effects of elevated CO_2 on ecosystems processes in a Chesapeake Bay wetland. *Australian Journal of Botany* 40: 579–95.

Drake, B. G., M. S. Muehe, G. Peresta, M. A. GonzalezMeler, and R. Matamala. 1996. Acclimation of photosynthesis, respiration and ecosystem carbon flux of a wetland on Chesapeake Bay, Maryland, to elevated atmospheric CO_2 concentration. *Plant and Soil* 187: 111–18.

Drew, M. C. 1992. Soil aeration and plant root metabolism. *Soil Science* 154: 259–68.

Drew, M. C., P. H. Saglio, and A. Pradet. 1985. Larger adenylate energy charge and ATP/ADP ratios in aerenchymatous roots of *Zea mays* in anaerobic media as a consequence of improved internal oxygen transport. *Planta* 165: 51–58.

Drexler, J. Z., and B. Bedford. 2002. Pathways of nutrient loading and impacts on plant diversity in a New York peatland. *Wetlands* 22: 263–81.

Dube, S., A. P. Plamondon, and R. L. Rothwell. 1995. Watering up after clear-cutting on forested wetlands of the St. Lawrence lowland. *Water Resources Research* 31: 1741–50.

Duever, M. J., J. E. Carlson, and L. A. Riopelle. 1984. Corkscrew Swamp: A virgin cypress strand. In *Cypress swamps,* eds. K. C. Ewel and H. T. Odum, 334–48. Gainesville, FL: University Presses of Florida.

Duever, M. J., J. F. Meeder, L. C. Meeder, and J. M. McCollom. 1994. The climate of south Florida and its role in shaping the Everglades ecosystem. In *Everglades: The ecosystem and its restoration,* eds. S. M. Davis and J. C. Ogden, 225–48. Boca Raton, FL: St. Lucie Press.

Duke, N. C. 1992. Mangrove floristics and biogeography. In *Tropical mangrove ecosystems,* eds. A. I. Robertson and D. M. Alongi, 63–100. Washington, D.C.: American Geophysical Union.

Dunn, C. P., and F. Stearns. 1987. A comparison of vegetation and soils in floodplain and basin forested wetlands of southeastern Wisconsin. *The American Midland Naturalist* 118: 375–84.

Dunne, T. and R. D. Black. 1970a. An experimental investigation of runoff production in permeable soils. *Water Resources Research* 6: 478–90.

———. 1970b. Partial area contributions to storm runoff in a small New England watershed. *Water Resources Research* 6: 1296–311.

Dunne, T., T. R. Moore, and C. H. Taylor 1975. Recognition and prediction of runoff-producing zones in humid regions. *Hydrological Science Bulletin* XX(3): 305–27.

Eason, G. W., and J. E. Fauth. 2001. Ecological correlates of anuran species richness in temporary pools: A field study in South Carolina, USA. *Israel Journal of Zoology* 47: 347–65.

Ebert, T. A., and M. L. Balko. 1987. Temporary pools as islands in space and in time—The biota of vernal pools in San Diego, Southern California, USA. *Archiv für Hydrobiologie* 110: 101–23.

Eddleman, W. R., and C. J. Conway. 1998. Clapper rail *(Rallus longirostris)*. In *The birds of North America,* No. 340, eds. A. Poole and F. Gill. Philadelphia, PA: The Birds of North America Inc.

Eertman, R. H. M., B. A. Kornman, E. Stikvoort, and H. Verbeek. 2002. Restoration of the Sieperda tidal marsh in the Scheldt estuary, the Netherlands. *Restoration Ecology* 10: 438–49.

Egan, D., and E. A. Howell, eds. 2001. *The historical ecology handbook.* Washington, D.C.: Island Press.

Egan, R. S., and P. W. C. Paton. 2004. Within-pond parameters affecting oviposition by wood frogs and spotted salamanders. *Wetlands* 24: 1–13.

Egerova, J., C. E. Proffitt, and S. E. Travis. 2003. Facilitation of survival and growth of *Baccharis halimifolia* L. by *Spartina alterniflora* Loisel. in a created Louisiana salt marsh. *Wetlands* 23: 250–56.

Ehrenfeld, J. G. 1995a. Microtopography and vegetation in Atlantic white cedar swamps: The effects of natural disturbances. *Canadian Journal of Botany* 73: 474–84.

———. 1995b. Microsite differences in surface substrate characteristics in *Chamaecyparis* swamps of the New Jersey Pinelands. *Wetlands* 15: 183–89.

———. 2000. Defining the limits of restoration: The need for realistic goals. *Restoration Ecology* 8: 2–9.

Ehrehfeld, J. G., and J. P. Schneider. 1991. *Chamaecyparis thyoides* wetlands and suburbanization: Effects on hydrology, water quality and plant community composition. *Journal of Applied Ecology* 28: 467–90.

Eklov, P. 2000. Chemical cues from multiple predator-prey interactions induce changes in behavior and growth of anuran larvae. *Oecologia* 123: 192–99.

Elcan, J. M., and S. R. Pezeshki. 2002. Effects of flooding on susceptibility of *Taxodium distichum* L. seedling to drought. *Photosynthetica* 40: 177–82.

Eliot, I., C. M. Finlayson, and P. Waterman. 1999. Predicted climate change, sea level rise and wetland management in the Australian wet-dry tropics. *Wetlands Ecology and Management* 7: 63–81.

Ellison, A. M., and E. J. Farnsworth. 1990. The ecology of Belizean mangrove-root fouling communities. I. Epibenthic fauna are barriers to isopod attack of red mangrove roots. *Journal of Experimental Marine Biology and Ecology* 142: 91–104.

———. 2001. Mangrove communities. In *Marine community ecology,* eds. M. D. Bertness, S. D. Gaines, and M. E. Hay, 423–42. Sunderland: Sinauer Associates Inc.

Ellison, A. M., E. J. Farnsworth, and R. E. Merkt. 1999. Origins of mangrove ecosystems and the mangrove biodiversity anomaly. *Global Ecology and Biogeography* 8: 95–115.

Ellison, A. M., E. J. Farnsworth, and R. R. Twilley. 1996. Facultative mutualism between red mangroves and root-fouling sponges in Belizean mangal. *Ecology* 77: 2431–44.

Emery, N. C., P. J. Ewanchuk, and M. D. Bertness. 2001. Competition and salt-marsh plant zonation: Stress tolerators may be dominant competitors. *Ecology* 82: 2471–85.

Emmerson, W. D., and L. E. McGwynne. 1992. Feeding and assimilation of mangrove leaves by the crab *Sesarma meinerti* de Man in relation to leaf-litter production in Mgazana, a warm-temperate southern African mangrove swamp. *Journal of Experimental Marine Biology and Ecology* 157 :41–53.

Ennos, A. R. 1993. The function and formation of buttresses. *Trends in Ecology and Evolution* 8: 350–51.

Entrekin, S. A., S. W. Golladay, and D. P. Batzer. 2001. The influence of plant community on chironomid secondary production in two wetland types: Cypress-gum swamps and grass-sedge marshes. *Archiv für Hydrobiologie* 152: 369–94.

Environmental Laboratory. 1987. *Corps of Engineers wetlands delineation manual*. Technical Report Y-87-1. Vicksburg, MS: U.S. Army Engineer Waterways Experiment Station.

Erickson, N. E., and D. M. Leslie, Jr. 1987. Soil-vegetation correlations in the Sandhills and Rainwater Basin wetlands of Nebraska. Biological Report 78(11). Washington, D.C.: U.S. Fish and Wildlife Service.

Eriksen, C. H., V. H. Resh, and K. W. Cummins. 1996. Aquaitc insect respiration. In *An introduction to the aquatic insects of North America*, eds. R. W. Merritt and K. W. Cummns, 29–40. Dubuque, IA: Kendall/Hunt Publishers.

Eriksson, P. G., and S. E. B. Weisner. 1996. Functional differences in epiphytic microbial communities in nutrient-rich freshwater ecosystems: An assay of denitrifying capacity. *Freshwater Biology* 36: 555–62.

Errington, P. L. 1963. *Muskrat populations*. Ames, IA: Iowa State University Press.

Ervin, G. N., and R. G. Wetzel. 2002. Influence of a dominant macrophyte, *Juncus effuses*, on wetland plant species richness, diversity, and community composition. *Oecologia* 130: 626–36.

———. 2003. An ecological perspective of allelochemical interference on land-water interface communities. *Plant Soil* 256: 13–28.

Espeland, E. M., S. N. Francoeur, and R. G. Wetzel. 2001. Influence of algal photosynthesis on biofilm bacterial production and associated glucosidase and xylosidase activities. *Microbial Ecology* 42: 524–30.

———. 2002. Microbial phosphatase in biofilms: A comparison of whole community enzyme activity and individual bacterial cell-surface phosphatase expression. *Archiv für Hydrobiologie* 153: 581–93.

Espeland, E. M., and R. G. Wetzel. 2001a. Effects of photosynthesis on bacterial photsphatase production in biofilms. *Microbial Ecology* 42: 328–37.

———. 2001b. Complexation, stabilization, and UV photolysis of extracellular and surface-bound glucosidase and alkaline phosphatase: Implications for biofilm microbiota. *Microbial Ecology* 42: 572–85.

Euliss, N. H., Jr., and D. M. Mushet. 1996. Water level fluctuations in wetlands as a function of landscape position in the prairie pothole region. *Wetlands* 16: 587–93.

Euliss, N. H., Jr., J. W. LaBaugh, L. H. Fredrickson, D. M. Mushet, M. K. Laubhan, G. A. Swanson, T. C. Winter, D. O. Rosenberry, and R. D. Nelson. 2004. The wetland continuum: A conceptual framework for interpreting biological studies. *Wetlands* 24: 448–58.

Ewanchuk, P. J., and M. D. Bertness. 2003. Recovery of a northern New England salt marsh plant community from icing. *Oecologia* 136: 616–26.

Ewel, K. C. 1998. Pondcypress swamps. In *Southern forested wetlands. Ecology and management,* eds. M. G. Messina and W. H. Conner, 405–20. Boca Raton, FL: Lewis Publishers.

Ewel, K. C., and L. P. Wickenheiser. 1988. Effect of swamp size on growth rates of cypress *(Taxodium distichum)* trees. *American Midland Naturalist* 120: 362–70.

Fabre, A. 1988. Experimental studies on some factors influencing phosphorus solubilization in connexion [sic] with the drawdown of a reservoir. *Hydrobiologia* 159: 153–58.

Fairchild, W., R. L. Lowe, and W. B. Richardson. 1985. Algal periphyton growth on nutrient-diffusing substrates: An in situ bioassay. *Ecology* 66: 465–72.

Falge, E., D. Baldocchi, J. Tenhunen, M. Aubinet, P. Bakwin, P. Berbigier, C. Bernhofer, et al. 2002. Seasonality of ecosystem respiration and gross primary production as derived from FLUXNET measurements. *Agricultural and Forest Meteorology* 113: 53–74.

Falkowski, P. G., and J. A. Raven. 1997. *Aquatic photosynthesis.* Oxford: Blackwell Science, 375 pp.

Fanning, D. S., and M. C. B. Fanning. 1989. *Soil morphology, genesis, and classification.* New York: John Wiley & Sons.

Farnell-Jackson, E. A., and A. K. Ward. 2003. Seasonal patterns of viruses, bacteria and dissolved organic carbon in a riverine wetland. *Freshwater Biology* 48: 841–51.

Farnsworth, E. J., and A. M. Ellison. 1991. Patterns of herbivory in Belizean mangrove swamps. *Biotropica* 23: 555–67.

Farnsworth, R. K., and E. S. Thompson. 1982. *Mean monthly, seasonal, and annual pan evaporation for the United States.* U.S. National Atmospheric and Oceanic Administration Technical Report NWS 34. Washington, D.C.

Fauth, J. E. 1999. Identifying potential keystone species from field data—An example from temporary ponds. *Ecology Letters* 2: 36–43.

Fazi, S., and L. Rossi 2000. Effects of macro-detritivore density on leaf detritus processing rates: A macrocosm experiment. *Hydrobiologia* 435: 127–34.

Federal Interagency Committee for Wetland Delineation. 1989. *Federal manual for identifying and delineating jurisdictional wetlands.* Cooperative technical publication, 76 pp. Washington, D.C.: U.S. Army Corps of Engineers, U.S. Environmental Protection Agency, U.S. Fish and Wildlife Service, and USDA Natural Resource Conservation Service.

Federal Register. 1994. *Definition of hydric soils.* USDA-NRCS, Vol. 59 (133)/Wed. July 13/p. 35681. Washington, D.C.: U.S. Government Printing Office.

Feller, I. C. 1995. Effects of nutrient enrichment on growth and herbivory of dwarf red mangrove *(Rhizophora mangle).* *Ecological Monographs* 65: 477–505.

Feller, I. C., and W. N. Mathis. 1997. Primary herbivory by wood-boring insects along an architectural gradient of *Rhizophora mangle. Biotropica* 29: 440–51.

Feller, I. C., and K. L. McKee. 1999. Light-gap creation in a Belizean mangrove forest by a wood-boring insect. *Biotropica* 31: 607–16.

Fellows, M. Q., and J. B. Zedler. 2005. Effects of the non-native grass, *Parapholis incurva* (Poaceae), on the rare and endangered hemiparasite, *Cordylanthus maritimus* subsp. *maritimus* (Scrophulariaceae). *Madroño* 52: 91–98.

Fenchel, T., and T. H. Blackburn. 1979. *Bacteria and mineral cycling*. London: Academic Press.

Fenchel, T. M. 1978. The ecology of micro and meio benthos. *Annual Review of Ecology and Systematics* 9: 99–121.

———. 1992. What ecologists can learn from microbes: Life beneath a square centimetre of sediment surface. *Functional Ecology* 6: 499–507.

Ferguson, B. K. 1998. *Introduction to stormwater*. New York: John Wiley and Sons.

Ferreira, C. S. 2002. Germinação e adaptações metabólicas e morfo-anatômicas em plântulas de *Himatanthus succuba* (Spruce) Wood., deambientes de várzea e terra firme na Amazônia Central. Master's thesis, Universidade do Amazonas, Instituto Nacional de Pesquisas da Amazônia, Manaus, Brazil.

Fetzer, S., F. Bak, and R. Conrad. 1993. Sensitivity of methanogenic bacteria from paddy soil to oxygen and desiccation. *FEMS Microbiology Ecology* 12: 107–15.

FICWD. 1989. Federal Manual for Identifying and Delineating Jurisdictional Wetlands. Federal Interagency Committee for Wetland Delineation: U.S. Army Corps of Engineers, U.S. Environmental Protection Agency, U.S. Fish and Wildlife Service, and U.S.D.A. Soil Conservation Service, Washington, D.C. Cooperative Technical Publication. 76 pp. plus appendices.

Figuerola, J., and A. J. Green. 2002. Dispersal of aquatic organisms by waterbirds: A review of past research and priorities for future studies. *Freshwater Biology* 47: 483–94.

Findlay, S. E. G., S. Dye, and K. A. Kuehn. 2002. Microbial growth and nitrogen retention in litter of *Phragmites australis* compared with *Typha angustifolia*. *Wetlands* 22: 616–25.

Finke, D. L., and R. F. Denno. 2004. Predator diversity dampens trophic cascades. *Nature* 429: 407–10.

Finlayson, C. M., and A. G. van der Valk. 1995. Wetland classification and inventory: A summary. *Vegetatio* 118: 185–92.

Finlayson, M., and M. Moser. 1991. *Wetlands*. Oxford, U.K.: International Waterfowl and Wetlands Research Bureau and Facts on File.

Fischer, W. R. 1988. Microbiological reactions of iron in soils. In *Iron in soils and clay minerals*, eds. J. W. Stucki, B. A. Goodman, and U. Schwertmann, NATO Advanced Study Institute Series C: Vol. 217. Boston: D. Reidel Publishing Company.

Fittkau, E. J. 1973. Artenmannigfaltigkeit amazonischer Lebensräume aus ökologischer Sicht. *Amazoniana* 4: 321–40.

———. 1982. Struktur, Funktion und Diversität zentralamazonischer Ökosysteme. *Archiv für Hydrobiologie* 95: 29–45.

FitzPatrick, E. A. 1980. *Soils. Their formation, classification and distribution*. London: Longman.

Fitzpatrick, R. W., E. Fritsch, and P. G. Self. 1996. Interpretation of soil features produced by ancient and modern processes in degraded landscapes. V. Development of saline sulfidic features in non-tidal seepage areas. *Geoderma* 69: 1–29.

Flora, M., and P. C. Rosendahl. 1982. Historical changes in the conductivity and ionic characteristics of the source water for Shark Slough, Everglades National Park, Florida. *Hydrobiologia* 97: 249–54.

Flowers, T. J. 1985. Physiology of halophytes. *Plant and Soil* 89: 41–56.

Flowers, T. J., P. F. Troke, and A. R. Yeo. 1977. The mechanism of salt tolerance in halophytes. *Annual Review of Plant Physiology* 28: 89–121.

Foote, A. L., J. A. Kadlec, and B. K. Campbell. 1988. Insect herbivory on an inland brackish wetland. *Wetlands* 8: 67–74.

Ford, M. A., and J. B. Grace. 1998. Effects of vertebrate herbivores on soil processes, plant biomass, litter accumulation and soil elevational changes in a coastal marsh. *Journal of Ecology* 86: 974–82.

Ford, P. W., P. I. Boon, and K. Lee. 2002. Methane and oxygen dynamics in a shallow floodplain lake: The significance of periodic stratification. *Hydrobiologia* 485: 97–110.

Forkner, R. E., and M. D. Hunter. 2000. What goes up must come down? Nutrient addition and predation pressure on oak insects. *Ecology* 81: 1588–1600.

Foster, W. A. 1984. The distribution of the sea-lavender aphid *Staticobium staticis* on a marine saltmarsh and its effect on host plant fitness. *Oikos* 42: 97–104.

Fowler, B. K., and C. Hershner. 1989. Primary production in CoHoke Swamp, a tidal freshwater wetland in Virginia. In *Freshwater wetlands and wildlife,* eds. R. R. Sharitz and J. W. Gibbons, 365–74. CONF-8603101, DOE Symposium Series No. 61. Oak Ridge, TN: Office of Scientific and Technical Information.

France, R. 1998. Estimating the assimilation of mangrove detritus by fiddler crabs in Laguna Joyuda, Puerto Rico, using dual stable isotopes. *Journal of Tropical Ecology* 14: 413–25.

Francis, B. M. 1994. *Toxic substances in the environment.* New York: John Wiley and Sons.

Francis, C., and F. Sheldon. 2002. River Red Gum (*Eucalyptus camaldulensis* Dehnh.) organic matter as a carbon source in the lower Darling River, Australia. *Hydrobiologia* 481: 113–24.

Francoeur, S. N., and R. L. Lowe. 1998. Effects of ambient ultraviolet radiation on littoral periphyton: Biomass accrual and taxon-specific responses. *Journal of Freshwater Ecology* 13: 29–37.

Francoeur, S. N., and R. G. Wetzel. 2003. Regulation of periphytic leucine-aminopeptidase activity. *Aquatic Microbial Ecology* 31: 249–58.

Frankforter, J. D. 1996. Nebraska wetland resources. In *National water summary on wetland resources,* comps. J. D. Fretwell, J. S. Williams, and P. J. Redman, 261–66. Water-Supply Paper 2425. Reston, VA: U.S. Geological Survey.

Franklin, E., J. Adis, and S. Woas. 1997. The oribatid mites. In *The Central Amazon floodplain. Ecology of a pulsing system,* ed. W. J. Junk, 331–49. *Ecological Studies* 126. Berlin, Germany: Springer.

Frederick, K. D., and P. H. Gleick. 1999. *Water and global climate change: Potential impacts on U.S. water resources.* Arlington, VA: Pew Center on Global Climate Change.

Fredrickson, L. H., and T. S. Taylor. 1982. Management of seasonally flooded impoundments for wildlife. Resources publication No. 148. Washington, D.C.: U.S. Fish Wildlife Service and U.S. Department of the Interior.

Freeman, B. J., and M. C. Freeman. 1985. Production of fishes in a sub-tropical ecosystem— The Okefenokee Swamp. *Limnology and Oceanography* 30: 686–92.

Freer, J., J. J. McDonnell, K. Beven, D. Burns, R. Hooper, B. Aulenbach, C. Kendall, and N. Peters. 2002. The role of bedrock topography on subsurface storm flow. *Water Resources Research* 38: 5-1–5-16.

Freeze, R. A., and J. A. Cherry. 1979. *Groundwater*. Englewood Cliffs, NJ: Prentice Hall.

Freidenburg, L. K., and D. K. Skelly. 2004. Microgeographical variation in thermal preference by an amphibian. *Ecology Letters* 7: 369–73.

Freitag, T., and J. I. Prosser. 2003. Community structure of ammonia-oxidizing bacteria within anoxic marine sediments. *Applied and Environmental Microbiology* 69: 1359–71.

Fretwell, J. D., J. S. Williams, and P. J. Redman. 1996. *National water summary on wetland resources*. U.S. Geological Survey Water-Supply Paper 2425. Washington, D.C.: U.S. Government Printing Office.Froend, R. H., R. C. C. Farrell, C. F. Wilkins, C. C. Wilson, and A. J. McComb. 1993. *Wetlands of the Swan Coastal Plain. Vol. 4. The effect of altered water regimes on wetland plants*. Perth, Australia: Water Authority of Western Australia.

Frost, C. C. 1987. Historical overview of Atlantic white cedar in the Carolinas. In *Atlantic white cedar wetlands*, ed. A. D. Laderman, 257–64. Boulder, CO: Westview Press, Boulder.

Fuhrman, J. A. 1999. Marine viruses and their biogeochemical and ecological effects. *Nature* 399: 541–48.

Furch, K., and W. J. Junk. 1997. Physicochemical conditions in the floodplains. In *The Central Amazon floodplain. Ecology of a pulsing system*, ed. W. J. Junk, 69–108. *Ecological Studies* 126. Berlin, Germany: Springer.

Furness, R. W., and J. J. D. Greenwood, eds. 1993. *Birds as monitors of environmental change*. London: Chapman and Hall.

Gabor, T. S., H. R. Murkin, M. P. Stainton, J. A. Broughen, and R. D. Titman. 1994. Nutrient additions to wetlands in the Interlake region of Manitoba, Canada: Effects of a single pulse addition in spring. *Hydrobiologia* 279/280: 497–510.

Gachter, R., and J. S. Meyer. 1993. The role of microorganisms in mobilization and fixation of phosphorus in sediments. *Hydrobiologia* 253: 103–21.

Gagliano, S. M. 1998. *Faulting, subsidence and land use in coastal Louisiana*. Baton Rouge, LA: Coastal Environments Inc.

Gagliano, S. M., K. J. Meyer-Arendt, and K. M. Wicker. 1981. Land loss in the Mississippi River Deltaic Plain. *Transactions Gulf Coast Association of Geological Societies* 32: 295–300.

Gaiser, E. E., J. H. Richards, J. C. Trexler, R. D. Jones, and D. L. Childers. 2005a. Periphyton responses to eutrophication in the Florida Everglades: Cross-system patterns of structural and compositional change. *Limnology and Oceanography* 50: 342–55.

Gaiser, E. E., J. C. Trexler, J. H. Richards, D. L. Childers, D. Lee, A. L. Edwards, L. J. Scinto, K. Jayachandran, G. B. Noe, and R. D. Jones. 2005b. Cascading ecological effects of low-level phosphorus enrichment in the Florida Everglades. *Journal of Environmental Quality* 34: 717–23.

Galand, P. E., H. Fritze, and K. Yrjala. 2003. Microsite-dependent changes in methanogenic populations in a boreal oligotrophic fen. *Environmental Microbiology* 5: 1133–43.

Galat, D. L., and I. Zweimüller. 2001. Conserving large-river fishes: Is the highway analogy an appropriate paradigm? *Journal of the North American Benthological Society* 20: 266–79.

Galatowitsch, S. M., N. O. Anderson, and P. D. Ascher. 1999. Invasiveness in wetland plants in temperate North America. *Wetlands* 19: 733–55.

Galatowitsch, S. M., and A. G. van der Valk. 1994. *Restoring prairie wetlands: An ecological approach*. Ames, IA: Iowa State University Press.

Galatowitsch, S. M., and A. G. van der Valk. 1996a. Characteristics of recently restored wetlands in the prairie pothole region. *Wetlands* 16: 75–83.

————. 1996b. The vegetation of restored and natural prairie wetlands. *Ecological Applications* 6: 102–12.

Galatowitsch, S. M., D. C. Whited, R. Lehtinen, J. Husveth, and K. Schik. 2000. The vegetation of wet meadows in relation to their land-use. *Environmental Monitoring and Assessment* 60: 121–44.

Gale, M. R., J. W. McLaughlin, M. F. Jurgenson, C. C. Trettin, T. Soelsepp, and P. O. Lyndon. 1998. Plant community responses to harvesting and post-harvest manipulations in a *Picea-Larix-Pinus* wetland with a mineral substrate. *Wetlands* 18: 150–59.

Gallardo, A., and J. Merino. 1993. Leaf decomposition in two Mediterranean ecosystems of southwest Spain: Influence of substrate quality. *Ecology* 74: 152–61.

GAO. 2001. *Wetlands protection: Assessments needed to determine effectiveness of in-lieu-fee mitigation.* GAO-01-325. Washington, D. C.: U. S. Government Accounting Office, 75 pp.

Gates, J. E., and L. W. Gysel. 1978. Avian nest dispersion and fledging success in field-forest ecotones. *Ecology* 59: 871–83.

Gates, P. W. 1968. *History of public land law development.* Washington, D. C.: Public Land Law Review Commission, U. S. Government Printing Office.

Gauer, U. 1997. The Collembola. In *The Central Amazon floodplain. Ecology of a pulsing system,* ed. W. J. Junk, 351–59. *Ecological Studies* 126. Berlin, Germany: Springer.

Gelwick, F. P., S. Akin, D. A. Arrington, and K. O. Winemiller. 2001. Fish assemblage structure in relation to environmental variation in a Texas Gulf coastal wetland. *Estuaries* 24: 285–96.

Gengarelly, L. M., and T. D. Lee. 2005. The role of microtopography and substrate in survival and growth of Atlantic white-cedar seedlings. *Forest Ecology and Management* 212: 135–44.

George, B., and D. P. Batzer. In review. Spatial and temporal variation of mercury levels in Okefenokee Swamp invertebrates (Southeast Georgia). *Environmental Toxicology and Chemistry.*

Gereta, E., and E. Wolanski. 1998. Wildlife-water quality interactions in the Serengeti National Park, Tanzania. *African Journal of Ecology* 36: 1–14.

Gersib, R. A. 1991. *Nebraska wetlands priority plan for inclusion in the 1991–1995 Nebraska State Comprehensive Outdoor Recreation Plan.* Lincoln, NE: Nebraska Game and Parks Commission.

GESAMP. 1996. *The contribution of science to integrated coastal management.* Reports and Studies No. 61. Rome, Italy: FAO, Food and Agriculture Organization of the United Nations.

Gessner, M. O. 1991. Differences in processing dynamics of fresh and dried leaf litter in a stream ecosystem. *Freshwater Biology* 26: 387–98.

Gessner, M. O., R. Chauvet, and M. Dobson. 1999. A perspective on leaf litter breakdown in streams. *Oikos* 85: 377–84.

Gessner, M. O., and J. Schwoerbel. 1989. Leaching kinetics of fresh leaf-litter with implications for the current concept of leaf-processing in streams. *Archiv für Hydrobiologie* 115: 81–90.

Gibbons, F., and J. Rowan. 1993. Soils in relation to vegetation in Victoria. In *Flora of Victoria. Volume 1. Introduction,* eds. D. B. Foreman and N. G. Walsh, 159–92. Melbourne, Australia: Inkata Press.

Gibbons, J. W. 2003. Terrestrial habitat: A vital component for herpetofauna of isolated wetlands. *Wetlands* 23: 630–35.

Gibbons, J. W., and R. D. Semlitsch. 1991. *Guide to amphibians and reptiles of the Savannah River Site*. Athens, GA: The University of Georgia Press.

Gibbs, J. P. 1993. Importance of small wetlands for the persistence of local populations of wetland-associated animals. *Wetlands* 13: 25–31.

Gilbert, B., and P. Frenzel. 1998. Rice roots and CH_4 oxidation: The activity of bacteria, their distribution and the microenvironment. *Soil Biology and Biochemistry* 30: 1903–16.

Giller, P. S., and N. Sangpradub. 1993. Predatory foraging behavior and activity patterns of larvae of two species of limnephilid cased caddis. *Oikos* 67: 351–57.

Gilman, K. 1994. *Hydrology and wetland conservation*. Chichester, U.K.: John Wiley and Sons.

GISD (Global Invasive Species Database). 2004. www.issg.org/database/species/search.asp?st= 100ss&fr=1&sts=).

Glaser, P. F., D. I. Siegel, E. A. Romanowicz, and Y. P. Shen. 1997. Regional linkages between raised bogs and the climate, groundwater, and landscape of north-western Minnesota. *Journal of Ecology* 85: 3–16.

Glaser, P. H., G. A. Wheeler, E. Gorham, and H. E. Wright. 1981. The patterned mires of the Red Lake peatland, northern Minnesota: Vegetation, water chemistry, and landforms. *Journal of Ecology* 69: 575–99.

Glazebrook, H. S., and A. I. Robertson. 1999. The effect of flooding and flood timing on leaf litter breakdown rates and nutrient dynamics in a river red gum *(Eucalyptus camaldulensis)* forest. *Australian Journal of Ecology* 24: 625–35.

Gleason, H. A. 1917. The structure and development of the plant association. *Bulletin of the Torrey Botanical Club* 44:463–481.

Gleason, P. J., and P. Stone. 1994. Age, origin, and landscape evolution of the Everglades peatland. In *Everglades: The ecosystem and its restoration,* eds. S. M. Davis and J. C. Ogden, 149–97. Boca Raton, FL: St. Lucie Press.

Glime, J. M., R. G. Wetzel, and B. J. Kennedy. 1982. The effects of bryophytes on succession from alkaline marsh to Sphagnum bog. *American Midland Naturalist* 108: 209–23.

Glinka, K. D. 1927. Dokuchaiev's ideas in the development of pedology and cognate sciences. In *Russian pedology. Invest. I. Acad. Sci. Leningrad, Russia,* 32 pp.

Glooschenko, W. A., C. Tarnocai, S. Zoltai, and V. Glooschenko. 1993. Wetlands of Canada and Greenland. In *Wetlands of the world I: Inventory, ecology and management,* eds. D. F. Whigham, D. Dykyjova, and S. Hejny, 415–514. Dordrecht, The Netherlands: Kluwer Adacemic Publishers.

Goldman, J. C., D. A. Caron, and M. R. Dennett. 1987. Regulation of gross growth efficiency and ammonium regeneration in bacteria by substrate C:N ratio. *Limnology and Oceanography* 32: 1239–52.

Gollier, C., B. Jullien, and N. Treich. 2000. Scientific progress and irreversibility: An economic interpretation of the "precautionary principle." *Journal of Public Economics* 75: 229–53.

Golterman, H. L. 1988. The calcium- and iron-bound phosphate phase diagram. *Hydrobiologia* 159: 149–51.

———. 1995. Theoretical aspects of the adsorption of ortho-phosphate onto iron-hydroxide. *Hydrobiologia* 315: 59–68.

Good, R. E., N. F. Good, and B. R. Frasco. 1982. A review of primary production and decomposition dynamics of the belowground marsh component. In *Estuarine comparisons,* ed. S. Kennedy, 139–57. New York: Academic Press.

Goodwin, T. M., and W. R. Marion. 1977. Occurrence of Florida red-bellied turtle eggs in north-central Florida alligator nests. *Florida Scientist* 40: 237–38.

Gopal, B. 1997. Biodiversity in inland aquatic ecosystems of India: An overview. *International Journal of Ecology and Environmental Sciences* 23: 305–13.

Gopal, B., and M. Chauhan. In press. Biodiversity and its conservation in Sunderban—a large mangrove ecosystem. *Aquatic Sciences.*

Gopal, B., and W. J. Junk. 2000. Biodiversity in wetlands: An introduction. In Biodiversity in wetlands: Assessment, function and conservation, eds. B. Gopal, W. J. Junk, and J. A. Davis, 1: 1–10. Leiden, The Netherlands: Backhuys Publishers.

Gopal, B., W. J. Junk, and J. A. Davis, eds. 2000. *Biodiversity in wetlands: Assessment, function and conservation.* Leiden, The Netherlands: Backhuys Publishers.

Gophen, M. 2000. Nutrient and plant dynamics in Lake Agmon wetlands (Hula Valley, Israel): A review with emphasis on *Typha domingensis* (1994–1999). *Hydrobiologia* 441: 25–36.

Goranson, C. E., C. K. Ho, and S. C. Pennings. 2004. Environmental gradients and herbivore feeding preferences in coastal salt marshes. *Oecologia* 140: 591–600.

Gorham, E. 1990. Biotic impoverishment in northern peatlands. In *The earth in transition: Patterns and processes of biotic impoverishment,* ed. G. M. Woodwell, 65–98. New York: Cambridge University Press.

———. 1991. Northern peatlands: Role in the carbon cycle and probable responses to climatic warming. *Ecological Applications* 1: 182–95.

Gorham, E., and L. Rochefort. 2003. Peatland restoration: A brief assessment with special reference to Sphagnum bogs. *Wetlands Ecology and Management* 11: 109–19.

Gorham, L. E., S. L. King, B. D. Keeland, and S. Mopper. 2002. Effects of canopy gaps and flooding on homopterans in a bottomland hardwood forest. *Wetlands* 22: 541–49.

Gornitz, V., S. Lebedeff, and J. Hansen. 1982. Global sea-level trend in the past century. *Science* 215: 611–14.

Gosselink, J. G. 1984. *The ecology of delta marshes of coastal Louisiana: A community profile.* FWS/OBS-84/09. Washington, D.C.: Office of Biological Services, U.S. Fish and Wildlife Service.

Gosselink, J. G., and R. E. Turner. 1978. The role of hydrology in freshwater wetland ecosystems. In *Freshwater wetlands. Ecological processes and management potential,* eds. R. E. Good, D. F. Whigham, and R. L. Simpson, 63–78. New York: Academic Press.

Gottschalk, G. 1986. Bacterial metabolism, 2d ed. New York: Springer-Verlag.

Gough, L. G., J. B. Grace, and K. L. Taylor. 1994. The relationship between species richness and community biomass: The importance of environmental variables. *Oikos* 70: 271–79.

Goulden, M. L., S. C. Wofsy, J. W. Harden, S. E. Trumbore, P. M. Crill, S. T. Gower, T. Fries, et al. 1998. Sensitivity of boreal forest carbon balance to soil thaw. *Science* 279: 214–17.

Goulding, M., M. L. Carvalho, and E. G. Ferreira. 1988. Rio Negro: Rich life in poor water. The Hague, The Netherlands: SPB Academic Publishing.

Goyer, R. A., G. J. Lenhard, and J. D. Smith. 1990. Insect herbivores of a bald-cypress/tupelo ecosystem. *Forest Ecology and Management* 33/34: 517–21.

Graca M. A. S., C. Cressa, M. O. Gessner, M. J. Feio, K. A. Callies, and C. Barrios. 2001. Food quality, feeding preferences, survival and growth of shredders from temperate and tropical streams. *Freshwater Biology* 46: 947–57.

Graca, M. A., S. Y. Newell, and R. T. Kneib. 2000. Grazing rates of organic matter and living fungal biomass of decaying *Spartina alterniflora* by three species of salt-marsh invertebrates. *Marine Biology* 136: 281–89.

Grace, J. B. 1987. The impact of preemption on the zonation of two *Typha* species along lakeshores. *Ecological Monographs* 57: 283–303.

———. 1993. The adaptive significance of clonal reproduction in angiosperms: An aquatic perspective. *Aquatic Botany* 44: 159–80

———. 2001. The roles of community biomass and species pools in the regulation of plant diversity. *Oikos* 92: 193–207.

Grace, J. B., and B. H. Pugesek. 1997. A structural equation model of plant species richness and its application to a coastal wetland. *The American Naturalist* 149: 436–60.

Grace, J. B., and R. G. Wetzel. 1978. The production biology of Eurasian Watermilfoil (*Myriophyllum spicatum* L.): A review. *Journal of Aquatic Plant Management* 16: 1–11.

———. 1981. Habitat partitioning and competitive displacement in cattails *(Typha):* Experimental field studies. *The American Naturalist* 118: 463–74.

———. 1982. Niche differentiation between two rhizomatous plant species: *Typha latifolia* and *Typha angustifolia*. *Canadian Journal of Botany* 60: 46–57.

Graf, W. L. 1988. Definition of flood plains along arid-region rivers. In *Flood geomorphology,* eds. V. R. Baker, R. C. Kochel, and P. C. Patton, 231–56. New York: John Wiley & Sons.

Graneli, W., and D. Solander. 1988. Influence of aquatic macrophytes on phosphorus cycling in lakes. *Hydrobiologia* 170: 245–66.

Grant, S. B., B. F. Sanders, A. B. Boehm, J. A. Redman, J. H. Kim, R. D. Morse, A. K. Chu, et al. 2001. Generation of enterococci bacteria in a coastal saltwater marsh and its impact on surf zone water quality. *Environmental Science and Technology* 35: 2, 407-2, 416.

Gray, M. J., L. M. Smith, and R. I. Leyva. 2004. Influence of agricultural landscape structure on a southern High Plains, USA, amphibian assemblage. *Landscape Ecology* 19: 719–29.

Green, A. J., J. Figuerola, and M. I. Sánchez. 2002. Implications of waterbird ecology for the dispersal of aquatic organisms. *Acta Oecologica* 23: 177–89.

Green, E. K., and S. M. Galatowitsch. 2001. Differences in wetland plant community establishment with additions of nitrate-N and invasive species (*Phalaris arundinacea* and *Typha xglauca*). *Canadian Journal of Botany–Revue Canadienne De Botanique* 79: 170–78.

Greenway, H., and R. Munns. 1980. Mechanisms of salt tolerance in non-halophytes. *Annual Review of Plant Physiology* 31: 149–90.

Greenway, S. C., and K. B. Storey. 2001. Effects of seasonal change and prolonged anoxia on metabolic enzymes of *Littorina littorea*. *Canadian Journal of Zoology* 79: 907–15.

Greenwood, R. J., A. B. Sargeant, D. H. Johnson, L. M. Cowardin, and T. L. Shaffer. 1995. Factors associated with duck nesting success in the prairie pothole region of Canada. *Wildlife Monographs* 128: 1–57.

Gribsholt, B., J. E. Kostka, and E. Kristensen. 2003. Impact of fiddler crabs and plant roots on sediment biogeochemistry in a Georgia saltmarsh. *Marine Ecology—Progress Series* 259: 237–51.

Grierson, P. F., N. B. Comerford, and E. J. Jokela. 1998. Phosphorus mineralization kinetics and response of microbial phosphorus to drying and rewetting in a Florida spodosol. *Soil Biology and Biochemistry* 30: 1323–31.

Grigal, D. F. 1985. *Sphagnum* production in forested bogs of northern Minnesota. *Canadian Journal of Botany* 63: 1024–27.

Grime, J. P. 1977. Evidence for the existence of three primary strategies in plants and its relevance to ecological and evolutionary theory. *The American Naturalist* 111: 1169–94.

———. 1979. *Plant strategies and vegetation processes.* Chichester, U.K.: John Wiley & Sons.

Grimes, B. G., M. T. Huish, J. H. Kerby, and D. Morgan. 1989. *Species profile: Life histories and environmental requirements of coastal fishes and invertebrates (mid-Atlantic)— Atlantic Marsh Fiddler.* United States and Wildlife Service Biological Report 82 (11.114). United States Army Corps of Engineers, TR EL-82-4.

Grimm, N. B. 1993. Implications of climate change for stream communities. In *Biotic interactions and global change,* eds. P. M. Kareiva, J. G. Kingsolver, and R. B. Huey, 293–314. Sunderland, MA: Sinauer Associates.

Groombridge, B., and M. Jenkins, eds. 1998. *Freshwater biodiversity. A preliminary global assessment.* WCMC Biodiversity Series 8. World Conservation Monitoring Centre. Cambridge, U.K.: World Conservation Press.

Grootjans, A. P., L. F. M. Fresco, C. C. de Leeuw, and P. C. Schipper. 1996. Degeneration of species-rich *Calthion palustris* hay meadows: Some considerations on the community concept. *Journal of Vegetation Science* 7: 185–94.

Gross, E. M. 1999. Allelopathy in benthic and littoral areas: Case studies on allelochemicals from benthic cyanobacteria and submersed macrophytes. In *Principles and practices in plant ecology: Allelochemical interactions,* eds. K. M. M. Inderjit, C. L. Dakshini, and C. L. Foy, 179–99. Boca Raton, FL: CRC Press.

Grubb, P. J. 1977. The maintenance of species-richness in plant communities: The importance of the regeneration niche. *Biological Reviews* 52: 107–45.

Grunfeld, S., and H. Brix. 1999. Methanogenesis and methane emissions: Effects of water table, substrate type and presence of *Phragmites australis. Aquatic Botany* 64: 63–75.

Gunderson, L. H. 1994. Vegetation of the Everglades: Determinants of community composition. In *Everglades: The ecosystem and its restoration,* eds. S. M. Davis and J. C. Ogden, 323–40. Boca Raton, FL: St. Lucie Press.

Gunderson, L. H., and W. F. Loftus. 1993. The Everglades. In *Biodiversity of the southeastern United States,* eds. W. H. Martin, S. G. Boyce, and A. C. Echternacht, 199–255. New York: John Wiley and Sons.

Guntenspergen, G. R., and B. A. Vairin, eds. 1998. *Vulnerability of coastal wetlands in the southeastern United States: Climate change research results, 1992–97.* U.S. Geological Survey, Biological Resources Division. Biological Science Report USGS/BRD/BSR—1998-0002, 105 pp.

Guthery, F. S., and F. C. Bryant. 1982. Status of playas in the southern Great Plains. *Wildlife Society Bulletin* 10: 309–17.

Guzy, G. S., and R. M. Andersen. 2001. *Memorandum: Supreme Court ruling concerning CWA jurisdiction over isolated waters.* Washington, D.C.: U.S. Environmental Protection Agency and U.S. Army Corps of Engineers.

Hacker, S. D., and M. D. Bertness. 1995. Morphological and physiological consequences of a positive plant interaction. *Ecology* 76: 2165–75.

———. 1999. Experimental evidence for factors maintaining plant species diversity in a New England salt marsh. *Ecology* 80: 2064–73.

Hacker, S. D., and S. D. Gaines. 1997. Some implications of direct positive interactions for community species diversity. *Ecology* 78: 1990–2003.

Haffer, J., and G. T. Prance. 2001. Climatic forcing of evolution in Amazonia during the Cenozoic: On the refuge theory of biotic differentiation. *Amazoniana* 16: 579–607.

Hails, A. J. 1996. *Wetlands, biodiversity and the Ramsar Convention. The role of the Convention on wetlands in the conservation and wise use of biodiversity.* Gland, Switzerland: Ramsar Convention Bureau; and New Delhi, India: Ministry of Environment and Forests, Govt. of India.

Hall, D. L., M. R. Willig, D. L. Moorhead, R. W. Sites, E. B. Fish, and T. R. Mollhagen. 2004. Aquatic macroinvertebrate diversity of playa wetlands: The role of landscape and island biogeographic characteristics. *Wetlands* 24: 77–91.

Halpin, P. N. 1997. Global climate change and natural-area protection: Management responses and research directions. *Ecological Applications* 7: 828–43.

Haltiner, J., J. B. Zedler, K. E. Boyer, G. D. Williams, and J. C. Callaway. 1997. Influence of physical processes on the design, functioning and evolution of restored tidal wetlands in California. *Wetlands Ecology and Management* 4: 73–91.

Hambright, K. D., and T. Zohary. 1999. The Hula Valley (Northern Israel wetlands rehabilitation project. In *An international perspective on wetland rehabilitation,* ed. W. Streever, 173–80. Boston: Kluwer Academic Publishers.

Hamer, A. J., S. J. Lane, and M. J. Maloney. 2002. Management of freshwater wetlands for the endangered green and golden bell frog *(Litoria aurea):* Roles of habitat determinants and space. *Biological Conservation* 106: 413–24.

Hamilton, S. K., W. M. Lewis, and S. J. Sippel. 1992. Energy-sources for aquatic animals in the Orinoco River floodplain—Evidence from stable isotopes. *Oecologia* 89: 324–30.

Hamilton, S. K., S. J. Sippel, D. F. Calheiros, and J. M. Melack. 1997. An anoxic event and other biogeochemical effects of the Pantanal wetland on the Paraguay River. *Limnology and Oceanography* 42: 257–72.

Hamilton, S. K., O. C. Souza, and M. E.Coutinho. 1998. Dynamics of floodplain inundation in the alluvial fan of the Taquari River (Pantanal, Brazil). *Verh. Internat. Verein. Limnol.* 26: 916–22.

Hammerson, G. A. 1994. Beaver *(Castor canadensis):* Ecosytem alterations, management, and monitoring. *Natural Areas Journal* 14: 44–57.

Handa, I. T., and R. L. Jefferies. 2000. Assisted revegetation trials in degraded salt-marshes. *Journal of Applied Ecology* 37: 944–58.

Hann, B. J. 1991. Invertebrate grazer-periphyton interaction in a eutrophic marsh pond. *Freshwater Biology* 26: 87–96.

Hansen, A. J., and F. di Castri. 1992. *Landscape boundaries: Consequences for biotic diversity and ecological flows. Ecological Studies* 92. Berlin, Germany: Springer.

Hanson, M. A., and M. G. Butler. 1994a. Responses to food-web manipulation in a shallow waterfowl lake. *Hydrobiologia* 280: 457–66.

————. 1994b. Responses of plankton, turbity, and macrophytes to biomanipulation in a shallow prairie lake. *Canadian Journal of Fisheries and Aquatic Sciences* 51: 1180–88.

Happell, J. D., and J. P. Chanton. 1993. Carbon remineralization in a north Florida swamp forest: Effects of water level on the pathways and rates of soil organic matter decomposition. *Global Biogeochemical Cycles* 7: 475–90.

Hardwick-Witman, M. N. 1985. Biological consequences of ice rafting in a New England salt marsh community. *Journal of Experimental Marine Biology and Ecology* 87: 283–98.

Harlin, M. M. 1973. Transfer of products between epiphytic marine algae and host plants. *Journal of Phycology* 9: 243–48.

Harold, F. M. 1986. *The vital force: A study of bioenergetics.* New York: W. H. Freeman and Company.

Harr, R. D. 1982. Fog drip in the Bull Run municipal Watershed, Oregon. *Water Resources Bulletin* 18: 785–89.

Hart, E. A., and J. R. Lovvorn. 2003. Algal vs. macrophyte inputs to food webs of inland saline wetlands. *Ecology* 84: 3317–26.

Hartman, J. M., H. Caswell, and I. Valiela. 1983. *Effects of wrack accumulation on salt marsh vegetation.* Proceedings of the 17th European Marine Biology Symposium. *Oceanologica Acta,* Brest, France, pp. 99–102.

Harvey, D. M. R., T. J. Flowers, and J. L. Hall. 1976. Localization of chloride in leaf cells of the halophyte *Suaeda maritiamu* by silver precipitation. *New Phytologist* 77: 319–23.

Haslam, S. M. 1970. The development of the annual population in *Phragmites communis* Trin. *Annuals of Botany* 34: 571–91.

Hatton, T. J., and R. A. Nulsen. 1999. Towards achieving functional ecosystem mimicry with respect to water cycling in southern Australian agriculture. *Agroforestry Systems* 45: 203–14.

Haukos, D. A., and L. M. Smith. 1994. The importance of playa wetlands to biodiversity of the southern High Plains. *Landscape and Urban Planning* 28: 83–98.

————. 1997. *Common flora of the playa lakes.* Lubbock, TX: Texas Tech University Press.

————. 2003. Past and future impacts of wetland regulations on playa ecology in the southern Great Plains. *Wetlands* 23: 577–89.

Havel, J. E., E. M. Eisenbacher, and A. A. Black. 2000. Diversity of crustacean zooplankton in riparian wetlands: Colonization and egg banks. *Aquatic Ecology* 34: 63–76.

Hayden, B. P., R. D. Dueser, J. T. Callahan, and H. H. Shugart. 1991. Long-term research at the Virginia Coast Reserve. *BioScience* 41: 310–18.

Hedlin, L. O., J. C. von Fischer, N. E. Ostrom, B. P. Kennedy, M. G. Brown, and G. P. Robertson. 1998. Thermodynamic constraints on nitrogen transformations and other biogeochemical processes at soil-stream interfaces. *Ecology* 79: 684–703.

Heimburg, K. 1984. Hydrology of north-central Florida cypress domes. In *Cypress swamps,* eds. K. C. Ewel and H. T. Odum, 72–82. Gainesville, FL: University Presses of Florida.

Heinselman, M. L. 1963. Forest sites, bog processes, and peatland types in the glacial Lake Agassiz region, Minnesota. *Ecological Monographs* 33: 327–74.

————. 1970. Landscape evolution and peatland types, and the Lake Agassiz Peatlands Natural Area, Minnesota. *Ecological Monographs* 40: 235–61.

————. 1975. Boreal peatlands in relation to environment. In *Coupling of land and water systems,* ed. D. Hasler, 83–103. New York: Springer-Verlag.

Helbling, E. W., and H. Zagarese, eds. 2003. *UV effects in aquatic organisms and ecosystems.* Comprehensive Series in Photochemical and Photobiological Sciences. Cambridge: European Society of Photobiology, 575 pp.

Henckel, T., U. Jackel, and R. Conrad. 2001. Vertical distribution of the methanotrophic community after drainage of rice field soil. *FEMS Microbiology Ecology* 34: 279–91.

Henderson, P. A., W. D. Hamilton, and W. G. R. Crampton. 1998. Evolution and diversity in Amazonian floodplain communities. In *Dynamics of tropical communities,* eds. D. M. Newbery, H. H. T. Prins, and N. D. Brown, 385–419. The 37th Symposium of the British Ecological Society, London 1998. Oxford, U.K.: Blackwell Science.

Herbst, G., and S. R. Reice. 1982. Comparative leaf litter decomposition in temporary and permanent streams in semi-arid regions of Israel. *Journal of Arid Environments* 5: 305–18.

Herdendorf, C. E. 1987. *The ecology of the coastal marshes of western Lake Erie: A community profile.* Washington, D.C.: U.S.D.I. Fish and Wildlife Service.

Herman, P. M. J., J. J. Middelberg, J. Widdows, C. H. Lucas, and C. H. R. Heip. 2000. Stable isotopes as trophic tracers: Combing field sampling and manipulative labeling of food resources for macrobenthos. *Marine Ecology—Progress Series* 204: 79–92.

Herwig, B. R., D. A. Soluk, J. M. Dettmers, and D. H. Wahl. 2004. Trophic structure and energy flow in backwater lakes of two large floodplain rivers using stable isotopes. *Canadian Journal of Fisheries and Aquatic Sciences* 61: 12–22.

Hewlett, J. D. 1982. *Principles of forest hydrology.* Athens, GA: University of Georgia Press.

Hewlett, J. D., and A. R. Hibbert. 1963. Moisture and energy conditions within a sloping soil mass during drainage. *Journal of Geophysical Research* 68: 1081–87.

———. 1967. Factors affecting the response of small watersheds to precipitation in humid areas. In *Forest hydrology,* eds. W. E. Sopper and H. W. Lull, 275–90. New York: Pergamon Press.

Hewson, I., and J. A. Fuhrman. 2004. Richness and diversity of bacterioplankton species along an estuarine gradient in Moreton Bay, Australia. *Applied and Environmental Microbiology* 70: 3, 425-3, 433.

Hey, D. L, D. McGuiness, M. N. Beorkrem, D. R. Conrad, and B. D. Hulsey. 2002. *Flood damage reduction in the Upper Mississippi River Basin: An ecological means.* Minneapolis, MN: The McKnight Foundation.

Hey, D. L., and N. S. Philippi. 1995. Flood reduction through wetland restoration: The Upper Mississippi River Basin as a case history. *Restoration Ecology* 3: 4–17.

———. 1999. *A case for wetland restoration.* New York: Wiley Interscience.

Hieber, M., and M. O. Gessner. 2002. Contribution of stream detritivores, fungi, and bacteria to leaf breakdown based on biomass estimates. *Ecology* 83: 1026–38.

Hierro, J. L., and R. M. Callaway. 2004. Allelopathy and exotic plant invasion. *Plant and Soil* 256: 29–39.

Hik, D. S., R. L. Jefferies, and A. R. E. Sinclair. 1992. Foraging by geese, isostatic uplift and asymmetry in the development of salt-marsh plant communities. *Journal of Ecology* 80: 395–406.

Hill, R. J., G. T. Prance, S. A. Mori, W. C. Steward, D. Shimabukuru, and J. Bernardi. 1978. Estudo eletroforético da dinâmica de variação genética em três taxa ribeirinhos ao longo do rio Solimões, América do Sul. *Acta Amazonica* 8: 183–99.

Hill, W. 1996. Effects of light. In *Algal ecology: Benthic algae in freshwater ecosystems,* eds. R. J. Stevenson, M. Bothwell, and R. L. Lowe, 121–48. New York: Academic Press.

Hobbs, R. J. 2004. Forum on restoration ecology: The challenge of social values and expectations. *Frontiers in Ecology and Environment* 2: 43–48.

Hobbs, R. J., and D. A. Norton. 1996. Towards a conceptual framework for restoration ecology. *Restoration Ecology* 4: 93–110.

Hobson, K. A. 1999. Tracing origins and migration of wildlife using stable isotopes: A review. *Oecologia* 120: 314–26.

Hodges, J. D. 1997. Development and ecology of bottomland hardwood sites. *Forest Ecology and Management* 90: 117–26.

Hodges, J. D. 1998. Minor alluvial floodplains. In *Southern forested wetlands ecology and management,* eds. M.G. Messina and W. H. Conner, 325–342. Boca Raton, FL: Lewis Publishers, CRC Press.

Höfer, H. 1997. The spider communities. In *The Central Amazon floodplain. Ecology of a pulsing system,* ed. W. J. Junk, 372–384. *Ecological Studies* 126. Berlin, Germany: Springer.

Holland, M. M. 1996. Wetlands and environmental gradients. In *Wetlands. Environmental gradients, boundaries, and buffers,* eds. G. Mulamoottil, B. G. Warner, and E. A. McBean, 19–43. Boca Raton, FL: Lewis Publishers.

Hollands, G. G., and D. W. Magee. 1985. A method for assessing the functions of wetlands. In *Proceedings of the National Wetland Assessment Symposium,* eds. J. Kusler and P. Riexinger, 108–18. Berne, NY: Association of Wetland Managers.

Hong, P. N., and H. T. San. 1993. *The mangroves of Vietnam.* Bangkok, Thailand: International Union for the Conservation of Nature.

Hoover, J. P. 2003. Decision rules for site fidelity in a migratory bird, the prothonotary warbler. *Ecology* 84: 416–30.

Hope, A. D. 1973. *Selected poems.* Sydney, Australia: Angus & Robertson.

Hopkinson, C. S., J. G. Gosselink, and R. T. Parrondo. 1980. Production of coastal Louisiana marsh plants calculated from phenometric techniques. *Ecology* 61: 1091–98.

Hornberger, G.M., J.P. Raffensperger, P.L. Wiberg, and K.N. Eshleman. 1998. *Elements of physical hydrology,* Johns Hopkins University Press, Figure 7.6, p. 153.

Horner, R. R., A. L. Azous, K. O. Richter, S. S. Cooke, L. E. Reinelt, and K. Ewing. 2001. Wetlands and stormwater management guidelines. In *Wetlands and urbanization: Implications for the future,* eds. A. L. Azous and R. R. Horner, 299–323. Boca Raton, FL: Lewis Publishers.

Horton, R. E. 1933. The role of infiltration in the hydrologic cycle. *Transactions of the American Geophysical Union* 14: 446–60.

Houlahan, J. E., and C. S. Findley. 2003. The effects of adjacent land use on wetland amphibian species richness and community composition. *Canadian Journal of Fisheries and Aquatic Sciences* 60: 1078–94.

Houlahan, J. E., C. S. Findley, B. R. Schmidt, A. H. Meyer, and S. L. Kuzmin. 2000. Quantitative evidence for global amphibian population declines. *Nature* 404: 752–55.

Howard, R. J. 1995. Increased salinity and water depth as constraints on growth of freshwater marsh plants. Ph.D. diss., Louisiana State University, Baton Rouge.

Howes, B. L., J. W. H. Dacey, and D. D. Goehringer. 1986. Factors controlling the growth form of *Spartina alterniflora:* Feedbacks between above-ground production, sediment oxidation, nitrogen and salinity. *Journal of Ecology* 74: 881–98.

Howes, B. L., R. W. Howarth, J. M. Teal, and I. Valiela. 1981. Oxidation-reduction potentials in a salt marsh: Spatial patterns and interactions with primary production. *Limnology and Oceanography* 26: 350–60.

Hruby, T., W. E. Cesanek, and K. E. Miller. 1995. Estimating relative wetland values for regional planning. *Wetlands* 15: 93–107.

Humphries, P., A. J. King, and J. D. Koehn. 1999. Fish, flows and flood plains: Links between freshwater fishes and their environment in the Murray-Darling River system, Australia. *Environmental Biology of Fishes* 56: 129–51.

Hunt, R. 1996. *Do created wetlands replace the wetlands that are destroyed?* USGS Fact Sheet FS-246–96.

Hunt, R. J., D. P. Krabbenhoft, and M. P. Anderson. 1997. Assessing hydrogeochemical heterogeneity in natural and constructed wetlands. *Biogeochemistry* 39: 271–93.

Hunt, R. J., J. F. Walker, and D. P. Krabbenhoft. 1999. Characterizing hydrology and the importance of ground-water discharge in natural and constructed wetlands. *Wetlands* 19: 458–72.

Hupp, C. R. 2000. Hydrology, geomorphology and vegetation of Coastal Plain rivers in the south-eastern USA. *Hydrological Processes* 14(16–17): 2991–3010.

Hurst, C. J., ed. 1997. *Manual of environmental microbiology.* Washington, D.C.: ASM Press.

Hurst, G. A., and T. R. Bourland. 1996. Breeding birds on a bottomland hardwood regeneration area on Delta National Forest. *Journal of Field Ornithology* 67: 181–87.

Hussain, U., and G. Acharya. 1994. *Mangroves of the Sundarbans, Volume 2: Bangladesh.* Gland, Switzerland: World Conservation Union.

Hutchens, J. J., D. P. Batzer, and E. Reese. 2004. Bioassessment of silvicultural impacts in streams and wetlands of the eastern United States. *Water, Air, and Soil Pollution: Focus* 4: 37–53.

Hutchinson, G. E. 1950. Biochemistry of vertebrate excretion. *Bulletin of the American Museum of Natural History* 96: 1–554.

———. 1959. Homage to Santa Rosalia or why are there so many kinds of animals? *American Naturalist* 93: 145–59.

Hyde, K. D. 1990. A comparison of the intertidal mycota of five mangrove tree species. *Asian Marine Biology* 7: 93–108.

Hyde, K. D., E. B. G. Jones, E. Leano, S. B. Pointing, A. D. Poonyth, and L. L. Vrijmoed. 1998. Role of fungi in marine ecosystems. *Biodiversity and Conservation* 7: 1147–61.

Iacobelli, A., and R. L. Jefferies. 1991. Inverse salinity gradients in coastal marshes and the death of stands of *Salix:* The effects of grubbing by geese. *Journal of Ecology* 79: 61–73.

Ingold, A., and D. C. Havill. 1984. The influence of sulphide on the distribution of higher plants in salt marshes. *Journal of Ecology* 72: 1043–1054.

IPCC (Intergovernmental Panel on Climate Change). 1995. *Climate change 1995: The science of climate change.* Eds. J. T. Houghton, L. G. Meira Filho, B. A. Callender, N. Harris, A. Kattenberg, and K. Maskell. New York: Cambridge University Press.

————. 2001. *Climate change 2001: The scientific basis*. Eds. J. T. Houghton, Y. Ding, D. J. Griggs, M. Noguer, P. J. van der Linden, X. Dai, K. Maskell, and C. A. Johnson. New York: Cambridge University Press.

Irion, G., W. J. Junk, and J. A. S. N. de Mello. 1997. The large central Amazonian river floodplains near Manaus: Geological, climatological, hydrological, and geomorphological aspects. In *The Central Amazon floodplain. Ecology of a pulsing system*, ed. W. J. Junk, 23–46. *Ecological Studies* 126. Berlin, Germany: Springer.

Irion, G., J. Müller, G. Keim, J. Nunes de Mello, and W. J. Junk. 1999. The late quaternary river and lake development in Central Amazonia. Extended abstract in the Abstract-Volume (CD-ROM) of the International Symposium on Hydrological and Geochemical Processes in Large-Scale River Basins, 1999, Manaus, Brazil.

Iriondo, M. H., and N. O. Garcia. 1993. Climatic variations in the Argentine plains during the last 18,000 years. *Palaeogeography, Palaeoclimatology, Palaeoecology* 101: 209–20.

ITAP (International Technical Advisory Panel). 2003. Building a scientific basis for restoration of the Mesopotamian Marshlands. Findings of the Restoration Planning Workshop of February 2003, convened by Eden Again Project, The Iraq Foundation, Washington, D.C.

Jackson, C. R. 1992. Hillslope infiltration and lateral downslope unsaturated flow. *Water Resources Research* 28: 2533–39.

Jackson, J. M. 1990. The status of nontidal, freshwater wetlands creation, restoration, and enhancement in the United States; mitigation effectiveness: Recap of the existing literature. Prepared for USEPA. Reno, NV: Desert Research Institute.

Jackson, M. B., and W. Armstrong. 1999. Formation of aerenchyma and the process of plant ventilation in relation to soil flooding and submergence. *Plant Biology* 1: 274–87.

Jackson, M. B., B. Herman, and A. Goodenough, 1982. An examination of the importance of ethanol in causing injury to flooded plants. *Plant, Cell and Environment* 5: 163–72.

Jacobsen, D., and N. Friberg. 1995. Food preference of the trichopteran larva *Anabolia nervosa* from two streams with different food availability. *Hydrobiologia* 308: 139–44.

Jacoby, J. M., D. D. Lynch, E. B. Welch, and M. A. Perkins. 1982. Internal loading of a shallow eutrophic lake. *Water Research* 16: 911–19.

Jannasch, H. W., and G. E. Jones. 1959. Bacterial populations in sea water as determined by different methods of enumeration. *Limnology and Oceanography* 4: 128–39.

Jefferies, R. L. 1988. Vegetational mosaics, plant-animal interactions and resources for plant growth. In *Plant evolutionary biology*, eds. L. D. Gottlieb and S. K. Jain, 431–369. London: Chapman and Hall.

Jefferies, R. L., T. Rudmik, and E. M. Dillon. 1979. Responses of halophytes to high salinities and low water potentials. *Plant Physiology* 64: 989–94.

Jeffries, M. 1994. Invertebrate communities and turnover in wetland ponds affected by drought. *Freshwater Biology* 32: 603–12.

Jehl, J. R., Jr. 1994. Changes in saline and alkaline lake avifauna in western North America in the past 159 years. In *A century of avifaunal change in western North America*, eds J. R. Jehl, Jr. and N. K. Johnson. *Studies in Avian Biology* 15:258-272.

Jenkins, D. G., and M. O. Underwood 1998. Zooplankton may not disperse readily in wind, rain, and waterfowl. *Hydrobiologia* 387/388: 15–21.

Jiang, S. C. 2001. *Vibrio cholera* in recreational beach waters and tributaries of southern California. *Hydrobiologia* 460: 157–64.

Jivoff, P. R., and K. W. Able. 2003. Evaluating salt marsh restoration in Delaware Bay: The response of blue crabs, *Callinectes sapidus*, at former salt hay farms. *Estuaries* 26: 709–19.

Johansson, A., and F. Johansson. 1992. Effects of different caddisfly case structures on predation by dragonfly larva. *Aquatic Insects* 14: 73–84.

Johansson, A., and A. N. Nilsson 1992. *Dystiscus latissimus* and *D. circumcinctus* (Cleopater, Dytiscideae) larvae as predators on three case-making caddis larvae. *Hydrobiologia* 248: 201–13.

Johnson, B. 2004. Wetland profiling: An approach to landscape and cumulative wetland impacts analysis. Report to U.S. Environmental Protection Agency, NHEERL Western Ecology Division, Corvallis, Oregon, and Colorado Geologic Survey.

Johnson, R. R. and C. H. Lowe. 1985. On the development of riparian ecology. In *Riparian ecosystems and their management: Reconciling conflicting uses,* eds. R. R. Johnson, C. D. Zieball, D. R. Patton, P. F. Ffollitt and R. H. Hamre, 112–16. General Technical Report RM-120. Washington, D.C.: U.S.D.A. Forest Service.

Johnson, R. L., and F. W. Shropshire. 1983. Bottomland hardwoods. In *Silviculture systems for the major forest types of the United States,* ed. R. M. Burns, 175–79. Agriculture Handbook 445, revised. Washington, D.C.: U.S.D.A. Forest Service.

Johnson, S. L., F. J. Swanson, G. E. Grant, and S. M. Wondzell. 2000. Riparian forest disturbances by a mountain flood—The influence of floated wood. *Hydrological Processes* 14: 3031–50.

Johnson, W. C., R. L. Burgess, and W. R. Keammerer. 1976. Forest overstory vegetation on the Missouri River floodplain in North Dakota. *Ecological Monographs* 46: 59–84.

Johnson, W. C., B. V. Millett, T. Gilmanov, R. A. Voldseth, G. Guntenspergen, and D. Naugle. 2005. Vulnerability of northern prairie wetlands to climate change. *BioScience.* 55:863–872.

Johnston, C. A., and R. J. Naiman. 1990. Aquatic patch creation in relation to beaver population trends. *Ecology* 71: 1617–21.

Johnston, S. G., P. G. Slavich, L. A. Sullivan, and P. Hirst. 2003. Artificial drainage of floodwaters from sulfidic backswamps: Effects on deoxygenation in an Australian estuary. *Marine and Freshwater Research* 54: 781–95.

Joly, C. A., and R. Brandle. 1995. Fermentation and adenylate metabolism of *Hedychium coronarium* J. G. Koenig (Zingiberaceae) and *Acorus calamus* L. (Araceae) under hypoxia and anoxia. *Functional Ecology* 9: 505–10.

Jones, C. G., J. H. Lawton, and M. Shachak. 1994. Organisms as ecosystem engineers. *Oikos* 69: 373–86.

Jones, J. G. 1979. *A guide to methods for estimating microbial numbers and biomass in fresh water.* Windemere, U.K.: Freshwater Biological Association.

Jones, R. H., and R. R. Sharitz. 1998. Survival and growth of woody plant seedlings in the understorey of floodplain forests in South Carolina. *Journal of Ecology* 86: 574–87.

Jordan, T. E., and I. Valiela. 1982. The nitrogen budget of the ribbed mussel, *Geukensia demissa,* and its significance in nitrogen flow in a New England salt marsh. *Limnology and Oceanography* 27: 75–90.

Jørgensen, B. B. 1977. Bacterial sulfate reduction within reduced microniches of oxidising marine sediments. *Marine Biology* 41: 7–17.

Jørgensen, B. B., and D. J. Des Marais. 1988. Optical properties of benthic photosynthetic communities: Fiber-optic studies of cyanobacterial mats. *Limnology and Oceanography* 33: 99–113.

Jørgensen, E. G. 1957. Diatom periodicity and silicon assimilation. *Dansk Botanisk Arkiv* 18(1), 54 pp.

Joyal, L. A., M. McCollough, and M. L. Hunter. 2001. Landscape ecology approaches to wetland species conservation: A case study of two turtle species in southern Maine. *Conservation Biology* 15: 1755–62.

Junk, W. J. 1980. Áreas inundáveis—Um desafio para limnologia. *Acta Amazonica* 10: 775–95.

———. 1985. Temporary fat storage, an adaptation of some fish species to the waterlevel fluctuations and related environmental changes of the Amazonian rivers. *Amazoniana* 9: 315–52.

———. 1989. Flood tolerance and tree distribution in central Amazonian floodplains. In *Tropical forests: Botanical dynamics, speciation and diversity*, eds. L. B. Holm-Nielsen, I. C. Nielsen, and H. Balslev, 47–64. London, U.K.: Academic Press.

———. 1993. Wetlands of tropical South America. In *Wetlands of the world*, eds. D. F. Whigham, S. Hejny, and D. Dykyjova, 679–739. Dordrecht, The Netherlands: Kluwer.

———. 2002. Long-term environmental trends and the future of tropical wetlands. *Environmental Conservation* 29: 414–35.

———. In press. Flood pulsing and the linkages between terrestrial, aquatic, and wetland Systems. *Verh. Internat. Verein. Limnol.*

Junk, W. J., P. B. Bayley, R. E. Sparks. 1989. The flood pulse concept in river-floodplain systems. *Special Publication of the Canadian Journal of Fisheries and Aquatic Sciences* 106: 110–27.

Junk, W. J., and V. M. F. da Silva. 1997. Mammals, reptiles and amphibians. In *The Central Amazon floodplain. Ecology of a pulsing system*, ed. W. J. Junk, 409–18. *Ecological Studies* 126 Berlin, Germany: Springer.

Junk, W. J., C. Nunes da Cunha, K. M. Wantzen, P. Petermann, C. Strüssmann, M. I. Marques, and J. Adis. In press. Comparative biodiversity value of large wetlands: The Pantanal of Mato Grosso, Brazil. *Aquatic Sciences.*

Junk, W. J., and M. T. F. Piedade. 1997. Plant life in the floodplain with spezial reference to herbaceous plants. In *The Central Amazon floodplain. Ecology of a pulsing system*, ed. W. J. Junk, 147–86. *Ecological Studies* 126. Berlin, Germany: Springer.

Junk, W. J, M. G. M. Soares, and F. M. Carvalho. 1983. Distribution of fish species in a lake of the Amazon River floodplain near Manaus (Lago Camaleão), with special reference to extreme oxygen conditions. *Amazoniana* 7: 397–431.

Junk, W. J, M. G. M. Soares, and U. Saint-Paul. 1997. The fish. In *The Central Amazon floodplain. Ecology of a pulsing system*, ed. W. J. Junk, 385–408. *Ecological Studies* 126. Berlin, Germany: Springer.

Junk, W. J., and K. M. Wantzen. 2004. The flood pulse concept: New aspects, approaches, and applications—An Update. In *Proceedings of the 2nd Large River Symposium (LARS)*, eds. R. Welcomme, and T. Petr, 117–49, Phnom Penh, Cambodia 2. RAP Publication 2004/16.

Food and Agriculture Organization & Mekong River Commission. FAO Regional Office for Asia and the Pacific, Bangkok.

Kadlec, J. A. 1962. Effects of a drawdown on a waterfowl impoundment. *Ecology* 43: 267–81.

Kadlec, J. A., and W. A. Wentz. 1974. *State-of-the-art survey and evaluation of marsh plant establishment techniques: Induced and natural.* Volume 1. Report on research. Fort Belvoir, VA: United States Army Coastal Engineering and Research Center.

Kahn, W. E., and R. G. Wetzel. 1999. Effects of ultraviolet radiation and microscale water level fluctuations on periphytic microbiota. *Microbial Ecology* 38: 253–63.

Kantrud, H. A., G. L. Krapu, and G. A. Swanson. 1989. Prairie basin wetlands of the Dakotas: A community profile. *U.S. Fish and Wildlife Servive Biological Report* 85(7.28), 116 pp.

Kantrud, H. A., J. B. Millar, and A. G. van der Valk. 1989. Vegetation of wetlands of the prairie pothole region. In *Northern Prairie Wetlands,* ed. A. G. van der Valk, 132–87. Ames, IA: Iowa State University Press.

Kao, C. M., J. Y. Wang, K. F. Chen, H. Y. Lee, and M. J. Wu. 2002. Non-point source pesticide removal by a mountainous wetland. *Water Science and Technology* 46: 199–206.

Karr, J. R., and E. W. Chu. 1999. *Restoring life in running waters: Better biological monitoring.* Washington, D.C.: Island Press.

Kathiresan, K., and B. L. Bingham. 2001. Biology of mangroves and mangrove ecosystems. *Advances in Marine Biology* 40: 81–251.

Kats, L. B., J. W. Petranka, and A. Sih. 1988. Antipredator defenses and the persistence of amphibian larvae with fishes. *Ecology* 69: 1865–70.

Kautsky, L. 1988. Life strategies of aquatic soft bottom macrophytes. *Oikos* 53: 126–35.

Keddy, P. A. 1992a. A pragmatic approach to functional ecology. *Functional Ecology* 6: 621–26.

———. 1992b. Assembly and response rules: Two goals for predictive community ecology. *Journal of Vegetation Science* 3: 157–64.

———. 1999. Wetland restoration: The potential for assembly rules in the service of conservation. *Wetlands* 19: 716–32.

———. 2000. Wetland Ecology. Principles and Conservation. Cambridge University Press, Cambridge, UK.

Keeley, J. E. 1979. Population differentiation along a flood frequency gradient: Physiological adaptations to flooding in *Nyssa sylvatica. Ecological Monographs* 49: 89–108.

Keer, G., and J. B. Zedler. 2002. Salt marsh canopy architecture differs with the number and composition of species. *Ecological Applications* 12: 456–73.

Keiper, J. B., and W. E. Walton. 2000. Biology and immature stages of *Brachydeutera sturevanti* (Diptera: Ephydridae), a hyponeustic generalist. *Annals of the Entomological Society of America* 93: 468–75.

Keleher, C. J., and F. J. Rahel. 1996. Thermal limits to salmonid distributions in the Rocky Mountain region and potential habitat loss due to global warming: A geographic information system (GIS) Approach. *Transactions of the American Fisheries Society* 125: 113.

Kellison, R. C., R. R. Braham, and E. J. Jones. 1998. Major alluvial floodplains. In *Southern forested wetlands. Ecology and management,* eds. M. G. Messina and W. H. Conner, 291–323. Boca Raton, FL: Lewis Publishers.

Kemp, P. F. 1990. The fate of benthic bacterial production. *Aquatic Sciences* 12: 109–25.

Kemp, P.F., B.F. Sherr, E.B. Sherr, and J.J. Cole, eds. 1993. *Handbook of methods in aquatic microbial ecology.* Boca Raton, FL: Lewis Publishers.

Kennamer, R.A. 2001. Relating climatological patterns to wetland conditions and wood duck production in the southeastern Atlantic Coastal Plain. *Wildlife Society Bulletin* 29: 1193–1205.

Kenney, L.P., and M.R. Burne. 2000. A field guide to the animals of vernal pools. Westborough, MA: Massachusetts Division of Fisheries and Wildlife, Natural Heritage and Endangered Species Program.

Kent, A.C., and R.W. Day. 1983. Population dynamics of an infaunal polychaete: The effect of predators and an adult-recruit interaction. *Journal of Experimental Marine Biology and Ecology* 73: 185–203.

Keough, J.R., C.A. Hagley, E. Ruzycki, and M. Sierzen. 1998. Delta C-13 composition of primary producers and the role of detritus in a freshwater coastal ecosystem. *Limnology and Oceanography* 43: 734–40.

Keough, J.R., T.A. Thompson, G.R. Guntenspergen, and D.A. Wilcox. 1999. Hydrogeomorphic factors and ecosystem responses in coastal wetlands of the Great Lakes. *Wetlands* 19: 821–34.

Kerbes, R.H., P.M. Kotanen, and R.L. Jefferies. 1990. Destruction of wetland habitats by lesser snow geese: A keystone species on the west coast of Hudson Bay. *Journal of Applied Ecology* 27: 242–58.

Kercher, S.M., and Zedler, J.B. 2004. Multiple disturbances accelerate invasion of reed canary grass (*Phalaris arundinacea* L.) in a mesocosm study. *Oecologia* 138: 455–64.

Kern, J., and A. Darwich. 1997. Nitrogen turnover in the várzea. In *The Central Amazon floodplain. Ecology of a pulsing system,* ed. W.J. Junk, 119–36. *Ecological Studies* 126. Berlin, Germany: Springer.

Kerr, J.B., and C.T. McElroy. 1993. Evidence for large upward trends of ultraviolet-B radiation linked to ozone depletion. *Science* 262: 1032–34.

Kesel, R.H. 1989. The role of the Mississippi River in wetland loss in southeastern Louisiana, USA. *Environmental Geology and Water Sciences* 13: 183–89.

Khoshmanesh, A., B.T. Hart, A. Duncan, and R. Beckett. 1999. Biotic uptake and release of phosphorus by a wetland sediment. *Environmental Technology* 20: 85–91.

Kiehl, K., I. Eischeid, S. Gettner, and J. Walter. 1996. Impact of different sheep grazing intensities on salt marsh vegetation in northern Germany. *Journal of Vegetation Science* 7: 99–106.

Kilgo, J.C., K.V. Miller, and W.P. Smith. 1999. Effects of group selection timber harvest in bottomland hardwoods on fall migrant birds. *Journal of Field Ornithology* 70: 404–13.

Kilgo, J.C., R.A. Sargent, B.R. Chapman, and K.V. Miller. 1998. Effect of stand width and adjacent habitat on breeding bird communities in bottomland hardwoods. *Journal of Wildlife Management* 62: 72–83.

King, A.J., A.I. Robertson, and M.R. Healey. 1997. Experimental manipulations of the biomass of introduced carp *(Cyprinus carpio)* in billabongs. 1. Impacts on water-column properties. *Marine and Freshwater Research* 48: 435–43.

King, J.K., S.M. Harmon, T.T. Fu, and J.B. Gladden. 2002. Mercury removal, methylmercury formation, and sulfate-reducing bacteria profiles in wetland mesocosms. *Chemosphere* 46: 859–70.

King, J. L., M. A. Simovich, and R. C. Brusca. 1996. Species richness, endemism and ecology of crustacean assemblages in northern California vernal pools. *Hydrobiologia* 328: 85–116.

King, R. S., and C. J. Richardson. 2002. Evaluating subsampling approaches and macroinvertebrate taxonomic resolution for wetland bioassessment. *Journal of the North American Benthological Society* 21: 150–71.

King, R. S., C. J. Richardson, D. L. Urban, and E. A. Romanowicz. 2004. Spatial dependency of vegetation-environment linkages in an anthropogenically influenced wetland ecosystem. *Ecosystems* 7: 75–97.

King, S. L., and B. D. Keeland. 1999. Evaluation of reforestation in the Lower Mississippi River Alluvial Valley. *Restoration Ecology* 7: 348–59.

King, S. L., J. P. Shepard, K. Ouchley, J. A. Neal and K. Ouchley. 2005. Bottomland hardwood forests: Past, present, and future. In *Ecology and management of bottomland hardwood systems: The state of our understanding,* eds. L. H. Fredrickson, S. L. King, and R. M. Kaminski, 1–17. Gaylord Memorial Laboratory Special Publication No. 10. Puxico, MO: University of Missouri-Columbia.

Kingsford, R. T., A. L. Curtin, and C. J. Porter. 1999. Water flows on Cooper Creek in arid Australia determine 'boom' and 'bust' periods for waterbirds. *Biological Conservation* 88: 231–48.

Kingsford, R. T., K. M. Jenkins, and J. L. Porter. 2004. Imposed hydrological stability on lakes in arid Australia and effects on waterbirds. *Ecology* 85: 2478–92.

Kingsford, R. T., and F. I. Norman. 2002. Australian waterbirds—Products of the continent's ecology. *Emu* 102: 47–69.

Kingsford, R. T., and J. L. Porter. 1993. Waterbirds of Lake Eyre, Australia. *Biological Conservation* 65: 141–51.

Kinzel, H. 1982. *Pflanzenokologie und Mineralstoffwechsel.* Stuttgart: Ulmer

Kirchman, D., ed. 2000. *Microbial ecology of the oceans.* New York: Wiley-Liss.

Kirk, J. T. O. 1994. *Light and photosynthesis in aquatic ecosystems,* 2d ed. Cambridge: Cambridge University Press, 509 pp.

Kirkman, L. K., P. C. Goebel, L. West, M. B. Drew, and B. J. Palik. 2000. Depressional wetland vegetation types: A question of plant community development. *Wetlands* 20: 373–85.

Kirkman, L. K. and R. R. Sharitz. 1993. Growth in controlled water regimes of three grasses common in freshwater wetlands of the southeastern USA. *Aquatic Botany* 44: 345–59.

———. 1994. Vegetation disturbance and maintenance of diversity in intermittently flooded Carolina bays in South Carolina. *Ecological Applications* 4: 177–88.

Kjerfve, B., and D. J. Macintosh. 1997. Climate change impacts on mangrove ecosystems. In *Mangrove ecosystem studies in Latin America and Africa,* eds. B. Kjerfve, L. D. Lacerda, and S. Diop, 1–7. Paris, France: UNESCO.

Klimanov, V. A., and A. A. Sirin. 1997. The dynamics of peat accumulation by mires of northern Eurasia during the last 3000 years. In *Northern forested wetlands ecology and management,* eds. C. C. Trettin, M. F. Jurgensen, D. F. Grigal, M. R. Gale, and J. K. Jeglum, 313–24. Boca Raton, FL: Lewis Publishers.

Kling, G. W., K. Hayhoe, L. B. Johnson, J. J. Magnuson, S. Polasky, S. K. Robinson, B. J. Shuter, M. M. Wander, D. J. Wuebbles, and D. R. Zak. 2003. Confronting climate change in the Great Lakes Region: Impacts on our communities and ecosystems. Report of the Union of Concerned Scientists, Cambridge Massachusetts and the Ecological Society of America, Washington, D.C., 104 pp.

Klopatek, J.M. 1974. Production of emergent macrophytes and their role in mineral cycling within a freshwater marsh. Master's thesis, University of Wisconsin, Milwaukee.

Klotzli, F., and A. P. Grootjans. 2001. Restoration of natural and semi-natural wetland systems in Central Europe: Progress and predictability of developments. *Restoration Ecology* 9: 209–19.

Kneib, R.T. 1997a. Early life stages of resident nekton in intertidal marshes. *Estuaries* 20: 214–30.

———. 1997b. The role of tidal marshes in the ecology of estuarine nekton. *Oceanography and Marine Biology: An Annual Review* 35: 163–229.

Kneib, R.T., and A. E. Stiven. 1982. Benthic invertebrate responses to size and density manipulations of the common mummichog, *Fundulus heteroclitus,* in an intertidal salt marsh. *Ecology* 63: 1518–32.

Kneitel, J.M., and T. E. Miller. 2003. Dispersal rates affect species composition in metacommunities of *Sarracenia purpurea* inquilines. *American Naturalist* 162: 165–171.

Knight, A. W., and R. L. Bottorf. 1984. The importance of riparian vegetation to stream ecosystems. In *California riparian ecosystems: Ecology, conservation and productive management,* eds. R. E. Warner and K. M. Hendrix, 160–67. Berkeley, CA: University of California Press.

Knutson, M.G., J. R. Sauer, D. A. Olsen, M. J. Mossman, L. M. Hemesath, and M. J. Lannoo. 1999. Effects of landscape composition and wetland fragmentation on frog and toad abundance and species richness in Iowa and Wisconsin, USA. *Conservation Biology* 13: 1437–46.

Koch, M. S., I. A. Mendelssohn, and K. L. McKee. 1990. Mechanism for the hydrogen sulfide-induced growth limitation in wetland macrophytes. *Limnol. Oceanogr.* 35:399–408.

Koch, M. S., and K. R. Reddy. 1992. Distribution of soil and plant nutrients along a trophic gradient in the Florida Everglades. *Soil Science Society of America* 56: 1492–99.

Koehn, J., A. Brumley, and P. Gehrke. 2000. *Managing the impacts of carp.* Canberra, Australia: Bureau of Rural Sciences.

Koerselman, W., and A. R.M. Meuleman. 1996. The vegetation N:P ratio: A new tool to detect the nature of nutrient limitation. *Journal of Applied Ecology* 33: 1441–50.

Koerselman, W., M. B. Vankerkhoven, and J. T. A. Verhoeven. 1993. Release of inorganic N, P and K in peat soils—Effect of temperature, water chemistry, and water-level. *Biogeochemistry* 20: 63–81.

Kohler, S. L., D. Corti, M. C. Slamecka, and D. W. Schneider. 1999. Prairie floodplain ponds: Mechanisms affecting invertebrate community structure. In *Invertebrates in freshwater wetlands of North America: Ecology and management,* eds. D. P. Batzer, R. B. Rader, and S. A. Wissinger, 711–30. New York: John Wiley and Sons.

Kolozsvary, M. B., and R. K. Swihart. 1999. Habitat fragmentation and the distribution of amphibians: Patch and landscape correlates in farmland. *Canadian Journal of Zoology* 77: 1288–99.

Kostka, J. E., B. Gribsholt, E. Petrie, D. Dalton, H. Skelton, and E. Kristensen. 2002. The rates and pathways of carbon oxidation in bioturbated saltmarsh sediments. *Limnology and Oceanography* 47: 230–40.

Kotanen, P. M., and R. L. Jefferies. 1997. Long-term destruction of sub-arctic wetland vegetation by lesser snow geese. *Ecoscience* 4: 179–82.

Kowalski, K. P., and D. A. Wilcox. 1999. Use of historical and geospatial data to guide the restoration of a Lake Erie coastal marsh. *Wetlands* 19: 858–68.

Kratzer, E. 2002. Aquatic macroinvertebrate assemblages of the Okefenokee Swamp, Georgia, USA. Master's thesis, University of Georgia, Athens.

Krebs, J. R. 1974. Colonial nesting and social feeding as strategies for exploiting food resources in the Great Blue Heron *(Ardea herodius)*. *Behaviour* 51: 99–131.

Kreibich, H., and J. Kern. 2003. Nitrogen fixation and denitrification in a floodplain forest near Manaus, Brazil. *Hydrological Processes* 17: 1431–41.

Krejci, M. E., and R. L. Lowe. 1986. Importance of sand grain mineralogy and topography in determining micro-spatial distribution of epipsammic diatoms. *Journal of the North American Benthological Society* 5: 211–20.

Kristjanson, J. K., and P. Schonheit. 1983. Why do sulfate-reducing bacteria outcompete methanogenic bacteria for susbstrates? *Oecologia* 60: 264–66.

Kroes, D., and M. M. Brinson. 2004. Occurrence of riverine wetlands on floodplains along a climatic gradient. *Wetlands* 24: 167–77.

Krumbein, W. E., and P. K. Swart. 1983. The microbial carbon cycle. In *Microbial geochemistry*, ed. W. E. Krumbein, 5–62. Oxford, U.K.: Blackwell Scientific.

Kubanek, J., W. Fenical, M. E. Hay, P. J. Brown, and N. Lindquist. 2000. Two antifeedant lignans from the freshwater macrophyte *Saururus cernuus*. *Phytochemistry* 54: 281–87.

Kühl, M., and B. B. Jørgensen. 1992. Spectral light measurements in microbenthic phototrophic communities with a fiber-optic microprobe coupled to a sensitive diode array detector. *Limnology and Oceanography* 37: 1813–23.

Kühl, M., and N. P. Revsbech. 2001. Biogeochemical microsensors for boundary layer studies. In *The benthic boundary layer*, eds. B. P. Boudreau and B. B. Jørgensen, 180–210. New York: Oxford University Press.

Kuhry, P. 1994. The role of fire in the development of *Sphagnum*-dominated peatlands in western boreal Canada. *Journal of Ecology* 82: 899–910.

Kuivila, K. M., J. W. Murray, and A. H. Devol. 1988. Methane production, sulfate reduction and competition for substrates in the sediments of Lake Washington. *Geochim et Cosmochimica Acta* 53: 409–16.

Kurz, H., and D. Demaree. 1934. Cypress buttresses and knees in relation to water and air. *Ecology* 15: 36–41.

Kus, B. E. 1998. Use of restored riparian habitat by the endangered Least Bell's Vireo *(Vireo bellii pusillus)*. *Restoration Ecology* 6: 75–82.

Kushlan, J. A. 1993. Colonial waterbirds as bioindicators of environmental change. *Colonial Waterbirds* 16: 223–51.

Kushlan, J. A., and H. Hafner. 2000. *Heron conservation*. London: Academic Press.

Kushlan, J. A., M. J. Steinkamp, K. C. Parsons, J. Capp, M. A. Cruz, M. Coulter, I. Davidson, et al. 2002. *Waterbird conservation for the Americas: The North American Waterbird Conservation Plan, Version 1*. Washington, D. C.: Waterbird Conservation for the Americas.

Kusler, J. 1992. Wetland delineation: An issue of science or politics. *Environment* 34: 7–11, 29–37.

Kusler, J. N. The SWANCC decision and state regulation of wetlands. Association of State Wetland Managers Inc., NY, 16 pp. www.aswm.org/fwp/swancc/index.htm

Kusler, J. A., and M. E. Kentula, eds. 1990. *Wetland creation and restoration: The status of the science.* Washington, D. C.: Island Press, 594 pp.

Kusler, J., and V. R. Burkett. 1999. Wetlands and climate change—Scientific approaches and management options. *National Wetlands Newsletter* 21: 1, 16–18.

Kvet, J., and S. Husak. 1978. Primary data on biomass and production estimates in typical stands of fishpond littoral plant communities. In *Pond littoral ecosystems,* eds. D. Dykyjová and J. Kvet, 211–16. Berlin: Springer-Verlag.

Kwak, T. J., and J. B. Zedler. 1997. Food web analysis of southern California coastal wetlands using multiple stable isotopes. *Oecologia* 110: 262–77.

LaBaugh, J. W. 1986a. Wetland ecosystem studies from a hydrologic perspective. *Water Resources Bulletin* 22:1–10.

———. 1986b. Limnological characteristics of selected lakes in the Nebraska sandhills, U.S.A., and their relation to chemical characteristics of adjacent groundwater. *Journal of Hydrology* 86: 279–98.

Laderman, A. D. 1989. *The ecology of the Atlantic white cedar wetlands: A community profile.* Biological Report 85(7.21). Washington, D. C.: U.S. Fish and Wildlife Service, 114 pp.

Laffaille, P., E. Feunteun, and J. C. Lefeuvre. 2000. Composition of fish communities in a European macrotidal salt marsh (the Mont Saint-Michel Bay, France). *Estuarine Coastal and Shelf Science* 51: 429–438.

Lafferty, K. D., C. C. Swift, and R. F. Ambrose. 1999. Extirpation and recolonization in a metapopulation of an endangered fish, the tidewater goby. *Conservation Biology* 1447–53.

LaGrange, T. 2001. The U.S. Supreme Court ruling on isolated wetlands and the implications for Nebraska wetlands. Briefing Paper. Lincoln, NE: Nebraska Game and Parks Commission.

Laidig, K. J., and R. A. Zampella. 1999. Community attributes of Atlantic white cedar *(Chamaecyparis thyoides)* swamps in disturbed and undisturbed pinelands watersheds. *Wetlands* 19: 35–49.

Lake, P. S., L. A. Barmuta, A. J. Boulton, I. C. Campbell, and R. M. St Clair. 1985. Australian streams and northern hemisphere stream ecology. *Proceedings of the Ecological Society of Australia* 14: 61–82.

Lamberti, G. A. 1996. The role of periphyton in benthic food webs. In *Algal ecology: Benthic algae in freshwater ecosystems,* eds. R. J. Stevenson, M. Bothwell, and R. L. Lowe, 533–72. New York: Academic Press.

Lamberti, G. A., and V. H. Resh. 1983. Stream periphyton and insect herbivores: An experimental study of grazing by a caddisfly population. *Ecology* 64: 1124–35.

Lambou, V. W. 1990. Importance of bottomland forest zones to fishes and fisheries: A case history. In *Ecological processes and cumulative impacts,* eds. J. G. Gosselink, L. C. Lee, and T. A. Muir, 125–93. Illustrated by Bottomland Hardwood Wetland Ecosystems. Chelsea, MI: Lewis Publishers Inc.

Lamers, L. P. M., S. J. Falla, E. M. Samborska, L. A. R. van Dulken, G. van Hengstum, and J. G. M. Roelofs. 2002. Factors controlling the extent of eutrophication and toxicity in sulfate-polluted freshwater wetlands. *Limnology and Oceanography* 47: 585–93.

Lamers, L. P. M., H. B. M. Tomassen, and J. G. M. Roelofs. 1998. Sulfate-induced eutrophication and phytotoxicity in freshwater wetlands. *Environmental Science and Technology* 32: 199–205.

Lampert, W., and U. Sommer. 1997. *Limnoecology: The ecology of lakes and streams*, trans. J. F. Haney. Oxford, U.K.: Oxford University Press.

Lange, W. 1976. Speculations on a possible essential function of the gelatinous sheath of blue-green algae. *Canadian Journal of Microbiology* 22: 1181–85.

Langellotto, G. A., and R. F. Denno 2001. Benefits of dispersal in patchy environments: Mate location by males of a wing-dimorphic insect. *Ecology* 82: 1870–78.

Langis, R., M. Zalejko, and J. B. Zedler. 1991. Nitrogen assessments in a constructed and a natural salt marsh of San Diego Bay, California. *Ecological Applications* 1: 40–51.

Larcher, W. 1995. *Physiological plant ecology: Ecophysiology and stress physiology of functional groups*, 3d ed. New York: Springer-Verlag.

Larkin, D. J., G. Vivian-Smith, and J. B. Zedler. 2006. Topographic heterogeneity theory and applications to ecological restoration. In *Foundations of restoration ecology*, eds. D. A. Falk, M. Palmer, and J. B. Zedler. Washington, D. C.: Island Press.

Larsen, J. A. 1982. *Ecology of the northern lowland bogs and conifer forests*. New York: Academic Press.

Larson, J. S., ed. 1976. *Models for assessment of freshwater wetlands*. Publication No. 32. Water Resources Research Center, University of Massachusetts, Amherst, MA.

Laubhan, M. K. 1995. Effects of prescribed fire on moist-soil vegetation and soil macronutrients. *Wetlands* 15: 159–66.

Le Mer, J., and P. Roger. 2001. Production, oxidation, emission and consumption of methane by soils: A review. *European Journal of Soil Biology* 37: 25–50.

Leclerc, H., L. Schwartzbrod, and E. Dei-Cas. 2002. Microbial agents associated with water-borne diseases. *Critical Reviews in Microbiology* 28: 371–409.

Lee, J. A., M. C. Press, and S. J. Woodin. 1986. Effects of NO_2 on aquatic ecosystems. In *Study for the environment and quality of life: Study on the need for an NO_2 long-term limit value for the protection of terrestrial and aquatic ecosystems*, 99–119. Luxembourg, Sweden: Commission of the European Communities.

Lee, S. Y. 1998. Ecological role of grapsid crabs in mangrove ecosystems: A review. *Marine and Freshwater Research* 49: 335–43.

Leeper, D. A., and B. E. Taylor. 1998. Insect emergence from a South Carolina (USA) temporary wetlands pond, with emphasis on the Chironomidae (Diptera). *Journal of the North American Benthological Society* 17: 54–72.

Lehtinen, R. M., and S. M. Galatowitsch. 2001. Colonization of restored wetlands by amphibians in Minnesota. *American Midland Naturalist* 145: 388–96.

Lehtinen, R. M., S. M. Galatowitsch, and J. R. Tester. 1999. Consequences of habitat loss and fragmentation for wetland amphibian assemblages. *Wetlands* 19: 1–12.

Leigh, D. S., P. Srivastava, and G. A. Brook. 2004. Late Pleistocene braided rivers of the Atlantic Coastal Plain, USA. *Quaternary Science Reviews* 23: 65–84.

Leips, J., M. G. McManus, and J. Travis. 2000. Response of treefrog larvae to drying ponds: Comparing temporary and permanent pond breeders. *Ecology* 81: 2997–3008.

Lemeur, R., and L. Zhang. 1990. Evaluation of three evapotranspiration models in terms of their applicability for an arid region. *Journal of Hydrology* 114: 395–411.

Leon-Quinto, T., A. de la Vega, A. Lozano, and S. Pastor. 2004. Summer mortality of water-birds in a Mediterranean wetland. *Waterbirds* 27: 46–53.

Leopold, A. 1933. *Game management.* New York: Scribners.

Lessmann, J. M., I. A. Mendelssohn, M. W. Hester, and K. L. McKee. 1997. Population variation in growth response to flooding of three marsh grasses. *Ecological Engineering* 8: 31–47.

Leuschner, C., and F. Schipka. 2004. *Klimawandel und Naturschutz in Deutschland.* Bonn, Germany: Bundesamt für Naturschutz.

Levin, L. A., D. F. Boesch, A. Covich, C. Dahm, C. Erseus, K. C. Ewel, R. T. Kneib, et al. 2001. The function of marine critical transition zones and the importance of sediment biodiversity. *Ecosystems* 4: 430–51.

Levine, J. M., J. S. Brewer, and M. D. Bertness. 1998. Nutrients, competition and plant zonation in a New England salt marsh. *Journal of Ecology* 86: 285–92.

Lewis, W. M., S. K. Hamilton, M. A. Rodríguez, J. F. Saunders, and M. A. Lasi. 2001. Foodweb analyses of the Orinoco floodplain based on production estimates and stable isotope data. *Journal of the North American Benthological Society* 20: 241–54.

Lide, R. F., V. G. Meentemeyer, J. E. Pinder III, and L. M. Beatty. 1995. Hydrology of a Carolina bay located on the upper Coastal Plain of western South Carolina. *Wetlands* 15: 47–57.

Lin, H. J., K. T. Shao, W. L. Chiou, C. J. W. Maa, H. L. Hsieh, W. L. Wu, L. L. Severinghaus, and Y. T. Wang. 2003. Biotic communities of freshwater marshes and mangroves in relation to saltwater incursions: Implications for wetland regulation. *Biodiversity and Conservation* 12: 647–65.

Lindeman, R. L. 1941. The developmental history of Cedar Creek Bog, Minnesota. *American Midland Naturalist* 25: 101–12.

———. 1942. The trophic-dynamic aspect of ecology. *Ecology* 23: 399–417.

Lindig-Cisneros, R., J. Desmond, K. Boyer, and J. B. Zedler. 2003. Wetland restoration thresholds: Can a degradation transition be reversed with increased effort? *Ecological Applications* 13: 193–205.

Lindig-Cisneros, R., and J. B. Zedler. 2002a. Relationships between canopy complexity and germination microsites for *Phalaris arundinacea* L. *Oecologia* 133: 159–67.

———. 2002b. Halophyte recruitment in a salt marsh restoration site. *Estuaries* 25: 1174–83.

Lindroth, A. 1985. Canopy conductance of coniferous forests related to climate. *Water Resources Research* 21: 297–304.

Lindsey, A. A., R. O. Petty, D. K. Sterlin, and W. V. Asdall. 1961. Vegetation and environment along the Wabash and Tippecanoe rivers. *Ecological Monographs* 31: 105–56.

Lipsky, A. 1997. *Narragansett Bay method: A manual for salt marsh evaluation.* Providence, RI: Save the Bay.

Littlehales, B., and W. A. Niering. 1991. *Wetlands of North America.* Charlottesville, VA: Thomasson-Grant.

Lock, M. A. 1993. Attached microbial communities in rivers. In *Aquatic microbiology,* ed. T. E. Ford, 113–38. Oxford: Blackwell Scientific.

Lock, M. A., R. R. Wallace, J. W. Costerton, and S. E. Charlton. 1984. River epilithon (biofilm): Toward a structural functional model. *Oikos* 42: 10–22.

Lockaby, B. G., J. Stanturf, and M. G. Messina. 1997. Effects of silvicultural activity on ecological processes in floodplain forests of the southern United States: A review of existing reports. *Forest Ecology and Management* 90: 93–100.

Lockaby, B.G., and M.R. Waldbridge. 1998. Biogeochemistry. In *Southern forested wetlands—Ecology and management*, eds. M.G. Messina and W.H. Conner, 149–72. Boca Raton, FL: Lewis Publishers.

Lodge, D.M. 1991. Herbivory on freshwater macrophytes. *Aquatic Botany* 41: 195–224.

Löffler, H. 1968. Tropical high-mountain lakes. Their distribution, ecology and zoogeographical importance. In *Geo-ecology of the mountainous regions of the tropical Americas*, ed. C. Troll, 57–76. Colloquium Geographicum, Band 9, Proceedings of the UNESCO Mexico Symposium August, 1-3, 1966, Mexico.

Lonard, R.I. and E.J. Clairain, Jr. 1985. Identification of methodologies for the assessment of wetland functions and values. In eds. J.A. Kusler and P. Riexinger, 66–72. Proc. National Wetland Assessment Symposium, Association of Wetland Managers, Portland, Maine, June 17–29, 1985.

Lonard, R.I., E.J. Clairain, Jr., R.T. Huffman, J.W. Hardy, L.D. Brown, P.E. Ballard, and J.W. Watts. 1981. *Analysis of methodologies used for the assessment of wetland values*. Washington, D.C.: U.S. Water Resources Council, 68 pp.

Lorah, M.M., and M.A. Voytek. 2004. Degradation of 1,1,2,2-tetrachloroethane and accumulation of vinyl chloride in wetland sediment microcosms and in situ porewater: Biogeochemical controls and associations with microbial communities. *Journal of Contaminant Hydrology* 70: 117–45.

Loreau, M., S. Naeem, P. Inchausti, J. Bengtsson, J.P. Grime, A. Hector, D.U. Hooper, et al. 2001. Biodiversity and ecosystem functioning: Current knowledge and future challenges. *Science* 294: 804–8.

Lorenz, R.C., M.E. Monaco, and C.E. Herdendorf. 1991. Minimum light requirements for substrate colonization by *Cladophora glomerata*. *Journal of Great Lakes Research* 17: 536–42.

Losee, R.F., and R.G. Wetzel. 1983. Selective light attenuation by the periphyton complex. In *Periphyton of freshwater ecosystems*, ed. G. Wetzel. *Developments in Hydrobiology* 17: 89–96.

———. 1993. Littoral flow rates within and around submersed macrophyte communities. *Freshwater Biology* 29: 7–17.

Lougheed, V.L., B. Crosbie, and P. Chow-Fraser. 1998. Predictions on the effect of common carp *(Cyprinus carpio)* exclusion on water quality, zooplankton, and submergent macrophytes in a Great Lakes wetlands. *Canadian Journal of Fisheries and Aquatic Sciences* 55: 1189–97.

Lougheed, V.L., T.S. Theysmeyer, T. Smith, and P. Chow-Fraser. 2004. Carp exclusion, food-web interactions, and the restoration of Cootes Paradise Marsh. *Journal of Great Lakes Research* 30: 44–57.

Lovley, D.R. 1987. Organic matter mineralization with the reduction of ferric iron: A review. *Geomicrobiology Journal* 5: 375–99.

———. 1991. Dissimilatory Fe(II) and Mn(IV) reduction. *Microbiological Reviews* 55: 259–87.

———. 1993. Anaerobes into heavy metal: Dissimilatory metal reduction in anoxic environments. *Trends in Ecology and Evolution* 8: 21–217.

Lovley, D.R., and E.J.P. Phillips. 1987. Competitive mechanisms for inhibition of sulfate reduction and methane production in the zone of ferric iron reduction in sediments. *Applied and Environmental Microbiology* 53: 2, 636-2, 641.

Lovvorn, J.R., W.W. Wolheim, and E.A. Hart. 1999. High plains wetlands of southeast Wyoming: Salinity, vegetation, and invertebrate communities. In *Invertebrates in freshwater wetlands of North America: Ecology and management*, eds. D.P. Batzer, R.D. Rader, and S.A. Wissinger, 603–34. New York: John Wiley and Sons.

Lugo, A.E. 1997. Old-growth mangrove forests in the United States. *Conservation Biology* 11: 11–20.

Lugo, A.E., M.M. Brinson, and S. Brown. 1990. Concepts in wetland ecology. In *Forested wetlands*, eds. A.E. Lugo, M.M. Brinson, and S. Brown, 53–85. Vol. 15 of Ecosystems of the World Series. Amsterdam: Elsevier Scientific Publishers.

Lugo, A.E., S. Brown, and M.M. Brinson. 1988. Forested wetlands in freshwater and saltwater environments. *Limnology and Oceanography* 33: 894–909.

Lugo, A.E., and C. Patterson Zucca. 1977. The impact of low temperature stress on mangrove structure and growth. *Tropical Ecology* 18: 149–61.

Lugo, A.E., and S.C. Snedaker. 1974. The ecology of mangroves. *Annual Review of Ecology and Systematics* 5: 39–64.

Lundkvist, E., J. Landin, and F. Karlsson. 2002. Dispersing diving beetles (Dytiscidae) in agricultural and urban landscapes in southeastern Sweden. *Annals Zoologica Fennici* 39: 109–23.

Luo, H.R., L.M. Smith, B.L. Allen, and D.A. Haukos. 1997. Effects of sedimentation on playa wetland volume. *Ecological Applications* 7: 247–52.

Luo, H.R., L.M. Smith, D.A. Haukos, and B.L. Allen. 1999. Sources of recently deposited sediments in playa wetlands. *Wetlands* 19(1): 176–81.

Luttge, U. 2002. Mangroves. In *Salinity: Environment—Plants—Molecules*, eds. A. Lauchli and U. Luttge, 113–35. Dordrecht, The Netherlands.

Lynch, J.J., T. O'Neil, and D.W. Lag. 1947. Management significance of damage by geese and muskrats to gulf coastal marshes. *Journal of Wildlife Management* 11: 50–76.

MacArthur, R.H., and E.O. Wilson. 1967. *The theory of island biogeography*. Princeton, NJ: Princeton University Press.

Macintosh, D.J., and E.C. Ashton. 2002. *A review of mangrove biodiversity conservation and management*. Final Report. Aarhus, Denmark: Centre for Tropical Ecosystems Research.

Mackay, R.J., and G.B. Wiggins. 1979. Ecological diversity in Trichoptera. *Annual Review of Entomology* 24: 185–208.

MacMahon, J. 1998. Empirical and theoretical ecology as a basis for restoration: An ecological success story. In *Successes, limitations, and frontiers in ecosystem science*, eds. M.L. Pace and P.M. Groffman, 220–46. New York: Springer-Verlag.

MacMillan, C. 1975. Adaptive differentiation to chilling in mangrove populations. In *Proceedings of the international symposium on biology and management of mangroves*, eds. G.E. Walsh, S.C. Snedaker and H.J. Teas, 62–68. Gainesville, FL: Institute of Food and Agricultural Sciences.

Madigan, M.T., J.M. Martinko, and J. Parker. 1997. *Brock's biology of microorganisms*, 8th ed. Upper Saddle River, NJ: Prentice Hall.

Madon, S.P., G.D. Williams, J.M. West, and J.B. Zedler. 2001. The importance of marsh access to growth of the California killifish, *Fundulus parvipinnis*, evaluated through bioenergetics modeling. *Ecological Modelling* 136: 149–65.

Mahoney, D. L., M. A. Mort, and B. E. Taylor. 1990. Species richness of calanoid copepods, clado-cerans and other branchiopods in Carolina bay temporary ponds. *American Midland Naturalist* 123: 244–58.

Main, A. R., M. J. Littlejohn, and A. K. Lee. 1959. Ecology of Australian frogs. In *Biogeography and ecology in Australia,* eds. A. Keast, R. L. Carocker, and C. S. Christian, 396–411. Den Haag, The Netherlands: W. Junk Publisher.

Malecki, R. A., B. Blossey, S. D. Hight, D. Schroeder, L. T. Kok, and J. R. Coulson. 1993. Biological control of purple loosestrife—A case for using insects as control agents, after rigorous screening, and for integrating release strategies with research. *Biosciences* 43: 680–86.

Mancil, E. 1969. Some historical and geographical notes on the cypress lumbering industry in Louisiana. *Louisiana Studies* 8: 14–25.

Mann, C. J., and R. G. Wetzel. 2000a. Hydrology of an impounded riverine wetland. I. Wetland sediment characteristics. *Wetlands* 20: 23–32.

———. 2000b. Hydrology of an impounded riverine wetland. II. Subsurface hydrology. *Wetlands* 20: 33–47.

Mann, M. E., R. S. Bradley, and M. K. Hughes. 1999. Northern Hemisphere temperatures during the past millennium: Inferences, uncertainties, and limitations. *Geophysical Research Letters* 26: 759–62.

Manny, B. A., R. G. Wetzel, and W. C. Johnson. 1975. Annual contribution of carbon, nitrogen and phopshorus by migrant Canada geese to a hardwater lake. *Verhandlungen Internationale Vereinigung für Theoretische und Angewandte Limnologie* 19: 949–51.

Mans, C., T. Denward, and L. J. Tranvik. 1998. Effects of solar radiation on aquatic macrophyte litter decomposition. *Oikos* 82: 51–58.

Maranger, R., and Bird, D. F. 1995. Viral abundance in aquatic systems: A comparison between marine and fresh waters. *Marine Ecology Progress Series* 121: 217–26.

Marchese, M. R., I. Escurra de Drago, and E. C. Drago. 2002. Benthic macroinvertebrates and physical habitat relationships in the Paraná River-floodplain system. In *The ecohydrology of South American rivers and wetlands,* ed. M. E. McClain, 113–32. IAHS Special Publication No. 6. Oxfordshire, U.K.: IAHS Press.

Margulis, L., and K. V. Schwartz. 1988. *Five kingdoms: An illustrated guide to the phyla of life on Earth,* 2d ed. New York: W. H. Freeman and Company.

Marklund, O., H. Sandsten, L. A. Hansson, and I. Blindow. 2002. Effects of waterfowl and fish on submerged vegetation and macroinvertebrates. *Freshwater Biology* 47: 2049–59.

Marquis, R. J., and C. J. Whelan. 1994. Insectivorous birds increase growth of white oak through consumption of leaf-chewing insects. *Ecology* 75: 2007–14.

Marschner, B., and K. Kalbitz. 2003. Controls of bioavailability and biodegradability of dissolved organic matter in soil. *Geoderma* 113: 211–35.

Marsh, A. S. 1999. How wetland plants respond to elevated carbon dioxide. *National Wetlands Newsletter* 21: 11–13.

Marsh, D. M., and P. C. Trenham. 2001. Metapopulation dynamics and amphibian conservation. *Conservation Biology* 15: 40–49.

Marshall, E. 1997. Apocalypse not (News and comment section). *Science* 278: 1004–6.

Martin, D. B., and W. A. Hartmann. 1987. The effect of cultivation on sediment composition and deposition in prairie pothole wetlands. *Water, Air, and Soil Pollution* 34: 45–53.

Martinez, L. M, A. Carranza M., and M. Garcia. 1999. Aquatic ecosystem pollution of the Ayuquila River, Sierra de Manantlán Biosphere Reserve, Mexico. In *Aquatic Ecosystems of Mexico: Status and scope,* eds. M. Munawar, S. Lawrence, I. F. Munawar, and D. Malley. Backhuys Publishers, Leiden, The Netherlands.

Martius, C. 1997. The termites. In *The Central Amazon floodplain. Ecology of a pulsing system,* ed. W. J. Junk, 362–71. *Ecological Studies* 126. Berlin, Germany: Springer.

Marumoto, T., J. P. E. Anderson, and K. H. Domsch. 1982a. Decomposition of ^{14}C and ^{15}N-labelled microbial cells in soil. *Soil Biology and Biochemistry* 14: 461–67.

———. 1982b. Mineralization of nutrients from soil microbial biomass. *Soil Biology and Biochemistry* 14: 469–75.

Mathieson, S., A. Cattrijsse, M. J. Costa, P. Drake, M. Elliott, J. Gardner, and J. Marchand. 2000. Fish assemblages of European tidal marshes: A comparison based on species, families and functional guilds. *Marine Ecology—Progress Series* 204: 225–42.

Mattoon, W. R. 1916. Water requirements and growth of young cypress. *Society of American Foresters Proceedings* 11: 192–97.

Maurer, D. A., and J. B. Zedler. 2002. Differential invasion of a wetland grass explained by tests of nutrients and light availability on establishment and vegetative growth. *Oecologia* 131: 279–88.

May, R. M. 1994. Conceptual aspects of the quantification of the extent of biological diversity. *Philosophical Transactions of the Royal Society, London* 345B: 13–20.

Mazerolle, M. J. 2001. Amphibian activity, movement patterns, and body size in fragmented peat bogs. *Journal of Herpetology* 35: 13–20.

Mbaiwa, J. E. 2003. The socio-economic and environmental impacts of tourism development on the Okavango Delta, north-western Botswana. *Journal of Arid Environments* 54: 447–67.

McAllister, L. S., B. E. Peniston, S. G. Leibowitz, B. Abbruzzese, and J. B. Hyman. 2000. A synoptic assessment for prioritizing wetland restoration efforts to optimize flood attenuation. *Wetlands* 20: 70–83.

McCall, T. C., T. P. Hodgman, D. R. Diefenbach, and R. B. Owen. 1994. Beaver populations and their relation to wetland habitat and breeding waterfowl in Maine. *Wetlands* 16: 163–72.

McCleery, K. 1999. When is a landscape natural? *Forest Landowner* 58: 28–31.

McCollum, S. A., and J. D. Leimberger. 1997. Predator-induced morphological changes in an amphibian: Predation by dragonflies affects tadpole color, shape, and growth rate. *Oecologia* 109: 615–21.

McCollum, S. A., and J. Van Buskirk. 1996. Costs and benefits of a predator-induced polyphenism in the gray treefrog *Hyla chrysoscelis. Evolution* 50: 583–93.

McComb, A. J., and S. Qiu. 1998. The effects of drying and reflooding on nutrient release from wetland sediments. In *Wetlands in a dry land: Understanding for management,* ed. W. D. Williams, 147–59. Canberra, Australia: Environment Australia.

McCraith, B. J., L. R. Gardner, D. S. Wethey, and W. S. Moore. 2003. The effect of fiddler crab burrowing on sediment mixing and radionuclide profiles along a topographic gradient in a southeastern salt marsh. *Journal of Marine Research* 61: 359–90.

McDowall, R. M. 1981. The relationships of Australian freshwater fishes. In *Ecological biogeography of Australia,* ed. A. Keast, 1253–73. The Hague, The Netherlands: W. Junk Publisher.

McIlhenny, E. A. 1935. *The alligator's life history.* Boston: Christopher Publishing House.

McIntosh, R. P. 1980. The background and some current problems of theoretical ecology. *Synthese* 43: 195–255.

McKee, K. L. 1996. Growth and physiological responses of neotropical mangrove seedlings to root zone hypoxia. *Tree Physiology* 16: 883–89.

McKee, K. L., I. A. Mendelssohn, and M. W. Hester. 1988. Reexamination of pore water sulfide concentrations and redox potentials near the aerial roots of *Rhizophora mangle* and *Avicennia germinans. American Journal of Botany* 75: 1352–59.

McKee, K. L., I. A. Mendelssohn, and M. Materne. 2004. Acute salt marsh dieback in the Mississippi River deltaic plain: A drought-induced phenomenon? *Global Ecology and Biogeography* 13: 65–73.

McKee, K. L., and W. H. Patrick, Jr. 1988. The relationship of smooth cordgrass *(Spartina alterniflora)* to tidal datums: A review. *Estuaries* 11: 143–51.

McKinley, K. R., and R. G. Wetzel. 1979. Photolithotrophy, photoheterotrophy, and chemoheterotrophy: Patterns of resource utilization on an annual and a diurnal basis within a pelagic microbial community. *Microbial Ecology* 5: 1–15.

McMahon, T. A., and B. L. Finlayson. 2003. Droughts and anti-droughts: The low flow hydrology of Australian rivers. *Freshwater Biology* 48: 1147–60.

Medland, V. L., and B. E. Taylor 2001. The strategies of emergence from diapause for cyclopoid copepods in a temporary pond. *Archiv für Hydrobiologie* 150: 329–49.

Meffe, G. K, and C. R. Carroll. 1997. *Principles of conservation biology,* 2d ed. Sunderland, MA: Sinauer Associates Inc.

Megonigal, J. P., W. H. Conner, S. Kroeger, and R. R. Sharitz. 1997. Aboveground production in southeastern floodplain forests: A test of the subsidy-stress hypothesis. *Ecology* 78: 370–84.

Melville, A. J., and R. M. Connelly. 2003. Spatial analysis of stable isotope data to determine primary sources of nutrition for fish. *Oecologia* 136: 499–507.

Mendelssohn, I. A., K. L. McKee, and W. H. Patrick, Jr. 1981. Oxygen deficiency in *Spartina alterniflora* roots: Metabolic adaptation to anoxia. *Science* 214: 439–41.

Mendelssohn, I. A., and J. T. Morris. 2000. Eco-physiological controls on the productivity of *Spartina alterniflora* Loisel. In *Concepts and controversies in tidal marsh ecology,* eds. M. P. Weinstein and D. A. Kreeger, 59–80. Dordrecht, The Netherlands: Kluwer Academic Publishers.

Mendelssohn, I. A., and M. T. Postek. 1982. Elemental analysis of deposits on the roots of *Spartina alterniflora* Loisel. *American Journal of Botany* 69: 904–12.

Menges, E. S., and D. M. Waller. 1983. Plant strategies in relation to elevation and light in floodplain herbs. *The American Naturalist* 122: 454–73.

Mensforth, L. J., and G. R. Walker. 1996. Root dynamics of *Melaleuca halmaturorum* in response to fluctuating saline groundwater. *Plant and Soil* 184: 75–84.

Mensing, D. M., S. M. Galatowitsch, and J. R. Tester. 1998. Anthropogenic effects on the biodiversity of riparian wetlands of a northern temperate landscape. *Journal of Environmental Management* 53: 349–77.

Menzel, M. A., T. C. Carter, J. M. Menzel, W. M. Ford, and B. R. Chapman. 2002. Effects of group selection silviculture on the spatial activity patterns of bats. *Forest Ecology and Management* 162: 209–18.

Mercier, F., and R. McNeil. 1994. Seasonal variations in intertidal density of invertebrate prey in a tropical lagoon and effects of shorebird predation. *Canadian Journal of Zoology* 72: 1755–63.

Metts, B. S., J. D. Lanham, and K. R. Russell. 2001. Evaluation of herpetofaunal communities on upland streams and beaver-impounded streams in the upper Piedmont of South Carolina. *American Midland Naturalist* 145: 54–65.

Michener, W. K., E. R. Blood, K. L. Bildstein, M. M. Brinson, and L. R. Gardner. 1997. Climate change, hurricanes and tropical storms, and rising sea level in coastal wetlands. *Ecological Applications* 7: 770–801.

Micsinai, A., A. K. Borsodi, V. Csengeri, A. Horvath, O. Oravecz, M. Nikolausz, M. N. Reskone, and K. Marialigeti. 2003. Rhizome-associated bacterial communities of healthy and declining reed stands in Lake Velencei, Hungary. *Hydrobiologia* 506: 707–13.

Middleton, B. 1999. *Wetland restoration, flood pulsing, and disturbance dynamics.* New York: John Wiley & Sons Inc.

Mihuc, T., and D. Toetz. 1994. Determination of diets of alpine insects using stable isotopes and gut analysis. *American Midland Naturalist* 131: 146–55.

Mihuc, T. B. 1997. The functional trophic role of lotic primary consumers: Generalist versus specialist strategies. *Freshwater Biology* 37: 455–62.

Milton, D. A., and A. H. Arthington. 1983. Reproduction and growth of *Craterocephalus marjoriae* and *C. stercusmuscarum* (Pisces:Atherinidae) in south-eastern Queensland, Australia. *Freshwater Biology* 13: 589–97.

———. 1984. Reproductive strategy and growth of the Crimson-spotted rainbowfish, *Melanotaenia splendida fluviatilis* (Castelnau) (Pisces: Melanotaeniidae) in south-eastern Queensland. *Australian Journal of Marine and Freshwater Research* 35: 75–83.

———. 1985. Reproductive strategy and growth of the Australian smelt, *Retropinna semoni* (Weber) (Pisces: Retropinnidae), and the olive perchlet, *Ambassis nigripinnis* (De Vis) (Pisces: Ambassidae), in Brisbane, south-eastern Queensland. *Australian Journal of Marine and Freshwater Research* 36: 329–41.

Minshall, G. W. 1988. Stream ecosystem theory: A global perspective. *Journal of the North American Benthololological Society* 7: 263–88.

Minshall, G. W., E. Hitchcock, and J. R. Barnes. 1991. Decomposition of rainbow trout *(Oncorhynchus mykiss)* carcasses in a forest stream ecosystem inhabited only by nonanadromous fish populations. *Canadian Journal of Fisheries and Aquatic Sciences* 48: 191–95.

Mitchell, A. M., and D. S. Baldwin. 1999. The effects of sediment desiccation on the potential for nitrification, denitrification, and methanogenesis in an Australian reservoir. *Hydrobiologia* 392: 3–11.

Mitchell, M. S., K. S. Karriker, E. J. Jones, and R. A. Lancia. 1995. Small mammal communities associated with pine plantation management of pocosins. *Journal of Wildlife Management* 59: 875–81.

Mitsch, W. J., J. W. Day, Jr., K. W. Gilliam, P. M. Groffman, D. L. Hey, G. W. Randall, and N. Wang. 2001. Reducing nitrogen loading to the Gulf of Mexico from the Mississippi River Basin: Strategies to counter a persistent ecological problem. *BioScience* 51: 373–88.

Mitsch, W. J., C. L. Dorge, and J. R. Wiemhoff. 1979. Ecosystem dynamics and a phosphorus budget of an alluvial cypress swamp in southern Illinois. *Ecology* 60: 1116–24.

Mitsch, W. J., and K. C. Ewel. 1979. Comparative biomass and growth of cypress in Florida wetlands. *American Midland Naturalist* 101: 417–26.

Mitsch, W. J. and J. G. Gosselink. 1993. *Wetlands, 2nd ed.* New York: Van Nostrand Reinhold.

Mitsch, W. J., and J. G. Gosselink. 2000. *Wetlands, 3d ed.* New York: John Wiley & Sons.

Mitsch, W. J., and W. G. Rust. 1984. Tree growth responses to flooding in a bottomland forest in northeastern Illinois. *Forest Science* 30: 499–510.

Mitsch, W. J., J. R. Taylor, and K. B. Benson. 1991. Estimating primary productivity of forested wetland communities in different hydrologic landscapes. *Landscape Ecology* 5: 75–92.

Mitsch, W. J., and R. F. Wilson. 1996. Improving the success of wetland creation and restoration with know-how, time and self-design. *Ecological Applications* 6: 77–83.

Mitsch, W. J., X. Wu, R. W. Nairn, P. E. Weihe, N. Wang, R. Deal, and C. E. Boucher. 1998. Creating and restoring wetlands. *BioScience* 48: 1019–30.

Moeller, R. G., J. M Burkholder, and R. G. Wetzel. 1988. Significance of sedimentary phosphorus to a submersed freshwater macrophyte (*Najas flexilis*) and its algal epiphytes. *Aquatic Botany* 32: 261–81.

Monk, L. S., K. V. Fagerstedt, and R.M.M. Crawford. 1987. Superoxide dismutase as an anaerobic polypeptide. *Plant Physiology* 85: 1016–1020.

Montague, C. L. 1980. A natural history of temperate western Atlantic fiddler crabs (genus *Uca*) with reference to their impact on the salt marsh. *Contributions Marine Science* 23: 25–55.

———. 1982. The influence of fiddler crab burrows and burrowing on metabolic processes in salt marsh sediments. In Estuarine comparisons, ed. V. S. Kennedy, 283–301. New York: Academic Press.

Monteith, J. L. 1965. Evaporation and environment. In *Proceedings of the 19th Symposium of the Society for Experimental Biology,* 205–33. New York: Cambridge University Press.

Moon, D. C., and P. Stiling. 2002. The influence of species identity and herbivore feeding mode on top-down and bottom-up effects in a salt marsh system. *Oecologia* 133: 243–53.

Moore, D. R. J., and P. A. Keddy. 1989. The relationship between species richness and standing crop in wetlands: The importance of scale. *Vegetatio* 79: 99–106.

Moore, D. R. J., P. A. Keddy, C. L. Gaudet, and I. C. Wisheu. 1989. Conservation of wetlands: Do infertile wetlands deserve a higher priority? *Biological Conservation* 47: 203–17.

Moore, P. D. 1990. Soils and ecology: Temperate wetlands. In *Wetlands: A threatened landscape,* ed. M. Williams, 95–114. Oxford, U.K.: Basil Blackwell.

Moore, P. D., and D. J. Bellamy. 1974. *Peatlands.* New York: Springer-Verlag.

Moore, T. R., and M. Dalva. 1997. Methane and carbon dioxide exchange potentials of peat soils in aerobic and anaerobic laboratory incubations. *Soil Biology and Biochemistry* 29: 1157–64.

Moore, T. R., and R. Knowles. 1989. The influence of water table levels on methane and carbon doxide emissions from peatland soils. *Canadian Journal of Soil Science* 69: 33–38.

Moore, T. R., N. T. Roulet, and J. M. Waddington. 1998. Uncertainty in predicting the effect of climate change on the carbon cycling of Canadian peatlands. *Climate Change* 40: 229–45.

Moorhead, K. K., and I. M. Rossell. 1998. Southern mountain fens. In *Southern forested wetlands. Ecology and management,* eds. M. G. Messina and W. H. Conner. Boca Raton, FL: Lewis Publishers.

Moorman, C. E., and D. C. Guynn. 2001. Effects of group-selection size on breeding bird habitat use in a bottomland forest. *Ecological Applications* 11: 1680–91.

Moorman, C. E., D. C. Guynn, and J. C. Kilgo. 2002. Hooded Warbler nesting success adjacent to group-selection and clearcut edges in a southeastern bottomland forest. *Condor* 104: 366–77.

Moriarty, D. J. W., and P. I. Boon. 1986. Interactions of seagrasses with sediment and water. In *Biology of seagrasses,* eds. A. W. D. Larkum, A. J. McComb, and S. A. Shepherd, 500–535. Amsterdam, The Netherlands: Elsevier.

Morin, P. J. 1981. Predatory salamanders reverse the outcome of competition among three species of anuran tadpoles. *Science* 212: 1284–86.

———. 1983a. Predation, competition, and the composition of larval anuran guilds. *Ecological Monographs* 53: 119–38.

———. 1983b. Competitive and predatory interactions in natural and experimental populations of *Notopthalmus viridescens dorsalis* and *Ambystoma tigrinum. Copeia* 1983: 628–39.

———. 1999. *Community ecology.* Oxford, U.K.: Blackwell Scientific.

Morin, P. J., H. M. Wilbur, and R. N. Harris. 1983. Salamander predations and the structure of experimental communities: Responses of *Notophthalmus* and microcrustacea. *Ecology* 64: 1420–37.

Morris, C. E., M. Bardin, O. Berge, P. Frey-Klett, N. Fromlin, H. Girardin, M. H. Guinebretiere, P. Lebaron, J. M. Thiery, and M. Troussellier. 2002. Microbial biodiversity: Approaches to experimental design and hypothesis testing in primary scientific literature from 1975 to 1999. *Microbiology and Molecular Biology Reviews* 66: 592–616.

Morris, J. T. 1991. Effects of nitrogen loading on wetland ecosystems with particular reference to atmospheric deposition. *Annual Review of Ecology and Systematics* 22: 257–79.

Morris, J. T., P. V. Sundareshwar, C. T. Nietch, B. Kjerfve, and D. R. Cahoon. 2002. Responses of coastal wetlands to rising sea level. *Ecology* 83: 2869–77.

Morris, K., P. C. Bailey, P. I. Boon, and I. Hughes, L. 2003a. Alternative stable states in the aquatic vegetation of shallow urban lakes. II. Catastrophic loss of aquatic plants consequent to nutrient enrichment. *Marine and Freshwater Research* 54: 201–15.

———. 2003b. Alternative stable states in the aquatic vegetation of shallow urban lakes. I. *Marine and Freshwater Research* 54: 185–200.

Morris, P. A., N. M. Hill, E. G. Reekie, and H. L. Hewlin. 2002. Lakeshore diversity and rarity relationships along interacting disturbance gradients: Catchment area, wave action and depth. *Biological Conservation* 106: 79–90.

Mortimer, C. H. 1941. The exchange of dissolved substances between mud and water in lakes. I. *Journal of Ecology* 29: 280–93.

Moss, B., and R. T. Leah. 1982. Changes in the ecosystem of a guanotrophic and brackish shallow lake in eastern England: Potential problems in its restoration. *Internationale Revue Gesampten Hydrobiologie* 67: 625–59.

Motzkin, G., W. A. Patterson III, and N. E. R. Drake. 1993. Fire history and vegetation dynamics of a *Chamaecyparis thyoides* wetland on Cape Cod, Massachusetts. *Journal of Ecology* 81: 391–402.

Moyle, P. B., and B. Herbold. 1987. Life-history patterns and community structure in stream fishes of western North America: Comparisons with eastern North America and Europe.

In *Community and evolutionary ecology of North American stream fishes: Comparisons with eastern North America and Europe,* eds. W. J. Matthews and D. C. Heins, 25–32. Norman, OK: University of Oklahoma Press.

Mulder, C. P. H., and R. W. Ruess. 1998. Effects of herbivory on arrowgrass: Interactions between geese, neighboring plants, and abiotic factors. *Ecological Monographs* 68: 275–93.

Mulhouse, J. M., L. E. Burbage, and R. R. Sharitz. 2005. Seed bank–vegetation relationships in herbaceous Carolina bays: Responses to climatic variability. *Wetlands* 25: 738–747.

Muller, K. L., G. G. Ganf, and P. I. Boon. 1994. Methane flux from beds of *Baumea arthrophylla* (Nees) Boeckler and *Triglochin procerum* R.Br. at Bool Lagoon, South Australia. *Australian Journal of Marine and Freshwater Research* 45: 1543–53.

Muller-Schwarze, D., and L. Sun. 2003. *The beaver: Natural history of a wetlands engineer.* Ithaca, NY: Cornell University Press.

Mullin, S. J., and R. J. Cooper. 2002. Barking up the wrong tree: Climbing performance of rat snakes and its implications for depredation of avian nests. *Canadian Journal of Zoology* 80: 591–95.

Mullin, S. J., W. H. N. Gutzke, G. D. Zenitsky, and R. J. Cooper. 2000. Home ranges of rat snakes (Colubridae: *Elaphe*) in different habitats. *Herpetological Review* 31: 20–22.

Murkin, H. R, and B. D. J. Batt. 1987. The interactions of vertebrates and invertebrates in peatlands and marshes. In *Aquatic insects of peatlands and marshes of Canada,* eds. D. M. Rosenberg and H. V. Danks, *Memoires of the Entomological Society of Canada* 140: 15–30.

Murkin, H. R., and P. J. Caldwell. 2000. Avian use of prairie wetlands. In *Prairie wetland ecology,* eds. H. R. Murkin, A. G. van der Valk, and W. R. Clark, 249–286. Ames, IA: Iowa State University Press.

Murkin, H. R., R. M. Kaminski, and R. D. Titman. 1982. Responses by dabbling ducks and aquatic invertebrates to an experimentally manipulated cattail marsh. *Canadian Journal of Zoology* 60: 2324–32.

Murkin, E. J., H. R. Murkin, and R. D. Titman. 1992. Nektonic invertebrate abundance and distribution at the emergent vegetation-open water interface in the Delta Marsh, Manitoba, Canada. *Wetlands* 12: 45–52.

Murkin, H. R., and L. C. M. Ross. 1999. Northern prairie marshes (Delta Marsh, Manitoba): I. Macroinvertebrate response to a simulated wet/dry cycle. In *Invertebrates in freshwater wetlands of North America: Ecology and management,* eds. D. P. Batzer, R. D. Rader, and S. A. Wissinger, 543–570. New York: John Wiley and Sons.

Murkin, H. R., A. G. van der Valk, and W. R. Clark, eds. 2000. *Prairie wetland ecology.* Ames, IA: Iowa State University Press.

Murphy, T., A. Lawson, C. Nalewajko, H. Murkin, L. Ross, K. Oguma, and T. MacIntyre. 2000. Algal toxins—Initiators of avian botulism? *Environmental Toxicology* 15: 558–67.

Muusze, B., J. Marcon, G. van der Thillart, and V. Almeida-Val. 1998. Hypoxia tolerance of Amazon fish: Respirometry and energy metabolism of the cichlid *Astronotus ocellatus*. *Comparative Biochemistry and Physiology A: Molecular and Integrative Physiology* 120: 151–56.

Naiman, R. J., and H. Decamps. 1990. *The ecology and management of aquatic-terrestrial ecotones.* Carnforth Hall, U.K.: Parthenon.

Naiman, R. J., C. A. Johnston, and J. C. Kelley 1988. Alteration of North American streams by beaver. *BioScience* 38: 753–62.

Naiman, R. J., G. Pinay, C. A. Johnston, and J. Pastor. 1994. Beaver influences on the long-term biogeochemical characteristics of boreal forest drainage networks. *Ecology* 75: 905–21.

National Audubon Society. 1993. *Saving wetlands: A citizens guide for action in the Mid Atlantic region.* Camp Hill, PA: National Audobon Society, 130 pp.

Navid, D. 1989. The international law of migratory species: The Ramsar Convention. *Natural Resources Journal* 29: 1001–16.

Neckles, H. A., H. R. Murkin, and J. A. Cooper. 1990. Influences of seasonal flooding on macroinvertebrate abundance in wetland habitats. *Freshwater Biology* 23: 311–22.

Neckles, H. A., and C. Neill. 1994. Hydrological control of litter decomposition in seasonally flooded prairie marshes. *Hydrobiologia* 286: 155–65.

Neely, R. K., and R. G. Wetzel. 1995. Simultaneous use of ^{14}C and ^{3}H to determine autotrophic production and bacterial protein production in periphyton. *Microbial Ecology* 30: 227–37.

Neiff, J. J. 1990. Ideas for an ecological interpretation of the Paraná. *Interciencia* 15: 424–41.

Neiff, J. J., and A. P. De Neiff. 1990. Litter fall, leaf decomposition and litter colonization of *Tessaria-integrifolia* Compositae in the Parana River floodplain. *Hydrobiologia* 203: 45–52.

Neill, C., and J. C. Cornwell 1992. Stable carbon, nitrogen, and sulfur isotopes in a prairie marsh food web. *Wetlands* 12: 217–24.

Neubauer, S. C., D. Emerson, and J. P. Megonigal. 2002. Life at the energetic edge: Kenetics of circumneutral iron oxidation by lithotrophic iron-oxidising bacteria isolated from the wetland-plant rhizosphere. *Applied and Environmental Microbiology* 68: 3988–95.

Newell, S. Y. 1993. Decomposition of shoots of a salt-marsh grass. *Advances in Microbial Ecology* 13: 301–26.

———. 1996. Established and potential impacts of eukaryotic mycelial decomposers in marine/terrestrial ecotones. *Journal of Experimental Marine Biology and Ecology* 200: 187–206.

———. 2003. Fungal content and activities in standing-decaying leaf blades of plants of the Georgia Coastal Ecosystems research area. *Aquatic Microbial Ecology* 32: 95–103.

Newell, S. Y., and F. Barlöcher. 1993. Removal of fungal and total organic-matter from decaying cordgrass leaves by shredder snails. *Journal of Experimental Marine Biology and Ecology* 171: 39–49.

Newman, B. D., A. R. Campbell, and B. P. Wilcox. 1998. Lateral subsurface flow pathways in a semiarid ponderosa pine hillslope. *Water Resources Research* 34: 3485–96.

Newman, M. C., and J. F. Schalles. 1990. The water chemistry of Carolina bays: A regional study. *Archive für Hydrobiologie* 118: 147–68.

Newman, R. M. 1991. Herbivory and detritivory on freshwater macrophytes by invertebtrates: A review. *Journal of the North American Benthological Society* 10: 89–114.

Newman, R. M., Z. Hanscom III, and W. C. Kerfoot. 1992. The watercress glucosinolate-myrosinase system: A feeding deterrent to caddisflies, snails, and amphipods. *Oecologia* 92: 1–7.

Newman, R. M., W. C. Kerfoot, and Z. Hanscom III. 1996a. Watercress allelochemical defends high-nitrogen foliage against consumption: Effects on freshwater invertebrate herbivores. *Ecology* 77: 2312–23.

Newman, S., J. B. Grace, and J. W. Koebel. 1996b. Effects of nutrients and hydroperiod on *Typha, Cladium,* and *Eleocharis:* Implications for Everglades restoration. *Ecological Applications* 6: 774–83.

Nienhuis, P. H., and R. S. E. W. Leuven. 2001. River restoration and flood protection: Controversy or synergism? *Hydrobiologia* 444: 85–99.

Niering, W. A. 1989. Wetland vegetation development. In *Wetlands ecology and conservation: Emphasis in Pennsylvania*, eds. S. K. Majumdar, R. P. Brooks, F. J. Brenner, and R. W. Tiner, 103–13. Easton, PA: Pennsylvania Academy of Science.

Nijssen, B., G. M. O'Donnell, A. F . Hamlet , and D. P. Lettenmaier. 2001. Hydrologic sensitivity of global rivers to climate change. *Climatic Change* 50: 143–75.

Nixon, S. W. 1995. Coastal marine eutrophication: A definition, social causes, and future concerns. *Ophelia* 41: 199–219.

———. 1997. Prehistoric nutrient inputs and productivity in Narragansett Bay. *Estuaries* 20: 253–61.

Noe, G. B., D. L. Childers, and R. D. Jones. 2001. Phosphorus biogeochemistry and the impact of phosphorus enrichment: Why is the Everglades so unique? *Ecosystems* 4: 603–24.

Nordhaus, I. 2004. Feeding ecology of the semi-terrestrial crab Ucides cordatus coradtus (Decapoda: Brachyura) in a mangrove forest in northern Brazil. Ph.D. diss., University of Bremen, Center for Tropical Marine Ecology, Germany.

Northcote, T. G. 1997. Why sea-run? An exploration into the migratory residency spectrum of coastal cutthroat trout. In *Sea-run cutthroat trout: Biology, management, and future conservation*, eds. D. Hall, P. A. Bisson, and R. E. Gresswell, 20–26. Corvallis, OR: American Fisheries Society.

Novak, J. M., K. F. Gaines, J. C. Cumbee, G. L. Mills, A. Rodriguez-Navarro, and C. S. Romanek. In press. Clapper rails as indicator species of estuarine marsh health. *Studies in Avian Biology*.

Novitzki, R. P., R. D. Smith, and J. D. Fretwell. 1995. Wetland functions, values, and assessment. In *National water summary on wetland resources*. U.S. Geological Survey Water-Supply Paper 2425. http://water.usgs.gov/nwsum/WSP2425/index.html.

NRC (National Research Council). 1995. *Wetlands: Characteristics and boundaries*. Washington, D.C.: National Academy Press.

———. 2001. *Compensating for wetland losses under the Clean Water Act*. Washington, D.C.: National Academy Press.

———. 2002. *Riparian areas: Functions and strategies for management*. Washington, D.C.: National Academy Press.

NRCS. 2002. Field indicators of hydric soils in the United States, Version 5.0, eds. G. W. Hurt, P. M. Whited, and R. F. Pringle. USDA, NRCS in cooperation with the National Technical Committee for Hydric Soils, Fort Worth, TX.

Nunes da Cunha, C., and W. J. Junk. 1999. Composição florística de capões e cordilleiras: Localização das espécies lenhosas quanto ao gradiente de inundação no Pantanal de Poconé, MT-Brasil. In *Anais do II Simpósio sobre Recursos Naturais e Socio-econômicos do Pantanal*, 17–28. Manejo e Conservação. 1996, EMBRAPA, Corumbá-MS, Brazil.

———. 2004. Year-to-year changes in water level drive the invasion of Vochysia divergens in Pantanal grasslands. *Applied Vegetation Science* 7: 103–10.

Nuttle, W. K. 1997. Measurement of wetland hydroperiod using harmonic analysis. *Wetlands* 17: 82–89.

O'Brien, E., and J. B. Zedler. In review. Accelerating the restoration of vegetation in a southern California salt marsh. *Wetlands Ecology and Management*.

O'Donnell, A. G., M. Goodfellow, and D. L. Hawksworth. 1994. Theoretical and practical aspects of the quantification of biodiversity among microrganisms. *Philosophical Transactions of the Royal Society, London* 345B: 65–73.

Odum, E. P. 1969. The strategy of ecosystem development. *Science* 164: 262–70.

———. 1971. *Fundamentals of ecology,* 3d ed. Philadelphia: W. B. Saunders.

———. 1981. Foreword. In *Wetlands of bottomland hardwood forests,* eds. J. R. Clark and J. Benforado, 8–10. Amsterdam, The Netherlands: Elsevier.

Odum, W. E. 1988. Comparative ecology of tidal freshwater and salt marshes. *Annual Review of Ecology and Systematics* 19: 147–76.

Odum, W. E., and E. J. Heald. 1975. The detritus based food web of an estuarine mangrove community. In *Estuarine research,* ed. L. E. Cronin, 265–86. New York: Academic Press.

Odum, W. E., T. J. Smith III, J. K. Hoover, and C. C. McIvor. 1984. *The ecology of tidal freshwater marshes of the United States East Coast: A community profile.* FWS/OBS-87/17. Washington, D.C.: U.S. Fish and Wildlife Service, 177 pp.

Oechel, W. C., S. J. Hastings, G. Vouritis, M. Jenkins, G. Riechers, and N. Grulke. 1993. Recent change of arctic tundra ecosystems from a net carbon-dioxide sink to a source. *Nature* 361: 520–23.

Oechel, W. C., G. L. Vourlitis, S. J. Hastings, R. C. Zulueta, L. Hinzman, and D. Kane. 2000. Acclimation of ecosystem CO_2 exchange in the Alaskan Arctic in response to decadal climate warming. *Nature* 406: 978–81.

Oertli, B. 1993. Leaf-litter processing and energy flow through macroinvertebrates in a woodland pond. *Oecologia* 96: 466–77.

Ogden, J. C. 1978. Recent population trends of colonial wading birds on the Atlantic and Gulf Coast Plains. In *Wading birds,* eds. A. Sprunt, J. C. Ogden, and S. Winckler, 137–53. National Audubon Society, New York.

———. 1994. A comparison of wading bird nesting colony dynamics as an indication of ecosystem conditions in the southern Everglades. In *Everglades, the ecosystem and its restoration,* eds. S. M. Davis and J. C. Ogden, 533–570. Delray, FL: St. Lucie Press.

Ohlendorf, H. M., R. L. Hothem, and D. Welsh. 1989. Nest success, cause-specific nest failure, and hatchability of aquatic birds at selenium-contaminated Kesterson Reservoir and a reference site. *Condor* 91: 787–96.

Okamura, B., and J. R. Freeland 2002. Gene flow and the evolutionary ecology of passively dispersing aquatic invertebrates. In *Dispersal ecology,* eds. J. M. Bullock, R. E. Kenward, and R. S. Hails, 194–216. Oxford, UK: Blackwell Science.

Olff, H., J. De Leeuw, J. P. Bakker, R. J. Platerink, H. J. Van Wijnen, and W. De Munck. 1997. Vegetation succession and herbivory in a salt marsh: Changes induced by sea level rise and silt deposition along an elevational gradient. *Journal of Ecology* 85: 799–814.

Olila, O. G., and K. R. Reddy. 1997. Influence of redox potential on phosphate-uptake by sediments in two sub-tropical eutrophic lakes. *Hydrobiologia* 345: 45–57.

Oliver, J. D., and T. Legovic. 1988. Okefenokee marshland before, during and after nutrient enrichment by a bird rookery. *Ecological Modelling* 43: 195–223.

Olmstead, K. L., R. F. Denno, T. C. Morton, and J. T. Romeo. 1997. Influence of *Prokelisia* planthoppers on amino acid composition and growth of *Spartina alterniflora. Journal of Chemical Ecology* 23: 303–21.

Onuf, C. P., J. M. Teal, and I. Valiela. 1977. Interactions of nutrients, plant growth and herbivory in a mangrove ecosystem. *Ecology* 58: 514–26.

Oquist, M., and I. Sundh. 1998. Effects of a transient oxic period on mineralization of organic matter to CH_4 and CO_2 in anoxic peat incubations. *Geomicrobiology Journal* 15: 325–33.

Orchard, V. A., and F. J. Cook. 1983. Relationship between soil respiration and soil moisture. *Soil Biology and Biochemistry* 15: 447–53.

Orme, A. R. 1990. Wetland morphology, hydrodynamics and sedimentation. In *Wetlands: A threatened landscape,* ed. M. Williams, 42–94. Oxford, U.K.: Basil Blackwell.

Ormerod, S. J., and S. J. Tyler. 1993. Birds as indicators of changes in water quality. In *Birds as monitors of environmental change,* eds. R. W. Furness and J. J. D. Greenwood, 179–216. London: Chapman and Hall.

Otsuki, A., and R. G. Wetzel. 1972. Coprecipitation of phosphate with carbonates in a marl lake. *Limnology and Oceanography* 17: 763–67.

Otte, M. L., and J. T. Morris. 1994. Dimethylsulphoniopropionate(DMSP) in *Spartina alterniflora* Loisel. *Aquatic Botany* 48: 239–59.

Otte, L. J. 1981. *Origin, development and maintenance of pocosin wetlands of North Carolina.* North Carolina Department of Natural Resources and Community Development. Unpublished report to the North Carolina Natural Heritage Program, Raleigh, NC.

Otto, C. 1983. Behavioural and physiological adaptations to a variable habitat in two species of case-making caddisfly larvae using different food. *Oikos* 41: 188–94.

Otto, C., and B. S. Svensson. 1980. The significance of case material selection for the survival of caddis larvae. *Journal of Animal Ecology* 49: 855–65.

Overpeck, J. T., P. J. Bartlein, and T. Webb III. 1991. Potential magnitude of future vegetation change in eastern North America: Comparisons with the past. *Science* 254: 692–95.

Paetzold, A., C. Schubert, and K. Tockner. 2005. Effects of riparian arthropod predation on aquatic insect emergence. *Journal of the North American Benthological Society* 24: 395–402.

Paijmans, K., R. W. Galloway, D. P. Faith, P. M. Fleming, H. A. Haantjens, P. C. Heyligers, J. D. Kalma, and E. Loffler. 1985. *Aspects of Australian wetlands.* CSIRO Australia Division of Water and Land Resources Technical Paper 44: 1–71.

Palik, B., D. P. Batzer, R. Buech, D. Nichols, K. Cease, L. Egeland, and E. W. Streblow. 2001. Seasonal pond characteristics across a chronosequence of adjacent forest ages in northern Minnesota, USA. *Wetlands* 2001: 532–42.

Palik, B., R. Buech, and L. Egeland. 2003. Using an ecological land hierarchy to predict seasonal-wetland abundance in upland forests. *Ecological Applications* 13: 1153–63.

Palmer, M. A., A. P. Covich, B. J. Findlay, J. Gilbert, K. D. Hyde, R. K. Johnson, T. Kairesalo, et al. 1997. Biodiversity and ecosystem processes in freshwater sediments. *Ambio* 26: 571–77.

Palmer, M. L., and F. J. Mazzotti. 2004. Structure of Everglades alligator holes. *Wetlands* 24: 115–22.

Parker, T. P. 1997. The scale of successional models and restoration objectives. *Restoration Ecology* 5: 301–06.

Parmenter, R. R., and V. A. Lamarra. 1991. Nutrient cycling in a freshwater marsh: The decomposition of fish and waterfowl carrion. *Limnology and Oceanography* 36: 976–87.

Parsons, L., and J. B. Zedler. 1997. Factors affecting reestablishment of an endangered annual plant at a California salt marsh. *Ecological Applications* 7: 253–67.

Partington, J. R. 1947. *Everyday chemistry*. London: MacMillan and Co.

Paton, P. W. C. 1994. The effect of edge on avian nest success: How strong is the evidence? *Conservation Biology* 8: 17–26.

Paton, P. W., and W. B. Crouch. 2002. Using the phenology of pond-breeding amphibians to develop conservation practices. *Conservation Biology* 16: 194–204.

Patrick, R. 1966. The Catherwood Foundation Peruvian-Amazon Expedition I. Limnological observations and discussion of results. *Monographs—The Academy of Natural Sciences of Philadelphia* 14: 5–28.

Patrick, W. H., Jr, and A. Jugsujinda. 1992. Sequential reduction and oxidation of inorganic nitrogen, manganese, and iron in flooded soil. *Soil Science Society of America Journal* 56: 1071–73.

Paul, B. J., and H. C. Duthie. 1988. Nutrient cycling in the epilithon of running waters. *Canadian Journal of Botany* 67: 2302–9.

Peacor, S. D., and E. E. Werner 1997. Trait-mediated indirect interactions in a simple aquatic community. *Ecology* 1146–56.

Pearcy, R. W., and S. L. Ustin. 1984. Effects of salinity on growth and photosynthesis of three California tidal marsh species. *Oecologia (Berlin)* 62: 68–73.

Pechmann, J. H. K., R. A. Estes, D. E. Scott, and J. W. Gibbons. 2001. Amphibian colonization and use of ponds created for trial mitigation of wetland loss. *Wetlands* 21: 93–111.

Pechmann, J. H. K., D. E. Scott, J. W. Gibbons, and R. D. Semlitsch. 1989. Influence of wetland hydroperiod on diversity and abundance of metamorphosing juvenile amphibians. *Wetlands Ecology and Management* 1: 3–11.

Pechmann, J. H. K, D. E. Scott, R. D. Semlitsch, J. P. Caldwell, L. J. Vitt, and J. W. Gibbons. 1991. Declining amphibian populations: The problem of separating human impacts from natural fluctuations. *Science* 253: 892–95.

Pedros-Alio, C., and R. Guerrero. 1994. Prokaryotology for the limnologist. In *Limnology now: A paradigm for planetary problems*, ed. R. Margalef, 37–57. Amsterdam: Elsevier.

Penfound, W. T. 1952. Southern swamps and marshes. *Botanical Review* 18: 413–46.

Penfound, W. T., and E. S. Hathaway. 1938. Plant communities in the marshlands of southeastern Louisiana. *Ecological Monographs* 8: 1–56.

Penman, H. L. 1948. Natural evaporation from open water, bare soil, and grass. *Royal Society of London Proceedings* Series A, 193: 120–45.

Pennings, S. C., and M. D. Bertness. 1999. Using latitudinal variation to examine effects of climate on coastal salt marsh pattern and process. *Current Topics in Wetland Biogeochemistry* 3: 100–111.

———. 2001. Salt marsh communities. In Marine community ecology, eds. M. D. Bertness, S. D. Gaines, and M. E. Hay. 289–316. Sunderland: Sinauer Associates Inc.

Pennings, S. C. and R. M. Callaway. 1992. Salt marsh plant zonation: The relative importance of competition and physical factors. *Ecology* 73: 681–90.

———. 1996. Impact of a parasitic plant on the structure and dynamics of salt marsh vegetation. *Ecology* 77: 1410–19.

Pennings, S. C., M. B. Grant, and M. D. Bertness. 2005. Plant zonation in low-latitude salt marshes: Disentangling the roles of flooding, salinity and competition. *Journal of Ecology* 93: 159–67.

Pennings, S. C., and C. L. Richards. 1998. Effects of wrack burial in salt-stressed habitats: *Batis maritima* in a southwest Atlantic salt marsh. *Ecography* 21: 630–38.

Pennings, S. C., E. R. Selig, L. T. Houser, and M. D. Bertness. 2003. Geographic variation in positive and negative interactions among salt marsh plants. *Ecology* 84: 1527–38.

Pennings, S. C., and B. R. Silliman. 2005. Linking biogeography and community ecology: Latitudinal variation in plant-herbivore interaction strength. *Ecology* 86: 2310–2319.

Pennings, S. C., E. L. Siska, and M. D. Bertness. 2001. Latitudinal differences in plant palatability in Atlantic coast salt marshes. *Ecology* 82: 1344–59.

Pennings, S. C., L. E. Stanton, and J. S. Brewer. 2002. Nutrient effects on the composition of salt marsh plant communities along the southern Atlantic and Gulf coasts of the United States. *Estuaries* 25: 1164–73.

Perison, D., J. Phelps, C. Pavel, and R. Kellison. 1997. The effects of timber harvest in a South Carolina blackwater bottomland. *Forest Ecology and Management* 90: 171–85.

Perry, D. A. 1994. *Forest ecosystems.* Baltimore: Johns Hopkins University Press.

Persing, D. H. 2004. Molecular microbiology: Diagnostic principles and practice. Washington, D.C.: American Society for Microbiology.

Perumalla, C. J., C. A. Peterson, and D. E. Enstone. 1990. A survey of angiosperm species to detect hypodermal Casparian bands. I. Roots with a uniseriate hypodermis and epidermis. *Botanical Journal of the Linnean Society* 103: 93–112.

Petermann, P. 1997. The birds. In *The Central Amazon floodplain. Ecology of a pulsing system,* ed. W. J. Junk, 419–54. *Ecological Studies* 126. Berlin, Germany: Springer.

Peters, V., and R. Conrad. 1995. Methanogenic and other strictly anaerobic bacteria in desert soil and other oxic soils. *Applied and Environmental Microbiology* 61: 1673–76.

Peterson, C. A., and C. J. Perumalla. 1990. A survey of angiosperm species to detect hypodermal Casparian bands. II. Roots with a multiseriate hypodermis and epidermis. *Botanical Journal of the Linnean Society* 103: 113–25.

Peterson, C. G. 1996. Response of benthic algal communities to natural physical disturbance. In *Algal ecology: Benthic algae in freshwater ecosystems,* eds. R. J. Stevenson, M. Bothwell, and R. L. Lowe, 375–402. New York: Academic Press.

Peterson, D. L., and G. L. Rolfe. 1982. Nutrient dynamics and decomposition of litterfall in floodplain and upland forests of central Illinois. *Forest Science* 28: 667–81.

Petranka, J. W., and C. A. Kennedy 1999. Pond tadpoles with generalized morphology: Is it time to reconsider their functional roles in aquatic communities? *Oecologia* 120: 621–31.

Petranka, J. W., C. A. Kennedy, and S. S. Murray. 2003. Response of amphibians to restoration of a of a southern Appalachian wetland: A long-term analysis of community dynamics. *Wetlands* 23: 1030–42.

Petrie, M., J. P. Rochon, G. Tori, R. Pederson, and T. Moorman. 2001. *The SWANCC decision: Implications for wetlands and waterfowl.* Memphis, TN: Ducks Unlimited.

Pezeshki, S. R., R. D. DeLaune, and W. H. Patrick, Jr. 1990. Flooding and saltwater intrusion: Potential effects on survival and productivity of wetland forests along the U.S. Gulf Coast. *Forest Ecology and Management* 33/34: 287–301.

Phelps, J. P., and R. A. Lancia. 1995. Effects of clearcut on the herpetofauna of a South Carolina bottomland swamp. *Brimleyana* 22: 31–45.

Pickett, S.T.A., J. Lolasa, J.J. Armesto, and S.L. Collins. 1989. The ecological concept of disturbance and its expression at various hierarchical scales. *Oikos* 54: 129–36.

Pickett, S.T.A,, and V.T. Parker. 1994. Avoiding the old pitfalls: Opportunities in a new discipline. *Restoration Ecology* 2: 75–79.

Piehler, M.F., C.A. Currin, R. Cassanova, and H.W. Paerl. 1998. Development and N-2-fixing activity of the benthic microbial community in transplanted *Spartina alterniflora* marshes in North Carolina. *Restoration Ecology* 6: 290–96.

Pip, E., and G.G.C. Robinson 1982a. A study of the seasonal dynamics of three phycoperiphytic communities using nuclear track microautoradiography. I. Inorganic carbon uptake. *Archiv für Hydrobiologie* 94: 341–71.

———. 1982b. A study of the seasonal dynamics of three phycoperiphytic communities using nuclear track microautoradiography. II. Organic carbon uptake. *Archiv für Hydrobiologie* 96: 47–64.

Pirow, R., C. Baumer, and R.J. Paul. 2001. Benefits of haemoglobin in the cladoceran crustacean *Daphnia magma*. *Journal of Experimental Biology* 204: 3425–41.

Podrabsky, J.E., J.F. Carpenter, and S.C. Hand. 2001. Survival of water stress in annual fish embryos: Dehydration avoidance and egg envelope amyloid fibers. *American Journal of Physiology—Regulatory Integrative and Comparative Physiology* 280: R123–R131.

Poff, N.L., J.D. Allan, M.B. Bain, J.R. Karr, K.L. Prestegaard, B.D. Richter, R.E. Sparks, and J.C. Stromberg. 1997. The natural flow regime: A paradigm for river conservation and restoration. *BioScience* 47: 769–84.

Poff, N.L., M.M. Brinson, and J.W. Day, Jr. 2002. *Potential impacts on inland freshwater and coastal wetland ecosystems in the United States.* Arlington, VA: Pew Center on Global Climate Change.

Poiani, K.A., and W.C. Johnson. 1991. Global warming and prairie wetlands. *BioScience* 41: 611–18.

Poiani, K.A., W.C. Johnson, G.A. Swanson, and T.C. Winter. 1996. Climate change and northern prairie wetlands: Simulations of long-term dynamics. *Limnology and Oceanography* 41: 871–81.

Pollard, P.C., I. Kioke, H. Mukai, and A.I. Robertson, eds. 1993. Tropical seagrass ecosystems: Structure and dynamics in the Indo-west Pacific. Melbourne, Australia: CSIRO.

Pomeroy, L.R., and R.G. Wiegert. 1981. The ecology of a salt marsh. New York: Springer-Verlag.

Ponnamperuma, F.N. 1972. The chemistry of submerged soils. *Advances in Agronomy* 24: 29–96.

———. 1984. Effects of flooding on soils. In *Flooding and plant growth,* ed. T.T. Kozlowski, 10–45. Orlando, FL: Academic Press.

Ponnamperuma, F.N., E.M. Tianco, and L. Teresita. 1967. Redox equilibria in flooded soils: I. The iron hydroxide systems. *Soil Science* 103: 374–82.

Portnoy, J.W. 1990. Gull contribution of phosphorus and nitrogen to a Cape Cod kettle pond. *Hydrobiologia* 202: 61–69.

Portnoy, J.W., and A.E. Giblin. 1997. Biogeochemical effects of seawater restoration to diked salt marshes. *Ecological Applications* 7: 1054–63.

Posey, M.H., and A.H. Hines. 1991. Complex predator-prey interactions within an estuarine benthic community. *Ecology* 72: 2155–69.

Post, D. M., J. P. Taylor, J. F. Kitchell, M. H. Olso, D. E. Schindler, and B. R. Herwig. 1998. The role of migratory waterfowl as nutrient vectors in a managed wetland. *Conservation Biology* 12: 910–21.

Pott, V. J., and A. Pott. 2000. Plantas aquáticas do Pantanal. EMBRAPA, Centro de Pesquisa Agropecuária do Pantanal, Corumbá, MS, Brazil.

Powell, J. A., and N. E. Zimmermann. 2004. Multiscale analysis of active seed dispersal contributes to resolving Reid's paradox. *Ecology* 85: 490–506.

Pringle, C. M. 1990. Nutrient spatial heterogeneity: Effects on community structure, physiognomy, and diversity of stream algae. *Ecology* 71: 905–20.

Prouty, W. F. 1952. Carolina bays and their origins. *Bulletin of the Geological Society of America* 63: 167–224.

Pruitt, B. A. 2001. Hydrologic and soil conditions across hydrogeomorphic settings. Ph.D. diss., University of Georgia, Athens.

Puckridge, J. T., F. Sheldon, K. F. Walker, and A. J. Boulton. 1998. Flow variability and the ecology of large rivers. *Marine and Freshwater Research* 49: 55–72.

Puckridge, J. T., K. F. Walker, and J. F. Costelloe. 2000. Hydrological persistence and the ecology of dryland rivers. *Regulated Rivers: Research and Management* 16: 385–402.

Pulliam, W. M. 1992. Methane emissions from cypress knees in a southeastern floodplain swamp. *Oecologia* 91: 126–28.

Purcell, S. L., and L. G. Goldsborough. 1995. The significance of waterfowl feces as a source of nutrients to algae in a prairie wetland. *UFS (Delta Marsh) Annual Report* 30: 43–51.

Putnam, J. A., G. M. Furnival, and J. S. McKnight. 1960. Management and inventory of southern hardwoods. Washington, DC: United States Department of Agriculture. USDA Agricultural Handbook 181.

Pywell, R. F., J. M. Bullock, D. B. Roy, L. Warman, K. J. Walker, and P. Rothery. 2003. Plant traits as predictors of performance in ecological restoration. *Journal of Applied Ecology* 40: 65–77.

Qiu, S., and A. J. McComb. 1994. Effects of oxygen concentration on phosphorus release from reflooded, air-dried wetland sediments. *Marine and Freshwater Research* 45: 1319–28.

———. 1995. The plankton and microbial contributions to phosphorus release from fresh and air-dried sediments. *Marine and Freshwater Research* 46: 1039–45.

Qiu, S., A. J. McComb, and R. W. Bell. 2002. Phosphorus-leaching from litterfall in wetland catchments of the Swan Coastal Plain, southwestern Australia. *Hydrobiologia* 472: 95–105.

Rabenhorst, M. C. 2001. Soils of tidal and fringing wetlands. In *Wetland soils, genesis, hydrology, landscapes, and classification,* eds. J. L. Richardson and M. J. Vepraskas, 301–16. New York: Lewis Publishers.

Rabenhurst M. C., and D. Swanson. 1999. Histosols. In *Handbook of soil science,* ed. M. E. Sumner, E183–209. New York: CRC Press.

Rader, R. B., and C. J. Richardson. 1994. Response of macroinvertebrates and small fish to nutrient enrichment in the northern Everglades. *Wetlands* 14: 134–46.

Rahel, F. J., C. J. Keleher, and J. L. Anderson. 1996. Habitat loss and population fragmentation for coldwater fishes in the Rocky Mountain region in response to climate warming. *Limnology and Oceanography* 41: 1116–23.

Ramberg, L., R. van Aarde, S. Ferreira, P. Hancock, T. Meyer, S. Ringrose, J. Sliva, J. Van As, and C. VanderPost. In press. Comparative biodiversity value of large wetlands: The Okavango Delta, Botswana. *Aquatic Sciences.*

Ramsar Convention Bureau. 1991. *Proceedings of the 4th Meeting of the Conference of Contracting Parties. Montreux, Switzerland.* Gland, Switzerland: Ramsar Convention Bureau.

Rand, T. A. 1999. Effects of environmental context on the susceptibility of *Atriplex patula* to attack by herbivorous beetles. *Oecologia* 121: 39–46.

Ranwell, D. S. 1961. *Spartina* salt marshes in southern England. I. The effects of sheep grazing at the upper limits of *Spartina* marsh in Bridgwater Bay. *Journal of Ecology* 49: 325–40.

Räsänen, M. E., J. S. Salo, and R. J. Kalliola. 1987. Fluvial perturbance in the western Amazon basin: Regulation by long-term Sub-Andean tectonics. *Science* 238: 1398–1401.

Rasmussen, J. B., and J. A. Downing. 1988. The spatial response of chironomid larvae to the predatory leech *Nephelopsis obscura. American Naturalist* 131: 14–21.

Ratering, S., and R. Conrad. 1998. Effects of short-term drainage and aeration on the production of methane in submerged rice soil. *Global Change Biology* 4: 397–407.

Ratti, J. T., A. M. Rocklage, J. H. Giudice, E. O. Garton, and D. P. Golner. 2001. Comparison of avian communities on restored and natural wetlands in North and South Dakota. *Journal of Wildlife Management* 65: 676–84.

Ray, H. L., A. M. Ray, and A. J. Rebertus. 2004. Rapid establishment of fish in isolated peatland beaver ponds. *Wetlands* 24: 399–405.

Reddy, K. R., and E. M. D'Angelo. 1994. Soil processes regulating water quality in wetlands. In *Global wetlands: Old and new,* ed. W. J. Mitsch, 309–24. Amsterdam: Elsevier.

Reddy, K. R., R. E. Jessup, and P. S. C. Rao. 1988. Nitrogen dynamics in a eutrophic lake sediment. *Hydrobiologia* 159: 177–88.

Reddy, K. R., and W. H. Patrick Jr. 1975. Effect of alternate aerobic and anaerobic conditions on redox potential, organic matter decomposition and nitrogen loss in a flooded soil. *Soil Biology and Biochemistry* 7: 87–94.

Reddy, K. R., R. G. Wetzel, and R. H. Kadlec. 2004. Biogeochemistry of phosphorus in wetlands. In *Biogeochemical cycling in wetland ecosystems.* Academic Press. In press.

Redfield, A. C. 1972. Development of a New England salt marsh. *Ecological Monographs* 42: 201–37.

Reed, P. B., Jr. 1988. National list of plant species that occur in wetlands: National summary. *U.S. Fish and Wildlife Service Biological Report* 88(24), 244 pp.

Reeder, B. C., and W. R. Eisner. 1994. Holocene biogeochemical and pollen history of a Lake Erie, Ohio, coastal wetland. *Ohio Journal of Science* 94: 87–93.

Rees, B. B., J. A. L. Bowman, and P. M. Schulte. 2001. Structure and sequence conservation of a putative hypoxia response element in the lactate dehydrogenase-gene of *Fundulus. Biological Bulletin* 200: 247–51.

Reese, E. G., and D. P. Batzer. In review. Invertebrate community structure along a floodplain continuum. *Freshwater Biology.*

Reichle, D. E. 1981. *Dynamic properties of forest ecosystems.* Cambridge: Cambridge University Press.

Reinelt, L. E., B. L. Taylor, and R. R. Horner. 2001. Morphology and hydrology. In *Wetlands and urbanization: Implications for the future,* eds. A. L. Azous and R. R. Horner, 221–235. Boca Raton, FL: Lewis Publishers.

Reiners, W. A. 1972. Structure and energetics of three Minnesota forests. *Ecological Monographs* 42: 71–94.

Reiter, P. 1996. Global warming and mosquito-borne disease in the USA. *The Lancet* 348: 622.

Rejmanek, M., C. Sasser, and G. W. Peterson. 1988. Hurricane-induced sediment deposition in a Gulf Coast marsh. *Estuarine, Coastal and Shelf Science* 27: 217–22.

Relyea, R. A. 2001. Morphological and behavioral plasticity in larval anurans in response to different predators. *Ecology* 80: 235–48.

Relyea, R. A., and E. E. Werner. 2000. Morphological plasticity of four larval anurans distributed along an environmental gradient. *Copeia* 2000: 178–90.

Resende, E. K. de, and S. S. Palmeira. 1999. Estrutura e dinâmica das comunidades de peixes da planicie inundável do Rio Miranda, Pantanal de Mato Grosso do Sul. Pages 249–81 in EMBRAPA, editor. Anais II Simpósio sobre Recursos Naturais e Sócio-econômicos do Pantanal, Manejo e Conservação. Empresa Brasileira de Pesquisa Agropecuária (EMBRAPA), Corumbá, Brazil.

Riber, H. H., and R. G. Wetzel. 1987. Boundary layer and internal diffusion effects on phosphorus fluxes in lake periphyton. *Limnology and Oceanography* 32: 1181–94.

Ricard, B., I. Couee, P. Raymond, P. H. Saglio, V. Saint-Ges, and A. Pradet. 1994. Plant metabolism under hypoxia and anoxia. *Plant Physiology and Biochemistry* 32: 1–10.

Richards, C. L., S. C. Pennings, and L. A. Donovan. 2005. Community-wide patterns of phenotypic variation in salt marsh plants. *Plant Ecology* 176: 263–73.

Richards, L. A. 1931. Capillary conduction of liquids through porous mediums. *Physics* 1: 318–33.

Richardson, C. J. 2003. Pocosins: Hydrologically isolated or integrated wetlands on the landscape? *Wetlands* 23: 563–76.

Richardson, C. J., R. Evans, and D. Carr. 1981. Pocosins: An ecosystem in transition. In *Pocosin wetlands,* ed. C. J. Richardson, 3–19. Stroudsburg, PA: Hutchinson Ross Publishing.

Richardson, C. J., and J. W. Gibbons. 1993. Pocosins, Carolina bays and mountain bogs. In *Biodiversity of the southeastern United States,* eds. W. H. Martin, S. G. Boyce, and A. C. Echternacht, 257–310. New York: John Wiley and Sons.

Richardson, C. J., and E. J. McCarthy. 1994. Effect of land development and forest management on hydrologic response in southeastern coastal wetlands: A review. *Wetlands* 14: 56–71.

Richardson, J. L, and M. J. Vepraskas. 2001. *Wetland Soils: Genesis, Hydrology, Landscapes, and Classification.* Boca Raton, FL: Lewis Publishers, CRC Press.

Richardson, J. S., and R. J. Mackay. 1984. A comparison of the life history and growth of *Limnephilus indivisus* (Trichoptera: Limnephilidae) in three temporary pools. *Archiv für Hydrobiologie* 99: 515–28.

Richardson, M. S., and R. C. Gatti. 1999. Prioritizing wetland restoration activity within a Wisconsin watershed using GIS modeling. *Journal of Soil and Water Conservation* 54: 537–42.

Richey, J. E., M. A. Perkins, and C. R. Goldman. 1975. Effects of kokanee salmon *(Oncorhynchus nerka)* decomposition on the ecology of a subalpine stream. *Journal of the Fisheries Research Board of Canada* 32: 817–20.

Richter, B. D., D. P. Braun, M. A. Mendelson, and L. L. Master. 1997. Threats to imperiled freshwater fauna. *Conservation Biology* 11: 1081–93.

Richter, D. D., and D. D. Markewitz. 2001. *Understanding soil change: Soil sustainability over millenia, centuries, and decades.* Cambridge, England: Cambridge University Press.

Richter, K. O. 1997. A simple gauge for water-level maxima and minima. *Restoration and Management Notes* 15: 60–63.

Ricklefs, R. E. 1969. An analysis of nesting mortality in birds. *Smithsonian Contributions in Zoology* 9:1–48.

Riekerk, H. 1985. Water quality effects of pine flat woods silviculture. *Journal of Soil and Water Conservation* 40: 306–9.

———. 1989a. Influence of silvicultural practices on the hydrology of pine flat woods in Florida. *Water Resources Research* 25: 713–19.

———. 1989b. Impacts of silviculture on flatwoods runoff, water quality, and nutrient budgets. *Water Resources Bulletin* 25: 73–79.

Riemann, B., and M. Sondergaard. 1986. Bacteria. In *Carbon dynamics in eutrophic, temperate lakes,* eds. B. Riemann and M. Sondergaard, 127–97. Amsterdam: Elsevier.

Risgaard-Petersen, N., S. Rysgaard, S. Nielsen, and N. P. Revsbech. 1994. Diurnal variation of denitrification and nitrification in sediments colonized by benthic microphytes. *Limnology and Oceanography* 39: 573–79.

Robb, J. T. 2002. Assessing wetland compensatory mitigation sites to aid in establishing mitigation ratios. *Wetlands* 22: 435–40.

Robertson, A. I., H. R. Healey, and A. J. King. 1997. Experimental manipulations of the biomass of introduced carp (*Cyprinus carpio*) in billabongs : 2. Impacts on benthic properties and processes. *Marine and Freshwater Research* 48: 445–454.

Robinson, S. K., F. R. Thompson, T. M. Donovan, D. R. Whitehead, and J. Faaborg. 1995. Regional forest fragmentation and the nesting success of migratory birds. *Science* 267: 1987–90.

Rochefort, L., D. H. Vitt, and S. E. Bayley. 1990. Growth, production, and decomposition dynamics of *Sphagnum* under natural and experimentally acidified conditions. *Ecology* 71: 1986–2000.

Rochow, T. F. 1994. *The effect of water table level changes on fresh-water marsh and cypress wetlands in the northern Tampa Bay region: A review.* Technical Report 1994-1. Brooksville, FL: Southwest Florida Water Management District.

Rocke, T. E., N. H. Euliss, and M. D. Samuel. 1999. Environmental characteristics associated with the occurrence of avian botulism in wetlands of a northern California refuge. *Journal of Wildlife Management* 63: 358–68.

Rocke, T. E., and M. D. Samuel. 1999. Water and sediment characteristics associated with avian botulism outbreaks in wetlands. *Journal of Wildlife Management* 63: 1249–60.

Roden, E. E. 2003. Diversion of electron flow from methanogenesis to crystalline Fe(III) oxide reduction in carbon-limited cultures of wetland sediment microorganisms. *Applied and Environmental Microbiology* 69: 5702–6.

Roden, E. E., and R. G. Wetzel. 2002. Kinetics of microbial Fe(III) oxide reduction in freshwater wetland sediments. *Limnology and Oceanography* 47: 198–211.

Rodewald, A. D. 2002. Nest predation in forested regions: Landscape and edge effects. *Journal of Wildlife Management* 66: 634–40.

Roehm, C. L., and N. T. Roulet 2003. Seasonal contribution of CO_2 fluxes in the annual C budget of a northern bog. *Global Biochemical Cycles* 17(1): Article 1029.

Rolauffs, P., D. Hering, and S. Lohse. 2001. Composition, invertebrate community and productivity of a beaver dam in comparison to other stream habitat types. *Hydrobiologia* 459: 201–12.

Rolls, E. 1981. *A million wild acres*. Ringwood, Australia: Penguin, p. 8

Rood, S. B., and J. M Mahoney. 1990. Collapse of riparian poplar forests downstream from dams in western prairies: Probable causes and prospects for mitigation. *Environmental Management* 14: 451–64.

Rosenberg, D. M., A. P. Weins, and B. Bilyj. 1988. Chironomidae (Diptera) of peatlands in northwestern Ontario, Canada. *Holarctic Ecology* 11: 19–31.

Rosendahl, P. C., and P. W. Rose. 1982. Freshwater flow rates and distribution within the Everglades marsh. In *Proceedings of the National Symposium on Freshwater Inflows to Estuaries*, eds. R. D. Cross and D. L. Williams, 385–401. Coastal Ecosystems Project. Washington, D.C.: U.S. Fish and Wildlife Service.

Roshier, D. A., P. H. Wheton, R. J. Allan, and A. I. Robertson. 2001. Distribution and persistence of temporary wetland habitats in arid Australia in relation to climate. *Austral Ecology* 26: 371–84.

Ross, J. L., P. I. Boon, P. Ford, and B. T. Hart. 1997. Detection and quantification with 16S rRNA probes of planktonic methylotrophic bacteria in a floodplain lake. *Microbial Ecology* 34: 97–108.

Ross, S. T., and J. A. Baker. 1983. The response of fishes to periodic spring floods in a southeastern stream. *American Midland Naturalist* 109: 1–14.

Rothe, J., and G. Gleixner. 2004. Application of stable nitrogen isotopes to investigate food-web development in regenerating ecosystems. In *Assembly rules and restoration ecology*, eds. V. M. Temperton, R. J. Hobbs, T. Nuttle, and S. Halle, 245–64. Washington, D.C.: Island Press.

Rothermel, B. B., and R. D. Semlitsch. 2002. An experimental investigation of landscape resistance of forest versus old-field habitats to emigrating juvenile amphibians. *Conservation Biology* 16: 1324–32.

Roulet, N. T. 2000. Peatlands, carbon storage, greenhouse gases and the Kyoto Protocol: Prospects and significance for Canada. *Wetlands* 20: 605–15.

Round, F. E. 1981. *The ecology of algae*. Cambridge: Cambridge University Press, 653 pp.

Rowcliffe, J. M., A. R. Watkinson, and W. J. Sutherland. 1998. Aggregative responses of brent geese on salt marsh and their impact on plant community dynamics. *Oecologia* 114: 417–26.

Rowe, C. L., and W. A. Dunson. 1995. Impacts of hydroperiod on growth and survival of larval amphibians in temporary ponds of central Pennsylvania, USA. *Oecologia* 102: 397–403.

Roy, V., J. Rule, and A. P. Plamondon. 2000. Establishment, growth, and survival of natural regeneration after clearcutting and drainage on forested wetlands. *Forest Ecology and Management* 129: 253–67.

Rozas, L. P., and T. J. Minello. 2001. Marsh terracing as a wetland restoration tool for creating fishery habitat. *Wetlands* 21: 327–41.

Ruello, N. V. 1976. Observations on some massive fish kills in Lake Eyre. *Australian Journal of Marine and Freshwater Research* 27: 667–72.

Ruess, R. W., D. S. Hik, and R. L. Jefferies. 1989. The role of lesser snow geese as nitrogen processors in a sub-arctic salt marsh. *Oecologia* 79: 23–29.

Ryan, T. J., and C. T. Winne. 2001. Effects of hydroperiod on metamorphosis in *Rana spehno-cephala. American Midlands Naturalist* 145: 46–53.

Ryder, D. S., and P. Horwitz. 1995. Seasonal water regimes and leaf litter processing in a wetland on the Swan Coastal Plain, western Australia. *Marine and Freshwater Research* 46: 1077–84.

Saglio, P. H., P. Raymond, and A. Pradet. 1980. Metabolic activity and energy charge of excised maize root tips under anoxia. *Plant Physiology* 66: 1053–57.

Saint-Paul, U., J. Zuanon, M. A. V. Correa, M. García, N. N. Fabré, U. Berger, and W. J. Junk. 2000. Fish communities in central Amazonian white- and blackwater floodplains. *Environmental Biology of Fishes* 57: 235–50.

Salgado, C. S., and S. C. Pennings. 2005. Latitudinal variation in palatability of salt-marsh plants: Are differences constitutive? *Ecology* 86: 1571–79.

Salinas, L. M., R. D. DeLaune, and W. H. Patrick, Jr. 1986. Changes occurring along a rapidly submerging coastal area: Louisiana, USA. *Journal of Coastal Research* 2: 269–84.

Salo, J. 1990. External processes influencing origin and maintenance of inland water/land ecotones. In *The ecology and management of aquatic-terrestrial ecotones,* eds. R. J. Naiman and H. Dechamps, 37–64. MAB series, Vol. 4. Paris: UNESCO; and U.K.: Parthenon Publishing.

Salo, J., R. Kalliola, I. Häkkinen, Y. Mäkinen, P. Niemelä, M. Puhakka, and P. D. Coley. 1986. River dynamics and the diversity of Amazon lowland forest. *Nature* 322: 254–58.

Salonius, P. O. 1983. Effects of air-drying on the respiration of forest soil microbial populations. *Soil Biology and Biochemistry* 15: 199–203.

Sammut, J. 2000. *An introduction to acid sulfate soils.* Canberra, Australia: Environment Australia.

Sanchez-Carrillo, S., and M. Alvarez-Cobelas. 2001. Nutrient dynamics and eutrophication patterns in a semi-arid wetland: The effects of fluctuating hydrology. *Water, Air, and Soil Pollution* 131: 97–118.

Sanchez-Carrillo, S., M. Alvarez-Cobelas, S. Cirujano, P. Riolobos, M. Moreno-Perez, and C. Rojo. 2000. Rainfall-driven changes in the biomass of a semi-arid wetland. *Verhandlungen Internationale Verieinigung Limnologie* 27: 1690–94.

Sand-Jensen, K., and J. R. Mebus. 1996. Fine-scale patterns of water velocity within macrophyte patches in streams. *Oikos* 76: 169–80.

Santamaria, L. 2002. Why are most aquatic plants widely distributed? Dispersal, clonal growth and small-scale heterogeneity in a stressful environment. *Acta Oecologia* 23: 137–54.

Santruckova, H., T. Picek, M. Simek, V. Bauer, J. Kopecky, L. Pechar, J. Lukavska, and H. Cizkova. 2001. Decomposition processes in soil of a healthy and a declining *Phragmites australis* stand. *Aquatic Botany* 69: 217–34.

Sanyal, P. 1999. Sundarbans—The larges mangrove diversity on globe. In *Sundarbans mangal,* eds. D. N. Guha Bakshi, P. Sanyal, and K. R. Naskar, 428–48. Calcutta, India: Naya Prokash.

Saracco, J. F., and J. A. Collazo. 1999. Predation on artificial nests along three edge types in a North Carolina bottomland hardwood forest. *Wilson Bulletin* 111: 541–49.

Sarker, S. U. 1989. Fish eating wildlife and some fishes of the Sundarbans, Bangladesh. *The Journal of Noami* 6: 17–29.

Sasser, C. E., and J. G. Gosselink. 1984. Vegetation and primary production in a floating freshwater marsh in Louisiana. *Aquatic Botany* 20: 245–55.

Saunders, G. W. 1972. The transformation of artificial detritus in lake waters. *Memorie di Istituto Italiano Idrobiologie* 29(Suppl.): 261–88.

Schafale, M. P., and A. S. Weakley. 1990. *Classification of the natural communities of North Carolina. Third Approximation.* Raleigh, NC: North Carolina Department of Environment, Health and Natural Resources.

Schäfer, S. A. 1998. Conflict and resolution: Impact of new taxa on phylogenetic studies of the neotropical Cascudinhos (Siluroidei: Loricariidae). In *Phylogeny and classification of neotropical fishes,* eds. L. R. Malabarba, R. E. Reis, R. P. Vari, Z. M. S. Lucena, and C. A. S. Lucena, 375–400. Porto Alegre, Brasil: EDIPUCRS.

Schalles, J. F. and D. J. Shure. Hydrology, community structure, and productivity patterns of a dystrophic Carolina bay wetland. *Ecological Monographs* 59: 365–385.

Scheffer, M. 1998. *Ecology of shallow lakes.* London: Chapman and Hall, 357 pp.

Schindler, D. W. 1998. A dim future for boreal waters and landscapes. *BioScience* 48: 157–64.

Schlesinger, W. H. 1977. Carbon balance in terrestrial detritus. *Annual Review of Ecology and Systematics* 8: 51–81.

———. 1978. Community structure, dyes, and nutrient ecology in the Okefenokee Cypress Swamp-Forest. *Ecological Monographs* 48: 43–65.

———. 1997. *Biogeochemistry: An analysis of global change.* New York: Academic Press.

Schneider, D. W., and T. M. Frost. 1996. Habitat duration and community structure in temporary ponds. *Journal of the North American Benthological Society* 15: 64–86.

Schneider, R. L., and R. R. Sharitz. 1988. Hydrochory and regeneration in a bald cypress–water tupelo swamp forest. *Ecology* 69: 1055–63.

Schoenberg, S. A., and J. D. Oliver. 1988. Temporal dynamics and spatial variation of algae in relation to hydrology and sediment characteristics in the Okefenokee Swamp, Georgia. *Hydrobiologia* 162: 123–33.

Scholander, P. F., H. T. Hammel, E. D. Bradstreet, and E. A. Hemmingsen. 1965. Sap pressure in vascular plants. *Science* 148: 339–46.

Scholz, O., and P. I. Boon. 2003. Biofilm development and extracellular enzyme activities on wood in billabongs of south-eastern Australia. *Freshwater Biology* 30: 359–68.

Scholz, O., B. Gawne, B. Ebner, and I. Ellis. 2002. The effects of drying and re-flooding on nutrient availability in ephemeral deflation basin lakes in western New South Wales, Australia. *River Research and Applications* 18: 185–96.

Schöngart, J., W. J. Junk, M. T. F. Piedade, J. M. Ayres, A. Hüttermann, and M. Worbes. 2004. Teleconnection between tree growth in the Amazonian floodplains and the El Niño–Southern oscillation effect. *Global Change Biology* 10: 683–92.

Schouten, S., M. Strous, M. M. M. Kuypers, W. I. C. Rijpstra, M. Baas, C. J. Schubert, M. S. M. Jetten, and J. S. S. Damste. 2004. Stable carbon isotopic fractionations associated with inorganic carbon fixation by anaerobic ammonium-oxidizing bacteria. *Applied and Environmental Microbiology* 70: 3, 785-3, 788.

Schrage, L. J., and J. A. Downing. 2004. Pathways of increased water clarity after fish removal from Ventura Marsh, a shallow, eutrophic wetland. *Hydrobiologia* 511: 215–31.

Scott, D. A. 1989. *A directory of Asian wetlands.* Gland, Switzerland, and Cambridge, U.K.: IUCN.

Scott, M. L., P. B. Shafroth, and G. T. Auble. 1999. Responses of riparian cottonwoods to alluvial water table declines. *Environmental Management* 23: 347–58.

Sculthorpe, C. D. 1967. *The biology of aquatic vascular plants.* London, U.K.: Edward Arnold.

Seabloom, E. W., and A. G. van der Valk. 2003. Plant diversity, composition, and invasion of restored and natural prairie pothole wetlands: Implications for restoration. *Wetlands* 23: 1–12.

Seago, J. L., Jr., C. A. Peterson, L. J. Kinsley, and J. Broderick. 2000. Development and structure of the root cortex in *Caltha palustris* L. and *Nymphaea odorata* Ait. *Annals of Botany* 86: 631–40.

Seago, J. L., Jr., O. Votrubova, A. Soukup, K. Stevens, D. E. Enstone, and L. Marsh. 2004. Development and structure of root aerenchyma in wetland flowering plants. In 7th INTECOL International Wetlands Conference, Utrecht, The Netherlands.

Segers, R. 1998. Methane production and methane consumption: A review of processes underlying wetland methane fluxes. *Biogeochemistry* 41: 23–51.

Seitzinger, S. P. 1988. Denitrification in freshwater and coastal marine ecosystems: Ecological and geochemical significance. *Limnology and Oceanography* 33: 702–24.

Selander, R. K. 1985. Protein polymorphism and the genetic structure of natural populations of bacteria. In *Population genetics and molecular evolution,* eds. T. Ohta and K. Aoki, 85–104. Berlin: Springer-Verlag.

Seliskar, D. M. 1985a. Effect of reciprocal transplanting between extremes of plant zones on morphometric plasticity of five plant species in an Oregon salt marsh. *Canadian Journal of Botany* 63: 2254–62.

———. 1985b. Morphometric variations of five tidal marsh halophytes along environmental gradients. *American Journal of Botany* 72: 1340–52.

Seliskar, D. M., J. L. Gallagher, D. M. Burdick, and L. A. Mutz. 2002. The regulation of ecosystem functions by ecotypic variation in the dominant plant: A *Spartina alterniflora* salt-marsh case study. *Journal of Ecology* 90: 1–11.

Semlitsch, R. D. 1987. Interactions between fish and salamander larvae: Costs of predator avoidance or competition? *Oecologia* 65: 305–13.

———. 1998. Biological delineation of terrestrial buffer zones for pond-breeding salamanders. *Conservation Biology* 12: 1113–19.

———. 2000. Principles for management of aquatic-breeding amphibians. *Journal of Wildlife Management* 64: 615–31.

Semlitsch, R. D., and J. R. Bodie. 1998. Are small isolated wetlands expendable? *Conservation Biology* 12: 1129–33.

———. 2003. Biological criteria for buffer zones around wetlands and riparian habitats for amphibians and reptiles. *Conservation Biology* 17: 1219–28.

Semlitsch, R. D., D. E. Scott, J. H. K. Pechmann, and J. W. Gibbons. 1996. Structure and dynamics of an amphibian community: Evidence from a 16-year study of a natural pond. In *Long-term studies of vertebrate communities,* eds. M. L. Cody and J. D. Smallwood, 217–48. New York: Academic Press.

Serrano, L. 1994. Sources, abundance and disappearance of polyphenolic compounds in temporary ponds of Donana National Park (south-western Spain). *Australian Journal of Marine and Freshwater Research* 45: 1555–64.

Serrano, L., and P. I. Boon. 1991. Effect of polyphenolic compounds on alkaline phosphatase activity: Its implication for phosphorus regeneration in Australian freshwaters. *Archiv für Hydrobiologie* 123: 1–20.

Serrano, L., M. D. Burgos, A. Diaz-Espejo, and J. Toja. 1999. Phosphorus inputs to wetlands following storm events after drought. *Wetlands* 19: 318–26.

Shaler, N. S. 1890. General account of the freshwater morasses of the United States, with a description of the Dismal Swamp District of Virginia and North Carolina. 10th Annual Report 1888–1889, 255–339. Washington, D.C.: U.S. Geological Survey.

Sharitz, R. R. 2003. Carolina bay wetlands: Unique habitats of the southeastern United States. *Wetlands* 23: 550–62.

Sharitz, R. R., and J. W. Gibbons. 1982. The ecology of southeastern shrub bogs (pocosins) and Carolina bays: A community profile.FWS/OBS-82/04. Washington, D.C.: U.S. Fish and Wildlife Service, Division of Biological Services, 93 pp.

Sharitz, R. R., and C. A. Gresham. 1998. Pocosins and Carolina bays. In *Southern forested wetlands. Ecology and management,* eds. M. G. Messina and W. H. Conner, 343–77. Boca Raton, FL: Lewis Publishers.

Sharitz, R. R., and W. J. Mitsch. 1993. Southern floodplain forests. In *Biodiversity of the southeastern United States,* eds. W. H. Martin, S. G. Boyce, and A. C. Echternacht, 311–72. New York: John Wiley and Sons.

Sharitz, R. R., R. L. Schneider, and L. C. Lee. 1990. Composition and regeneration of a disturbed river floodplain forest in South Carolina. In *Ecological processes and cumulative impacts: Illustrated by bottomland hardwood wetland ecosystems,* eds. J. G. Gosselink, L. C. Lee and T. A. Muir, 195–218. Chelsea, MI: Lewis Publishers Inc.

Sharitz, R. R., M. R. Vaitkus, and A. E. Cook. 1993. Hurricane damage to an old-growth floodplain forest in the Southeast. In *Proceedings of the Seventh Southern Silvicultural Research Conference,* ed. J. C. Brissette, 203–10. U.S. Forest Service General Technical Report 50–93. New Orleans, LA.

Shaver, G. R., L. C. Johnson, D. H. Cades, G. Murray, J. A. Laundre, E. B. Rastetter, K. J. Nadelhoffer, and A. E. Giblin. 1998. Biomass and CO_2 flux in wet sedge tundras: Responses to nutrients, temperature and light. *Ecological Monographs* 68: 75–97.

Shaw, E. M. 1988. *Hydrology in practice,* 2d ed. London, U.K.: Van Nostrand-Reinhold.

Shaw, S. P., and C. G. Fredine. 1956. *Wetlands of the United States.* Circular 39. Washington, D.C.: U.S. Fish and Wildlife Service.

Sheffield, R. M., T. W. Birch, W. H. McWilliams, and J. B. Tansey. 1998. *Chamaecyparis thyoides* (Atlantic white cedar) in the United States. In *Coastally restricted forests,* ed. A. D. Laderman, 111–23. New York: Oxford University Press.

Sherry, T. W., and R. T. Holmes. 1995. Summer versus winter limitation of populations: What are the issues and what is the evidence? In *Ecology and management of neotropical migratory birds,* eds. T. E. Martin and D. M. Finch, 85–120. New York: Oxford University Press.

Shipley, B., P. A. Keddy, C. Gaudet, and D. R. J. Moore. 1991. A model of species density in shoreline vegetation. *Ecology* 72: 1658–67.

Shreffler, D. K., C. A. Simenstad, and R. M. Thom. 1992. Foraging by juvenile salmon in a restored estuarine wetland. *Estuaries* 15: 204–13.

Shumway, S. W., and M. D. Bertness. 1994. Patch size effects on marsh plant secondary succession mechanisms. *Ecology* 75: 564–8.

Shuttleworth, W. J. 1992. Evaporation. *Handbook of hydrology,* ed. D. R. Maidment. 4.1–4.53. New York: McGraw Hill.

Sick, H. 1967. Hochwasserbedingte Vogelwanderungen in den neuweltlichen Tropen. *Die Vogelwarte* 24: 1–6.

Sidle, W. C., L. Arihood, and R. Bayless. 2000. Isotope hydrology dynamics of riverine wetlands in the Kankakee Watershed, Indiana. *Journal of the American Water Resources Association* 36: 771–90.

Siegel, D. I. 1983. Ground water and evolution of patterned mires, glacial Lake Agassiz peatlands, northern Minnesota. *Journal of Ecology* 71: 913–21.

Siegel, D. I., and P. H. Glaser. 1987. Groundwater flow in the bog/fen complex, Lost River Peatland, northern Minnesota. *Journal of Ecology* 75: 743–54.

Siemens, D. H., S. H. Garner, T. Mitchell-Olds, and R. M. Callaway. 2002. Cost of defense in the context of plant competition: *Brassica rapa* may grow and defend. *Ecology* 83: 505–17

Silberbauer, M. J., and M. J. King. 1991. The distribution of wetlands in the south-western Cape Province, South Africa. *Southern African Journal of Aquatic Sciences* 17: 65–81.

Silliman, B. R., and M. D. Bertness. 2002. A trophic cascade regulates salt marsh primary production. *Proceedings of the National Academy of Sciences USA* 99: 10500–505.

———. 2004. Shoreline development drives invasion of *Phragmites australis* and the loss of plant diversity on New England salt marshes.*Conservation Biology* 18: 1424–34.

Silliman, B. R., and S. Y. Newell. 2003. Fungal farming in a snail. *Procceedings of the National Academy of Sciences USA* 100: 15643–48.

Silliman, B. R., and J. C. Zieman. 2001. Top-down control of *Spartina alterniflora* production by periwinkle grazing in a Virginia salt marsh. *Ecology* 82: 2830–45.

Simberloff, D. J., D. Doak, M. Groom, S. Trombulak, A. Dogbson, S. Gatewood, M. Soule, M. Gilpin, C. Martinez del Rio, and L. Mills. 1999. Regional and continental restoration. In *Continental conservation: Scientific foundations of regional reserve networks,* eds. M. E. Soule and J. Terborgh, 65–98. Washington, D.C.: Island Press.

Simberloff, D. J., and B. Von Holle. 1999. Positive interactions of nonindigenous species: Invasional meltdown? *Biological Invasions* 1: 21–32.

Simberloff, D. S., and E. O. Wilson. 1970. Experimental zoogeography of islands—a 2-year record of colonization. *Ecology* 51: 934.

Simenstad, C. A., and R. M. Thom. 1996. Functional equivalency trajectories of the restored Gog-Le-Hi-Te estuarine wetland. *Ecological Applications* 6: 38–56.

Simmons R. E., C. Boix-Hinzen, K. N. Barnes, A. M. Jarvis, and A. Robertson. 1998. Important bird areas of Namibia. In *The important bird areas of southern Africa,* ed. K. N. Barnes, 295–332. Johannesburg, South Africa: Birdlife South Africa.

Simon, J. 2002. Enzymology and bioenergetics of respiratory nitrite ammonification. *FEMS Microbiology Reviews* 26: 285–309.

Simpson, R. L., R. E. Good, M. A. Leck, and D. F. Whigham. 1983. The ecology of freshwater tidal wetlands. *BioScience* 33: 255–59.

Sinclair, A. R. E., S. Mduma, and J. S. Brashares. 2003. Patterns of predation in a diverse predator-prey system. *Nature* 425: 288–90.

Singer, D. K., S. T. Jackson, B. J. Madsen, and D. A. Wilcox. 1996. Differentiating climatic and successional influences on long-term development of a marsh. *Ecology* 77: 1765–78.

Sinsabaugh, R. L., and C. M. Foreman. 2003. Integrating dissolved organic matter metabolism and microbial diversity: An overview of conceptual models. In *Aquatic ecosystems. Interactivity of dissolved organic matter,* eds. S. Findlay and R. L. Sinsabaugh, 425–54. Amsterdam: Academic Press.

Skelly, D. K., E. E. Werner, and S. A. Cortwright. 1999. Long-term distributional dynamics of a Michigan amphibian assemblage. *Ecology* 80: 2326–37.

Skelly, D. M. 1995. A behavioral trade-off and its consequences for the distribution of *Pseudacris* treefrog larvae. *Ecology* 76: 150–64.

Skelly, D. M. 1997. Tadpole communities. *American Scientist* 85: 36–45.

Smart, R. M., and J. W. Barko. 1980. Nitrogen nutrition and salinity tolerance of *Distichlis spicata* and *Spartina alterniflora*. *Ecology* 61: 630–38.

Smirnov, V. V., and K. Tretyakov. 1998. Changes in aquatic plant communities on the island of Vallam due to invasion by the muskrat *Ondatra zibethicus* L. (Rodentia, Mammalia). *Biodiversity and Conservation* 7: 673–90.

Smith, D. H., J. D. Madsen, K. L. Dickson, and T. L. Beitinger. 2002. Nutrient effects on autofragmentation of *Myriophyllum spicatum*. *Aquatic Botany* 74: 1–17.

Smith, L. C., G. M. MacDonald, A. A. Velichko, D. W. Beilman, O. K. Borisova, K. E. Frey, K. V. Kremenetski, and Y. Sheng. 2004. Siberian peatlands a net carbon sink and global methane source since the early Holocene. *Science* 303: 353–56.

Smith, L. M., and D. A. Haukos. 2002. Floral diversity in relation to playa wetland area and watershed disturbance. *Conservation Biology* 16: 964–74.

Smith, L. M., and J. A. Kadlec. 1985. Predictions of vegetation change following fire in a Great Salt Lake marsh. *Aquatic Botany* 21: 43–51.

Smith, R. D. 1994. Hydrogeomorphic approach to assessing wetland functions developed under the Corps' research program. *The Wetlands Research Program Bulletin* 4(3).

———. 2001. Hydrogeomorphic approach to assessing wetland functions: Guidelines for developing regional guidebooks. Chapter 3, Developing a Reference Wetland System, ERDC/ EL TR-01-29. Vicksburg, MS: U.S. Army Engineer Research and Development Center.

Smith, R. D., A. Ammann, C. Bartoldus, and M. M. Brinson. 1995. An approach for assessing wetland functions using hydrogeomorphic classification, reference wetlands, and functional indices. Technical Report WRP-DE-9. Vicksburg, MS: U.S. Army Corps of Engineers Waterways Experiment Station.

Smith, R. D., and J. S. Wakeley. 2001. Hydrogeomorphic approach to assessing wetland functions: Guidelines for developing regional guidebooks. Chapter 4, Developing Assessment Models, ERDC/EL TR-01-30. Vicksburg, MS: U.S. Army Engineer Research and Development Center.

Smith, T. J. III. 1992. Forest structure. In Tropical mangrove ecosystems, eds. A. I. Robertson and D. M. Alongi, 101–36. Washington, D.C.: American Geophysical Union.

Smith, T. J. III, K. G. Boto, S. D. Frusher, and R. L. Giddins. 1991. Keystone species and mangrove forest dynamics: The influence of burrowing by crabs on soil nutrient status and forest productivity. *Estuarine, Coastal and Shelf Science* 33: 419–32.

Smith, T. J. III, H. T. Chan, C. C. McIvor, and M. B. Robblee. 1989. Comparisons of seed predation in tropical tidal forests from three continents. *Ecology* 70: 146–51.

Smith, T. J. III, and W. E. Odum. 1981. The effects of grazing by snow geese on coastal salt marshes. *Ecology* 62: 98–106.

Smith, T. J. III., M. B. Robblee, H. R. Wanless, and T. W. Doyle. 1994. Mangroves, hurricanes, and lightning strikes. *BioScience* 44: 256–62.

Smits, A. J. M. 1990. Alcohol dehydrogenase isozymes in the roots of some nymphaeid isoetid macrophytes. Adaptations to hypoxic sediment conditions? *Aquatic Botany* 38: 19–27.

Snedaker, S. C., and E. J. Lahmann. 1988. Mangrove understorey absence: A consequence of evolution. *Journal of Tropical Ecology* 4: 311–14.

Snodgrass, J. W. 1997. Temporal and spatial dynamics of beaver-created patches as influenced by management practices in a south-eastern North American landscape. *Journal of Applied Ecology* 34: 1043–56.

Snodgrass, J. W., A. L. Bryan, and J. Burger. 2000. Development of expectations of larval amphibian assemblage structure in southeastern depression wetlands. *Ecological Applications* 10: 1219–29.

Snodgrass, J. W., A. L. Bryan, R. F. Lide, and G. M. Smith. 1996. Factors affecting the occurrence and structure of fish assemblages in isolated wetlands of the upper coastal plain, U.S.A. *Canadian Journal of Fisheries and Aquatic Sciences* 53: 443–54.

Snodgrass, J. W., M. J. Komoroski, A. L. Bryan, and J. Burger. 2000. Relationships among isolated wetland size, hydroperiod, and amphibian species richness: Implications for wetland regulations. *Conservation Biology* 14: 414–19.

Snodgrass, J. W., and G. K. Meffe. 1998. Influence of beavers on stream fish assemblages: Effects of pond age and watershed position. *Ecology* 79: 928–42.

Society for Ecological Restoration (SER) Science and Policy Working Group. 2002. The SER primer on ecological restoration. www.ser.org/.

Sorenson, L. G., R. Goldberg, T. L. Root, and M. G. Anderson. 1998. Potential effects of global warming on waterfowl populations breeding in the northern Great Plains. *Climatic Change* 40: 343–69.

Sorensen, L. H. 1974. Rate of decomposition of organic matter in soil as influenced by repeated air drying-rewetting and repeated addition of organic material. *Soil Biology and Biochemistry* 6: 287–92.

Sorrell, B. K. 2004. Regulation of root anaerobiosis and carbon translocation by light and root aeration in *Isotes alpinus*. *Plant Cell and Environment* 27: 1102–11.

Sorrell, B. K, and P. I. Boon. 1994. Convective gas flow in *Eleocharis phacelata* R. Br.: Methane transport and release from wetlands. *Aquatic Botany* 47: 197–212.

Sorrell, B. K., H. Brix, and P. I. Boon. 1994. Modelling of *in situ* oxygen transport and aerobic metabolism in the hydrophyte *Eleocharis phacelata* R. Br. *Proceedings of the Royal Society of Edinburgh* 102B: 367–72.

Sorrell, B. K., I. A. Mendelssohn, K. L. McKee, and R. A. Woods. 2000. Ecophysiology of wetland plant roots: A modeling comparison of aeration in relation to species distribution. *Annals of Botany* 86:675–685.

Soulides, D. A., and F. E. Allison. 1961. Effect of drying and freezing soils on carbon dioxide production, available mineral nutrients, aggregation and bacterial populations. *Soil Science* 91: 291–98.

Sparks, R. E., P. B. Bayley, S. L. Kohler, and L. L. Osborne. 1990. Disturbance and recovery of large floodplain rivers. *Environmental Management* 14: 699–709.

Sparling, G. P., T. W. Speir, and K. N. Whale. 1985. Changes in microbial biomass carbon, ATP content, soil phospho-monoesterase and phospho-diesterase activity following air-drying of soils. *Soil Biology and Biochemistry* 18: 363–70.

Sprunt, A., J. C. Ogden, and S. Winkler, eds. 1978. *Wading birds*. New York: National Audubon Society.

Stallard, R. F. 1998. Terrestrial sedimentation and the carbon cycle: Coupling weathering and erosion to carbon burial. *Global Biogeochemical Cycles* 12: 231–57.

Stanford, J. A. 1998. Rivers in the landscape: Introduction to the special issue on riparian and groundwater ecology. *Freshwater Biology* 40: 402–6.

Stanford, J. A., J. V. Ward, and B. K. Ellis. 1994. Ecology of the alluvial aquifers of the Flathead River, Montana. In *Groundwater ecology*, eds. J. Gibert, D. L. Danielopol, and J. A. Stanford, 313–47. London, U.K.: Aquatic Ecology Series, Academic Press.

Stanley, E. H., M. D. Johnson, and A. K. Ward. 2003. Evaluating the influence of macrophytes on algal and bacterial production in multiple habitats of a freshwater wetland. *Limnology and Oceanography* 48: 1101–11.

Steinman, A. D. 1996. Effects of grazers on freshwater benthic algae. In *Algal ecology: Benthic algae in freshwater ecosystems*, eds. R. J. Stevenson, M. Bothwell, and R. Lowe, 341–73. New York: Academic Press.

Stevaux, J. C. 2000. Climatic events during the late Pleistocene and Holocene in the upper Parana River: Correlation with NE Argentina and South-Central Brazil. *Quaternary International* 72: 73–85.

Steven, D. D., and M. M. Toner. 2004. Vegetation of upper Coastal Plain depressional wetlands: Environmental templates and wetland dynamics within a landscape framework. *Wetlands* 24: 23–42.

Stevens, L. E., T. J. Ayers, J. B. Bennett, K. Christensen, M. J. C. Kearsley, V. J. Meretsky, A. M. Phillips III, et al. 2001. Planned flooding and Colorado River riparian trade-offs downstream from Glen Canyon Dam, Arizona. *Ecological Applications* 11: 701–10.

Stevenson, B. S., S. A. Eichorst, J. T. Wertz, T. M. Schmidt, and J. A. Breznak. 2004. New strategies for cultivation and detection of previously uncultured microbes. *Applied and Environmental Microbiology* 70: 4, 748-4, 755.

Stevenson, I. L. 1956. Some observations on the microbial activity in remoistened air-dry soils. *Plant and Soil* 8: 170–82.

Stewart, J. B., and L. W. Gay. 1989. Preliminary modeling of transpiration from the FIFE site in Kansas. *Agricultural and Forest Meteorology* 48: 305–15.

Stiassny, M. L. J. 1999. The medium is the message: Freshwater biodiversity in peril. In *The living planet in crisis: Biodiversity science and policy*, eds. J. Cracraft and F. T. Grifa, 53–71. New York: Columbia University Press.

Stoltzfus, D. L., and R. E. Good. 1998. Plant community structure in *Chamaecyparis thyoides* swamps in the New Jersey Pinelands Biosphere Reserve, USA. In *Coastally restricted forests*, ed. A. D. Laderman, 142–55. New York: Oxford University Press.

Storey, R. G., R. R. Fulthorpe, and D. D. Williams. 1999. Perspectives and predictions on the microbial ecology of the hyporheic zone. *Freshwater Biology* 41: 119–30.

Streever, W. J., K. M. Portier, and T. L. Crisman. 1996. A comparison of dipterans from ten created and ten natural wetlands. *Wetlands* 16: 416–28.

Stribling, J. M., and J. C. Cornwell. 1997. Identification of important primary producers in a Chesapeake Bay tidal creek system using stable isotopes of carbon and sulfur. *Estuaries* 20: 77–85.

Stumpf, R. P., and J. W. Haines. 1998. Variations in tidal level in the Gulf of Mexico and implications for tidal wetlands. *Estuarine, Coastal and Shelf Science* 46: 165–73.

Sturman, A. P., and N. J. Tapper. 1996. *The weather and climate of Australia and New Zealand.* Melbourne, Australia: Oxford University Press, 476 pp.

Suding, K. N., K. L. Gross, and G. Houseman. 2003. Alternative states and positive feedbacks in restoration ecology. *Trends in Ecology and Evolution* 19: 46–53.

Sullivan, M. J., and C. A. Currin. 2000. Community structure and functional dynamics of benthic microalgae in salt marshes. In *Concepts and controversies in tidal marsh ecology,* eds. M. P. Weinstein and D. A. Kreeger, 81–106. Dordrecht, The Netherlands: Kluwer Academic Publishers.

Sun, G., H. Riekerk, and L. V. Korhnak. 2000. Groundwater table rise after forest harvesting on cypress-pine flatwoods in Florida. *Wetlands* 20: 101–12.

Sundareshwar, P. V., J. T. Morris, E. K. Koepfler, and B. Fornwalt. 2003. Phosphorus limitation of coastal ecosystem processes. *Science* 299: 563–65.

Sutter, R. D., and R. Kral. 1994. The ecology, status, and conservation of two non-alluvial wetland communities in the South Atlantic and eastern Gulf Coastal Plain, USA. *Biological Conservation* 68: 235–43.

Swanson, G. A., and H. F. Duebbert. 1989. Wetland habitats of waterfowl in the prairie pothole region. In *Northern prairie wetlands,* ed. A. G. van der Valk, 228–67. Ames, IA: Iowa State University Press.

Sweeney, B. W., J. K. Jackson, J. D. Newbold, and D. H. Funk. 1992. Climate change and the life histories and biogeography of aquatic insects in eastern North America. In *Global climate change and freshwater ecosystems,* eds. P. Firth and S. G. Fisher, 143–76. New York: Springer-Verlag.

Swiadek, J. W. 1997. The impacts of Hurricane Andrew on mangrove coasts in southern Florida: A review. *Journal of Coastal Research* 13: 242–45.

Szumigalski, A. R., and S. E. Bayley. 1996. Net above-ground primary production along a bog-rich fen gradient in central Alberta, Canada. *Wetlands* 16: 467–76.

Taft, O. W., M. A. Colwell, C. R. Isola, and R. J. Safran. 2002. Waterbird responses to experimental drawdown: Implications for the multispecific management of wetland mosaics. *Journal of Applied Ecology* 39: 987–1001.

Takaya, N., M. A. B. Catalan-Sakairi, Y. Sakaguchi, I. Kato, Z. Zhuo, and H. Shoun. 2003. Aerobic denitrifying bacteria that produce low levels of nitrous oxide. *Applied and Environmental Microbiology* 69: 3152–57.

Tan, L. W., and R. J. Shiel. 1993. Responses of billabong rotifer communities to inundation. *Hydrobiologia* 255/256: 361–69.

Tangen, B. A., M. G. Butler, and M. J. Ell. 2003. Weak correspondence between macroinvertebrate assemblages and land use in prairie pothole region wetlands, USA. *Wetlands* 23: 104–15.

Tate, C. M., and M. E. Gurtz. 1986. Comparisons of mass loss, nutrients, and invertebrates associated with elm leaf litter decomposition in perennial and intermittent reaches of tallgrass prairie streams. *Southwestern Naturalist* 31: 511–20.

Taylor, B. E., D. A. Leeper, M. A. McClure, and A. E. DeBaise. 1999. Carolina bays: Ecology of aquatic invertebrates and perspectives on conservation. In *Invertebrates in freshwater wet-*

lands of North America, eds. D. P. Batzer, R. B. Rader, and S. A. Wissinger, 167–96. *Ecology and Management*. New York: John Wiley & Sons Inc.

Taylor, B. E., and D. E. Scott. 1997. Effects of larval density dependence on population dynamics of *Ambystoma opacum*. *Herpetologica* 53: 132–45.

Taylor, B. E., G. A. Wyngaard, and D. L. Mahoney. 1990. Hatching of *Diaptomus stagnalis* eggs from a temporary pond after a prolonged dry period. *Archiv für Hydrobiolgie* 117: 271–78.

Taylor, B. R. 1998. Air-drying depresses rates of leaf litter decomposition. *Soil Biology and Biochemistry* 30: 403–12.

Taylor, B. R., and F. Barlocher. 1996. Variable effects of air-drying on leaching losses from tree leaf litter. *Hydrobiologia* 325: 173–82.

Taylor, K. L., J. B. Grace, G. R. Guntenspergen, and A. L. Foote. 1994. The interactive effects of herbivory and fire on an oligohaline marsh, Little Lake, Louisiana, USA. *Wetlands* 14: 82–87.

Taylor, B. R., and D. Parkinson. 1988. Does repeated wetting and drying accelerate decay of leaf litter? *Soil Biology and Biochemistry* 20: 647–56.

Teal, J. M. 1962. Energy flow in the salt marsh ecosystem of Georgia. *Ecology* 43: 614–24.

Teal, J. M., and J. Kanwisher. 1961. Gas exchange in a Georgia salt marsh. *Limnology and Oceanography* 6: 388–99.

Thamdrup, B. 2000. Bacterial manganese and iron reduction in aquatic sediments. *Advances in Microbial Ecology* 16: 41–84.

Theron, J., and T. E. Cloete. 2000. Molecular techniques for determining microbial diversity and community structure in natural environments. *Critical Reviews in Microbiology* 26: 37–57.

———. 2002. Emerging waterborne infections: Contributing factors, agents, and detection tools. *Critical Reviews in Microbiology* 28: 1–26.

Thingstad, T. F., and F. Rassoulzadegan. 1999. Conceptual models for the biogeochemical role of the photic zone food web, with particular reference to the Mediterranean Sea. *Progress in Oceanography* 44: 271–86.

Thom, R. M. 2000. Adaptive management of coastal ecosystem restoration projects. *Ecological Engineering* 15: 365–72.

Thomas, B. E., and R. M. Connolly. 2001. Fish use of subtropical saltmarshes in Queensland, Australia: relationships with vegetation, water depth and distance onto the marsh. *Marine Ecology – Progress Series* 209: 275–288.

Thompson, A. L., and C. S. Luthin. 2004. *Wetland restoration handbook for Wisconsin landowners*. Madison, WI: Bureau of Integrated Science Services, Wisconsin Department of Natural Resources.

Thompson, G. B., and B. G. Drake. 1994. Insects and fungi on a C-3 sedge and a C-4 grass exposed to elevated atmospheric CO_2 concentrations in open-top chambers in the field. *Plant Cell and Environment* 17: 1161–67.

Thormann, M. N., and S. E. Bayley. 1997. Aboveground net primary productivity along a bog-fen-marsh gradient in southern boreal Alberta, Canada. *Ecoscience* 4: 374–84.

Thornthwaite, C. W., and F. K. Hare. 1965. The loss of water to the air. *Agricultural Meteorology, Meteorological Monographs* 6(28): 163–80.

Tiedje, J. M., J. Sorensen, and Y. Y. Chang. 1981. Assimilatory and dissimilatory nitrate reduction: Perspectives and methodology for simultaneous measurement of several nitrogen cycle processes. *Ecological Bulletin (Stockholm)* 33: 331–42.

Tiner, R. W. 1984. *Wetlands of the United States: Current status and recent trends.* Washington, D.C.: United States Department of Interior, Fish and Wildlife Service.

———. 1991. The concept of hydrophyte for wetland identification. *BioScience* 41: 236–47.

———. 1995. Wetland definitions and classification in the United States. In *National water summary on wetland resources.* U.S. Geological Survey Water-Supply Paper 2425. http://water.usgs.gov/nwsum/WSP2425/index.html.

———. 1998. In search of swampland: A wetland sourcebook for the Northeast. Piscataway, NJ: Rutgers University Press.

———. 1999. Wetland indicators: *A guide to wetland identification, delineation, classification, and mapping.* Boca Raton, FL: Lewis Publishers.

———. 2003. Geographically isolated wetlands of the United States. *Wetlands* 23: 494–516.

Tiner, R. W., H. C. Bergquist, G. P. DeAlessio, and M. J. Starr. 2002. Geographically isolated wetlands: A preliminary assessment of their characteristics and status in selected areas of the United States. Hadley, MA: U.S.D.I. Fish and Wildlife Service, Northeast Region.

Titus, J. G. 1986. Greenhouse effect, sea level rise, and coastal zone management. *Coastal Zone Management* 14: 147–71.

Tockner, K., F. Malard, and J. V. Ward. 2000. An extension of the flood pulse concept. *Hydrological Processes* 14: 2861–83.

Tockner, K., F. Schiemer, C. Baumgartner, G. Kum, E. Weigand, I. Zweimuller, and J. V. Ward. 1999. The Danube restoration project: Species diversity patterns across connectivity gradients in the floodplain system. *Regulated Rivers—Research & Management* 15: 245–58.

Tomlinson, P. B. 1986. *The botany of mangroves.* Cambridge, U.K.: Cambridge University Press.

Toong, Y. C., D. A. Schooley, and F. C. Baker. 1988. Isolation of insect juvenile hormone III from a plant. *Nature* 333: 170–71.

Tori, G. M., S. McLeod, K. McKnight, T. Moorman, and F. A. Reid. 2002. Wetland conservation and ducks unlimited: Real world approaches to multispecies management. *Waterbirds* 25 (Suppl. 2): 115–21.

Torsvik, V., J. Goksoyr, and F. L. Daae. 1990. High diversity of DNA of soil bacteria. *Applied and Environmental Microbiology* 56: 782–87.

Toth, L. A., J. W. Koebel, Jr., A. G. Warne, and J. Chamberlain. 2002. Implications of reestablishing prolonged flood pulse characteristics for the Kissimmee River and floodplain ecosystem. *Flood pulsing in wetlands: Restoring the natural hydrological balance,* ed. B. Middleton, 191–221. New York: John Wiley & Sons Inc.

Trenham, P. C., W. D. Koenig, J. J. Mossman, S. L. Stark, and L. A. Jagger. 2003. Regional dynamics of wetland-breeding frogs and toads: Turnover and synchrony. *Ecological Applications* 12: 1522–32.

Trnka, S., and J. B. Zedler. 2000. Site conditions, not parental phenotype, determine the height of *Spartina foliosa.* *Estuaries* 23: 572–82.

Tromp van Meerveld, I., and J. J. McDonnell. In review. The fill and spill hypothesis: An explanation for observed threshold behavior in subsurface stormflow. *Water Resources Research.*

Tuchman, N. C. 1996. The role of heterotrophy in algae. In *Algal ecology: Benthic algae in freshwater ecosystems,* eds. R. J. Stevenson, M. Bothwell, and R. Lowe, 299–319. New York: Academic Press.

Tuchman, N. C., K. A. Wahtera, R. G. Wetzel, and J. A. Teeri. 2003a. Elevated atmospheric CO_2 alters leaf litter quality for stream ecosystems: An in situ leaf decomposition study— decomposition of elevated CO_2-altered leaf litter. *Hydrobiologia* 495: 203–11.

Tuchman, N. C., K. A. Wahtera, R. G. Wetzel, N. M. Russo, G. M. Kilbane, L. M. Sasso, and J. A. Teeri. 2003b. Nutritional quality of leaf detritus altered by elevated atmospheric CO_2: Effects on development of mosquito larvae. *Freshwater Biology* 48: 1432–39.

Tuchman, N. C., R. G. Wetzel, S. T. Rier, K. A. Wahtera, and J. A. Teeri. 2002. Elevated atmospheric CO_2 lowers leaf litter nutritional quality for stream ecosystem food webs. *Global Change Biology* 8: 163–70.

Tucker, P., S. Dominelli, S. Nichols, M. van der Wielen, and M. Siebentritt. 2003. *Your wetland: Supporting information.* Renmark, Australia: Australian Landscape Trust.

Turner, A. M., J. C. Trexler, C. J. Jordan, S. J. Slack, P. Geddes, J. H. Chick, and W. F. Loftus. 1999. Targeting ecosystem features for conservation: Standing crops in the Florida Everglades. *Conservation Biology* 13: 898–911.

Turner, B. L., J. P. Dreissen, P. M. Haygarth, and I. D. McKelvie. 2003. Potential contribution of lysed bacterial cells to phosphorus solubilisation in two rewetted Australian pasture soils. *Soil Biology and Biochemistry* 35: 187–89.

Turner, M. G. 1987. Effects of grazing by feral horses, clipping, trampling, and burning on a Georgia salt marsh. *Estuaries* 10: 54–60.

Turner, R. E. 1976. Geographic variations in salt marsh macrophyte production: A review. *Contributions in Marine Science* 20: 47–68.

———. 1997. Wetland loss in the northern Gulf of Mexico: Multiple working hypotheses. *Estuaries* 20: 1–13.

———. 2001. Estimating the indirect effects of hydrologic change on wetland loss: If the earth is curved, then how would we know it? *Estuaries* 24: 639–46.

———. 2004. Coastal wetland subsidence arising from local hydrologic manipulations. *Estuaries* 27: 265–72.

Turner, R. E., A. Redmond, and J. B. Zedler. 2001. Count it by acre or function—Mitigation adds up to net loss of wetlands. *National Wetlands Newsletter* 23(6): 5–6, 14–16.

Turner, S. D., and C. F. Friese. 1998. Plant-mycorrhizal community dynamics associated with a moisture gradient within a rehabilitated prairie fen. *Restoration Ecology* 6: 44–51.

Twedt, D. J., R. R. Wilson, J. L. Henne-Kerr, and R. B. Hamilton. 2001. Nest survival of forest birds in the Mississippi Alluvial Valley. *Journal of Wildlife Management* 65: 450–60.

Twilley, R. R., R. H. Chen, and T. Hargis. 1992. Carbon sinks in mangroves and their implications to carbon budget of tropical coastal ecosystems. *Water, Air, and Soil Pollution* 64: 265–88.

Twolan-Strutt, L., and P. A. Keddy. 1996. Above- and below-ground competition intensity in two contrasting wetland plant communities. *Ecology* 77: 259–70.

USACE Waterways Experiment Station. 1988. *The Wetland Evaluation Technique (WET): A technique for assessing wetland functions and values.* Environmental effects of dredging, Technical Notes EEDP-03-4. Vicksburg, MS.

USDA. 1999. *Soil taxonomy: A basic system of soil classification for making and interpreting soil surveys,* 2d ed. USDA Natural Resources Conservation Service Agriculture Handbook Number 436. Washington, D.C.: U.S. Government Printing Office.

USDA. 2003. *Keys to Soil Taxonomy*, 9th ed. United States Department of Agriculture, Natural Resources Conservation Service. U.S. Government Printing Office, Washington, D.C.

USDA NRCS. 2005. Guidance on conducting wetland determinations for the Food Security Act and Section 404 of the Clean Water Act: Key points—February 25, 2005. U.S. Department of Agriculture, Natural Resources Conservation Service, Highly Erodible Land and Wetland Conservation (HELC/WC) Compliance Provisions white paper. www.nrcs.usda.gov/PROGRAMS/compliance/

USEPA. 1992a. *The guardian: Origins of the EPA.* EPA Historical Publication-1. Washington, D.C.: U.S. Environmental Protection Agency. www.epa.gov/history/publications/print/origins.htm

———. 1992b. *Agriculture and wetlands: Finding common ground.* EPA 503/9-92/003A. Washington, D.C.: U.S. Environmental Protection Agency, Office of Water.

USEPA and USDOA. 1998. *Guidance for Corps and EPA field offices regarding Clean Water Act Section 404 jurisdiction over isolated waters in light of* United States v. James J. Wilson, 7 pp. Washington, D.C.: U.S. Environmental Protection Agency; Office of Wetlands, Oceans, and Watersheds; and U.S. Department of Army, Army Corps of Engineers.

USFWS. 1980. *Ecological services manual* (101–104 ESM). Washington, D.C.: U.S. Fish and Wildlife Service, Division of Ecological Services. Unnumbered. http://www.fws.gov/policy/esmindex.html

———. 1988. Endangered and threatened wildlife and plants, determination of threatened status for Boltonia decurrens (decurrent false aster). *Federal Register* 53: 45858–61.

———. 2002. *National Wetlands Inventory: A strategy for the 21st century.* Washington, D.C.: U.S. Fish and Wildlife Service. http://wetlands.fws.gov/

———. 2003. *Digest of federal resource laws.* Washington, D.C.: U.S. Fish and Wildlife Service, Division of Congressional and Legislative Affairs. http://laws.fws.gov/

Valiela, I., G. Collins, J. Kremer, K. Lajtha, M. Geist, B. Seely, J. Brawley, and C. H. Sham. 1997. Nitrogen loading from coastal watersheds to receiving estuaries: New method and application. *Ecological Applications* 7: 358–80.

Valiela, I., K. Foreman, M. LaMontagne, D. Hersh, J. Costa, P. Peckol, B. DeMeo-Andreson, et al. 1992. Couplings of watersheds and coastal waters: Sources and consequences of nutrient enrichment in Waquoit Bay, Massachusetts. *Estuaries* 15: 443–57.

Valiela, I., and J. M. Teal. 1974. Nutrient limitation in salt marsh vegetation. In *Ecology of halophytes,* eds. R. J. Reimold and W. H. Queen, 347–563. New York: Academic Press Inc.

Valiela, I., J. M. Teal, and W. G. Deuser. 1978. The nature of growth forms in the salt marsh grass *Spartina alterniflora. The American Naturalist* 112: 461–70.

Van Breemen, N. 1975. Acidification and deacidification of coastal plain soils as a result of periodic flooding. *Soil Science Society of America Proceedings* 39: 1153–57.

Van Buskirk, J. 2000. The costs of an inducible defense in anuran larvae. *Ecology* 81: 2813–21.

Van Cleve, K., F. S. Chapin III, C. T. Dyrness, and L. A. Viereck. 1991. Element cycling in taiga forests: State-factor control. *BioScience* 41: 78–88.

van Dam, R., R. G. Habiba, and M. Finlayson. 2002. Climate change and wetlands: Impacts, adaptation and mitigation. Ramsar COP8 DOC. 11: Climate Change and Wetlands. 8th Meeting of the Conference of the Contracting Parties to the Convention on Wetlands, Valencia, Spain, 18–26 November 2002.

van der Hammen, T., and H. Hooghiemstra. 2000. Neogene and quaternary history of vegetation, climate, and plant diversity in Amazonia. *Quaternary Science Reviews* 19: 725–42.

van der Hoek, D., and W. G. Braakhekke. 1998. Restoration of soil chemical conditions of fen-meadow plant communities by water management in the Netherlands. In *European wet grasslands: Biodiversity, management and restoration,* eds. C. B. Joyce and P. M. Wade, 265–75. London: John Wiley & Sons.

van der Putten, W. H. 1997. Die-back of *Phragmites australis* in European wetlands: An overview of the European research programme on reed die-back and progression. *Aquatic Botany* 59: 263–75.

van der Valk, A. G. 1981. Succession in wetlands: A Gleasonian approach. *Ecology* 62: 688–96.

———. 1987. Vegetation dynamics of freshwater wetlands: A selective review of the literature. *Archiv für Hydrobiologie* 27: 27–39.

van der Valk, A. G., and L. C. Bliss. 1971. Hydrarch succession and net primary production of oxbow lakes in central Alberta. *Canadian Journal of Botany* 49: 1177–99.

van der Valk, A. G, T. L. Bremholm, and E. Gordon. 1999. The restoration of sedge meadows: Seed viability, seed germination requirements, and seedling growth of *Carex* species. *Wetlands* 19: 756–64.

van der Valk, A. G., and C. B. Davis. 1978a. The role of seed banks in the vegetation dynamics of prairie glacial marshes. *Ecology* 59: 322–35.

———. 1978b. Primary production of prairie glacial marshes. In *Freshwater wetlands: Ecological processes and management potential,* eds. R. E. Good, D. F. Whigham, and R L. Simpson, 21–37. New York: Academic Press.

———. 1979. A reconstruction of the recent vegetational history of a prairie marsh, Eagle Lake, Iowa, from its seed bank. *Aquatic Botany* 6: 29–51.

van der Valk, A. G., and R. L. Pederson. 2003. The SWANCC decision and its implications for prairie potholes. *Wetlands* 23: 590–96.

van der Wal, R., P. Kunst, and R. Drent. 1998. Interactions between hare and Brent goose in a salt marsh system: Evidence for food competition? *Oecologia* 117: 227–34.

van Duren I. C., D. Boeye, and A. P. Grootjans. 1997. Nutrient limitations in an extant and drained poor fen: Implications for restoration. *Plant Ecology* 133: 91–100.

van Ginniken, V. J. T., P. van Caubergh, M. Nieveen, P. Balm, G. van den Thillart, and A. Addink. 1998. Influence of hypoxia exposure on the energy metabolism of common carp (*Cyprinus carpio* L.). *Netherlands Journal of Zoology* 48: 65–82.

Van, T. K., G. S. Wheeler, and T. D. Center. 1998. Competitive interactions between *Hydrilla* (*Hydrilla verticillata*) and *Vallisneria* (*Vallisneria americana*) as influenced by insect herbivory. *Biological Control* 11: 185–92.

Vanni, M. J. 2002. Nutrient cycling by animals in freshwater ecosystems. *Annual Review of Ecology and Systematics* 33: 341–370.

Vannote, R. L., G. W. Minshall, K. W. Cummins, J. R. Sedell, and C. E. Cushing. 1980. The river continuum concept. *Canadian Journal of Fisheries and Aquatic Sciences* 37: 130–37.

Veltman, R. 2002. Effect of stormwater pulsing on wetland vegetation. Master's thesis, University of Wisconsin, Madison.

Venberg, W. B., and F. J. Vernberg. 1972. *Environmental physiology of marine animals.* New York: Springer-Verlag.

Veneman, P. L. M., M. J. Vepraskas, and J. Bouma. 1976. The physical significance of soil mottling in a Wisconsin toposequence. *Geoderma* 15: 103–18.

Vepraskas, M. J. 1992. *Redoximorphic features for identifying aquic conditions.* Technical Bulletin No. 301. Raleigh, NC: North Carolina Agricultural Research Service, North Carolina State University.

Verhoeven, J. T. A., E. Maltby, and M. B. Schmitz. 1990. Nitrogen and phosphorus mineralization in fens and bogs. *Journal of Ecology* 78: 713–26.

Vershinin, A. V., and Rozanov, A. G. 1983. The platinum electrode as an indicator of redox environment in marine sediments. *Marine Chemistry* 14: 1–15.

Vileisis, A. 1997. *Discovering the unknown landscape: A history of America's wetlands.* Washington, D.C.: Island Press, 433 pp.

Viljugrein, H., N. C. Stenseth, G. W. Smith, and G. H. Steinbakk. 2005. Density dependence in North American ducks. *Ecology* 86: 245–254.

Virgl, J. A., and F. Messier. 1996. Population structure, distribution, and demography of muskrats during the ice-free period under contrasting water fluctuations. *Ecoscience* 3: 54–62.

Vitousek, P. M. 1994. Beyond global warming: Ecology and global change. *Ecology* 75: 1861–76.

Vitt, D. H., L. A. Halsey, I. E. Bauer, and C. Campbell. 2000. Spatial and temporal trends in carbon storage of peatlands of continental western Canada through the Holocene. *Canadian Journal of Earth Science* 37: 683–93.

Voesenek, L. A. C. J., and C. W. P. M. Blom. 1999. Stimulated shoot elongation: A mechanism of semiaquatic plants to avoid submergence stress. Plant responses to environmental stresses: From phytohormones to genome reorganization, ed. H. R. Lerner, 431–48. New York: Marcel Dekker Inc.

Vohland, K. 1999. Untersuchungen zu Anpassung und Artbildung bei *Pycnotropis tida* (Diplopoda: Polydesmida: Aphelidesmidae: Amplininae) in amazonischen Überschwemmungswäldern. Ph.D. diss., University of Kiel, Kiel, Germany.

Vohland, K., and J. Adis. 1999. Life history of Pycnotropis tida (Diplopoda: Polydesmida: Aphelidesmidae) from seasonally inundated forest in Amazonia (Brazil and Peru). *Pedobiologia* 43: 231–44.

Vymazal, J. 1995. *Algae and element cycling in wetlands.* Boca Raton, FL: Lewis Publishers.

Wackett, L. P., A. G. Dodge, and L. B. M. Ellis. 2004. Microbial genomics and the periodic table. *Applied and Environmental Microbiology* 70: 647–55.

Waisel, Y. 1972. *Biology of halophytes.* New York: Academic Press.

Waiser, M. J. 2001. Nutrient limitation of pelagic bacteria and phytoplankton in four prairie wetlands. *Archiv für Hydrobiologie* 150: 435–55.

Wakeley, J. S., and R. D. Smith. 2001. *Hydrogeomorphic approach to assessing wetland functions: Guidelines for developing regional guidebooks.* Chapter 7, Verifying, Field Testing, and Validating Assessment Models, ERDC/EL TR-01-31. Vicksburg, MS: U.S. Army Engineer Research and Development Center.

Walbridge, M. R. 1994. Plant community composition and surface water chemistry of fen peatlands in West Virginia's Appalachian Plateau. *Water, Air and Soil Pollution* 77: 247–69.

Walker, D. 1970. Direction and rate in some British post-glacial hydroseres. In *Studies in the vegetational history of the British Isles,* eds. D. Walker and R. G. West, 117–39. Cambridge, U.K.: Cambridge University Press.

Walker, J., and R. K. Peet. 1983. Composition and species diversity of pine-wiregrass savannas of the Green Swamp, North Carolina. *Vegetatio* 55: 163–79.

Walker, P. H. 1972. Seasonal and stratigraphic controls in coastal floodplain soils. *Australian Journal of Soil Research* 10: 127–42.

Wallace, J. B., and J. O'Hop. 1985. Life on a fast pad: Waterlily beetle impact on water lilies. *Ecology* 66: 1534–44.

Wallach, R., and D. Zaslavsky. 1991. Lateral flow in a layered profile of an infinite uniform slope. *Water Resources Research* 27: 1809–18.

Walshe, B. M. 1950. The function of hemoglobin on *Chironomus plumosus* under natural conditions. *Journal of Experimental Biology* 24: 343–51.

Wantzen, K. M., E. Drago, and C. J. da Silva. 2005. Aquatic habitats of the Upper Paraguay River-Floodplain-System and parts of the Pantanal (Brazil). *Ecohydrology and Hydrobiology* 5: 107–126.

Wantzen, K. M., and W. J. Junk. 2000. The importance of stream-wetland-systems for biodiversity: A tropical perspective. In Biodiversity in wetlands: Assessment, function and conservation, eds. B. Gopal, W. J. Junk, and J. A. Davies, 11–34. Leiden, The Netherlands: Backhuys.

Wantzen, K. M., F. A. Machado, M. Voss, H. Boriss, and W. J. Junk. 2002a. Flood pulse-induced isotopic changes in fish of the Pantanal wetland, Brazil. *Aquatic Sciences* 64: 251.

———. 2002b. Seasonal isotopic shifts in fish of the Pantanal wetland, Brazil. *Aquatic Sciences* 64: 239–51.

Wantzen, K. M., and R. Wagner. 2006. Detritus processing by shredders: A tropical-temperate comparison. *Journal of the North American Benthological Society* 25:214–230.

Ward, G. M. 1998. A preliminary analysis of hydrodynamic characteristics of a small lotic wetland ecosystem. *Verhandlungen Internationale Vereinigung Limnologie* 26: 1373–76.

Ward, J. V., K. Tockner, and F. Schiemer. 1999. Biodiversity of floodplain river ecosystems: Ecotones and connectivity. *Regulated Rivers: Research and Management* 15: 125–39.

Ward, P., and A. Zahavi. 1973. The importance of certain assemblages of birds as "information centres" for food finding. *Ibis* 115: 517–34.

Warner, B. G., and C. D. A. Rubec, eds. 1997. The Canadian Wetland Classification System. National Wetlands Working Group, Wetlands Research Centre, University of Waterloo, Waterloo, Ontario.

Warren, L. A., and E. A. Haack. 2001. Biogeochemical controls on metal behaviour in freshwater environments. *Earth-Science Letters* 54: 261–20.

Warren, R. S., P. E. Fell, R. Rozsa, A H. Brawley, A. C. Orsted, E. T. Olsen, V. Swamy, and W. A. Niering. 2002. Salt marsh restoration in Connecticut: 20 years of science and management. *Restoration Ecology* 10: 497–513.

Warren, S. D., H. L. Black, D. A. Eastmond, and W. H. Whaley. 1988. Structural function of buttresses of *Tachigalia versicolor*. *Ecology* 69: 532–36.

Watson, A., K. D. Stephen, D. B. Nedwell, and J. R. M. Arah. 1997. Oxidation of methane in peat: Kinetics of CH_4 and O_2 removal and the role of plant roots. *Soil Biology and Biochemistry* 29: 1257–67.

Watson, T. 2001. Developers rush to build in wetlands after ruling. *USA Today*, December 6, 2002.

Watts, C. J. 2000. Seasonal phosphorus release from exposed, re-inundated littoral sediments from two Australian reservoirs. *Hydrobiologia* 431: 27–39.

WDNR (Wisconsin Department of Natural Resources). 2002. Identifying wetland management opportunities in the Milwaukee River Basin. DNR PUB-SS-975. Madison, Wisconsin.

Weber, G. E. 1997. Causes of hydrochemical seasonality of major cations in Lago Camaleão, a Central Amazonian floodplain lake. *Verhandlungen Internationale Vereinigung für theoretische und angewandte Limnologie* 26: 408–11.

Weber, L. M., and S. M. Haig. 1997. Shorebird-prey interactions in South Carolina coastal soft sediments. *Canadian Journal of Zoology* 75: 245–52.

Weinbauer, M. G. 2004. Ecology of prokaryotic viruses. *FEMS Microbiology Reviews* 28: 127–81.

Weinhold, C. E., and A. G. van der Valk. 1989. The impact of duration of drainage on the seed banks of northern prairie wetlands. *Canadian Journal of Botany* 67: 1878–84.

Weiss, J. V., D. Emerson, S. M. Backer, and J. P. Megonigal. 2003. Enumeration of Fe(II)-oxidizing and Fe(III)-reducing bacteria in the root zone of wetland plants: Implications for a rhizosphere iron cycle. *Biogeochemistry* 64: 77–96.

Weiss, J. V., D. Emerson, and J. P. Megonigal. 2004. Geochemical control of microbial Fe(III) reduction potential in wetlands: Comparison of the rhizosphere to non-rhizosphere soil. *FEMS Microbiology Ecology* 48: 89–100.

Welcomme, R. L. 1985. River fisheries. FAO Fish. Tech. Pap. 262, Food and Agriculture Organization of the United Nations, Rome, Italy.

Welcomme, R. L., and A. Halls. 2001. Some considerations on the effects of differences in flood patterns on fish populations. *Ecohydrology and Hydrobiology* 1: 313–21.

Wellborn, G. A., D. K. Skelly, and E. E. Werner. 1996. Mechanisms creating community structure across a freshwater habitat gradient. *Annual Review of Ecology and Systematics* 27: 337–63.

Weller, M. W. 1978. Management of freshwater marshes for wildlife. In Freshwater wetlands: Ecological processes and management potential, eds. R. E. Good, D. F. Whigham, and R. L. Simpson, 267–84. New York: Academic Press.

Wells, R. M. G., M. J. Hudson, and T. Brittain. 1981. Function of the hemoglobin and the gas bubble in the backswimmer *Anisops assimilis* (Hemiptera: Notonectidae). *Journal of Comparative Physiology* 142: 515–22.

Werner, E. E. 1992. Competitive interactions between wood frog and northern leopard frog larvae: The influence of size and activity. *Copeia* 1992: 26–35.

Werner E. E., and K. S. Glennemeier 1999. Influence of forest canopy on the breeding pond distributions for several amphibian pond species. *Copeia* 1999: 1–112.

Werner, E. E., and M. A. McPeek. 1994. Direct and indirect effects of predators on two anuran species along an environmental gradient. *Ecology* 75: 1368–82.

Werner, K. J., and J. B. Zedler. 2002. How sedge meadow soils, microtopography, and vegetation respond to sedimentation. *Wetlands* 22: 451–66.

West, J., G. D. Williams, S. P. Madon, and J. B. Zedler. 2003. Integrating spatial and temporal variability into the analysis of fish food web linkages in Tijuana Estuary. *Environmental Biology of Fishes* 67: 297–309.

West, J. M., and J. B. Zedler. 2000. Marsh-creek connectivity: Fish use of a salt marsh in southern California. *Estuaries* 23: 699–710.

West-Eberhard, M. J. 1989. Phenotypic plasticity and the origin of diversity. Annual Review of Ecology and Systematics 20: 249-278.

Westlake, D. F. 1963. Comparisons of plant production. *Biological Reviews* 38: 385–425.

Wettstein, W., and B. Schmid. 1999. Conservation of arthropod diversity in montane wetlands: Effects of altitude, habitat quality and habitat fragmentation on butterflies and grasshoppers. *Journal of Applied Ecology* 36: 363–73.

Wetzel, P. R., A. G. van der Valk, and L. A. Toth. 2001. Restoration of wetland vegetation on the Kissimmee River floodplain: Potential role of seed banks. *Wetlands* 21: 189–98.

Wetzel, R. G. 1979. The role of the littoral zone and detritus in lake metabolism. In *Symposium on lake metabolism and lake management,* eds. G. E. Likens, W. Rodhe, and C. Serruya. *Archiv für Hydrobiologie Beihreit. Ergebnisse der Limnologie* 13: 145–61.

———. 1983. *Limnology,* 2d ed. Philadelphia, PA: W. B. Saunders.

———. 1989. Wetland and littoral interfaces of lakes: Productivity and nutrient regulation in the Lawrence Lake ecosystem. In *Freshwater wetlands and wildlife,* eds. R. R. Sharitz and J. W. Gibbons, 283–302. DOE Symposium Series 61. Oak Ridge, TN: US DOE Office Scientific Technical Information.

———. 1990. Land-water interfaces: Metabolic and limnological regulators. Edgardo Baldi Memorial Lecture. 24th Congress Societas Internationalis Limnologiae. *Verhandlungen Internationale Vereinigung Limnologie* 24: 6–24.

———. 1993. Microcommunities and microgradients: Linking nutrient regeneration and high sustained aquatic primary production. *Netherlands Journal of Aquatic Ecology* 27: 3–9.

———. 1995. Death, detritus, and energy flow in aquatic ecosystems. *Freshwater Biology* 33: 83–89.

———. 1996. Benthic algae and nutrient cycling in standing freshwater ecosystems. In *Algal ecology: Benthic algae in freshwater ecosystems,* eds. R. J. Stevenson, M. Bothwell, and R. Lowe, 641–67. New York: Academic Press.

———. 1999a. Plants and water in and adjacent to lakes. In *Eco-hydrology: Plants and water in terrestrial and aquatic environments,* eds. A. J. Baird and R. L. Wilby, 269–99. London: Routledge.

———. 1999b. Organic phosphorus mineralization in soils and sediments. In *Phosphorus biogeochemistry in Florida ecosystems,* ed. K. R. Reddy, 225–45. Boca Raton, FL: Lewis Publishers.

———. 2001. *Limnology: Lake and river ecosystems.* San Diego: Academic Press, 1066 pp.

———. 2002. Dissolved organic carbon: Detrital energetics, metabolic regulators, and drivers of ecosystem stability of aquatic ecosystems. In *Aquatic ecosystems: Interactivity of dissolved organic matter,* eds. S. Findlay and R. Sinsabaugh, 455–77. San Diego: Academic Press.

———. 2003. Solar radiation as an ecosystem modulator. In *UV effects in aquatic organisms and ecosystems,* eds. E. W. Helbling and H. Zagarese, 3–18. Comprehensive Series in Photochemical and Photobiological Sciences. Cambridge: European Society of Photobiology.

Wetzel, R. G., E. S. Brammer, and C. Forsberg. 1984. Photosynthesis of submersed macrophytes in acidified lakes. I. Carbon fluxes and recycling of CO_2 in *Juncus bulbosus* L. *Aquatic Botany* 19: 329–42.

Wetzel, R. G., and A. Otsuki. 1974. Allochthonous organic carbon of a marl lake. *Archiv für Hydrobiologie* 73: 31–56.

Wetzel, R. G., A. K. Ward, and M. Stock. 1997. Effects of natural dissolved organic matter on mucilaginous matrices of biofilm communities. *Archiv für Hydrobiologie* 139: 289–99.

Whalen, P. J., L. A. Toth, J. W. Koebel, and P. K. Strayer. 2002. Kissimmee River restoration: A case study. *Water Science and Technology* 45: 55–62.

Wharton, C. H., and M. M. Brinson. 1979. Characteristics of southeastern river systems. In *Strategies for protection and management of floodplain wetlands and other riparian ecosystems*, tech. coords. R. R. Johnson and J. F. McCormick, 32–40. Publication GTR-WO-12. Washington, D.C.: U.S.D.A. Forest Service.

Wharton, C. H., W. M. Kitchens, E. C. Pendleton, and T. W. Sipe. 1982. *The ecology of bottomland hardwood swamps of the Southeast: A community profile*. FWS/OBS-81/37. Biological Services Program. Washington, D.C.: U.S. Fish and Wildlife Service.

Wheeler, B. D. 1999. Water and plants in freshwater wetlands. In *Eco-hydrology. Plants and water in terrestrial and aquatic environments*, eds. A. J. Baird and R. L. Wilby, 127–80. London: Routledge.

Wheeler, B. D., and M. C. F. Proctor. 2000. Ecological gradients, subdivisions and terminology of north-west European mires. *Journal of Ecology* 88: 187–203.

Whigham, D. F., and C. J. Richardson. 1988. Soil and plant chemistry of an Atlantic white cedar wetland on the Inner Coastal Plain of Maryland. *Canadian Journal of Botany* 66: 568–76.

Whiles, M. R., and B. S. Goldowitz. 2001. Hydrologic influences on insect emergence production from central Platte River wetlands. *Ecological Applications* 11: 1829–42.

Whiles, M. R., B. S. Goldowitz, and R. E. Charlton. 1999. Life history and production of a semiterrestrial limnephilid caddisfly in an intermittent Platte River wetland. *Journal of the North American Benthological Society* 18: 533–544.

White, D. A., T. E. Weis, J. M. Trapani, and L. B. Thien. 1978. Productivity and decomposition of the dominant salt marsh plants in Louisiana. *Ecology* 59: 751–759.

Whisenant, S. G. 1999. *Repairing damaged wildlands: A process-orientated, landscape-scale approach*. Cambridge, U.K.: Cambridge University Press.

White, G. 1789. *The natural history of Selborne*. Wordsworth Classics edition of 1996, edited by G. Allen and illustrated by E. H. New. Ware, U.K.: Wordsworth Editions.

White, I., D. Melville, B. P. Wilson, and J. Sammut. 1997. Reducing acidic discharges from coastal wetlands in eastern Australia. *Wetlands Ecology and Management* 5: 55–72.

White, P. S. 1994. Synthesis: Vegetation pattern and process in the Everglades ecosystem. In *Everglades: The ecosystem and its restoration*, eds. S. M. Davis and J. C. Ogden, 445–58. Boca Raton, FL: St. Lucie Press.

Whiteman, H. H., and S. A. Wissinger. 2004. Multiple hypotheses for population fluctuations: The importance of long-term data sets for amphibian conservation. In *Conservation status of North American amphibians*, ed. M. J. Lannoo. In press.

Whiteman, H. H., S. A. Wissinger, and A. J. Bohonak. 1996. Seasonal movement patterns and diet in a subalpine population of the tiger salamander, *Ambystoma tigrinum nebulosum*. *Canadian Journal of Zoology* 72: 1780–87.

Whiteman, H. W. 1994. Evolution of facultative paedomorphosis in salamanders. *Quarterly Review of Biology* 69: 205–11.

Whitham, T. G., W. P. Young, G. D. Martinsen, C. A. Gehring, J. A. Schweitzer, S. M . Shuster, G. M. Wimp, et al. 2003. Community and ecosystem genetics: A consequence of the extended phenotype. *Ecology* 84: 559–73.

Whittaker, R. H. 1967. Gradient analysis of vegetation. *Biological Reviews* 42: 207–64.

Wieder, R. K., J. R. Yavitt, G. E. Lang, and C. A. Bennett. 1989. Above-ground net primary production at Big Run Bog, West Virginia. *Castanea* 54: 209–16.

Wiggins G. B. 1973. A contribution to the biology of caddisflies (Trichoptera) in temporary pools. Life Science Contributions of Royal Ontario Museum. 88:1–28.

———. 1996. *Larvae of the North American caddisflies (Trichoptera)*, 2d ed. Toronto, ON, Canada: University of Toronto Press.

Wiggins, G. B., R. J. Mackay, and I. M. Smith. 1980. Evolutionary and ecological strategies of animals in annual temporary pools. *Archiv für Hydrobiologie Supplement* 58: 97–206.

Wigley, T. B., and T. H. Roberts. 1994. A review of wildlife changes in southern bottomland hardwoods due to forest management practices. *Wetlands* 14: 41–48.

Wilbur, H. M., and J. E. Fauth. 1990. Experimental aquatic food webs: Interactions between two predators and two prey. *American Naturalist* 135: 176–204.

Wilcove, D. S. 1985. Nest predation in forest tracts and the decline of migratory songbirds. *Ecology* 66: 1211–14.

Wilcox, D. A. 1995. Wetland and aquatic macrophytes as indicators of anthropogenic hydrologic disturbance. *Natural Areas Journal* 15: 240–48.

Wilcox, D. A., J. E. Meeker, P. L. Hudson, B. J. Armitage, M. G. Black, and D. G. Uzarski. 2002. Hydrologic variability and the application of Index of Biotic Integrity metrics to wetlands: A Great Lakes evaluation. *Wetlands* 22: 588–615.

Wilcox, D. A., and T. H. Simonin. 1987. A chronosequence of aquatic macrophyte communities in dune ponds. *Aquatic Botany* 28: 227–42.

Wilcox, D. A., and T. H. Whillans. 1999. Techniques for restoration of disturbed coastal wetlands of the Great Lakes. *Wetlands* 19: 835–57.

Wilcox, J. 2004. Challenges of replacing reed canary grass (*Phalaris arundinacea* L.) with native species. M. S. Thesis, University of Wisconsin, Madison.

Wilhite, L. P., and J. R. Toliver. 1990. *Taxodium distichum* (L.) Rich. Baldcypress. In *Silvics of North America, Volume 1, Conifers*, tech. coords. R. M. Burns and B. H. Honkala, 563–72. Agricultural Handbook 654. Washington, D.C.: U.S.D.A. Forest Service.

Williams, D. D. 1987. *The ecology of temporary waters*. Portland, OR: Timber Press.

———. 1996. Environmental constraints in temporary fresh waters, and their consequences for insect fauna. *Journal of the North American Benthological Society* 15: 634–50.

Williams, D. D., A. F. Tavares, and E. Bryant. 1987. Respiratory device or camouflage? A case for the caddisfly. *Oikos* 50: 42–52.

Williams, D. M., and T. M. Embley. 1996. Microbial diversity: Domains and kingdoms. *Annual Review of Ecology and Systematics* 27: 569–95.

Williams, J. D. H., J. K. Syer, S. S. Shulka, and R. F. Harris. 1971. Levels of inorganic and total phosphorus in lake sediments as related to other sediment parameters. *Environmental Science and Technology* 5: 1113–20.

Williams, W. D. 1988. Limnological imbalances: An antipodean viewpoint. *Freshwater Biology* 20: 407–20.

———. 1998a. Dryland wetlands. In *Wetlands for the future*, eds. A. J. McComb and J. A. Davis, 33–47. Adelaide, Australia: Gleneagles Publishing.

———. 1998b. *Guidelines of lake management. Volume 6. Management of inland saline waters.* Shiga, Japan: International Lake Environment Committee Foundation.

Willink, P. W., B. Chernoff, L. E. Alonso, J. R. Montanbault, and R. Lourival. 2000. A biological assessment of the aquatic ecosystems of the Pantanal, Mato Grosso do Sul, Brazil, RAP Bulletin of Biological Assessment 18. Washington, D.C.: Conservation International.

Wilson, B. P., I. White, and M. D. Melville. 1999a. Floodplain hydrology, acid discharge and change in water quality associated with a drained acid sulfate soil. *Marine and Freshwater Research* 50: 149–57.

Wilson, D. M., W. Fenical, M. Hay, N. Lindquist, and R. Bolser. 1999b. Habenariol, a freshwater feeding deterrent from the aquatic orchid *Haberaria repens* (Orchidaceae). *Phytochemistry* 50: 1333–36.

Wilson, J. B., W. McG. King, M. T. Sykes, and T. R. Partridge. 1996. Vegetation zonation as related to the salt tolerance of species of brackish riverbanks. *Canadian Journal of Botany* 74: 1079–85.

Wilson, R. R., and R. J. Cooper. 1998. Acadian Flycatcher nest placement: Does placement influence reproductive success? *Condor* 100: 673–79.

Wilson, S. D., and P. A. Keddy. 1986. Species competitive ability and position along a natural stress/disturbance gradient. *Ecology* 67: 1236–42.

Wilson, W. H. 1989. Predation and the mediation of intraspecific competition in an in faunal community in the Bay of Fundy. *Journal of Experimental Marine Biology and Ecology* 132: 221–45.

Wimpenny, J. W. T., and R. Colasanti. 1997. A unifying hypothesis for the structure of microbial biofilms based on cellular automation models. *FEMS Microbiology and Ecology* 22: 1–16.

Winemiller, K. O. 1991. Ecomorphological diversification in lowland freshwater fish assemblages from five biotic regions. *Ecological Monographs* 61: 343–65.

Winter, T. C. 1981. Uncertainties in estimating the water balance of lakes. *Water Resources Bulletin* 17: 82–115.

———. 1986. Effect of ground-water recharge on configuration of the water table beneath sand dunes and on seepage in lakes in the sandhills of Nebraska, U.S.A. *Journal of Hydrology* 86: 221–37.

———. 1989. Hydrological studies of wetlands in the northern prairie. In *Northern prairie wetlands*, ed. A. G. van der Valk, 16–54. Ames, IA: Iowa State University Press.

———. 2000. The vulnerability of wetlands to climate change: A hydrologic landscape perspective. *Journal of the American Water Resources Association* 36: 305–11.

Winter, T. C., and D. O. Rosenberry. 1995. The interaction of groundwater with prairie pothole wetlands in the Cottonwood Lake area, east-central North Dakota, 1979–1990. *Wetlands* 15: 193–211.

Winterbourn, M. J. 1971. The life histories and trophic relationships of the Trichoptera of Marion Lake, British Columbia. *Canadian Journal of Zoology* 49: 623–35.

Wisheu, I. C., and P. A. Keddy. 1989. Species richness-standing crop relationships along four lakeshore gradients: Constraints on the general model. *Canadian Journal of Botany* 67: 1609–17.

———. 1992. Competition and centrifugal organization of plant communities: Theories and tests. *Journal of Vegetation Science* 3: 147–56.

Wissinger, S. A. 1997. Cyclic colonization and predictable disturbance: A template for biological control in ephemeral crop systems. *Biological Control* 10: 1–15.

———. 1999. Ecology of wetland invertebrates: Synthesis and applications for conservation and management. In *Invertebrates in freshwater wetlands of North America: Ecology and management,* eds. D. P. Batzer, R. D. Rader, and S. A. Wissinger, 1043–86. New York: John Wiley and Sons.

Wissinger, S. A., A. J. Bohonak, H. H. Whiteman, and W. S. Brown. 1999a. Subalpine wetlands in Colorado: Habitat permanence, salamander predation, and invertebrate communities. In *Invertebrates in freshwater wetlands of North America: Ecology and management,* eds. D. P. Batzer, R. D. Rader, and S. A. Wissinger, 757–90. New York: John Wiley and Sons.

Wissinger, S. A., W. S. Brown, and J. E. Jannot. 2003. Caddisfly life histories along permanence gradients in high-elevation wetlands in Colorado (USA). *Freshwater Biology* 48: 255–70.

Wissinger, S. A., C. Eldermire, and J. C. Whissel. 2004a. The role of cases in reducing aggression and cannibalism among caddisflies in temporary wetlands. *Wetlands* 24: 777–83.

Wissinger S. A., and Gallagher, L. J. 1999. Beaver pond wetlands in western Pennsylvania: Modes of colonization and succession after drought. In *Invertebrates in freshwater wetlands of North America: Ecology and management,* eds. D. P. Batzer, R. D. Rader, and S. A. Wissinger, 333–62. New York: John Wiley & Sons.

Wissinger, S. A., J. Steinmetz, J. S. Alexander, and W. S. Brown. 2004b. Larval cannibalism, time constraints, and adult fitness in caddisflies that inhabit temporary wetlands. *Oecologia* 138: 39–47.

Wissinger, S. A., J. C. Whissel, C. Eldermire, and W. S. Brown. 2006. Predator defense along a permanence gradient: roles of case structure, behavior, and developmental phenology in caddisflies. *Oecologia* 147: 667–678.

Wissinger S. A., H. H. Whiteman, G. B. Sparks, G. L. Rouse, and W. S. Brown. 1999b. Trade-offs between competitive superiority and vulnerability to predation in caddisflies along a permanence gradient in subalpine wetlands. *Ecology* 80: 2102–16.

Wittmann, F., W. J. Junk, and D. Anhuf. 2002. Tree species distribution and community structure of Central Amazonian várzea forests by remote-sensing techniques. *Journal of Tropical Ecology* 18: 805–20.

Wium-Andersen, S. 1987. Allelopathy among aquatic plants. *Archiv für Hydrobiologie* 27: 167–72.

Woese, C., and G. E. Fox 1977. Phylogenetic structure of the prokaryotic domain: The primary kingdoms. *Proceedings of the National Academy of Sciences, USA* 74: 5088–90.

Wold, A. K. F., and A. E. Hershey. 1999. Effects of salmon carcass decomposition on biofilm growth and wood decomposition. *Canadian Journal of Fisheries and Aquatic Sciences* 56: 767–73.

Wolf, H. G., and J. Adis. 1992. Genetic differentiation between populations of *Neomachilellus scandens* (Meinertellidae, Arachae-ognatha, Insecta) inhabiting neighbouring forests in Central Amazonia. *Verhandlungen der naturwissenschaftlichen Vereinigung Hamburg* 33: 5–13.

Wommack, K. E., and R. R. Colwell. 2000. Virioplankton: Viruses in aquatic systems. *Microbiology and Molecular Biology Review* 64: 69–114.

Wong, M. K. M., T. K. Goh, I. J. Hodgkiss, K. D. Hyde, V. M. Ranghoo, C. K. M. Tsui, W. H. Ho, W. S. W. Wong, and T. K. Yuen. 1998. Role of fungi in freshwater ecosystems. *Biodiversity and Conservation* 7: 1187–1206.

Woo, I., and J. B. Zedler. 2002. Can nutrients alone shift a sedge meadow towards dominance by the invasive *Typha* x *glauca*? *Wetlands* 22: 509–21.

Wood, A. P., J. P. Aurikko, and D. P. Kelly. 2004. A challenge for 21st century molecular biology and biochemistry: What are the causes of obligate autotrophy and methanotrophy? *FEMS Microbiology Reviews* 28: 335–52.

Wood, L. A. 1999. Short-term effects of timber management on prothonotary warbler breeding biology. Master's thesis, University of Georgia, Athens.

Wood, L. V. 2004. Don't be mislead: CWA jurisdiction extends to all non-navigable tributaries of the traditional navigable waters and to their adjacent wetlands (a response to the Virginia Albrecht/Stephen Nickelsburg ELR article, to the Fifth Circuit's decision in re Needham and to the Supreme Court's dicta in SWANCC. *Environmental Law Reporter News & Analysis* 34: 10187–217. Washington, D.C.: Environmental Law Institute.

Woodhouse, C. A. 2004. A paleo perspective on hydroclimatic variability in the western United States. *Aquatic Sciences* 66: 346–56.

Wright, J. P., W. S. C. Gurney, and C. G. Jones. 2004. Patch dynamics in a landscape modified by ecosystem engineers. *Oikos* 105: 336–48.

Wrubleski, D. A. 1999. Northern prairie marshes (Delta Marsh, Manitoba): II. Chrinomidae (Diptera) responses to changing plant communities in newly flooded habitats. In *Invertebrates in freshwater wetlands of North America: Ecology and management,* eds. D. P. Batzer, R. D. Rader, and S. A. Wissinger, 571–602. New York: John Wiley and Sons.

Wrubleski, D. A. 2005. Chironomidae (Diptera) responses to the experimental flooding of prairie marshes. *Wetlands* 25: 200–209.

Wrubleski, D. A., and D. M. Rosenberg. 1990. The Chironomidae of Bone Pile Pond, Delta Marsh, Manitoba, Canada. *Wetlands* 10: 243–275.

Yahner, R. H. 1988. Changes in wildlife communities near edges. *Conservation Biology* 2: 333–39.

Yao, H., and R. Conrad. 2000. Effect of temperature on reduction of iron and production of carbon dioxide and methane in anoxic wetland rice soils. *Biology and Fertility of Soils* 32: 135–41.

Yates, R. F. K., and F. P. Day, Jr. 1983. Decay rates and nutrient dynamics in confined and unconfined leaf litter in the Great Dismal Swamp. *American Midland Naturalist* 110: 37–45.

Yu, Z., M. R. Turetsky, I. D. Campbell, and D. H. Vitt. 2001. Modelling long-term peatland dynamics. II. Processes and rates as inferred from litter and peat-core data. *Ecological Modelling* 145: 159–73.

Yu, Z., D. H. Vitt, I. D. Campbell, and M. J. Apps. 2003. Understanding Holocene peat accumulation pattern of continental fens in western Canada. *Canadian Journal of Botany* 81: 267–79.

Yulianto, E., W. S. Sukapti, A. T. Rahardjo, D. Noeradi, D. A. Siregar, P. Suparan, and K. Hirakawa. 2004. Mangrove shoreline responses to Holocene environmental change, Makassar Strait, Indonesia. *Review of Palaeobotany and Palynology* 131: 251–68.

Yurewicz, K. L. 2004. A growth-mortality tradeoff in larval salamanders and the coexistence of intraguild predators and prey. *Oecologia* 138: 102–11.

Zajic, J. E. 1969. *Microbial biogeochemistry*. New York: Academic Press.

Zamora-Munoz, C., and B. W. Svensson. 1996. Survival of caddis larvae in relation to their case material in a group of temporary and permanent pools. *Freshwater Biology* 36: 23–31.

Zaslavsky, D., and G. Sinai. 1981a. Surface hydrology IV—Flow in sloping, layered soil. *Journal of the Hydraulics Division, ASCE*. Vol. 107, No. HY1, Proc. Paper 15961, 53–64.

———. 1981b. Surface hydrology V—In-surface transient flow. *Journal of the Hydraulics Division, ASCE*. Vol. 107, No. HY1, Proc. Paper 15961, 65–93.

Zedler, J. B. 1966. Buena Vista Marsh in historical perspective. Master's thesis, University of Wisconsin, Madison.

———. 1980. Algae mat productivity: Comparisons in a salt marsh. *Estuaries* 3: 122–31.

———. 1993. Canopy architecture of natural and planted cordgrass marshes: Selecting habitat evaluation criteria. *Ecological Applications* 3: 123–38.

———. 1998. Replacing endangered species habitat: The acid test of wetland ecology. In *Conservation biology for the coming age*, eds. P. L. Fiedler and P. M. Kareiva, 364–79. New York: Chapman and Hall.

———. 1999. The ecological restoration spectrum. In *An international perspective on wetland rehabilitation*, ed. W. Streever, 301–18. Dordrecht, The Netherlands: Kluwer Academic Press.

———. 2000. Progress in wetland restoration ecology. *Trends in Ecology and Evolution* 15: 4027.

———, ed. 2001. *Handbook for restoring tidal wetlands*. Marine Science Series. Boca Raton, FL: CRC Press LLC.

———. 2003. Wetlands at your service: Reducing impacts of agriculture at the watershed scale. *Frontiers in Ecology and Environment* 1: 65–72.

Zedler, J. B. 2005. Restoration ecology: Principles from field tests of theory. *San Francisco Estuary and Watershed Science*. On line at: http://repositories.cdlib.org/jmie/sfews/vol3/iss2/art4.

Zedler, J. B., and P. A. Beare. 1986. Temporal variability of salt marsh vegetation: The role of low-salinity gaps and environmental stress. In *Estuarine variability*, ed. D. A. Wolfe, 295–306. San Diego, CA: Academic Press.

Zedler, J. B., and J. C. Callaway. 1999. Tracking wetland restoration: Do mitigation sites follow desired trajectories? *Restoration Ecology* 7: 69–73.

———. 2000. Evaluating the progress of engineered tidal wetlands. *Ecological Engineering* 15: 211–25.

———. 2003. Adaptive restoration: A strategic approach for integrating research into restoration projects. In *Managing for healthy ecosystems*, eds. D. J. Rapport, W. L. Lasley, D. E. Rolston, N. O. Nielsen, C. O. Qualset, and A. B. Damania, 167–74. Boca Raton, FL: Lewis Publishers.

Zedler, J. B., J. C. Callaway, J. Desmond, G. Vivian-Smith, G. Williams, G. Sullivan, A. Brewster, and B. Bradshaw. 1999. Californian salt marsh vegetation: An improved model of spatial pattern. *Ecosystems* 2: 19–35.

Zedler, J. B., M. Fellows, and S. Trnka. 1998. Wastelands to wetlands: Links between habitat protection and ecosystem science. In *Successes, limitations and frontiers in ecosystem science*, eds. P. Groffman and M. Pace, 69–112. New York: Springer-Verlag.

Zedler, J. B., and S. Kercher. 2004. Causes and consequences of invasive plants in wetlands: Opportunities, opportunists, and outcomes. *Critical Reviews in Plant Sciences* 23: 431–52.

Zedler, J.B., H.N. Morzaria-Luna, and K. Ward. 2003. The challenge of restoring vegetation on tidal, hypersaline substrates. *Plant and Soil* 253: 259–73.

Zedler, J.B., and A. Powell. 1993. Problems in managing coastal wetlands: Complexities, compromises, and concerns. *Oceanus* 36: 19–28.

Zedler, P.H. 1987. *The ecology of southern California vernal pools: A community profile.* Washington, D.C.: U.S. Fish and Wildlife Service, Biological Report 85(7.11).

———. 2003. Vernal pools and the concept of "isolated wetlands." *Wetlands* 23: 597–607.

Zerm, M., J. Adis, W. Paarmann, M.A. Amorim, and C.R.V. da Fonseca. 2001. On habitat specificity, life cycles, and guild structure in tiger beetles of Central Amazonia (Brazil) (Coleoptera: Cicindelidae). *Entomologia Generalis* 25: 141–54.

Zimmer, K.D., M.A. Hanson, and M.G. Butler. 2000. Factors influencing invertebrate communities in prairie wetlands: A multivariate approach. *Canadian Journal of Fisheries and Aquatic Sciences* 57: 76–85.

———. 2002. Effects of fathead minnows and restoration on prairie wetland ecosystems. *Freshwater Biology* 47: 2071–86.

INDEX

Note: Organisms are included only if significant information is presented, and they are listed by their most widely used name, either common or scientific.